THE CORRESPONDENCE OF

HENRY EDWARD MANNING
AND
WILLIAM EWART GLADSTONE

THE CORRESPONDENCE OF

HENRY EDWARD MANNING AND WILLIAM EWART GLADSTONE

THE COMPLETE CORRESPONDENCE 1833–1891

VOLUME II
1844–1853

EDITED BY

PETER C. ERB

OXFORD
UNIVERSITY PRESS

OXFORD
UNIVERSITY PRESS

Great Clarendon Street, Oxford, OX2 6DP,
United Kingdom

Oxford University Press is a department of the University of Oxford.
It furthers the University's objective of excellence in research, scholarship,
and education by publishing worldwide. Oxford is a registered trade mark of
Oxford University Press in the UK and in certain other countries

© Peter C. Erb 2013

British Library Cataloguing in Publication Data

Data available

ISBN 978–0–19–957733–0 (Hbk.)
978–0–19–957731–6 (Set)

Printed in Great Britain by
the MPG Printgroup, UK

CONTENTS

Volume I: 1833–1844

Abbreviations	ix
Introduction	xiii

SECTION I

Initial Contacts: 1833–1836	3

SECTION II: PRELUDES TO POWER

1. Early Reflections on Church and State: February 1837–July 1837	21
2. Opposing the Commission: September 1837–March 1838	64
3. *The State in its Relations with the Church* and Interlude in Rome: May 1838–July 1839	106
4. Church Principles in Theory and Practice: February–November 1840	143
5. Archdeaconry and Board of Trade: December 1840–November 1841	197
Addendum to Section II	231

SECTION III: THE STRAIN OF TRACTARIAN IDEALS

1. The Jerusalem Bishopric and the Oxford Poetry Professorship: November 1841–January 1842	249
2. *The Unity of the Church*: February–September 1842	302
3. Church Discipline and the Problem of Education: October 1842–June 1843	313
Addenda to Section III	350

SECTION IV: CONFRONTING
THE ROMEWARDS MOVEMENT

1. Pusey's Sermon on the Eucharist: June–October 1843   377
2. Newman's Crisis and Resignation: October–November 1843   385
3. New and Lost Opportunities: November–December 1843   407
4. Facing Old Realities: January–October 1844   440

Addenda to Section IV   475

Volume II: 1844–1853

SECTION V: THE IMPLICATIONS OF
CATHOLIC CONCERNS

1. The Debate over Ward and Maynooth: October
   1844–February 1845   3
2. Aftermath: February–August 1845   60

Addenda to Section V   102

SECTION VI: READJUSTMENTS
AND REVISIONS

1. After Newman's Conversion: October–November 1845   163
2. Secretary for the Colonies: December 1845–February 1846   174
3. Renewed Reflections on Church and State: March–June 1846   188

Addendum to Section VI   212

SECTION VII: CHARTING NEW
DIRECTIONS

1. 'From Oxford to Rome': August 1846–August 1847   219
2. Manning's Second Interlude in Rome: January 1848–July 1849 258
3. The Lincoln Affair: July–October 1849   281

Addenda to Section VII   305

SECTION VIII: THE GORHAM CRISIS

1. The Problem of Response: November 1849–April 1850   319
2. *The Royal Supremacy* and a Proposed Engagement:
   April–June 1850   351

3. *The Appellate Jurisdiction*: June–September 1850   380
4. The Growth of Separation: September–October 1850   414
5. Gladstone to Italy and Manning's Resignation:
   November 1850–April 1851   435

Addenda to Section VIII   467

SECTION IX: EPILOGUE

June 1851–August 1853   505
Addendum to Section IX   518

Volume III: 1861–1875

SECTION X: REACQUAINTANCE AND REALIGNMENT

1. Initial Meeting: March 1861–December 1862   3
2. Italian and English Concerns: April–December 1864   22
3. Ireland and other Church–State Issues: January–March 1865   47
4. The Problem of Education: May–July 1865   59
5. Episcopal Authority and Commons Leadership:
   July 1865–September 1866   66
6. Ireland Again: February 1867–March 1868   95
7. Detente: April–November 1868   113

SECTION XI: ARCHBISHOP AND PRIME MINISTER

1. Ireland and Disestablishment: December 1868–July 1869   143
2. Viewing Rome and the Council: September–November 1869   166
3. The Irish Land Bill: January–March 1870   185
4. Interpreting Rome and Vatican I: April–July 1870   199
5. The Italian Problem: July 1870–May 1871   212
6. Education in a Changed Perspective: June–December 1871   272
7. The Struggle in Rome: February 1872–February 1873   289
8. Irish Universities and Education: February 1873–August 1874   335
9. The Vaticanism Controversy: November 1874–February 1875   390

Addenda to Section XI   419

Volume IV: 1882–1891

SECTION XII: THE FINAL DECADE

1. Initial Forays: January 1882–June 1884   3
2. Ireland, Science, and Scripture: November 1885–March 1886   20
3. Planning Biographies: June 1887–November 1888   41
4. Final Reflections: March 1889–November 1891   58
Addenda to Section XII   121

APPENDICES: THE VATICANISM TRACTS
AND CONTROVERSY

1. 'Preface' to W. E. Gladstone's *Rome and the Newest Fashions
   in Religion* (1875)   135
2. W. E. Gladstone, *The Vatican Decrees in Their Bearing on
   Civil Allegiance: A Political Expostulation* (1874 and 1875 editions)   142
3. W. E. Gladstone, *Vaticanism: An Answer to Reproofs &
   Replies* (1875 edition)   187
4. H. E. Manning, *The Vatican Decrees in Their Bearing on Civil
   Allegiance* (1875)   278
5. The Vaticanism Controversy: A Bibliography   391

Bibliography   395
Index   497

ABBREVIATIONS

Sigla for correspondence: All letters are identified and cited by date, the first two numerals indicating the year (in the nineteenth century), the second two the month, and the last two the day, followed by letter references to author and addressee; thus, 330809mg indicates that the letter was written 1833, August 9, by Manning to Gladstone.

Autobiographica	Royal Commission on Historical Manuscripts, *The Prime Ministers' Papers: W. E. Gladstone*, ed. John Brooke and Mary Sorensen (4 vols.; London: Her Majesty's Stationery Office, 1971–81): 1. *Autobiographica*; 2. *Autobiographical Memoranda, 1832–1845*; 3. *Autobiographical Memoranda, 1845–1866*; 4. *Autobiographical Memoranda, 1868–1894*
Bassett	*Gladstone to his Wife*, ed. A. Tilney Bassett (London: Methuen, 1936)
Bertie	David M. Bertie, *Scottish Episcopal Clergy 1689–2000* (Edinburgh: T & T Clark, 2000)
BL	British Library, London
Boase	Frederic Boase, *Modern English Biography: Containing many thousand concise Memoirs of Persons who have died since the Year 1850* (6 vols.; Truro: Netherton & Worth, 1892–1921)
Bodl.	Bodleian Library, Oxford
Chadwick	Owen Chadwick, *The Victorian Church* (2 vols.; 3rd edn.; London: Adam & Charles Black, 1971)
Chapeau	Alphonse Chapeau, 'La Vie anglicane de Manning' (unpub. doctoral thesis, Paris, Sorbonne, 1955)
CP	Chapeau Papers, Angers, France
DNB	*Dictionary of National Biography* (electronic source; Oxford: Oxford University Press, 2004–9)

DS	*Enchiridion symbolorum: definitionum et declarationum de rebus fidei et morum*, ed. Heinrich Denzinger and Adolf Schoenmetzer (Barcelona: Herder, 1965)
EHD	*English Historical Documents*, ed. Douglas C. Smith. All references are to vol. xii (1), 1833–74, ed. G. M. Young and W. D. Handcock (London: Eyre & Spottiswoode, 1956)
Foster	*Alumni Oxonienses: The Members of the University of Oxford, 1715–1886. Their parentage, birthplace, and year of birth, with a record of their degrees. Being the matriculation register of the University*, ed. Joseph Foster (4 vols.; Oxford and London: Parker, 1891)
GD	*The Gladstone Diaries*, ed. M. R. D. Foot and H. C. G. Matthew (14 vols.; Oxford: Oxford University Press, 1968–94)
Gibson	Edmund Gibson, *Corpus Juris Ecclesiastici Anglicani: Or, The Statutes, Constitutions, Canons, Rubricks and Articles, of the Church of England* (London: J. Baskett, 1713)
Gillow	Joseph Gillow, *A Literary and Biographical History, or Biographical Dictionary of the English Catholics from the Breach with Rome, in 1534, to the Present Time* (5 vols.; London: Burns & Oates, 1885)
Gleanings	W. E. Gladstone, *Gleanings of Past Years* (7 vols.; London: John Murray, 1879)
Hansard	*British Parliamentary Debates*, 3rd series, 1830–91
Later Gleanings	W. E. Gladstone, *Later Gleanings. A New Series of Gleanings of Past Years* (London: John Murray, 1897)
'Later Reminiscences'	MS notations by Henry Edward Manning, begun 'Vatican. 18 February 1878', preserved with Chapeau Papers, Angers, France
Lathbury	*Correspondence on Church and Religion of William Ewart Gladstone*. Selected and arranged by D. C. Lathbury (2 vols.; London: Macmillan, 1910)
LD	*The Letters and Diaries of John Henry Newman*, ed. Charles Stephen Dessain, Ian Ker, et al. (31 vols.; London: John Nelson; Oxford: Oxford University Press, 1961–2006)

Leslie	Shane Leslie, *Henry Edward Manning: His Life and Labours* (London: Burns, Oates & Washbourne, 1921)
Leslie transcript	Shane Leslie transcripts of Gladstone correspondence, preserved with CP, Angers, France
Liddon	Henry Parry Liddon, *Life of Edward Bouverie Pusey*, ed. J. O. Johnston and Robert J. Wilson (4 vols.; London: Longmans, Green, 1893–7)
Morley	John Morley, *The Life of William Ewart Gladstone* (3 vols.; London: Macmillan, 1903)
Morley transcript	John Morley transcripts of Gladstone correspondence preserved at St Deiniol's Library, Hawarden
NLS	The National Library of Scotland, Edinburgh
NLW	The National Library of Wales, Aberystwyth
Ornsby	Robert Ornsby, *Memoirs of James Robert Hope-Scott of Abbotsford, D.C.L., Q.C.* (2 vols.; London: John Murray, 1884)
PG	*Patrologiae cursus completus: seu Bibliotheca universalis, integra, uniformis, commoda, oeconomica, omnium SS. Patrum, doctorum, scriptorumque ecclesiasticorum, sive latinorum, sive graecorum, qui ab aevo apostolico ad aetatem Innocentii III (ann. 1216) pro latinis, et ad Concilii Florentini tempora (ann. 1439) pro graecis floruerunt. Series graeca* (166 vols.; Paris, 1857–65)
PHL	Pusey House Library, Oxford
Pitts	Pitts Theology Library, Emory University, Atlanta, Ga
PL	*Patrologiae cursus completus: seu Bibliotheca universalis, integra, uniformis, commoda, oeconomica, omnium SS. Patrum, doctorum, scriptorumque ecclesiasticorum, latinorum, sive graecorum, qui ab aevo apostolico ad aetatem Innocentii III (ann. 1216) pro latinis, et ad Concilii Florentini tempora (ann. 1439) pro graecis floruerunt. Series latina* (221vols.; Paris, 1844–64)
PP	British Parliamentary Papers
PRO	Public Record Office, London
Purcell	Edmund Sheridan Purcell, *Life of Cardinal Manning: Archbishop of Westminster* (2 vols.; London: Macmillan & Co., 1895; 2nd edn. 1896)

PurGl	Gladstone's annotations in his copy of Edmund Sheridan Purcell, *Life of Cardinal Manning: Archbishop of Westminster* (2 vols.; London: Macmillan & Co., 1895), preserved at St. Deiniol's Library, Hawarden
SDL	St. Deiniol's Library, Hawarden
SN	William Anderson, *The Scottish Nation; or, the Surnames, Families, Literature, Honours, and Biographical History of the People of Scotland* (3 vols.; Edinburgh: A. Fullarton, 1876)
Stenton	Michael Stenton, *Who's Who of British Members of Parliament* (2 vols.; vol. ii with Stephen Lees; Hassocks: Harvester, 1976–8)
Tanner	Norman P. Tanner, *Decrees of the Ecumenical Councils* (2 vols.; London: Sheed & Ward, 1990)

SECTION V

The Implications of Catholic Concerns

1. The Debate over Ward and Maynooth: October 1844–February 1845

441014mg

Lavington. Oct[ober] 14. 1844.

My dear Gladstone,

Since I wrote to you I have been ten days in Normandy, quietly enjoying myself in the Churches. I went from Rouen by Caen, Bayeux, St. Lo, Coutances, Arranches to Mt. S[t]. Michel & S[t]. Malo, and made a very pleasant sally.[a] On my return, I found your letter, & thank you truly for it.

Your view of the question, I put, is what I anticipated, and I feel satisfied that it is the right course. It may be difficult, & a fine matter.

This sad contest at Oxford is & will be fruitful of evil: & Hooks ill-starred letter[b] has left a mark nothing will efface. I have seen a private letter from Dalgairns,[c] who reflects Newman's mind, and the upshot of it is that, they accept this as a breach between themselves, & the 'Anglocatholics', as they call them. He says they have known the breach to be inevitable, & are glad that it has come from the other side $\kappa.\tau.\lambda.$[d] All this is to be lamented: and

[a] Manning was at Dieppe on 26 September 1844 where he wrote to his mother indicating that he was on his way to Rouen the following day and that he was meeting Henry Wilberforce to spend the remaining time with him. He returned home on 5 October, when he again wrote to his mother (Bodl. MS Eng. lett. c. 652, 489–92; cf. H. Wilberforce to Gladstone, 9 Oct. 1844 [BL Add. MS 44361, 262]).

[b] Hook's letter on the Vice-Chancellor election at Oxford appeared in *The Times*, 7 October 1844, 5c, and in the *English Churchman*, 10 October (641) with replies. The critical passage read: 'The number of persons who will protest [the election of Dr Symons as Vice-Chancellor] is, I apprehend, reduced very nearly to those who advocate the extreme opinions of Mr. Ward, and who form what is called the Romanizing party in the Church.' Cf. Hook's earlier letter of 15 December 1841 to Gladstone which criticized Tractarian activity (Stephens [1885], i. 130–7).

[c] Not located. John Dobrée Dalgairns (1818–76; *DNB*) studied at Exeter College, Oxford, joined Newman at Littlemore in 1842, and was received into the Roman Catholic Church, September 1845, later becoming an Oratorian priest.

[d] Etc.

seems as if things are ripening fast for some worse issue. It is a fault of every age to magnify its own events—& yet I cannot but feel that the English Church is entering upon a trial wholly new: and under conditions wholly changed. This makes our difficulties greater. What exact basis in the history of the last 300 years can we form upon? And when I look for the men to guide us, when had we fewer?

Have you read Ward's book?[e] It is the most Luther-like protest I have ever read:[f] and yet how sorely true is[1] his exposure of our miserable defects in all branches of theological science,[2] discipline, & practice. I feel to have settled down into the conviction that our only hope is in the next race of clergy. A devout, united, self-denying laity with an indevout, disunited, relaxed Clergy is impossible. And what are we doing to form a new race of Pastors? Literally worse than nothing. The Universities are labouring to debase the very standard of the Priestly & Pastoral character, while they profess to be providing Clerical Education. What can be more fatal than a proposal to prepare men for holy orders in a place where they offer the Holy Communion only so often, in every year, as will shield men from self excommunication? And the Academies are looked upon as the standard of truth, & devotion for the Church. All this comes of the blindness of the Episcopate to the real sores & wants of our system. I cannot refrain from saying this, when I see Bishops putting from them a duty which is almost identical with their highest functions. I mean that of rearing & ripening a body of Pastors under their own eye.

I suppose that our duty is to 'possess our souls in patience'.[g] But it is a perplexing dispensation when the Church cannot bear her diseases, & will not have her remedies.

---

[e] William George Ward, *The Ideal of the Christian Church Considered in Comparison with Ensuing Practice, containing a Defence of Certain Articles in the British Critic in Reply to Remarks on them in Mr. Palmer's 'Narrative'* (London: James Toovey, 1844). On the background to the controversy at the time see 431119mg.

[f] According to Wilfrid Ward, his father, William George Ward, met Manning for the first time on the afternoon after Ward's degradation. The two entered into a conversation in which Ward said that Lutheranism was the equivalent of atheism and Manning replied: 'The most Lutheran book I have ever read was called *The Ideal of the Christian Church*' (Ward [1889], 344n.). Manning had earlier expressed to Ward his reservations regarding the work. Note his letter to Ward on 15 February 1843 in which he asks for clarification on a statement Ward had made that 'the High Church theology "as an intellectual statement leads lower than Atheism itself" ' (Bodl. MS Eng. lett. c. 662, 21–2).

[g] Luke 21: 19.

I hope you have enjoyed your holiday. When you come up to London I shall try to see you.[h]

Meanwhile, with kindest regards to Mrs. Gladstone & my Godson, believe me

Yours very aff[ectionate]ly

H. E. Manning

P.S. You will find in Carlton Terrace a copy of some University Sermons.[i] More will be sent tomorrow.

H.E.M.

[[Pitts; Chapeau, 94, 149–50]]

441023mg

Oct[ober] 23. 1844.

Lavington.

Confidential

My dear Gladstone,

The Bishop gave his Charge yesterday.[a] There was nothing, under *limitations of my own*, that I could not receive.

But I suffered another person to request that it should be printed.

This is not according to the view I had originally taken in correspondence with you.

But when it came to the point I shrunk from the danger of compromising the perfect integrity of word & deed which I pray God I may be always[3] preserved in.

I feel sure that my limitations of his words the Bishop would not admit: & that [th]e popular understanding of his words w[oul]d be his & not mine.

What made this more than ever trying was that the Bishop addressed me in public in a tone of confidence & regard beyond all that I could have imagined from a man hitherto both distant, & reserved. To this I answered, & his reply went further. If ever there was a moment when it seemed ungenerous & ungrateful to do what I have done it was then. All that I can

---

[h] Gladstone had been at Fasque since 9 August 1844 (*GD* iii. 395). He returned to London 28 October (ibid. 409).

[i] Henry Edward Manning, *Sermons Preached before the University of Oxford* (Oxford: John Henry Parker; London: G. F. and J. Rivington, 1844c).

[a] See 440916mg.

recur to is the consciousness that I sacrificed all other thoughts & feelings to keep my conscience clear before God & man.

Today I have written the plainest & most open letter I c[oul]d write to the Bishop.[b] I do not inclose the copy to you because without his permission I told him I sh[oul]d not make it known.

It is a crisis in our relations: & will be decisive which way soever it turn.

Believe me, my dear Gladstone,
Your ever aff[ectionatel]y
H. E. Manning

P.S. I hope I have done something for the case you wrote of in your last letter.[c] You shall hear from me in a week about it. I sh[oul]d be most glad to serve such a purpose. I fear the training School proper is quite impossible: as the rules are very strict (of necessity). I am trying in Chichester.

H.E.M.

The Right Hon[oura]ble
W. E. Gladstone[4]

[[Pitts; Chapeau, 95, 151]]

[[On 2 November 1844 Gladstone informed Catherine of the postscript to Manning's 23 October letter: 'Manning has promised to let me know whether he can do any thing about Rebecca in a few days. I do not know whether there is any use in my seeing her forthwith—but if you think so either tell her to call any morning about ten or let me have her address' (SDL, Gladstone–Glynne MS 770, 50–1, 51). Three days later, on 5 November, before his reception of Manning's letter of the same day, Gladstone wrote to Catherine once more:

Today Rebecca Ayscough called & I had some conversation with her. As to religion she really has no particular leaning to the Methodists, and is simply in the state in which most other people are, that is without definite and clear convictions respecting the Church. She attends Church now, & would gladly continue to do so waiting further opportunity & information—

I have not heard from Manning but I have not much hope through him: & unless the Oak Farm Schools[d] were to afford her an opening I see nothing likely at present except service & as to service I know nowhere to look for an opening except our own, because we are the people that know most of her & ought therefore to take the risk rather than others. (ibid. 54–5, 54)]]

---

[b] The draft of Manning's letter is preserved in Bodl. MS Eng. lett. c. 653, 556–62 and is printed in the Addenda to this Section.

[c] On Gladstone's request see 441012gm.

[d] On the Oak Farm Schools, founded by the brick and iron works firm there, see *Minutes of the Committee of Council on Education, with Appendices, 1847–1848* (2 vols.; London: W. Clowes & Sons, 1848), ii. 135. On their eventual demise see 480312gm.

441105mg

Nov[ember] 5. 1844.

My dear Gladstone,

I think I could make the following arrangement for the young person you wrote about.

At a cost of about £ 18…a year (which is very little more than the Training School) she might lodge in a trustworthy house in Chichester, & receive the religious care of Mrs. Lockhart,[a] (mother of the poor man who joined the Roman Church) & instruction[5] from persons who carry on a school, of an upper kind, under Mrs. Lockhart's direction.[6] I think I c[oul]d find an elderly and steadfast person in whose house she would be under a salutary discipline.

But such a plan involves expence: & before I move further, I sh[oul]d like to know how you are disposed to consider of it.

The Training School is impossible.

I need not add that I would put her under the guidance of an excellent Pastor: & would at times, see her myself.

You will I know be glad to hear that I received from my Bishop a straightforward and exceedingly kind reply.[b] It was more than I could have expected & all I could wish. And our correspondence on business has fallen into its old channel, with if any change, a change to fuller confidence. This of course is grateful to me, as I felt that I had risked everything.

Strange rumours about Newman keep floating about. It is a terrible suspense: & makes one almost impatient.

In matters of practical judgment I feel more & more unable to think Pusey to be right. He is persevering, on a large scale, with R[oman] C[atholic] books of devotion: the end of which he seems blind to.[c]

Believe me,

Ever yours aff[ectionatel]y

H. E. Manning

The Right Hon[oura]ble
W. E. Gladstone

[[Pitts; Chapeau, 96, 152]]

---

[a] On Martha (Jacob) Lockhart and her son and daughter see 431127mg.

[b] For letter see Addenda to this Section.

[c] Manning took up the question of translations of Roman Catholic books in his correspondence with Pusey at this time. In a postscript to a letter written to Manning early in January 1845, Pusey responded to the issue. See Addenda to this Section.

441105gm[a]

Whitehall
Nov[ember] 5. [18]44.

My dear Manning

I should have written to you before but that I have been awaiting the further letter promised from you with respect to the young woman on whose case I wrote.[b] I think she is an excellent subject but feels deeply and painfully the want of regular means of help for her. However the more signal is the mercy by which God has thus far supported her.

From the report of your Bishop's Charge in the newspaper[c] I cannot doubt that your course though painful was right. The fact that you could put a sound construction on his language was not enough if it naturally bore an unsound one, especially in the case where the impression of the moment upon others was so much to be regarded.

I congratulate you on R[obert] Phillimore's appointment[d]—

I expect to leave town on Monday the 11th and return on Tuesday the nineteenth.[e]

Believe me aff[ectiona]tely yours
W. E. Gladstone

Venerable

Archdeacon Manning.

[[BL Add. MS 44247, 222–3; Morley transcript; cf. Chapeau, 307]]

[[On 6 November 1844 Gladstone wrote to Catherine, enclosing Manning's letter of the previous day: 'I send you a note from Manning about Rebecca which please to return. He has been very kind & has taken great pains—but I do not see that his plan would provide either for systematic training as a school teacher or for regular and steady occupation of any other kind. Pray tell me what you think' (SDL, Glynne–Gladstone MS 770, 56–7, 56).

On 8 November he wrote to Catherine again:

---

[a] 'Wrote to . . . Manning' (*GD* iii. 411).

[b] On the same day as he wrote this letter Gladstone 'saw Rebecca Ayscough' (ibid. 411).

[c] The *Charge* was published in *The Times*, 24 October 1844, 5j–6b. Following a discussion of the Chichester Training School and the poor, the Bishop reflected on the Tractarian movement, stating that its 'founders had no other intention at first than to raise a barrier against the threatening aspect with which the state appeared at the time to view the Church', that they went too far (the Editor indicates that the allusion is to Ward), and that he hopes that some of their usages might be corrected.

[d] Phillimore was appointed Chancellor of the Diocese of Chichester on 29 October 1844.

[e] Gladstone left for Hagley on 11 November and returned to London on 19 November 1844 (*GD* iii. 412, 413).

It appears to me that there is a difficulty about Manning's plan for Rebecca to which
you have not addressed viz. that it does not shew any means of constant occupation—
she would be a lodger in one home, would receive the religious care of a person in
another, and would receive instructions from persons in a third who carry on an
'Upper'[7] kind of school—now I rather incline to think that a system without the
regular & methodical routine of daily duty would however excellent & trustworthy the
persons be a dangerous one.... But if you think differently I am quite willing you
should do it but in that case I should ask you to complete it with Manning as I think it
would be rather offensive in me to accept his plan & express distrust of it—I am not
sure however how Rebecca w[oul]d take it: its indefiniteness as to occupation might
frighten her. However I write to Manning today to ask him how this w[oul]d be, and
ask him to answer me at Hagley. (SDL, Glynne–Gladstone MS 770, 60–1, 60)]]

441108gm[a]

London Nov[ember] 8. [18]44

My dear Manning

I think we could manage the affair of Rebecca Ayscough as far as money
is concerned but there is one difficulty that occurs to me & that is the want,
so far as I understand the plan you have so kindly concocted, not of any
occupation, but of steady regular and full occupation which seems to me
under the circumstances the first condition of safety—Would the persons
who carry on the school you mention be in a condition to give her instruction in such a way as to make her day's work, & this throughout this year?
You will I think understand me and be able to tell me how this is—as a
lodger I conclude she would have nothing to do, but if sufficient occupation
could be made up between learning as a pupil and assisting in housework or
needlework or any thing else, I think both my wife & her sister would be very
much for our availing ourselves of the opening you give.—

[8]Please answer me to Hagley, Stourbridge—

Again the rumour about Newman seems to have blown over—I do not
think any one can judge how short, or how long, this interval may be—

I have just been subscribing to what they call a μονή[b] or college at Leeds,
under Pusey's auspices.[c] It was intended I suppose to avoid any alarming
name but I suspect people will say μονὴ is the short for monastery.
However this I think is all right & unless they put a Romanising spirit

---

[a] 'Wrote to ... Manning' (ibid. 411).

[b] Residence, monastery; used by Tractarians as the term for monastic establishment.

[c] Following the death of his wife in 1839 Pusey was in regular correspondence with
Hook over the building of a church in Leeds as a memorial to her. By 1841 the project was
in place, but the building went slowly and the consecration of St Saviour's was finally held

into it nothing is more likely to allay the feverish thirst of that class of men which appears to be going over by driblets—

Is your Deans Sermon on receiving a Romish convert to be seen or is it a secret[d]— The narrative of Ciocci, reviewed in the Dublin, is curious[e]—

Ever aff[ectiona]tely yours

W. E. Gladstone

[[BL Add. MS 44247, 224–5; Morley transcript; cf. Chapeau, 307]]

[[On 9 November 1844, Gladstone wrote again to Catherine:

Manning writes[f] offering to come to C[arlton] H[ouse] T[errace] for a day on the 25th[g] if I am alone—which he can do very well. I have been subscribing money to an establishment in Leeds, connected with the new Church of Holy Cross [later, St Saviour's], which is to be somewhat like that Hook made known to us—& as is said under excellent direction. (SDL, Glynne–Gladstone MS 770, 62–3, 63)]]

on 28 October 1845. The Leeds work was the subject of a number of letters between Manning and Pusey in September, October, and November 1845 and again in January 1847 when difficulties arose as a result of secessions to Rome and continuing opposition to Puseyite practices there. (See PHL MS Manning–Pusey, Nos. 23, 24, 26, 34, and Bodl. MS Eng. lett. c. 654, 274, 280–1, 290–1; PHL MS, Liddon transcriptions, Pusey–Manning, Nov. 1845.) On St Saviour's see John Hungerford Pollen, *Narrative of Five Years at St. Saviour's, Leeds: to which is added, An Extract from the 'Christian Remembrancer' for January, 1850* (Oxford: J. Vincent, 1851), Liddon, ii. 466–514 and iii. 112–36, and Yates (1975).

    [d] George Chandler, Dean of Chichester Cathedral and Rector of All Soul's, Mary-Le-Bone, *A Sermon Preached in the Cathedral Church of Chichester, on the Occasion of Publicly Receiving into the Church a Convert [C. F. Viganti] from the Church of Rome* (Chichester: William Hayley Mason, 1843). Gladstone read the work on 24 November 1844 (*GD* iii. 413). As indicated in the Preface Viganti, born in 1813, had become a priest in the Franciscan Order in 1836, was laicized by Pope Gregory XVI, and travelled to Switzerland and France where he was a member of a French Protestant congregation for several years. On coming to England he was in communion with the Church of England for twelve months at Brighton. The Sermon concludes with a six-page 'Form for Admitting Converts from the Church of Rome, and such as shall renounce their errors'.

    [e] Raffaelli Ciocci, 'formerly a Benedictine and Cistercian Monk, Student and Hon. Librarian of the Papal College of San Bernardo alle Terme Diodeziane in Rome', *A Narrative of Iniquities and Barbarities Practiced at Rome in the Nineteenth Century* (London, 1844) was reviewed along with M. A. Tierny, *A Letter to the Very Rev. G. Chandler, D. C. L., Dean of Chichester, &c., Containing some Remarks on his Sermon Preached in the Cathedral Church of Chichester, on Sunday, Oct[ober] 15, 1843, 'on the Occasion of Publicly Receiving into the Church a Convert from the Church of Rome'* (London: C. Dolman, 1844), in *Dublin Review* 33 (Sept. 1844), 252–89. Gladstone began to read the Ciocci book on 5 November and completed it on 8 November 1844 (*GD* iii. 411–12).

    [f] Not located.   [g] See 441114gm.

441110mg

Nov[ember] 10. 1844.

My dear Gladstone,

I intended constant employment for Rebecca Ayscough without which I should have little hope of good. And I think it can be so managed, but will let you know more in detail before you decide.

You shall have a copy of the Dean's Sermon which alas, is no secret. The whole was an unsatisfactory affair. You see my name in the D[ublin] R[eview] in connection with L'Herminez.[a] I am sorry to say the writer of

[a] In his review of Chandler's *Sermon* (see 441108gm), the reviewer comments on the reception of Mr Viganti: 'the good people of Chichester seem to have a peculiar affection, a peculiar attraction, for the rejected of Catholicity'. Some time earlier a M. L'Herminez, a Cambray priest had gone to Rome, married, and worked as a teacher. 'Of course, his true character was there unknown, until he met with the high-church Archdeacon of Chichester, Mr. Manning; from whom we should have expected better things than encouragement to a violator of his ecclesiastical engagements' (255–6). L'Herminez's reception was reported in the *English Churchman* on 26 October (682) and 2 November 1843 (690; including the Bishop's comments at the time and details on the liturgy). See *LD* vii. 163 (Newman to Marriott, 8 Oct. 1839) and the Bishop of London's letter to Manning of 18 May 1840, stating that unless Herminez abjured the Church of Rome, he could not be accepted as a clergyman of the Church of England (Lambeth Palace, Blomfield Papers, 25: 33–4). Thereafter, Manning seems to have befriended the former Catholic priest, helping him gain a placement in the Lavington area. Defending his actions in a letter of 11 November 1842 he outlines his role in the affair thus:

Mr. L'Herminez resolution to come to England was taken, and executed unknown to me. He had been some weeks in England before I heard of it.

His renunciation of the Roman Communion, & reception into the Church of England were made unknown to me, & to my surprize when I heard it: for though I had known his opinions during my stay in Rome, respecting that portion of the Church, I did not know of his design of offering himself to be received in the English.

I am responsible for endeavouring to maintain him & his family, and for inducing him to seek employment at Chichester where, I believed, I had more measures than in any other place of aiding him. He has never been countenanced by me in speaking against the Roman Church. I have used my endeavours to prevent it.

Since his miserable fall, I have had no intercourse with him except so far as the Apostle commands Rom XII. 20. & in the avowed character of Pastor dealing with a professing penitent. It was I that extorted from him a confession of his guilt.

I am responsible for advising not more for his sake than for the sake of those he injured that his offences should not be made public. I am still of the same opinion. Since his offence, I have recommended him to no one, but on the contrary have watched against his admission into families.

Mr. Tierney's paragraph [in a letter sent to Manning] in which he speaks of 'sheltering', & of the motives which he imagines to lead to such a course, it is perhaps not unnatural he should write, especially as the above facts are unknown to him.

the Pamphlet knew better than he wrote. I had nothing to do with his admission into the English Church. It was all over before I so much as knew of it. But it suited Mr. Tierney's[b] purposes to write by insinuation, & he has misled the Reviewer.

I have not read ab[ou]t Ciocci but will look at it.

Ever yours affect[ionate]ly
H. E. Manning

The Right Hon[oura]ble
W. E. Gladstone
[[Pitts; Chapeau, 97, 152–3]]

441114gm[a]

Hagley
Nov[ember] 14. 1844.

My dear Manning

I waited for your answer to my letter before replying to your note of the 8th about the visit of the 25th[b]—my answer is that I shall be very glad to have you, only you must put up with very primitive fare as a housemaid is my cook and my rooms are clad in white sheets.

I have been writing an article on Ward's book,[c] avoiding almost entirely his theology but severely censuring his rash methods of decision & censure

---

I should have read his letter with more pleasure if it had not been tinged with a little feeling of suspicion, which though rational & venial, has led him to wrong some to whom he seems to refer. (BL Add MS 39948, 158–61)

   [b] See 441108gm.
   [a] 'Wrote to . . . Manning' (*GD* iii. 412).
   [b] Not located; Gladstone met with Manning on 26, 27, and 29 November 1844. Their second meeting dealt with the case of 'R. Ayscough', their third with Gladstone's article on Ward (*GD* iii. 415–16).
   [c] On 22 September 1844, Gladstone 'read Ward (& ruminated & wrote on him)' (*GD* iii. 402). The draft (see BL Add. MS 44683, 167–216, which includes sections removed in the debate over the publication) was developed into a full review, 'Ward's *Ideal of the Christian Church*', *Quarterly Review* 75 (Dec. 1844), 149–200 (see also *Gleanings* v. 81; on Gladstone's role as a *Quarterly Review* contributor see Parker [1955]). Gladstone was reading Ward from 29 September to 12 October (*GD* iii. 403–5). After meeting with Ward on 2 November and discussing Ward's *Ideal* with Rowland Williams the next day, Gladstone began to write on the volume on 5 November and continued to work on his article 13–19 November, sending it off on 20 November, and revising his draft on 24 November (*GD* iii. 411–13). See 441014mg above. Williams (1817–70), educated at King's College, Cambridge, elected a Fellow, 1839, and appointed a classical tutor, had opposed the union of the St Asaph and

without examination—I intend to offer it to the Quarterly but I should be very desirous to have your judgement upon it—

I am to be here all Monday—back to town please God on Tuesday morning.[d]

We await with interest the further information you promise respecting employment for Rebecca.

Ever aff[ectiona]tely yours
W. E. Gladstone

Venerable
Archdeacon Manning.

I think we have given you to understand clearly that Rebecca cannot be said to be neutral as to connection with the Church—so that nothing in that respect would be found ready made, everything is still to be done.

[[BL Add. MS 44247, 226–7; Morley transcript; Purcell, i. 295; cf Chapeau, 308]]

441115mg

Nov[ember] 15. 1844.
Lavington.

My dear Gladstone,

1. I send you a copy of the Deans Sermon, wh[ich] you may keep.
2. And also a reply from Mrs. Lockhart,[a] whose absence from home hinders the matter of Rebecca Ayscough. Mrs. Lockhart is at 31 Cadogan Place, & would communicate, if you like with you direct. You will see that she is naturally & rightly anxious on one point, on which you will be able to satisfy her—I mean the disposition of this young womans mind towards repentance: & with what confidence you could advise her admission into a family. Would you like to see Mrs. Lockhart in London?

Bangor bishoprics. In 1850 he was appointed Vice-President of St David's, Lampeter and Select Preacher at Cambridge, 1854–62, and was embroiled in a legal battle over heretical views because of his review of Bunsen's writing in *Essays and Reviews* (London: J. W. Parker, 1861). See *DNB* and Shea and Whitla (2000), *passim*.

[d] On 19 November 1844 Gladstone travelled '8 A. M.–3 P. M. Hagley to B[oard] of T[rade] by omnibus & Train & carriage' (*GD* iii. 413).

[a] Not located.

3. The third letter I send you in the same confidence in which I sent Archdeacon Marriotts first letter[9] some time ago.[b] You will see that it is a copy of a letter to the Archbishop of Canterbury detailing an interview with Lord Stanley.[c]

I wish to repeat that no one knows that I have sent this to you: & I look for no reply but the return of it: unless you like to express any view upon it. All I wish is to state the deep concern with which I look upon the subject. I am disposed to go great lengths in putting myself into the position from which a Politician may look at the subject, & to acquiesce in any securities which Government may reasonably take for the due discharge of Spiritual functions in the Chaplains appointed for the care of the Convicts. But there is a higher principle which must be first regarded, I mean the order of the Church from which those Chaplains derive their office, & under which alone their ministrations can be exercised. This is not a colonial, but an universal question for the Church of England. Nothing but the informal securities held by the Church at home, in the shape of public opinion, & the personal influence of its members, enables it to endure the radically vicious system under which its Clergy minister as Chaplains in Gaols & Poor Houses. Very little is wanting to open this whole question. I set nothing upon Lord Stanleys replies about changing the law, & about employing Wesleyans &c. They escaped in haste, or from inconsideration. A moments reflection would tell him what the attempt to substitute Wesleyans for the Clergy of the Church would produce, at home. It would be hard to find a matter so comprehensive in its appeal to first principles and so kindling to the highest & best feelings of the whole Church in England. He would lay a bond upon the conscience of every man to raise the most direct, and energetic opposition.

I will not say any more about this because to you it is quite needless: & because I have not a moments thought that Lord Stanley would venture on such a course. There would not be wanting men to counsel it, for I believe Stephen w[oul]d not stick to do so: but Lord Stanley has to look more afield than Stephen and he knows what w[oul]d be the political & religious consequences of a contest between the Church & the State on a principle which is no less than vital to the Church.

[b] See 440713mg.

[c] Not located. Stanley was at the time Secretary for War and the Colonies, a position Gladstone would undertake in December 1845.

Would to God, that at last Statesmen would deal openly, & generously with the Church. You know I am not blind to what may be said against it: but it is madness to go on as if the State were the salt to preserve the Church from corruption.

However this is enough for the present so I will come to an end.

Believe me,
Ever yours aff[ectionate]ly
H. E. Manning

The Right Hon[oura]ble
W. E. Gladstone
[[Pitts; Chapeau, 98, 153–4]]

441117gm[a]

Hagley Sunday
Nov[ember] 17. [18]44

My dear Manning

I can readily answer your challenge & Mrs. Lockhart's about Rebecca Ayscough—but you have had a great deal of trouble[10] about this matter, and I think my best course is to write to Mrs. Lockhart directly, giving the assurance she desires—& requesting her which I do to communicate further with you—

You will understand that we should much prefer for moral reasons her being in a situation where she should earn her own support or a part of it, if it were to be had—but on the score of money there is no difficulty—& I only wait for what you may announce.

Now as to Archdeacon Marriott's letter. I do not feel that it puts me in possession of all the facts of the case. You have cancelled (I fear) your engagement for the 25th but I hope that you may be in town about that time[b]—and perhaps you will then explain to me orally, or otherwise write, what are the points really at issue. You will readily believe I can have little hesitation in forming an opinion upon the alternative of employing Weslyans, but your object in naming this is not in order that opinions may pass from me to you, and I on my part am[11] very anxious to get a view of the case.

I have done my Article on Ward. It is to go to Lockhart but I cannot form an idea whether he will be afraid of it. Nothing but the publication of such a book would have put me in case to offer an article on such a subject to the Quarterly—I am very anxious you sh[oul]d see it. Believe me,

---

[a] 'Wrote to ... Manning' (*GD* iii. 413).   [b] See 441114gm.

Aff[ectiona]tely yours
W. E. Gladstone

I hope I have said how deeply and truly we are obliged by your kindness in
the matter of Rebecca.

Venerable

Archdeacon Manning

[[BL Add. MS 44247, 228–9; Morley transcript; Purcell, i. 295; cf. Chapeau, 308]]

441120mg

Nov[ember] 20. 1844.
Lavington

My dear Gladstone,

This week has been & is a busy one to me but I hope I may be able to be
in London on Monday next.[a] I shall have very great interest in going over
your review of Ward's Book.[b] It has mooted more in every way than any
book we have yet had.

I send you a most intensely & painfully interesting letter from Newman.
I am thinking of trying to get him to come to me simply to relax his mind if
he can.[c]

As to Archdeacon Marriotts letter I will endeavour to have the whole
case for you next week.

At this moment I have not time to write more, than to say that I shall
with great pleasure do all I can in the matter of Rebecca Ayscough, & am
glad you will communicate with Mrs. Lockhart.

Believe me,
Affect[ionate]ly yours
H. E. Manning

The Right Hon[oura]ble
W. E. Gladstone

[[Pitts; Chapeau, 99, 154–5]]

[Enclosure: Newman to Manning]

---

[a] 25 November 1844. See 441117gm.

[b] Manning considered the review with Gladstone between 9.30 and 11.30 on the
morning of 29 November 1844 (*GD* iii. 416).

[c] Newman's letter was sent in response to one from Manning of 13 November 1844 in
which Manning expressed concern over news he heard that Newman was ill. On 23 November 1844 Manning wrote, inviting Newman to Lavington, but the latter declined the following
day (*LD* x. 432–3: correspondence in Birmingham Oratory MS Newman–Manning).

Littlemore, Nov[ember] 16, [18]44.

My dear Manning

I am going through what must be gone through,—& my trust only is that every day of pain is so much from the necessary draught which must be exhausted. There is no fear (humanly speaking) of my moving for a long time yet. This has got out without my intending it, but it is all well.

As far as I know myself, my one great distress is the perplexity, unsettlement, alarm, scepticism, which I am causing to so many, and the loss of kind feeling and good opinion on the part of so many, known[12] and unknown, who have wished well to me. And of those two sources of pain, it[13] is the former is the constant, urgent, unmitigated one. I had for days a literal ache all about my heart, and from time to time all the complaints[14] of the Psalmist seem[15] to belong to me.

And, as far as I know myself, my one paramount reason for contemplating a change is my deep, unvarying conviction that our Church is in schism and my salvation depends on my joining the Church of Rome. I may use arguments *ad hominem* to this person or that, but I am not conscious of resentment, or disgust, at anything that has happened to me. I have no visions whatever of hope, no schemes of action, in any other sphere more suited to me. I have no existing sympathies with Roman Catholics. I hardly ever, even abroad, was at one of their services.—I know none of them. I do not like what I hear of them.

And then, how much I am giving up in so many ways.—and to me sacrifices irreparable, not only from my age, when[16] people hate changing, but from my especial love of old associations and the pleasures of memory.

Nor am I conscious of any feeling, enthusiastic or heroic, of pleasure in the sacrifice; I have nothing to support me here.

What keeps me yet is what has kept me long—a fear that I am under a delusion—but the conviction remains firm under all circumstances, in all frames of mind.

And this most serious feeling is growing on me, viz. that the reasons, for which I believe *as much* as our system teaches, *must* lead me to believe more, and not to believe more, is to fall back into scepticism.

A thousand thanks for your most kind and consoling letter, though I have not yet spoken of it. It was a great gift.

Ever yours affectionately,
John H. Newman

[[Purcell, i. 258–9; *Apologia* (Svaglic edn.), 206–7; *LD* x. 412–13: original owned by George Barton, Worcester, Mass., a photostat of which is preserved in the Birmingham Oratory.]]

[[On 21 November 1844 after receiving it, Gladstone sent the Newman letter to Catherine as he had others:

I inclose for your perusal another letter of N[ewman']s which Manning has sent me: it removes immediate alarm, but confirms that which is ulterior—remember it is strictly secret & send it back to me by return of post. But it is melancholy to see so great a mind pressed in such a manner: it is however the letter of a great man. (SDL, Glynne–Gladstone MS 770, 66–7, 66)]]

441123gm[a]

Whitehall
Nov[ember] 23. [18]44.

My dear Manning

I return to you N[ewman]'s letter & need hardly specify with what deep & what painful interest I have read it. In a recent note to me he has disclosed a small part of the same feeling[b]—this you shall see & hear about when you come up—

---

[a] 'Wrote to . . . Manning' (*GD* iii. 414).

[b] Newman had written to Gladstone on 12 November 1844 apologizing for not taking up a matter concerning which Gladstone had questioned him. It was not, he wrote, 'as if I had not continually had the subject in mind—but on such very grave and anxious matters I should be much gratified if I could suggest anything as a subject for your reflection.' He was 'much tired,' he wrote, with seeing through the printing of his *Athanasius* 'and, if it is not impertinent to state a matter so personal, I fear my spirits are just now a little affected, by the continued or rather continuous attacks which have been made upon me for so many years, and from so many quarters at once' (BL Add. MS 44361, 286–7, 286; cf. *LD* x. 420). Gladstone responded on 16 November:

Hagley Stourbridge
Nov[ember] 16.1844

My dear Mr. Newman

It was I must own too much to expect from you that you should devote to the subject of my letter the time and thought necessary for the solution of the great problems it involves. I feel very sincerely obliged by the kindness with which you entertained it, and it will be a great gain to me to use it if any time you give us the opportunity of testing and of rectifying the conclusion that under her actions of daily experience are fixing themselves in my mind by any thoughts of yours.

The subject however of your own mental suffering under a course of continued attacks and imputations, by touching upon which you have (permit me to say) honoured me, is one of so deep an interest that rather than pass it by in silence I must risk the appearance at least of obtrusiveness.

In the sphere with which I am conversant I do not think there is an auspicious person who does not during his active career receive in above fifty fold more than in commendation and encouragement: and it is ever particularly characteristic of that sphere, that no small part of the whole obloquy comes, & under the conditions of our constitution must come from alienated or suspecting friends. But public men look for their earthly reward in the ultimate verdict of the community upon their motives and their acts.

Do not suppose for a moment that I mean to compare the trial in this case (of which also I speak more as an observer than a participant) with yours: but however it may be absolutely less, does not the reward also fall short in more than a curriculum proportion.

The servants of the public are treated like those of individuals: who blame them for faults from hour to hour, but early praise them at all until they are gone, & thus memory does them justice.

Clearly one material difference which is in their favour for the moment—they are usually supported by a party, or by a section of a party: but this kind of support it has been the direct tendency of your own teaching to discourage—you have yourself therefore lessened the number of the visible signs of sympathy, regard, & reverence: but the substance though latent is I should hope greater & not smaller on that account.

I will not however pursue this further, for although I confine myself to the region [illegible word] motives, even there I feel my words imply presumption. But there can be no sufficient reason, I think, to prevent my simply expressing as one among thousands of members of the church our sentiments towards you. I write without the advantage of reading your works in the light of your example: with a far more imperfect sense of them than I might and ought to have attained: and under the difficulty that I am able to follow you without particular services. But I give utterance to the sense of many, of many whose names you may never have heard, in fervently acknowledging that you have laid upon us a debt that can not easily be overstated, & can never be cancelled. Nothing would cause me deeper or more permanent pain, than if in the course of my own perhaps rash dealings in these matters, I should have added either by acts, or by words, or by unbefitting silence, one grain to your anxieties: and it is a much more material reflection, and one which I trust may not be evil of emulation, that many (as I at least am persuaded) of those to whom you have been a messenger of good work among their duties to the Church & God to offer up constant prayer for you: prayer which surely has reward and still receives its answer both as respects yourself, and wherein in the clear though chequered progress of the work to which your life has been described.

Pray for us if you can, & interpret with indulgence this intrusion for which you have yourself given the occasion though I will say a warrant.

Believe me my dear Mr. Newman
Most sincerely yours
W. E. Gladstone

Rev. J. H. Newman (Birmingham Oratory MS Newman–Manning)

Newman replied, 18 November, commenting on his situation: 'I do not think I should mind the attacks of ever so many, if I had anything to fall back upon. But for a long time past I have nothing—I cannot fall back upon Bishops, or upon rubrics, or upon Articles, or upon Reformers, or upon our theology, or upon usage. Nothing present, nothing past, nothing in books serves as an appeal—and thus I must stand by myself or seek external support. It is not the clamour against me that troubles me in itself; Dî me terrent, et Jupiter hostis' [The gods frighten me, and Jupiter, the enemy: Virgil, *Aeneid*, 12. 895. Cf. use in *Apologia* (Svaglic edn.), 158]. This feeling has for a long while made me wish to lay down my arms and keep to myself—though it could not lead to anything beyond this (BL Add. MS 44361, 290–1; *LD* x. 420).

You should not fail to read Oakeleys remarkable letter in the English Churchman: he calls Ward's a wonderful book[c]—but I confess I think it partly wonderful in a different sense for its temerity and harsh judgments upon insufficient grounds. The $\_\theta os$[d] of it is, to me, very very far below that of Oakeley or of Newman.

When do you come up? I *may* be out of town Thursday, or Friday, or both—Next[17] Saturday evening to Monday morning I *must* be at Windsor.[e] Do not dream of coming to satisfy me but I have much more to say than I can discharge in such a scrape of time as alone I can vindicate for writing to you from the dense crowd of other occupations—I am at this moment hard pressed— By the bye I see you speak of Monday: after one I fear I shall be engaged until late at night[f]—but either then or the next morning we[18] may talk.

Lockhart[g] inserts my article: but has certain amendments to suggest. I look much for your aid about it. I have done it God knows conscientiously—& I think Mr. Ward deserves to be well whipped for his mode of going to work: my object is while handling that sharply, to deal gently with his opinions & to say nothing that can estrange his friends.

[c] Frederick Oakeley, 'Letter to a Roman Catholic Friend', 18 November 1844, *English Churchman*, 21 November, 744: 'that wonderful book, the "Ideal of a Christian Church"!' On 23 November Gladstone wrote Catherine: 'Manning comes up on Monday [25 November]. . . . Oakeley's letter is very remarkable: far far above the tone of Ward's I think, and though strong here & there how infinitely gentler and more modest. He *does not give up* the historical & ecclesiastical argument—and by no means builds upon conscience in W[ard']s manner' (SDL, Glynne–Gladstone MS 770, 70–1, 71). Note Gladstone's annotation 'no' to Purcell's remark that Oakeley had been 'an intimate friend' of Gladstone's 'from their Oxford days until his conversion in 1845' (PurGl i. 314).

[d] Moral disposition.

[e] Gladstone was in London at the time. On Friday, 24 November 1844, he met Catherine at the train, intending to go with her to Windsor, but the appointment was postponed (*GD* iii. 416; Morley, i. 273).

[f] On 23 November 1844, Gladstone indicated to his wife that Manning was coming to London 'on Monday [25 November]', but he was occupied on that day, as he notes to Manning, from 12.30 a.m., with Board of Trade, Cabinet meetings, and a dinner in the evening with Sir Robert Peel (*GD* iii. 415).

[g] John Gibson Lockhart (1794–1854; *DNB*), editor of the *Quarterly Review*, was the son-in-law and biographer of Walter Scott and the future father-in-law of James Hope.

I wonder what these Oxford wiseacres will do with him. After the affair of Pusey's Sermon[h] one can not but tremble: but may God avert mischief.

Ever aff[ectiona]tely yours

W. E. Gladstone

I have not yet been civil enough to thank you for your Sermons:[i] I am sorry to say I still look *forward* to reading them.

[[BL Add. MS 44247, 230–1; Morley transcript; Purcell, i. 259, 295; cf. Chapeau, 308–9]]

441124mg

Lavington. Nov[ember] 24. 1844

My dear Gladstone,

I will come to you at ½ p[as]t 9 Tuesday Morning, if on getting to London I do not find a letter fixing that hour for another engagement.

Oakeleys letter is remarkable. There is much good in it.

I have written trying to persuade Newman to come to me & stay awhile at Lavington.[a]

The Oxford people have need to look very sharp at the work they are about: or they will infallibly do mischief. I really think Puseys sermon was open to a friendly & fair criticism, which it w[oul]d have met with if they had not outraged heaven & earth.

Ever yours affect[ionate]ly

H. E. Manning

P.S. If you have written anything lately in the English Churchman I found you out.[b]

H.E.M.

The Right Hon[oura]ble
W. E. Gladstone[19]

[[Pitts; Chapeau, 100, 155]]

[[On Tuesday, 26 November 1844, Gladstone met with Manning as arranged: '9½–1 Conv[ersation] with Manning' (*GD* iii. 415). On the same day Gladstone wrote to

---

[h] On Pusey's University Sermon, *The Holy Eucharist a Comfort to the Penitent. A Sermon Preached before the University, in the Cathedral Church of Christ, in Oxford, on the Fourth Sunday after Easter* (Oxford: John Henry Parker, 1843), and the controversy thereafter, see Introduction, pp. xlviii ff.

[i] On 1 December 1844 Gladstone finished reading Manning's *University Sermons* (*GD* iii. 416; see 441014mg) which he had begun on 25 November (ibid. 414).

[a] On Manning's invitations see Enclosure in 441202mg.

[b] Reference perhaps to the *English Churchman*, 24 November 1844, 746, which carried a letter dated 18 November 1844 and signed 'Conformity and Uniformity', deploring those who oppose 'innovations' and 'novelties', and commenting that the terms are not applicable to 'a return to the rules of the Church'.

Catherine: 'Manning was with me all this morning: he is well, & is to come back tomorrow, & to see Rebecca Ayscough when I hope that matter will be wound up' (SDL, Glynne–Gladstone MS 770, 77–8, 78; see also Morley, i. 273). On 27 November he noted in his Diary: 'Saw Manning—R. Ayscough' (*GD* iii. 415) and on the same day reported the meeting to Catherine: 'Manning saw Rebecca at our house today when I came away. I am to see him again on Friday morning. He has got my article in type to look at. It is fearfully long—& must be abridged' (SDL, Glynne–Gladstone MS 770, 79–80, 80). The meeting on Friday, 29 November occurred as planned: 'Saw Manning 9½–11½ on my Article &c.' (*GD* iii. 416).]]

441201mg

Lavington. Dec[ember] 1. 1844.

My dear Gladstone

1. The inclosed letter from Mrs. Lockhart will settle all about Rebecca. She may come as soon as you will. I hope all will succeed to our wishes.

2. The passage ab[ou]t our Indian Empire in Wards Book is the first half of p. 388.[a]

3. The inclosed letter of Newmans is sad—it shews that things are shaping themselves into definite measures: & that he is preparing for the last step.

Also it is a warning to you & to me to make up our minds as to the relation of Ward & the University.

I have no time to write more, though I have two or three matters to add. One is ab[ou]t your sentence on desuetude, custom & law &c.[b]

But I can only add that I shall be ready to do anything you desire ab[ou]t Rebecca Asycough's journey, if I can be of use.

Believe me,
Ever yours aff[ectionatel]y
H. E. Manning

[a] '...when the most grave and serious doubts have been entertained, whether the principles on which our Indian Empire has been acquired, or on which it is retained, are justifiable on grounds of Christian morality, or whether we are not, as a nation, daily committing a grievous sin in our demeanour towards the subjects of that Empire; any such conception, as the duty of a national Church to protest (if so be) against a national sin, seems never to have practically found admittance into the mind of either Church or nation' (W. G. Ward, *Ideal* [1845], 388). Note Gladstone's response in his article: 'In another place Mr. Ward intimates that, if we had a pure Church, it is probable that there would have been an ecclesiastical inquiry into the means by which we have acquired and by which we hold our Indian empire (p. 388)' (Gladstone, 'Ward's *Ideal*', 167; *Gleanings*, v. 113).

[b] Sentence appears to have been removed in final version of Gladstone's article.

The Right Hon[oura]ble
W. E. Gladstone[20]
[[Pitts; Chapeau, 101, 155–6]]
[Enclosure: Mrs Lockhart to Manning, undated]
My dear Archdeacon

I have just had a conversation with Mrs Jardine about Rebecca Ays-cough and she is perfectly willing to undertake the charge and I am sure you would greatly approve the very right & Christian principles by which she is activated in doing this—She thinks that 5 £ a quarter would pay for her board lodging & schooling and if she finds her useful in the house and family she might afterwards be able to require less—Mrs Jardine will willing *pay* her for any needle work she may be able to do, and this money might be used for clothing. I have agreed with Mrs Jardine that she is to be employed in any way in which her own daughters assist and as they have no servant they will of course be fully occupied. I should add that she is no *to serve in the* [*sic*] I hope at any time—If Mrs Jardine is informed of the day Rebecca is to arrive she will meet her at the Coach—I need not tell you that I have known Mrs. Jardine very well for these years and in circumstances of great trial and have the very highest dependence in her sense & principles.

Believe me dear Mr. Archdeacon
Yours gratefully & affectionately
M. Lockhart

[[Bodl. MS Eng. lett. c. 663, 210–11]]
[Enclosure 2: Newman to Manning[c]]

Littlemore. Nov[ember] 24. 1844

My dear Manning

Nothing should I like better, but it is not possible now. We are so few here, that I cannot run away, were I inclined. Advent too is coming—and after Christmas I have already settled to go to Mrs Bowden at St. Leonard's.[d]

Since I wrote, I have been obliged to go to Wootten[e]—but I believe he has already set right the immediate occasion of my doing so. I know I am not quite well, but I have had a very trying year, or at least six months.

---

[c] In answer to Manning's invitation to Newman on 23 November 1844 that he come for a rest to Lavington (Birmingham Oratory MS Newman–Manning).

[d] Elizabeth Bowden (1805–96), the wife of John William Bowden (1798–1844; *DNB*), was a strong supporter of Newman. She converted to the Roman Catholic Church in 1846.

[e] Dr John Wootten (d. 1847), educated at Balliol College, Oxford, D.Med., 1826, was a physician in Oxford and active supporter of the Tractarians (Foster).

My intention is, if nothing comes upon[21] me, which I cannot foresee, to remain quietly in statu quo[f] for a considerable time, trusting that my friends will kindly remember me and my trial in their prayers. And I should give up my fellowship sometime before anything further took place.

But talking of fellowship, it may give up me, for, I suppose, our Provost w[oul]d make what use he can of the new Hebdomadal act against Ward. It is said to be very strong, but will not be published until February. I suppose Convocation will be called in.

Ever y[ou]rs affectionately

John H. Newman

[[*LD* x. 433: Birmingham Oratory MS Newman–Manning, No. 21; *Apologia* (Svaglic edn.), 207]]

441202gm[a]

Whitehall

Dec[ember] 2. [18]44.

My dear Manning

I return Newman's letter. It is a step in advance, towards the precipice: but it still remains impossible to say how many more paces may remain between him & its edge.

Friday has passed:[b] but I do not see in the newspapers that there has been any publication at Oxford. God grant they may keep straight: but I have no confidence in the judgment of the Heads from the extraordinary maladroitness of their previous steps.

Not knowing anything of the Chichester Coaches I have been rather puzzled to find out what would be the proper conveyance: & I may not have chosen right but I have desired her[c] to go down by the 'Duke of Richmond' at 9 on Wednesday morning,[d] & have written to Mrs. Lockhart to request that she may be met.[e]

---

[f] In my present state.

[a] 'Wrote to . . . Manning—Mrs Lockhart—R. Ayscough' (*GD* iii. 416).

[b] 29 November 1844 at a meeting of the Oxford College Heads; rumours had been circulating since October that the Heads were to censure Ward's *Ideal*.

[c] Rebecca Ayscough.

[d] 4 December 1844.

[e] Letter not located.

From the expression 'schooling' I think there may be some misunderstanding—but perhaps it refers to branches of teaching beyond those which are merely primary.

Ever aff[ectiona]tely yours
W. E. Gladstone

Venerable
Archdeacon Manning
I retain Mrs. Lockhart's letter which I think you intended me to do.
[[BL Add. MS 44247, 232–3; Morley transcript; cf. Chapeau, 308[b]]]

441203gm[a]

Private

Whitehall
Dec[ember] 3. [18]44

My dear Manning

Here is a curious note from Lockhart throwing me over. I am however one of those soldiers who do not know when they are beat: and I have written an answer[b] to say that I do not wish to pronounce upon *Mr. Ward's* position: but seek three things—to show

1. That the process of mobbing people out by invective & *private* interpretations is bad.

2. That the Ch[urch] of E[ngland] does not make assent to the proceedings of the Reformation a term of communion—

3. That before even judicial proceedings in one sense, due consideration should be had, what judicial proceedings in another sense consistency may entail, if that game be begun—

I may have to act before I can hear from you: the pinch is this that I fear there is no other medicine for me worth having—I cannot stand the F[oreign] & C[olonial Quarterly] any longer: my own writings are leaden enough but the platina of that Review would sink even cork.

---

[a] 'Wrote to . . . Manning' (*GD* iii. 417).

[b] Not located. On 18 December 1844 Lockhart wrote to Gladstone acknowledging receipt of a 'packet', indicating that Gladstone's article would need to be cut, and apologizing for the delay in writing since he had been ill. See also Lockhart to Gladstone 21 December 1844 and 6 January 184 (BL Add. MS 44237, 371–6).

There is no reason for submitting to all degrees of mutilation: but as at present minded, I shall be compliant in details[22] if he will let me retain the argument (2) and certainly not otherwise.

Pray advise me for the chance of being in time—& say whatever occurs—

I imagine L[ockhart] *has been advised* since he wrote his first note.

Ever aff[ectiona]tely yours
W. E. Gladstone

Venerable Archdeacon Manning

Pray weigh L[ockhart']s words well. The problem is what residuum is sufficient to make it right to go on? and something depends on this, whether I should have the right *subsequently to publish entire* in a separate form. Might I offer L[ockhart] free scope on those terms?

[[BL Add. MS 44247, 234–5; Morley transcript; Lathbury, i. 307–8; cf. Purcell, i. 296, Lathbury, i. 305]]

[Enclosure]

(copy) Mr Lockhart to Mr Murray

Dec[ember] 2. 1844.

My dear Murray,[c]

I dare say both you, and still more Mr. Gladstone, have been thinking me very negligent in not communicating sooner on the subject of the article on Ward. Of course it was necessary for me to study not only the article (which I could not do till it was in type) and the Book, which I had but hastily read on its first appearance, and finally the Articles & Canons of the Church themselves—very seriously—before I could venture to submit my suggestions as to a paper so distinguished by every literary merit, and evincing such profound thought on most momentous topics.

I have now endeavoured to do all this, under a very painful sense of my own inadequacy for such a task; and I am extremely concerned to say that in my opinion the Quarterly Review could not adopt what I fear may have been a very principal part in Mr. Gladstone's own view, of the article on Mr. Ward.

The question whether a man of his opinions holding his position in the Church & the University ought to withdraw from the Church of England is one of his own conscience.

The question whether such a man, so placed, as an Instructor of youth, ought or ought not to be expelled or censured, is a question for the

---

[c] For Gladstone's reply to Murray, see Lathbury, i. 306–7.

Authorities of the Church and the University. I cannot think the Q[uarterly] R[eview] could enter into the discussion of this question without laying itself open—as a journal conducted almost entirely by laymen—to a sort of censure which it would be very unwise for us to provoke. If Mr. G[ladstone] were willing to let the opening paragraphs be modified somewhat, and the concluding disposition on Mr. Wards position be omitted, I am sure his Article would be not only a prodigious ornament to the Review, but productive of vast good to the Church and the public mind. In this case I should still have not a few alterations in phraseology to suggest in the review part; but I am so much afraid that what I must in conscience omit is what the writer would not consent to my omitting, that until you shall have found an opportunity of submitting my general notion, and ascertaining in what light Mr. G[ladstone] regards it, it would be idle and presumptuous in me to go into the minor details.

Sincerely yours
(signed) J. Lockhart

[[BL Add. MS 44247, 236; Morley transcript]]

441204mg

Lavington. Dec[ember] 4. 1844.

My dear Gladstone,

You did not tell me to send back the copy of Lockhart's letter. I therefore keep it for further thoughts. But I write at once to give what I can.

I think Lockhart's note is intended to express the σκληρόν μαλθακῶς,[a] & that he proposes terms which he knows pretty well you cannot come into.

The effect of your article, without the last division, would be highly censorious, & repulsive and I think would do great harm, (1) as a mere article, and (2) still more as coming from you. Your Article on the Prospects of the Church I take as the *Ethical* basis on which you may rest your present censure without driving Ward & his like from you. But if the *protective* part of it be cut off it will cancel your last attempt in the F[oreign] & C[olonial] Quarterly.[b] This in a general way.

But as a question of truth, & principle I think it most important to get well & strongly stated the fact that assent to the Reformation is no term of Communion. I conceive that this is wholly remitted to the individual conscience: and the person[23] remanded to the judgment of God: e.g. at

---

[a] To speak hard words softly. Sophocles, *Oedipus at Colonos*, 774.
[b] 'Present aspect of the Church'. See 431030gm.

the time of the Reformation, & in[24] the 11th year of Q[ueen] Elizabeth no layman that had the will to stay in the Communion of the E[nglish] Church was cast out.[c] They that left us went out of themselves: They that would abide were suffered to abide without scrutiny as to their interior opinions. I know of no terms of lay-communion, but the Apostles Creed, which is the condition of reception into the Church, & a good life, which is the condition of approaching the Altar. The superadding of terms is precisely what we complain of in the Roman Church.

The question of what Lockhart ought or ought not to publish in the Q[uarterl]y R[eview] is distinct from the question what *you* ought or ought not suffer him to publish from your hand. It must be known to be yours, & on you, and through you on, in proportion to your hold on certain minds, it will recoil on the Church. My notion therefore is

1. That I would concede almost any amount of mutilation in detail.
2. That I would concede no mutilation of the *whole as a whole*, in its part, *relations & proportions*, & *balance*.

On this depends the whole character of the Article & of the impression it will make.

In saying this I do not speak of the Philosophy of conscience, which I could wish you to work out more fully: & not to put your view in jeopardy by a narrow exhibition of it.

But by this time you have probably decided the matter.

As to publishing the Article elsewhere or in a separate form, it seems to me that you would no longer be free to do so if Lockhart were to publish it in any form.

And the mischief I have supposed would be done by Lockhart's act: & would compromise the good of anything you could do afterwards. Would the [Chris]t[ia]n Remembrancer suit you?

I think there can be no doubt that he had been advised. The premisses he gives of Articles & Canons are vague enough: and work enough for a fortnight.

Ever affect[ionate]ly yours
H. E. Manning

The Right Hon[oura]ble
W. E. Gladstone
[[Pitts; Chapeau, 102, 156–7]]

---

[c] That is, following the 1569 revolt (with the support of Pope Pius V) against Elizabeth I to reinstate Roman Catholicism in England, and the Pope's bull, 'Regnans in excelsis', excommunicating Elizabeth in 1570.

441206gm[a]

Whitehall

Dec[ember] 6. [18]44.

My dear Manning

It costs me no effort to thank you for your valuable letter—for I had substantially arrived at its conclusions before I read it, & I was much fortified in them by your concurrence. I saw Lockhart yesterday and likewise I have performed upon the paper that most irksome labour of modifying & in particular places rewriting[b]—the basis of our concordat is that my argument is to be conferred to the case of simple communion and that I am to let alone[25] the questions connected with the special obligations of subscription[c]—

In some respects he has improved the article by his remarks which in general were very acute. In others I am conscious that it has lost: still I think that on the whole it will carry quite as much pith as the readers of the Quarterly will bear, and though it does not represent my entire mind upon the subject, yet neither does it misrepresent it: and I retain at least the seed of everything I had said or could say—

At the same time we may break down after all when the time for considering the revises arrives—we thought however yesterday that we understood one another—

Lockhart had consulted no one—this I have set him at liberty to do.

---

[a] 'Wrote to...Manning' (*GD* iii. 417).

[b] Gladstone 'Spent most of the evening [of 4 Dec. 1844] in carefully reviewing my article in determining on the practicality of meeting Lockhart's terms', and on 5 December he was 'Busy much of the day in a visit to Lockhart & correcting & modifying my article at home' (*GD* iii. 417). Following the meeting and Gladstone's revisions, relations between the two men improved. See Lockhart's comments on 18, 19, and 21 January 1845 on the *From Oxford to Rome* article (BL Add. MS 44237, 371–4) and on 6 and 10 January 1845 on a later article by Gladstone on Blanco White (ibid. 375–7; 'Life of Mr. Blanco White [by himself]', *Quarterly Review* 76 [June 1845], 164–203; repr. *Gleanings*, ii. 1–64).

[c] Note Gladstone's comments in the final form of his article: 'It is not necessary to enter in this place upon the question, what is or is not consistent with Subscription to the Articles. For, in the first place, that is a matter for the cognisance of constituted tribunals. The subject is too grave, especially under present circumstances, to be considered except in full detail; and as it is out of our power so to deal with it, we hold it an absolute duty to refrain alike from pronouncing and from insinuating an opinion upon it, in the hope that it will be reserved entire for its proper judges' (Gladstone, 'Ward's *Ideal*', 190–1; *Gleanings*, v. 153).

The main difficulty now[26] is the length. He will not consent to part with any of the discussion on conscience:[d] and I cannot tell where else to prune materially—

He is much struck with the talent of Ward's book.

Ever aff[ectiona]tely yours
W. E. Gladstone

Venerable
Archdeacon Manning

Keep the copy. I have shown my corrected proofs to Northcote[e] whose judgment I think acute and sound—& he approves.[f]

[[BL Add. MS 44247, 237–8; Morley transcript; Lathbury, i. 308–9; cf. Chapeau, 308 [b]]]

441220mg

Lavington. Dec[ember] 20. 1844.

Private

My dear Gladstone,

Let me know when you can what you have to say on the following first thoughts about this Oxford Statute.[27]

First & generally, I see[28] no greater felicity in these than in the former proceedings of the Hebdomadal Board.[a29]

They propose—

---

[d] That is, sect. III of the eventual article: Gladstone, 'Ward's *Ideal*', 181ff.; *Gleanings*, v. 138ff.

[e] Gladstone wrote to Northcote on 17 and 19 December 1844 (*GD* iii. 419). Stafford Henry Northcote (1818–87; *DNB*), educated at Balliol College, Oxford, served as Gladstone's private secretary as President of the Board of Trade, financial secretary to the Treasury, 1859, President of the Board of Trade, 1866, and continued to hold senior Parliamentary posts, serving as Chancellor of the Exchequer, 1874–80, Leader of the Commons, 1880–5, and Foreign Secretary, 1886–7.

[f] On 6 December 1844 Gladstone notes 'Completed my revision & launched my art[icle] once more—taking Northcote's opinion on it' (*GD* iii. 417).

[a] Manning's reference is to the statement by the Vice-Chancellor, Symons, issued on 13 December 1844 ('Whereas it is notoriously reputed and believed throughout the University that a book entitled "The Ideal of the Christian Church" . . .' [Oxford: Baxter, 1841]). For details see Introduction.

I. First as to[30] Ward.

    (1) To pronounce certain parts of[31] his book inconsistent with the Articles.

    (2) To attaint him of bad faith.

    (3) To deprive him of his degrees.

II. Next as to[32] subscription.

    (1) To declare the sense in wh[ich] the Articles are to be subscribed.[33]

    (2) to give the Vice Chancellor a standing ordeal to be used at discretion.

Now as to Ward.

I will reserve (1) & (3) as the only real points. All the rest of the proceedings seem to me false or mischievous.[34]

The (2d) I cannot affirm.[35] It is as bad as Wards own treatment of the Reformers. He has invoked it on himself, & is an example of 'With what measure ye mete &c.'[b] I believe him[36] to be a boisterous, honest Lutheran.[c37]

Even tho' I w[oul]d[38] go all lengths with[39] (1) & (3) I w[oul]d not vote for them in combination with (2).

Next as to Subscription.

The Statute is either equivalent[40] to the declarations of the Church on this point:[41] or it says less[42] or more.

It seems to me therefore to be[43] either needless, or dangerous.

The preface to the Articles says they shall be taken in the 'true' 'usual' 'literal' 'plain'[44] 'grammatical' sense.[d45]

I know of no other criteria *given by the Church* to fix their meaning—or their *original*, i.e. *actual* sense.

And I know of no tribunal confident to add either new *criteria*, or new & *living expositions* but the Church in Synod.[46]

The Statute goes on to say[47] 'and now are proposed by the University'.

What[48] is that *University* sense? How & where declared? Where lodged? How secured from fluctuations?[49]

---

  [b] Matt. 7: 2.

  [c] See 441014mg.

  [d] '...though some differences have been raised, yet We take comfort in this, that all Clergymen...agree in the true, usual, literal meaning of the said Articles....And that no man hereafter shall either print, or preach, to draw the Article aside any way, but shall submit to it in the plain and full meaning thereof, and...shall take it in the literal and grammatical sense' (Declaration to Articles of Religion, Book of Common Prayer).

They seem to think that they have[50] something like the crown which never dies?

All this seems to me headlong work.

And if this is bad, the ordeal is worse.[51] How do I know in what sense Ogilvie & Hampden, Routh & Hawkins agree to propose the articles for my subscription?[52]

So much by way of objection.

The more I think about[53] it the more these principles seem to commend themselves[54] to me.

1. That the Church of England repels no one[55] holding Roman Doctrine[56] inwardly from her Communion.

2. That in proposing Articles for subscription she takes the *only* security *possible in the first instance,* ag[ain]st admitting persons minus recte sentientes[e] *among* her *teachers.*

3. That so long as they do not molest her by *propagating* any thing at variance with[57] the 'full usual,[58] and literal' meaning of the Articles, she does not molest them for their interior opinions.[59]

4. That if they do molest her, she may animadvert on them.[60] This is the remedy or corrective, i.e. the security in the 2d instance.[61]

If[62] the Heads had contented themselves with affirming

1. That Ward had *propagated* matter at variance with the articles.[63]

2. That for that act the[64] University ought to withdraw his degrees, supposing the power.

They w[oul]d have done their work.[65]

Now they have opened a world of difficulties for their own supporters.[66]

Really[67] with Dalton,[f] & Everett[g] before ones eyes, there is, after all, something (however tenable in logic) ethically bad.[68]

---

[e] Those thinking less correctly.

[f] John Dalton (1766–1844), Professor of New College, Manchester, 1793–9, was a member of the British Association which was meeting at Oxford in June of 1832 and was awarded an honourary DCL with three other 'men of science' on 21 June of that year. See *DNB* and Liddon, i. 219.

[g] The *English Churchman* of 29 June 1843 (415) reported on the 28 June Convocation at Oxford and noted the uproar in the Sheldonian since Edward Everett, the American ambassador, was proposed for an honorary degree and the 'impression arose that [Everett] had been a Unitarian leader and editor of a Unitarian Review'. See also *Hebdomadal Board Minutes* (Oxford University Archives WPγ [24] 6), 51, on the 26 June meeting at which the

I[69] said at the beginning that I w[oul]d reserve (1) & (2)[70] of the First head, because with the ten first years of Q[ueen][71] Elizabeths reign & with B[isho]p Goodman[h] before ones eyes there is something yet to be considered.

Let me know how these things bear your sifting.[72]

Believe me,
Ever y[ou]rs aff[ectionatel]y
H.E.M.

The Right Hon[oura]ble
W. E. Gladstone

[[Pitts (draft and copy); Chapeau, 103, 157–61]]

441224gm[a]

Hawarden. Dec[ember] 24.
Christmas Eve. 1844.

My dear Manning

I had almost begun a letter to you concerning these new and formidable freaks of the Hebdomadal Board: you have anticipated me, and I have no more to do than to subscribe my *ditto* to what you have written. What spirit of dementation possesses these our guides and governors in the University? At the same time I cannot help thinking that it was the palpable error committed in the case of the Vice-Chancellorship[b] on the other side which has emboldened them to the present pitch.

---

degree was proposed, Oxford *Register of Convocation, 1837–1845* (Oxford University Archives, NEP/Subtus) for the report on the matter, and (interleaved into the *Register*) a letter by Charles Marriott of 3 July 1843 protesting the conferring of the degree. Everett was granted the degree. See also Tuckwell (1909), 157. Edward Everett (1794–1865), a Unitarian clergyman, was educated at Harvard, held a doctorate from Göttingen, 1817, and was appointed Professor of Greek Literature at Harvard in 1819. He served as a Member of the American Congress, 1825–35, Governor of Massachusetts, 1836–9, and was American minister at the Court of St James, 1841–5, before returning to an active political life in the United States. For details see Johnson and Malone (1928–36), vi. 23–226.

[h] Godfrey Goodman (1583–1656; *DNB*), appointed Bishop of Gloucester by Charles I, consecrated 1625, and deposed in 1639. He was Catholic in his leaning, an intimate of Franciscus a Santa Clara (Christopher Davenport; see 441228mg) and in the mid-1630s was openly suspected of being a Roman Catholic.

[a] 'Wrote to Manning' (*GD* iii. 421).

[b] See 440920gm.

It is scarcely possible however to conceive that so foolish a measure as the new test[c] can be carried. Of course one should reserve one's own freedom of action, and allow for the liberty of others: but I cannot avoid supposing that there will be a powerful and general rally on this occasion—

After much discussion and much correction my article on Ward appears.[d] I think it has suffered all that I could possibly have admitted: and in one or two places the argument is reduced almost to tatters, by a second revision which it underwent after the criticisms of other parties, the first having been the consequence of Lockhart's own. Still I rather anticipate you will be of the opinion that I decided rightly in letting it retain its place. There are things standing in it that I shall be very glad to see in the Quarterly Review.

Ever aff[ectiona]tely yours
W. E. Gladstone

Venerable
Archdeacon Manning
A blessed Christmas to you.

[[BL Add. MS 44247, 239–40; Morley transcript; Purcell, i. 296; cf. Chapeau, 309]]

441228mg

Lavington. Holy Innocents Day. 1844.

My dear Gladstone,

I am glad to have your assent to what I wrote about the Oxford Censure & Statute. I should like to have your mind also upon the two points which I reserved in my last letter, i.e.

1. Whether or no the parts alleged from Wards book be at variance with the 39 Articles?

And if so—

---

[c] That is, the Test oath printed in 'Whereas it is notoriously reputed . . .' of 13 December 1844, proposing to change Titulus XVII, Sectio III of the Statutes of the University so as to exclude anyone who wished to subscribe to the Thirty-Nine Articles in the sense Newman proposed in *Tract 90*. The final published announcement, dated 23 January 1845, stated that the Test had been removed, but was circulated with another on 4 February, containing the proposal to censure *Tract 90*.

[d] On 10 December 1844, after a meeting with Lockhart, Gladstone notes that he 'revised my Article afterwards—& started it afresh' (*GD* iii. 418) and on 20 December he spent '3 or 4 hours in (I hope) the last revision of my article' (ibid. 420).

2. Whether it be a wise & equitable measure to deprive him of his degrees?

Now as to the first:

Ward covers the whole question by avowing 1. that he holds the whole Roman doctrine. 2. that there is nothing hindering a man so holding, from subscribing the 39 Articles. His principle is this, that what the Articles condemn as Roman doctrine is not Roman doctrine, but error which the Roman Church equally condemns. This is Santa Claras principle who says of Article XXII that it condemns 'doctrinam falso nobis imputatam', e.g.[73] the invocation of Saints—'explevit impiam, et gentilitiam doctrinam falso Ecclesiae imputatam', and Transubstantiation—Art[icle]s XXVIII 'Debet glossari hic articulus: eos scilicit solum condemnare antiquum errorem Capharnaitarum &c.' And so throughout.[a]

---

[a] See Franciscus a Sancta Clara (Dr Christopher Davenport [1595–1680]), *Paraphrastica Expositio Articulorum Confessionis Anglicanae: The Articles of the Anglican Church paraphrastically considered and explained. . . . Reprinted from the Edition in Latin of 1646*, trans. and ed. Frederick George Lee (London: John T. Hayes, 1865). The passage concerning Article 22 (as treated in the paraphrasis to Article 37) to which Manning refers reads:

The sum of the matter is, that the Anglican Confession has decided nothing against the faith; but has condemned an impious heathen notion, falsely imputed to the Church. In exactly the same manner, they reject not purgatory, indulgences, the worshipping of relics and images in itself, but as before the *Romish doctrine* on all these points—that is, a doctrine falsely imputed to us. (ibid. 40)

The paraphrasis to Article 27 reads in full:

Debet igitur glossari hic Articulus; eos scilicet solum condemnare antiquum errorem Capharnaïtarum, sc. carnalem praesentiam Christi, id est, quasi Christus modo naturali seu carnali hic existeret, et dentibus nostris masticetur.

(The Article ought, then, to be explained thus: that the authors only condemn the old error of the Capharnaïtes, namely the carnal presence of Christ, that is as though Christ was present in the Sacrament in a natural or carnal manner, and were chewed with the teeth. [Ibid., 58].) The *Paraphrastica* was a supplement to Davenport's main work, *Deus, natura, gratia: sive tractatus de praedestinatione, de meritis peccatorum remissione, seu justificatione, et denique de sanctorum invocatione; ubi ad trutinam Fidei Catholicae examinature confessio Anglicana . . .* (2nd edn.; Lyons: Antoine Chard, 1634).

Davenport was educated at Merton College, Oxford, converted to Catholicism and admitted to Douai, 1616, joined the Franciscan order, 1617, joined the English Recollects, and after studying at Salamanca, went to England as a missioner and chaplain to Queen Henrietta Maria. Well respected at court, he was committed to the union of the Anglican and Roman Catholic churches, and worked for toleration of Roman Catholicism during the Cromwellian period, gaining favour at court once again following the Restoration. For details see *DNB* and Dockery (1960).

The question then simply is whether or no the Church of England has rightly understood, & stated the doctrine of the Roman Church?

I heartily wish Ward or any man would prove that we had nothing but a delusion of our own to condemn. He sh[oul]d have all my help in the undertaking. I w[oul]d not cross it with a straw.

But how will this stand with the whole doctrinal action of the reign of Q[ueen] Mary to omit Edward & Elizabeth: with the whole, continuous controversy of the 16th & 17th centuries on both sides, both accepting the Articles, as fair enunciations of the points in[74] dispute, and attacking & defending them accordingly.

I never heard that Andrewes & Perron wrangled about terms, or were deceived in their enunciations.[b] They simply contested the truth or falsehood of propositions accepted as definitions on both sides.

Forbes[c] & Montague, not to name Thorndike the closest approximators to the Roman doctrine, never dream of a mere verbal controversy: and on the points in question no Romanist that ever I heard alleged that they were fighting shadows.

I know of no Romanist that ever ventured on Santa Claras line, but he, & I think I am right in saying that his so doing brought him under direct disfavour in his own Communion.

If Ward be right where is the charge of heresy ag[ain]st the definitions[75] of the English Ch[urch] or the point of Transubstantiation?

But it really seems to me idle to argue the point.

In Strypes Eliz[abeth] c. 39 on the propositions offered by Dorman a R[oman] C[atholic] ag[ain]st Jewel of which the 2d is,

'That the people was[76] then (i.e. in the first 600 years) taught to believe that Christs body is really, substantially, corporally, carnally or naturally in the Sacrament.'[d]

---

[b] See Lancelot Andrewes, *Two Answers to Cardinall Perron and Two Speeches in the Starr Chamber* (London: Printed by Felix Kyngston for Richard Badger and Andrew Hebb, 1629) and as repr. in Lancelot Andrews, *Two Answers to Cardinal Perron, and other Miscellaneous Works*, ed. James Bliss (Oxford: John Henry Parker, 1854), 1–80. Jacques-Davy Du Perron (1556–1618) was a French convert from Calvinism, theologian, diplomat, and controversialist.

[c] William Forbes (1585–1634; *DNB*), was educated at Marischal College, lecturing there, 1601–6. He ministered throughout his life at various Scottish parishes, maintaining a High Church position, and shortly before his death was appointed Bishop of Edinburgh by Charles I, 1634.

[d] John Strype, *The Annals of the Reformation and Establishment of Religion, and other Various Occurrences in the Church of England during Queen Elizabeth's Happy Reign* (Oxford: Clarendon, 1824), i pt. II ch. 39 p. 113, quotes Dorman: 'That the people was taught to believe, that

'

I never heard that he, & his like were reproved by the Roman Church for exceeding her doctrine at that time.

But I do believe that a great purification, & filtering of thought & conceptions has gone on, under the force of the Reformation, in the Roman Communion, & that they have indefinitely approached the doctrine of the real presence as held by the Church of England. It would be a task as easy as it would be uncharitable to set in conflict their earlier & later writers. e.g. Bellarmine[e] & Wiseman.

Oakeley in his pamphlet on Tract 90[f] relies much on the fact that R[oman] Catholics subscribed the Articles at the beginning of the reign of Eliz[abe]th. He mentions by name 'the celebrated John Bridgewater' p.13, note 6.[g] But he does not add that Bridgewater afterwards went over to the R[oman] C[atholics] though Strype mentions it in the place he quotes. Another named by Strype is White, who (or some other White) was reproved by a Romanist for 'dissembling in religion &c.' on account of

Christ's body is really, substantially, corporally, carnally, or naturally, in the sacrament.' See Thomas Dorman, *A Proufe of Certeyne Articles in Religion, denied by M. Ivell, sett forth in defence of the Catholyke belief* . . . (Antwerp: Ioh. Latus, 1564), 80[v]. Note Manning's copy (in possession of Dr Sheridan Gilley) of *The Faith of Catholics, Confirmed by Scripture and Attested by the Fathers of the First Five Centuries of the Church*, compiled by Joseph Berington and J. Kirk (London: Joseph Booker, 1830), extensively annotated in respect to this topic, p. 220.

[e] Robert Bellarmine (1542–1621) entered the Society of Jesus, 1560, studying at Padua and Louvain, appointed to a chair of controversial theology at the Roman College, 1576, served on the Vulgate revision committee, Rector of the Roman College, 1592, Provincial of Naples, 1595, theologian to Clement VIII, 1597, appointed to the Congregation de Auxiliis, 1599, fulfilling various roles for the papacy from 1605, particularly in the debates over the oath imposed on Catholics during the reign of James I and the Galileo case.

[f] Frederick Oakeley, *The Subject of Tract XC. Examined, in Connection with the History of the Thirty-Nine Articles, and the Statements of Certain English Divines: to Which is Added, the Case of Bishop Montague, in the Reign of King James I* (London: J. G. F. & J. Rivington, 1841). Cf. 450426mg. For details on Manning's historical discussion with Oakeley at the time see Addenda to this Section.

[g] Manning depended heavily on Oakeley's treatise in writing this letter. For John Bridgewater (also, Aquapontanus; b. 1532, Rector of Lincoln College, Oxford, 1563–74, when he fled to Douai, supporting English Catholics abroad) see ibid. 13 n. 6 which also cites Strype ch. 28. Note as well Oakeley's use of Franciscus a Sancta Clara, i.e. the Franciscan Christopher Davenport, *Expositio paraphrastica confessionis anglicae* (35–6), the Andrewes and Perron correspondence (53–8), and the extensive use of Forbes, Montague, and Thorndike on invocation of saints (58–61), reverence to images and relics (61–5), and immediate state of perfection (66–71).

subscribing. Strype, c. 38. Feckenham, Abbot of Westminster,[h] who con-
formed under Henry VIII Edw[ard] VI. Q[ueen] Mary stood out under
Eliz[abeth] and assigned among other reasons the removal of the prayers
to Saints &c.[i]

So that upon the whole I cannot put the subscribing of the Romanists
any higher than Feckenhams subscription & conformity under H[enry]
VIII. Ed[ward] VI. & Q[ueen] Mary. Can we make of it more than a
yielding produced. 1. by the ascendency of the Reformation 2. the inaction
(for the 1st 10 years) of the Pope. 3. the severe penal Laws?

I confess it does not satisfy me. The subscription of the R[oman]
C[atholic]s seems simple concession, or surrender.

What makes me the more think that they submitted to the Reformation
on its own terms, is that the *imponens*[j] was then a living, speaking, & what is
much more *governing* being.

And I cannot but hold

1. that the animus imponentis[k] is the first axiomatic principle of all
   oaths, covenants, & subscriptions.

2. that it was so held & acted on at the Reformation e.g. the Oath of
   Supremacy wh[ich] is parallel with the Articles.

I think these things certain

1. that when the 'animus' is known the subscriber is bound.

2. that where uncertain, he has his liberty.

This seems enough for the present use.

[h] John de Feckenham (1510–84; *DNB*) was early admitted to Evesham Monastery and
educated at Gloucester Hall (Worcester College), Oxford, left the University on the
dissolution of his Abbey in 1539, served for a decade as Rector of Solihull, Warwickshire,
domestic chaplain to Bishop Bell of Worcester and thereafter to Bishop Bonner of London.
On Bonner's deprivation Feckenham was imprisoned in the Tower of London, although
released to participate in a conference on the Eucharist. Released under Mary he was often
called upon to work for the conversion of Protestants. In 1556 he was appointed Abbot of
Westminster. He was deprived under Elizabeth, imprisoned in the Tower, 1570–4, after
which he was released.

[i] See Strype, *Annals*, i pt. II, Appendix, ix, 431ff. which provides a text of Feckenham's
speech. See also ibid. i pt. I, 109–10.

[j] The one imposing [an oath].

[k] The intention of the imposer.

Whatever liberty there be in details it is undeniable that the 39 Articles are Anti-Arian.

Whatever liberty in details the 39 Articles are anti-Roman.

If you have Waterlands works look at 'The Case of Arian Subscription.' Vol.II.[l] wh[ich] by the way was invoked the other day ag[ain]st Hampden.[m]

Thus far there can be no doubt of the animus imponentis as read in the light of the political, Ecclesiastical, controversial history of the 16th Century. I therefore come to the conclusion—

1. That they who refused to subscribe refused because the Articles are Anti-Roman.

2. That they who did subscribe, subscribed because they succumbed.

And this makes me feel unable to refuse assent to the censure on certain parts of Wards Book.

Nevertheless I cannot vote for it: because it is mixed up with a censure on his interior state which I do not believe to be true.

If without seeming to negative the censure upon his book I c[oul]d vote against the censure on his person I sh[oul]d do so.

The next point is the deprival of degrees.

This seems to me precipitate justice. Deprival of degrees is an ultimate punishment: a last penalty not to be inflicted in the first instance.

I think a censure on the Book enough for the present—both to vindicate the rule of subscription, & to animadvert upon the person.

Moreover with Hampdens case before us[77] (acknowledging all differences) I sh[oul]d not incline to proceed at once to extremes.

Also Everetts degree seriously compromises the $\tilde{\eta}\theta o\varsigma$[n] of the University in relation to degrees as expressions of moral or doctrinal complacency.

I feel strongly inclined to vote against this point. If the votes had been

1. that the book is censurable.

2. that the writer be incapacitated for University functions.

[l] Daniel Waterland, *The Case of Arian Subscription Considered: And the Several Pleas and Excuses for it Particularly Examined and Confuted*, in *The Works of the Rev. Daniel Waterland, D. D., to Which is Prefixed a Review of the Author's Life and Writings by William van Mildert* (6 vols.; Oxford: Oxford University Press, 1843), ii. 259–363.

[m] Manning is here referring to a printed circular, 'The following Abstract of Dr. Waterland's "Case of Arian Subscription"...' (Oxford: Baxter, n.d.).

[n] Moral disposition.

I should have been forced to concur.

If you have patience to get through this letter I must love you for it.

Ever yours affect[ionate]ly

H. E. Manning

The Right Hon[oura]ble
W. E. Gladstone

[[Pitts original and copy (the latter in a second hand); Chapeau, 104, 161–5]]

441231mg

Lavington. Dec[ember] 31. 1844.

My dear Gladstone,

You will like to see the inclosed letter of Hooks.[a]

I cannot but say to you that there is a tone which does not altogether chime with my feeling towards either the so-called Evangelicals or the Roman Church.

However he is a tone nearer & has done a great work for us under God: & I both honor & love him.

I wish I c[oul]d feel that his remarks on Pusey were groundless.

With great misgiving I am meditating, in some way, to open the matter to him. His[78] preface to Surin is to me really[79] distressing.[b]

Ever yours aff[ectionate]ly

H. E. Manning

the Right Hon[oura]ble
W. E. Gladstone

[[Pitts; Chapeau, 105, 165]]

450102gm[a]

Hawarden
Jan[uary] 2. 1845

My dear Manning

Dr. Hook has a certain rudeness in these matters: but after all on the main practical question he is right. As to Pusey I have not read his Preface

---

ᵃ Not located.

ᵇ F. Surin, *The Foundations of the Spiritual Life Drawn from the Book of The Imitation of Christ, Translated from the French, and Adapted to the Use of the English Church* (London: A. D. Innes & Co. [1844]; preface by E.B.P., dated Vigil of St James [24 July], 1844). See 441105mg and Addenda to this Section.

ᵃ 'Wrote to Manning' (*GD* iii. 423).

to Surin: but I have been seriously stumbled by some of the things which he has left in his Avrillon's Advent;[b] though he calls it 'adapted', I fear I am not quite 'adapted' to it—

I mean however that Hook is right in the positive part of his sentiments (like so many other men): if he contemplates any public reprobation of Newman, I think it would be a great error.

For my part I shall be very glad that you and he should bolt this matter of the Oxford proposals to the bran[c]—& shall have the strongest predispositions to concur with you—

I have written rather largely upon them to S[amuel] Wilberforce[d]—in answer to queries from him—from memory I think my sense is this—

1. that as yet I can form *no* final opinion—but for the present,

2. I think Ward's propositions censurable in themselves—

3. Before voting them so, must inquire what *other* censurable propositions are tolerated—

4. Have great difficulty in declaring them a breach of faith,

5. and therefore in degrading—

(NB. Should they not give him an Honorary Deg[ree] ... After Everett?)

6. Have a score of difficulties about the Test[e] —& do not know anything of the argument for it.

I agree with you that the articles bear evidence of the intention to hit the Church of Rome and fasten upon *her* the charge of error—upon some of her current notions and practices, blasphemy and impiety—but with a great tenderness for those *germs* of idea, out of[80] the corrupt following of which the said notions and practices have sprung—

I agree with you *eminently* in your doctrine of *filtration*.[f] You quote Dorman[81] who uses the word 'carnally'—now Bossuet explicitly denies a 'présence

---

[b] Jean Baptiste Avrillon, *A Guide for Passing Advent Holily, in Which is Found for Each Day, a Practice, a Meditation, Thoughts upon Portions of the Holy Scripture for the Season* (London: James Burns, 1844). On the controversy see also Liddon, ii. 393ff.

[c] On the phrase see 431024.

[d] Gladstone's lengthy letter of 29 December 1844 is preserved in Bodl. MS Wilberforce d. 35, 30–7 (copy: BL Add. MS 44343, 49–63). On Purcell's comment that Wilberforce was 'the most distinguished orator of the day' (i. 269), Gladstone notes in his copy of the biography 'not quite' (PurGl, ibid.)

[e] See 441224gm.

[f] See 441228mg and Manning's reference to 'filtering'.

charnelle'[g]—I thought Ward good on that particular point as to agree-ment[h]—intention to agree is another thing. I am not sure however of your whole assertion that subscribers were mere succumbers.

It sometimes occurs to me, though the question may seem a strange one—how far was the Reformation, but[82] especially the Continental Reformation, designed by God, in the region of final causes, for *that* purification of the Roman Church which it has actually realised? The English Reformation we yet hope has a higher kind of purification to accomplish in the rest of the Church.

Perhaps you would like your letter of 28th[83][i] to be returned—If so pray let me know.

I am very sorry to hear that the English Review has tumbled into the pit—and defends the Test[j]—but I have not yet seen their argument for it about which I endeavour to maintain the same feeling as one has about an undiscovered land—it may be a reality but I have not the least conception what—i.e. specifically what: *generally*, it is easy enough to show that there are dangers, & that remedies are wanted.

Ever affe[ctiona]tely yours
W. E. Gladstone

Venerable
Archdeacon Manning

[[BL Add. MS 44247, 241–3; Morley transcript; Purcell, i. 297; cf. Chapeau, 309]]

[g] Note, in particular, Jacques Benigné Bossuet's opposition to Protestant characteriza-tions of Catholic teaching on the real presence in *Histoire des variations des églises proetestantes* (4 vols.; Paris: Guillaume Desprez, 1740), sects. 3: 4, 4: 9. And cf. the same passages in the translation, *The History of the Variations of the Protestant Churches* (2 vols.; Dublin: Richard Coyne, 1829).

[h] Ward's explicit discussion on the nature of 'agreement' in subscribing to The Thirty-Nine Articles is developed with respect to the Sacrament in his *A Few Words*, 28–31, and with respect to the framers of the Articles in *A Few Words More*, emphasizing that the Framers did not exclude the position taken in *Tract 90*. In his *An Address to Members of Convocation in Protest against the Proposed Statute* (London: James Toovey, 1845), released later in January 1845, Ward took up the specific section from the *Ideal* in which he had referred to the Eucharist as 'carnally pressed' by his opponents and the nature of his agreement on this point (pp. xi–xii).

[i] The letter on Holy Innocents' Day, 441228mg.

[j] See 'Jelf's Bampton Lectures', *English Review* 4 (Dec. 1844), 460–72, 470–2, which defends the Test; by use of 'we' the author (Palmer, on Gladstone's suspicion; see 450105gm) reflects editorial policy.

450105gm[a]

Hawarden NW
Sunday Jan[uary] 5. 1845

My dear Manning

I have expressed to you the disinclination which as a general rule I feel to the practice of not voting upon a definite and important question—such as the first of those to be proposed at Oxford. And I see it stated in the Christian Remembrancer p. 137[b] that there is nothing to prevent any one from proposing an amendment except that the V[ice] C[hancellor] may then dissolve the House. Now I do not think this forms an objection in the particular case—and the question which I wish to have considered is this: why should not you or some other propose an amendment to such an effect as this (which is very nearly in the sense of[84] your letters of Dec[ember] 20 & 28)

That the propositions cited from Ward's work (not saying *each and all*) were censurable upon the ground of variance with the articles & otherwise: and

That the writer be incapacitated from teaching functions in the University until he should have given satisfaction to it.

This would in my view be going to the very farthest allowable point against Ward—and in my own mind I should prefer the first of these only.

In all probability such an amendment if allowed to be put would be rejected—but after its rejection I would freely vote against the first proposition[c] on account of its impugning Ward's good faith: which I should think a severe course even in the strictest state of discipline, & our state intolerable.

If the amendment were not put the whole thing would fall to the ground by the dissolution of the Convocation—assuming always that the Christian Remembrancer is correct.

The argument for the Test in the English Review—written I fear by Palmer—is deplorable in itself, & besides ought never to have appeared in that publication—

---

[a] 'Wrote to Manning' (*GD* iii. 424).

[b] 'The Vice Chancellorship of Dr. Wynter', *Christian Rembrancer* 47 (Jan. 1845), 133–87. Gladstone read the *Christian Rembrancer* on 4 January 1845 (*GD* iii. 422).

[c] On the proposition enumerated here and by Manning in the following letters see Introduction, liiiff.

Do not answer me until it is convenient. Something must be done to bring men together—you will know when you are mature enough to say anything to me—I expect to be in London on the 9th, and again on the 11th,[d] to remain probably—

Believe me aff[ectiona]tely yours

W. E. Gladstone

Venerable

Archdeacon Manning

[[BL Add. MS 44247, 244–5; Morley transcript; Purcell, i. 297–8; cf. Chapeau, 309]]

450107gm[a]

Hawarden Jan[uary] 7. 1845.

My dear Manning

I hope, or rather fear, to be in town on Thursday[b] morning—and perhaps you will either come at 9½ to breakfast, or to converse at any time not later than eleven—I wrote to you on Sunday[c] broaching the notion of an amendment.

I think it would be a great advantage if you were to see Badeley or some lawyer whose advice would be valuable—Hope can scarcely have arrived but he was to leave Rome after Christmas and fly back.[d]

Aff[ectiona]tely yours

W. E. Gladstone

Leave word at C[arlton] H[ouse] T[errace] tomorrow when I am to expect you, if you conveniently can.

[[BL Add. MS 44247, 246; Morley transcript; cf. Chapeau, 310]]

[[The meeting on Thursday, 9 January 1845, occurred as planned: 'Saw Manning 10–12 on Oxf[ord] proposals.' In addition to this Gladstone discussed with Manning 'my own position; & intended arrangement of the prayers' (*GD* iii. 424; see *Autobiographica*, ii. 186, 196, 198). The 'position' of which they spoke was that faced by him in the Government's forthcoming proposal to increase and make permanent the grant to the Roman Catholic educational institution at Maynooth, an action that conflicted with the principles Gladstone had expressed in his *The State in its Relations with the Church* (*GD* iii. 424–5). To his wife Gladstone wrote on 9 January that he saw 'Manning for

---

[d] Gladstone left Hawarden for London on the evening of 8 January 1845, was at Windsor and Eton late on 9 January, returned to London on 11 January (*GD* iii. 424–5).

[a] 'wrote to... Manning' (ibid. 424).

[b] 9 January 1845.

[c] Sunday, 5 January 1845; 450105gm.

[d] Hope was on an extensive tour of the Continent with Badeley from September 1844 to the first week of January 1845 inclusive. See Ornsby, ii. 49–64.

two hours this morning and let the cat out of the bag to him in part' (SDL, Glynne–Gladstone MS 770, 97–8, 98; Morley, i. 274), noting the matter to her again on 14 January: 'There is a certain Maynooth bill in preparation, and when that appears for decision my time will probably have come, but I am quite ignorant when it will be forthcoming' (SDL, Glynne–Gladstone MS 770; Morley, i. 275).]]

450116mg

Lavington. Jan[uar]y 16. 1845

My dear Gladstone,

I send you the inclosed in confidence. Newman, it seems, feels your article on Ward sensitively.

As to the amendment I have made no way. The Dean of Chichester did not incline to it.[a] Badeley was against it:[b] and I had myself already begun to doubt of it.

Woodgate will have got out his declaration in a day or two:[c] & under the cover of that I think men will vote decisively against the censure.

You shall however hear from me again about it.

What an exposure is there about Puseys Sermon.

I have been thinking much of our last conversation, but I must see more in detail before I sh[oul]d like to affirm or deny the minor premiss.

Ever yours affect[ionate]ly,

H. E. Manning.

P.S. I will send your Family Prayers by Monday morning.[d]

HEM.

The Right Hon[oura]ble
W. E. Gladstone.

[[Pitts]]

[Enclosure]

[a] Correspondence not located.

[b] Correspondence not located.

[c] Manning was in contact with Henry Arthur Woodgate on the Ward issue on 30 December 1844, indicating that although he thought the book was censurable, he believed the charge against Ward to be unjust. See Bodl. MS Eng. lett. c. 662, 9–10, and Henry Arthur Woodgate, *Reasons for Voting against the Measures to be Proposed in Convocation on Feb[ruary] 13, 1845* (London: James Burns, 1845) and cf. the same author's *An Earnest Appeal to Members of the Oxford Convocation, on the Proposed Assumption of Ecclesiastical Powers by the University* (London: James Burns, 1845; preface dated 1 February 1845). Woodgate (1801–74) was educated at St John's College, Oxford, and held a Fellowship there which he resigned in 1837 to become Rector of Belbroughton, Worcestershire (Boase, iii. 1484).

[d] A manuscript by Gladstone, 'An Arrangement of Prayers from the Liturgy of the Church of England for Domestic Use', from 1845 includes as an interpolated correction a

Jan[uary] 15. 1845

My dear Friend,

I really think that you have no choice about W[ar]d's book, i.e. you must act somehow, & then do what you see right besides. These are not days for neutrality. Either it is a wrong & oppressive measure, or it is a very necessary one; this sensitiveness to Romanism & insensitiveness to every heresy is a deep disease: a person might be a Sabellian, Nestorian, Mono-physite, or whatever separate or combined heresy besides, & the majority w[oul]d think it absolutely indifferent; if he hold any shade of the belief in Purgatory, people w[oul]d all be in arms. Dr. Tait[e] has truly noticed that I, with others, tried to bring the Statute of the 6 Doctors[f] to bear ag[ain]st Dr. H[ampden], & it was turned ag[ain]st myself, i.e. the heads, some few excepted, were indifferent to the cartloads of heresies in his B[ampton] L[ectures] but thought they could not demolish too promptly any state-ment of the doctrine of the H[oly] E[ucharist] higher than they were accustomed to.

I have had a little correspondence with O[akeley] about y[ou]r vote.[g] I wished to find out whether he, as W[ard]'s friend, w[oul]d rather you voted and wrote ag[ain]st W[ard]'s sentence, & ag[ain]st his book or did neither. I understand that y[ou]rs was a personal feeling of reluctance to write ag[ain]st W[ard] now, but that you felt you c[oul]d not vote ag[ain]st

---

leaf from a letter in Manning's hand that reads: 'It has been sometime thought that by daily saying the prayers of the Church, reverence for them may be lessened, & a full sense of their depth and meaning impaired. This Collection is founded upon a directly opposite suppos-ition. Nevertheless, no censure is thereby intended on those whose experience seems to lead them to the other view' (BL Add. MS 44683, 221; full text by Gladstone, fos. 217–23). The volume appeared as W. E. Gladstone (ed.), *A Manual of Prayers From the Liturgy: Arranged for Family Use* (London: John Murray, 1845).

[e] Archibald Campbell Tait (1811–82) was raised a Presbyterian, educated at Glasgow University, joined the Church of England, entered Balliol College, Oxford, and was elected a Fellow there, 1834; he was one of the Four Tutors opposing *Tract 90* in 1841, Headmaster of Rugby, 1842, Dean of Carlisle, 1849, Bishop of London, 1856, and Archbishop of Canterbury, 1868. For details see *DNB* and Marsh (1969).

[f] See 430625mg.

[g] On 21 December 1844 Oakeley wrote to Pusey commenting: 'Archd[eaco]n Manning writes me that he is wavering. I am not much surprised' (PHL MS Oakeley to Pusey 1838–40, No. 32; the Pusey correspondence is not located). See also Marriott to Pusey, Sunday after Christmas, 1844: 'Even Manning doubts whether he can vote *for* Ward, but I think that he will come to the conclusion that he can, as he states nearly sufficient ground for it in his letter' (PHL MS PUS 136/15).

the statute without doing so. I meant to say to O[akeley] that over and above your objections to the book you dislike its ἦθος.[h] He has, in part, misunderstood me. I have written again. You know how much you feel you ought to say about W[ard]'s book, at such a moment as this. I sh[oul]d have thought a simple declaimer enough, & that it was better not to write when people are so excited. And recollect your words are always very heavy. You have none in your armory but 16 pounders. I have not read Gl[adstone's] article: N[ewman] felt it very grievous to choose just this moment for it: it is like sinking a drowning man. I hope Gl[adstone], since he writes so strongly ag[ain]st W[ard], will vote as decidedly ag[ain]st injustice and untruth.

I am to be at Chich[ester] tomorrow, but I ought, if I can, to be back here on Fr[iday],[i] for I am just sending up a rejoinder to the Prov[ost], and if I am not back for the Friday's post, two days may be lost, which in this sharp-shooting may be of moment. For it is taken for granted that all one does is evil until the contrary is proved.

I have recollected, since I spoke to you, that altho' I have no doubt whatever of the meaning of the 3rd Proposition wh[ich] I spoke of, the Prov[ost] afterwards interpreted it thus—'I do not believe that, holding as you do, that the consecrated elements are also Christ's Body and Blood, you mean that they will enable any other than the *faithful* and worthy Communicant to partake of [Chris]t.' I never heard that any ever did: however, I am quite certain that the words proposed to me meant what I said to you.

y[ou]r affec[tiona]te friend
EBP

[[Bodl. MS Eng. lett. c. 654, 249–50]]

450118gm[a]

Whitehall
Jan[uary] 18. 1845.

My dear Manning

I thank you very much for sending me Pusey's note, on my own account. I[85] at once wrote an explanation to Newman of the reasons which made me persevere even when I had become aware of what was intended at

---

[h] Moral disposition.
[i] 17 January 1845.
[a] 'Wrote to . . . Manning' (*GD* iii. 427).

Oxford.[b] A most kind and temperate comment by Keble, in the way of objection, has today been sent to me by Rogers[c]—

As to amendment, *I* have no strong feeling for it, except as preferable, if practicable, to not voting at all: and I seem to myself to be quite prepared to say non placet[d] to both the remaining propositions. I treat the Test as gone. S[amuel] Wilberforce writes to me to that effect, after a correspondence[86] with the Vice Chancellor.[e] This seems to me conclusive, although the intention is kept, as it appears, very secret—& consequently I am not believed when I propagate this notion. The *formal* resolution to abandon cannot yet take place, as the Hebdomadal Board has not met—

I am glad to find that several pens are in motion—

Pusey's note gives me the impression that he is in better spirits—

I have read the Preface to Surin:[f] and the whole former part of it I am bound to say with great admiration: the latter not without it, though there seems to me to be more room for question there.

Thanks for the promise of the Family Prayers. If you are to write to me on other matters, Deh non tardar.[g]

We saw Hope this morning: looking quite fat and uncatholic.[h]

Ever aff[ectiona]tely yours

W. E. Gladstone

Venerable

Archdeacon Manning

[[BL Add. MS 44247, 247–8; Morley transcript; cf. Chapeau, 310]]

[b] On 17 January 1845 Gladstone wrote to Newman; the letter opens by stating directly his knowledge of Pusey's letter: 'I have learned, through a note of Dr. Pusey's to Manning, that the Article in the *Quarterly Review* upon Ward's book written by me, should not in your judgment have been produced at a moment like this, when so much influence and so much passion are arrayed against him' (*LD* x. 496–7: Birmingham Oratory MS Newman–Gladstone; BL Add. MS 44362, 26–9; Lathbury, i. 312–24). Correspondence continued on the issue; see Newman's reply with criticisms, 22 January (ibid. 32–3 [*LD* x. 503]) and 24 January (ibid. 39 [*LD* x. 510]), to Gladstone's 'full' answer of 23 January (Birmingham Oratory MS Newman–Gladstone).

[c] Keble's letter to Rogers and forwarded to Gladstone is preserved in BL Add. MS 44362, 15–20.

[d] [To say] it does not please, i.e. to cast a negative ballot.

[e] See Wilberforce to Gladstone, 7 and 14 January 1845, and Gladstone's response of 16 January (BL Add. MS 44343, 66–74).

[f] Gladstone read the preface on 12 January 1845 (*GD* iii. 426). See 441231mg.

[g] 'Deh! viene, non tardar (Pray, come, do not delay)', Mozart, *Le Nozze di Figaro*, Act iv. Note C. R. L. Fletcher's ([1908], 39) later comment on Gladstone's love of opera.

[h] Gladstone 'Saw Hope…m[ornin]g' (*GD* iii. 427). Cf. comment on Hope in 461207gm.

450118mg[a]
or Eucharistical to be said as the 21st in the Commination Service?

I do not know that I have anything more worthy of saying.

Ever yours affect[ionate]ly
H. E. Manning

[[Pitts; Gladstone's annotation: Jan[uary] 18 H. E. Manning (The Prayers); Chapeau filed the fragment with the 18 June 1844 letter.]]

450119mga

Lavington. Jan[uar]y 19. 1845.

My dear Gladstone,

After the best thoughts I can give to the matter and supposing my facts correct & sufficient, I do not see what there is to make you change your present position.[aa]

It is not a question of right or wrong as in the sight of God for in all the *subject-matter* of the question you are already committed: and have no doubting conscience.

The question is this—Would such a measure as you described so clash with your recorded opinions, as to overturn the character, & confidence which rest upon them.

On one side it may be said that it would, because at this moment your recorded opinions, which are the terms of compact with public confidence, do not avow, but rather deny, that the paternal office of the State has ceased among us to restrict its religious actions to the Church. The readers of your Books may perhaps hold you to the rigid theory of Church & State.

But on the other hand it seems to me that your whole Parliamentary & political standing supply what your books have not formally stated. First: the present Government has inherited & adopted much of the policy of the late Government in respect to the Church. And next, it has originated measures of its own in the same direction.

You stand before the country at this moment as a partaker in the following acts.

1. The Committee of the Privy Council on Education with its acts, & grants to Dissenters.

2. The religious policy of Government in the colonies which covers every anomaly.

---

[a] All that remains of the letter is the final leaf, treating Gladstone's 'Family Prayers'.

[aa] That is, regarding the Maynooth grant.

3. The National Education in Ireland: with its accident, the refusal of grants to the Church Education Society.[b]

4. The Charitable bequests Act which seems to me to go beyond any increase of an existing money-vote.[c]

5. The annual grant to Maynooth.

You say this was part of a compact as the sum paid to the Hindoos by the Indian Government.[d]

But if it be not a malum per se[e] the facts I refer to seem to me to cover not only an increase of the same grant, but the formation of like Institutions.

I may have overlooked distinctions as the case is in matter not perfectly[87] known to me: but if my facts hold, my belief is that no loss of public character or confidence w[oul]d follow on a participation in the supposed measure.

My belief is that no such loss would be incurred by any policy terminating on religious bodies external to the Church so long as that policy does not directly & at once derogate from, or despoil the Church:—

But that men will judge you by your policy terminating on the Church itself.

A policy which should threaten the integrity of the Church by latitudinarian or Erastian measures: or by repressing its spiritual energies; & obstructing its free action & development, especially if contemporaneous with such a policy as is the question of this letter, would bring on you the loss of I know not what. I am only writing argumentative as you will see.

---

[b] The Kildare Place Society (earlier The Dublin Education Society) had received Government grants for its work in popular education in Ireland since 1813 until it was superseded by the Board of National Education in Ireland in 1831. Its schools were mainly in Ulster. See Sturt (1967), 64, and Hurt (1971), 26. See also 'A Bill to amend the Acts for the Education of Persons professing the Roman Catholic Religion, and for the better Government of the Seminary Establishment at Maynooth for the Education of such Persons', PP 1841 (171.) ii. 569, and 'A Bill to provide for the recovery by Summary Process, of Sums due to the teachers of Schools in Ireland', PP 1843 (578.) iv. 475; PP 1844 (44.) iv. 635. Cf. 'A Bill to enable Her Majesty to endow New Colleges for the Advancement of Learning in Ireland', PP 1845 (299.) (400.) i. 357, 365.

[c] 'An Act for the more effectual Application of Charitable Donations and Bequests in Ireland' (PP 1843 [180.] i. 425, PP 1844 [529.] [570.] i. 103; Note the discussion in the House of Lords, 25 June and 22 July 1844 [7 & 8 Victoria, c. 97 (1844)]). For details see Kerr (1982), 110–51.

[d] See 'Correspondence and Papers relative to the Education of Natives', PP 1831–2 (in 735–I) ix. 395.

[e] Evil in itself.

On the whole my impression is that no new or distinctive question has arisen, always supposing that you have no doubting conscience as to your present position, & that my facts are correct.

May God who is only wise guide us in these sifting days. Questions, powers,[88] & principles wh[ich] have been pent up more or less these three hundred years, have burst upon us, & are demanding of every man a deliberate choice of aye or no. Believe me,

Ever your attached friend,
H. E. Manning

The Right Hon[oura]ble
W. E. Gladstone

P.S. Pusey has been staying a day with me:[f] and I never felt more powerfully the real saintliness of his temper. There is something about him which, I have seen in no man except Newman: & in him far less than in Pusey. It leaves one with a feeling of shame, & fear, and awe at one's own state.

In point also of opinion & judgment I never found more to go along with in him. His whole tone forbids him to take Wards line.

He confirmed what I had heard of the withdrawal of the Statute. What an exposure of ill-counsel, & misrule it is.

H.E.M.

[[Pitts; Chapeau, 107, 165–7]]

450119mgb

Lavington. Jan[uar]y 19. 1845.

My dear Gladstone,

I add another note today to what I wrote last night.

First to send you the inclosed[a] from a Son of Sir L. Shadwells to Pusey[89]—which is miserable. 'For the iniquity of a land many are the Princes thereof'.[b]

---

[f] Manning refers to the visit in a letter to Pusey, 23 January 1845 (PHL MS Manning to Pusey, No. 17): 'It was a great happiness to me to see you here. God has indeed blessed me with a quiet which is unspeakably soothing. W[oul]d I c[oul]d use it as he w[oul]d have me: & not enjoy it only. Some time ago I asked Newman to come & stay here: from a sort of persuasion that a place so still c[oul]d not but refresh him, & recall old days, & hopes. But he c[oul]d not come. It was with great joy that I found you c[oul]d feel with me in my belief & trust about the Church of England. I know of nothing, but the power of something above myself that gives me so confiding and steadfast a feeling in the midst of all our conflicts, and losses. But it seems that I could as soon doubt of my own life.'

[a] Not located.
[b] Cf. Prov. 28: 2.

And next to say that Wilberforce writes me word^c that the V[ice]
C[hancellor] makes some address to him a condition of withdrawing the
Statute.

W[ilberforce] sends me an address which I cannot sign: & there is no
need. Heaps of names are ready to hand.

I will read the preface to Surin again. My objections were—

1. The endorsement of R[oman] C[atholic] Saints. S[t]. Alphonsus
   Lig[uori] S[t]. Ignatius Loyola.^d

2. The adoption of the visions and raptures &c. in the lives of Saints.^e

3. The opening of the case of possession, &c.^f

All peace be with you today.

On the greater matter I have still many thoughts wh[ich] I will put down
to-night.

Ever yours affec[tionate]ly
H. E. Manning

[[Pitts; Chapeau, 106, 165]]

450121gm^a

Secret

Whitehall
Jan[uary] 21. [18]45.

My dear Manning

I like very much your advice upon the Prayers: and I am glad you have
untied the labyrinthine sentence—

By the bye I hope you observed that I sacrificed my 'stolid' on the altar
of friendship.^b

I return Shadwell's extraordinary letter—not the most fit to be shown to
Newman.^c The V[ice] C[hancellor']s proposition was indeed an astounding one, & there are *some* good answers—

---

^c Not located.

^d See Surin, Preface, pp. xx–xxii. Alphonsus Liguori (1696–1787) was a Redemptorist
and widely influential moral theologian, and Ignatius Loyola (1491–1556) the founder of
the Society of Jesus.

^e See ibid. pp. xlvii–xlviii.

^f Ibid. pp. xl–xlv.

^a 'Wrote to . . . Manning' (*GD* iii. 426).

^b Reference to an editorial suggestion by Manning.

^c Newman's 'fitness' as understood by Gladstone was indicated to Manning a short time
later on 9 February 1845, when Newman wrote that he had 'no interest about next

Your account of Pusey is very refreshing.

I thank you much for your letter of counsel: but yet I cannot come to it. My recorded opinions, you justly say, are the terms of compact with public confidence. The circumstances you enumerate on the other hand may perhaps prove that I have already done what should entail the forfeiture— but it is only on the supposition of having nothing more to give up that they could release me from my engagements.

As to positive action towards the Church that is[90] what yet remains worth thinking of. But the time has not come for doing much good in that sense: and it will never come till there is a lull in our internal dissensions, of which I by no means despair when I consider that at this moment the pressing danger arises from the comparatively small question of two or three rubrics, from an error in judgment (as I think) of two Prelates (London & Exeter) & from the incomparable villainy of the Times.[d]

As to your particulars

1. I am not on the Committee of Education—Dissenters may get the benefit of its grants but not commonly *as such*—

2. Colonial policy is by many stages more remote from the seat of life—

Thursday's result' and suffered 'ills which Heads of Houses can neither augment nor cure' (*LD* x. 540–1: Newman to Manning, Bodl. MS Eng. lett. c. 654, 56–7; Purcell, i. 305). Newman's letter was in answer to an earlier one by Manning (6 Feb. 1845) in which Manning assured Newman of his support in the forthcoming censure. (See Birmingham Oratory MS Newman–Manning.)

[d] Pressed by extreme Tractarian practices such as those of Oakeley at Margaret Chapel, Blomfield published his *A Charge Delivered to the Clergy of the Diocese of London at the Visitation in October, MDCCCXLII* (London: B. Fellows, 1842) of 10 October 1842. In it, while opposing *Tract 90* and other Tractarian practices, he nevertheless recommended, among other things, that the priest wear a surplice at the morning service and that one should bow at the mention of the name of Jesus in the liturgy. *The Times* reported that he supported members of the Oxford Movement (*The Times*, 12 Oct. 1842, 3d; 19 Oct., 4b–c). When such recommended practices were initiated in Tottenham and Ware, disputes arose and continued. Similar difficulties between congregation and parish priest resulted in the diocese of Exeter when Bishop Phillpotts supported the highly exacting priest, Walter Blunt, on 19 November 1844. On the latter case see *The Times*, 15 November, 6a, 16 November, 8e, 19 November, 6a, 20 November, 8g. See also the report on the two bishops in *The Times*, 26 November, 5c. Manning wrote to Phillpotts, expressing his support and sympathy for the Bishop on 30 December 1844, and the two continued correspondence on the matter through February 1845 (Exeter Cathedral Library MS ED/11, 423–7). For a general discussion see Chadwick (1966), i. 212–21, and Galloway (1999), 43–66, 128–31.

3. The National Education was the assertion of negatives—and in principle was much akin to the much older system of Kildare Place.[e]

4. The Charitable Bequests Act is a measure of permissions—

5. The grant to Maynooth I have often described—

Whatever there be in *theory*, practically the intended increase will be an immense advance. Can you deny this?

Aff[ectiona]tely yours
W. E. Gladstone

Venerable
Archdeacon Manning
There is no doubt that the Test is *gone*.[f]

[[BL Add. MS 44247, 249–50; Morley transcript; cf. Chapeau, 311]]

450123mg

Lavington. Jan[uar]y 23. 1845.
Night.

My dear Gladstone,

I cannot deny that the intended increase[a] will be an immense advance. It must affect the relative strength, & position of the two Churches: & produce, in the end, consequences greater than can, perhaps, be foreseen.

Again I cannot deny that public opinion judges more by the *quantity* than by the principle of a measure.

I am inclined to think that your position has actually explained away your written compacts with public confidence without losing it. And you seem to incline to the same view. Now whether this be done by word, or by act in effect, it is all one.

There is however one point on which I am less able to judge.

Public confidence means confidence both in & out of Parliament.

And the confidence of men in Parliament for the most part creates confidence out of Parliament.

---

[e] See 450119mg.

[f] The printed announcement circulated on 23 January 1845 omitted the 'Test' section. See 450102gm. The *Christian Rembrancer* 47 (Jan. 1845, 188–200) included an article, 'The Proposed Oxford Test'. The Test was withdrawn while the article was at proof stage.

[a] As projected by the Bill in support of Maynooth College. See 'A Bill to amend Acts passed in Ireland for the better Education of Persons professing the Roman-catholic Religion, and for the better government of the College established at Maynooth for the Education of such Persons; and also Act passed for amending said Acts' (PP 1845 [189.] iv. 361).

I can chiefly[91] speak of that confidence which is (1) out of Parliament and (2) not affected by the feeling of trust or mistrust reflected by Parliament: but created by *yourself.*

I feel to need more data in experience & knowledge of men to know how it w[oul]d be regarded within your own sphere. This you must supply.

Limiting myself to the simple general confidence out of Parliament, I am not disposed to change the conclusion of my last letters.

I will not go again over the particulars: nor will I refer at all to any not applying directly to Ireland: though the others affect you in the vague public judgment even more.

The answers you make on earth I must allow to be fair in argument: but in effect the Charitable bequests Act goes far to found a new status for the R[oman] C[atholic] Church in Ireland: & thereby to change the relation of the two Churches: And the refusal of a grant to the Irish Church for education is:

1. A difference in regard to the Church in Ireland as compared with the Church in England which violates the public sense of the union of the two Churches.

2. A real violation of this principle of Establishment so far as that includes aid in extending & propagating the truth as held by the Church.

This touches the quick of your published system.

However the first question is how would you be affected within your own sphere? If I knew this I would feel less misgiving in speaking of all effects out of it.

Ever yours affect[ionatel]y
H. E. Manning.

The Right Hon[oura]ble
W. E. Gladstone
P.S. I said I would write again & finally about the Amendment: & I add this Postscript to say that, I feel quite decided that it is better not attempted. On reflection I feel that in addition to my previous view of the injustice and inordinate, & one sided enmity of the censures, that they are unstatutable, & illegal: & on the whole I [End of MS]
[[Pitts]]

450130gm[a]

Private

Whitehall
Jan[uary] 30. 1845

My dear Manning

It is virtually[92] all over and I am out: but, so far as this is concerned, with a clear judgment and a sound conscience. I am sure I should have broken 'the terms of my compact with public confidence'—'I thank thee for that word.'[b] It might not have been discovered now: but my sin would have found me out hereafter and at some vital moment, if I had as a member of the Government been party to a proposal reopening so much of the great question of Church and State, in principle almost reconstructing their relation for Ireland, and depend upon it seriously modifying the aspect of the case for England also—

Do you know that daily intercourse and cooperation with men upon matters of great anxiety and moment interweaves much of one's being with theirs, and parting with them, leaving them under the pressure of their work and setting myself free, feels I think much like dying: more like it than if I were turning my back altogether upon public life.

I have received great kindness & so far as personal sentiments are concerned I believe they are well among us as they can be.

Believe me
Aff[ectiona]tely yours
W. E. Gladstone

Hope is wholly with me. The affair has got into the Times today[c]—no one knows how.

[[BL Add. MS 44247, 251–2; Morley transcript; Lathbury, i. 67–8; Morley, i. 276; cf. Chapeau, 311]]

---

[a] 'Wrote to ... Manning' (*GD* iii. 430).

[b] Cf. Shakespeare, *The Merchant of Venice*, iv. i: 'I thank thee, Jew, for teaching me that word.'

[c] *The Times*, 30 January 1845, 4a notes changes in 'the present Administration ... much discussed and confidently anticipated. ... The most unforeseen and significant is the resignation and retirement of the President of the Board of Trade. Mr. Gladstone's name has been connected, from the moment of his first appearance in the world, with opinions of a very decided character on several important questions which have no reference whatever to his particular duties. ... But these speculative opinions are reported to have divided the hon. Gentleman from his colleagues on some of the most important matters likely to be brought before Parliament. And we hope we may infer that those measures ... will afford a sufficient compensation for the loss of so active a public servant as Mr Gladstone.'

450131mg

Lavington. Jan[uar]y 31. 1845.

My dear Gladstone,

I have not the shadow of a doubt that you are right: & I feel as if a weight were suddenly taken off me.

With my imperfect lights I felt ill at ease about it. I am always afraid of my first impressions, which are almost always for steps, which on reflection often appear naked, & extreme. In our first conversation I was conscious of this feeling: & my two letters were[93] to castigate it so far as was possible. But I could get no further than the hypothetical way in which I put it. And you have done that which I feel from my soul to be the safer, & wiser & higher part.

ὁ διακρινόμενος ἐὰν φάγῃ κατακέκριται[a94]

For your future course I have hardly a thought or care. You have been upon a present probation which in one act sums up all a man's whole moral life in the sight of God & man. And you have well done in it.

For this reason I say nothing of consequences or effects public, or personal: all these are things of another category and often mix in perniciously to colour, or complicate our intentions.

This has been a trial in the higher region of what is right.

I am sure you must have many painful feelings of a private kind.

Next to daily cooperation, and the offices of brotherhood in works of charity & Faith, I can conceive nothing more uniting than great common anxieties, responsibility, contests, and the whole warfare of public life. How could I doubt that you would part with the kindliest personal feelings, and with a great increased respect, & confidence?

God bless you, my dear Gladstone, you have been, & ever shall be in my prayers, such as they are, day by day.

Ever yours affect[ionate]ly
H. E. Manning

The Right Hon[oura]ble
W. E. Gladstone
[[Pitts; Chapeau, 108, 167–8]]

---

[a] He who has doubts is condemned, if he eats. Rom. 14: 23.

450206mg

Lavington. Feb[ruar]y 6. 1845

My dear Gladstone,

I have read your explanation with great interest, & Sir R[obert] Peels speech which is most honourable, & kind.[a] It seems to stand well in every way.

But my object in writing now is to say that I shall, I trust, be in London on Monday next.[b] Shall you be disengaged at ¼ to 10 on Tuesday? If so I w[oul]d come (having breakfasted): subject only to one possible hindrance from a Dentist[95] appointment: which however I shall know in a day, & will communicate.[c]

The fight at Oxford thickens. I almost hope that their precipitation in proposing this censure on Tract 90 may go far to defeat it: we are ἐπὶ ξυροῦ ἀκμῆς.[d] You see my Bishop among the requisitionists ag[ain]st Tract 90.[e]

While your deliberations were pending & pressing, I abstained from saying a word about the present confusion in the Church. But I earnestly desire some time to speak of it. We are nearer to the breakers on that side than people seem aware.

The whole case seems to me like Cabul[f] over again. If certain persons do not destroy the Church by misgovernment, and non-government, it is Heaven only that will save it.

Believe me,
Ever yours aff[ectionatel]y
H. E. Manning

[a] On Tuesday, 4 February 1845, the day before Ash Wednesday, Gladstone faced the House of Commons with the official word on his resignation from the Cabinet: 'Ruminated on the dangers of my expl[anatio]n right and left: & it made me unusually nervous. H[ouse] of C[ommons] 4½–9 [(Hansard, lxxvii. 77)]. I was kindly spoken of and heard: & I hope attained practically the purposes I had in view [on railway reform, then under discussion]: but I think the H[ouse] felt that the last part [announcing the resignation] by taking away the sting reduced the matter to flatness' (*GD* iii. 431). Gladstone was immediately answered by Peel. (Hansard, lxxvii. 77 [Gladstone], 82 [Peel]; see also *The Times*, 5 February, 4a–b). For discussion see Morley, i. 270–81.

[b] 10 February 1845.

[c] Gladstone annotated the letter on 8 February 1845: 'shall be happy to see him as proposed' and the meeting took place on Tuesday, 11 February (*GD* iii. 433).

[d] On the razor's edge. Homer, *Iliad*, 10. 173.

[e] The Heads had agreed to the censure of Newman's *Tract 90*, following the Convocation.

[f] See 1 Kgs. 9: 11ff.: For gold and cedar, Solomon gave Hiram of Tyre twenty cities 'which pleased him not', designating them as 'the land of Cabul', interpreted by Josephus and others as 'unpleasant' or 'unfruitful'.

The Right Hon[oura]ble
W. E. Gladstone

[[Pitts; Chapeau, 109, 168]]

[[On 11 February 1845 Gladstone 'Saw Hope & Manning 10–12 on Oxford matters: & we agreed [foreseeing the eventual outcome?] to a Declaration of Thanks to the Proctors' (*GD* iii. 433; cf. *English Churchman* 3 (13 Mar. 1845), 163–4, which prints the Declaration with over 500 signatures, and Chadwick, i. 210). There is a memorandum in Gladstone's hand found among Hope's papers:

We the u[nder]s[igned] M[embers] of C[onvocation], understanding that you have resolved to put your negative upon the Proposal relating to the Ninetieth Tract in Convocation on Thursday, the 13th instant, beg leave to tender to you our cordial thanks for a determination which we consider to have been demanded by the principles of our Academical Constit[utio]n.

W.E.G.

Manning and self. Feb[ruar]y. 11, '45.

J.R.H. (NLS MS 3673, 45; Ornsby, 36)

The following day he travelled to Oxford and on 13 February (see *GD* iii. 433) Ward was degraded by 777 to 386 at a vote held in the Sheldonian Theatre, but the Proctors vetoed the vote on censuring *Tract 90*. Manning recalled the event, in later life, thus:[g]

I remember well going up to Oxford with Gladstone; it was a bitterly cold day in March: snow was on the ground. There was an immense assemblage; great excitement; members of Convocation had come up from all parts of the country, the majority evidently hostile to Ward. As the sentence of Ward's degradation was announced, turning to Mr. Gladstone, by whose side I was standing, I said ? ? ?. [*sic*][h] The ominous words were heard. Men turned to look at us, and (he added with a smile) we were too well known not to be recognised. (Purcell, i. 299)

---

[g] For details of the event see Oxford *Register of Convocation, 1837–1845* (Oxford University Archives, NEP/Subtus), 489–91, on the 13 February Convocation, and *Hebdomadal Board Minutes* (Oxford University Archives WPγ (24) 6), 78–9 (29 Nov. 1844), 81 (9 Dec.), 82 (16 Dec.), 83 (20 and 23 Jan. 1845), 86 (10 Feb. 1845), and circulars numbers 32 and 33. Interleaved at p. 84 is a 28 January letter in favour of the censure signed by the bishops of Llandaff and Chichester, Hallam, Garbett, and others.

[h] According to Francis de Pressensé, *Cardinal Manning*, trans. E. Ingall (London: William Heinemann, 1897), 117–18: 'The day when he [Manning] had been present at the degradation of Ward by the University of Oxford, he turned towards Gladstone and said in a low voice, "this is the beginning of sorrows." He knew not then what a true prophet he was. While Gladstone (who had enough confidence in him to write: "I begin to think that, on a matter of importance, I cannot differ from you") wished "the trumpet to give no uncertain sound".' For some of Gladstone's correspondence on the Ward case see Lathbury, i. 314–27.

On Saturday, 15 February Gladstone met with Manning once more (*GD* iii. 434) and for the following three days was caught up with a close correspondence with Pusey on possible protests Gladstone might make to the Archbishop.[i]]]

2. Aftermath: February–August 1845

450219mg

Lavington. Feb[ruary] 19. 1845

Private

My dear Gladstone,

I wish for your advice on a point of practice which needs judgment. You see the decision in the Arches against Stone Altars.[a]

I have two, one in each of my Churches, put up within two years. There are four more at least in this Archdeaconry.

Shall I,

1. Leave them as they are: or

2. Ask the Bishops wishes & direction:[96] or

3. Take them down proprio motu.[b]

---

[i] See BL Add. MS 44281, 28–37, PHL MS Gladstone to Pusey, Nos. 3, 4, 5, 6, and i. 134–96. Cf. Bodl. MS Eng. lett. c. 654, 252–3.

[a] On 6 February 1845 *English Churchman* carried a detailed article (82–4) on the decision of Herbert Jenner Fust against the maintenance of stone altars on 31 January 1845 in the Court of Arches in the case of *Faulkner* v. *Litchfield and Stearn* (J. E. P. Robertson [ed.], *The Judgment of the Rt. Hon. Sir Herbert Jenner Fust, Kt. Dean of the Arches, &c. &c. &c. in the Case of Faulkner v. Litchfield and Stearn, on the 31st January 1845* [London: William Benning, 1845]). Earlier, the churchwardens of the Church of the Holy Sepulchre in Cambridge applied for permission to repair and renovate their building which involved work on a stone altar and credence table. The minister, Faulkner, opposed the action and the case eventually came to the Arches Court where a decision was reached on 31 January 1845 against the church-wardens, Litchfield and Stearns. Among the materials presented to Fust was Francis Close, *The Restoration of Churches is the Restoration of Popery, Proved and Illustrated from the Authenticated Publications of the 'Cambridge Camden Society': A Sermon Preached in the Parish Church, Cheltenham, on Tuesday, November 5th, 1844* (London: Hatchard, Hamilton, Adams, 1844). See White (1962), 66, 136–8, 163, Rose (1966), and Chandler (1995), 47–8. Herbert Jenner Fust (1778–1852; *DNB*) was educated at Trinity Hall, Cambridge, called to the bar, 1800, appointed King's Advocate General, 1828, Vicar General to the Archbishop of Canterbury, 1832, and Principal of the Court of Arches and Judge of the Prerogative Court of Canterbury, 1834.

[b] By an act of one's own initiative.

The question involves what is due (1) to the Bishop, i.e. the Church in him.

   2. to the Archdeaconry.

   3. to myself as an Ordinary in it.

I will add nothing to this letter.

Ever affect[ionatel]y yours

H. E. Manning

The Right Hon[oura]ble
W. E. Gladstone
[[Pitts; Chapeau, 110, 169]]

450220gm[a]

13 C[arlton] H[ouse] Terrace

Feb[ruary] 20. [18]45.

My dear Manning

It is still I suppose possible that the *Fust* judgment in the Cambridge case may be brought before a Court of Appeal: & therefore I should think any proceeding under it altogether premature.

But even if this were not so, or still more, even if it had been affirmed upon appeal, I should presume that the right course was to let them remain as they are when they exist, only not to erect new ones—

Sir H. Fust's judgment *may* be law but it is at all events no better law than the rubrics—you as ordinary must be cognisant of an hundred cases in which usage or the status quo prevails[97] against them, and no process is commenced. Why should his judgment be of greater force? A judgment can only bring the point to which it relates up to the level of the clear written statute & cannot surely by possibility carry it one jot higher.

Besides this in the case of altars the *argumentum ab inconvenienti*[b] is not wholly inconsiderable—

And, more especially, I should wait for proceedings in the principal Churches. Here is Westminster Abbey with its stone altars undisturbed, &[98] I presume some Cathedrals or at all events considerable Churches. There are quite enough to cover you *pagans*, even if the former considerations carried no force, whereas I confess they seem to me quite sufficient for the matter immediately in hand.

---

[a] 'Wrote to Manning' (*GD* iii. 435).

[b] The argument from inconvenience.

This unhappy letter of Oakeley's to the V[ice] C[hancellor][c] has brought the Bishop down upon him and I am fearful of a crisis at least as regards the charge of the Chapel: we are considering whether anything can be done.

I do not think the Heads at Oxford intend any fresh measure against Tract 90 & Pusey seems to be coming over to that opinion.[d]

Ever aff[ectiona]tely yours

W. E. Gladstone

Venerable

Archdeacon Manning

I found many horrors in Hare[e] as I read on: but many parts of truths also.

[[BL Add. MS 44247, 253–4; Morley transcript; cf. Chapeau, 312]]

450221mg

Lavington. Feb[ruar]y 21. 1845.

My dear Gladstone,

Many thanks for your opinion which falls in with my own thoughts, & fully satisfies me.[a]

---

[c] In a printed letter dated Balliol College, Oxford, 14 February 1845, Oakeley reiterated a statement he had earlier made in his pamphlet on *Tract 90*, namely, that he had 'no wish to remain a member of the University, or a Minister of the Church of England, under false colours. I claim the right which has already been asserted in another quarter, of *holding*, (as distinct from teaching,) *all Roman doctrine*, and that, notwithstanding my Subscription to the Thirty-nine Articles.' On 20 February, Gladstone was reading in proof Oakeley's *A Letter to the Bishop of London on a Subject Connected with the Recent Proceedings at Oxford* (London: James Toovey, 1845) (*GD* iii. 435).

[d] See Pusey to Gladstone, 16, 18, 19 February 1845 (BL Add. MS 44281, 28–32, 33–7) and Gladstone to Pusey, 20 February (PHL MS Gladstone to Pusey, No. 5).

[e] Gladstone was reading Julius C. Hare, *The Unity of the Church; A Sermon Preacht at St. Peter's Church, Brighton, on Thursday, December 10, 1840, at the Annual Meeting of the Chichester Diocesan Association: With Some Introductory Remarks on Uniformity* (London: John W. Parker, 1845) on 12 February 1845 (*GD* iii. 433).

[a] Following Gladstone's response, however, Manning complied with the order at some point before October 1845 when Pusey, particularly disturbed because of the implications for the final completion of St Saviour's, Leeds (Liddon, ii. 483ff.), wrote to him:

Are you at liberty to tell me any thing about your stone Altar[?] I suppose that in pulling it down, you acted upon some injunction of the Bishop's. It has caused great dismay in minds you w[oul]d not think of and would respect. These acts shock people. It seems to them as if no protest could be kept up at all. One said to me, 'What you try to build up, M[anning] pulls down.' It seems to them as if the nearest friends c[oul]d not act together. . . . I know personally you w[oul]d do everything better than I; but I dread your line being to keep things smooth; whereas I am convinced it is much better to let B[isho]ps do wrong things, than make ourselves parties to them. I sh[oul]d have resisted the B[isho]p's order to pull down a stone Altar as long as I c[oul]d &, at last, if he did (wh[ich] I believe is illegal) he sh[oul]d have done it himself. No great harm w[oul]d have been done by an act of the B[isho]p of Ch[ichester]; great harm is done by our seeming concurrence in it. I know a very valuable clergyman, older than yourself, who is very much troubled at it. It makes him despond. (Bodl. MS Eng. lett. c. 654, 277–8)

On 10 October 1845 Manning answered:

My dear Friend,

I have just time before starting for London to give you the reasons why I removed the Stone Altars in my Churches.—They are as follows.

1. Because I believe the matter to be indifferent, & to involve neither doctrine nor principle.
2. Because an Ecclesiastical Tribunal (it matters not by whom nor on what reasons) has given a decision, which until *legally* set aside (i.e. by process of law) is law.
3. Because I am myself an administrator of Eccles[iastica]l law, and should weaken my whole ground by placing myself even in apparent variance to a tribunal to wh[ich] I am liable to be compelled to proceed to fulfill my own duties.

I am especially bound to uphold the force, & obligation of Eccl[esiastical] decisions as such. These were my sole reasons, in fact. The act originated with me, & my intention was unknown to the Bishop until I communicated it.

But there are other subsidiary reasons any one of which would lead me to remove them.

1. If the Bishop had expressed his judgment & wish to that effect, I sh[oul]d have done so, and have been glad to comply with a desire in days when obedience is obtained only by penalty.
2. If any persons had through ignorance, and suchlike causes conceived offence, I should on St. Paul's rule [1 Cor. 8: 13] have been bound to do an act wh[ich] infringed no principle, & sacrificed chiefly if not me, my own preferences.
3. If any persons are in danger of thinking a principle to be at stake, I feel it is well by such an act, to add my testimony to your written arguments.

I am compelled to finish. And can only add first my affectionate thanks for your asking me, & then my wish that you should make any use you like (except publish) of this letter. May He keep us from greater difficulties, & I shall be at peace. All I can do is to follow such poor light as I have, & to remit myself to his compassion.

Believe me, my dear Friend,
Yours most affe[ctionatel]y, HEM
(PHL MS Manning to Pusey, No. 25)

Note Marriott's letter to Pusey on St Thomas's Day, 1845: 'I am glad to find that Manning's altars are still stone ones in the sense of the Church. That being so I am satisfied with his reasons. It certainly is not wise unnecessarily to state a doctrine on a ritual point in which English law is probably against us' (PHL MS PUS 136/44).

I send you a letter of the Rector of Exeter.[b] You will find in it nothing you do not know, I conceive, already.

The process of whipping the country for names to the address of thanks to the Proctors needs some tact and discernment, lest it should be too exact a revelation of our strength: unless that be found very great, & decisive.

Oakeley is running a mad career. It is like his private letters, with which I have not troubled you: but if you sh[oul]d like to see what has passed on the subject of Roman subscription, to which he refers in a note to his last[c] but I do not know how many letters, I will send them to you.

I hope to be in London on Wednesday next[d] & to stay till Saturday.

As to Hare I really feel a 'religio'[e] in speaking. I have a sincere feeling of affection for him: & he has for me much more than I deserve. He has in some ways the mind of a Poet: and a gift of beautiful English, in which when not deformed by conceits, I delight. He has also some great truths and axioms of truth (as in the thing you are reading) with which I go all lengths. But there are two things in which his defects are almost unequalled in any man I know, I mean in logical connection of reasoning, and in practical judgment. My close intimacy personal & official[f] has given me abundant opportunities of knowing this.

As to the whole question of uniformity you may judge what it means in his mouth by one fact.

A Clergyman who heard him read in at [*sic*] the Cathedral at Chichester told me that he counted 24 alterations, most of them verbal & fanciful, in the prayers. Some time afterwards I myself heard him make 8 or 9 in the Evening Service. They were chiefly like his spelling 'preacht, & toucht,' & the like. You can hardly conceive how these petty fancifulnesses hinder the good he might do: and I add with a great feeling of sorrow, that for some time past he has not contributed to unite the Diocese.

The Jerusalem Bishopric as I told you at the time was the beginning of a new[99] and a *disconnecting* tone. The publication you are reading has had the same effects.[g]

But to drop this matter which I never speak of without reluctance.

---

[b] Correspondence not located. Joseph Loscombe Richards (1798–1854), educated at Exeter College, Oxford, was appointed tutor there, 1822, and served as rector from 1838 to his death (Boase, iii. 140).

[c] See 4502003om in Addenda to this Section.

[d] 26 February 1845.

[e] Pious misgiving.

[f] That is, as colleagues in the Chichester Diocesan Association.

[g] That is, Hare, *The Unity of the Church*. See 450221mg.

As to the whole question of rubrics &c. now in contest,[h] I feel so firmly persuaded that there is a plain and (if anything can be) certain way to allay & reconcile the Church as a body, that I would willingly incur any responsibility in the attempt. If these trifling, & foolish strifes be permitted to hurt the English Church, it will only be because she is wounded in the house of her friends.

I have had going on under my eye as great an example of the blindness, and inefficiency of our Church government as can be easily found.

If any disturbance arise in these parts, it will be by contagion from a peculiar of Canterbury.[i]

Believe me,
Ever affect[ionate]ly yours
H. E. Manning

The Right Hon[oura]ble
W. E. Gladstone
[[Pitts; Chapeau, 111, 169–70]]
[[Gladstone 'saw Manning' on 27 February 1845 (*GD* iii. 437).]]

450304mg

Lavington. March 4. 1845.

My dear Gladstone,
You have heard this very sorrowful news about poor Rebecca Ayscough.[a]

---

[h] Note on this matter the latter study of Benjamin Harrison, *An Historical Inquiry into the true Interpretation of the Rubrics in the Book of Common Prayer, respecting the Sermon and the Communion Service* (London: Francis & John Rivington, 1845). Manning wrote to thank him for his work on 29 July 1845 (Pitts).

[i] A peculiar is a parish controlled from outside its normal diocesan boundaries; in this case, however, it is probably playing on the position of Benjamin Harrison (1808–87; *DNB*), Domestic Chaplain to William Howley, Archbishop of Canterbury, 1843–8, and Canon of Canterbury and Archdeacon of Maidstone, 1845–7.

[a] On 4 March 1845, Gladstone recorded that 'We were sadly shocked with the account received today of Rebecca Ayscough' (*GD* iii. 438). The case, it appears, eventually rectified itself. On 21 April 1851 Catherine Gladstone informed Gladstone: 'I have encouraging tidings of poor *Rebecca Ascough* now Rebecca Daly from Mr. Spencer Drummond who writes from Brighton begging to see me about her & wishing to come here by a day ticket—so may we not hope some of the good seed sown has ripened? This has pleased me and will you' (SDL, Glynne–Gladstone MS 612). The following day, 22 April, she wrote again: 'Mr. S. Drummond has been here about poor Rebecca. I mean to write to Mrs. Tennant—My fear is lest *his* low church views should interfere, but still I cant think as they will as he seemed so grateful for the interest I expressed, & is waiting to hear again from us[.] in the mean time he watches over the poor girl & gets needle work from her' (ibid.).

I have little to add to it except the inclosed note[b] left, by her in her room, when she went away on Sunday:[c] and to say that facts have come to my knowledge since this went which, taken alone, would have determined me to the measure I took of sending her without a day's delay from Chichester.

My reasons for acting so peremptorily are:

First consideration for Mrs. Lockhart on whom such a responsibility ought not to rest.

Next for the sake of the school, the children in it & their Parents.

And lastly, above all for the sake of the young daughters of the family where she lodged to whom I now find she has been a most dangerous familiar.

It now appears, & by her own confession, that she has spoken to them of her past life, not in the way of repentance: and has become the channel of perilous knowledge to them.

So much for my reasons. I immediately took steps to send her to the care of my sister, Mrs. Carey, a woman above all praise, who lives a life of mercy & alms deeds. I should be glad if you w[oul]d make this an occasion of calling to see her. I ought to say she is my half-sister, though to one so good I can recognize nothing less than the closest relations.

She will do your bidding about Rebecca.

As to the poor girl, I must add two things.

First there is no evidence of actual sin at this time.

And next, her return appears to have been her own act: & so far as we can yet see, appears to be a mastery over the temptation.

Both these things still give hope.

But she will need an exact penitential discipline, & a long course of very real & searching repentance.

Do you remember that when you spoke of her after I had first seen her, I did not readily answer? It may have escaped you, but I had from the first very great anxieties about her, knowing how fearful are the passive effects of such a life as hers, short as it may have been. I believe she desires to be delivered from the power which is still upon her: that it still holds her fearfully I am compelled to believe.

It is altogether a sad case: for there is about her something that has won the kindly feelings of everyone.

I know nothing short of the Magdalen Hospital that will with any sufficient hope of a lasting restoration, meet her case.

---

[b] Not located.   [c] 2 March 1845.

May I ask of you to discharge Mrs. Carey of her responsibility as soon as you are able. Her address is 44 Cadogan Place.

I have written this in a matter of fact way as the exigency of the case requires: but I cannot help saying with what unfeigned sorrow I have done it, & how I share in the pain you will both feel after all your kindness & solicitude for this poor soul.

Believe me,
Ever yours affect[ionate]ly
H. E. Manning

The Right Hon[oura]ble
W. E. Gladstone
[[Pitts; Chapeau, 112, 171–2]]

450316mg

Lavington. Palm Sunday 1845.

My dear Gladstone,

The inclosed was not intended to travel to me much less to you, but it is no breach of trust to send it. There is very little in it, but even that, I had not time today to transcribe.

I fear poor Rebecca Ayscough has practised great deceit, & has at times deceived even herself. She *seems* now just dropping through into the pit again: but I hope you will not be '*weary* in well doing.'[a] The poor girl may yet be saved.

I have been in correspondence with the Master of Balliol about No. 90.[b] He professes himself satisfied with the past censures: & not disposed to move again.

When you have time I should like to have from you your view of Oakeley's case as a *practical* question in its bearing upon the Church of England hereafter.

His friends have seemed to me to dwell exclusively on two points: 1. his own personal usefulness. 2. the unsettlement of other minds likely to follow in any act of the Church adverse to his claim. I want a broader consideration of the question, & would exclude the *present & personal* consequences of such an act.

---

[a] Gal. 6: 9; 1 Thess. 3: 13.

[b] Richard Jenkyns (1782–1854; *DNB*), educated at Balliol College, Oxford, was appointed tutor, 1813, bursar, 1814, Master of the School, 1809, public examiner, 1811–12, and Master of Balliol, 1819, which position he held until his death, serving as Dean of Wells, 1845–8. On his tenure as Master and his antagonism to the Tractarians see Jones (1997), 180–200.

Believe me,
Yours ever affect[ionate]ly
H. E. Manning

The Right Hon[oura]ble
W. E. Gladstone
[[BL Add. MS 44247, 255–6]]
[Enclosure[c]]

My dear Archdeacon,

As I am happy in every opportunity of holding communication with one for whom I entertain so high a regard as yourself I have to thank, instead of blaming[100] you, for what you are pleased to call freedom in writing to me. However dangerous may [be][101] the modes of interpreting the 39 Articles suggested by Tract 90,[102] I consider that Tract to have been *directly* condemned by the decision of the Hebdomadal Board in 1841 and again[103] indirectly[104] by[105] a considerable majority of Members of Convocation on the 13th of Feb[ruary] last. The sentences upon[106] Mr Ward in the 1st Proposition submitted to Convocation on that occasion cannot[107] be fairly considered any of themselves[108] an actual condemnation of the principles inculcated by the author of Tract 90.—[109] I therefore[110] for one am quite[111] satisfied with the consequential declaration of the sentiments of the University on that point. But in thus giving my own opinion I cannot answer for the opinions of[112] those for whom the requisition[113] may be addressed, calling for a further notice of the obnoxious publication.[114] I may however[115] venture to remark that the spirit of the requisitionists is perhaps[116] naturally excited by the efforts[117] which have been studiously & successfully[118] made to obtain signatures to an address of thanks to the Proctors for the interposition of their veto.

With regard to the alarum which you[119] endeavour to create in my mind by the threatened exposure of the A[rch]b[isho]p of Dublin, I must say that serious as may be the blow inflicted on the Church by the censure of one in so exalted a station, yet I doubt not that,[120] if a case deserving of such a notice were to be clearly made out against the A[rch]b[isho]p of D[ublin] which equally with Mr. W[ard]'s affected[121] the indignity of our Academical Statutes, the University would not shrink from its duty in vindicating the Truth.—Till you mentioned it[122] I had not indeed heard

---

[c] The letter to Manning was the result of the latter's earlier letter to Jenkyns of 6 March 1845. For this and related correspondence as well as details on the possible censure of Whately, Archbishop of Dublin, see Addenda to this Section.

of the A[rch]b[isho]p of D[ublin]'s recent publication. You will perhaps allow me[123] to correct a mistake into which you have fallen, in suggesting that the A[rch]b[isho]p of D[ublin] had by his counsel *promoted the late measures*. I can truly say that[124] these[125] measures[126] were wholly independent of[127] his part,[128] being[129] neither suggested by him in the first instance nor afterwards aided[130] of his advice. It is true that the A[rch]b[isho]p early in the last term[131] wrote to the V[ice] C[hancellor] on the subject [of] the Religious opinions. Mr. W[ard]'s case had been previously[132] taken up by several members of the Hebdomadal Board & no subsequent communication was made to them by the A[rch]b[isho]p of D[ublin].[133]

Believe me to be, regards with every kind wish[134]

Y[ou]rs faithfully

RJ

[[Private collection of Mr Richard Jenkyns, Lady Margaret Hall, Oxford; copy at Balliol Library MS Jenkins]]

450317gm[a]

13 C[arlton] H[ouse] Terrace

March 17. [18]45

My dear Manning

Your letter and Mr. Browne's[b] have been at Hagley which has delayed my acknowledgement and I have also been most closely occupied with a many-figured commercial pamphlet[c] and otherwise:

The disclosures about poor Rebecca were indeed extremely painful and at the first moment produced the effect of surprise: but I quite agree with you and think that in such cases nothing can justly surprise when we consider how deep the canker eats. But still I also believe with you the general intention of her will to be upright & therefore hope the best: I have written to Mrs. Browne.[d] My wife has seen Mrs Carey & been delighted with her not to add that we are much beholden to her kindness in getting Rebecca placed in an institution. I was not able to call on her but I now feel that I know her.

[a] 'Wrote to Manning' (*GD* iii. 441).

[b] Not located.

[c] W. E. Gladstone, *Remarks upon Recent Commercial Legislation: Suggested by the Expository Statement of the Revenue from Customs, and Other Papers Lately Submitted to Parliament* (London: John Murray, 1845; preface dated 15 Mar. 1845).

[d] Not located; no reference in *GD.*

I return Dr. Richards's note.[e] The Second Requisitionists[f] will I think
build a wall to break their own heads against. I find S[amuel] Wilberforce,[g]
Tyler,[h] Saunders,[i] utterly averse to the revival of that movement: and
considering the class they represent I am convinced that the majority of
the University is against it.

But Oakeley has sadly complicated these vexed affairs. The B[isho]p of
London told me 1. how bitterly he regretted the challenge 2. that he & all
the B[isho]ps (probably meaning those in London?) were convinced it
must be taken up 3. that if he could not get on in the Arches Court he
would act as Diocesan and suspend or rather withdraw his license—I was
also painfully impressed with the belief that he had nothing like a measured theological view of the case—in the meantime I think O[akeley]
becomes more tenacious. Last night at Margaret Chapel[j] I heard him for

[e] Joseph L. Richards, Rector of Exeter College. See 450221mg.

[f] That is, those who wished to renew the censure of Newman's *Tract 90*.

[g] Cf. Wilberforce to Gladstone, 2 and 14 January 1845 (BL Add. MS 44343, 66–7,
68–9). On the basis of the earlier letter Gladstone could have concluded that Wilberforce
opposed any attempt at a censure of *Tract 90*.

[h] Revd James Endell Tyler declared his intention to Gladstone on 12 February 1845 to
vote against Ward, but expressed his great relief that the Proctors had intervened in the case
of Newman and *Tract 90* (BL Add. MS 44362, 89–90).

[i] Augustus Page Saunders (1801–78; tutor at Christ Church, Oxford, Headmaster of
Charterhouse, 1832, and Dean of Peterborough, 1853 [Boase, iii. 418]) wrote to Gladstone,
6 March 1845 (BL Add. MS 44362, 111–12).

[j] Palm Sunday, 16 March 1845 (*GD* iii. 441). On Gladstone's relationship to the
Fraternity at the Margaret Chapel see John E. Acland, *A Layman's Life in the Days of the
Tractarian Movement: In Memoriam Arthur [Acland] Troyte* (London: James Parker, 1904), 172–7,
and note Gladstone's latter comment on 23 February 1845, when he '[w]orked on the
contemplated applicat[io]n of the Engagement to myself which may God guide and
prosper.' See the Gladstone memorandum (Lambeth MS, 1846[?]): The Engagement
(founded by the Aclands in 1844 and lasting into 1852) had the following rules: '1. Some
regular works of charity. 2. Attendance on the daily service. 3. Observance of the fasts of the
Church. 4. Observance of the hours of prayer (9,12,3). 5. Special prayers for the unity of the
Church and the conversion of unbelievers at some hour: also for the other persons engaged.
6. Rule of number of hours to be spent in sleep and recreation. 7. Meditation and morning
prayers—self-examination with evening. 8. To fix a portion of income for mercy and piety.
9. To consider with a practical view the direction of the Church concerning confession and
absolution. 10. Failing any spiritual director to follow the judgment of one or more of those
engaged in the case of breach of rule. 11. If unable to perform (1) contribute funds instead.
12. To meet, compare results, and consider amendments' (*GD* iii. 435–6; see Morley, i. 99f.)
and compare Manning's reference to 'sharing the discipline', 500905mg. According to
John E. Acland (1904), 172–7, the Engagement was first established by July 1844 and
included among its members: Frederic Rogers (Lord Blachford); Thomas Henry Haddan

the first time in his Sermon advert in detail to the[135] religious movement of the time, and distinguish the *earlier & less healthful* from the *later & more healthful* stages of its development. He is now evidently wedded in heart to this controversy of his own, which is a bad sign for our peace.

In the midst of my writing I have got your note.[k] My wife will wish to send the note to her sister—my post is too heavy today to allow me to say more about Oakeley—I wish you all the blessings of the season & remain

Aff[ectiona]tely yours
W. E. Gladstone

Archdeacon Manning

[[BL Add. MS 44247, 257–8; Morley transcript; Purcell, i. 300]]

450319mg

Lavington. March 19. 1845.

My dear Gladstone,

You may have time this Easter to read the inclosed[a] on which I should like to have your mind.

I have for some time past felt that something had gone out of course in Margaret Street.[b] I have missed the tone of calm persuasion and charitable

---

(1814–73, educated at Brasenose College, Oxford, called to the bar, 1841, first editor of *The Guardian* [*DNB*]); Thomas Dyke Acland; Edwin Richard Windham Wyndham-Quin (Lord Adare, 1812–71, educated at Trinity College, Dublin, served as a Conservative MP for Glamorganshire, 1837–50, with other Irish High Churchmen attracted to the Tractarians through William Sewell, received into the Roman Catholic Church, 1855; *DNB*); John T. Coleridge; Roundell Palmer; Mathew Rhodes; Thomas Moorsom; William Monsell (1812–94, 1st Baron Emly, educated at Oriel College, Oxford, MP for Limerick, and held a number of offices with Liberal governments, received into the Roman Catholic Church, 1850; *DNB*); A. H. D. Acland; W. E. Gladstone; Robert Campbell; William Butterfield (1814–1900, trained as an architect in Worcester and early attached to the Cambridge Camden Society, designing churches throughout the century according to the Society's principles, including the redesign of All Saint's, Margaret Street, 1859 [*DNB*; Thompson (1971)]); Robert Brett (1808–74, surgeon, educated at St. George's Hospital, London, founder of the Guild of St Luke (medical men working with clergy), Vice-President of the London Union, 1850, a founder and Vice-President of the English Church Union, 1860 [*DNB*; Boase, i. 391]).

[k] That is, 450317mg.

[a] Not located; Manning appears to have included part of his correspondence with Oakeley, December 1844–February 1845. For full correspondence see Addenda to this Section.

[b] Manning wrote to Oakeley concerning his reservations. Oakeley 'fanc[ied] to see a definite line in our Church on two opposite sides, but not on the space between' late in 1844

judgment which I used to perceive there, & have ever seen in Newman, & Pusey.

Of late a sharp, querulous, challenging note has been sounded. Private letters are my chief proofs of this, though Oakeleys public acts are enough. I have not troubled you with them, & they need a longer preface than I can offer to write.

May all the sadder and the brighter blessings of these next days be with you.

Ever yours affect[ionatel]y

H.E. Manning

P.S. Let me have your Pamphlet. Remember I am a Free Trader in wool.[c]

H.E.M.

[[Pitts; Chapeau, 113, 171]]

450331gm[a]

13 Carlton H[ouse] Terrace

M[ar]ch. 31. 1845

My dear Manning

I have been in hopes of finding time to consider at least with some of the care which it deserves your historical letter to Oakeley—but it has not yet been found nor have I any immediate prospect of it. Of my general concurrence you are aware.

This new appointment to Ely is not I fear a good appointment,[b] though the spirit in which it is made is a good one: I mean the desire to appoint a moderate & safe, as well as a learned & good man. But a man may be learned & good, & yet a cipher for the purposes of direction in these

---

and drew from him an animated and lengthy response (Oakeley to Manning, 12 December 1844, Bodl. MS Eng. lett. c. 654, 58–64). The debate between the two men continued in a series of letters through 3 February 1845 (ibid. 65–102). Manning also wrote to Pusey what he described as 'a painful letter' on 5 March 1845 which expressed his concerns about Oakeley (see PHL MS Manning to Pusey, No. 19).

  [c] Pun on the parish of Woolavington, of which Manning's parish of West Lavington remained a detached portion until 1851 (see Salzman [1963], 65). The reference is to Gladstone's *Remarks upon Recent Commercial Legislation* (see 450317gm).

  [a] 'Wrote to . . . Manning' (*GD* iii. 444).

  [b] Joseph Allen, Bishop of Ely, died 20 March 1845; the death was announced in the *English Churchman* on 27 March (190). Thomas Turton (1780–1864; *DNB*), Dean of Peterborough, was nominated, 28 March, and consecrated 4 May. A controversialist, Turton was know for his conflicts with, among others, Edward Copleston on predestination, Lord Brougham on natural theology, and Nicolas Wiseman on the Eucharist.

difficult & crooked times. There is a rumour that Dr. Bull goes to[136] Westminster.[c]

With regard to my pamphlet you little know what you ask for. I will only consent on these terms: when you come to see me you shall look into it for one minute and if after that you desire to possess it, it shall be yours.

The Prayers are just out.[d]

I am very happy to see a Fourth Edition of your Sermons.[e]

Maynooth is close at hand— God guide us all safely through it.[f]

The dimensions of the question are palpably swelling every day. In the House of Commons I do not doubt there is a large majority in its favour and the Lords will not resist—but farther than this I do not pretend to see into the matter.

Believe me
Aff[ectiona]tely yours
W.E. Gladstone

Venerable
Archdeacon Manning

[[BL Add. MS 44247, 259–60; Morley transcript; cf. Purcell, i. 300]]

[[Maynooth remained firmly on Gladstone's mind throughout this period and on 9 April 1845 he 'saw Manning on Maynooth—the movement to Rome &c.' for two hours between 11 a.m. and 1.30 p.m. (*GD* iii. 446).]]

450413mg

Lavington. April 13. 1845.
Sunday night.

My dear Gladstone,

I was not able to come on the chance of seeing you yesterday morning, as I left London by an early train. Tomorrow I shall be all day engaged, & I must therefore write tonight or lose another day.

---

[c] John Bull (d. 1858) was educated at Christ Church, Oxford, and following several pastorates was appointed a canon of Christ Church Cathedral in 1830, a position which he held to his death (Boase, i. 468).

[d] Gladstone's *A Manual of Prayers From the Liturgy*. See 450116mg.

[e] Reference is to Henry Edward Manning, *Sermons* [vol. i] (London: James Burns, 1845*a*).

[f] Once freed from his association with the Cabinet and acting as an independent Member in the House, Gladstone supported the Maynooth grant. See *The Times*'s reports on his re-entry in favour of Maynooth, 7 March 1845, 4j, 8 March, 6f, 31 March, 3b.

I heard your explanation on Friday night with great interest.[a] So far as I can judge the House seemed to receive it very well: and I cannot doubt that the course you have taken will confirm the belief which I have never heard so much as breathed on, of your sensitive integrity of purpose.

As a speech it was far the best I have heard from you, & I thought it very real, & able.

So much about it for this particular occasion.

I have been reproaching myself more than once for saying to you so abruptly what I said in Grosvenor Square,[b] on the brink of such a debate as that of Friday night. But it seemed to me to be well to say it for the very reason that such a debate was coming, & that you were especially marked in it.

I, therefore, set myself on Friday to watch what you said with a view to better understanding what was meant by others.

It is of course most rash to judge by one speech, but such remarks as I made I will give, only premising that I feel how little weight anything of mine on the subject ought to have.

Your speech seemed to me to be perfectly clear in its entire intellectual statement.

Every several argument seemed to me to be equally clear.

The whole series of arguments I seemed to find in order, and place.

I am, therefore, persuaded that there was no mental indistinctness.

Neither did I find any indistinctness[137] of expression: for it seemed to me to be expressed with great exactness, & point.

And yet I fancy that I can perceive some reasons for the sort of criticism I retailed to you.

First as regards the person who made it to me, it did not escape me that he was never five minutes still the whole night: I saw him all over the house a dozen times, & that while you were speaking.

So much for that part of the affair.

---

[a] On Friday, 11 April 1845 Gladstone spoke in the House of Commons 'under 1 ½ hour on Maynooth: most defectively but I hope without any great positive error' (*GD* iii. 447; Hansard, lxxxix. 520, 556; *The Times*, 12 Apr., 3c–4a). The speech was later published as *Substance of a Speech for the Second Reading of the Maynooth College Bill, in the House of Commons, on Friday, April 11, 1845* (London: John Murray, 1845; dated 16 Apr. 1845). Note also his letter to his constituents on the matter as published in *The Times*, 19 April, 7d. For details see Kerr (1982), 193–289, and Cornish (1995), 99–105.

[b] i.e. the meeting of 9 April 1845, a Wednesday, two days before Gladstone's speech on Friday, 11 April.

But the following things occur to me on thinking your speech over.

I. As to the matter of it.

(1) The several arguments were so elaborated as to diminish the unity of effect. Elaborating detailed arguments has always seemed to me to be a great feature and force in your mind, & with this strong habit it is difficult to keep details in subordination. I could more easily say for what *reasons*, than for *what reason* you support the Bill. Though there be many reasons yet, I suppose, subordination w[oul]d give them the unity & effect of one.

(2) The strongest arguments seemed to me to be those in refutation of the reasons on[138] which you did *not* rest your conclusion, & they left more impression on my mind that[139] the arguments on which you did found your vote.

(3) It seemed to me that the strong tendency of your mind to fine & abstract distinction shewed itself not prominently at all in the speech and yet it moulded your forms of argument.

I really hardly like to venture a criticism but it always seems to me to be necessary to have some one, or one chief reason to enunciate in a fixed proposition, & to state, & re-state it at the beginning, middle, & end of an argument addressed to many & therefore to not a few dull and inattentive minds.

II. Next as to expression.

(1) I seemed to feel that your sentences were long and too continuous. Wherever your broke them up & spoke in single, or at most in double propositions the effect appeared immediately perceptible. Few people can follow a sustained mental process in their own minds, & still less in another. And to tie country gentlemen to the train of yours, is like dragging them at the tail of a wild-horse.

(2) The diction seemed to me to be latinistic, and I cannot help thinking that Latin has an appearance of refinement & abstraction about it (as compared with the family of Saxon words) which passes to the matter.

Besides the Latin English has a stiffness and want of idiom which is less akin to our common ears.

Now I have risked all this with a freedom which I have no claim to except on the score of our tried friendship, and my desire to see the[140] powers it has pleased God to give you unfolding themselves year by year into a greater force of persuasion, & control. You remember in the De Oratore how much is made of a popular style both in language & argument.[c]

---

[c] Among other passages in Cicero's *On the Orator*, note 2, xlii (178), treating the need for the orator to gain the favour of the audience.

I suppose the use of the[141] *actual average words*, & *thoughts* of the people spoken to must be the means & conditions of convincing & persuading them. And to a mind under the discipline of yours this is like a new language & a new logic, a sort of approximate system, not perfectly exact, but the most exact that can be employed.

Accept all this at least as an intended offering of a lively & kind interest.

I cannot end[142] without asking you to let me know so far as you may how your explanation was received by the Government.

Believe me,

My dear Gladstone,

Yours ever affect[ionate]ly,

H. E. Manning.

The Right Hon[oura]ble

W. E. Gladstone

M.P.

[[Pitts; Chapeau, 114, 173–5; Gladstone's annotation on the letter indicates he took the matter seriously:

1. The details not in due subordination

2. The confutative arguments left the strongest impression

3. Want of a fixed chief reason to annunciate & [illegible word] upon

4. Sentences too long ($\lambda\epsilon\xi\iota\varsigma$ $\dot{\epsilon}\iota\rho o\mu\acute{\epsilon}\nu\eta$?[d])

5. diction latinistic.]]

450416gm[a]

13 Carlton H[ouse] Terrace

Ap[ril] 16. 1845

My dear Manning

I thank you heartily for every part of your letter, except the sentence in which you half-excuse yourself for your freedom; either on Wednesday last,[b] or in your letter itself, it was alike acceptable and valuable.[143]

You have made five particular criticisms to four of which I agree wholly and to the fifth with a qualification: I have little more to do than to digest and apply them.

Refinements, and abstractions, and long sentences, I have tried to get rid of though it may surprise you to hear it—I am sensible that I have not yet succeeded, particularly as to the first and last.

---

[d] Fastened together in strings.   [a] 'Wrote to Manning' (*GD* iii. 448).

[b] See 450413mg. Reference is to the Wednesday meeting of 9 April 1845.

You must however recollect that a subject of this kind is one of large discourse looking before and after: and I do not think it would be wise to handle it simply with a view to the immediate debate: nor consequently with that degree of submission to the dispositions of the hearer, which in a mere debate would be advisable.

For example, to lay the permanent groundwork of my argument no part was so essential as what I said respecting the incapacity of 'Protestantism' to afford us a religious ground of legislative action.[c] But yet it was open as an argument in debate to every possible objection. Obviously it would enlist against me the sympathies of nineteen twentieths of my hearers: it had a dangerous affinity of sound to the most violent & paradoxical

---

[c] Note Gladstone's comments: 'I now come, Sir, to that which I think is an objection springing out of a religious sentiment, and entitled to profound respect on that account, as well as on account of the numbers of persons by whom it is entertained. I mean the objection of those who would propose, as the rule of the future policy of the State, that we should recognise as admissible to public support all the forms of Protestantism, without making any specific exception, but should at the same time hold as disqualified all that is in the communion of the Church of Rome. Now, Sir, I am bound frankly and plainly to avow, that I cannot understand nor adopt this principle, either as a principle of the Constitution, or as a principle of religion. I cannot in the first place understand that there is an essential alliance between the law and the Constitution on the one hand, and an undefined and negative idea, such as that which is indicated by the term Protestantism, on the other. But do not let me do an injustice, nor seem to glance at that which I have not in my view. I am very far indeed from asserting that the phrase Protestantism, as it is used by individuals, is necessarily or always indefinite. It is in many minds any thing rather than a negative idea. With them, so far from being confined to mere negation, and to a protest against opinions or practices that they disclaim, it is the exponent of a definite and positive belief in the truths of the Christian revelation, on which those who employ it are content to build their individual hope of salvation. Of these I do not speak, but of the signification which the term Protestantism will be found practically, and I fear inevitably, to bear, if it is adopted as the legal definition comprising all forms of Christianity which are to be admissible to the favour of the State, and excluding those which are to be disqualified. In this point of view I deny that the constitution of the country recognises all that bears the name of Protestant, and nothing that does not bear it. It is provided indeed by law that the Sovereign of the United Kingdom cannot be other than a Protestant; but this general term acquires a defined and positive sense, from the further provision of the law which requires that the Sovereign shall also be a communicant of the Church of England. I admit that the law does not recognise the religion of the Church of England alone; there is also an alliance formed by Statute between it and the Presbyterian Church Establishment of Scotland. That Establishment, therefore, professes a Protestantism which is known to the Constitution. But here we are dealing with what is definite; what is known to the State, embodied in written instruments, and incapable of alteration, except with the knowledge and consent of the State' (Hansard, lxxxix. 540–2).

propositions lately broached among our Romanisers: it partook of the nature of refinement & of abstraction, and the distinction between Protestantism as a true expression in many cases by the individual of a fixed belief, and Protestantism as a constitutional definition of sound & allowable religion, is one that it would take months to hammer into the minds of an assembly of Englishmen. While I was upon this part of the subject I was acutely conscious of being within an inch of losing the House altogether & irrecoverably. In fact I am sorry to say the multiplicity of relations involved is such, that I feel as if I had escaped from a devouring flood when I have got through a speech of that kind in the sorriest and shabbiest manner: and for half the way through it I am always on the brink of utter confusion—

This is said not so much in qualification of any *one* of your definite remarks, as in order to establish *de jure*[144] a general class of exceptions from the rule of using the 'actual average words' &c. of the hearers. But *de facto* I must stand, for such occasions, on a broader excuse: the incapacity of the brain to do its work.

The Archbishop of Canterbury writes me a very kind approving note upon the 'Manual of Prayers'—and makes the very suggestion that you made with regard to Psalms.[d] I am only distrustful of my fitness to make the selection—

Ever aff[ectiona]tely yours
W. E. Gladstone

Murray will send you a copy of my Speech.[e]
Venerable
Archdeacon Manning
[[BL Add. MS 44247, 261–3; Morley transcript; cf. Chapeau, 313]]

450418mg

Lavington. April 18. 1845.

My dear Gladstone,

I have just read Smythe's speech on Wednesday night:[a] & a very clever & foolish one it is. Somehow I cannot help writing to you, for though I do not

---

[d] Archbishop of Canterbury to Gladstone, 15 April 1845 (BL Add. MS 44362, 147–8) suggests that in the second edition Gladstone include extracts from the Psalms.

[e] William E. Gladstone, *Substance of a Speech for the Second Reading of the Maynooth College Bill.*

[a] George Augustus Frederick Smythe (1818–57; *DNB*), MP for Canterbury, 1851–2, spoke on Maynooth at the second reading of the Bill, commenting that Gladstone's speech supporting the Bill on 16 April 1845 was 'a good cause...defended by a bad apology' (Hansard, lxxix. 833; comment on 838; *The Times*, 17 Apr., 4c).

imagine that such attacks make any deep impression, yet both in their circumstances, & consequences they are painful.

In the course your mind has taken on this subject since you entered Parliament I can recall almost chronologically the growth of juster & deeper principles which will solve nearly all the mixed questions of your future life.

The misconstruction, and railing of this moment will soon be over. It is full of solace even now that no man has assailed your personal or political integrity. The most that has been charged on you is the not knowing your own mind, or having changed it, or having left office for no sufficient reason, or being hampered by an impracticable Theory.

God grant I may never deserve a worse imputation than all these taken at once. The true reading of your case seems to me to be clear as light.

You had to find your highest principles after you had entered into public life.

You found, & defended them in writing, after they had been really though for the most part covertly abandoned by the Legislature.

They are as absolutely impracticable under the conditions of the Civil Power at this moment, as they are absolutely true in themselves.

The course of Legislation has been slowly disclosing the inevitable consequences of the acts of 1828.1829.[b]

The Theory outlived those years because facts only strained, but did not subvert it.

It is now acknowledged as a rule of Legislature to be[145] subverted, and you have been brought to what is in effect an epoch in your political life.

Happy is the man who with whatsoever cost & pain passes through such an epoch with a character of unsullied integrity. This I trust, my dear friend, God helping you,[146] will be your lot. Indeed it is so already.

I call it an epoch for this reason. Look at the question as I may, I can read it in no way but this.

The British Empire has converted the principle of universal toleration into the principle of universal support of such religious bodies as either by number, organization, or political weight are definite & strong enough to force themselves upon the cognizance of the Civil Power.

This is universal in the Colonies.

It is now being recognized in Ireland.

---

[b] 'The Repeal of the Corporation and Test Acts' (9 George IV c. 17 [1828]) and 'The Catholic Emancipation Act' (10 George IV c. 7 [1829]).

And it will be at some time, however distant, admitted in England.

In fact we are gravitating towards the same political idea as France.

These Maynooth debates have swept away every check upon their political theory except the principle of gradual application, for the sake of our existing institutions in Ireland, & England. In fact it is the question of Free-Trade, & our existing commerce over again.

This leads me to one word in supplement to my last letter, & suggested by your reply.

I entirely agree in all your qualifications in regard to your speech of Friday last. Indeed I intended to supply them. It was evident to me that you did not desire and were bound not, to state your affirmative arguments a whit more strongly than the occasion absolutely forced[147] from you. The movement that way has momentum enough already. And to shew a practical limit to it was part of your object.

Moreover I quite feel as all that I have written will shew that, the importance of that speech in regard to its effect on the house there is altogether as nothing compared to its unspeakable importance as the basis of your acts hereafter.

And now I have only two more things to say for which as your last letter *chode*[c] my words of apology I will make none, though you will see how I shall use my freedom.

I am anxious for two points.

The one that your return to Office be as long delayed, within limits of discretion, as may be.

The other that you will for a while suffer *us* to bear the weight & brunt of our theological strife.

You cannot misunderstand my drift in either of these, less in the latter than[148] the former.

Down to this time you have done a good work in the line which recalls our letters of years ago. Both by word & deed you have rallied the members of the Church.

The time is come when they must do the same for you: & you may fairly, & I think wisely give yourself to preparing for the broader, and more life-&-death questions which will break inevitably upon the Irish & English Churches.

You will serve them better in power, or in Parliament the more you reserve yourself to meet them upon the basis on[149] which henceforward, alas, I believe will be the career of public events.

[c] Chided (archaic).

I need not guard myself from seeming to breathe a thought that should withdraw you from our ever-increasing devotion of life to Christ & His Church among us.

And I cannot, in this letter at least, attempt to state what course appears to me open to you for the sake of the Church after this epoch has passed.

Such thoughts as I can put together in due time I will.

May God ever guide, & keep you to the end.

Believe me,
Ever your affectionately,
H. E. Manning.

The Right Hon[oura]ble
W. E. Gladstone
[[Pitts; Chapeau, 115, 175–7]]

450426gm[a]

13 C[arlton] H[ouse] Terrace
Ap[ril] 26. 1845.

My dear Manning

I *am* anxious but not about my own reputation, nor about Maynooth—my cares have reference to the future fortunes of the Irish Church. I have always looked upon the Maynooth measure as what is called buying time: a process that presupposes the approach of the period of surrender. Whether or not time will be actually gained as the result of the measure—or whether the thing given & the thing sought will both be lost is I think very doubtful.

What we pay however I do not consider to consist chiefly in the £17,000 a year: but in the cession we make of most important parts of the argument for the maintenance of the Church in Ireland.

That you should feel anxious on my account about Smythe's speech is another proof of your friendship but also of the fact that you do not[150] breathe the air of politics. It makes no impression upon me whatever. Perhaps taken with some other speeches & with the desire I find time to entertain out of doors it entails upon me the duty of spending ten minutes in explanation—but it is not of such materials (though I do not mean to underrate the speech, it was a very clever one) that the burdens of my walk of life are made up—

---

[a] 'Wrote to . . . Manning' (*GD* iii. 450).

Newman sent me a letter giving his own explanation of my position—it was admirably done. Of course you shall see it.[b]

And now as to your two precepts. I can say nothing about my disposition to return to office (let alone that of other people to recall me) until my mind is made up what policy ought to be adopted & maintained with regard to the Irish Church as the guide of future years. You need not therefore be afraid of anything precipitate on that subject: I do not anticipate anything early. Your precept would have even more value if it were more defined, but more defined it cannot well be since the due measure of its application must be determined by courts. However I think I enter into the spirit of it.

So likewise of the second. I am ready to admit that the things I have done with regard to the Church, which I think are three (the Article in 1843,[c] the signature in Pusey's case,[d] and the Hawkins correspondence[e]) were all of them on some accounts very undesirable—The worst of it is that the least desirable (the 2d & 3d) were the most necessary—& done under what seemed an absolute pressure of duty. I fervently trust no such occasion may recur.

> Believe me ever
> Aff[ectiona]tely yours
> W. E. Gladstone

Venerable
Archd[eaco]n Manning

I am a *brute* for not having thanked you for giving me so much time & valuable thought.

[[BL Add. MS 44247, 264–7; Morley transcript; Purcell, i. 301; cf. Chapeau, 313]]

---

[b] On the correspondence between the two men at this time see Addenda to this Section.

[c] 'Present Aspect of the Church', *Foreign and Colonial Review* 4 (Oct. 1843), 552–603; *Gleanings*, i. 1–80. See 431030gm.

[d] See 430625mg.

[e] On 6, 7, 8, and 10 February 1845 Gladstone wrote to Hawkins, Provost of Oriel, on the proposed censure against *Tract 90*, and on 12 February he wrote to thank him for the Proctors' veto (Oriel College Library MS Gladstone–Hawkins Correspondence, GL1–5). Hawkins wrote to Gladstone 7, 8, 10, 11 February (ibid. GL65–8). Cf. Gladstone to Pusey, 10 February, regarding the information he had received from Hawkins on the Proctors' veto (ibid. GL97).

450429mg

Lavington. April 29. 1845.

My dear Gladstone,

I write to say that I hope to be in London on Tuesday[a] for a few days.

And as I am writing I will add, that I can understand how my letter might look as if I made more of Smythe's speech than I really intended. I think I know fairly well what such things and especially in this instance, are worth.

The fact is I was thinking only of you: & that made me say nothing about the Irish Church.

Do you know that the consequences of this measure about Maynooth, have so come out on reflection that I am shaken as to the line I, at least, ought to pursue.

Do not feel bound to answer this letter.

My reasons are these.

1. The Maynooth Grant, as you have said, disposes, so far as the Legislature is concerned, of the religious objection[151] to any measure of endowment in favour of the R[oman] C[atholic] Church in Ireland.

2. This abandons the whole *active* theory of the Reformation in Ireland at least.

It abandons the whole *active* theory of 'the duty of Godly Princes &c'[b] as the Regale was expounded at the Reformation. It abandons the whole notion of the Irish Church acting on the Irish people according to the idea of the Reformation.

It lays the beginnings of the old contests of Provisors over again between the Regale & Pontificate in Ireland.

So far I say nothing of its effect on the existing status of the Irish Church.

---

[a] 6 May 1845.

[b] See Article 37 of the Thirty Nine Articles, 'Of the Civil Magistrates': 'Where we attribute to the King's Majesty the chief government, by which Titles we understand the minds of some slanderous folks to be offended; we give not to our Princes the ministering either of God's Word, or of the Sacraments, the which thing the Injunctions also lately set forth by Elizabeth our Queen to most plainly testify; but that only prerogative, which we see to have been given always to all godly Princes in holy Scriptures by God himself; that is, that they should rule all estates and degrees committed to their charge by God, whether they be Ecclesiastical or Temporal, and restrain with the civil sword the stubborn and evil-doers.'

3. But the abandonment of the Reformation theory will inevitably bring on the breaking up of the Status which rests upon it, & can be justified by that theory alone.

As you say the Irish Church will be surrendered. I think it is ceded covertly already. And that the force of events, facts, and popular will makes its support impossible.

You may go on calling it the Irish Church, & the Established Church, & the Church of the Civil Power, i.e. of the Crown, but it is a mere phrase.

The *work of the XVI Century* is undone in Ireland.

It is a question of *first* principles.

So much for Ireland.

Now for England.

You will have disposed of the religious objection[152] (I thank thee) for the same course in England.

It may creep & crawl instead of fly.

It will have to contend against a protestant populace, & Protestant Landlords, & a numerical majority.

But as a question of *principle* it is gone.

As a question of policy, & administration, & of Legislative *volition*, you may keep up the Ecclesiastical Status of England, but what is sauce for the goose is sauce for the Gander.

I see in the present State Policy, of which this Maynooth grant is the Pilot-fish,[c] a repeal of the Religious & Civil *principles* on which the Crown & the Parliament founded their acts in the Reformation of Edward, & Elizabeth.

Now for the question of practice. What line ought to be taken? & what line can be?

I seem to see three courses open to individuals.

1. To vote for Money Grants to the Churches of England, & Ireland on the unabandoned theory of the Reformation, & to vote against all grants to all other religious bodies.

2. To vote for Money Grants to all religious bodies according to the present course of Legislation.

3. To vote against all Money Grants to all religious bodies equally the Church included.

---

[c] A tropical fish, common in the Mediterranean, that accompanies ships or larger fish.

As to the two first I shall say nothing because the first, seems to me impossible, and perhaps inconsistent with the present obligations of Political Justice: the second, has too many to speak for it already.

The third is ultra-radical. But I am in doubt whether it is not the safest course of the three.

1. For in the first place it divests the State of at least its *active*[153] quasi-ecclesiastical character, which is the greatest danger the Church has in that quarter. The State is professedly Ecclesiastical, and avowedly not religious. It has destroyed its conscience, & yet it is our guide.

2. Next it is a *principle*, & capable of simple enunciation, & liable to no modification except direct infraction or repeal: it is no question of measure & comparative claims or forces.

3. It is perfectly consistent with these two principles of government.

    (1) The preservation of all existing endowments to all endowed bodies equally of which the Dissenters Endowment Bill is a violent confirmation.[d]

    (2) The inducement to new Endowments, of which the Bounty-board-borrowing bill[e] is a mean example, & the Charitable Bequests Act a fair and established precedent.

This seems to me a principle round which mens consciences & hearts can rally. It appears to me to be tolerant, and in strict accordance with the fairest & most equitable spirit of mutual charity and concession. It is a principle simply conservative of old endowments. It reduces any attempt to alienate them to the best and simplest form in which they can be defended. And it rests the further development, & destiny of the Church & its antagonists upon the true forces which ought to determine them, faith charity, self-denial, zeal and the suggestions of God's spirit.

If the Constantine theory is to be abandoned let us at least have a free appeal to the Great Head of the Church.

Now I can see at once objections to be made to this on the score of 1. political prudence. 2. consideration of the state of property in Ireland.

---

[d] 'Bill for the Regulation of Suits relating to Meeting-houses, and other property held for religious Purposes by persons Dissenting from the United Church of England and Ireland...' See 440409mg.

[e] 'A Bill to make better provision for the spiritual care of populous parishes'. PP 1843 (274.) i. 445, resulting in 6 and 7 Victoria c. 37, allowing borrowing from the Queen Anne's Bounty.

3. practical dangers in the state of parties in & out of Parliament. 4. the possibility of weakening the actual conservative powers by strengthening a theory against which they are committed, and many more.

Yet after all, the objections are drawn from matter which is remote from, & inferior to the great principles which are at stake on the other side.

However I will write no more; I only added the last paragraph on Aristotles rule of προεπίπληξις.[f]

All I will say is that I think I see an answer to each of the supposed objections.

Believe me,
Ever yours affect[ionate]ly
H. E. Manning.

The Right Hon[oura]ble
W. E. Gladstone

[[Pitts (original and copy); Chapeau, 116, 177–80]]

[[On the following Wednesday, 7 May 1845, Gladstone 'saw Manning' (*GD* iii. 453). On 24 May Gladstone 'Saw Manning 10½–1½—active conv[ersation] on Irish & English Church & all the questions now open.'[g] The following day, 25 May, he went to 'St. Paul's Co[vent] G[arden] 11 (to hear Manning for the first time: high Toned, full of thought, & very impressive[)].' That evening he 'read Manning on Missions', that is, *The Missions of the Church From the Third Number of the English Review (for October, 1844)*, repr. for Private Circulation (London, 1845)[h] (*GD* iii. 456). On 29 May he saw Manning again (*GD* iii. 437) and on 1 June was with him: '3–6½ to St. Mark's with Manning—conv[ersation] chiefly on the Ac[ademic] Coll[eges] Bill' ('A Bill to enable H[er] M[ajesty] to endow new Colleges for the Advancement of Learning in Ireland', PP 1845 [299.] i. 357; 9 May 1845), Newman's forthcoming resignation of his Fellowship ('Littlemore catastrophe'), 'and disposal of my property' (*GD* iii. 458). The two men met again on 16 June 'on N[ewman] & Ch[urch] matters' and on 17 June Gladstone had 'Judge Coleridge, R. Wilberforce, & Manning to breakfast for a consultation respecting N[ewman]—We decided that an appeal from his friends to reconcile himself out of England would be very desirable: and C[oleridge] and M[anning] undertook to write to Keble and Pusey accordingly.' On the same day he held a separate meeting with Manning 'on letter to Sir R. Peel & Ch[urch] matters' (*GD* iii. 461).]]

---

[f] First to be blamed. See Aristotle, *Rhetoric*, 1408b2, referring to a common adage that any speaker going beyond where he ought should blame himself first. The application of the principle did not, for Manning, limit access to requests of government offices. See his letters of 17 and 26 June 1845, requesting a position in the Colonial Office for the needy son of a recently deceased personal friend (BL Add. MS 40872, 213–14 and 226–7).

[g] Gladstone's concerns at the time are perhaps made most evident in his letter to Hope of 15 May 1845, for which see Addenda to this Section.

[h] Gladstone's slightly annotated copy is preserved in SDL, F 25/ Mann2c.

450629mg

Lavington. Feast of S[t]. Peter
1845

My dear Gladstone,

I see your Blanco White goes off on Wednesday,[a] & my charge explodes on Tuesday.[b] I have spent labour in vain at it, and it is a caput mortuum.[c] After all my intentions, desires, & endeavours to do what I told you I wished[154] to do, it has come almost to nothing. The fear of precipitating rocks on our heads, the fear of hurting friends dear to us: & of increasing the 'preternatural suspicion': or of seeming egotistical, self conscious & apologetic; or of mooting differences: or of offending by μείωσις[d] & by not cursing our Roman Sister all these & a thousand more have simmered my mess down to a rapid, colorless, tasteless pot-wash.

And now it is too late to begin again.

Believe me,
Ever yours affec[tionate]ly
H. E. Manning

The Right Hon[oura]ble
W. E. Gladstone

P.S. My Sister-in-law has just received a sorrow of great and exceeding sharpness. Her Father Sir Richard Jackson, to whom from the early loss of

---

[a] Wednesday, 3 July 1845. The reference is to William E. Gladstone, '*Life of Mr. Blanco White* [by himself]', *Quarterly Review* 76 (June 1845), 164–203.

[b] Tuesday, 2 July 1845. The address was published with some additional remarks as *A Charge Delivered at the Ordinary Visitation of the Archdeaconry of Chichester in July, 1845* (London: John Murray, 1845; note the unannotated copy among the Gladstone Tracts at NLW [SDL, GTM/ F 175/ 7]). It reviewed the usefulness of the 'Act for better regulating the Offices of Lecturers and Paris Clerks' (7 & 8 Victoria, c. 59 [1844]) and the dangers to the Church's independence in the 'Bill to consolidate the Jurisdiction of the several Ecclesiastical Courts in England and Wales into one Court; and to enlarge the Powers and Authorities of such Court; and to alter and amend the Law in certain matters Ecclesiastical, introduced 25 April 1845' (PP 1845 [431.] iii. 63; 1 July), commenting particularly on its implications for marriage law, and expressing Manning's hope that the Bill will be 'laid aside for a more mature reflection' (21; note Hope's similar concerns [Ornsby, iii. 37ff.]). Discussion of a third Bill of the session, the Parochial Settlement Bill ('A Bill to consolidate and amend the Laws relating to Parochial Settlement, and to the removal of the Poor', PP 1844 [606.] iv. 33, PP 1845 [36.] iv. 455), led Manning into a discussion of Parish unions, which 'must greatly weaken the relation between the pastor and his flock' and 'tend to make the homes of our poor less fixed and stationary' (26). A final lengthy section comments with regret on the misuse of funds in Benefit societies and provides suggestions by which such societies and parish holidays can be improved for the benefit of the working poor.

[c] Worthless residue (literally 'head of the dead').   [d] Degrading.

her mother she has been unusually attached, after six years absence in Canada, is dead.[e] The Messenger bringing these tidings came by the ship that sh[oul]d have brought him home to her. Such is life & its joys. O life. O World.[155]

H.E.M.

[[Pitts; Chapeau, 117, 180–1]]

[[On 4 July 1845 Gladstone saw Manning on Church matters (*GD* iii. 466).]]

450712mg

Lavington. July 12.
1845.

My dear Gladstone,

I send you the last pages of my Charge,[a] and should feel very thankful if you would read them over. If you could do so before Post on Monday it would be a double kindness.

You shall have the whole, I hope, in a day or two.

Ever yours affect[ionate]ly
H. E. Manning

The Right Hon[oura]ble
W. E. Gladstone

[[Pitts; Chapeau, 118, 181]]

450714gm[aa]

13 C[arlton] H[ouse] T[errace] July 14. [18]45

My dear Manning

My anticipations were anything but low: yet as usual you surpass them. I put down hastily in pencil on the margin such trumpery remarks in detail as occurred to me.

I inclose to you today, partly with reference to your *Note* a curious communication I have received today from a very good friend in Paris. Pray return it to me as soon as you conveniently can—it is not yet answered.

---

[e] Manning's brother Charles John (1799–1880) married Catherine Jackson (d. 1859) in 1828. Her father, Richard Downes Jackson (1777–1845) arrived in Canada in October 1839 as Commander-in-Chief of the military forces in British North America, and served intermittently as administrator of Lower Canada and of the united Province of Canada. In 1845 he requested a return to England to be with his daughters, but died unexpectedly on 9 June 1845 in Montreal as his replacement was arriving. See Hillmer and Cooke in Halpenny and Hamelin (1988), vii. 440–1. On the Manning family see E. S. Purcell, 'Episodes in the Life of Cardinal Manning in his Anglican Days', *Dublin Review* 110 (1892), 391–2.

[a] Draft of Manning's 1845 *Charge*.   [aa] 'Wrote to . . . Manning' (*GD* iii. 468).

I happen to have rather a heavy bit of Parliamentary work in hand so I am obliged to write briefly.

Ever your aff[ectiona]te friend

WEG

I *could* not do it for the regular post.

[[BL Add. MS 44247, 268; addressed overleaf: Archdeacon Manning Lavington Petworth; postmarked: july 15 1845; Morley transcript; cf. Chapeau, 314]]

[Enclosure]

Eugiens Les Baines Paris

11 July 1845

My dear Gladstone

Since we came to Paris I have been much interested in the case of a young Romish priest who by his own study under better guidance has become convinced of the errors of his church & having derived assistance from the sermons of B[isho]p Lushcombe[b] came to him for advice. He has happily determined to avoid the rock on which the Evangelical congregations of France have split, whose congress this season in the vain hope of forming some common centre of amalgamation expand the fundamental falacy [*sic*] of their constitutions in the absence of all proper authority. He is now therefore in full communion with the Church of England & the Bishop has arranged the accompanying articles from our own as the basis of the experiment. The moment is favourable after the congress I have mentioned & the breakup of the Jesuits in France, which will dispose the Government how to agree the more readily, a large congregation is already assured & there is good reason to believe that if the start is successful a number of priests some well qualified to judge calculate 40 in Paris alone would be ready to join who are restrained by the dread of absolute want on leaving their present situations without a refuge, for whom congregations would not be wanting. Thro' the liberality of Col[one]l Beckwith,[c] who is present gone to England to make the case

---

[b] Matthew Henry Thornhill Luscombe (1775–1846), educated at Trinity College, Cambridge, was Missionary Bishop in Europe, 1825–46, in the Scottish Episcopal Church after serving as Chaplain to the Duke of Cambridge and at Caen and Paris, France. His sermons, *L'Église Romaine comparée avec la Bible, les Pères de l'Église et l'Église Anglicaine, en six sermons* (Paris, 1839) appeared in the English translation of H. P. Wright as *The Church of Rome Compared with the Bible, The Fathers of the Church, and the Church of England* (London: Potter, 1841). For details see *DNB* and Bertie (2000).

[c] Colonel John Charles Beckwith (1789–1862) had fought in the Battle of Waterloo, was wounded, and later settled among the Waldensians in the Piedmont. See *DNB* and Gladstone's comments on him on 6 March 1832 (*GD* i. 442–3).

known[,] the liturgy changed from the old tu-toi version[d] is now being printed & a site has been secured but the funds for the building is [*sic*] wanting & on that point I now bring the matter under your notice. A very small sum will do in this country & I really believe under God's blessing it is an experiment likely to bring forth most important results to the Church of England favoring a much sounder basis of fraternity than the Prussian alliance into which we rushed with such avidity in the establishment of the Jerusalem Episcopate. It is resolved that clinging to our own liturgy to be daily said & eschewing every thing approaching to idolatry the Roman catholic ceremonies are to be retained as far as possible to accommodate to the utmost those who are to leave that form while as you will observe the articles avoid every subject of dispute which is not essential to the communion. Pray let us know whether you think any support could be obtained for building. The chapel as a commencement at present is most devoutly to be wished. We have come out here a few leagues from Paris to try the sulphurous douches for L[ad]y Harriet who has been free for some time from the excessive pain she formerly endured but is exceedingly weak from the remedy or seton[e] which to a delicate person is a very irritating thing. The congestion is I fear far from being subdued & the sight is entirely gone at present & from what has gone tho' my hopes are very faint of any improvement. We think of Paris for the winter. I have good acc[oun]ts from Thomas[f] at Fettercairn. Kind regards. Y[ours] truly John S. Forbes.[g]

[[BL Add. MS 44362, 251–2]]

450716mg

                                                                        Lavington. July 16. 1845.
My dear Gladstone,

I thank you much for your promptness & kindness. It was a shame to tax you: but I felt anxious. I have taken up all your marginals. It will be sent you, I hope, this week. You will see I have risked some law, & ethics about marriage & now that the Bill is postponed[a] I am tempted to do something

---

[d] That is, a version using personal-familiar rather than formal language.

[e] A thread drawn through the skin to allow a discharge of fluid.

[f] Thomas Gladstone.

[g] John Stuart Hepburn Forbes (1804–66), 8th Baronet of Pitsligo, lived at Fettercairn (*GD* ii. 55).

[a] On the debate over the Bastard Children Bill and its postponement see Hansard, lxxxi. 235.

in a separate form. But I dread opening the foundations of morals. It is an overwisdom which destroys ones ἄρχαι.[b] The inclosed letter is very interesting.[c] Is it credible that 40 Priests in Paris have lost their stirrups? I have not ventured to hint at anything of this sort: for the less that is said at present the better. I wonder whether your correspondent knows Dupins Commonitorium (Appendix III to Maclane's Mosheim vol VI).[d] Can no wise & silent man go over to Paris?

What a book is Blanco Whites.[e] I have not read your Article & am waiting till I have read the book.

It seems to me:

1. That his faith had never any deeper root than in the intellect, & and that only by passive reception.

2. That he was a victim of morbid selfconsciousness, equivalent to intense vanity if not vanity outright.

But the book proves that we must lay down our *science of proof*, or the Roman infallibility will do dreadful havock. Believe me ever,

Yours affect[ionate]ly,
H. E. Manning.

The R[igh]t Hon[ourabl]e
W. E. Gladstone
[[Pitts; Chapeau, 119, 181]]
[[Gladstone read Manning's *Charge* on 20 July 1845 (*GD* iii. 470)[f]]]

450731mg

Lavington. July 31. 1845.

My dear Gladstone,

Will you oblige me by reading the inclosed note of Puseys, & giving me your mind on the last point about 'love of Rome'. It seems to me to be a fair opportunity of expressing something I feel in the uncircumspect way in

---

[b] First principles.

[c] i.e. the letter of Forbes to Gladstone. See 45014gm.

[d] John Lawrence Mosheim, *An Ecclesiastical History, Ancient and Modern from the Birth of Christ to the Beginning of the Eighteenth Century.* For details see 400714mg. In the controversy with Wake, Du Pin drew up a paper, *Commonitorium de modis ineundae pacis inter Ecclesias Anglicanam et Gallicanam.*

[e] *The Life of Joseph Blanco White, written by himself, with Portions of his Correspondence*, ed. John Hamilton Thom (3 vols; London: J. Chapman, 1845).

[f] Gladstone's annotated presentation copy is preserved in SDL, F25Man2i.

which he writes & speaks—rather in private than public. I have sometimes a feeling of fear that he will be overawed, through his great tenderness of mind, into saying or doing something which will affect his own peace.

I feel it very painful to say anything of the sort to him, & always think that I am the 'avvocato del Diavolo'.[a]

What is it he would have? Shall I ask him? It will be one way to lead him to feel the unpractical nature of his wishes, & feelings.

What a book is Blanco White's! I am in the third vol[ume] and it grinds, and gores one.

Ever yours affect[ionatel]y,
H. E. Manning.

The Right Hon[oura]ble
W. E. Gladstone
[[Pitts; Chapeau, 120, 182]]
[Enclosure Pusey to Manning, 29 July 1845]

My dear Friend,

Thank you for y[ou]r full letter. As I may not have time to enter into it by this post, I w[oul]d first consult you on another matter on wh[ich] I have been consulted, & wh[ich] relating to an oath, is very serious. The oath is

Ego N. N. juro ac teste Deo promitto me veram Christi religionem omni animo amplexurum (? [*sic*] what does this mean?)[156] scripturae auctoritatem hominum judiciis praepositurum, regulam vitae et summam fidei ex verbo Dei petiturum: caetera quae ex verbo Dei non proba[n]tur pro humanis habiturum: au[c]toritatem regiam in hominibus summam et externorum episcoporum jurisdictionis minime subjectum existimaturum: et contrarias[157] verbo Dei opiniones omni voluntate ac Mente refusaturum: vera consuetis, scripta non scriptis in religionis causa antehabituarum.[b]

---

[a] The devil's advocate.

[b] Ego r R iuro ac Deo teste promitto me veram Christi religionem omni animo amplexurum, scripturae auctoritatem hominum iudiciis praepositurum, regulam vite et summam fidei ex verbo dei petiturum, caetera que ex verbo dei non probantur pro humanis habiturum, auctoritatem regiam in hominibus summam et externorum episcoporum iurisdictionem minime subiectam estimaturum et contrarias verbo dei opiniones omni voluntate ac mente refutu[tat]rum vera consuetis scripta non scriptis, in religionis causa antehabiturum, theolgiam mihi finem studiorum propositurum, et sacros ordines cum tempus his statutis praescriptum advenerit, suscepturum, aut a Collegio discessurum. De inde me omnia huius Collegii statuta, leges ritus atque laudabiles consuetudines quae ad me pertinebunt servaturum. Item me huic Collegio fidelem et benevolum futurum ei

This oath is taken at admission to scholarships & fellowships of Trin[ity] Coll[ege,] Camb[ridge]. I am consulted^c about the line I have underlined, whether it contains the Protestant doctrine, that the Bible is the rule of faith.

et omnibus sociis ac discipulis atque etiam magistro eiusdem non solum dum in eo vixero, sed etiam postea pro virili cum opus sit benevolentiam et opem praestaturum nullum Collegio dam[p]num incommodumve unquam allaturum alio cum consilio contiones, coniurationes, insidias facta et dicta quae Collegium detrimento et infamia afficiant quantum potero repulsurum ac officiariis Collegii qui de eiusmodi rebus cognoscere, ac decidere debent remi[s]ciaturum. Et si propter aliquod crimen inter maiora crimina numeratum, e Collegio per consensum magistri et maioris partis octo seniorum eo modo, quo in capite de maioribus criminibus dederatum est, expulso fuero, me neque ad alium iudicium iudices non apellaturum aut magistro Collegii aut socio alicui litem aut actionem unquam in posterum ea de causa intertaturum [*sic*] neque ullam unquam dispensationem contra hoc meum iuramentum quaesiturum aut ab aliis quaesitam et oblatam accepturum. Tum magistro, vicemagistro, senioribus reliquisque oficiariis in omnibus legitimis honest-ique rebus morem gesturum et dignam debitaque reverentiam eis et honorem delaturum. (Elizabethan Statutes, 9 Aug. 1561, Trinity College Library, Trinity College, Cambridge.) (I r R swear and with God as witness promise that I will embrace the true religion of Christ with all my soul; that I will place the authority of scripture before the judgements of men; that I will seek from the word of God a rule of life and compendium of faith; that I will hold the rest—whatever is not proved by the word of God—to be human matters; that I will esteem the royal authority to be the highest among men and the jurisdiction of external bishops to be minimally subordinate; that I will refute with all my will and mind opinions contrary to the word of God; that I will prefer true to customary things, written to unwritten; that I will propose for myself theology as the end of studies; and that I will receive holy orders when the time prescribed by these statutes arrives, or I shall withdraw from the College. I swear and promise that thereafter, I will keep all the statutes of this College: all of its laws, ceremonies, and the praiseworthy customs that pertain to me. Likewise, I promise that I will be faithful and devoted to this College; that I will offer goodwill and assistance to it and to all colleagues and students and also to the master of the same, not only as long as I shall live in it, but also afterwards, to the best of my ability, when there is need; that I will never bring any harm or inconvenience upon the College; that as far as I am able I will work against meetings with another deliberating body, conspiracies, plots, words and deeds that afflict the College with injury and infamy; and that I will consult with officials of the College who know about things of this kind and ought to decide about them. And if on account of some offence numbered among the major offences I shall be expelled from the College by the consent of the master and of the greater part of eight seniors in the way in which it is given in the chapter concerning the major offenses, I promise that I will not summon the judges to another verdict, nor will I ever in future bring a lawsuit or legal action against the master of the College or any colleague concerning this case; nor will I ever seek any dispensation from this oath of mine, or accept any dispensation sought or offered by others. Moreover I promise to oblige the master, the vice-master, and the rest of the senior officials in all legitimate and upright matters, and to render to them worthy and due reverence and honour. [Trans. Tina Marshall.])

^c No correspondence located.

Now what strikes me is, on the one side, that the whole is very Protestant and I sh[oul]d have more difficulty about other words as that I 'would account as human whatever is not proved by the word of God'; for, if e.g. prayers for the departed can be proved from S[t]. Paul's prayer for Onesiphorus,[d] 'the intercession of saints for the Church on earth', m[igh]t be difficult to prove (altho' that too m[igh]t lie in the 'Lord, how long?'[e]) & yet certainly I c[oul]d not account it among 'humana.' The person who asks me w[oul]d doubtless not account 'Invocation' such; for wh[ich] I suppose nothing can be alleged from H[oly] Scr[ipture], & yet considering the earliness of such practice in some degree, and again the consent of the whole present Church, except ourselves, neither c[oul]d I look upon it as a thing to be stigmatized, as the word 'humana' does. It is one thing to take up for one's self a practice discommended by the system in wh[ich] one is placed; another, to reject it formally.

The only thing wh[ich] strikes me, on the other hand, is the use of all these futures, petiturum, habiturum, &c as tho' this was not in any sense to be regarded as a declaration of belief, but as a line of conduct to be pursued, & so that it relates rather to public teaching instruction &c than to any opinions held. W[oul]d not all declarations as to opinion or doctrine be in the present, of acts &c be in the future?

The person writing is a scholar of Trin[ity] and as a scholar has taken the oath without scruple. The only scruple he names is the underlined part, wh[ich] I do not, in itself, feel as of any difficulty, because all *the* faith must come from H[oly] Scr[ipture], & the former of the oath never can have meant that any individual was to 'draw it' for himself, or to supersede the office of the Church. He is a layman.

His questions are 1) c[oul]d he take the oath anew, sh[oul]d he be elected fellow 'wh[ich] is highly improbable the 1st time of trial', but still it w[oul]d be absurd to stand, if he c[oul]d not take the oath. 2) If he c[oul]d not take it anew, may he keep his scholarship wh[ich] he received upon taking it?

Altogether, the question to what degree subscription once made still binds, perplexes people: I was surprised by the decision with wh[ich] a very conscientious simple-hearted, clear person both felt that he c[oul]d remain where he was, (a curate) & yet w[oul]d not go elsewhere where he must sign the Art[icle]s anew. To myself, I own the tone of the Art[icle]s i.e. those wh[ich] relate to Rome, are uncomfortable as a whole; I do not like

---

[d] 2 Tim. 1: 16–18.   [e] Rev. 6: 10.

their ἦθος,[f] although there is no *one* wh[ich] causes me any scruple, & directed as we are by our Church to the Fathers, I feel myself on quite safe ground, throwing myself into them, using their language, holding their beliefs. Such parts of the Articles as teach positively are to me valuable, e.g. as securing the truth against Pelagianism. Of much I heartily wish we were rid; & my own comfort is in feeling how we can live among the fathers, as so being satisfied that we are one Church with them, & not thinking about the Reformation, or any things then done, but only of God's good Providence, in saving us from harm we m[igh]t have run into, & His Fatherly care since.

This reminds me to ask, what was the exact meaning of y[ou]r words that you 'could not occupy the position I do.' It was at the Brighton station. Did it mean that you c[oul]d not believe, as I do, that the later Roman saints were favoured by God, as they are related in Butler (taking this as a whole not as to details)[g] & not receive the whole system wh[ich] they embraced; or that you must, if you did receive it, consider their Church as *the* Catholic Church, i.e. is it in faith or practice that you think my ground inconsistent[?]

I have just been preaching on Phil 3. 15, 16 which led me, at the close, to apply it to your state of confusion as to belief. I thought it gave 3 rules: 1) hold the truth whereto you have attained; 2) grow in life by it; 3) walk on by the rule of faith, & what you do not now see, 'God will reveal unto you'[h]— 'If any man will do His will &c.'[i]

Now, has the Huntingtonian system[j] (as N[ewman] says with reference to S[t]. Martin's vision) 'the print of the nails?[k] 2) have they not left the

---

[f] Moral disposition.

[g] Alban Butler, *The Lives of the Primitive Fathers, Martyrs, and other Principal Saints: Compiled from Original Monuments, and Other Authentic Records . . .* (12 vols.; Edinburgh: J. P. Coglane, 1799–1800).

[h] Phil. 3: 15.

[i] John 7: 17.

[j] That is, the 'Connection' of Selina Hastings, Countess of Huntingdon (1707–91; *DNB*), a group of Calvinistically oriented Whitfieldian Methodists. See John Henry Newman, 'Selina, Countess of Huntingdon', *British Critic* 28 (Oct. 1840), 263–95; *Essays Critical and Historical* (London: Basil Montagu Pickering, 1871), i. 386–424.

[k] 'The application of the vision to St. Martin's age is obvious; I suppose it means in this day, that Christ comes not in pride of intellect, or reputation for ability. These are the glittering robes in which Satan is now arraying. *Many spirits are abroad; more are issuing from the pit.* The credentials which they display are the precious gifts of the mind, beauty, richness, depth, originality. Christian, look hard at them with Marin in silence, and then ask for the print of the nails' (the closing passage to John Henry Newman, *Church of the Fathers* [London: J. G. F. & J. Rivington, 1840], 414). Note also the use of the passage in W. G. Ward (1844), 268.

rule, instead of walking on by it? 3) Can one deny the reality of spiritual convictions, though they are counterfeits?

Thank you for your Charge. While it is in a cheering tone, is there quite love enough for the Roman Church? 'If one member suffer &c.'[1] You must think that those who 'renounce Romanism' and join the Arian Protestants in France are wrong. Ronge &c,[m] I suppose deny the doctrine of the Trinity altogether; one section certainly. It seems a movement, developing more rapidly than usual into extreme evil. Perhaps you meant this by your words 'of a truly alarming kind.' The note seems to say, 'If we are in a storm so are our neighbours, therefore do not despond about yourselves.' This w[oul]d be true were we only losing the secular and half-believers, but we are threatened with the loss of so many of our most devotional minds. This may be the necessary accompaniment of restoration from a deep fall in our state both of doctrine & life in the last century, but it is a heavy sign. We are so far worse off than our neighbours, if we suffer both ways; cannot by the vitality of the Church retain many who are good, or turn bad into good. However you do not put forth strongly that we are sick, & what you say of chastenings must do good. I only desiderated more love for Rome. When the battle with infidelity & rebellion comes, we must be on the same side.

> With kindest thanks—in haste.
> Your affec[tiona]te
> EBP

[[Bodl. MS Eng. lett. c. 654, 268–9[n]]]

---

[1] 1 Cor. 12: 26.

[m] Pusey's reference is to a note on p. 57 of Manning's 1845 *Charge* and to his closing enconium on The Church of England as 'a true and living member of the Holy Catholic Church' (56). The note comments on the signs of conflict, 'some of a truly alarming kind', in every 'branch of the Roman Catholic communion in the North and West of Europe'. In France 'ten parishes have almost unanimously renounced Romanism'. Johannes Ronge (1813–87; *DNB*) was a priest in Grottau before he was removed from his post in 1843 and excommunicated in 1844 for liberal tendencies in his publications. He was supportive of democratic movements in 1848, was forced as a result to flee the country, and visited London for a time. On his return in 1861 he pastored 'German Catholic' communities in Breslau and elsewhere. On Ronge and his adaptation of the Confession of Faith see *The Times*, 21 February 1845, 6f.

[n] For Manning's reply (Lavington. 30 July 1845) see PHL MS Manning–Pusey, No. 21 (cf. Purcell, i. 308), the text of which reads:

As you may wish to answer your correspondent without delay, I send you such as I can: but must keep the rest of your letter for another day: for I am at the point of going to an engagement.

450801gm[a]

London Aug[ust] 1. [18]45

My dear Manning

I thank you very much for your congratulations on our second daughter's birth,[b] and my wife is not less pleased with it. Through God's mercy they are both doing all very well. The process of recovery or rather the commencement of nursing has always been attended in my wifes case with some difficulty: but we are in hopes that it is overcome & that all will now go smoothly.[c] If so we may leave town in three weeks. I ought however to tell you that I do not think we shall be able to go to Scotland early in the year: it may even be the middle of November.[d] And I do not think our

The only question raised is as to the clause 'summam fidei ex verbo dei &c'

Of course it is a duty not to suggest any difficulty wh[ich] a man does not feel.

As to that clause I do not see why he sh[oul]d scruple at it.

No doubt 'verbum Dei' then means 'scriptum.'

This is giving it the most strongest [*sic*] interpretation.

And then the clause seems to me the equivalent to S[t]. Irenaeus' words.

'quod quidem tunc praeconiaverunt, (apostoli) postea vero per Dei voluntatem in Scripturis nobis tradiderunt fundamentum et columnam fidei nostrae futurum' [Irenaeus, *Against the Heresies*,] lib. III c. 1 ['which they did at one time proclaim in public, and later by the will of God handed down to us in the Scriptures to better ground the pillar of our faith.']

The oath says '*summam* fidei,' wh[ich] I take to be equivalent to the 'fundamentum fidei' or Creed.

Also it appears to me

1. That the oath predicates nothing of other troubles e.g. the inspiration of Holy Scripture, & any others not invoked in the 'Summa.'

2. That 'humana' must also be confined to other doctrines ['truths' overscored] claiming to be part of the 'fundamentum.

S. Irenaeus w[oul]d call them 'humana,' i.e. not flowing from the preaching or writing of the Apostles as part of the 'Summa.' They need not therefore be false, for all truths are not in the 'Summa' nor in Holy Scripture as Hooker argues.

I send this in obedience to you.

Believe me,

Yours ever aff[ectionatel]y

H.E.M.

For further correspondence on the issue see Addenda to this Section.

[a] 'Wrote to Manning' (*GD* iii. 473).

[b] Letter not located; Catherine Jesse Gladstone (1845–50) was born on Sunday, 27 July 1845 (*GD* iii. 472).

[c] On Catherine Gladstone's ongoing difficulties with pregnancies and nursing, see Marlow (1977), 30, 35–49, 57, 64, 71–80.

[d] The Gladstones were able to leave for Hawarden on 21 August 1845 (*GD* iii. 477) and for Scotland earlier than he anticipated, on 1 September (ibid. 479).

going *as a body* even then is quite beyond doubt. Your presence would of course be as acceptable at that late season as in a more propitious one: but it would not be equally fair to urge the visit upon you.

I have read & return Pusey's note. That one should entertain love for the Church of Rome in respect of her virtues & her glories is of course right & obligatory: but one is equally bound under the circumstances of the English Church in direct antagonism with Rome to keep clearly in view their very fearful opposites. I do not recollect that in your charge (which however is gone to the binders) you have made any dissertation upon the latter: if you had, some compensating exhibition of the former might have been desiderated. But I am afraid onesidedness as to the Church of Rome is becoming an article of religion with Dr. Pusey. I can well understand the personal advantage of keeping clear of the whole function of censure as such: but if parties came forward as teachers of others, and in that capacity they profess however laudable their sentiments of affection towards the Church of Rome, it seems to me that they are absolutely bound to take into their calculation the effect of what they write, upon the minds of others and to adjust it so as to produce a true *general* effect. This I find in you but not in Dr. Pusey's later writings.

Acland tells me he hears a report that N[ewman] has refused to go abroad[e]—& also a strange reason for it (which I do not quite believe) that he will not risk his life by crossing the sea until he is reconciled.

Believe me ever
Aff[ectiona]tely yours
W. E. Gladstone

Venerable
Archdeacon Manning

[[BL Add. MS 44247, 269–70; Morley transcript; Lathbury, i. 347–8; cf. Morley, i. 317–18; cf. Chapeau, 314]]

450811gm[a]

13 Carlton H[ouse] Terrace
Aug[ust] 11. 1845.

My dear Manning

We have a small case of conscience for you.

My wife, who thank God gets on most prosperously, is anxious to go to Hawarden to make a better recovery: & to go as soon as possible for the

---

[e] Gladstone met with Acland on 1 August 1845, before writing to Manning (ibid. 473).

[a] 'Wrote to . . . Manning' (*GD* iii. 475).

change is material to her.[158] She has a feeling in favour of baptizing our little child *there*: & there is the recommendation that we might there have two of three sponsors (the third being out of the country) present, whereas in town we could have none. And so it stood arranged: but a doubt came across me whether, although the risk of travelling be now only infinitesimal, we should be justified in incurring it without having our infant baptized first.

This has perhaps occurred to me in consequence of a sentiment I have heard ascribed to Newman which sounded to me strange & whimsical: that he could not accept the suggestion to go abroad in order to effect his transition, because he would not cross the sea unreconciled—I do not see in such a case the distinction between sea & land: were it a balloon one could understand it.

However will you kindly let us know what you think in our case: I think we shall act upon your advice: you are certainly a *probable doctor*. By the bye it is plain to me from the letter to Colonel Wyndham that you have got to your old tricks & have been poisoning the mind of a *third* bishop of Chichester.[b]

My wife shall read this before it goes—that she may see if she can make any further point for the move—which we trust may be in the latter half of next week, either way.

Ever your aff[ectiona]te friend
W. E. Gladstone

Venerable
Archdeacon Manning

Baby will not be three weeks old until next Sunday & the time at which we hope to get out of town is before the expiration of the month—

---

[b] On 17 July 1845 the Bishop of Chichester wrote to Manning indicating that he had 'received a letter from Col. C. Wyndham, which I enclose, and replied to it in a letter which, with his consent, is to be published. It goes to Mason [the Chichester printer] today' (Bodl. MS Eng. lett. c. 653, 584). The correspondence was the result of a petition to the Bishop from Thomas Clayton, a churchwarden of Shoreham, who with 117 others opposed the Tractarian innovations by the parish priest, Mr Wheeler. After discussing the matter with the priest, the Bishop wrote to the petitioners pro forma through Colonel Wyndham. According to *The Times*, which printed a copy of the letter on 31 July (8f.) the letter left the 'questions untouched and the people dissatisfied. A second letter directly to Clayton at Shoreham on 25 July (printed in *The Times*, 8 August, 6a) calls for evidence of 'innovations'. On the role of the Cambridge Camden Society in the matter see Chandler (1995), 47. Colonel Charles Wyndham (1796–1866) was MP for West Sussex, 1841–7 (Boase, iii. 1539).

There is a *chance* of our going to Scotland in September but it is entirely uncertain.

[[BL Add. MS 44247, 271–2; Morley transcript; cf. Chapeau, 314]]

450814mg

Lavington. Aug[ust] 14. 1845.

My dear Gladstone,

I came home yesterday from Easton[a] near Winchester and found your letter after Post-time.

If you had not put this case to me, I doubt if the thought would have occurred to my mind.

But having occurred I have a sort of fear lest by disregarding it, any of the infinite casualties of life should follow.

I think that our Forefathers would have advised that your little one should be baptized before it makes its first journey in the world.

Certainly if they had seen the panting, bellowing, fiery beast in the entrails of which your child is to shake its way to Chester they would have baptised it with all speed.

On the whole I think solid peace of mind, and wise, though perhaps overcautious, circumspection will do well to outweigh the happiness of having friends about you.

Without therefore pretending to argue the case I should say it is better to have your child baptised before you go. Cannot you combine it with her mothers thanksgiving, & so make the act one, & rest both on the same fitness.[b]

My Bishop (with occasional steps which I cannot account for) has been acting excellently. His letter to Shoreham is better than that to Col[onel] Wyndham.

I have one of these cases on me at this moment—a negotiation apparently concluded happily, wantonly violated, & a country gentleman writing to me like a passionate child.[c]

These things make my heart ache, for I have enough on me in other ways.[159] I do not shrink or repine: but I sigh for rest both of body & of spirit. Sometimes I feel deeply sorrowful.

---

[a] The home of George Dudley and Sophia Ryder.

[b] The Gladstones took Manning's advice and the child was baptized in London on 19 August 1845 (*GD* iii. 477).

[c] Correspondence not located.

You are right about Scotland for this year. It will be better hereafter. The season is growing sere[d] and I see little chance of much holiday. So let me hope to see Fasque when your Church is consecrated.

I have read your article on Blanco White with great pleasure. It is very good: & suggests much.

With my love to your wife and your children.

Believe me,
Yours ever affect[ionatel]y
H. E. Manning

The Right Hon[oura]ble
W. E. Gladstone

[[Pitts; Chapeau, 121, 182–3]]

[[On 4 September 1845 Manning indicated in a letter to his mother that he was going for a two week-trip to Dieppe and Paris to visit George and Sophia Dudley Ryder (Bodl. MS Eng. lett. 652, 499–502). On 25 September Gladstone travelled from Dover to Calais (*GD* iii. 484), and then on to Germany in aid of his sister, Helen. On 5 October he recorded reference to Manning in his meeting with Johann Joseph Ignaz von Döllinger:

He [Döllinger] had read my article on Ward, and said certainly Ward could not complain of it.

He had read Manning on the Unity of the Church, and admired it as a work of talent, but thought it quite unsatisfactory because it did not make out the case of internal unity of doctrine in the English Church, of which he thought we must feel the want much more acutely than the want of external unity (Lathbury, ii. 390; *Autobiographica*, iii. 7; see also *GD* iii. 486 and 541127sm).

On 19 October, he wrote to Catherine:

Of all the men we have in the Church of England Manning is the one to take the lead—he has not exactly Newman's peculiar gifts, but he has one which for a long time, not less than six or seven years, I have not been able to find in N[ewman] or his immediate friends—namely *wisdom*. And I think he has looked before & after, & knows his own mind, which N[ewman] it seems did not for many years after he had been a distinguished and powerful teacher of religion. God who made him can make for us if need be others like him. There is material enough in England, of every human gift, if only within the Divine gifts of faith, love, & zeal, to bring it out (SDL, Glynne–Gladstone MS 770; 142–4, 143; Bassett [1936], 66).]]

---

[d] Withering, drying up.

ADDENDA TO SECTION V

Manning to the Bishop of Chichester: October 1844

441023mc

Lavington. Oct[ober] 23. 1844

My dear Lord,

The[160] unvarying kindness I have[161] always received from you, and the[162] public expressions of esteem, & regard with which you addressed me yesterday lead me to throw myself with perfect openness upon your Lordship's great forbearance.[163] You may have observed last night that I did not claim for myself the privilege in which I might have taken precedence in requesting of your Lordship the publication of your Charge. I earnestly desire permission to state the reasons of my allowing[164] any[165] person to[166] be beforehand with me in that act lest I sh[oul]d seem wanting to y[ou]r L[or]d[shi]p rather in attachment or gratitude. It was not, so far as one hearing enables me to speak,[167] because anything was said by your Lordship yesterday in which (with limitations) I could not concur. There was nothing that was not measured & charitable, nothing that with y[ou]r L[or]d[shi]p's feelings & duties c[oul]d[168] have said. In the whole excepting two or three passages, I felt myself gladly & thankfully to agree—[169]and even of the passages excepted I feel that there is a sense in which I c[oul]d receive them all.

But I could not satisfy myself that your Lordship intended them in[170] that sense.

Nor that they w[oul]d generally[171] would as such be so limited and understood.

I felt myself, therefore, in the[172] trying position of choosing one of three alternatives, namely: to risk the perfect integrity of word & deed, which I pray God ever always to preserve in me, by seeming to[173] express consent: or to guard integrity by words which might have the painful effect of implying the existence of differences towards my Bishop, I have[174] always made it a point of conscience to avoid in myself in such ways, or lastly[175] to suffer the privilege I might have claimed[176] to be enjoyed by another: and to[177] bear myself any blame which might attach to a seeming omission on my part.

Of these I could not hesitate to choose the last.

But I never knew how much pain it w[oul]d cut[178] till your Lordship overcame me by the words of Fatherly kindness with which you addressed me in the presence of [179] my brethren.[180] All I can do now is to throw myself upon your great[181] consideration. Indeed, my dear Lord, I had rather offend you ever by a mistaken feeling of[182] sincerity: than be inwardly conscious of not deserving your esteem by any compromise of truth. This w [oul]d be worst of all: and would[183] take from me the only thing which day by day stands to me in the stead of the charities of home and those blessings which God has been pleased to give me and[184] I mean the consciousness[185] that I have no aim but to serve Him in singleness of heart in serving the Church in which I am [illegible word]. I have written with the openness of heart that a son would use to a Father[186] and I feel something to assure me that your Lordship will receive this letter as a Father from a Son. That I may bring this letter to an end, I will omit all that I w[oul]d further say.[187]

As no official duty & I believe no[188] any customary usage w[oul]d[189] require[190] my attendance at Storrington my not being there would excite no remark among[191] the Clergy in visitation.[192]

I will interpret your answer in the affirmative but will also hold myself in readiness to be present if you should write to that effect by Post tonight. And lastly, let me assure your Lordship that I shall not feel myself at liberty without y[ou]r permission to[193] make the contents of this letter known.[194] Suffer me to[195] beg to be ever remembered in your prayers & to expect that in mine such as they are your Lordship is never forgotten. May I beg you to believe that I am, my dear Lord, your obed[ien]t & attentive Servant.

HEM

[196]I heard nothing but what was measured & charitable: nothing that with your Lordships feelings and duties combined could have been left unsaid. Allow me even to add that I thought I c[ould] trace marks of[197] forbearance and regard to the feelings of others in the way in wh[ich][198] the[199] losses prominent at this time were approached and passed on.

[[Bodl. MS Eng. lett. c. 653, 556–62]]

441023cm

Palace Chichester
23 Oct[ober] 1844

My Dear Archdeacon,

I have only a moment in which to say that I appreciate every motive and feeling disclosed in your letter, and that I see no reason why I should request you to do what is not necessary in attending Storrington. I pray I may never so far forget [Christ]ian principles as not to give credit to everyone, until he has openly forfeited it, for conscientiousness and integrity.

Your faithful Brother
A. T. Chichester

Ven[era]ble Archdeacon Manning
[[Ibid. 564–5)]]

Pusey on Ward and Roman Catholic Books of Devotion: January 1845

441215pm

15. Dec[ember]
3rd. S[unday] in Advent. 1844.

My dear Friend,

I cannot doubt which side you will take this time, but it is of moment that your choice shall be known early, for it is a bellum internecinum,[a] threatening with excision, root and branch, all with whom you have acted here and most whom you love.

Perhaps you have not yet seen what is proposed—1) to declare certain passages in Ward's book to have been inconsistent with good faith in his signing the Articles when he became B.A. and M.A. (when, I suspect, he was a Liberal); 2) to 'degrade' him; 3) to empower the Vice Chancellor to propose to any suspected persons to declare solemnly that he will sign the Articles in that sense in which they were 'primitus editos esse et nunc mihi ab Univ[esitate] propositos tanquam opinionum mearum certum ac indubitum signum.'[b]

Now this is at once contrary to what Laud won for us against the Puritans and the H[ouse] of C[ommons] that we should sign them in this 'grammatical sense' without reference to the private opinions of any one but according to the analogy of the faith.

3. [200] The first part is vague enough: by whom were they primitos editos, the Ref[ormers] or the Convocation who, commanded us to Cath[olic] Antiq[uity]? What the test of their meaning, public or private documents, or our Formularies; if the Ref[ormers], their individual opinions or their appeal to Cath[olic] Antiq[uity]? &c. &c. All this might leave us ample scope and would have been

---

[a] Internecine war.

[b] '[In the sense I believe they were] originally published and not proposed to me by the University as the certain and indubitable sign of my views,' as stated in the proposed test oath in 'Whereas it is notoriously reputed and believed throughout the University that a book entitled "The Ideal of the Christian Church" ...' (Oxford: Baxter, 1841), unpaginated p. 4.

sufficient for me who seek but for Cath[olic] Antiq[uity]. But it is plain that the 'proposers' (if these be the Heads) do not mean this, for they must mean some one definite sense, else the signature could be no certum-opinionum signum. And that sense one knows to be Ultra Protestant. Again, who is the University? i.e. has Convocation in accepting this test, the same meaning as the Heads in proposing it? If it unhappily did so, I feel sure that it would not. But overtly it would commit itself to the Heads, and we must go by overt acts.

The result would be, that persons who see clearly and with scrupulous minds, could not sign it; certainly not without such grave appearance of dishonesty as could be sinful. Yet how much there is to entangle people as that our being swept clean away would be far the least evil. One should most dread people signing with half-doubting consciences or signing and then suspecting themselves afterwards. What fearful evil the Clergy did themselves by persuading themselves, they might take these tests after 1688, contrary to their previous convictions, which, I suppose, was one great reason why our Church sank so rapidly from the best estate to her worst.

I think our complete extermination from this place would be the least evil.

But apart from us, and personal feeling, there seems the great constitutional question.

What right have the University to change the test, contrary to Laud's rule, when the Bishops are silent, and to limit the meaning of all the Articles to their own?

Then also, as I said, the great moral mischief and hardship of ambiguous tests.

I too have long felt that (except overt heresy as D[r]. H[ampden]'s) we need the greatest sympathy and charity for each other. I recollect that I never could bring myself to point out, at least to press, how inconsistent the Low Church teaching is with the Baptismal Service, lest any, feeling it, should leave the Church. I have longed to conciliate them, to meet them, hoping that God might draw them to fuller truth. (However, too much of self.) But now, in this critical state of things, we seem to need the utmost tolerance of each other's consciences, bearing and forbearing, as in a 'crisis' in the human body, the physician stands still, and leaves all to God. When wind and wave are so on our vessel, any motion may overset it.

And so as to Ward, I think it shocking to pronounce on his conscience when so very much has been tolerated. I am sure he is conscientious. It is absolutely shocking to endure him when Milman and Whately etc have been passed by. Then his practical chapters are slowly being acted upon in and ascending to our Church, and are opening people's eyes to great defects in their way of going on. He is thus a very great benefactor to us.

However, I need only state facts to you, who can judge better than I.

If we escape, it is God's great mercy, for things are hard against us. The excitement about Ward, the panic, the confusion in the Church, the bringing on all these questions on the same day are all against us. You then will not fail to pray for us here, against whom this blow is directed, and to ask others to pray for our Church and for us.

Ever your affect[ionat]e friend

E.B.P.

When you see your own way clearly, I wish you would try to influence Hook, for he is so excited that I dread exceedingly the part he may take: and indeed it is an occasion to put forth all your influence any way.

441227mp

Lavington. Feast of St. John's Eve

[27 December 1844.[a]]

My dear Friend,

I have not answered your letter sooner, because I wished to make up my mind once for all on the subject of the votes I shall give in the matter of Wards Book and the proposed statute.

Things reach me slowly here and your letter and Marriotts gave me the first intelligence that anything was afoot. I shall steadfastly vote against the

---

[a] Note also Manning's comments to another friend on the same day:

Lavington. Feast of St. J[ohn] Ev[angelist] [27 December] 1844.

My dear Friend,

In my note yesterday I forgot to answer ab[ou]t the Oxford business.

I shall vote with all decision ag[ain]st the Statute on Subscription in all its parts.

As towards book I shall

1. either *not* vote at all—because tho' I think it open to the censure, I can not join in charging him with bad faith. I believe him boisterously & contemptuously honest. And I think this deprival of degrees an ultimate penalty not to be inflicted in the first instance.

2. or I shall vote ag[ain]st it simply to protect the person from an untrue charge and a sentence prematurely severe.

Ever yours aff[ectionatel]y

H. E. Manning (Pitts)

proposed statute on subscription in all its parts. And will write as you desire to Hook to that effect.

As to the part relating to Ward's book and degrees, if I vote at all upon those I shall vote against them. But I have these reasons which induce me to think that I shall not vote at all.

I am forced to admit that certain parts of his Book are, in my belief, at variance with the 39 articles. And I think that propagation of certain of his opinions is a legitimate subject of censure by the University.

If the proposed votes simply affirmed this much I should feel compelled to assent.

But they attaint him also of bad faith, which I altogether refuse to believe as a true charge.

It is not necessary for me to say what moral faults his book seems to me to exhibit in full breadth: but certainly that of dishonesty seems excluded by an opposite which is not therefore a virtue.

And again the deprival of degrees seems to me to be a capital and ultimate penalty not to be inflicted except in the last instance especially after the precedent of Dr. Hampden. I do not at all know how far what I have said on this latter point falls in with your own judgement. I have said it as markedly as I could both because I feel that we owe to each other for our sincere brotherly love's sake, the clearest expression of our convictions and because I should feel most thankful to you if you would state to me anything you feel against it. I will give it the fullest and best consideration I can. I feel day by day that nothing but the hand of God can lead us out of our present straits. And that feeling drives me to my altar and to my flock, where I thank God, something higher and stronger than all evidence and reasoning assures me what our Church is and Who is in it.

That every blessing, if not every joy of Christmas be with you is my heartfelt prayer.

Believe me
Yours ever affectionately
H.E.M.

4501pm

[early in January 1845.]

My dear Friend,

Thank you for your full letter, and for wishing to have my opinion on anything. I do not mean that you are not uniformly kind about every thing, only as to my own unfitness for anything.

I have misgivings about W[ard]'s temper in this. I fear he has been hurrying on a crisis on some view of his own, which no man had any right to do. However, this is only an expression of fear that things may go on ill, if the crisis be brought about in a wrong way, as I too contributed to it by my opinion as to the late matter as to the V[ice] C[hancellor]. I hope however, it is on the whole a merciful overruling, and that the Provost of Oriel has been allowed to overshoot his own mark, and that the defeat of the test will restore things a little. It is always comfortable to be in the defensive. Yet it is a tremendous crisis, and the results beyond all calculation. It is the most decisive conflict fought yet, and minds are most stirred. I dread over sanguineness on our side.

As to Ward's book, I know not what to call contrary to the Articles, with the fact, as I understand, that the R[oman] C[atholic]'s were intended to remain among us. And then I deprecate exceedingly judging of other men's consciences and honesty, as you also do. I never could share that dry hard way in which people used to speak of the Low Church, until they came to unite themselves with them, in order to precipitate us; how it was said that people who do not hold Baptismal Regeneration should leave the Church. I always dreaded it, and was glad that we were held together anyhow. And strange as it seems in the abstract, how people could use that prayer in the Baptismal Service 'We give Thee hearty thanks'[a] who did not believe any of the whole system of doctrine which it expresses, still one could not but see that certain individuals were honest, and so wished neither to point out to them the untenableness of their position, nor that they should see it. If we were held together, one felt undoubtingly that Moses' Rod would devour the rest,[b] and so was only anxious that we should be kept on in one. And now with regard to others. One sees God's Hand certainly in the whole, and so Gamaliel's advice[c] seems the only council to be followed. I dare form no judgement as to others, the more since I see far more reality among those who go far beyond myself, than in most of those who, as to the system with regard to St. Mary, are more where I am. There is an intrinsic shallowness in mere Anglicans of this day

---

[a] 'We yield thee hearty thanks, most merciful Father, that it hath pleased thee to regenerate *this Infant* with Thy Holy Spirit, to receive *him* as thine own *Child* by adoption, and to incorporate *him* into thy Holy Church' (closing prayer for 'The Ministration of Publick Baptism of Infants', Book of Common Prayer).

[b] Cf. Exod. 7: 9 ff.

[c] Acts 5: 34–9, in which Gamaliel advises that prosecution be set aside, 'for if this counsel or this work be of men, it will come to nought'.

and I think an inconsistency in most of our writers, some very few excepted, which makes me unwilling to speak against others. I see not with whom I sympathise, except very few. I can throw myself wholly into Antiquity and rest there: thankful that I never felt disturbed about our Church, and seeing a great deal of good being developed in her and of her: but what form it will ultimately take, I feel wholly incompetent to anticipate and so can take part against nothing but overt heresy, as D[r]. H[ampden]'s. I am not more drawn than formerly to the system as to St. Mary, but I feel that the Anti-Romanizing temper and language jar exceedingly with me.

Thus much for explicitness sake. With regard to the actual measures against Ward; I meant in voting against them to say some few words in the name of myself and, as is probable, others, that I did not make the passages my own. This, I hoped, might be a relief to some who might not like to speak in Convocation themselves. But by that time probably, it will be generally understood. This surely removes the only ground for not voting against 1 and 2. One should only wish not to seem to affirm what one does not. But if there are distinct grounds for not passing even No. 1, the matter is not cured by not voting at all. 1) Since you think the imputation of dishonesty untrue, it is seriously surely a matter of justice to vote against it. One has no right to acquiesce in an untrue assertion as to one's neighbour, when one has the power to hinder it. 2) I do not see if No. 1 is passed, how the University is not committed to regard every one of those extracts as contrary to 'good faith' in the signature of the Articles. But this is to erect an opinion as to a very complex historical event, the Reformation, into a matter of doctrine. And yet I suppose, the more people look into the Reformation, however God may have overruled it, the less sympathy they have with almost everything about it, and the people engaged in it. It seems to cut us off from repentance of what was amiss in it, thus to bind up our Articles with it. And it is, I think, a very grave act to commit ourselves formally to that about which there was so much of ill. 3) (which applies still more to No. 2) if the University once takes the line of condemning errors in her individual members, then she makes herself guilty as to all past & present neglects. Truly, ye 'do allow the deeds of your fathers'[d] I can easily understand that we can be in a state of weakness & confusion; that the powers of the Church in speaking out against unsound doctrine should be in a state of abeyance; that we must bear with everything, lest we

---

[d] Luke 11: 48.

should do more harm than good. We cannot refine the waters ourselves, but must wait until they be calmed & settled. But if we do claim to exercise true power, then we convict one ourselves, if we use it in lesser cases only; pass by the A[rch]b[isho]p of Dublin's Sabellianism[e] and attack Ward. It implies absolute dullness as to the faith to attack a rival Communion and be careless as to what the whole Church has condemned as contrary to the Faith in the Holy Trinity. 4) Ward is doing us a great deal of practical good, on principles of our Church, it is shocking to learn of one and condemn him at once.

I think very much with C[harles] M[arriott] that if you follow out your own letter you must vote against the measures against Ward. It comes to this at the very best; in your judgment, a person is indicted for a wrong offense and to be punished with extreme and disproportionate severity. And are you to sit by each and acquiesce in it?

I fully appreciate your difficulties in your position; but there must be some way out of them. They would come simply to this; that your act must be liable to be misunderstood, and this of course ought to be avoided. But there must be means for this. Whether you should write an explanation, I know not; but certainly in a case of such extreme moment, a person is not to sit still, because there is some difficulty in moving.

All blessings of this new eventful year be with you. I do trust there is more prayer and so more hope. I have been suggesting to earnest persons to ask others to use some form daily 'for our Church amid her distractions and those perplexed in her' as (at least, since many are too busy for longer forms) the Lord's Prayer thrice in honour of the SS. Trin[ity] and with this intention, and perhaps Ps[alm] 130 or any other. Something as fervent as they can and persevering. Can you give any suggestions.

Ever your most affect[ionat]e
E.B.P.

I do think all the critical state of people's minds, (I do not mean at Oxford, but everywhere, women as much as men, widows, wives, and unmarried women) a great reason against any new line of action, as against Ward's book. Surely when the wind blows hard upon us, and the vessel can hardly bear up, is not the time for adding canvass, or, if we could, letting out all the winds of Oolus' cave.[f]

---

[e] See Richard Whately, *Essays [Second Series] on Some of the Difficulties in the Writings of the Apostle Paul and in other Parts of the New Testament* (5th rev. and enlarged edn.; London: B. Fellowes, 1845); see particularly Essay ix, 'On the Influence of the Holy Spirit', 317–86.

[f] See Virgil, *Aeneid*, 1. 50–9, and cf. Homer, *Odyssey*, 10. 67.

I add this question on a separate paper, in case you should like to shew the other to Gladstone or any other. Miss. L[ockhart] has all but finished her Italian work for me and I engaged not to give her any more employment of this sort, without your consent. My own conviction is that whatever peril she might ever be in would not be in the least increased by employment of this sort, but rather that her mind is kept the more tranquil. All those terrible reports and doubts about others is what so shakes people, with the fierce Ultra-Protestant spirit which is continually jarring and bidding people 'Begone'. Ultra-Protestants have all along done more harm in unsettling people than any other. I am not sure that I may not inadvertently have occasioned Miss. L[ockhart] to assist Miss. E[llacombe] in learning Spanish. Miss. E[llacombe] is about Rodriguez, which is full of practical wisdom. I did not mean it. But I should like to have an answer to give, as I am pledged to you.

Miss Ellacombe promises much for 'the Home':[g] she is so very tractable, obedient, humble, real, enthusiastic too which with other qualities to correct etc, is needed to begin such places. I did not understand your misgiving not about the plan, that 'such things force themselves'. Miss E[llacombe] (perhaps you know, between ourselves) was very urgent with her father to let her begin such a plan and invite others, which was the first of my knowing anything of her: N[ewman] and I wrote to quiet her. It is now with her father's acquiescence. D[odsworth] has been pining for it, and has great depth of character. I hear from some, daughters of a clergyman in important office,[h] who beg to be servants, 'being fit for no more responsible employment'. Surely this increasing longing is a seeming token on God's part. I know of between 20 and 30 who are longing for such Institutions, though held back in part for the present by engagements of duty. And this has sprung up of late. Is not this longing a call?

[[PHL, Liddon transcripts]]

---

[g] The home for 'fallen women' established by the Anglican Sisters of St Mary the Virgin at Wantage. Jane Ellacombe was the daughter of Henry Thomas Ellacombe (1790–1885; *DNB*) and joined Pusey's Sisterhood at Regent's Park as Sister Anne.

[h] The Misses Terrot, daughters of Charles Hughes Terrot (1790–1872; *DNB*). Terrot was educated at Trinity College, Cambridge, elected a Fellow, 1813, appointed Dean of Edinburgh and Fife, 1839, Bishop of Edinburgh, 1841, and served as primus of the Scottish Episcopal Church, 1857–62. Terrot's daughter Sarah Anne joined Pusey's Sisterhood of the Holy Cross (Park Village Sisterhood), 1845, and later worked as a nurse in the Crimea.

450109pm

Thursday the Octave of the
Epiphany 1845

My dear Friend,

I did not leave B[adeley].'s rooms until 6 yesterday.[a] The result you will
probably have seen. This is probably only the first instalment.

You could not say anything but what is kind and tender. I wished to have
seen you very much, in order to say more, thinking I had left you with an
impression beyond the truth. But it is long to say by letter; I do not feel my
position in the least altered: what has impressed me in the Roman Church
is the self-discipline, and the blessings bestowed upon it. It is so strongly
said in Roman Catholic books that those vouchsafements are not to be
received as revelations of faith, but to be received as subordinate to it, that
they do not disturb me.

I may also have given you a wrong impression as to the state of persons
I spoke of. I do not mean that such as I was thinking of depend solely on
individuals; many, I suppose, *have* in a period of unrest, or for some time,
and then come to feel and know the gifts lodged in our Church for
themselves; individuals have been (and are perhaps to many now) a
resting-place for the time, as the Samaritan woman, or even miracles,
'until the Day Star arise in their hearts'.[b] What I rather meant was, that
I thought people who would be employed in these translations would
be of such humble minds, that they would not act for themselves, nor
be disturbed as long as they are under guidance, i.e. that they were not
endangered.

Of course, it would be quite distinct whether it was good for a person
that Roman doctrine should pass through their mind or they be familiar-
ized with it. Miss L[ockhart]'s present employment if she has any, would be
about Rodriguez, whom you probably know, who is full of practical

---

[a] Despairing of further correspondence with the Bishop of Oxford over his suspension
from preaching at the university as a result of his Sermon on the Eucharist in 1843, Pusey
decided in late 1844 to appeal yet again to the Vice-Chancellor's court, travelling in
January to London from Brighton to consult with Badeley concerning a possible suit. See
Liddon, 361ff. In an open letter of 8 January 1845 to Edward Hawkins, Provost of Oriel
and Vice-Chancellor, published in the *English Churchman*, 10 January 1845, 31, Pusey
declared that he was not asked to 'explain' his position in 1843 as Hawkins had suggested.
Hawkins responded the same day, hoping that there could be an end of the matter. For
relevant correspondence and Pusey's 4 and 8 January drafts of his letter see PHL MS
Pusey's Suspension 1843 (unpaginated).

[b] 2 Pet. 1: 19.

wisdom, and has very little of Roman doctrine, I believe, nothing of that which is with us the great stumbling-block, the doctrine about St. Mary. If she is so employed, it was not my doing, except incidentally in giving it to Miss E[llacombe]; but I feel that if you think it best for Miss L[ockhart], I ought to stop it, and she will have the blessing resulting from obedience.

I am obliged, my dear friend, to be equally confident about the line as to Roman Catholic books: whether I should execute such a plan rightly or without involving evil, is another matter. I had much rather it was in your hands, or in others: but I do think it absolutely necessary, in order to deepen devotion and practical duty among us. I feel confident that when these are deepened, things will come right in the end.

Ever your affect[ionat]e and obliged

E.B.P.

Th[ursday] in Oct[ave] of the Epiphany. 1845.

[[Bodl. MS Eng. lett. c. 654, 246–8]]

Manning and Richard Jenkyns: March 1845

450306mj

Lavington March 6, 1845

My dear Master,

For some time past I have been wishing, & intending to write to you on a subject of no little interest to all members of the University, & indeed to the University itself, I mean the possible renewal of the requisition to the Hebdomadal Board against the 90th Tract, in the Tracts for the Times.

I do not know what your opinions have been on this subject, & I therefore can write the more freely.

It is for those who promote the requisition for a censure on that Tract to consider what will be the effect of their attempt.

Facts have lately proved that a very large number of members of Convocation will vote against such a censure. And it is to be considered whether such an event, taken alone, does not put the cause they wish to save in a worse case than before.

But it is even supposable that any proposed censure may be rejected; & I can here join with them in saying (whatsoever be my opinion of the Tract in question) that I should be sorry to see any apparent sanction given to a publication of that kind by the University of Oxford. Untrue as such a notion would be, the country would believe a rejection of the censure to be equivalent to an adoption of the Tract.

But my chief object in writing to you is to communicate a danger which I think, imminent & more serious.

You may be aware that there has long existed a hardly restrained desire to bring the writings of the Archbishop of Dublin under public censure in the University.

This desire has been powerfully stimulated; first by his having re-published in this year, 1845, an Essay 'on Christian Self denial' taken from his book on the difficulties in the writing of St. Paul.[a] In which essay are interpretations of the most direct Sabellian appearance: And next by his being understood to have been a promoter, by counsel, of some of the late measures at Oxford.

Now there is no need of pointing out the sore scandal to the whole Church which must ensue upon the question of heterodoxy being raised in the person of an Archbishop: or the difficulty the Hebdomadal Board would find after consenting to renew the censure on the 90th Tract in refusing a censure on the Archbishop's writings, on any principle which the public sense of equity will acknowledge to be just.

Moreover, I fear that this most peremptory refusal would ultimately have little avail: for my fears are that such a refusal could have two consequences, & both of them disastrous; the one that of exciting a severe examination, & public censure of the Archbishop's writings: the other of bringing again upon the Hebdomadal Board the same requisition re-indorsed by the whole weight which such a public excitement must inevitably add to it. It would be difficult in such a case to refuse a second time.

How shall I excuse myself to you for venturing to write with this freedom? I am very sensible of the risk I run of seeming to exceed all bounds which your kindness has permitted to me: but the subject is one of such moment both to the University & the Church, & the dangers which beset the path on which the requisitionists against the 90th Tract would have us enter are so great, that I must throw myself upon the confidence which you have so kindly reposed in my for my justification.

At such a moment as this it seems to me that our safety in going may lie in the old warning μὴ κινεῖν [*sic*] καμαρίαν κ.τ.λ.[b]

---

[a] Richard Whately, *Essay on Christian Self-Denial As Appended to the Fifth Edition of 'Essays on Some of the Difficulties in the Writings of the Apostle Paul'* (London: B. Fellowes, 1845*b*).

[b] Do not rouse Camarina [it is best left alone]. The city of Camarina was encircled with a swamp for protection; the line is the response of the Delphic Oracle when queried regarding a proposal to drain the area. See *The Greek Anthology*, bk. 9. 685. Cf. *Aeneid* 3. 701 and John Henry Newman, *The Idea of a University Defined and Illustrated, I. In Nine Discourses Delivered to the Catholics of Dublin, II. In Occasional Lectures and Essays Addressed to Members of the Catholic University* (Ker edn., 1976), 321.

Believe me
My dear Master,
Yours very faithfully
·H. E. Manning

The Rev[eren]d
The Master of Balliol

450315mj

Lavington March 15. 1845

My dear Master,

I returned home from our Diocesan Committee only last night, or I should have thanked you sooner for your very kind letter. After writing to you I was almost afraid that I had taken too large a freedom but your answer, which is like your kindness to me these many years past has removed my apprehension.

In my last letter I did not state my opinion of Tract ninety, because it seemed to me irrelevant to the matter then in hand.

But I will do so freely so far as a letter can carry it, and so far as a general statement will admit of.

After the best consideration I can give to it, the tract seems to me to be based on the principle adopted by the Church of England in the whole process of the Reformation, and formally enunciated by the Synod of London in 1571.[a]

I find in it a[n] express[201] recognition of the animus imponentis[b] as the first law of subscription: an acknowledgment of the anti-Roman sense of the articles directed against Rome: and a distinction between Catholic and Roman Catholic so as to cover, & include no principles of interpretation which were not maintained & justified by Bishop Andrewes in his anti-Roman controversies.

Thus far I have spoken only of the *principle* of the Tract.

As to details, I seem to see in it:

1. Particulars in which this principle has been *missapplied* or *exceeded*.

2. Expositions which seem to me incorrect.

3. Expressions relating to the Church which I regret to see.

---

[a] The Thirty-Nine Articles, for which assent was formally required in 1571.

[b] The intention of the imposer.

Without going into a length for which neither of us are at sufficient leisure, I can do little more than send you the above remarks which in turn come to their conclusion.

It appears to me that the Tract is open to a discriminating, & critical censure on Theological & historical grounds, in its details, but in its principle I do not see how it is to be condemned without involving our greatest divines, our formularies, and the Church of England itself.

From this, you will readily see (why all other reasons apart) I could not but oppose the recently published censure.

I have answered you, My dear Master, with the frankness & gladness, with which I feel bound always to meet any wish of yours that may be in my power,

Believe me,
With much regard,
Yours very faithfully
H. E. Manning

[[Private Collection of Richard Jenkins]]

Manning and Oakeley[a]

441212om

74. Margaret Street
12th [December] 1844.

My dear Archdeacon Manning

I thank you much for the kind present of your University Sermons, and especially for the note which prepared me for it. In the Sermons—I am sure, at any rate, to find all that seriousness and considerateness, in union with high intellectual qualities, can sense—and I only wish I could convey to you how very painful it ever is to me to find myself forced in pausing, when I so much long to follow.

Your note which I feel so much kinder than I deserve, hardly seems to leave me any alternative but that of endeavouring to account to you for my backwardness—where I seem to withhold from the course which you and others whose friendship I should value—and from yourself, so far as you are in my feelings identified with it—the full content of sympathy with which I should wish to regard both it and you. Yet it can only be, I assure you, under a very surpassing sense of the duty and great advantage of the natural openness, that I venture upon what may be as ever so much as the

---

[a] For a general discussion of the correspondence see Galloway (1999), 160–3.

faintest appearance of disrespect towards one so much my superior in many of those points which go to constitute a claim upon my veneration, as well as a motive to acquiesce in his judgement.

Shall I then bring myself to say, that what seems to me so arrogant, and so injurious,—that I fancy to see a definite line in our Church on two opposite sides, but not in the space between? When, then, I find yourself, for instance, expressing what I may call theological sympathy with me, I am led to fear some compromise on my part and absolutely shrink from the temptation which closer intercourse might involve to an increase of the suffered mischief. So far as I know my own view, and so far as I know yours, I do really believe, that in spite of whatever apparent points of connection, they are at the most not different merely, but contrary. I should be very reluctant indeed to enter upon proofs of this statement and yet I feel it harsh and abrupt to make it without suggesting some idea of the sort of grounds upon which I seem to myself ab[ou]t to justify it. I suppose then that upon such *very* fundamental questions, as (for example) that of the moral and theological character of the Eng[lish] Reformation—the abstract and essential nature of the great Lutheran tenet—the standard of orthodoxy—the conditions (as distinct from the object) of Catholic unity, our minds and hearts, could each see into the other's—apart from that actual and in some inscrutable disguise which causes partly natural, partly due to circumstances such as peculiarities of temperament, position, and the like, have a tendency to throw over deep and real feelings—we sh[oul]d find them so unlike, as to be convinced that, on which ever side truth lies (a point not necessary to the question) a relation of intimacy, as distinct from one of mutual kindness, would bring with it all the evils of a 'false position.' Were you to kindly urge upon myself, or upon others (so far) like myself, in letters, or in personal intercourse, the extent of your fellow feeling with us, I, for my own part, feel myself in this strait, that, to respond, seems hypocrisy, and to keep silent, sadness—and the only remaining course is that which I am taking, of free explanation: What I seem to feel is—that I have got hold of a notion—however miserably inadequate to the subject— of a 'something' definite, consistent, most real, most influential,—a 'something' which vindicates to itself my whole mind—colours all my views— regulates all my sympathies—determines all my movements—a something which—'si quantum cuperem, possem quoque'[a]!—would make all feeling enthusiastic and all action energetic. And I cannot but fancy, that did you

---

[a] If only I had strength equal to my desire (Horace, *Epistles*, 2. 1. 257).

share this one pervading, informing, animating idea, which has taken hold of me, you must have given such distinct unequivocal expression to your feelings before the world, as would utterly preclude your being popularly identified (whether rightly or wrongly—still as a fact) with those who have spoken certainly in no unconfused language of this intense, deep-rooted hostility to the line of action and sentiment, with which the latter N[umber]s of the British Critic, with the comment in them of Ward's book, w[oul]d be accounted the symbol. I really do feel, that public opinion is in this case a sufficient test, especially in days so watchful and critical as these. Intense feeling will find its vent sooner or later; and of course in saying that your feeling in one direction is not intense, I am merely stating, at most, a fact, not hasarding a reflection. Whether these differences within our Church which one so wishes to the last moment to believe superficial, are, or are not so (as you, I know, with more charity & hopefullness think that they are, and as I and others have long feared that they are not[)]—this, time will shew, or rather, I shall say, *is* shewing. Some of those who have hitherto acted in common, are evidently drawing off one way, some the other—as circumstances quite naturally, & without any effort bring certain lines (on whichever tests) into distinctive shape. Thus—the B[ritish] Critic does *not* prove a searching test—but things are not allowed to remain in that equivocal position. Palmer attacks the British Critic—and Ward, in any self defense against the most serious imput-ation—is obliged to explain himself—All this brings out Newman, Pusey, Hook &c in new, more distinct, and, in some respects, divergent points of view. Hook gives utterance to what must have been *very* intense and oppressive feeling in 'his fuller' letter at the time of the Oxford business (in which contest by the bye I took no part)—Pusey with whom Hook had previously very much identified himself does not seem, (from the way in which he speaks in his last preface to Surin) to shun this feeling at all events—one side talks of 'idolatry' when the other seems to hope devo-tion—Then comes the projected attack on Ward and his book—which seems likely still more to bring matters to an issue—and to force people in taking their sides—or keeping aloof from a very central contest.

It is unpleasant to speak of actual things and actual people—but it is necessary for illustration.

With the strong and overpowering conviction that the present struggle is between two lively and vigorous principles lying at the root of an immense map of superincumbent materials which hide them from view and tend to perplex our notions about them, the *one* course which I can*not* appreciate is the neutral one. I feel all that is late said for it, on the score of dutifullness, moderation, charity, abstinence from exciting circumstances; I feel (I think) the temptation on the other side, to restlessness, precipitancy, presumption, meddling; I feel, again, that those in the low planes of our Church are no judges of the trials which beset them in the high places. I feel all this not insignificantly, though I dare say indifferently—still it does come home to me that, at whatever risk of seeming conceited, exclusive, unfriendly, (and I am far from being insensible to my danger in these & such points) still—while my Church allows me, I must try to follow out my own line with however few companions, and forgo the opportunity of much improving intercourse, and the advantages of external union, rather than expose myself to the temptation of making concessions which I might afterwards regret, or of disputing where I ought to listen, or—last not least—of prejudicing a cause of which I am morally satisfied, by taking part in arguments to which (especially which I sit in the habits of the greatest intimacy). I am intellectually unequal.

I trust, my dear Mr Archdeacon, that in this very candid exposé of my *whole* feeling on a subject, I have abstained from every expression which might appear inconsistent with high respect and consideration.

Believe me
Yours very truly and faithfully
Frederick Oakeley

[[Bodl. MS Eng. lett. c. 654, 58–64; addressed: The Ven[era]ble Archdeacon Manning]]

441215mo

Lavington 3 Sunday Adv[en]t 1844.

My dear Oakeley,

I take your last letter as an invitation to use the same frankness towards you as you used towards me and I very gladly accept it.

Let me first tell you what drew my first letter from me. I had received a statement of what passed lately on the subject of your relation to the pastoral charge about Margaret Chapel[a] and I thought you had been saddened & distressed at it. The old, & kindly recollections of our slight though not short acquaintance recurred to me, and I sent the book & the letter as a simple expression of a friendly feeling. I designed my letter to distinguish between a sympathy with you personally, & a participation in

---

[a] On Blomfield's *Charge* see 450121mg and cf. Gladstone's comments on the Bishop of London's 'regret' in 450317gm.

your opinions. I have no copy of it: but I believe the distinction is not doubtful. This was the whole aim, drift & reach of my communication. I am careful to say this because I know that some gifts are ἄδωρα δῶρα οὐκ ὀνήσιμα[b] and the notion of compromise or solicitation of intimacy at the cost of sincerity & truth, I trust we may both have faithfullness to reject.

I am, however, truly glad that I should have drawn from you your last letter: because it will I trust help me to enter into myself, & to reconsider the grounds of my present convictions both in matters of judgement & practice. We meet with too few admonitions to mistrust ourselves: and I thankfully accept what you have said I feel sure that I do, indeed, need more of intensity in every thing, and I trust I may have your prayers, that it may be given me.

There are some points in your letter on which I should wish to say a few words, but I can only hope to do so in a very short, & abrupt way, or this letter would exceed all due bounds.

You say that there are 'two lively & vigorous principles' now in contest, & that the 'one' course which 'you' cannot appreciate is the 'neutral one.' These two principles, are, I conceive, in your view the Protestant, & the Catholic, understanding the latter in the sense in which you believe it, including the criteria given in your letter respecting the Engl[ish] Ref[ormatio]n, & the conditions of Catholic unity &c. No doubt to you any one who does not embrace one of these two lines must seem 'neutral', and neutral in one sense he must be, in that he takes neither as a true principle, or exposition of fact. And in this sense, I am not unwilling to a great extent not only to confess to, but to recommend neutrality.

But such a neutrality would not be the result of indifference or want of intense feeling but from regard to birth, & fact, and for the sake of guarding against a misdirection of earnestness which is done to others, & deeper principles. With you, I believe, there are only two principles, only two tenable & consistent positions, (so far as that can be said of two positions of which one must be false) namely the Catholic & the Protestant. And I should feel like you that any one who embraced neither was neutral whether from want of light or of intensity of feeling I cannot say.

The question therefore between you & me can only be as to the nature of the true Catholic principle.

---

[b] Gifts which are no gifts and of no profit (Sophocles, *Ajax*, 665).

And here as it seems to me, you have adopted arbitrary, and perhaps to me, inadmissible criteria. For instance, I think the statement that the Engl[ish] Reformation was simply [a] political movement contrary to historical fact. I believe its moral & theological character to be in great measure evil: but I with equal strength of conviction believe the position in which it has placed us to be tenable: and that we have cause to be thankful to God for great, and extraordinary mercies in the over-ruling & result of it. Unless you hold the whole both in act, & principle, & result to be unmixed evil, I should think we differ only in degree, but you may hold more than I am aware of.

Again, as to the great Lutheran tenet—so far as I understand it, I wholly reject it. I think what Moehler says of it to be true, that taken without its qualifications it is pregnant with heretical consequences: taken with them it loses its differentia & becomes simply a bad statement of truth.[c] And yet in the principle you have laid down in your answer to Mr Bird,[d] for comparing the Engl[ish] & Foreign Reformations, I sh[oul]d think the language, I have seen applied to Luther to be contrary to the moral facts of this case. It does not appear to me therefore how this can be raised to the character of a test of difference or contrariety in principle.

On the other two points however, i.e. the conditions of unity, & the standard of orthodoxy I can readily see though not believe it likely that a direct contrariety sh[oul]d exist: that is to say if the view taken by you on

---

[c] See John Adam Moehler, *Symbolism; Or, Exposition of the Doctrinal Differences between Catholics and Protestants, as Evidenced by Their Symbolical Writings*, trans. James Burton Robertson (2 vols.; London: Charles Dolman, 1843), pt. II, ch. 1 sect. liv: 'When, accordingly, we speak of an incomplete development of the principles of primitive Protestantism; or, when we say that the consistent development of the same was even rejected and assailed by the Reformers; we advert to those doctrines, which could and must be deduced from their one-sided supernaturalism; if we are justified in supposing, that a doctrine once put forth, being in itself pregnant and important, is sure to find some souls ready to devote themselves to it, with all their energy, and own its sway without reserve. The fundamental principles of the Reformers, was, that without any human co-operation, the Divine Spirit penetrates into the soul of the true Christian, and that the latter, in his relation to the former, is with respect to all religious feeling, thought, and will, perfectly passive.'

[d] Frederick Oakeley, *Explanation of a Passage on an Article in Certain Works of Bishop Jewel, Published in the British Critic for July 1841, in a Letter to the Reverend C. S. Bird, Author of 'A Plea for the Reformed Church'* (London: J. G. F. & J. Rivington, 1842) in opposition to Charles Smith Bird (1795–1862; educated at Trinity College, Cambridge, a staunchly Evangelical priest and writer; *DNB*), *A Plea for the Reformed Church; Or, Observations on a Plain and Most Important Declaration of the Tractarians, in the British Critic for July, 1841* (London: J. Hatchard, 1841).

the other two points be the Roman. If it be not I can conceive differences of degree but not of principle.

Believe me in saying this, I have no desire, much as I yearn for unity, to make out that we agree, or to offer sympathy or approximation to your theological views.

I make no scruple in saying that I find myself under deep & governing convictions which set my conscience in direct resistance to some of the, alas, most prominent points of the Roman system of which I will instance only the necessity of communion with Rome, the theory of infallibility which is pleaded for the doctrinal definitions of the Roman Church, & the worship of the Blessed Virgin as it is permitted & practiced in that communion.

Now if in what I have said you find no difference in principle, then my position, however inactive it may be in it, is not neutral.

If you do find difference of principle my position seems to me to be only neutral in the sense in which the English Church is neither Lutheran nor Roman.

Whether the position of the English Church be a true & a tenable position is another question. For me, & for the present it is only necessary to say that I have made no advance towards holding the points above instanced as held by the Church of Rome. If I be in error may God of His mercy open my eyes to see it: & let me have your prayers that I may receive my sight. Under my present convictions which are not hasty, nor without thought, and such reading, as I am capable of,[202] with some personal observation I feel that, I should commit a deadly sin both in leaving the English, & in entering the Roman Church. I thank God I have no feeling of doubt as to the life & reality of the English Church. I raise the deepest doubts, misgivings, & fears about the safety of the[203] Roman.

And as I have this feeling about the English Church as a whole so I can never use, or sympathize in language which suggests doubts of its life & reality—Moreover as, I feel what I have said about the Roman Church as a whole I can never, by word or deed, approximate it, or promote its system, or lead others by the remotest conscious influence to do so.

Both of these lines seem to me wavering, inconsistent, & mischievous: & the worst sort of neutrality which is irresolution.[204]

To them who believe that Catholic & Roman are not convertible terms, the unprotestantizing of the English Church does not signify the Romanizing of it. I can heartily embrace your word but not in this latter sense.

[[Bodl. MS Eng. lett. c. 654, 65–71]]

450125mo

Lavington Conversion of St. Paul 1845

My dear Oakeley,

According to your desire I send you some of[205] the reasons why it seems to me that your historical argument[a] falls short of its object.

The conclusion you propose to establish as I understand it, is that Roman Catholics being, & continuing such in doctrine[206] subscribed the 39 Articles in the beginning of Q[ueen] Elizabeths reign.

The passages you quote in proof of this are

1. 'Against Papists['] (says Fuller[b] &c. Page 29 of y[ou]r Pamphlet[c]

2. 'Hitherto (i.e. till AD 1570. &c'. from Fuller also Page 29[d]

3. 'Their moderation is no less visible &c.' from Heylin Pages 39. 40[e]

Taken from Strypes Grindall in the note to page 29 does not refer to the 39 Articles.[f] I am not aware of any other passages, quoted in your Pamphlet, relating to[207] subscription to the 39 Articles.

---

[a] As enunciated in Frederick Oakeley, *The Subject of Tract XC Historically Examined, with a View of Ascertaining the Object with Which the Articles of the Church of England were Put Out, and the Sense in Which They are Allowed to be Subscribed*... (2nd rev. edn.; London: James Toovey, 1845; preface dated 23 Dec. 1844).

[b] Thomas Fuller, *The Church History of Britain from the Birth of Jesus Christ until the Year MDCXLVIII* (new edn., 3 vols.; London: Thomas Tegg, 1837). On the moderate historian Thomas Fuller (1607/08–1661) see *DNB* and O'Day (1986), 38–41.

[c] Oakeley, *Subject of Tract XC*, 29 loosely quotes Thomas Fuller, bk. 9, 13 Elizabeth, sect. 30 as follows: 'Against Papists... [ellipses *sic*] it was enacted that to write, print &c. *that the Queen was a heretic* &c. should be judged *treason. Against Non-Conformists*, it was provided that every Priest or Minister should, before the Nativity of Christ next following, declare his assent, and subscribe, to all the Articles of Religion agreed on in the Convocation of 1562, under pain of deprivation.'

[d] Oakeley, *Subject of Tract XC*, 29, loosely quotes Thomas Fuller, bk. 9, 13 Elizabeth, sect. 30 thus: 'Hitherto (i.e. till A.D. 1570) Papists generally without regret repaired to the places of divine service, and were present at our prayers, sermons, and *Sacraments*.... [ellipses *sic*] In which sense one may say, that *the whole land was of one language and one speech*.... [ellipses *sic*] Hitherto the English Papists *slept in a whole skin, and so might have continued* had they not wilfully torn it themselves.'

[e] For the relevant section of Oakeley's very loose translation of Peter Heylyn, *Ecclesia Restaurata. The History of the Church of England Controversy Containing the Beginning, Progress, and Success of it*... (London: Printed by R.B. for H. Twyford, J. Place, and T. Basset, 1674), 39–40. See 450131mo. On Peter Heylyn (1599–1662) as a respondent to Thomas Fuller and an opponent of Puritan historiography see *DNB* and O'Day (1986), 32–42.

[f] Oakeley, *Subject of Tract XC*, 29, loosely quotes John Strype, *The History of the Life and Acts of the Most Reverent Father in God Edmund Grindall* (Oxford: Clarendon, 1821), 98, as follows: 'Of the subscribers (to Queen Eliz[abeth's] injunctions to conformity)... [ellipses *sic*] there

It seems to me that these reach no further than to show

1. That Roman Catholics continued in the *communion* of the Church of England

2. That they were not vexed by the Civil Power for their religion, i.e. for their belief, but for their politics.

3. That certain who as Strype says '*complied* with the Popish religion, & were dignified in the Church' in Q[ueen] Mary's reign (Strype Ref: vol[208] 1. c. 28[g]) or as Heylin says '*possibly some* also which were *inclined* rather to the old religion'[209] & subscribed among the members of the Lower House of Convocation.[h]

I am not aware of any proof you have[210] adduced[211] which goes beyond these conclusions: which, it seems to me,[212] amount to no more than that these subscribers succumbed & complied with the Reformation.

I can find no indication that Strype, Fuller or Heylin understood or intended anything more than this.[213] It is hardly necessary to refer to any passages: but Strype's way of telling it[214] (Annals 1. c. 28)[215] Fuller's contrast of the Articles and the Definitions of Trent[216] B. IX. p. 72 s. 54.[i] & Heylin's Preface to the Articles Hist[ory of the] Ref[ormation,] 350.[j217] sufficiently show this their view.

1. That[218] Roman Catholics continued[219] in the Communion of the Ch[urch] of E[n]g[land], & [']came to the *places of Div[ine] Service, prayers, sermons, & sacraments*'[220] is[221] well known.

And it seems significant that often as this was said (eg. Q[ueen] Elizabeths declaration in the Star Chamber. Strype Hist. Ref[ormation] 1. c. 57.[k]) there is not a word[222] to raise it above *lay-communion*. Can you refer me[223] to any

were many who had said Mass in Queen Mary's time, and such as would not change their custom of old Pater Nosters.'

[g] Strype, *Annals*, i. 491, indicates that some of the subscribers were exiles during Mary's reign, some lived 'obscurely' during the period, and some 'lastly, in that reign complied with the popish religion, and were dignified in the church'.

[h] Heylyn, *Ecclesia restaurata*, 331.

[i] Thomas Fuller, bk. 9, 5 Elizabeth, sect. 54, 469, provides a very brief contrast: 'Truth and falsehood starting in some sort together... many of the Decrees [of Trent] begin with lying, and all conclude with cursing... whilst these our Articles, like the still voice, only plainly express the positive truth.'

[j] Heylyn, *Ecclesia restaurata*, 350, preface to the comparative table of the 1552 and 1562 Articles.

[k] Strype, *Annals*, i. 391–7.

such expression? This uniform omission seems to imply that anything more than communion[224] was not conceived possible. There is not the smallest sign[225] that any such persons were in the ministry of the Church: but even supposing there were, still it would not prove the point you have in view,[226] because during those 9 or 10 years i.e. till 1570, *Subscription to the Articles was not enforced on the Clergy at large.* It was not required till 1571.[227]

2. That they were not vexed by the Civil Power for their religion, i.e. for their belief, but for their politics is also most certain. And it is to this & not to their religious condition[228] that Fuller refers when he says 'Hitherto the English Papists slept in a whole skin, and so might have continued had they not wilfully torn it themselves.'[1] This is proved by the context for he goes on to speak of the Penal laws following on the rebellions in the north, the Pope's bull of excommunication, &c. Their 'whole skin' refers to their safety in our *communion*, & quietness: but I see nothing further. And this is confirmed by the Declaration of Q[ueen] Elizabeth quoted before in wh[ich] she[229] disclaims[230] 'inquisition of any mens consciences so long as they shall observe her laws in their open deeds' i.e. 'coming to Church to common prayer and divine service.' Strype H[istory of the] Ref[ormation] 1. c. 57.[m]

3. That certain persons who 'complied' under Q[ueen] Mary or were 'inclined' to the old religion subscribed in[231] the Lower House of convocation is clear.

But this surely comes short of your conclusion. It seems to me that the case of Feckenham, Abbot of Westminster may be taken as[232] an example of the changes of these times.

Strype says (Hist. Ref: 1. 45 & Appendix) that he complied under Henry VIII, Edward VI, & Q[ueen] Mary, but under Q[ueen] Elizabeth though he was willing to take the oath of Supremacy, he stood out in points of religion & worship, & did not comply.[n]

This appears to be a sample of[233] the religious history of the four reigns: & this[234] is not said[235] of the 'unscrupulousness of the Roman Catholics' in respect of oaths &c. (p. 31)[o] but applies to both sides.

[1]   See Oakeley, *Subject of Tract* XC, 29, loosely quoting Fuller, bk. 9, 13.

[m]   Loose paraphrase of Strype, *Annals*, i. 391.

[n]   Ibid. 186.

[o]   Oakeley, *Subject of Tract XC*, 31: 'And if the "unscrupulousness of Roman Catholics" in respect of oaths, and other civil obligations, be urged as the ground of the insufficiency of our formularies as means of excluding them, then it must be shown, *why they were eventually excluded*, for that they did refuse *some* tests, is undeniable.'

Under Henry VIII then, two parties were alternatively in the ascendant eg the King's book the B[isho]ps book[236] the six Articles[P] &c.

Under Edward VI. the Reformers had it all their own way.

Under Mary the Roman Catholics were in absolute power.

Under Elizabeth the Reformation was again supreme.

All through these four reigns there was a large[237] compliant body which yielded to the[238] governing powers.

It appears to me that those who subscribed the[239] 39 Articles[240] simply assented to or[241] complied with the Reformation under Elizabeth as they or others had in[242] the changes of Edward & Mary.

And the reasons which incline me to this[243] belief[244] are:

First, because the non-complying Romanists had been already deprived in the year 1560, a year before the Articles were proposed in Convocation. The oath[245] of supremacy had sifted the Clergy, & what remained were made up[246] either of men more or less sympathising in the[247] reformation or complying with it. B[isho]p Short seems to state the case correctly[248] when he says 'The rest of the Clergy generally complied with the changes wh[ich] were established by law, as indeed they had frequently done before: for of 9,400 beneficed men in England there were but 14 Bishops, 6 Abbots, 12 Deans 12 *Arch*deacons 15 heads of Colleges, 50 Prebendaries, 80 Rectors making a total of 189 who refused to take the oath of suprem-acy.' History of the Ch[urch][q249] Lingard also says the oath of supremacy 'was deemed equivalent to a renunciation of the Catholic Creed' (Hist. vol. VII. p. 316)[r] and this explains one passage you quote from Fuller where he says 'Against *Papists* it was enacted &c. against *nonconformists* &c.' This was not the Oath of supremacy, for that[250] was required[251] in 1560 but a new statute[252] of pains & penalties in 1571 on the withdrawal of the R[oman] C[atholic] from Divine worship,[253] the northern[254] rebellion, the excommunication of the Queen & the like.[255] See Fuller Eliz[abeth]

[P] 'The King's Book' (1543) was a revision of 'The Bishop's Book' (1537), a compilation on the Creed, the seven Sacraments, and other central theological matters. The 'Six Articles' were promulgated against Protestant tendencies by Henry VIII in 1539. For texts see *Formularies of Faith put forth by Authority during the Reign of Henry VIII*, ed. Charles Lloyd (Oxford: Clarendon, 1825).

[q] Thomas Vowler Short (1790–1872; educated and tutor at Christ Church, Oxford, Bishop of Sodor and Man, 1841, and of St Asaph, 1846 [*DNB*]), *A Sketch of the History of the Church of England to the Revolution of 1688* (2 vols.; Oxford: S. Collingwood, 1837), i. 349.

[r] John Lingard, *The History of England from the First Invasion by the Romans* (4th edn., 13 vols.; London: Baldwin & Cradock, 1838).

p. 98 The Papists Fuller speaks of were[256] not *in* the Church but *out* of it. The 39 Articles were not tendered to them because[257] they were not *in* the Church: against non conformists subscription[258] was enforced because they continued in the Church. The Articles were enforced on all Clergymen officiating in the Church. The Papists have spoken of more external & political adversaries of the Government & therefore no mention is made of doctrine or religion. The Civil power used its own weapons.[259] This seems to me to prove the reverse of your conclusion. I mean that the articles were not tendered to them because other tests[260] were needed & *because* it was certain and manifest that they c[ou]ld not subscribe them.

(2) And next as to the subscription of the lower House of Convocation.

The Upper House was unanimous because the Recusant Bishops were deprived.

The Recusant Members[261] of the lower House had been deprived also, namely, 12 Deans, 12 Archdeacons (i.e. 24 out of 143 the number of the whole L[ower] H[ouse]) & of the 50 Prebendaries many it is likely were Proctors. At all counts all the Lower House as it was when it met had taken the[262] oath of Supremacy were so far compliant. It is said in your Pamphlet[263] 'Many' 'who were Roman Catholics subscribed.' p. 30.[s]

This seems to me to go beyond the premises. Strype says who *'complied'* under Q[ueen] Mary:[t] & Heylin *'inclined'* to the old religion.[u] But this falls a great way short of calling them *Roman Catholics* in the sense required[264] for your conclusion. No doubt among those that took the oath of Supremacy there were some[265] that had 'complied' under Q[ueen] Mary; & were 'inclined' to the old religion, and did yet fully tho' reluctantly[266] yield to the Reformation when it c[ou]ld no longer [be] resisted.

Then again as to the[267] number. You say 'Many.' Heylin says *'possibly some'*. Strype names *five* & adds '& diverse others.'

In a note p. 30[268] you quote John Bridgewater as having subscribed.[269] ([Strype, Annals of the] Ref[ormation,] I. c. 28).

---

[s] Oakeley, *Subject of Tract XC*, 30: 'It farther appears, that many members of the Lower House of Convocation, who were Roman Catholics subscribed the Articles under revision in 1562,' footnoting this statement: 'Strype (Ann[als] of Ref[ormation] c. xxviii) gives their names: and, among them, we find the celebrated John Bridgewater, (called in Latin, Aquapontanus) who, in 1582, published the Treatise called 'Concertatio Ecclesiae Catholicae in Angliâ.'

[t] See above Strype, *Annals*, i. 491.

[u] See above Heylyn, *Ecclesia restaurata*, 331.

But[270] in the same paragraph you quote Strype[271] adds that 'after divers years' he '*turned* Papist'.[v]

Of another, Strype says, he was reproved by Gregory Martin[w] a Roman Catholic 'for following the world, or dissembling in religion against his conscience & knowledge.' (See Postscript[x]) This seems to me to reduce the facts both in respect to the number of subscribers and of the moral force of their example[272] to a low standard.

So far as I know I believe that on both sides such subscriptions were looked upon as a compliance, with the ruling power.

It was not for nine years after this that subscription was enforced on the clergy at large.

And during these nine years the whole doctrinal controversy was hotly maintained.[273]

The Articles were attacked the[274] next year after their publication i.e. in 1563 by Rastell[y] nephew to Sir Thomas More.[z] (Fuller's Eliz[abeth] 75.[aa]) to say nothing of the controversies of Harding,[bb] Sandon, Dorman,[cc] Stapleton,[dd] &c.

Also before 1571 the R[oman] C[atholic] Colleges were formed abroad for the English Mission emissaries were at work all over England: the two

---

[v]   Strype, *Annals*, i. 492.

[w]   Martin, Gregory (1542?–82; *DNB*), Roman Catholic priest, Bible translator, and controversialist, was a Fellow of St John's College, Oxford, before his flight to the Continent in 1569.

[x]   Strype, *Annals*, i. 492.

[y]   John Rastell (d. 1536), *The Exposicions of the Termes of the Lawes of England: With Diuers Propre Rules and Principles of the Lawe, as Well Out of the Bookes of Maister Littleton, as of Other: Gathered Both in French and English, for Yong Men Very Necessary: Whereunto are Added the Olde Tenures* (London: Richardi Tottell, 1563).

[z]   On Sir Thomas More (1478–1535; *DNB*), Chancellor to Henry VII and executed for refusing to sign the Oath of Supremacy.

[aa] Thomas Fuller discusses the William Rastall incident and his opposition with Jewell in bk. 9, 5 Elizabeth, sect. 64.

[bb] Thomas Harding (1516–72; *DNB*), educated at New College, Oxford, upheld Reformed principles during the reign of Edward VI, but turned back to Catholicism under Mary, was deprived of offices under Elizabeth, and carried on extensive controversies, particularly with John Jewel thereafter.

[cc] Thomas Dorman (d. 1557; *DNB*), educated at New College, Oxford, elected a Fellow at All Soul's, Oxford under Mary, and on the coronation of Elizabeth fled to the Continent, from where he continued to write controversial treatises against the Protestants.

[dd] The Catholic controversialist Thomas Stapleton (1535–98; *DNB*), was educated at New College, Oxford, and fled to the Continent on the advent of Elizabeth.

churches[275] were already in conflict on matter of doctrine: this seems to be a comment on the Articles at the date of their publication.

These are some of the reasons why it seems to me that the proofs you have offered fall short of your conclusion. They show that certain persons who 'complied' under Q[ueen] Mary, & some 'inclined' to the old religion acquiesced in the Reformation under Elizabeth: but they do not appear to me to prove that Roman Catholics, being & continuing such in doctrine subscribed the 39 articles: or that the examples given by Strype, indicate the signing of the 39 articles by persons holding[276] Roman doctrines.

Can you refer me to any Historian or Divine of either side who has maintained your view in this particular?

I would beg you to observe two things:

1. That I have[277] not undertaken[278] to prove a negative, but only to show the points in which your arguments seem to fail.

2. That I have[279] spoken[280] only of the *historical* argument as distinct from Santa Claras system[281] & from all *theological* questions. All that I[282] will add is the same request made to me,[283] you will truly oblige me by[284] pointing out where I appear to you to miss of the two. If I may say so much of myself, I have no bias, inclination, or desire but for the truth what &[285] wheresoever it be. It is no pleasure for me to seem to cross an argument for[286] approximation between those who are mutually divided.[287] I desire agreements and not differences but I dread the thought of resting upon a false persuasion believing that truth always indicates itself at last to them that have wronged it.

Believe me, my dear Oakeley

Yours very truly

H.E.M.

P.S. In his History of Cambridge p. 142 Fuller says 'Philip Barker D[octor] of D[ivinity] Provost of King's College being a zealous Pap[is]t had hitherto so *concealed* his relig[io]n, that he was not only the first Eccl[e-siastical] person on whom Q[ueen] E[lizabeth] bestowed preferment, but also being V[ice] C[hancellor] of C[ambridge] commendably discharged the place, without any *discovery of his opinions*. But now being questioned for his Rel[i]g[io]n, not wishing to abide the trial he fled beyond the seas.'[ee] This was ab[ou]t 1570–1.

[ee] Thomas Fuller, *The History of the University of Cambridge from the Conquest to the Year 1634*, ed. Marmaduke Prickett and Thomas Wright (Cambridge: J. & J. J. Deighton and T. Stevenson), 271.

Unless he was a member of Con[vocatio]n (wh[ich] is not likely, & his name is not in the list of subscribers in Strype) he had never signed the 39 articles wh[ich] were not enforced till 1571 on the Clergy, & not till much later in the University. But at 1570–1 were about to be enforced. The concealment of his opinion falls in with Gregory Martins view wh[ich] so far as I know has always been the view of the R[oman] C[atholics] as well as of the English Ch[urch].

[[Bodl. MS Eng. lett. c. 654, 73–9 (draft); 80–3 (fair copy to '... prove a negative but only')]]

450127om

London
27 Jan[uary] 1845

My dear Archdeacon Manning,

I am exceedingly obliged by your paper on the Articles, which deserves my best attention, and shall review it with the least possible delay. I only regret that I read your remarks in manuscript and not in print. I am indeed most glad that you have stated to me the grounds on which you demur to my argument; and if it be indeed unsound, then I most sincerely wish it to be publicly exposed, as I have reason to know that a considerable number of persons are resting upon it. Without my books, and with only a very imperfect recollection of the paragraph by which I satisfied myself at the time of the inquiry, I am quite unable to say more at this moment than that your objections ardently require to be carefully considered.

Whether the Historical part of the argument for Roman Catholic Subscription be so material as that its failure must be decisive on the *practical* point in question, this I will not go so far as to say without a great deal more consideration. That it is *very* important, however, I certainly do feel because 1) The language of the[288] Articles does seem to me to require the comment of evidence to the comprehensive intentions of the Framers; (and this with a view not only to *Roman* Catholic subscription but to what is in outline Catholic subscription altogether) and thus I am anxious to be able to prove à posteriori as well as à priori that they were framed with a view to comprehension—by shewing, that as it was likely the Ref[ormers] sh[oul]d aim at comprehending *R[oman]* Catholics, so in fact they succeeded in their aim—2) because I am prepared to acknowledge that there is a lack, if not an absence of evidence to prove that since 1571 the Articles have ever been subscribed in the *full Roman Catholic* sense, *Forbes's* seems to me the strongest case.[a]

---

[a] William Forbes (1585–1634).

3) —and in drawing upon 1) Newman at the close of N[umber] 90 seems to feel the *historical* proof necessary to *his* argument; and much more of course must it be to Santa Clara's.

After all, however, there is one (apparently) very strong argument on our side[289] which I have implied in my preface to the 2d Ed[itio]n of my Pamphlet & which Ward has drawn out at page 43 of his Defence,[b] and this argument would I think remain in force, even although all your objections to my statements of fact sh[oul]d prove to be[290] well founded. If the articles were framed with a comprehensive object at all (and this I take to be an *acknowledged* historical fact) must they not have been meant to let in *Roman* Catholics? What other Catholics existed at this time more Catholic than the Reformers themselves? No one I suppose would deny that Ar[ch]b[isho]p Laud went further in Catholicism than B[isho]p Ridley, the least Protestant of the Reformers.[c] Do you not then prove *too much* in disproving that the inclusion of Roman Catholics was designed, for how then can you shew that it was intended to include such as Laud? I should really be most glad to know what you feel on this point though it is asking a great deal; but it would be a kindness to me if you would even indicate the view upon which you think it may be met.

You will readily conceive how interesting to me is this whole subject at the present moment. And I agree with you of course most fully upon the importance of ascertaining the grounds on which we are resting & binding others to such. These are certainly not 'one or two' only, as Keble says,[d] in his very kind and interesting pamphlet, but very many more who if the question of subscription in the Roman Catholic sense be determined in the negative, whether authoritatively, or as proceeds satisfactory to their own conclusions, are preferred to part with the Articles and not with the

---

[b] Ward, *Address to Members of Convocation*, 43, argues against the position that the Articles are believed in so far as they agree with Holy Scripture, noting the furore over Article 21 and adding that many, like Palmer, in fact support Ecumenical Councils as infallible.

[c] Nicolas Ridley (1502–55; *DNB*), Bishop of London, martyred with Cranmer under Mary Tudor.

[d] John Keble, 'The Case of Catholic Subscription to the Thirty-Nine Articles Considered, with especial Reference to the Duties and Difficulties of English Catholics in the Present Crisis, in a Letter to the Hon. Mr. Justice Coleridge' (London: unpublished, 1841), 29–30: 'It does seem to me that...loyalty to the Church, her Creed and her Order both, could only be maintained by one of the two of the following courses [that is, to stay in the Church and defend one's position, or to resign and therefore accept that the Articles cannot be subscribed to in the manner Catholic Christians wish].'

Roman doctrine. But they are also most anxious to find honest ways of reconciling the Articles with the Roman doctrine—and it is anything but charitable and fair in those who demur to the reasons they have put out, to keep them in ignorance of the nature, as well as the fact, of their objections. And this is why I thank you so much for the assistance you have given me.

Believe me, My dear Archdeacon Manning

Your ever truly & obliged

Frederick Oakeley

[[Bodl. MS Eng. lett. c. 654, 84–8; addressed: The Venerable Archdeacon Manning Lavington Petworth, Sussex; postmarked: zpd 27 ja 1845; **petworth aja 23 1845**]]

450128mo

L[avington] J[anuary] 28 [18]45

My d[ear] O[akeley]

I beg you to acc[ep]t my thanks for y[ou]r lett[er] r[e]c[eive]d this ins[tant]. In my last I omitted the case of D[r] R[ichard] Marshall com-[mented on] by Strype Vol. 1. c. 36.[a]

In fear that my last lett[e]r sh[oul]d not be entirely clear I wish to report that the only question there spoken of is whether the evidence you have given be enough to shew that R[oman] C[atholic]s did as such subscribe the Articles.

I did not mention to say

1. That there may not be more evidence in known losses

2. That whether there be evidence or no, they did not as such subscribe

3. That the intention of the Framers & imposers was out of prospect to include them

4. That they would not have subscribed if causes distinct from the substance & wording of the Articles had not diverted them.

5. That the articles are in contradiction with the Trid[entine] definitions. On all these & many more like points I have written.

As many of these we shall perhaps find ourselves more than you may think. Even supposing therefore that your historical arguments, so far as I have

---

[a] Strype, *Annals*, i. 48–9. Richard Marshall, Dean of Christ Church and a convinced Roman Catholic, publically retracted under Edward, but returned to his former religious positions under Mary.

gone, are incapable of suff[icien]t proof that w[oul]d not bear on the practical issue you speak of by any necessity.

I have only time to add that my reasons for not putting anything of the sub[ject] in print has been a sincere[291] & I trust a charitable desire not to shake anything which men such as yourself conscientiously believe.

Believe me my d[ear] O[akeley]

Yours very truly

HEM

I write this just going to Chich[este]r. In the course of this week I shall write again on the question you put ab[ou]t A[rch]b[isho]p Laud.

[[Bodl. MS Eng. lett. c. 654, 89–90]]

450131mo

Lavington Jan[uary] 31. 1845.

My dear Oakeley,

I have been looking to see what evidence there is for saying that the Articles were framed with a view to comprehending 'Catholics' in any sense. If this c[oul]d be shown certainly those Catholics c[oul]d be no other than Roman Catholics.

But I am not able to find evidence of that supposition. In saying this, I am bound to say that, I am very insufficiently versed in anything beyond the common histories of Collier, Strype, Fuller &c. I should be most willing to be convinced, & to change my opinion on seeing further proof to the contrary.

I can find no such comprehensive intention in 1552 & very little in 1562.

1. As to 1552, wh[ich] seems to be the decisive period, for the Articles were then framed, I see no[292] evidence that the comprehension of Roman Catholics was aimed at. The idea of the Articles seems taken from the Foreign Protestant Confessions.

They bear internal marks of agreement with the Augsburgh Confession. Cranmer invited foreign reformers to assist in some general convention for the publication of definitions.

And in his letter to Calvin gives as his reason: 'Adversarii nostri habent nunc Tridenti sua concilia, ut errores stabiliant, et nos piam Synodum congregare negligemus ut errores refutare, dogmata repurgare et propagare possimus? Illi περὶ τῆς ἀρτολαρσίας (ut audio) decreta condunt quaere nos omnem lapidem movere debemus, non solum ut alios adversus hanc idololatriam muniamus, sed etiam ut ipsi in doctrina hujus sacramenti consentiamus.' March 20. 1552. (works: vol. I. 346.)[a]

The Reformation under Edw[ar]d VI was at that time at its height & so far as I can see the only comprehension was:

1. To include all who went with the Reformation from Cranmer to Ridley
2. To put no bar in the way of those who c[oul]d just acquiesce though they would not forward the movement.

The fact that Cranmer's controversy with Gardiner took place the year before 1551, seems to prove that the two Theological[293] Systems were already in direct collision.

Thus far I see no evidence of an aim to comprehend Roman Catholics

2. Next as to 1562. The Articles were substantially & almost wholly unchanged so that no new design had scope to work in.

There are I think only three changes then made, which bear on the present point.

(1) In the XXII Article the '*Scolasticorum* doctrina' is exchanged for 'doctrina *Romanensium*' w[hic]h does not look like relaxation.[b]

(2) The long paragraph in the XXVIII respecting the 'corporal presence' was omitted.[c]

---

[a] *The Remains of Thomas Cranmer*, collected and arranged by Henry Jenkins (4 vols.; Oxford: Oxford University Press, 1833), i. 346. 'Our adversaries are now holding their councils at Trent for the establishment of their errors; and shall we neglect to call together a godly synod, for the refutation of error, and for restoring and propagating the truth? They are, as I am informed, making decrees respecting the worship of the host: wherefore we ought to leave no stone unturned, not only that we may guard others against this idolatry, but also that we may ourselves come to an agreement upon the doctrine of this sacrament' (Thomas Cranmer, *Works*, ed. John Edmund Cox [2 vols. Cambridge: Cambridge University Press, 1846], ii. 431–2).

[b] See Gilbert [Burnet], Bishop of Sarum, *An Exposition of the Thirty-Nine Articles of the Church of England*, rev. and corrected by James R. Page (London: Scott, Webster & Geary, 1837), on Article XXII, 284: 'What is here called the *Romish doctrine* is there [in the Edward VI Articles] called the *doctrine of schoolmen*. The plain reason of this is, that these errors were not so fully espoused by the body of the Roman Church, when the Articles were first published, so that some writers that softened matters threw them upon the schoolmen, and therefore the Article was cautiously worded.' See also Newman, *Remarks on Certain Passages in the Thirty-Nine Articles. Tract Ninety*, 25 in which he directs attention to the 'doctrina Romanensium' specifically in those terms.

[c] See Gilbert [Burnet], *Exposition of the Thirty-Nine Articles*, on Article XXVIII, 402, for the section from the Edward VI Article that denied 'the Real and Bodily Presence' and was omitted in the Elizabethan Articles.

Burnet in his Expos[ition] of the Articles thinks this was done with the view of comprehending Roman Catholics. In his History of the Reform[atio]n P[ar]t III b. VI he thinks it was also done with a regard to Lutherans[d]— Nevertheless from the tone of that day it is more likely that his first supposition was the true one.

> (3) The third change was the omission of the four last Articles on the 1 resurrection, 2 intermediate state, 3 millennium, 4 universal salvation: which omission is evidently what Heylin points at in the passage you quote in y[ou]r 39. page. Indeed he expressly says so in his '[second]ly in not stuffing &c. . . . *as they omitted* &c'.[e]

Your other question is how can it be[294] shown that it was intended to include such as Laud.

It does not seem to me necessary to undertake any proof at all as to such an intention. It is simply a question of fact.

Laud found the Articles wide enough for him.

Newman seems to put the matter exactly in saying 'our Articles the offspring of an uncatholic age are through God's good providence, to say the least not uncatholic.'[f]

I do not pretend to explain how it happened that the Articles were more catholic than their framers.

Indeed, true as it may be of some, I do not know that it is so of all. I could not venture to say that there were not men fully as Catholic as Laud, who may have combined to modify, or balance, or restrain the definitions of the Articles—

Also I am inclined to think that the Reformers though they may have had little sympathy with the Patristic or Scholastic definitions, had a

---

[d] Gilbert Burnet, *The History of the Reformation of the Church of England* (6 vols.; Oxford: Oxford University Press, 1829), pt. III, bk. VI, pp. 578–9.

[e] Frederick Oakeley, *Subject of Tract XC* . . . (2nd edn., 1845), 39, offers a very loose and at times paraphrased section from Peter Heylyn, *Ecclesia Restaurata. The History of the Church of England Controversy Containing the Beginning, Progress, and Success of it* . . . (London: Printed by R.B. for H. Twyford, J. Place, and T. Basset, 1674), 331. The relevant passage in Oakeley reads as follows: '2ndly, *in not stuffing [sic] the Articles with conclusions theological* [Heylyn: in not suffering the Book of Articles with all Conclusion Theological], in which a latitude of judgement was to be allowed, as far as was consistent with peace and charity. As they omitted many whole Articles in King Edward's book, and qualified the expressions in some others, so were they generally very sparing of anything which was merely matter of modality, or *de modo* only . . . [ellipses *sic*] *which rules being carefully observed by all the bishops, it was no wonder that they passed their votes without contradiction*.'

[f] Newman, *Remarks on Certain Passages in the Thirty-Nine Articles*, 4.

considerable knowledge of them; & that they were thereby kept within limits recognized[295] by the Church. And of this I take Sancta Clara's view as a confirmation but I have no need now to go into any further questions than, whether there appears any evidence of an *intention* to include Roman Catholics; & if not, how it is that Laud is not excluded.

On the whole I am disposed to think

1. That the Reformers, as for convenience I have gone on calling the Bishops & those of[296] Edw[ar]d VI reign, were sounder, as a body, than you seem to feel.

2. That they probably, & under God happily, framed a document more Catholic in substance than the conditions under wh[ich] it was framed w[oul]d lead us to expect.

I have written all this with a full sense how much more I ought to know of the subject before I venture to speak with confidence. I can only assure you that, I shall instantly yield to any correction or proofs unknown to me. I have no wish but the wish you expressed at first: & I am thankful to have an opportunity of obtaining any clearer or fuller[297] lights on this subject.

Believe me
My dear Oakeley
Yours very truly
H.E.M.

(Copy)
[[Bodl. MS Eng. lett. c. 654, 91–6]]

Theses

1. That the 39. Articles are Anti-Roman in intention, and essence

2. That they are Anti-Roman in intention, but not in essence, only in appearance

3. That they are Anti-Roman in intention, & essence, but not anti-tridentine

4. That they were intended to be essentially anti-Roman, & anti-Tridentine

5. That they were intended essentially to be neither but only to look so

6. That they condemn only what the Ch[urch] of R[ome] condemns

7. That what they call R[oma]n doctrine is not R[oma]n doctrine.

Principles

1. That the Imponens intended to exclude Roman subscription, & has succeeded in terminarum[g]
2. That he intended, & has failed
3. That he intended to include Roman subscription & has succeeded in term[inaru]m.

[[Bodl. MS Eng. lett. c. 654, 98]]

450203om

74 Margaret St.

3. Feb[ruary] 1845

My dear Archdeacon Manning

You have done me a great kindness and I am sure also that in the end you will be found to have done a service to a good cause by looking so far into the historical question touching the purposes and effects of the Articles. I hear that [Arthur Penrhyn] Stanley[a] of University [College] whom I know to be better read in the history of that time than most men is also looking into the subject and will probably publish.[a] His view I understand is that the Articles were not intended as Tests at all; but as mere manifestoes of opinion, or expositions of the Anglican view: he, like yourself, disputes some of my positions; and when his pamphlet or work appears I hope to go into the whole subject both of his objections & of yours and to come out with a Defence of my position.

At the moment I will say that your *last* ground seems to me[298] to be less tenable than your former: I think it may very fairly be agreed that in many cases the Roman Catholics who assented to the Articles were low fellows, though I do not think it can be shown to have been so in every case, but that there are plain exceptions. I think *nothing* of its being said that a man

---

[g] In respect to the furthest point.

[a] Arthur Penrhyn Stanley (1815–81) was educated at Rugby and Balliol College, Oxford, elected a Fellow, University College, Oxford, 1838, appointed as a tutor at University College, 1843, Canon at Canterbury Cathedral, 1851, Regius Professor of Ecclesiastical History at Oxford, 1856, Dean of Westminster Abbey, 1864. For details see *DNB*, George Granville Bradley, *Recollections of Arthur Penrhyn Stanley, Dean of Westminster: Three Lectures Delivered in Edinburgh in November 1882* (London: John Murray, 1883), Rowland Edmund Prothero, *The Life and Correspondence of Arthur Penrhyn Stanley*, with the co-operation and sanction of G. G. Bradley (2 vols.; London: John Murray, 1893), *Letters and Verses of Arthur Penrhyn Stanley, D.D: Between the Years 1829 and 1881*, ed. Rowland E. Prothero (London: John Murray, 1895), Baillie (1930), Hammond (1987).

who assented 'afterwards became' a 'Papist' i.e. acknowledged the Papal supremacy in addition to 'holding all Roman doctrines.' If a future historian were describing the case of one among ourselves[299] who now assents to the Articles in the Roman sense & hereafter enters the Roman Communion in a foreign country, he w[oul]d discount the case just as one of the cases to which you refer is discounted.

But as to a new arg[ument], the comprehensiveness of intention, this I think it will be difficult to establish; though I have not yet gone into your objections and so am not saying this as in opposition to them. But I see you think the Articles are modelled upon the Conf[ession] of Aug[sburg]. Now I remember looking into the Conf[ession] of Augsburg & other Protestant Conf[essions] 3 years ago, and feeling that my case was greatly strengthened by the comparison. It seemed to me the sort of difference between the eloquent speech of an earnest man feeling his way & being sure of less he asks: and the cautious Document of one or more men feeling that he & or they had objections to meet and objections to include.

But I rejoice at any rate that the subjects bode fair to be discussed. I am sure that everything will do good which draws attention to the history of that time; and it is likely to be discussed so amicably and with so single an aim at truth that the good will act I am sure viz counterbalanced as that of controversy in general is so [illegible word] be.

[300]This Historical quarter w[oul]d be very unlike all others, of the same kind, if it did not admit of two sides, or if it *did* admit of being ruled unquestionably. But at last, our position in favour of our own mode of subscription is not *grounded* upon the truth of the historical view, though it w[oul]d be helped by it. If, upon y[ou]r hypothesis, A[rch]b[isho]p Laud c[oul]d sign Articles which were drawn up with no eye to his opinions; so can we. I do not at all grant that any interpretation by wh[ich] a man can satisfy his conscience is therefore honest. But when persons declare in face of day in what sense they subscribe & the Imponens (whoever it be) accepts that sense, or does not prohibit it, I consider it fully competent to those persons to remain in the Univ[ersity] or the Ministry of the Ch[urch] of England. But this indeed I do not understand you to question.

Ever yours very truly
Frederick Oakeley

[[Bodl. MS Eng. lett. c. 654, 99–102]]

Newman on Gladstone's Resignation

450418ng

Littlemore. April 18. 1845

My dear Mr. Gladstone,

I should not venture to incroach upon your time with this note of mine, but for your letters to me last autumn, which make me read with great interest of course everything which is in the Papers about you, and encourage me to think that you will not think me intrusive.

As various persons ask me what I understand is your present position, I will put down what I conceive it to be—and I will beg you to correct my account of it just as much or just as little as you please, and to determine, as you think best, whether I shall say I have your authority for any statements you may kindly make in your answer, or not.

Unless words always look cold & formal on paper, I should not think of saying, (what I really hope it will not even come into your passing thoughts to doubt,) how great interest I feel in the line of thought which is at present engaging your mind & how sure I am you will be conducted to right conclusions. Nor is there anything to startle or distress me in what you are reported to have said in the house.

I say then—'Mr. Gladstone has said the State *ought* to have a conscience—but it has not a conscience. Can *he* give it a conscience? Is he to impose his own conscience on the State? he would be very glad to do so if it would thereby become the State's conscience. But this is absurd—He must deal with the facts. It has a thousand consciences, as being, in its legislative and executive capacities, the aggregate of a hundred minds—that is, it has no conscience.[']

You will say, 'Well, the obvious thing would be if the State has not a conscience that he should cease to be answerable for it.' So he has—he has retired from the Ministry. While he thought he could believe it had a conscience, till he was forced to give up what it was his duty to cherish as long as ever he could, the notion that the British Empire was a subject and servant of the Kingdom of Christ,—he served the State. Now that he finds this to be a mere dream, much as it ought to be otherwise, much as it once was otherwise, he has said, 'I cannot serve such a mistress.'

'But really,' I continue, 'do you in your heart mean to say that he *should* absolutely and for ever give up the State & country. I hope not—I do not think he has so committed himself. That the conclusion he has come to is a very grave one, and not consistent with his going on blindly in the din and hurry of business, without having principles to guide him, I admit, and this

I conceive is his reason for at once retiring from the Ministry, that he may contemplate the state of things calmly and from without. But I really cannot pronounce, nor can you, nor can he perhaps at once, what is a Christian's duty under these new circumstances—whether to remain in retirement from public affairs or not. Retirement however could not be done by halves. If he is absolutely to give up all management of public affairs, he must retire not only from the Ministry, but from Parliament.

'I see another reason for his retiring from the Ministry. The public thought that they had in his book a pledge that the government would not take such a step with respect to Maynooth as is now before the country. Had he continued in the Ministry, he would, to a certain extent, have been misleading the country.

'You say "he made some show of seeing his way in public for he gave advice—He said it would be well for all parties to yield something. To see his way and to give advice is as if he had found some principle to go on." I did not so understand him. I thought he distinctly stated he had not yet found a principle—But he gave that advice which facts, or what he called circumstances, made necessary—and which, if followed out, will, it is to be hoped, lead to some basis of principle, which we do not see at present.'

This letter has run to a greater length than I had expected—but I thought I would do my best to bring out the impression which your speech has given me of your meaning.

I am
My dear Mr. Gladstone
Very truly yours
John H. Newman

[[BL Add. MS 44362, 160–1; *LD* x. 629–31]]

450419gn

13, Carlton H[ouse] Terrace,
April 19. [18]45

My dear Mr. Newman,

You have expressed with great accuracy the view which I take of the question of Church and State as a whole enveloping in it the particular question as to Maynooth that at present agitates England.

According to the old European & Christian civilisation (to go no farther back) the State was a family and the governors had the position and the duties of parents. According to the modern notion, the State is a Club: the government is the organ of the influences predominating in the body.

Where its spirit is hard what has been called the tyranny of the majority rules with a high hand. Where its spirit is more gentle, as it can scarcely fail to be in every State founded upon the ancient basis, other sentiments entertained by bodies[301] of sensible magnitude besides those of the mere majority find their way into & are represented in the action of the State.

With us the State is neither a family nor a club: but it is on its path of transition from the former to the latter. It is less like a Club than America, or than France: it is less like a family (I mean as to duties not as to their fulfilment) than Austria or than Russia. The public men of the present day are, I must not conceal it from myself, engaged in regulating & qualifying, & some of them in retarding, this transition. But the work proceeds; and as to that work regarded as a whole, and its results, I view them with great alarm.

The State cannot be said now to have a conscience, at least not by me, inasmuch as I think it acts, & acts wilfully, & intends to go on acting, in such a way as no conscience, that is no personal conscience (which is the only real form of one) can endure. But the State still continues to act, in many ways, *as if* it had a conscience. The Christian figure of our institutions still remains though marred by the most incongruous associations. There are therefore actual relations of the State to Religion, I mean to determinate religion, which still subsist and retain much vitality, and offer opportunities of good in proportion to it: however they may be surrounded with violent moral contradictions. For the sake of these opportunities I think that public life is tolerable & in my case as it at present stands obligatory. But it is like serving for Leah afterwards to win Rachel.[a]

I have clung to the notion of a conscience, and a Catholic conscience, in the State, until that idea has become in the general mind so feeble, as to be absolutely inappreciable in the movement of public affairs. I do not know whether there is one man opposing the Maynooth Bill upon that principle. When I have found myself the last man in the ship, I think that I am free to leave it.

But some persons will say a principle is not to be regarded as a ship which may be left in extreme necessity: it is a witness for truth & power & life belong to it as such. Then my answer is I do not think that any theory of government is in this sense a principle. My language has always been, 'Here is the genuine & proper theory of government as to religion: hold it as long as you can, & as far as you can.' Government must subsist; and if not as (in strictness) it ought, then as it may.

At this point comes in the question whether the work of government has not therefore become absolutely unclean, & whether it should not be abjured. That is a very difficult question, I mean the first part of it. Upon the whole, for specific reasons, I have made up my mind in the negative: not with an entire conviction, perhaps but as the better of the two alternatives before me. But most emphatically do I agree with that sentence of your letter: retirement to have anything like its full meaning must be retirement from Parliament as well as office.

I am quite unable I confess to give any definition of the abstract character of the acts of a State while it is much like ours in its course of transition. I understand that when it has come to be a Club it acts like a clock: a good or a bad one as the case may be. When it was in its early & normal condition it acted or should have acted like a man, or even more like an archangel. In our case the ancient principle of reverence to truth, the supreme law of the State in its higher condition, is crossed & intercepted by the law of representation & equality of claims according to number & will, the supreme law of the State in its lower condition, when the hand of Death is palsying it by however slow degrees. In the sense therefore of incapacity to give a moral definition of acts in which I myself concur, I am at fault: a serious difficulty.

But, as to the course which offers to my mind the only alternative other than that of retirement, I have framed my general idea of it. It is, in all those cases where the State acts *as if* it had a conscience, to maintain that standard as nearly as we can: and in other cases to take social justice according to the lower but now prevalent idea for a guide. 'A principle' I can hardly presume to call this. In the House of Commons there is unfortunately no word with which such liberties are taken. But it is a sort of general rule though planted I grant upon ground infirm enough.

I do not know that I should have the least difficulty in subscribing your letter as it stands: & I could much rather say ditto to you than do your work over again in my own language. Still I thought I should convey to you less of my own mind by merely stating assent, than by placing before you my view in a positive & distinct form, so as to enable you to judge how far I really fulfil your meaning, and likewise what my own is worth.

You will perceive that much of what I have said here is not fit to be said in public: especially for this great reason, that the demonstration in detail of the necessity for giving ground, & all strong statements of that necessity, enhance the evil from which they flow. This is a difficulty with me: higher interests require me to run the hazard of misapprehensions wh[ich] in other circumstances it w[oul]d be a duty to try to obviate. I may now try it, but it is with my hands tied.

A copy of my speech will be sent to you by the publisher. If you take the pains to read you will find it probably less obscure than the report in the newspapers. In the meantime I am exceedingly thankful both for the interest you express & for the very valuable statement which you have put into my mouth. I cannot ask you to pursue the subject farther: but I am sure you will understand that it is not from any other motive than the fear of intrusion upon you.

Believe me, etc.,
W.E.G.

J. H. Newman
[[BL Add. MS 44362, 166–71; *LD* x. 632–3; Lathbury, i. 71–4]]

Gladstone to Hope, 15 May 1845

450515gh

13 Carlton House Terrace
Thursday Night
May 15 [18]45.

Private.
My dear Hope,

In 1838 you lent me that generous and powerful aid in the preparation of my book for the press, to which I owe it that the defects and faults of the work fell short of absolutely disqualifying it for its purpose. From that time I began to form not only high but definite anticipations of the services which you would render to the Church in the deep and searching processes through which she has had and yet has to pass. These anticipations, however, did not rest only upon my own wishes, or on the hopes which benefits already received might have led me to form. In the commencement of 1840, in the very room where we talked to-night, you voluntarily, & somewhat solemnly, tendered to me the assurance that at all times [you would] be ready to cooperate with me in furtherance of the welfare of the Church, and you placed no limit on the extent of such cooperation. I had no title to expect, & had not expected, a promise so heartstirring, but I set upon it a value scarcely to be described, & it ever after entered as an element of the first importance into all my views of the future course of public affairs in their bearing upon religion.

The prospects of a great crisis in the destinies of the Church as it is related to the State[302] which were then remote, are now in much closer view, and we seem to see even the remaining steps one by one which are to bring us into immediate contact with it.

In the midst of the most painful oppression of heart, under a deep conviction that the civil power is moving itself further & further from God, and in a word beneath a pressure of anxieties not personal so heavy as to reduce to perfect insignificance the anxieties connected with the personal question whether I & any who may think similarly shall make utter shipwreck come of what is commonly termed public character in the effort, I am fastened down to the conviction that it is the duty of us who are in public affairs to remain where we are, and not effectually to separate ourselves from a general course which we believe to be our tendency to evil, for the sake of the Church of God, & of the great opportunities, the gigantic opportunities of good or evil to the Church, which the course of events seems (humanly speaking) certain to open up.

If the time shall ever come (which I look upon as extremely uncertain, but I think if it comes at all it will be before the lapse of many years) when I am called upon to use any of those opportunities, it would be my duty to look to you for aid under the promise to which I have referred, unless in the meantime you shall as deliberately & solemnly withdraw that promise as you first made it. I will not describe at length how your withdrawal of it would increase that sense of desolation which, as matters now stand, often approaches to being intolerable: I only speak of it as a matter of fact, & I am anxious you should know that I look to it as one of the very weightiest kind, under a title which you have given me.

You would of course cancel it upon the conviction that it involved sin on your part: with anything less than that conviction I do not expect that you will cancel it; and I am, on the contrary persuaded that you will struggle against pain, depression, disgust, & even against doubt touching the very root of our position, for the fulfillment of actual *duties* which the post you actually occupy in the Church of God, taken in connection with your faculties & attainments, may assign to you.

I have no obligation, & no title apart from obligation, to say more on that subject. It is with a weaker claim upon your attention, that I mention today a few words in relation to such doubts.

They may conceivably arise in any given case either from the view of the actual state & tendency of a Church, or from a conviction that there has been a separation of it from the body of our Lord—as the title of a man to salvation would be called in question either by his living in flagrant sin, or by the discovery of his never having been baptised or of his having been excommunicated.

I can hardly think that any man of sober judgement can, certainly I have heard of none who does. I do not say doubt but realise and affirm his doubts in regard to the Church of England, upon the footing of her present state including in her state her tendencies. For instance, to take some particular subjects that are among the sorest: if we speak of rarity of devotion, no year elapses without the establishment of new daily services in this city—two, that I know of, at this end of it, within the last six months. If we speak of ascetic institutions, one has opened this very month within two miles of us; and you probably know of our effort among young men living in the world to commence something of life by rule under[303] mutual engagement—but if you doubt, & if you will let me, I will take care that you are duly informed respecting it. If we speak of the want of heroic self devotion, I do seriously declare, that most of those who have recently gone out to our Colonial Bishoprics, have gone as it seems to me, in the frame and spirit of Apostles, and have left all for their Lord's sake in as true and as high a sense as the Church has ever known.

I put it to you however that the state of the Church, which you know much better than I do, not only is not a disproof to any mind in sobriety of her character as a Church, but that it makes a very forcible and authoritative appeal to all who are in her path & under her allegiance to be zealous and enthusiastic on her behalf, an appeal which to tell you the truth I believe you own & obey, even if your language at a particular moment is to a contrary effect.

You have given me lessons, that I have taken thankfully: believe I do it in the payment of a debt, if I tell you that your mind & intellect, to which I look up with reverence under a consciousness of immense inferiority, are much under the dominion, whether it be known or not known to yourself, of an agency lower than their own, more blind, more variable, more difficult to call inwardly to account & make to answer for itself; the agency, I mean, of painful and disheartening impressions; impressions which have an unhappy & powerful tendency to realise the very worst of what they picture. Of this fact I have repeatedly noted the signs in you.

Moving to the other grounds upon which we might assume the responsibility of releasing ourselves from the service of the Church, namely the supposition of a separation, I am at the greatest loss to answer the following queries, every one of which (& probably more but I write on the moment) I should be forced to put even if I believed that every material step taken at the Reformation was a wrong one.

1. So far as the declarations of the English Church against *doctrines* received elsewhere are concerned, how can they destroy her being as a Church until they have been formally condemned, & contumaciously adhered to by her nowithstanding that condemnation?

2. So far as the rejection of the Pope's 'jurisdiction' is concerned, is it seriously to be held that no societies are the body of Christ unless they be under that jurisdiction? Are we at once to cut off from that Body *one half* of the whole Christian world? Can we deliberately look (say) the Russian Church in the face and apply this anathema against it? Can we attain one point without going yet further? What was the condition of the British Bishops & their Churches whom St. Augustine found in England—who had existed for centuries there, who had never been in communion with the Pope, and who were not all brought into communion with him (to say nothing upon the degree & kind of his jurisdiction at that time) for *six hundred years* after St. Augustine's arrival? Is the proposition anything less than humourous, that those Bishops and Churches were cut off from the Redeemer, & that individuals in them were at liberty to quit them, to disown their authority, or to refuse them any other than a cold and passive obedience?

3. But if not, how is it possible that the rejection of papal jurisdiction, even if for argument's sake it were granted to be evil, & wholly evil, & the cause & root of other evils, could be such an evil as to cut off this Church from her Head?

4. None can say that the Church of England has excommunicated and anathematised the Pope & the Church of Rome. The Russian Church has done this—& acts upon it by rebaptising. Does it not seem that (though *possibly* we might escape sentence on the ground of separation while the cause under it) it is inconceivable that it should invite us if it leaves her scatheless?

I will not [illegible word] these questions further; indeed they are objectionable to me, on the ground that they seem to make admissions which come for argument's sake I am loath to make.

Having made these demands upon you, let me say a few words on the state of my own mind & views of the Church of Rome.

I can conceive scarcely a nobler vocation than that of one of the sentinels of the Church of England on the side looking towards the Church of Rome; whose duty it is to maintain defence there but to maintain it in love. It seems to me one of the greatest of human achievements to do all that faithfulness requires in indicating & declaring the dangers of the Roman system, and yet to do all that justice as well as Christian love & the tender recollection of our Lord's departing prayer no less imperatively demand in exchanging whatever might be a new obstacle to reunion, and in humanising the exalted spirits which that Church has formed, and the glorious deeds she has done.

Of all men I should be the most impotent[a] though powerfully attracted towards it; for I am paralysed by the conflict between the fear of bringing a railing accusation[b] against the work of the Holy Ghost in her on the one hand[304] and the sense of most frightful evils on the other,[305] most intimately associated with her actual system, & to all appearance cherished in deadly embrace by herself, with a further sense that a blindness to these evils, a total misconception not merely of their amount but of their relation to her system, seems, as God's latest & sharpened judgement against us for our sins, to have overshadowed some among our holiest minds. I see in the Church of Rome the very best and the very worst of the Churches of Christ. It is no new discovery; if it were it would not be my sentiment. It is clearly and strongly pronounced as to substance[306] in Dante, that prodigy of humankind; I will not go to any other great names but one. No one has more consciously stated at least a great part and a vital one of the case than Newman in the Sentences (1841) where he declares that the actual system of the Church of Rome goes far to substitute the Blessed Virgin, the Saints, & Purgatory for the Trinity and Heaven and Hell.[c] Of this he has since stated his retraction. Then comes in this peculiarity. I firmly believe that the rules of the Church of England would have put down the heresy & latitudinarianism that range within her, if they could. But on the other hand it seems from history & living experience that authority is resolutely set on the side of those equally awful evils which have a freer scope within the Roman Church.

I can well conceive a far more perfect system than that of the English Church as it is on paper—but even from that I am infinitely distant; and

---

[a] Cf. 1 Cor. 15: 19.

[b] Cf. 2 Pet. 2: 11.

[c] John Henry Newman, *A Letter Addressed to the Rev. R. W. Jelf, D.D., Canon of Christ Church in Explanation of the Ninetieth Tract in the Series Called The Tracts for the Times* (Oxford: J. H. Parker, 1841), 5.

yet if a man may rely upon inward & spiritual facts, of which we may have at least as sure knowledge as sensible objects, I say with immoveable conviction, we have in the Church of England, even amongst her mutilated institutions, large & free access to our Lord & a communion with him sufficient to form in ourselves, as I have plainly seen it form in others, all the lineaments of His Divine Image: and how *can* things be right if while we drink the blessed lifegiving stream, we disown the channel that brings it and suffer our hearts to wander & our hands to be slack?

It may be that this fatal sentiment, which touches one and another as God permits, shall continue to spread; that our best hopes of realising a Catholic system for ourselves and our children in this mourning Church shall one by one be smitten down; that the elements of life will be withdrawn from us (as God has heretofore suffered other & greater Churches and less sinful men to be destroyed) by degrees, and more and more space cleared for the ravages of the heretical principle that abides among us: and that as Rome has fearfully ripened the harvest of unbelief in the lands of her unchecked dominion, so she may prepare it here also by exhausting the Church of England of her life and power. Up to this time, these accursed mischiefs can scarcely be said to have begun. Those who have gone are to be deplored indeed on many grounds, but they were not the men who have led and formed the inmost mind of the Church of England in the generation passing by, nor the men that were to form it in the generation that is coming on. It will no longer be wholly thus, if God shall permit the calamity of Newman's abandonment of the Church to descend upon us. If that comes, which I do not yet regard as certain, what extent of evil will follow, is an awful secret of the future; I fear the worst from an Anticatholic reaction, fortified by such evidence as the history of the period from 1833 will have placed in its hands. But be that as it may it will indeed be an appalling result if the fairest hopes that these three hundred years have yielded not only for England but for the ultimate reunion of Christendom shall[307] finally be blighted by the agency of the very man who was the principal instrument employed in calling them into existence, and of those who call him their spiritual father. Nor will it be less mysterious and wonderful if the Church of Rome which at this moment quakes in every country where it is dominant, in which the French Revolution ripened and which the actual pain is a result, shall display among us a power for evil which she cannot evoke for good, and shall destroy us while she is engaged in a struggle of life and death, but not a triumphant struggle, with unbelief abroad. It is true our sphere is small, our strength is but weakness, our hopes are only in the Lord; and yet they are such, that it is no presumption I think to declare it proved by experience that they are beyond the reach of fatal harm from any *other* quarter.

I should have been glad to have got your advice on some points connected with the Maynooth question on Monday next, but I will not introduce here any demand on your kindness—the claims of this letter on your attention, be they great or small, and you are their only judge, rest upon wholly different grounds.

God bless and guide you, and prosper the work of your hands.

Ever your aff[ectiona]te friend,
W. E. Gladstone.

[[NLS MS 3673, 54–9]]

Manning and Pusey on 'Love for Rome'

450808mp

Lavington. Aug[ust] 8. 1845.

My dear Friend,

One part of your last letter[a] I have thought much upon since I received it, and have at last made up my mind to venture upon writing to you about it.

I must, however, bespeak your wanted kindness lest you should think that I am venturing to express an opinion too freely about yourself. I feel most unwilling and unfit to do so and if I seem to do it, believe me, it is only because I can hardly say what I wish about myself without at least implying something in regard to you.

In your last letter you say that what you desiderate in the end of what I wrote to you is 'love for Rome'.

I have been trying to understand what is your exact meaning. But I am not able to say what could have been expressed in that context or at that time, or to those I addressed and without irrelevance under the circumstances of my then duties.

I have a sort of feeling that if you would put yourself into my place you will realize it we should be of one mind. I will, therefore dismiss this part of the subject being of no great importance.

It is, however, of much importance to have a clear view if possible of what is our duty in regard to the Church of Rome.

---

[a] Pusey to Manning, 29 July 1845, the enclosure in 450731mg.

In my endeavour to say what I feel about it:

1. We owe to the Church of Rome a pure Christian charity—as to a member of the Catholic body: we owe the same also to the Churches of the East. I do not find you expressing the latter feeling and that seems to me the cause why you are misunderstood to have not a charity to the whole Body of Christ but a partial fondness and leaning to the Roman Church.

2. We owe to the Church of Rome a special kind of charity because there are in it things of which we dare not ourselves partake.

We are bound to use no language which can arrest the course of spiritual and intellectual purification which I trust and believe is advancing in parts or in individuals of that Communion.

One Roman Catholic and some time ago [said] of certain Oxford men. 'They are forging new chains for themselves and rivetting ours.'

This seems to me to be the effect of an undecided and weak tone: and to be highly wanting in charity.

3. We owe it in charity to the whole Church and to the Roman inclusively to do all we can to deepen and perfect the spiritual life of the English Church: and however many things we may learn them, there are some of God's great mercies, which they may learn of us.

Now one powerful obstruction to the very work in which you are spending yourself arises. I believe, out of the tone you have adopted toward the Church of Rome. Will you forgive me if I say that it seems to me to be not charity but want of decision. The effect of them as I have had the opportunity of observing among the Parochial Clergy is to make them withdraw in doubt and misgiving.

4. We owe above all the largest and tenderest charity to our own Church and unless we do more than express it, I mean unless we act upon it and are governed by it, I am led to doubt the reality of our more enlarged view of charity. Is it not like the Philosophical benevolence which embraces nations and neglects kindred, and yearns after strangers while it slights the ties of home and blood?

Now what are the facts but these.

The Church of Rome for 300 years has devised our extinction. It is now undermining us. Suppose your own brother to believe that he was divinely inspired to destroy you. The highest duties would bind you to decisive, firm, and circumspect precaution.

Now a tone of love such as you speak of seems to me to bind you also to speak plainly of the broad and glaring evils of the Roman system. Are you prepared to do this? If not, it seems to me that the most powerful warnings of charity forbid you to use a tone which cannot but lay asleep the consciences of many for whom by writing and publishing you make yourself responsible. Already in many minds, all caution has been broken down: and I find minds not of men only but women giving themselves up passively and wholly to Roman books and theories for it cannot be unsafe to follow one whom they have been taught without misgiving to love.

The state to what I find persons come (and I speak with instances in my mind) is this: Not only will they not bear to hear that this Roman religion is wrong in anything, but they cannot endure to hear that we are right for by implication that means that Rome is wrong. I know of no words to express the state to which some minds have been brought than by saying that they have been taught to 'go wandering after' anything and everything that Romanists say and do: Even their errors and follies and some that are sharply reproved among themselves. I write this to the undecided and faltering tone in which people have of late suffered themselves to write.

No doubt the reaction from old and exaggerated prejudice is one cause: and now we are far advanced in the other extreme. To my ear it is a simple cant: and I firmly believe is both censured and despised by some of the best Roman Catholics as being unreal and injurious to themselves.

Another most hurtful effect of this is the recoil it produces among our own brethren. Some are fairly set adrift by it, and are driven into Puritan-ism embittered by fear, or into doubts provoked as in Blanco White by believing that the end of all positive Christianity is Rome. I really believe that the gains by such a line of unguarded tenderness towards the Church of Rome are Protestantism, and Rationalism; and the lovers are the Church of England in which the Catholic element is weakened or the Church of Rome in which the uncatholic is strengthened. It is impossible to get half what I would say in a letter. I will therefore only add that I believe that the best hope of building up the spiritual life of the English Church, and so of bringing about a reconciliation of our Church with those from whom we are unhappily estranged in a clear, firm, unambigu-ous tone as regard the points at issue, and the surest way to defeat these desires and to abandon souls on both sides to danger and shipwreck is to mistake indecision for charity.

And now, my dear Friend, I do not know that I can give you a stronger proof of my attachment than by sending this letter: for nothing less than a true friendship could venture to speak so plainly with a confidence that it will be read with patience and kindness.

May God of His great love guide us in our way.

Believe me, My dear Friend.

Yours very affect[ionately],

H. E. Manning

[[PHL MS Manning–Pusey, No. 22]]

ENDNOTES TO SECTION V

1. is] inserted, replacing overscored: are
2. in all . . . science] Chapeau omits
3. be always] Chapeau: always be
4. The . . . Gladstone] on first page
5. instruction] Chapeau: instructions
6. direction] Chapeau: directions
7. sch] overscored
8. Again] overscored
9. letter] Chapeau: letters
10. of] overscored
11. am] corrected freeman
12. known] Barton original: 'unknown' corrected to 'known'
13. Barton original: it] inserted
14. complaints] Barton original: inserted, replacing overscored: and
15. seem] Barton original: corrected from: seemed
16. Barton original: changed from which
17. Next] inserted
18. we] written over: you
19. The . . . Gladstone] on first page
20. The . . . Gladstone] on first page
21. comes upon] inserted, replacing overscored: happens to
22. in details] inserted
23. is] overscored
24. in] inserted, relacing overscored: at
25. f] overscored
26. now] inserted
27. Let . . . Statute] draft: I have not attempted yet to decide finally about this Oxford Statute: but some things which have occurred to me as tending to a decision, I should like to have your thoughts upon.
28. see] draft: so

29. than . . . Board] draft: proceedings of the Hebdomadal Board than in their former
30. to] draft: regards
31. certain parts of] draft omits
32. to] draft: regards
33. subscribed] Chapeau: submitted
34. I will . . . mischievous] draft: I will reserve the (1)st & (3)d points as being the great and only questions: and because I have more to say about them than I can write now. Moreover they seem to me to be the only parts of the statute which need to have been entertained by the H[ebdomadal] Board.
35. The . . . affirm] draft: On the (2d) I do not hesitate to say I cannot, & dare not affirm it.
36. It is . . . him] draft: The worst ethical part of Wards book, i.e. his evil speaking of the good faith of the Reformers is not worse than this. He has involved the judgment on himself, with what measure ye mete &c.' & yet I cannot do ill because he has done it. With 50 manifest faults I do not believe 'mala fides' to be one. He seems to me
37. draft adds: Now in this the Heads have split their own supporters.
38. wd] draft: were to
39. with] draft: in
40. draft adds: in this point
41. on this point] draft omits
42. less] written over: more
43. It . . . to be] draft: It seems to me therefore to be
44. draft adds: 'full'
45. sense] draft: meaning & sense
46. And I . . . Synod] draft: I take *these* to be the *criteria* of the sense & meaning originally intended, & I do not know how to find it otherwise.
47. to say] draft omits
48. What] draft: But what
49. How is it . . . fluctuations] draft: How is it to [be] secured from mutability?
50. They seem to think that they have] draft: Is it
51. And . . . worse] draft: And if so what is to be said of the ordeal?
52. for my subscription] draft: to me
53. of] draft: about
54. to commend themselves] Chapeau omits
55. one] draft: man
56. Doctrine] draft: opinions
57. at variance with] draft: contrary, or inconsistent to
58. usual] Chapeau: moral. Draft omits: and
59. for their interior opinions] draft omits
60. animadvert on them] draft omits

61. This... instance] draft: This is her security in the 2d instance, the corrective & remedial proceeding.
62. If] draft: Now if
63. That... articles] draft: That by propagating Roman doctrine Ward had gainsayed the Articles.
64. That... the] draft: That for such act of gainsaying this
65. more wisely & surely] draft adds
66. supporters] draft friends
67. really] draft: But really
68. something... bad] draft: something ethically bad, tho' tenable in logic
69. I] draft: Now I
70. I w[oul]d reserve (1) & (2)] draft: I reserved the 1st & 3d points
71. Q[ueen]] draft omits
72. bear your sifting] draft: strike you. I write them freely because I wish to test them [being: overscored] by a second judgment.
73. e.g.] Chapeau: i.e.
74. in] Chapeau: of
75. definitions] Chapeau: definitions
76. was] Chapeau: were
77. before us] inserted
78. last] overscored
79. really] Chapeau omits
80. which] overscored
81. Dorman] Morley: Darmon
82. but] written over: our
83. of 28th] inserted
84. your two propositions in] overscored
85. I] corrected from: It
86. correspondence] corrected from illegible word
87. perfectly] Chapeau: fully
88. powers] Chapeau: principles
89. From a... Pusey] inserted
90. is] corrected from: it
91. chiefly] inserted, replacing overscored: only
92. and] overscored
93. then] overscored
94. ho... kekritai] Chapeau omits
95. &] overscored
96. direction] Chapeau: directions
97. prevails] is [illegible word] overscored
98. &] MS: & &
99. new] Chapeau: raw
100. instead of blaming] inserted, replacing overscored: rather than blame

101. However dangerous may] inserted, replacing overscored: You withhold
     your own opinion on Tract 90. Whatsoever may be the serious danger of
102. In an additional pencilled revision, Jenkyns enclosed 'However dangerous...
     Tract 90' in square brackets and entered a revision in the margin, the first section
     of which (illegible) he wrote over in pen: 'Note [illegible word] that absence.' The
     pencil annotation which follows reads: reserve I should gladly have been
     informed learnt of your opinion ['of your opinion' replacing illegible overscored
     words] inter[pret]ing Tract 90—I cannot but omit?
103. again] inserted
104. condemned] inserted and overscored
105. the a mo] overscored
106. sentences upon] inserted replacing: condemnation of
107. must] overscored
108. any of themselves] inserted replacing overscored: as
109. And I must own that] inserted in pencil
110. therefore] in pencilled parentheses
111. quite] inserted
112. the opinions of] inserted
113. to which you allude by what you allude & calling] overscored
114. calling for a further notice of the obnoxious publication.] inserted in margin,
     replacing overscored: & which calls for further notice for Convocation of the
     obnoxious publication.
115. however] inserted
116. perhaps] inserted
117. efforts] inserted, replacing overscored: successful endeavours
118. studiously and successfully] inserted
119. suggest to] overscored
120. doubt not that] overscored in pencil and within pencilled parentheses and
     inserted in pencil: am prepared. Pencilled marginalia at this point reads: to
     my own duty fearlessly, nor do I doubt that the U[niversity] w[oul]d be
     equally prepared to do
121. affected] corrected from: affecting
122. Till you mentioned it] inserted
123. perhaps allow me] inserted, replacing overscored: however permit me
124. I can myself truly say that] inserted
125. these] corrected from: They
126. measures] inserted
127. any communication from] overscored
128. &] overscored
129. being] inserted
130. aided] inserted, replacing overscored: assisted forwarded
131. early in the last term] inserted

132. It is true that ... previously] inserted in margin replacing overscored: It is true that he addressed a letter to the V. C. in relation to letters testimonial from this University, but Mr. W's case Mr. W's case had

133. & no ... D[ublin]]] inserted in margin, replacing overscored: before the V. C. who would have deemed any interference of the A[rch]b[ishop] in the matter out of place from the A[rch]b[ishop] relative to letters testimonial & no subsequent communication of any kind was to the best of my knowledge made by the A[rch]b[ishop].

134. & I] pencilled

135. existing] overscored

136. Ely] overscored

137. Neither did I find any indistinctness] Chapeau omits

138. on] inserted

139. that] *sic*; Chapeau: than

140. the] inserted, replacing overscored: your

141. use of the] inserted

142. by] overscored

143. either on ... valuable] inserted

144. *de jure*] inserted

145. acknowledged ... be] inserted

146. you] Chapeau omits

147. forced] Chapeau: forces

148. Chapeau adds: in

149. on] inserted

150. live] overscored

151. objection] Chapeau: objections

152. objection] Chapeau: objections

153. at least its *active*] overscored

154. wished] Chapeau: wish

155. Such ... World] inserted

156. (? what does this mean?)] inserted

157. MS: contrario

158. for the ... her] inserted

159. But] overscored

160. uniform

161. ever] overscored

162. open] overscored

163. in asking permission From all that I] overscored

164. another] overscored

165. other] overscored

166. be do so] overscored

167. that] overscored

168. have been] overscored

169. but] overscored
170. such a] overscored
171. interpretations apprehensions of them would not be more excluded] overscored
172. very] overscored
173. imply] overscored
174. ever] overscored
175. of] overscored
176. for myself] overscored
177. exp] overscored
178. me] overscored
179. the Clergy] overscored
180. In reply I cd say express but a very small part of the feelings I have] overscored
181. un unvarying] overscored
182. in integrity] overscored
183. affect me] overscored
184. of earthly blessings] overscored
185. before God] overscored
186. And that I may not make this letter bring this letter to an end, I would only beg that your Lordship will receive the impression not understand that in the Charge of yesterday there was anything that I could not with limitations of general terms accept. I say repeat this that I may not do myself the wrong of allowing your Lordship to suppose that the letter is] overscored
187. only add [illegible word] a forward] overscored
188. nor] overscored
189. make] overscored
190. me] overscored
191. tomorrow] overscored
192. to be requisite Might it not [*twenty inserted and overscored illegible words*] were to give up the pleasure of attending your Lordship there tomorrow] overscored
193. communicate this] overscored
194. That our father in Heaven may ever bless, strengthen and help you in the daily prayers of your Lordship.] overscored
195. ask] overscored
196. There was indeed] overscored
197. the] overscored
198. yr Lordship] overscored
199. prominent] overscored
200. 3.] corrected from MS: 2.
201. express] inserted, replacing overscored: formal
202. as I am capable of] inserted
203. safety of the] inserted

204. which is irresolution] inserted
205. some of] inserted
206. did] overscored
207. the] overscored
208. Vol.] inserted
209. did] overscored
210. you have] inserted
211. by you] overscored
212. it seems to me] inserted
213. than this] inserted
214. seems enough] overscored
215. and for the others] overscored
216. contrast . . . Trent] inserted
217. seem plain. sufficiently enough] overscored
218. the As to the continuance of the] overscored
219. continued] inserted
220. in the Communion . . . sacraments] inserted in copy
221. no question] overscored
222. that] overscored
223. me] inserted
224. more than communion] inserted to replace overscored 'more'
225. is not . . . sign] inserted, replacing overscored: seems no proof of him
226. the point . . . view] inserted replacing overscored: any thing
227. There is not . . . 1571] section indicated by Manning to be placed here from original position below following: prayer & divine service Strype H. Ref. 1. c. 57
228. & not . . . condition] inserted replacing overscored: credulity
229. in wh[ich] she] inserted
230. 's' replaces overscored: ing
231. in] inserted replacing overscored: with
232. may . . . as] inserted replacing overscored: is
233. be a example of] inserted, replacing overscored: illustrate
234. this] inserted replacing overscored: what I say
235. said] inserted
236. the King's . . . book] inserted
237. & act] overscored
238. It supreme] overscored
239. the] inserted, replacing overscored: were
240. under Elizabeth] inserted
241. assented to or] inserted
242. in] inserted, replacing overscored: to
243. this] inserted
244. belief] revised from: believe. this] overscored

245. The Oath] inserted, replacing overscored: What
246. made up] inserted
247. men ... the] inserted, replacing overscored: reformers or
248. correctly] inserted
249. History of the Ch[urch]] inserted, replacing overscored: And then
250. for that] inserted, replacing overscored: which
251. required] inserted, replacing overscored: conform
252. stature] inserted, replacing overscored: act
253. the Church] overscored
254. northern] inserted
255. the Excommunication ... like] inserted in copy
256. where] inserted, replacing overscored: when
257. because] inserted, replacing overscored: for
258. subscription] inserted; they] inserted
259. The Civil power used its own weapons.] inserted
260. other tests] inserted
261. The Recusant members] inserted
262. had been deprived ... the] inserted, replacing overscored: was confessed ostensibly compliant because all had taken the Oath of Supremacy
263. It is ... Pamphlet] inserted, replacing overscored: You may
264. required] inserted, replacing overscored: intended
265. some] inserted, replacing overscored: those
266. fully ... reluctantly] inserted
267. the] inserted
268. p. 30] inserted
269. It may be that possibly he did. But Strype does not say so. He names him in a separate paragraph not only that he was as having been a [illegible word] of that time] overscored
270. And] overscored
271. you quote Strype] inserted
272. example] inserted, replacing overscored: act
273. maintained] inserted, replacing overscored: opened
274. very] overscored
275. churches] inserted, replacing overscored: parties
276. Those] overscored
277. have] inserted, replacing overscored: am
278. undertaken] corrected from: undertaking
279. have] inserted, replacing overscored: am
280. spoken] corrected from: speaking
281. system] inserted, replacing overscored: view
282. only] overscored
283. that] overscored
284. truly oblige me by] inserted

285. what &] inserted
286. argument for] inserted, replacing overscored: scheme of
287. those who ... divided] inserted
288. language of the] inserted
289. on our side] inserted; four illegible words overscored
290. sh[oul]d prove to be] inserted, replacing overscored: seem
291. desire not to] overscored
292. No] inserted, replacing overscored: the
293. theological] inserted
294. proved] overscored
295. recognized] inserted, replacing overscored: acknowledged
296. King] overscored
297. fuller] inserted, replacing overscored: further
298. to me] inserted
299. among ourselves] inserted
300. In the mean time] overscored
301. entertained by bodies] inserted and corrected in pencil
302. as it is related to the State] inserted
303. of life by rule under] inserted replacing overscored illegible word
304. in her on the one hand] inserted
305. on the other] inserted
306. as to substance] inserted
307. ultimately] overscored

SECTION VI

Readjustments and Revisions

1. After Newman's Conversion:
October–November 1845

451020gm[a]

Baden-Baden Oct[ober] 20, 1845.

My dear Manning

A few words in this day of trouble must pass from me to you; for your own sake I wish you had been with me here at the time of Newman's secession.[b] To see the R[oman] Church on the defensive against Ronge, rationalism, and thought tending towards rationalism within its own pale, is in the nature of a correction to that half-heartedness and despondency which is almost forced upon us at home by the contemplation of our own difficulties.

The state of things in this country is sad. At Munich I have seen a good deal of Dr. Döllinger that is a good deal relatively to the time I spent there, something under a week. He does not make much of Ronge's movement: but looks very grave upon the tendencies of thought in general. He is a

---

[a] 'Wrote to...Manning' (*GD* iii. 490).

[b] On 8 October 1845 Newman informed Manning of his intention to enter into the 'One True Fold' when Father Dominic arrived (*LD* lxi. 8). Manning replied on 14 October (Birmingham Oratory MS Newman–Manning; Purcell, i. 309–10). To Purcell's comment that 'On Newman's conversion not only the leadership, but to a large extent the propelling force of the Tractarian movement passed away from Oxford' Gladstone comments 'yes' (PurGl i. 319).

Wilfred Meynell reports a confused and in all likelihood apocryphal story that he heard of the event in the 1880s: 'Mr. Gladstone, full of distress and doubt, went down to Lavington to ask Manning whether all these secessions, culminating in Newman's, were separate testimonies to Rome, or had the seceders any one "note" by which they could be explained in a group. The Archdeacon, who was always ready with an answer, and generally to excellent purpose, made reply: "Yes, there is one note of all these men—want of truth"' (Meynell, 'Reminiscences of Cardinal Manning', *Contemporary Review* 61 (1892), 182, and Arthur Wollston Hutton, *Cardinal Manning* [London: Methuen, 1892], 252; cf. comments on 'want of truth' in 451121gm and 941017gr). When Meynell questioned both men concerning the story in 1888, neither could recall the incident, although Gladstone, some time later, reported it and cited Meynell as his source. See Wilfred Meynell, 'Mr. Gladstone and the Roman Church', *Nineteenth Century* 44 (July 1898), 21–2.

great lover of England, a mild judge of our religion, & a delightful man. Almost all I see drives my sympathies into the Roman Camp—that is *quoad* German matters.[c] Elsewhere there are pious individuals, and even parties and schools of a certain amount of orthodoxy, but it is there alone I think that we can anticipate with confidence the essential & permanent maintenance of *the Truth*—and as to additions and abuses, they do not occupy the same position here as in some other places, e.g. I have before me the 18th edition of a popular prayer book in which it says that there are still many abuses in the invocation of Saints, that the honour paid to them is of the same kind as that paid to holy men—the B[lessed] V[irgin] is included—that invocation is permitted; not commanded—that they are simply men & can *give* us nothing—that we are not bound to believe any reputed saint to be such—(here in a note the book denies the infallibility of the Pope in matters of faith) & so on— Now I do not mean that there is any one thing wonderful—but conceive such a book distributed in Italy for popular use— The author is an official person, & the work has the approbation of the 'episcopal Vicariate at Bruchsal.'[d]

But now to England. Is there to be any firm and intelligible declaration from Pusey? I read the *first* Wingfield letter of his[e] before leaving England—from a subsequent one I have seen an extract on the subject of the peculiar Roman doctrines[f]—which was *not*, I think, of a kind to

[c] Gladstone arrived in Munich early on 30 September 1845 and met with Döllinger on that day, 1, 4, and 5 October (*GD* iii. 85–487). Cf. Manning's letter to Edward Coleridge (1800–83; Assistant Master of Eton [Boase, iv. 712]), 28 October, in which he writes: 'A letter from Gladstone, dated Baden Baden tells me what I partly knew before, that Döllinger, one of the most eminent German Catholics, looks with far deeper anxiety on the tendencies in the mind in the German Church than on the confusion of... Ronge' (West Sussex Record Office MS Par. 122/7/3).

[d] On 19 October 1845 Gladstone was reading Philip Joseph von Brunner, *Gebetbuch für aufgeklärte katholische Christen* (18th rev. edn.; Heilbronn: Classische Buchhandlung, 1845). For further details on Gladstone's reading at this time see Erb (1997), 451.

[e] On 18 September 1845, the *English Churchman* carried a report on (595) and a letter from (597) William F. Wingfield, who as a result of the decision in the Stone Altars Case (see 450219mg) announced that he had withdrawn from the Church of England. Pusey replied in the same journal, 25 September (611) and Wingfield wrote again on 16 October (663). Pusey held that a Eucharistic Sacrifice could still be offered by the priest despite the judgment, whereas Wingfield linked the two issues and interpreted the decision as a rejection of High Church Eucharistic theology.

[f] Reference perhaps to the discussion regarding the rebaptism of recent converts by Roman Catholics whose adherents on the Continent in particular questioned Anglican baptismal practices (*English Churchman* [16 Oct. 1845], 664).

do good at a time when men want to be rallied. I at one time thought of inclosing to you for your use or not, according to your judgment, a letter to him expressing a very strong hope that it was his intention, upon the occasion of Newman's secession, to make some declaration of such a kind as will settle and compose men's minds, or at least tend that way, with a view to the future.[g] No such effect as this is produced by shewing that after infinite question one can just make out a case for remaining in the Church of England. Surely we must not always and only dwell upon negatives, but a little revive in people's minds the idea of the Apostolical authority that is over us, & the obligations it entails. I wish Pusey were to spend some time here—I think he would be the better in his public tone for it. I do not want any worldly wisdom distinct from the wisdom of the Gospel, but I do desire and pray that the trumpet shall not give an uncertain sound, inasmuch as men are certainly called upon to prepare themselves for the battle. It is possible that you may be at work on this subject with him. If you are, pray say as much of this to him in my name as you like, or as little, or none at all.

It may appear strange, but I have almost a feeling of disappointment at not seeing more secessions with Newman, because it looks as if they were *to follow.* Now, as we are undergoing an amputation, we must desire it should be done at once; the feverish excitement attending the prolongation of the process is far worse, because it has the effect of destroying confidence within the Church, and of disqualifying so many for the active and resolute performance of duty. However, I suppose and hope that Newman's book will bring all this to a head, and that persons are waiting for that in order to declare themselves. It is sad and bitter, but a sweep now, and after that some repose, is, in the choice of evils, that which we should seek from the mercy of God.

Then the conviction always returns upon me that, as the Church of England, being a reality, is not dependent upon this or that individual, the immediate duty is, when one secedes, simply to think of the supplying his place, as a rear rank man steps forward when his front rank man falls in battle. And what does England and its Church want? Certainly nothing of

---

[g] The 16 October 1845 issue of the *English Churchman* announced Newman's secession and printed a letter from Pusey for Anglican readers in the face of it (660; see also Liddon, ii. 460–3). So popular was the letter that it was reprinted in the *English Churchman* on 20 October (692). The letter in which Gladstone suggested to Pusey that he have something prepared to explain Newman's secession is not located. See Liddon, ii. 459–65.

all that the ordinary powers and appliances of human nature can supply: nothing but the development of spiritual gifts, and of the Divine life within us. Have we men ready to devote themselves in mind and body and in all they have to the work of God? If not, it is all over with us—but if so, then every question that remains is subsidiary, and every difficulty surmountable.

I wished to have written to you upon some other points, but my thoughts are too crude. Only I have a strong impression that Puseyism (the name must be used after that so much idiosyncrasy, so many elements which are not simply and truly those of the Church, have been mixed in it) has not up to this time been able to accomplish more than a very small fraction indeed of its work as an evangelising power. Where is the secret of the power of preaching? Who has got that? Why have we, in the matter of the rubrics, been putting the cart before the horse? Who can *restore* spiritual life by ceremonial? I have seen churches where the clergyman has not the smallest idea of reverence in himself and his own manner, though every accessory is provided with accuracy and with liberal love. Now, if I must choose *between* the two, give me a reverent clergyman, whose voice, countenance, manner, movement, tell me incessantly of the presence of God, and I will give you all the rest. In every (material) church we have this one central element in our power: no churchwardens can make that into a complaint, it may be had without bowing or crossing, though it might be better with them. How little of it do we really possess! The truth is, English hardness is yet upon us, we have not enough yet been bruised and chastened. When by holiness we have learned the fulness of love, shall not the glory of God appear?

Forgive my writing in haste—*you* will understand me. I am here with my sister—my stay is too uncertain to let me ask you to write. I *hope* to be at Hagley in the end of next week.[h]

Your aff[ectiona]te friend
W. E. Gladstone

Archd[eaco]n Manning.

[[BL Add. MS 44247, 273–4; Morley transcript; Lathbury, i. 348–50; Purcell, i. 312–13[i]]]

---

[h] Gladstone returned to London from the Continent only on 18 November 1845 and was at Hagley the following day (*GD* iii. 497).

[i] Purcell's introduction to this letter states that Gladstone 'was on more intimate terms with Newman than Manning', a passage that Gladstone annotates in his copy of Purcell with 'no' (PurGl, ibid.).

451029mg

Lavington. Oct[ober] 29. 1845.

My dear Gladstone,

Your letter was a real comfort to me: for since Newman left us I have had little or no communication with anyone able to say what I seem to desire. I knew you were abroad: but I did not know where, and did not feel able to write a letter in uncertainty where to send it.

I am not surprized at the smallness of the number who have followed him: for I always thought that it w[oul]d be smaller than we were prepared for. My chief fear is for the unsettlement which will for a long time spread itself in our best minds.

But before going on it w[oul]d be unnatural not to say something of dear Newman. What do I not owe him? No living man has so powerfully affected me: and there is no mind I have so reverenced. It was so unlike those round him—so discerning, masculine, real, and self-controlled, such a perfect absence of formation, and artificial habits. His whole course is fearful to me—& though I seem to feel a clear and undoubting conviction that he has by some mysterious inclination swerved from truth in the points which divide us—his course has about it a strange fascination. All I can do is still to love, & pray for him which I do very earnestly.

I cannot but feel that it is a fact which must have its consequences ethical, & intellectual in our relation to Rome: and decidedly for good.

They must learn to understand, & appreciate us more truly: & I trust to love us more which they have done but little as yet.

And now for our own Church and work. I do not scruple to say to you, that I am less & less able to enter into Puseys mode of speaking & judging. If his course is practically wise, I am altogether unfit to judge of it. To me it seems far other than I should think wise or safe at this or any time. It is a painful, and almost a hateful task to say anything of one who is so tender, loving, & devoted: but I have seemed to see from the beginning a tendency to excess in statement, and in act, which alarms me for the steadfastness of his own mind, & of those drawn within his range. I cannot but feel this about his truly valuable tract on Baptism:[a] & the more I have lately read of Roman Theology, the more I feel it of his sermon on the Eucharistical

---

[a] See E. B. Pusey, *Tracts for the Times. Tract 67 [24 August 1835], Tract 68 [29 September 1835], Tract 69 [18 October 1835]: Scriptural Views of Holy Baptism.* Cf. John Henry Newman, *Tracts for the Times. Tract 82 [1 November, 1837]. 'Letter to a Magazine on the Subject of Dr. Pusey's tract on Baptism'.*

Sacrifice.[b] I believe Bossuet would have thought it inaccurate, & over-wrought. I can hardly venture to say with what anxiety I look to his future course. He seems to me to want *foresight* both in practice & reasoning, & I feel that he is entangling himself, & others in positions out of which there is no natural pass but in a fearful direction. He does not mean this or know it: but his whole negative tone is a proof of great, and even conscious embarrassment. The undeserved affection he has always shewn me, which I sincerely reciprocate, makes all this a subject of heavy thoughts day by day.

The account you send of the German Prayer Book is very hopeful. It is just what is contained in Veron's Rule of Faith:[c] after reading which one says, 'then what is all this contention about?' These distinct advances prove many things, as that the Council of Trent was a real Reformation: & is doing its work still: & that the best fruit of the Protestant reformation will be seen in the Catholic Church. It also strongly justifies our position, & Divines: & gives great hope for the future.

Certainly no lover of the Faith will desire to see the *affirmative* powers of the Roman Church weakened anywhere. I often think that all will be at last reduced to the simple opposition of the negative, & affirmative principles, & that we & Rome shall be thereby united.

It is a grave question for a far-sighted English Statesman whether the stability & perpetuity of our Empire will not ultimately depend on the affirmative & constructive powers of the English & Roman Churches. This view seems to suggest an idea against which I could fore-shorten Maynooth, & an alarming policy for Ireland.

But I am getting out of my whereabouts into yours.

Farewell: I hope this will greet you in safety with my welcome.

Ever your affect[ionat]e friend

H. E. Manning

The Right Hon[oura]ble W. E. Gladstone

[[Pitts; Chapeau, 122, 183–5]]

---

[b] E. B. Pusey, *The Holy Eucharist, a Comfort to the Penitent. A Sermon Preached before the University, in the Cathedral Church of Christ, Oxford, on the Fourth Sunday after Easter* (Oxford: John Henry Parker, 1843).

[c] Francis Véron, *The Rule of Catholic Faith; or, the Principles and Doctrines of the Catholic Church, Discriminated from the Opinion of the Schools, and from Popular Errors and Mis-statements*, trans. J. Waterworth (Birmingham: R. P. Stone, 1833).

451030mg

Lavington. Oct[ober] 30. 1845.

My dear Gladstone,

I have been turning over in my mind the subject at the end of the letter I wrote you last night, and should like to put it down, & have your judgment about it.

It seems to me that the perpetuity of a State depends upon its moral unity, which may be either perfect, or predominant i.e. in the ruling majority. That where as with us it is only a predominant unity, there must exist one or more antagonist, disuniting forces at work. This seems to me to describe our old Ecclesiastical Status, and the Dissenters Roman & Protestant.

Now I leave all political, & economical causes out of view for a while. These set aside, it seems to me that the moral unity of a people will always be the result of some Agent which affirms positive truths & moral laws, and associates men on some principle of organization. This is of course the Church. No dissenting body fulfils this definition, because it bases its teaching on indiv[idua]l judgment, & its organization on the individual will. It is therefore the moral opposite of the constructive & perpetuating principle, & is destructive or exhaustive.

Now it seems to me that there are two bodies at home, & in our Colonies the continual agency of which is to associate and hold people in unity & to perpetuate that unity by succession: of course I mean the Churches of England & Rome.

I see no basis of construction or perpetuity but one or both of these. I say both, first because I think they might be & ought to be conservative of each other, & next because think what we may, we have both to deal with, e.g. in Ireland.

It appears to me an axiom of political science, that the constructive forces of a people (truth & righteousness permitting) ought to be strengthened & developed.

I see no hope of political perpetuity for us if the exhaustive processes are stimulated.

Now after this prose come to Ireland.

It seems to me, but I say it as yet only, as Eneas Sylvius did hypothetiκῶς,[a] that political equity and [Chris]t[ia]n moderation recommend the attempt to organize Ireland as a R[oman] C[atholic] nation. We have tried to convert & to govern it: & have failed. It seems like fighting

---

[a] Last three letters only in Greek script: hypothetically.

against gravitation. What is left but to stimulate & develop its own organization upon its own constructive principles which are those of the R[oman] C[atholic] Church?

But, pari passu,[b] the Legislature must develop the organization of the English Church & the branch of it in Ireland.

And the latter in a truly Irish mode.

I am coming to look at it in this way.

A Church must be either a missionary or a ministering Church.

The Ch[urch] in Ireland is not a ministering Church (except partially) having no flock to minister to.

A missionary Church it can never be as an Establishment with Endowments. Conceive John Héké & his N[ew] Zealanders paying rent Charge.[c] The Irish Church I am told lacks the spiritual & ethical properties of a Missionary Church. Certainly it lacks the external conditions.

Now I do not like the idea of reductions & retrenchments.

But why not let the Irish Church withdraw itself into the original attitude of a Missionary Church? Why not:

1. Continue all revenues as needed for actual care of souls.

2. Preserve all Sees.

3. As the Clergy of Parishes having no care of souls, die off, absorb these benefices into the See.

4. Create a numerous body of Cathedral Clergy in every See.

5. Create Collegiate Churches in all Towns where there are Protestants.

6. Found in such[1] Cathedral Professorships: and require Candidates for Holy Orders to read & live there under training for __ years.

7. Found in the Cathedral Cities & large towns Prebendal schools for the Laity.

---

[b] With equal pace. Note Gladstone's later quip of 19 February 1890 on the plan for parallel Scottish and Irish Parliaments: 'There is no doctrine of greater danger than that of *pari passu* applied to the method of legislation in the House of Commons. The only practical way of illustrating it is that which was employed by Mr Bright when he said it was like driving six omnibuses abreast down Parklane' (Hansard, clxvii. 721).

[c] *The Times*, 30 October 1845, 3f, published a letter (8 May) from the Governor of New Zealand, reporting the defeat of the native insurgents against the government and the flight of the insurgent chief, John Héké and others. A fuller article on Héké appeared on 6 December 1845, 3e. For details see H. W. Tucker, *Memoir of the Life and Episcopate of George Augustus Selwyn, D.D.* (2 vols.; London: Wells Gardner, Darton, 1879), i. 169, and Hight (1933), 127–8.

8. Charge the Clergy of the Cathedral or Collegiate Churches with the duty of officiating in Parishes where there may be individuals, or families of the Irish Church still scattered.

In fact do in Ireland what the R[oman] C[atholic]s since the Reformation & now most systematically, & effectively have done in England. In this way I believe the Spiritual strength of the Irish Church w[oul]d be greatly increased; & its powers of organization & self-perpetuation wonderfully developed. I sh[oul]d expect also, that it would act upon the intellectual state of Ireland & thereby on the Roman Church, much as Protestantism has done in Germany.

In this way a beneficial application w[oul]d be found for the Eccl[esiastical] revenues without alienation to secular uses: and this w[oul]d be only just as a correlative to an act endowing the R[oman] C[atholic] clergy. Some wise measures to sustain & strengthen the spiritual action of the Church in Ireland are absolutely necessary to make it safe to confer on the R[oman] C[atholic] Church, the social position which it seems certain to obtain.

I leave England out altogether, as a subject too large to be taken except alone. The more I think of it, the more convinced I am that the Church as it now exists is inadequate to its work,[2] & that the attempt to repress it within the sphere & proportions of its present organization is fatal. The Roman Church c[oul]d desire no more ἥ κεν γηθήσαι πρίαμος.[d]

Now I will make an end. What I have said is, I have no doubt, very crude. But the subject is most difficult, & perilous.

Ever yours affect[ionatel]y
H. E. Manning

The Right Hon[oura]ble
W. E. Gladstone
P.S. In the last English Review you will see an Article to shew that the Irish Church is on the increase.[e] I am not able to judge of the facts.

Of course in all I have written, I suppose the Church to recast herself. I am not invoking the Civil Power. Such a course would give the death-blow to the Irish Church as a Spiritual, & Catholic body.

H.E.M.

[[Pitts; Chapeau, 123, 185–7]]

---

[d] Priam truly would rejoice. Homer, *Iliad*, 1. 255.
[e] 'The Church in Ireland', *English Review* 7 (Oct. 1845), 24–72, and cf. 'Sir Robert Peel's Government of Ireland' (ibid. 173–209).

451121gm[a]

Hagley Stourbridge
Nov[ember] 21. 1845.

My dear Manning

I received your letters here yesterday from my wife's hands. As to Ireland I should like to talk about that rather than write: I am too crude for the latter.

My chief object in writing is to suggest to you the possibility that you may have to entertain the idea of answering Newman's book.[b]

---

[a] 'Wrote to . . . H. E. Manning' (*GD* iii. 497).

[b] Newman, *Essay on the Development of Christian Doctrine* (London: James Toovey, 1845). Note Manning's later recollection of 16 June 1847 in a letter to his curate, Charles John Laprimaudaye: 'When Newman's book was published, Gladstone urged me to answer it. I declined pledging myself; but it forced me again into the two same subjects (Unity and Infallibility) to which I have continued to give all the thought and reading I can. And I am bound to say that I could not republish either of the two books as they stand. They are inaccurate in some *facts*, incomplete as compared with the truth of the case, and concede some of the main *points* I intended to deny' (Bodl. MS Eng. lett. c. 662, 106–7; Purcell, i. 318–19, 470). According to Purcell, i. 318, Gladstone later recalled: that 'it was quite true that, on the publication of Newman's *Essay on Development*, he had strongly pressed Manning to write a refutation of the book, and that he had undertaken to do so. Manning [. . .] was however not strong enough to grapple with Newman. Manning was an ecclesiastical statesman; very ascetic, but not a theologian, nor deeply read. [. . .] I may now tell you, what I had during the Cardinal's lifetime advisedly withheld. Newman's secession, followed by that of so many others, not at Oxford only, but all over the country, presented an intellectual difficulty which I was unable to solve. What was the common bond of union, the common principle, which led men of intellect so different, of such opposite characters, acting under circumstances and with surroundings so various, to come to one and the same conclusion? [. . .] I remember as if it were yesterday, the house, the room, Manning's attitude as, standing before me, I put to him that question. His answer was slow and deliberate: "Their common bond is their want of truth." I was surprised beyond measure and startled at Manning's judgment.' Cf. comments on 'want of truth' in 451020gm and 941017gr. Charles John Laprimaudaye (1807–58) was educated at St John's College, Oxford, served as a curate to his father in Leyton, Essex, and from 1847 served in the same capacity to Manning, to whom he was also confessor. He was received into the Roman Catholic Church in 1850, followed by his wife and nine children. On the death of his wife (Anne Francesca, b. 1812, sister of John Gellibrand Hubbard [1805–89], 1st Baron Addington) in 1854 he joined the Oblates of St Charles and travelled to Rome to study for the priesthood, where he died of smallpox. On Gladstone's own notion of development in his *Church Principles* (1842) and its relation to Newman's see Nicholls (1978). On Gladstone's later exploration of the matter see BL Add. MS 44736, 265–333.

Toovey[c] told me it would probably be out next Monday, and I have asked him to send me a copy of it as early as he can. After reading it I may have to write to you again on the subject. It will probably be a real and a subtle argument, backed by great knowledge and it must not if so be allowed to pass unnoticed nor should the task be left to those who will do mischief—

All I will now say is this: if upon reading it you entertain the notion that you can do it, do not lose a moment in making known your intention among friends and let it appear to the public as soon as you have made any progress that will warrant an advertisement.

You will think I travel rather fast: but this is all hypothetical.

Oakeley's is a sad production[d]—very unworthy of him, except in the spirit which seems to me gentle and good.

I grieve much over the loss of Faber[e]—He was evidently a man who understood working the popular *side* of this religious movement, which has for the most part been left to shift for itself.

I have no doubt that many persons are waiting for Newman's book & mean to say Aye or No after reading it. In haste, I am always

Aff[ectiona]tely yours
W.E.G.

Thank God all are well here.

[[BL Add. MS 44247, 275–6; Morley transcript; Purcell, i. 313–14; cf. Chapeau, 315]]

[c] James Toovey (1813–93), London publisher and bookseller, was received as a Roman Catholic, 1846 (Boase, iii. 988, and William James Gordon-Gorman, *Converts to Rome: A Biographical List of the More Notable Converts to the Catholic Church in the United Kingdom During the last Sixty Years* (London: Sands, 1910), 272).

[d] F. Oakeley, *A Letter on Submitting to the Catholic Church. Addressed to a Friend* (London: James Toovey, 1845). Gladstone read it on 18 November 1845 (*GD* iii. 497).

[e] Frederick William Faber (1814–63) was educated at Balliol College and University College, Oxford, elected a Fellow at University College, Oxford, 1837, appointed rector of Elton, 1842, and was received into the Catholic Church on 11 November 1845. He was ordained priest, 1847, and joined the Oratorians, 1849, serving as Father Superior, 1850 to his death. See *DNB* and John Edward Bowden, *The Life and Letters of Frederick William Faber* (London: Thomas Richardson & Son, 1869), 238, and Addington (1974), 130.

2. Secretary for the Colonies:
December 1845–February 1846

451223gm

13 Carlton H[ouse] Terrace
Dec[ember] 23. [18]45.

My dear Manning

The whirl of events which has been so rapid within the last few weeks has dragged me within its circle. I could have wished to tell it you sooner— today I became Secretary for the Colonies.[a]

I had been long on the point of writing to you—Newman's book interests me deeply, shakes me not at all.[b] I think he places Christianity on the edge of a precipice: from whence a bold & strong hand would throw it over.

Your mind I am sure has been at work upon it: but do not hurry to tell me the results—I trust to see them ripen.

It is vain for me in a few hurried moments to tell you either my reasons or my feelings in my recent act. Suffice it to say the latter are rather disponding, the former clear before me and imperative in their operation. I have endeavoured to judge upon the present crisis as it stood on Sunday evening when it was first presented to me. My instincts of ease, & study too

---

[a] Gladstone was approached two days earlier, on Sunday evening, 21 December 1845. He accepted the offer the following day (*GD* iii. 506; see Morley, i. 285). Manning had just turned down an invitation from the Archbishop of York to be his Subalmoner, since, as he told his mother on 9 December it would take him away from his parishioners at Lavington from Maundy Thursday to Easter Monday and 'This [the position of subalmoner] is not a higher, not an equal spiritual duty' (Bodl. MS Eng. lett. c. 652, 503–6). Likewise to Robert Wilberforce he wrote on 25 December: 'The reason I assigned is a true, real, and sufficient reason. I feel that I owe it to my flock and to my own soul to avoid absence and distraction at the season of Passion week & Easter.... The Lincoln's Inn affair convinced me that my duty is to have only one field and one work' (Bodl. MS Eng. lett. c. 655, 32). Cf. also his letter to Dodsworth (ibid. 658, 40–1) and his detailed personal analysis on making the decision from the time he received the invitation on 4 December and his continuing turmoil over his decision for the first two months of the following year as printed in Purcell, i. 277–83.

[b] On 28 November 1845 Gladstone 'Received & went to work on Newman's book: with some tho' not enough sense of the seriousness of the task; I pray God to guide my mind in it. His own appeal at the end did me this good.' He read the book over the next three days, finishing it on 1 December, when he began to reread Newman's *On the Prophetical Office of the Church, Viewed Relatively to Romanism and Popular Protestantism* (2nd edn.; London: J. G. & F. Rivington, 1838) (*GD* iii. 499) and continued to read and write on Newman's *Essay on Development* until 17 December (ibid. 499–503).

in my lazy droning fashion, recoiled. But I believe I have obeyed the call of what is for the present at least my profession, and if so it is the call of God, whose aid I trust has been given me.

I am fearfully weak for the office, fearfully unworthy. You know my need—I have no occasion then to *press* myself on your remembrance in your prayers.

Ever aff[ectiona]tely yours
W. E. Gladstone

Many thanks for your Sermons which I have just received—a blessed Christmas to you—you will not have this until that happy morning.
Venerable H. E. Manning

Thanks too for your note D[ec]. 24.[c]

[[BL Add. MS 44247, 277–8; Morley transcript; Purcell, i. 315]]

451226mg

Lavington. Feast of St. Stephan. 1845

My dear Gladstone,

Newmans Book is a subject I could not begin upon yesterday: and now all I can say must be παχυλῶς καὶ τύπω.[a]

I have read it once with an extraordinary interest, I remember no book that so held my attention fast from beginning to end. It seemed as if the doubts, difficulties, and problems of the last ten years were suddenly brought to a focus external to my own mind, with the strength & light of another mind to whose powers I felt as nothing. It seemed to swallow me up with all the thoughts of years.

But in the end I feel where I was. There are some things which go before all reasoning, & survive all objections: of the former kind as[3] I feel, is the invocation of God alone, & of the latter, the reality of the English Church.

The Book seems to me to be an admission that the Roman Pontificate, & the Invocation of the Blessed Virgin cannot be proved by the 'quod semper'.[b] The idea of development shews that a case must be made for after ages.

---

[c] Not located; the postscript is in the hand of Catherine Gladstone.

[a] Roughly and in outline. Cf. Aristotle, *Nicomachean Ethics*, 1094b20: '[We must be content in speaking of such subjects . . . to indicate the truth] roughly and in outline.'

[b] See Newman's definition: 'the *dictum* of Vincent of Lerins, that revealed and Apostolic doctrine is "quod semper, quod ubique, quod ab omnibus [what has been held always, everywhere, by all]," a principle infallibly separating, on the whole field of history, authoritative doctrine from opinion' (*An Essay on the Development of Doctrine* [London: Longman, Green & Co., 1888], 10). Cf. also Newman, *Essay on the Development of Christian Doctrine* (1845), 12.

On the whole, then, the great debate is where it was: with this gain. Even Newman has hardly[4] moved its limits in advance against us. The evident & vast difficulty with which he had to wrestle comes out in a multitude of ways.

Having said this I cannot but add that 'the blast of the terrible ones is as a storm against the wall'.[c] The Book is to me wonderful. In some things very unlike him. The English is latinized—& the style abrupt in parts,[5] & even odd & freakish, implying, I fancy, the perils of a solitary, & intense intellect. Some things made me uncomfortable, & reminded me of people who have been affected by strange causes. Other parts, for breadth, depth, splendour, fullness, & beauty are almost beyond compare. The awful passage on St. Mary pp. 405,6. 'Thus there was, &c.'[d] has no parallel that I know except the Paradiso C.XXXIII 'Vergine Madre figlia del tuo Figlio &c.'[e] The whole book exhibits an intellectual compass, & *movement*[6] belonging to an order of minds wh[ich] live in a region above the reach of all except a few. And I anticipate great but very various effects from it. I think it will provoke some to scepticism, & more to doubts about the Blessed Trinity: not a few will it send, year by year, to Rome. I am afraid it will open a running sore in our poor body.

One thing which makes it singularly formidable is the elevation of tone, and high, reverent, charitable, treatment of the Church of England, & the Theology 'dear to memory'.[f]

---

[c] Isa. 25: 4.

[d] 'Thus there was "a wonder in heaven:" [Rev. 12: 1] a throne was seen, far above all other created powers, mediatorial, intercessory; a title archetypal; a crown bright as the morning star; a glory issuing from the Eternal Throne; robes pure as the heavens; and a sceptre over all; and who was the predestined heir of that Majesty? Who was that Wisdom, and what was her name, "the Mother of fair love, and fear, and holy hope," "exalted like a palm-tree in Engaddi, and a rose-plant in Jericho," "created from the beginning before the world" in God's everlasting counsels, and "in Jerusalem was her power"? The vision is found in the Apocalypse, a Woman clothed with the sun, and the moon under her feet, and upon her head a crown of twelve stars. The votaries of Mary do not exceed the true faith, unless the blasphemers of her Son came up to it. The Church of Rome is not idolatrous, unless Arianism is orthodoxy' (Newman, *Essay on the Development of Christian Doctrine* [1845], 405–6).

[e] Virgin mother, daughter of your Son. Dante, *Paradisio*, 33. 1.

[f] See Newman, *Development of Christian Doctrine* (1845), 127, on the earlier divines 'dear to memory'.

Having said this much you will see that we come out nearly at the same conclusion.

As you referred in your last letter but one to myself, I will say that on the best consideration I can give, it seems that I ought to take this question, & not leave it till I can shut it up for life. You know what I mean, for we have often talked about re-opening first principles; & the necessity of decisions open to no re-view.

With this feeling I have been for some time working in the direction of Newmans book, but I should deserve to make a fool of myself if I were to put together certain obvious things without a real examination of details. The man & the Book, & the subject, and the probation of our own conscience all make it a duty to go through with it to the best of the power with which we are entrusted.

I cannot but feel that the Roman controversy in Newmans hands demands a treatment different from the treatment we should give it in Wisemans. Our old controversialists will not serve. Like old muskets they kick dangerously. Newmans book seems to me to demand of us a higher Theology, as the public events of the last 15 years demand a new Church organization. It is with this view that I feel I cannot do things for the nonce, or patch an inconsistent theory. By all this I do not mean that I venture to hope to do more than find ultimate positions in which I can stand & work for life, in my poor way. For anything more I daily feel a painful sense of insufficiency.[g]

And now to make an end, though I have much to say, I will only add one sad word more. A letter this morning tells me privately that Isaac Williams life is as good as given over. He is a blessed man, humble, holy, & devout— Sit anima mea &c.[h] With kind regards,

Yours ever affect[ionate]ly
H. E. Manning

[[Pitts; Chapeau, 124, 188–9]]

---

[g] Newman's book was still firmly in Manning's mind at the end of the month. On 30 December 1845 he wrote to Robert Wilberforce on the subject. See Addendum to this Section.

[h] Might it be so with my soul. On Williams's illness at the time and his eventual recovery see *LD* xii. 57, 66, 68–70, 74, and 150. See also Jones (1971), 71.

451228gm[a]

Private

Hawarden Sunday
Dec[embe]r 28. 1845.

My dear Manning

I have got your note about Newman's book, on which I shall be very
brief. First I am more sanguine than you about the ultimate issue: I am
persuaded that Bishop Butler if he were alive would in his quiet way tear[7]
the whole *argument* into shreds wonderful as is the *book*,[8] so that one should
wonder where it had been. Secondly I am heartily glad you are at work
upon it, & I augur that you will find your confidence grow as you proceed.
May God be with you in the task. I have myself put down certain notes
upon it: if I can connect them sufficiently, on some Sunday or Sundays, to
give a *hope* of their being of any use to you, they shall be sent you. Lastly
I agree about the passage which you call awful respecting the Blessed
Virgin: to me it realises both senses of that word, it is both sublime and
frightful. Perhaps however I am applying this latter epithet to something
beyond the limits of what you quote—to the general doctrine & the
expressions contained in two or three pages.[b]

But I write requesting your Sermons, & in their bearing on myself.
I have read this morning with delight & I hope not without profit those
numbered xvi–xviii:[c] certainly with great sympathy & concurrence as to all

---

[a] 'Wrote to H. E. Manning...Read Manning's Serm[ons]' (*GD* iii. 508).

[b] Cf. Gladstone's comments to Robert Wilberforce two days later, on 30 December 1845:
I hope that Newman's book will be carefully and resolutely answered. How well he could
do it himself in another state of mind. It is a wonderful work, but most wonderful because it
is so grand a structure erected out of materials in many places so flimsy. Anxious,
ill-considered, and founded on grounds that cannot bear the closest scrutiny, on much
worse than none at all.

His work of dealing with the Eastern Church is really more or less than shutting his eyes
to it. I am persuaded he had it in his mind when he wrote a passage where he says that
under certain circumstances men ought to refuse even to look at adverse facts. (Bodl. MS
Wilberforce c. 67, 12–13)

[c] See note a above; Manning, *Sermons. Volume the Second* (London: James Burns, 1845*a*),
305–60; Sermon XVI, 'Devotion Possible in the Busiest Life'; Sermon XVII, 'Prayer a
Mark of True Holiness'; Sermon XVIII, 'Short Devotions a Hindrance to Prayer'. On
Gladstone's sensitivity to Manning's sermons, note that he may have considered Manning
in part as a spiritual director. See *Memoirs* of Sir Almeric Fitzroy (2 vols.; London:
Hutchinson, n.d.), ii. 587: '[18 February 1914] He [Morley] was much interested to hear
that Shane Leslie was writing a Life of Manning as a counterblast to Purcell, and had in his

principles & general positions, except that I do not *know* your justification for the passage in p. 347 beginning 'it were rather true to say'[9] I write however rather for confession than for criticism.[d]

You teach that daily prayers, the observance of fast & festival, & considerable application of time to private devotion & to Scripture ought not to be omitted e.g. by me: because great as is the difficulty the need is enhanced in the same proportion, the balance is the same.[e]

You think, very charitably, that ordinary persons, of such who have a right general intention in respect to religion give an hour & a half (pp 352,3) to its direct duties: & if they add attendance at both daily services, raising it to three, you consider that still a scanty allowance (355) while some 16 or 17 are given to sleep food and recreation.[f]

Now I cannot deny this position with respect to the increase of the need: that you cannot overstate: but I think there are two ways in which God is wont to provide a remedy for real & lawful need, one by augmenting supply, the other by intercepting the natural & ordinary[10] consequences of the deficiency.

I am desirous really to look the question full in the face: & then I come to the conclusion that if[11] I were to include the daily service now in my list of daily duties, my next step ought to be resignation.

Let me describe to you what has been at former times, when *in London and in Office*, the very narrow measure of my stated religious observances: on weekdays I cannot estimate the one family prayer together with morning & evening prayer at more than three quarters of an hour, even if so much. Sunday is reserved with rare exceptions for religious employments: and it was my practice in general to receive the holy communion weekly.

hands Manning's note-book on cases of conscience submitted to his judgment while still in the Anglican Church, in which communications from Mr. Gladstone, who seems to have treated him as his director, were frequent.'

[d] The passage to which Gladstone refers reads: 'It were rather true to say, that no man's life was ever yet so broken in upon, and taken from him by labour, and care, and the importunity of others, as His; and yet He is to us a perfect example of devotion' (ibid. 347; Sermon XVIII, 'Short Devotions a Hindrance to Prayer').

[e] Ibid. 348–50; cf. 'They who live in the world are so far from being released from stricter habits of private devotion, that they, above all, need them most. The busier their daily thoughts, the greater need of recollection at night. The more closely the world presses upon them all day long, the more need is there for them to break loose from it, and to give themselves up again to God, when the day is done' (348).

[f] Gladstone here bases his calculations on Manning's in ibid. 352–5, but note Manning's summation: 'Not so much as three hours for God, and one-and-twenty for ourselves' (355).

Of daily services except a little before & after Easter, not one in a fortnight, perhaps one in a month. Different individuals have different degrees of facility in supplying the lack of regular devotion by that which is occasional: but it is hard for one to measure this resolve in his own case.

I cannot well estimate, on the other hand, the amount of relaxation which used then to accrue to me. Last year I endeavoured in town[12] to apply a rule to the distribution of my hours & took ten for sleep food and recreation, understanding this last word so as to include *whatever* really refreshes mind or body[13] or has a fair chance of doing so. Now my exigencies for sleep are great: as long as I rise feeling like a stone, I do not think there is too much, and this is the general description of my waking sense in office & during the Session: but I consider 7½ hours the least I ought then to have and I should be better with eight. I know the old stories about retrenching sleep & how people have deceived themselves: with me it may be so, but I think it is not. I have never summed up my figures but my impression is that last year upon the average I was under & not over the ten for the particulars named,[14] I should say between 9 & 10. But last year was a holiday year as to pressure upon mind & body, in comparison with those that preceded it. Further, people are very different as to the rate at which they expend their vigour during their work—my habit, perhaps my misfortune, is, & peculiarly with work that I dislike, to labour at the very top of my strength, so that after five or six hours of my office I was frequently in a state of great exhaustion. How can you apply the duty of saving time for prayer out of sleep and recreation to a man in these circumstances?

Again take fasting. I had begun to form to myself some ideas upon this head: but I felt, though without a positive decision to that effect, that I could not & must not apply them if I should come again into political activity.[g]10 I speak now of fasting in quantity, fasting in nutrition: as to fasting in quality, I see that the argument is even strengthened, subject only to the exception that in times of mental anxiety it becomes impossible to receive much healthy food with[15] which a sound appetite would have no difficulty. The fact is undoubted: it is extremely hard to keep the bodily frame *up* to its work under the twofold condition of activity in Office & in Parliament—I take it then that to fast in the usual sense would generally be a sin & not a duty—I make a little exception for the time immediately preceding Easter, as then there is a short remission of Parliamentary duties.

---

[g] On Manning's influence on Gladstone regarding fasting, see the notes in Gladstone's later memoranda 'H.E.M.' as indicated by Bebbington (2004), 101.

I need not perhaps say more now. You see my argument with you, and that I differ, it may be, when the pinch comes upon myself. But I speak freely, in order to give scope for opposite reasoning—in order that I may be convicted if possible, as then I hope also to be convinced.

There is the greatest difference, as I find, between simple occupation however intense, and occupation with anxiety as its perpetual accompaniment. Serious reading & hard writing even for the same number of hours that my now imminent duties may absorb, I for one can bear without feeling that I am living too fast; but when that one element of habitual anxiety is added, nature is spurred on beyond her own pace under an excessive burden, & vital forces waste rapidly away. I should be more suspicious of myself than I now am in the argument I have made, were it not that I have had experience of occupation in both forms and know the gulf between them.

I ought to have added the other *sting* of official situations combined with[16] Parliament. It is the sad irregularity of one's life. The only fixed points are prayers & breakfast in the morning: & Sunday at the beginning of the week. It is Sunday I am convinced that has kept me alive and well, even to a marvel, in times of considerable labour, for I must not conceal from you even though you may think it a sad *bathos*, that I have never at any time been prevented by illness from attending either Parliament or my office—the only experience I have had of the dangers from which I argue, in results, has been in weakness and exhaustion from the brain downwards—it is impossible for me to be thankful enough for the exemptions I enjoy, especially when I see far stronger constitutions, constitutions truly Herculean, breaking down around me. I hope I may be preserved from the guilt and ingratitude of indulging sensual sloth under the mask of wise & necessary precautions.

Do not trouble yourself to write at length—but revolve these matters in the casuistical chamber of the mind—& either before or when we meet give me an opinion which I trust will be frank & fearless.

There is one retrenchment I could make: it would be to take from activity outwards in matter of religion, in order to give to prayer. But I have given a misdescription. What I could economise is chiefly reading: but reading nowadays I almost always shall have to resort to, at least so it was before, by way of repose. Devotion is by far the best sedative to excitement: but then it requires great & sustained exertion (to speak humanly & under the supposition of the Divine grace) or else powerful external helps, or both. Those mere dregs of the natural energies which too often are all that occupation leaves, are fit for little beyond *passivity*: only for reading when not severe.

Reading all this you may the more easily understand my tone sometimes about public life as a whole.—

Joy to you at this blessed time & at all times.

Your aff[ectiona]te friend

W. E. Gladstone

Ven[erable]

H. E. Manning

[[BL Add. MS 44247, 279–84; Morley transcript; Lathbury, ii. 266–70; Purcell, i. 315, 436–8; cf. Chapeau, 315–16]]

460103mg

Lavington. Jan[uar]y 3. 1846.

My dear Gladstone,

I will endeavour to answer your bidding to the best of my power: but the great peculiarity of your case makes it difficult.

You will observe that in what I have said I have laid on no injunctions. All I attempted was to exhibit certain great spiritual facts and tendencies: and thereby to get a theory in which particular cases may be located by special treatment: as you will see in pp 73. 74. 'Lastly, &c.'[a]

Your case stands almost alone. Other men labour as much, but only a few have also public responsibility such as yours, which is more consuming than labour.

You tell me to speak what I feel, and I will, therefore, say that what I should fear in such a case as yours would be two things 1. failure of health. 2. intellectual activity of an amount, & continuity adverse to the devotional affections, which are extensively passive.

Now this is no reason for resignation or retirement from a labour to which God has manifestly called you. But it needs a special treatment: & yet not so much in the amount of time given to religious exercises as in the kind & conduct of them.

As to time—from what I know of you & from what you say I would not suggest much change. I should be afraid of rules which might become burdensome, or being broken, give rise to scruples, or to relaxation of self discipline.

---

[a] Manning, *Sermons* (1845*a*), Sermon IV, 'Fasting a Means to Christian Perfection' (56–75): 'Lastly, as to the particular rules by which this duty is to be limited and directed, I cannot attempt to say any thing; partly because it is hardly possible to be particular without provoking objections to the principle from those to whom the instances will not apply' (73–4).

The Order of Jesuits seem to give an admonition to men who labour in the world. They are neither bound to austerities, nor to the service of the Choir. And this is much the course I should think marked out for you. First I believe you need all the sleep you take. And with your habits a full suspension of cerebral action is necessary.

Next you remember your wife & I enjoined you to take more exercise.

Nevertheless it w[oul]d be well to take an unbroken half hour in private in the morning: and a quarter of an hour at night.

Daily service seems to me next to impossible. If our Churches were more in number, always open, & the services more continuous it would be an easier and a very blessed practice to go even for a few minutes, on your way to or from your Office. But this unhappily is not ours. The distance of the Churches, & length of the Service makes it as good as impossible, and I should not scruple to say that you are not tied to 'the service of the Choir'.

You do already make your Family Prayers a stated and well-considered act and to this it w[oul]d be well to give even increased attention, as being the representative of the daily Offices of the Church.

Now this will not greatly increase the length of time you give already.

It appears to me that in your case it is not so much the length of time as the kind of religious exercises that you must chiefly look to.

You have two things, especially[17] to watch against and to counteract, one the tendency to forget yourself in external activity, and the other the hardening, and deadening effect of the intellect upon the soul, as for instance upon the sense of compunction, & perception of the tenderness of the love of God. Continued intellectual activity dries up the affections of the mind, & religion becomes a 'lumen siccum'[b] inhabiting the conscience, & the will, & but faintly moving the desires and sympathies of the spiritual nature. Of course the effect of this would spread over ones whole life; and give a tone to ones prayers, which a quarter of an hour more or less do little to correct.

What seems necessary, therefore, in such a life as yours is what old devotional writers call 'Recollection', & mental prayer. Perhaps the shortest way of expressing what I mean is to refer you to Rodriguez on Christian

[b] Dry light. See Francis Bacon, *The Advancement of Learning*, bk. II, sect. XII: 'So generally men taste well knowledges that are drenched in flesh and blood, civil history, morality, policy, about which men's affections, praises, fortunes do turn and are conversant; but this same lumen siccum doth parch and offend most men's watery and soft natures,' Francis Bacon (1561–1626), *The Works of Francis Bacon, Baron of Verulam, Viscount St. Albans* (10 vols.; London: W. Baynes & Son, 1824), i. 131.

Perfection. Vol. 1. Treatise 5. p 234 in my edition (Dublin).[c] There will be found in the course of the busiest day moments when a man may pause for never so short a time and recollect himself. It would be well to make some few & very light rules such as the saying of single sentences by way of suffrage. For this no time, place, or posture need be a hindrance. I believe by such an interior habit an[18] increased devotional intention in[19] morning & nightly prayers would soon be perceptible. Something of the kind is needed, for it is hardly possible that the mind which is for all its waking hours, with a very small reserve, always active, stimulated & discursive can at the bidding of our will suddenly subside into the stationary and suspended state implied by[20] acts of devotion.

Prayer is the concentrated expression of habitual aspirations.[21]

It is remarkable that we have come to limit the meaning of devotion to prayer, & prayer to supplication, or recital of petitions. Whereas devotion includes meditation in which the mind is active within the compass of it may be a single truth, & supplication which is meditation with desire and prayer in its largest sense of aspiration; in which last[22] the intellect has less share than the affections, and what share it has is rather by passive perception than discursive thoughts.

I need not suggest to you any particular means of recollection, because your own habits of self discipline will supply you. There are many light practices which have great power: and they are of a kind which would be easily interwoven even with your hours of official work.

I believe you are already in the habit of having some one devotional book for daily reading, & of dating it as you read on day by day.

I need not name the *receiving* of the Holy Communion *as often as possible.*[23]

The only other point you mention is, I think, Fasting. There can be no doubt that you are discharged from it as a literal precept. With the drain on your vital strength your fasting ought to be for recollection rather than self-discipline: & in quality rather than in quantity. Very slight things suffice in this matter, especially when a man's habit is temperate as yours is.

Thus far I have been speaking without reference to the[24] grace which God bestows signally upon all who spend themselves in works of their calling. He not only intercepts, & diverts the ill effects of labour to a great degree, but converts it into a direct means of subduing & strengthening the

[c] Alonso Rodriguez, *The Practice of Christian and Religious Perfection, Written in Spanish*... trans. Sir John Warner (3 vols.; Dublin: Richard Coyne, 1840–3). The page cited by Manning opens Rodriguez's fifth treatise, an extensive study on the practice of prayer.

conscience & will. In fact work is a kind of prayer. It is a worship of obedience and is greatly blessed.

I feel that I have written very vaguely: but I could hardly do otherwise without going into details beyond what your letter would justify or, I believe, your case require.

There is no need that I should assure you that these suggestions are not all I offer for you. I should be very ungrateful if in the peace I enjoy from the turmoil of the world I were not to pray, as well as I can, for those who are in the midst of its noise & conflict.

That you may be kept in it & from it is my daily desire.

Believe me,
My dear Gladstone,
Your affect[ionat]e friend,
H. E. Manning

The Right Hon[oura]ble
W. E. Gladstone
P.S. I expect to be in London on Thursday,[d] & if you are in C[arlton] H[ouse] T[errace] I sh[oul]d be tempted to stay over Sunday. Let me have a line at 44 Cadogan Place.

HEM.

[[Pitts; Chapeau, 125, 189–92]]

460108gm[a]

13 C[arlton] H[ouse] T[errace]
Jan[uary] 8. [18]46.

Here I am—I fear I have no disposable time except enough for a glance & shaking hands before Sunday—but on Sunday I shall be very glad indeed if you are forthcoming.

Yours aff[ectiona]tely
W.E.G.

Ven[erable]
H. E. Manning

[[BL Add. MS 44247, 285; Morley transcript]]

[[Gladstone met with Manning on 9 January, and on Sunday, 11 January 1846 he spent '[t]he whole day with Manning until ev[enin]g Church (full of exercise with delight, & it should have been also profit) except H[elen]'s matters' (*GD* iii. 512). Gladstone indicates that he read Manning's *Sermons* on 11 January, and again on the following Sundays, 18, 25 January, 1, 8, and 15 February when he 'Finished Manning's very valuable volume of Sermons' (ibid. 512, 514–19).]]

---

[d] 8 January 1846. See 460108gm.   [a] No indication of correspondence in *GD*.

460224mg

Lavington. Shrove Tuesday 1846

My dear Gladstone,

The coming in of Lent reminds me of our last letters: & I have a wish to send you a book which seems to me, as I read it, to be wonderful for its masculine character and elevation—I mean the *Paradisus Animae*.[a] I have therefore written to Dolman & desired him to send a copy to C[arlton] H[ouse] Terrace. Not knowing whether you have any dealings with Romans I have desired him to direct it[25] to me. It may therefore be well to tell Hampton[b] to house it when it comes. Will you accept it as a *Shrove* offering. I have found it useful to read one page a day: & it is so divided as to make it easy. The structure of the Book is significant, & good.

Of course you know Fenelons Oeuvres Spirituelles.[c] They are the best I know for people whose life & labour is in the world: especially in the gentle severity with which he puts one's self-love to death.

May this Lent be full of good to you, & of healing, if of sadness.

Believe me,

Ever yours affect[ionatel]y

H. E. Manning

The Right Hon[oura]ble
W. E. Gladstone
[[Pitts; Chapeau, 126, 192–3]]

460225gm[a]

C[olonial] O[ffice] Feb[ruary] 25. [18]46.

My dear Manning

I never deal with Dolman or any of his tribe: but then I have special reasons for avoiding it; they refer[26] to my sister.[b]

---

[a] See Jacob Merlo Horstius (1597–1644), *Paradise for the Christian Soul, Compiled by M. J. Horst. Part IV, The Practice of Virtue* (London: James Burns, 1845), a translation of *Paradisus animæ christianæ: lectissimis omnigenæ pietatis delitiis amoenus, studio et operâ Jacobi Merlo Horstii...Edition: Nova editio; àmendis innumeris expurgata...* (Malines: Typographia Hanicquiana, 1840). Gladstone began to read the book on Ash Wednesday, 25 February 1846 (*GD* iii. 521), using it almost daily throughout Lent to Easter Saturday, 5 April 1846 (ibid. 521–31) and sporadically thereafter (cf. 17 April; ibid. 532).

[b] Gladstone's butler (see *GD* iv. 395).

[c] *Œuvres spirituelles de [François de Salignac de la Mothe] Fénélon, contenant son traité de l'existence de Dieu et ses lettres sur la religion; nouvelle édition...par M. de Grenoude* (Paris: A. Royer, 1843). No indication of Gladstone's reading of the work in *GD*.

[a] 'Wrote to...H. E. Manning' (*GD* iii. 521).

[b] Note the crises faced by the Gladstone family at the time: the Lunacy Commissioners had met on 9 January 1846 to hear Helen Gladstone's complaint that she was

I thank you very much for your remembrance of me, and I hope your good intentions may not be wholly disappointed. I am happy for the present in having continued free from the burden of Parliamentary attendance, & in still remaining so—yet even with that I have found the pressure on me quite sufficient for my limited powers. Lyttelton's health having crippled him for some time, & even still requiring care, though thank God he is now well & likely I hope to continue so.[c]

The political atmosphere is (What is called) gloomy. From all I hear of the temper of the House of Commons, I think there will be a disposition to put out the Gov[ernmen]t after if not before the passing of this measure— and what lies beyond is mere chaos. Were expulsion from office final by a fundamental law, this prospect would not be a very disagreeable one—

I have no immediate prospect of a seat—& Lincoln you see is doomed to join me.[d]

I shall not be sorry if circumstances should lead me soon to make a clean breast by saying all I have to say upon the Irish Church—

Moberlys Preface[e] seems to me decidedly good—The first thing I have seen in print that was worthy of its subject. Much of the mine however still remains unwrought. I trust your labours prosper & remain

Always aff[ectiona]tely yours
W. E. Gladstone

Ven[erable]
Archdeacon Manning

illegally confined by her family. See 'Minutes of the Commissioners in Lunacy', PRO, MH 50/1, 146ff.

[c] On Lyttelton's ongoing battle with depression and his eventual suicide see Aswith (1975) and Fletcher (1997), *passim*.

[d] On 15 February 1846 Lincoln wrote to Gladstone, 'In the event of my being beaten in the Southern Division (an event to all appearances very probably) they want me to stand in the Northern' (University of Nottingham MS NeC 11, 685). Gladstone wrote to Lincoln on 16 February indicating his sorrow to hear that Lincoln's prospects in South Nottingham-shire were not good (BL Add. MS 44262, 64–6; cf. Gladstone to Lincoln, 24 February and 6 June, ibid. 68–9, 72–3). Lincoln did lose the seat; see Munsell (1985), 60–5. On Gladstone's own seat, see 470818mg.

[e] George Moberly, *The Sayings of the Great Forty Days, between the Resurrection and Ascension, Regarded as the Outlines of the Kingdom of God: in Five Discourses: with an Examination of Mr. Newman's Theory of Developments* (3rd edn.; London: Francis & John Rivington, 1846). George Moberly (1803–85; *DNB*) was a Fellow at Balliol College, 1826–34, Headmaster of Winchester College, 1835–66, and was consecrated Bishop of Salisbury, 1869.

P.S. I do not think I have seen or written to you since finishing your Volume of Sermons: but I really do not know when I read one that [contained] so much good in it for *me*—and I am very glad to find others find it equally suitable. I think there are traces of some of our conversations in it. My wife is now busy upon the volume.

[[BL Add. MS 44247, 286–7; Morley transcript; cf. Chapeau, 316]]

3. Renewed Reflections on Church and State: March–June 1846

460306mg

Lavington. March 6. 1846.

My dear Gladstone,

Last night[27] I came home from Hursley where I spent the day before with Keble. I was glad to find him calm, & firm, and I have no fear about him. He has not read Newman's book, &[28] does not mean to read it: partly for his own sake & partly for Newman's.

But of the principle of development so far as he knows it he speaks without reserve or hesitation. One thing wh[ich] has confirmed him more than any other is the admonition contained in the moral σημεια[a] attaching to the last secessions. He seems shocked, & alarmed at them.

His new book is all in type & will be soon out—it is about 350 pages.[b]

Now—I am made curious by your mention of the Irish Church to know what you have come to.

I cannot hide from myself that the question of the Irish Church will split Churchmen in England fearfully. Maynooth has done it already to a great extent. The Protestant, Establishment, Conservative, anti Roman Churchmen will all go together: and any man who gives up the Reformation theory in Ireland will be deposed from his hold on the Church in England, being such as it is now, & so long as it continues such.

Nevertheless fiat justicia[c]—if justice be there to be done.

The payment of the R[oman] C[atholic] Priests w[oul]d be better endured though at best but ill.

[a] Signs.

[b] [John Keble,] *Lyra Innocentium: Thoughts in Verse on Christian Children, their Ways, and their Privileges* (Oxford: John Henry Parker, 1846) is an octavo volume, viii + 354 pp.

[c] Let justice be done: the phrase by which the King endorsed a 'Writ of Error' allowing a criminal case to be taken to a court of appeal.

I see no one likely to know anything (by the way I have an appointment at Goodwood[d] tomorrow) but it somehow seems to me that the Gov[ernmen]t cannot go on after this Bill.[e] What strikes me is that there remains no sufficiently great point of opposition to L[or]d John [Russell] & his [party] upon which Sir R[obert] P[eel] can by his favours or their fears re-constitute a body of supporters. And that this would be found at a general election. It would seem likely that the two antagonist parties w[oul]d both be stronger in the next Parliament, but that there is no intermediate constituency to return, in any numbers,[29] such politicians as you have all become—that in fact, as N[ewman] said, you must go on or go back.[f] Is there anything in this?

To go to matters nearer home, after many tentatives I have today gone off the slips, & launched out to try what I can do on the science of proof in Theology. I am a long way off from Development, & do not know when I shall come in sight. Somehow I cannot satisfy myself either with objecting to anything without offering a substitute—nor with taking a point, such as development—which is a property and not an entity. But what will come of it, if anything, &, if anything, when, I have no notion. Certainly not for a long time.

I am thankful if you have found anything for yourself in the Sermons. I am perfectly sure there must be many traces of our conversations. It c[oul]d not be otherwise: & I can often detect them. In one I am able to point out the time & place: do you remember our talking about alms & luxury coming from St. Marks by Chester Square? The minutes are in the sermon about worldly cares.[g]

With kind regards to your wife, believe me,
Ever yours affec[tionate]ly
H. E. Manning

The Right Hon[oura]ble
W. E. Gladstone
[[Pitts; Chapeau, 127, 193–4]]

---

[d] Perhaps Molecomb House, Goodwood, Sussex, the home of Charles Lennox (1791–1860; *DNB*), 5th Duke of Richmond and Lennox, Lord Lieutenant of Sussex.

[e] Peel's Bill on the Corn Laws. See 460309mg.

[f] See Newman in the Enclosure to 441120mg: 'this most serious feeling is growing on me, viz. that the reasons, for which I believe *as much* as our system teaches, *must* lead me to believe more, and not to believe more, is to fall back into scepticism'.

[g] Henry E. Manning, *Sermons* (1842*b*), Sermon VI, 'Worldly Care', 95–116.

460308gm[a]

13 C[arlton] H[ouse] Terrace
Sunday M[ar]ch 8. [18]46

My dear Manning

Your account of Keble is comforting. I am sorry to say I hear that both R[obert] Williams[b] & Sergeant Bellasis[c30] are in a very uncertain state, but I cannot say I know it. Toovey the bookseller[d] it seems has been smitten. We should pray first I suppose that no more may go, & next 'That which thou doest do quickly'[e]—the Church of England cannot acquire a clear self-consciousness till this dismal series is at an end. It *is* a dismal series: we are unhappy in losing them, but the evil they do is greatest in itself. I hope you will not hurry your proceedings about Newman's book: for its remoter consequences are more serious, surely, than those which are immediate.

I have read as yet only the Preface to Dr. Pusey's Sermon & I confess myself much shocked at his allusion in a note to 'Mr. Newman's valuable Sermon'[f] —not that the words express an untruth, but the whole circumstances considered they appear to me little less than an outrage upon decency. His cannot be the mind which is to afford the mold to form future minds for the governments[31] of the fortunes of the Church of England: his personal character is a great light for all, but his character & proceedings as a member of the body suggest much matter for regret.

---

[a] 'Wrote to Manning' (*GD* iii. 523).

[b] Robert Williams (1811–90), a Tractarian and MP for Dorchester, 1835–41. As early as 1841 Williams had conversed with Gladstone on Roman Catholicism. On 25 February 1841 Gladstone notes 'A painful conv[ersation] 1½ hour at night with R. Williams. May God hold him safe' (*GD* iii. 86; cf. also ibid. 528, 540). See Gladstone to Williams (26 Feb. 1841) regarding the conversation of the previous evening on the Blessed Virgin and other matters (BL Add. MS 44357, 285–6).

[c] Edward Bellasis (1800–73) was educated at the Inner Temple and was called to the bar in 1824, served as Justice of the Peace for Middlesex and Westminster, and was active throughout his life as a parliamentary counsel. He was eventually received into the Catholic Church on 28 September 1850. For details see Boase, i. 233 and Adams (1977).

[d] James Toovey was received into the Roman Catholic Church in 1846 (*DNB*, Gordon-Gorman [1910], 272).

[e] John 13: 27.

[f] On the day of writing (*GD* iii. 523) Gladstone was reading E. B. Pusey, *Entire Absolution of the Penitent. A Sermon, Mostly Preached Before the University, in the Cathedral Church of Christ, in Oxford, on the Fourth Sunday after Epiphany* (Oxford: John Henry Parker, 1846); see p. xix, note, which directs readers to 'Mr. Newman's valuable Sermon, "Dangers to the Penitent" in the "Sermons on the Subjects of the Day" '. See Sermon 4 in *Sermons, Bearing on Subjects of the Day* (Oxford, 1843*a*).

I see I have written foolishly as if it were to be supposed that an individual is to give form to the future mind of the Church among us: I did not mean it: what has happened to Newman ought at least to rid us of that delusion.

I have not arrived at any set form of opinion concerning the Irish Church. The question that pursues me is this: can social justice, which of course varies in its form & application according to the conditions of political society, warrant the permanent maintenance of the Irish Church as it is? I have not yet been able to find the grounds of an affirmative answer: but it is only right that I should not conclude in the negative till the whole time left me for consideration shall have elapsed. My intention is never again to pledge myself at an Election on the subject—should it come next week—As to my book I believe people could show from it if they choose that I am bound after Maynooth, so far as consistency binds, to strip the Irish Church. The silver hairs of that indeed most Reverend old man the Primate move me: I have been reading his Charge today[g]—but it does not answer my question. I wish I could get a synodical decision in favour of my retirement from public life. For I profess to remain there (to myself) for the service of the Church; and my views of the mode of serving her are getting so fearfully wide of those generally current that even *if* they be sound they may become wholly unavailable.

Your speculations on the fate of the Gov[ernmen]t are I think very reasonable. We shall I expect have another crisis before six months are over. I have however not the least idea what the issue of it will be.

In the meantime I feel most distinctly that I am now in a position where good is to be done—if only we have the heart to do it. Certainly the very thing one should wish is to try certain things in the Colonies—for ulterior use at home when the day of need comes.

Believe me always
Aff[ectiona]tely yours
W. E. Gladstone

Venerable
H. E. Manning

[[BL Add. MS 44247, 289–2; Morley transcript; Lathbury, i. 350–1; Purcell, i. 316–17; cf. Morley, i. 323; Chapeau, 316–17]]

---

[g] On the day of writing Gladstone was reading John George Beresford, Archbishop of Armagh, *A Charge Delivered at his Annual Visitation, 1845* (London: John W. Parker, 1845), which called for a defence of the Established Church in Ireland (*GD* iii. 523).

460309mg

Lavington. March 9. 1846.

My dear Gladstone,

I see that Sir Robert Peel on Friday night expressed his intention of discussing on the second reading of the Bill relating to the Importation of Corn the effect of that measure on the Tithe property.[a]

Hitherto I have not wished to trouble you about this point: but as it is mooted it is not too soon to say that I am very anxious about it, and feel that something must be done to avert a very serious national evil, I mean the impoverishment of the Parochial Clergy.

On the whole subject of the corn Laws I can but take my premises from others. If Sir Robert Peel is right (and I feel well disposed to trust his knowledge & judgment) in saying that a reduction in the price of corn will neither reduce the rent of the Landlord nor the wages of the Labourer, then I have little difficulty in coming to the conclusion that the proposed change will be a great *general* benefit.

The compensation for reduction of price being in the increase of produce.

But it is precisely this compensation from the benefit of which the Tithe owner is excluded.

The rent Charges are calculated on two quantities one fixed, & one variable. The variable is average price the fixed is the amount of produce.

The Tithe Owner therefore will share in the operation of this measure only on the side of loss by reduction of price.

Suppose the prices of grain to be reduced one third he is one third poorer a rent charge of £ 300 a year will fall to £ 200. And there is no provision for compensation.

A reduction in general prices is not enough, for that will be only a partial & indirect benefit whereas the reduction of the Rent Charge is direct and extends over the whole sphere.

It is not for me to suggest remedies: but I can see no fair one but releasing the fixed quantity, & making it variable. The objection to this might be lessened by requiring a longer average of years.

But in that proportion the Tithe owner suffers.

---

[a] Peel's speech on Friday, 6 March 1846 (Hansard, lxxxiv. 71) was reported in *The Times*, 7 May, 3c. For the discussion that followed the introduction of the 'Bill to amend the Laws relating to the Importation of Corn' (PP 1846 [111.] i. 423; 9 Mar. 1846), see Hansard, lxxxiv. 786, and that on 13 May, ibid. 1010.

Another partial remedy might be found in exempting the Tithe, at least Clerical, from its present heavy burdens: for instance: the value of Lavington was last year (gross) £ s. d. 210.. 0.. 0

The Poor Rate	21..16.. 6
Property Tax	5..16.. 5
Way Rate	7.. 5.. 6
	34..18.. 5
Add window Tax	10..13.. 0
	45..11.. 5 45..11.. 5

£164.. 8.. 7

From this are deductions of Ecclesiastical dues &c. not less,[32] with repairs of Chancel &c., than[33] about £7. or 10 a year: so that one fourth is absorbed before the Incumbent can begin to subsist upon the benefice. This in a class of men who seldom possess private property, & are precluded from all common & secular[34] modes of acquiring income is very severe.

I need not add anything on the vital importance of this matter except this only. We have about 14,000 Clergy—they are already poor to embarrassment. We need *at least* 3000 more, & it is at this crisis that an impoverishment perhaps of one fourth or even one third hangs over them.

I assume that the price of grain must fall or else I do not see who is to gain by the Repeal of the Restrictive duties.

Believe me,
My dear Gladstone,
Yours affect[ionatel]y
H. E. Manning

P.S. I hope to see you next week.[b] On Monday I am to be at the B[isho]p of Oxford.[c]

H.E.M.

The Right Hon[oura]ble
W. E. Gladstone
[[Pitts; Chapeau, 128, 194–6]]

---

[b] See 460311gm and 460402mg.
[c] Samuel Wilberforce, to be visited 16 March 1846.

460310gm[a]

13 C[arlton] H[ouse] Terrace
M[ar]ch 10: [18]46.

My dear Manning

I do not yet know the precise view which Sir Robert Peel takes of the bearing of the Corn Law Repeal on the property of the Tithe Owner. But your view of the relation in which he stands to the measure is not to be disputed. If the price falls the landlord & the farmer may compensate themselves by increasing production: & though this increase in the first instance causes a still further fall of price, yet by pushing the process to a certain point they may have such an augmentation in quantity as to cover the whole loss in proportionate return. Whereas both parts of this process, both the importation of corn from abroad, and also the efforts of the producer at home to retrieve his position, concur in the[35] point that they damage the owner of tithe.

I think however it is very uncertain whether there will be any great fall of prices in the long run under a system of free trade. To talk of their falling to the continental level is it seems to me absurd: as much so as to predict that the composition of forces will[36] produce not a diagonal but the elongation of the line in which one of them has been moving. I think it is *possible* that we may see a very great reduction in the price of corn, but not likely in any way, and only in one way possible, that one way being a vast increase in the home growth, caused by the general application of the energy of the English mind, under the pressures of competition, to a pursuit which has hitherto attracted a comparatively small share of it.

But the question arises, what will Parliament do to secure the tithe owner. And now I must answer you according to my own individual expectation. I think Parliament will in this view do nothing. Parliament will hold him to the letter of his bond under the Commutation Act.[b] He will never escape from that bond: he will never see the conditions of that Act altered in his favour. He cannot, in these days, swim up the stream.

Another thing Parliament may do—I hope will do: that is raise the standard of rating generally to a point somewhat near the real value. This would be a considerable relief to the tithe owner. I do not by any means

---

[a] 'Wrote to Manning' (*GD* iii. 524).

[b] Note the eventual bill, 'A Bill to amend the Acts for the Commutation of Tithes in England and Wales', PP 1846 (627.) iv. 465; 14 August 1846, addressing 6 & 7 William IV c.71, 'An Act for the Commutation of Tithes in England and Wales', which commuted tithes in kind for moneys.

abandon the hope of it—but if this is done it will not be for the sake of relieving the tithe owner; nor even for the sake of doing him justice so much as because this kind of rating is more conformable than the old & lax system to the economical spirit of the time.

Should matters turn out better than I expect you will remember that I am not of a sanguine habit of mind in these things. But my opinion is that the Church, as a proprietress, enjoyed her last victory on the day when the Ecclesiastical Commissioners resolved to run out the leases & take the full value of the Estates either in sale or letting. That was done under a combination of favourable circumstances: here we have a combination of such as are in the same sense adverse.

I see but two modes in which the available resources of the Church are likely to receive material increase—over and above certain modes of increase now in operation under statutes or other arrangements already formed. There are 1. the Episcopal & all of the capitular[37c] Estates, and 2. the free and systematic resort to voluntary contributions.

As to the first I am afraid I am right in the supposition that the old spendthrift modes of managing Ecclesiastical Estates are still generally in vigour, so far as relates to Bishops and to many Chapters: that there is still, to this extent, the same inducement to provide for the life interests of actual holders by waste of prospective resources, and that so long as it continues it must; one may almost say it ought, to produce the same effects.

In my opinion it is visionary as matter of fact, & unwarrantable as matter of right, to ask Parliament to interpose for any purpose which regards the Church *in formâ pauperis*[d] until she has thoroughly husbanded her own pecuniary means & applied them to the best advantage. There may be some remote risk in centralising the management of Episcopal & capitular estates, there may be some derogation to temporal dignity in interposing such a system of control over & above the will of life-incumbents, as is necessary for thrift: let us have as little of these evils as possible, but we must I think & ought to have that of which they may be the accompaniments—a thorough excision of the old system of management & a *bonâ fide* effort to obtain from the property all it can be justly made to yield.

But what next? Supposing this done?—can the Church then seek for public aid? I think not. She would be met at the door of Parliament 1. by the allegation that half of the population of the United Kingdom do not belong to the Communion: 2. by the question who are you & what are you? The first of these constitutes a formidable opposition—the second is

---

[c] That is, of the Cathedral chapter.　　　[d] In the form of a pauper.

far more formidable, it would carry division & with division dismay into her own ranks. She has become in the popular view so hybrid; her mind is so variously apprehended on this side & on that; the just jealousies of the people of England have been so fearfully aroused by the development of Romanising elements among her members, that she is no longer an unity for the purposes of political combat.

But the evil does not stop there. Neither you nor I should much lament shutting the door upon the prospect of Parliamentary Church Extension. The sorer evil, for which also the late movers to the Church of Rome have also in my belief mainly to answer, is that they have brought into fatal prejudice & disrepute that most innocent, most simple, most effective, nay let me add for so it is that somewhat Protestant and Presbyterian mode of supplying the wants of the Church, by Church-like[38] appeal to the voluntary liberality of her members. The sore point in the use of the offertory seems to be, collection from pew to pew—the common practice, I believe, of multitudes of Presbyterian congregations every Sunday in Scotland. But being favoured here[39] by those who favour Rome, & who favour her as Rome, it seems to be now placed under general ban, to hold its ground in some places where it had been introduced before the general[40] suspicion of Romanism put the Church in a flame, but the hopes of its progress & extensive prevalence to be indefinitely postponed. This is very sad and very disheartening. Nor do I think we shall live to see this prejudice effectually removed, except by new modes of action. The last twelve or fifteen years have I think afforded us an example of what Froude declared the Reformation to be—the limb is badly set & must be broken again, before it can get sound.[e] In some way or other the Church must descend into the ranks of the people and find her strength there, and build up from that level. If she can really unfold great energies in that region, prejudices among the classes having property will be too weak to hold their ground. Asceticism itself provided it be an active & missionary asceticism, will become a source of popular as well as of inward strength. To some this would seem at the best very remote speculation: but I confess that whatever it may be where I look deliberately at it and compare it with other modes & schemes of human improvement now in vogue, as[41] to its utilitarian aspect, the question arises why does not every one who wishes well or thinks that he wishes well to his kind, betake himself to this path of duty?

---

[e] *Remains of the Late Reverend Richard Hurrell Froude, M. A. Fellow of Oriel College, Oxford* (2 vols.; London: J. G. & F. Rivington, 1838), i. 433: 'The Reformation was a limb badly set—it must be broken again in order to be righted.'

But I have gone at length into these subjects led by your letter and rather to the prejudice of the immediate claims upon my time. I am glad to hear you are coming to London. It now seems likely that in about a fortnight I may become a Candidate for Wigan[f]—with a prospect of a quiet Election—

Believe me always
Aff[ectiona]tely yours
W. E. Gladstone

Venerable
H. E. Manning

There is one point I should have noticed—there *may* be great gain in the repeal of restrictive duties without any fall of price: that is if it should lead at once (as we may hope it will lead) to increased trade, increased means of consumption or demand, & increased production or supply. Increase of trade would give the labouring[42] community greater means of paying for food and would enable them to conserve more even at the same price.

[[BL Add. MS 44247, 293–6; (copy) ibid. 44528, 23; Lathbury, ii. 270–2; cf. Chapeau, 317]]

460311gm[a]

13 C[arlton] H[ouse] Terrace
M[ar]ch 11. [18]46.

My dear Manning

I am glad to hear you take part at the meeting for the S[ociety for the] P[ropagation of the] G[ospel] on Tuesday next.[b] Will it interfere with this if I ask you & you agree to dine with me on Monday to meet Rogers only and converse upon Colonial Church matters?

Aff[ectiona]tely yours
W.E.G.

[[BL Add. MS 44247, 297; Morley transcript]]

---

[f] On accepting the position of Secretary of State for War and the Colonies, Gladstone gave up his seat for Newark. The suggestion was that he run for Wigan, where it appeared that the Member would be unseated, but Gladstone eventually decided not to run and remained out of the Commons, although retaining his secretaryship and Cabinet post until the election in 1847 when he ran for the Oxford seat. See Morley, i. 287–8 and 470818mg.

[a] 'Wrote to ... Manning' (*GD* iii. 524).

[b] On Tuesday, 17 March 1846, a meeting was held at Mansion House in London to encourage the Church in the colonies. See *The Times*, 18 March, 5e, and *The Guardian*, 18 March, 140, which notes that Manning moved that a subscription fund be established 'to encourage the spread of public worship and religious instruction in the colonies'.

460313mg

Lavington. March 13. 1846.

My dear Gladstone,

I shall have great pleasure in dining with you on Monday.

My old Family relations with the city, & the wishes of others made me promise to be at the Mansion House next Tuesday. I had thought of asking you (but w[oul]d not trouble you with a letter) whether there is anything you w[oul]d wish to have said: or any fact stated.

I have thought much of your last letter, & in some points hope to shew cause to have better heart for the Church—if that is our centres are multiplied, & our organization drawn closer.

But all this must wait til we meet with an hours leisure.

Believe me,
Ever your aff[ectionatel]y
H. E. Manning.

[[Pitts]]

[[On 16 March 1846 Gladstone had 'Manning & Rogers to dinner. We discussed the questions relating to the Colonial Church & R[oger]'s intended position—also the subject of the Irish Church—until near 12' (*GD* iii. 525). On 20 March Gladstone 'Saw Manning 11¼–2 on Church & personal matters—a very intense conversation' (ibid. 526; cf. Purcell, i. 318).]]

460402mg

Lavington. April 2. 1846.
(After Post)

My dear Gladstone,

Our last conversation has been much in my thoughts, & I will tell you, as shortly as I can, what seems to me to be a just conclusion.

The great choice men have to make is whether they be called to serve God in a sacred or secular state.

This choice you took when you laid aside the thought of taking Holy Orders.

Having chosen the secular state you entered Parliament, with a purpose of serving the Church in that sphere. I designedly put it in this order because Parliament is a specific form of the secular state, & in choosing the species you had already in the order of[43] moral election, if not of time, chosen the genus.

Now the question here first arising is whether a man may enter Parliament with a defined view, & leave it when that is either accomplished, or shewn to be impossible.

Clearly in principle he may. He will then serve God, & the Church in other specific forms of the secular state.

But, as a matter of fact, this is not your case.

For though you may have entered public life with a view of your own, the Providence of God has laid on you many claims binding you to the specific sphere you have entered.

I will put an extreme case. Suppose you were convinced that there is no more to be done in Parliament for the Church, I should think it still your duty to abide in your present sphere until some *positive* reason (for this is only negative) should require you to withdraw.

You went there with a view of your own, it may please God to keep you there for a purpose of His. You aimed at serving[44] the Church, & He may detain you to serve the common welfare of our social state—a lower office but necessary, & if laid on you by Him, your duty & probation.

Now to this you will perhaps say that public life is not your 'home'.

Cannings life[a] has always been to me very instructive. He is a great example of the difficulty with which a man without the presumptions of alliance, & hereditary standing can maintain himself. But he lived when the climate of Parliament was highly aristocratic, & all his political relations were with those who were sensitive at the rise of powers without blood.

Times are as much altered as Parliament is. And this was never, in any great degree, true of any party except the old Tories. It is less true of the Conservatives, and least of all with the class of Politicians who are evidently gathering for the next permanent administration.

To be plain—It is impossible that the Tory section of the Conservatives can make a lasting, if any, Government. And such men as L[or]d Dalhousie,[b] Herbert[c] & the like are bound to public life & have a right to you.

---

[a] George Canning (1770–1827) was educated at Christ Church, Oxford, served as an MP from 1794 (Liverpool, Gladstone's family's riding, 1812–22), as a Liberal Foreign Secretary, 1807–9, 1822–7, and as Prime Minister, 1827, strongly favouring Catholic emancipation. On Gladstone's early acquaintance with him see Matthew (1999), 8–9. For details see *DNB*, Dixon (1976), Hinde (1973), Marshall (1938), Petrie (1946), and Temperley (1968).

[b] Lord James Andrew Broun Ramsay (1812–60; *DNB*), 10th Earl of Dalhousie, 1838, was educated at Christ Church, Oxford, served as MP for Haddingtonshire, 1837–8, and was appointed Viceroy of India, 1848–56.

[c] Sidney Herbert (1810–61), 1st Baron Herbert of Lea, was educated at Oriel College, Oxford, and served as MP for South Wiltshire from 1832, was Secretary to the Admiralty, 1841–5, War Secretary, 1845–6, 1852–5, 1859–60, and Secretary of State for the Colonies, 1855. See *DNB* and Stanmore (1906).

Therefore home or no, public life is your *place* call it what you will. But I have been going on the lowest, and very untrue suppositions.

Four or five years may as you say go far to shew what is & what is not possible to be done for the Church in regard to direct measures.

But neither your life nor the life of your boy will touch the period when the Church of England will be out of reach of mischief-issuing from Parliament. The old Church system is too broad & deep in England to be disposed of. It will take a long time to bring us to the condition of the Church in France. And even then there is an immense work to be done by men of heavier metal than Montalembert.

Now to fulfil my promise of being short.

I think:

1. That tho' lawful in *principle* it was probably not intended in *fact* for you to define your original intention.

2. That the events of your Public life have bound you by other bonds to the wheel.

3. That your 'home' topos is not true.

4. That the Church will have a work to be done by public men whether aggressive or defensive for one or more generations.

5. That it is dangerous to admit the thought of terminableness. It can hardly fail to affect the tone & energy of the will.

6. That our first duty is to realize our present position: for no other exists to us. What is future is no more *ours*, than what is non-existent. I see I must take another sheet, & so I will add—

7. Lastly that I think your time is not yet come. You have worked under, & for a high, & able Leader who has stood between you, & the sympathies of those who have longed to draw nearer to you: & to whom you really belong.[45]

I do not say this as if it could have been otherwise. But as a fact you have been compelled to forego much of your own personal hold on public feeling created by your character, acts, & writing, to hold your present high public office. I think you have done rightly as I have always said. But this cannot always be. There is evidently a change coming. Whether by voluntary act or no you will stand in Parliament more simply on your own responsibility,[46] & will before long. And the opinions of young men are the opinions of the next generation.

There is a great game to be played yet in England in which the young men of the last ten years will be forced to bear if not a forward part at least the heaviest brunt. And I seem to myself to see in your career a preparation for involving you in the fray. I do not like to say anything of Sir Robert Peel of whom I have a very high esteem in many ways: but one thing he has failed to do I mean to gain the attachment or[47] trust of the Church. And the higher you have risen with him, the more you have come under this momentary shadow.

I have written more than enough: but I would still go on: and yet, perhaps, it will be best to come to an end.

Only do not give way to the thought that *your* end is coming. *The* end of a public *policy* which has given the Church neither freedom nor support, which would neither help it, nor let it help itself is coming: though things may be worse before they are better.

It has pleased God that a generous, and distinguished Friend should guide you upwards in public life, but I do not believe that your public life is either to end with his, or to be the continuance of his policy towards the Church.

Forgive me all this: & believe me
Ever your affectionate Friend,
H. E. Manning

The Right Hon[oura]ble
W. E. Gladstone
[[Pitts; Chapeau, 129, 196–8]]

460405gm[a]

13 C[arlton] H[ouse] Terrace
Palm S[unday]. Ap[ril] 5. [18]46.

My dear Manning

Whether it be because my egoism is more peculiarly engaged in this case or from what other reason soever, I have rarely read an argument opposed to my conviction with so little movement of mind under its pressure, as that contained in your letter of the 2d.

I see the force of reasonings against an alteration of the choice made for the direction of the general course of a man's life, without new and distinct signs to warrant it. But this force bears the other way. I am contending against being driven from my original choice and you to drive me from it.

---

[a] 'Wrote to Manning' (*GD* iii. 529; cf Morley, i. 323–4).

I speak of the formal not the material choice: the identity of external semblance I grant is with you. If you contend on the contrary that the work of serving the Church is one to be always done in Parliament, I reply first on the proposition itself that the power of such service is rapidly evanescing (and that the first person who serves the Church effectually once will I fear *ipso facto* disqualify himself from serving her further there)— secondly whether this be true or not at least it is in substance[48] my original and never shaken conviction—

If you were to look, though I should be sorry to entail upon you such a penalty, to the last Chapter of my book[b] you would see that my difficulty must hereafter be to furnish those who ask it with a reason for my remaining—that no reason of a political nature can possibly suffice— that indeed it is scarcely possible for anyone viewing the case from a distance even now to acquit me either of having written rashly and wildly or else of having abandoned what I had professed in a very solemn manner. Rely upon it, it will not be enough to answer I am pledged to my contemporaries and co-party-men. That fact may hamper me as a fact, but it cannot sustain me as a reason.

I think that towards the end of your letter you have unconsciously given me what I ask for. You say that Sir R[obert] Peel's policy will neither help the Church, nor let her help herself. Suppose that policy gone by, and another in vogue, which *will* let her help herself—this work of emancipation, so to speak qualified & partial as it must & ought to be, may extend over a very long period of time: but it may not, my impression is that in the same hands it will not: till it either ends absolutely, or ends & that manifestly so far as I am concerned, my first[49] choice binds me to the place where I stand, but so soon as that is over, the force of original & never abandoned election, whatever that may be, draws me away from it.

I do not think that any policy can as matter of fact be adopted which will do more *in quantity* for the Church than Sir Robert Peel's, that is to say which shall make larger demands in her name on the 'spirit of the age'! Of this as a substantial truth I am firmly convinced. The question with me is whether the Church may not with a portion of her gold (by which I mean civil and secular privilege generally) buy what she wants and loves more than gold: whether without greatly altering in practice her political

---

[b] Chapter X. The ulterior Tendencies of the Movement towards the Dissolution of the Connection [between the State and the Church], in W. E. Gladstone, *The State in its Relations with the Church* (2 vols.; London: John Murray, 1841).

position she may not wisely make concessions, which shall have the effect of allaying jealousies that now prevent compliance with her reasonable demands appertaining to her immediate office, and in return for these obtain not absolute freedom nor any thing like it, but any present freedom that she may need and be able to have, and the guarantee of more in future, in a proportion to her future needs and capacities.

I could write down in a few lines the measures, after the adoption of which I should be prepared to say to a young man entering life, if you wish to serve the Church do it in the sanctuary and not in Parliament (unless he were otherwise determined by his station, and not always then—it must depend surely upon the nature and strength of his inward vocation—) & should not think it at all absurd to say the same thing to some who have already placed themselves in this[50] latter sphere. For when the end is attained of 'letting the Church help herself' and when it is recognised that active help can no longer be given, the function of serving the Church in the State, such as it was according to the old idea, dies of itself, and what remains of duty is of a character essentially different.

It is the essential change now in progress from the Catholic to the infidel idea of the State which is the determining element in my estimate of this matter and which I think has no place in yours. For I hold and believe that when that transition has once been effected, the State never can come back to the Catholic idea by means of any agency from within itself—that if at all it must be by a sort of re-conversion from without. I am not of those (excellent as I think them) who say remain & bear witness for the truth— there is a place where witness is ever to be borne for truth, that is to say for full and absolute truth but it is not there.

I can conceive an American, who intended to be the servant of the Church, and who should enter into Congress for the purpose if it should have happened that essential interests of the Church were brought into immediate contact with public policy. The questions might occupy many years in coming to issue: he might have spent the best part of his life upon them: but this and the conventional sense attached to it surely[51] could not form a law of duty binding him for the remainder.

There is so much more to say which I cannot now put down that I blame myself for writing anything: yet it could not be withheld. But indeed I shall not be contented in this matter unless you end by coming to my way of thinking (which however I suspect is nearer yours than appears in my crude and imperfect manner of discussing the question)—for with me the conclusion itself & the views on which it is built are really the result of more steady & *seasoned* observation and reflection, with more of the signs of a lawful process of thought about them, than almost anything that I know within me. And recollect I am not arguing for any act or decision which shall anticipate the course of events; but merely to be allowed to follow it. Again I think your statement is the very reverse of the fact when you say that at the highest a *positive* reason for removal is wanting: the positive reasons are many & strong, but especially the one is with me the fact that I am all along standing upon an original intention, never altered, though[52] always as now subject to the issue of certain suppositions. Indeed it *may* happen that my political death may soon arrive. I may find that when the indeterminate impressions now upon my mind about the Irish Church take form & articulation, the result may be fatal to my capacity of doing any good in political life: not because of the greatness of the change alone, but because of its sinister alliance with that suspicion of leaning to the Church of Rome & therefore of treachery which now & for many years must attach not without presumptions of justice to those whose names have ever been associated with that Oxford constellation of which the chief light is now put out for the Church of England and blazes for her (I fear it must be said) determined foe.

There is a greater difficulty in the way than that of Parliamentary alliances: it is the relation to the Queen and the Monarchy in which a man insensibly comes to stand. She is the venerable shadow of a long line of Kings that were kings indeed: the very name of the English monarchy is to those who stand about it a great and sacred trust, but even this idea never has stood before me as a barrier because *non tali auxilio*[c]—it would be ridiculous in me to suppose either that in these times the Throne can be maintained, i.e. the balance of the question[53] of its maintenance can require to be cast in its favour, by a single person, or that if it did I could be that unit. But I dismiss the first as much as the latter notion. It stands upon general approval and affection, & those public sentiments will not & do not want organs.

Believe me, with many thanks,

Aff[ectiona]tely yours

W. E. Gladstone

Venerable

H. E. Manning

[[BL Add. MS 44247, 298–305; Morley transcript; Morley, i. 323–4; cf. Chapeau, 318]]

---

[c] Not for such aid. In Virgil, *Aeneid*, 2. 501, Hecuba on seeing Priam armed responds: non tali auxilio . . . tempus eget (the time does not call for such aid).

460417mg

Lavington. April 17. 1846.

My dear Gladstone,

Your letter has filled me with a multitude of thoughts, and I hardly know where to begin.

I have conceded to you that a man may make such an original election as you claim for yourself.

The only practical questions are:

1. Have subsequent events laid you under the yoke for life, or no?

2. Can there cease in our life, to be work for the Church, at least defensive in the sphere of Parliament, or public life?

On the former I still feel that, I should answer affirmatively. On this, however, I am open to conviction.

But I am ready to merge the former question in the latter, and say, when the day comes that the Church can no longer be served either positively, or defensively in Parliament, τὸ κατ᾽ ἐμέ[a] you are free to withdraw. I will go further. I should for your sake rejoice at your retirement from the world. This brings us *practically* to at least a *working agreement.*

On the latter question, then, which is in effect the only question remaining I will say that I can also conceive a speedy end to the service of the Church in Public Life.

But then it would be by a revolution—an overthrow of our national order. This *might* happen abruptly. I do not expect it: because I do not see the elements of a sufficiently active force: and I can see that the classes making up Society in England have mutually given hostages, & bail, & have been bound over too strongly & reciprocally to keep the peace.

Nevertheless I see slow poisons enough in operation to bring about any result hereafter.

My belief is that you & I shall go to our rest leaving the *Established Church* much where it is.

1. It has the whole 'vis inertiae'[b] of England in its favour.

2. All public, & domestic traditions are founded on it.

3. The mighty prejudice against Rome, & Dissent is its supporter.

4. It is really and deeply loved by individuals of great learning, power, piety, & social weight.

---

[a] As for me; cf. Rom. 1: 15: as for me [I am eager].   [b] Inactive energy.

5. It has the masses of the poor in agricultural districts with it.

6. The intellect, science, learning of England is de facto in its communion to a great & disproportioned extent.

This alone w[oul]d carry its present status beyond our day.

7. There is a real growth of the Catholic, or semi-catholic element in the Church. It is more loved as a Church & less as an Establishment than perhaps at any time since the Reformation, unless we except 1648 to 1660.[c]

8. The universal settlement of Land & property is bound up with its endowments.

These & many more reasons lead me to think that (unless the earth be shaken) you and I shall go to our rest leaving the *Establishment*[54] between life & death, as now & always.

If this be so you are on Ixions wheel,[d] or your Sessions will be those of Theseus.[e]

However I see an auxiliary which may come to your release.

If the purely Spiritual element in the Church itself gain strength, certain changes will come from within, & bring all its political relations to an issue.

For instance the restoration of Spiritual discipline (without which the health if not the life of the Church will one day be impossible) will extinguish Church-rates, & shake the whole Tithe endowment.

I am prepared to give Church Rates at once to obtain a free, & righteous exercise of spiritual correction.

This is becoming a grave matter in my mind.

At this moment I might be required to bury (if he sh[oul]d die)[55] with the full Christian Offices a man who committed an aggravated rape, being a married man, on a girl of 15, about a month ago.

It does not signify talking of the Courts not having pronounced him excommunicate. The instinct of the populace righteously abhors such technical defenses of sacrilege.

---

[c] The period of the Puritan Interregnum.

[d] The murderer of his father-in-law, Ixion, was punished by Zeus by being bound to a wheel that turned forever.

[e] From the time he had gained enough strength to raise the rock under which his father had placed sandals and sword for him, the Greek hero, Theseus, performed great deeds, slaying evildoers, the rampaging bull of Marathon, and the Minotaur in Crete.

However this is only by the way.

You say you think you could write down the measures which would wind up the work of the Church in Parliament.

I think I could make my list, but it would give you no hope of escaping from public life.

Whatever settlement you may devise, will need perpetual, & vigilant protection so long as there is a Parliament at Westminster.

But to come to a nearer question.

I think you are probably right in saying that the Irish Church Question may put it beyond your power to serve the Church again.

I cannot say with what anxiety I look to this subject. My impression of the effect of Irish Church questions on England has always, I think, been more anxious & foreboding than yours.

We seem to be between parallels made up of crises, and it appears as if the Will of God is that we should be brought to an issue of first principles.

But I will not go into this. If we could talk we should agree. Some words in your letter I should not have written: as well as in one a few weeks ago.

I will only add that the Jerusalem Bishopric seems to be assuming a decidedly worse aspect: & I dread its effect on Hope & many more.[f]

Believe me,
Ever yours affect[ionate]ly
H.E. Manning

[[Pitts; Chapeau, 130, 199–201]]

---

[f] Hope's religious concerns had begun sometime earlier. Note Gladstone's letter to him 7 December 1845: 'As to your habit of searching for broad, by which I think you mean determinate and satisfying, views, is it not in great part a temptation? Of course I mean by satisfying not simply such as ought to satisfy, but such as answer all the mind's demand. For my part I do not find in *other* departments of life and action, that such standing ground is as matter of fact ordinarily vouchsafed to us. There comes in Butler's position, so truly broad and so deeply rooted in the essential laws, that the God of nature and of life is also the God of salvation; and in the many mansions, not of our rest, but of our school, we must expect a correspondence of character. Think of this if I have made it intelligible: at the same time do not suppose I advance it as a complete reply. But I believe it cuts very deep' (NLS MS 3673, 84–7, 85).

460419gm[a]

13 C[arlton] H[ouse] Terrace
Sunday Ap[ril] 19 [18]46

My dear Manning

It is not without some compunction that I continue this correspondence, which though so burdensome you have kindly entered into on my account. But we make progress and as it is called see daylight.

I blame myself for never having clearly stated to you the original and cardinal ideas upon which I proceed. Had I done this thoroughly, we should sooner have found out our real proximity of view. But the truth is that to deal properly with a question of this kind requires certain mental habits as well as will, and those habits with me[56] never well matured are now of course utterly disorganised.

Still let me repair one omission, & beg you to observe I am not claiming privilege or relief—first of all because that possibility of change in my outward career which is all that I claim may never realise itself—secondly because the claim rests upon a different basis, namely on this that the process which I am now actively engaged in carrying on is a process of lowering the religious tone of the State, letting it down, de-moralising it, i.e. stripping it of its ethical character, and assisting its transition into one which is mechanical. This it is which makes me feel that the 'burden of proof' lies on the side of the argument for remaining in public life; & that the purposes which warrant it for me—i.e. for one in whose public life office or executive gov[ernmen]t is an element—must be very strong and very special in order to make good the conclusion.

I agree with you that in all probability the Church will hold her nationality, in substance, beyond our day: I think she will hold it as long as the monarchy subsists & that that will last when we are gone, though it is difficult to look at the little Prince of Wales without a sigh.

So long, undoubtedly, the Church will want political and parliamentary defence. But it is quite another question, in what form that defence can be best conducted. I have seen the popular cause of Ireland at its strongest when the popular leaders have even contumaciously absented themselves from the business of the House of Commons. The Dissenters have no members for Universities but their real representation is better organised, by far, in proportion to its weight, than that of the Church: and yet it is not

---

[a] 'Wrote to Manning' (*GD* iii. 532). 'I inclose a letter from Manning with my answer' (Gladstone to Catherine, 19 Apr. [SDL, Glynne–Gladstone MS 770, 228]).

formally organised at all. A knot of men professing & claiming everything, engaged in constant resistance and protest, like Montalembert & τῆς περὶ αὐτὸν[b] in France, permit to view a method of advocacy which may be well united to a country like France, and to a state of acute active hostility between the Church & the State. But that is not likely to be our case for a long time to come. And my belief is that strength with the people will for our day at least be the only effectual defence of the Church in the H [ouse] of Commons, as the want of it is now her weakness there. It is not every thing which calls itself a defence that is really such. There are kinds of defence that excite jealousies far beyond their power to repel and thus cause more danger than no defence at all. As the Church grows out of doors, she will be more felt in doors. She has already as you justly say the educated classes: therefore she has the *personnel* of Parliament: what she needs is beyond it, to make the *personnel* effective—but I cannot conceive the possibility of her lacking the means of representation in that region in full proportion to that which is to be represented, & which now I think demands the application to speak generally of all available energies for its replenishment.

These truths must be held 'in solution' but the day for them to be 'precipitated' may be nearer, or may be farther, than any rational conjecture now formed would serve to show.

My impression has been that Hope is beyond being affected by the Jerusalem Bishopric either one way or the other: but if you think otherwise & particularly if you know anything to the contrary it is a fact so important that I hope you will give your mind to the case & consider what you can do towards bringing Gobat's case[c] out fully. From some little things lately seen and heard I have comforted myself with the belief that Hope's mind was more settled—

[b] Those around him.

[c] Protests were again raised regarding the Jerusalem Bishopric when Samuel Gobat (1799–1879), a Swiss missionary to Abyssinia, was appointed to succeed Bishop Alexander on the latter's death in November 1845. Gobat was suspected by Pusey since he had refused to anathematize Nestorius or Eutyches. See *Documents Connected with the Foundation of the Anglican Bishopric in Jerusalem; and with The Protest against Bishop Gobat's Proselytism* (London: John Masters, 1853), 9–15 (the protest of the Bishop of Exeter against Gobat's consecration on 25 May 1846) and Liddon, iii. 70ff. Note also the later discussion surrounding the work of the Gobat Protest Committee in *The Guardian* (1856), 260. On Gobat see Samuel Gobat, *Samuel Gobat, Bishop of Jerusalem. His Life and Work: A Biographical Sketch, Drawn Chiefly from his Own Journals*, preface by the Earl of Shaftesbury, trans. Sarah M. S. (Clarke) Pereira (London: J. Nisbet, 1885). On concerns about Hope's religious directions at the time see 461207gm.

If your dissent from 'some^57 things' in my letters had been a moral one,
I hope you would have pointed them out—or that you will do so now—
But if otherwise I will not give you the trouble—

Believe me always,
Aff[ectiona]tely yours
W. E. Gladstone

Venerable
Archdeacon Manning

[[BL Add. MS 44247, 306–10; Morley transcript; Lathbury, ii. 272–4; cf. Morley,
i. 324–5; cf. Chapeau, 318–19]]

460420mg

Lavington. April 20.
1846.

My dear Gladstone,

This letter needs no answer unless you like to give one.

But I feel unwilling not to comply with the request of the writer of the
inclosed. It is from Mr. Blunt of the Colonial Office,^a who is in some
apprehensions of changes in the Office which may unfavourably affect
him. I send his letter as the best way of letting him speak for himself. What
I have known of him, long ago in my old Downing Street days, has left a
kindly recollection on my mind which is strengthened by the memory of
his brothers personal excellence.

I have a delicacy in speaking to you on these things, for I have a general
'religio'^b about the exercise of all administrative functions to which I am
not personally related.

Believe me
Yours aff[ectionate]ly
H. E. Manning

The Right Hon[oura]ble
W. E. Gladstone

---

^a Not located. Gladstone's note on the letter reads: 'Mr. Blunt has no cause for alarm.
I have written to him to say so Ap[ril] 21. done.' Gladstone wrote to Samuel Jasper Blunt
the following day, 21 April 1846, from 13 Carlton House Terrace: 'I have learned through
Archdeacon Manning that you are apprehensive of such changes in the Colonial Office as
may injuriously affect your interests', and assured him that such were not the case (BL Add.
MS 44528, 38; *GD* iii. 532). In his listing of letters received Gladstone notes under 20 April
1846 a letter from Manning, 'Mr Blunt C[olonial] O[ffice]' (BL Add. MS 44556, 50^v–51^r).
^b Piety.

P.S. Did I tell you that I shall be, please God, at 78 Eaton Square[c] on Monday next?

HEM

[[BL Add. MS 44247, 311]]

[[On 26 April 1846, Gladstone 'read Manning's ninth sermon to Lady L[yttelton] and C[atherine]' (*GD* iii. 533), but he did not meet with Manning until 1 May from 10 to 12.30 a.m. (ibid. 534). On 12 May, Gladstone visited the B[isho]p of Exeter and 'stated my general view of Church & State Policy for the time to come in wh[ich] he was disposed to concur' (ibid. 537). At some point during this time Gladstone read Manning's *Christ's Presence. The Support of Faith. A Sermon Preached at the Foundling Hospital, On Sunday, May 3, 1846* (London: John W. Parker, 1846).[d]]]

460612mg

Lavington. Petworth
June 12. 1846.

My dear Gladstone,

I write you a few words to say that I hope to be at 78 Eaton Square tomorrow.

Sunday morning I shall be at Kings College, & late in the Ev[enin]g out of London if you are free between whiles that is to say from 2 to 5, I should be able to come to C[arlton] H[ouse] T[errace].[a] A line by your Secretary aye or no will suffice me.

I have been thinking much of you: though other things & these heavy in my own family have been my chief thought of late.

There is I suppose no doubt of the majority against Government. And that will whip the top, & make it go faster than ever. If the Opposition come in all Church questions will be precipitated many years in advance. And, I believe, the Protectionists are quite ready to transfer the Clergy from the Rent Charge to the Consolidated Fund.[b]

If public events bring on great changes of this kind from without before we have prepared the Church spiritually more maturely, & extensively than at present from within, there is no hope of holding long together. And

---

[c] Manning resided at 78 Eaton Square regularly in the spring and summer of 1846, during April and early May (see Manning to his tailor, 31 March 1846 [Pitts]), in June and July on preaching assignments (see Manning to Revd W. H. Brookfield, 12 June 1846 and 23 June 1848 [Pitts]).

[d] Gladstone's slightly annotated copy is preserved in SDL F 25/ Mann 2e.

[a] Gladstone was able to meet with Manning 'on Church matters' on Sunday, 14 June 1846 (*GD* iii. 544).

[b] See *The Times*, 15 April 1846, 6d, on the protectionist landlords at Northfleet on refusal of the rate.

when we remember that all real and extensive spiritual unity must descend from the Episcopate, & that an united one, I can only shelter myself by shutting my eyes, & hoping. I remember trying to believe that the ruin hanging over my dear Fathers house would never descend, but it did come.

Believe me,

My dear Gladstone,

Ever yours aff[ectionate]ly

H. E. Manning

The Right Hon[oura]ble

W. E. Gladstone

[[Pitts; Chapeau, 131, 201]]

[[On 12 July 1846, Gladstone read 'Manning aloud at night prayers' (*GD* iii. 537). On 29 June, he wrote to Badeley from the Colonial Office:

Manning intimated to me that he was busied in some manner about a Tasmanian College and wished to send me something —I said 'be quick' or something to that effect.

But it would not be possible for me to take any official step upon the paper you have transmitted, without knowing from whom it comes, and in what capacity those act who send it—I wonder he did not perceive.

Of course there is no step other than official that could be of any advantage.

I do not know where he is or I w[oul]d send the paper to him—as it is I can only return it that you may send it to him or some other person who can act on behalf of the promoters. (Morley transcript)

The Butler v. Purcell trial records indicate that Gladstone also wrote to Manning on 29 June.[c]]]

ADDENDUM TO SECTION VI

Manning on Newman's *Development*: December 1845

451230mw

[30 December 1845]

...Now about better things—if I can call Newman's Book Good. It seems to me a wonderful intellectual work, sceptical in one sense, as all estimates of evidence must be, e.g. It is most probable that the world was created as it is is less so that it was self-made, or is eternal. I am not sure that it is more sceptical really than Butler for all conviction rests on a

---

[c] Among the Gladstone Tracts at NLW is an unannotated copy of Henry Edward Manning, *The Work of the Comforter: A Sermon in Behalf of the King's College Hospital, Preached in the Chapel of the College, on Sunday, June 14, 1846* (London: John W. Parker, 1846), SDL, GTM/ F 183/9, that he may have read at this time.

balance of *intellectual* reasons, apart from the spiritual consciousness. The infallibility of Truth, whether in the Church or the Scriptures rests on moral i.e. scientific imperfect evidence. And yet it is the highest source of conviction.

Still Newman's mind is subtil even to excess & to us seems certainly sceptical.

After reading the book, I am left where I was found by it.

I do not believe in the fact of development in the Roman & Lutheran sense for they are both alike with the advantage on the Roman side.

I believe

1. that the Faith was perfected 'uno afflatu' by the Inspiration of the Apostles.[a]

2. that it has existed *ideally* perfect in the illuminated reason of the Church from then till now.

3. that development as in the Creeds has been logical, & virtual, not ideal or *conceptual*.

4. that the spiritual perceptions of the Church thro' contemplation & devotion have become more *intense* but always within the same focus.

5. that the facts, and documents of Revelation have been *codified*, harmonized, distributed, & cast into a scientific order, capable of scientific expression.

But that the omer of Manna (as S[t]. Irenaeus says of the Regula Fidei) is in quantity unchanged.[b] 'He that gathereth much hath nothing over, &c.' [Exod. 16: 18; 2 Cor. 8: 15].

---

[a] Note the shift in this regard from Manning's position in his *The Unity of the Church* (London: John Murray, 1842), 119:

We must remember, then, that the point is not to be decided by quoting the first acts of the apostles, immediately after our Lord's ascension, when they were on the threshold of their ministry. He that searches for dogmatic proofs (for the co-optation of Matthias is a practical one) of the apostolical succession at the time the Apostles were only themselves succeeding to the sole apostolate of our Lord, must have a mind strangely exacting, or eccentric in its reasoning process: or he that looks to find from the beginning of the Gospel an entire hierarchy, with all its supplements and complements of order and office, must have a mind as strangely unskilled in the analogies of God's works. The notion that the Church was perfected in all its organic parts, *uno apostolorum afflatu*, by the first breath of St. Peter and the Apostles, has no foundation in the testimony either of inspired or uninspired history. On the contrary, not only the analogy of all God's inanimate and animate works, but also His earlier dispensations, would lead us beforehand to look for what in Holy Scripture we find.

[b] Irenaeus, *Against the Heresies*, 1. 9. 4 refers to the canon of faith as unchangeable.

I have very slightly touched on this in my last University Sermon.[c] Tell me what you say of it.

I hope it will hold: for if not I do not see the end.

Is it not strange that the Lutherans, & Lutheranizers οἵ τότε καὶ οἵ [νέοι] νῦν[d] hold a development? Is it not the refuge for the destitute who can find no shelter in antiquity?

Have you seen Trench's Hulsean Lectures?[e] It is a delightful book earnest stirring, & eloquent with a fine masculine imagination. But his theory of development is to me fatal. It seems to me as if the thought of the Regula Fidei, & the tradition of dogma, & the whole oral confession of the Faith seldom if ever crossed his mind. It is Scripture & the Student: & the internal needs of mans spirit developing Scripture by demands upon it. There are more true things put in an untenable way than in any recent book I have seen.

If there be such a principle of development at all Newman has it against him 1000 to 1. It is no good to say Lutheran developments are *in Scripture* & Roman not. It begs the question. And then—Quo judice?[f]

Certainly with me the Councils of the Church, even of the West, even in Trent as against the private spirit.

Now this brings me to our dear Brother. I am jealous of the influence of Maurice over him: & I am fearful in some points even of Trench's; high as it is for he is a noble fellow. But I found S[?] evidently full of Trench's theory of development: After sifting, for some time, he acquiesced in what I have stated above. Whether he enunciated this or that at Oxford I do not know. I love him very dearly &, as I am able, pray for him.

But let it pass only between our own minds, I feel that he is *afloat*, & I dread the direction he may be wafted in.

---

[c] See Manning's 'The Gift of Illumination', in his *Sermons Preached before the University of Oxford* (1844c), 151–81, in which there is an allusion to Irenaeus, *Against the Heresies*, 1. 9. 4 and a reference to 1. 10 on 156.

[d] Those of that day and those of this. Cf. Athanasius, *On the Dionysian Sentences*, 3: 'The Jews of that day and the new Jews of the present day', in *Select Treatises of S. Athanasius, Archbishop of Alexandria, in Controversy with the Arians*, trans. J. H. Newman with notes and indices, A Library of Fathers of the Holy Catholic Church 8 and 19 (Oxford: J. H. Parker, 1842–4), 19. 391–2n.

[e] Richard Chenevix Trench, *The Fitness of Holy Scripture for Unfolding the Spiritual Life of Man: Being the Hulsean Lectures for the Year M. DCCC. XLV* (Cambridge: Macmillan, Barclay, & MacMillan, 1845).

[f] By what judge?

I say this because I feel for myself that nothing but a deep & solid foundation such as the Catholic Ch[urch] has laid (as in St. Thomas ag[ainst] Melchior Cano, &c) can help a man from intellectual uncertainty & fluctuation. So it is with me. I have never found rest for my foot till I began to see the foundation of Systematic Theology: and I feel appalled at the thought how little I *know* i.e. in its *principles*.

To come back to N[ewman]'s book. There are some things wh[ich] go before all arguments—e.g. the Invocation of God alone—& some that survive all objections—e.g. the reality of the English Church: and these come through the book unhurt....

[[Bodl. MS Eng. lett. c. 655, 33–7]]

ENDNOTES TO SECTION VI

1. such] Chapeau: each
2. work] Chapeau: works
3. as] Chapeau omits
4. Hardly] Leslie: not
5. Parts] Leslie: points
6. which] overscored
7. tear] corrected from illegible word
8. wonderful . . . book] inserted
9. But] overscored
10. natural & ordinary] inserted
11. if] inserted
12. in town] inserted
13. mind or body] inserted
14. for the . . . named] inserted
15. with] inserted
16. with] inserted
17. especially] inserted, replacing overscored: chiefly
18. an] inserted, replacing overscored: the
19. in] inserted, replacing overscored: of
20. the] overscored
21. Prayer . . . aspirations] inserted
22. last] inserted
23. I need . . . *possible*] inserted
24. the] inserted, replacing overscored: you
25. direct it] Chapeau: send direct
26. *originally*: referring
27. late] overscored
28. &] Chapeau omits

29. numbers] Chapeau; number
30. Bellasis] Morley: Bellairs
31. governments] Morley: government
32. than] overscored
33. than] inserted, replacing overscored: of
34. common & secular] inserted
35. illegible word overscored
36. will] inserted
37. & all . . . capitular] inserted
38. Church-like] inserted
39. here] inserted
40. general] inserted
41. match its te] overscored
42. or] overscored
43. of] Chapeau: or
44. serving] Chapeau: saving
45. & . . . belong] inserted
46. responsibility] inserted, replacing overscored: judgment
47. or] Chapeau: &
48. in substance] inserted
49. first] inserted
50. this] corrected from their
51. surely] written over: shortly
52. though] inserted
53. of the question] inserted
54. *Establishment*] inserted
55. (if . . . die)] inserted
56. w] overscored
57. 'some] inserted

SECTION VII

Charting New Directions

1. 'From Oxford to Rome': August 1846–August 1847

460814gm[a]

Fasque Aug[ust] 14. 1846.

My dear Manning

We arrived here from Hawarden the night before last,[b] and I write to perform the unwelcome duty of apprising you that my Father's Chapel will not be ready for consecration for the next two months, at the earliest: we fear indeed it may not be ready during the present year.[c] It was but fair that I should make this known to you, as the Consecration was the bait which we held out to you, and undoubtedly your presence *then* would be of an especial value. But it will be most welcome to my Father and to us if you are disposed to take us as we are—and all times are equally suitable so far as we are concerned. My wife and I expect to remain here until the winter.

I have heard nothing of late about the notion of a gathering to lay the first stone of the Chapel at Trinity College. That subject was left altogether in Wordsworth's hands[d] and you probably may be better informed of his movements than I am. I only wait, ready to attend if summoned.

---

[a] 'Wrote to Manning' (*GD* iii. 565).

[b] On 12 August 1846 the Gladstones arrived from Glasgow: 'Children very lively. Went to see the Chapel with my Father' (ibid.).

[c] Reference is to the chapel on the Gladstone estate at Fasque. It opened 18 October 1846. See 461207gm.

[d] The ceremony took place at 2.00 p.m. at Glenalmond on 8 September 1846 (*GD* iii. 570). Christopher Wordsworth delivered an opening address and assisted in laying the first stone for the Chapel of the 'Scotch College' project undertaken earlier by Gladstone and Hope. Among others, Bishops Skinner of Aberdeen and Moir of Brehen were also present at the ceremony (Wordsworth, *Annals* [1893], 317). See below 460831gm. A circular for Trinity College, Glenalmond, Perthshire, was issued July 1846 requesting subscriptions (BL Add. MS 44796, 22). For clippings and circulars regarding the College see SDL, Gladstone–Glynne MSS 1362 and 1672.

I suppose however W[ordsworth] will come to Scotland in the first week of Sept[embe]r because the Bishops hold their Synod at that time in Edinburgh.[e]

Barring sugar, in regard to which however the new Gov[ernmen]t have only done what we were bound to expect from them, I think they have made a good start.[f] Indeed if their aspect shall remain for another twelve month as Conservative as it now is we shall see the radical party fall away from them and they must depend upon the support of former opponents. For my own part neither approving of their former conduct as a Government, nor of the *manner* in which they recently obtained power, I could not profess to have confidence in them; but on the other hand I am not dissatisfied with what has appeared of their general views and intentions, and the only subject of *immediate* moment on which I feel any apprehension is their disposal of Church patronage. I see no indication as yet of anything but sobriety in the Foreign and Colonial Offices, in which more than in any other departments fears of a disposition to extravagate might have been entertained—

Believe me always
Affectionately yours
W. E. Gladstone

Venerable
Archdeacon Manning

Your Charge[g] has come to my house: (many thanks) not yet to my hand—

[[BL Add. MS 44247, 312–13; Morley transcript]]

---

[e] See Gladstone's letter to Wordsworth of 16 June 1846, inviting the latter's presence in the first week in September 'when the Episcopal Synod is held' (Lambeth Palace MS 1823, 94–5, 95).

[f] On the collapse of the Peel ministry in June,1846, Lord John Russell formed a government on 6 July and was able to pass legislation on sugar duties before the close of the session in August, eliminating the distinction between foreign free-grown and slave-grown sugar and reducing the duties on both. For details see Hansard, lxxxviii. 99 (27 July 1846) and Spencer Walpole, *The Life of Lord John Russell* (2 vols.; London: Longmans, Green, 1889), i. 429–30.

[g] Henry Edward Manning, *A Charge Delivered at the Ordinary Visitation of the Archdeaconry of Chichester in July, 1846* (London: John Murray, 1846). Gladstone's annotated copy is preserved in SDL, F25Man2e.

460828mg

Lavington
Aug[ust] 28. 1846.

My dear Gladstone,

The very thought of throwing off the South & all its cares and troubles,[1] & coming to Scotland makes my heart beat:[a] but I fear that it is impossible. Yet I will not give up the hope for ten days, during which I am fixed here. After that I shall see my way more clearly but I am as good as hopeless about it. Do not think of me or change any plan or purpose lest I should fail after all. It would be a great pleasure to me for I have never been over the border.

I am glad to see what you say of the Gov[ernmen]t. Lord John Russells statements have seemed to me to be very well & wisely conceived: and so far as I am able to speak, I should think he is likely to be a valuable minister, in political matters properly so called.

As to the Church I have so much greater fear for it from itself that I do not much think of the Gov[ernmen]t. You have often said that year by year there is an increase of personal religion & a decrease of the Ecclesiastical principle in Parliament. I seem to see the same in the Church. There is an increase of real devotion in individuals, but a decrease of *corporate* improvement. I have a fear amounting to a belief that the Church of England must split asunder, the 'diversa et adversa sentientes'[b] must be absorbed by a higher unity or parted. Absorption seems impossible: and the passive traditions of the Established Church are broken as green withs.[c]

With my love to Mrs. Gladstone & your children, believe me,
Always your affectionately
H. E. Manning

Pray offer my compliments, & kind regards to your Father.[2]

The Right Hon[oura]ble

W. E. Gladstone[3]

[[Pitts; Chapeau, 132, 202]]

---

[a] In his annotations to Purcell's biography, note Gladstone's 'ma' to Purcell's comment that Manning had little interest in 'the ancient glories of the Catholic Church in Scotland' (PurGl i. 289).

[b] Those sensing diverse and adverse things. Augustine, *On the City of God*, 18. 51. 1 (PL 41. 613): 'philosophos inter se diversa et adversa sentientes' (philosophers, sensing among themselves diverse and adverse things). Cf. ibid. 18. 41. 2 (PL 41. 601): 'qui diversa et adversa senserunt' (who sense diverse and adverse things), and *On True Religion* 1. 1. 1 (PL 34. 102).

[c] Cf. Judg. 16: 7: 'And Samson said [to Delilah], if they bind me with seven green withs [bowstrings] . . . Then shall I be weak.' Manning outlined his fears for the Church of England in greater detail in his personal diaries at the time. Compare his comments in this letter and Gladstone's reactions in 460831gm with the diary entries of August 1846, where he lists the organic and functional problems with the Church of England (Purcell, i. 483).

460831gm[a]

PRIVATE

Fasque Fettercairn
Aug[ust] 31. [18]46.

My dear Manning

I write to tell you that the foundation stone of the Chapel of Trinity
College is to be laid on the 8th of September.[b] I do not know however
whether this inducement could bring you to undertake so long a journey.
So far as we are concerned I should at any time be glad to see you on a visit
to my Father—but it is only fair to you to state that there is a reason the
other way, I mean the presence of my poor sister in the house,[c] whose
change of religious profession combined with some other points of character make it a delicate matter for clergymen in your position to manage
common intercourse with her. I am not sure however that she will be here
ten days or a fortnight hence.

There is another passage in your letter that makes me write. 'I have a
fear amounting to a belief that the Church of England must split asunder.'
Now I will not dwell on my own strong conviction the other way though
nothing can be more firm in my mind than the opposite idea that the
Church of England has not been marked off this way & that way for
naught, that she will live through her struggles, and that she has a *great*
providential destiny before her—I will say little in the way of argument.
But recollect that for a century and a half (a much longer period than any
for which the puritanical, or individual, and the Catholic principles have
been in conflict *within* the Church of England) Jansenists[d] and antiJanse-
nists dwelt and propagated themselves within the Church of Rome, with
the unity of wolf and lamb:[e] their differences[4] were not absorbed by the
force of the Church: they were in full vigour when the French Revolution
burst upon them both and when the breach between the nation and the
Church was so wide that the separation between them became insignificant, & the subsequent hostility of State and Church caused ultimately the

---

  [a] 'Wrote to Manning' (*GD* iii. 569).

  [b] See 460814gm.

  [c] Helen Gladstone was still at Fasque on 24 September 1846 (*GD* iii. 573), but had left by
5 October when Gladstone wrote to her (ibid. 575). She returned 1 December (ibid. 586).

  [d] The Roman Catholic theological school originating with Cornelius Jansen (1510–76),
emphasizing human depravity.

  [e] Cf. Isa. 11: 6 and 65: 25.

fusion together of the two sections.—But I will more rely on reminding you that your present impressions are entirely at variance with those of six or seven months ago—I begin now to think that on a matter of magnitude I cannot differ from you: so I have the most immediate interest in your opinion as I have a presentiment of its proving to be mine too if it be indeed yours—hence this intolerance on my part—

Our Chapel thank God will we trust[5] be opened though not consecrated in October[f]—we want a temporary clergyman for three months. Do you happen to know of any available person? Your aff[ectiona]te friend

W. E. Gladstone

Ven[erable] Archdeacon Manning

[[BL Add. MS 44247, 314–15; Morley transcript; Lathbury, i. 352–3; Purcell, i. 317; Cf. Morley, i. 325, Chapeau, 319]]

[[Gladstone 'read Manning's Charge' on 27 September 1846 (*GD* iii. 574).]]

461201mg

Lavington Petworth
Dec[ember] 1. 1846.

My dear Gladstone,

In my last letter I promised to write to you again in a certain time: and with a full recollection of that promise I have failed to do so. It is, however, I hope, & believe, the first time I have broken my word with you. I have no excuse to offer.[6] After writing to you I left home, and the subjects we stirred in our last letters were great, and grew by delay, & I felt less inclined to try the impossible feat of conjuring them into a letter: the times of the Genii, or as Mr. Lane will have it, the Jinns being past.[a]

This being so I leave myself at your mercy, seeming to have said contradictory things at the two ends of the same six months. Not that I confess it any more than Aneas Sylvius did when he was made Pope.[b]

---

[f] The Chapel was opened 18 October 1846. See 461207gm.

[a] Edward William Lane, *An Account of the Manners and Customs of the Egyptians, Written in Egypt during the Years 1833, -34 and -35* (2 vols.; London: Charles Knight, 1836), 283–90.

[b] Aeneas Sylvius (1405–64), Italian humanist, conciliar and papal negotiator, was elected Pope as Pius II, 1458. In his Bull, *Execrabilis*, 1460, he defended papal authority, rejecting his earlier conciliar theories, and several years later wrote in another Bull, *In minoribus agentes*, 1463: 'Aeneam rejicite, Pium recipite' (You reject Aeneas, you accept Pius), *Bullarum diplomatum et privilegiorum sanctorum Romanorum pontificum Taurinensis editio: locupletior facta collectione novissima plurium brevium, epistolarum, decretorum actorumque S. Sedis a S. Leone Magno usque ad praesens cura et studio collegii adlecti Romae virorum s. theologiae et ss. canonum peritorum quam*

Let me enter one plea.

Speaking *politically*, as we did last winter, I think the Church of England in its present status will see out our day. This I said in bar of your supposing the public life of a Churchman might determine in a few years.

Speaking *theologically*, & of the interior life of this Church I seem to see a visible increase in the activity & antagonism of two irreconcilable elements in laity, Priesthood, & Episcopate.

I cannot maintain the thesis that this contradiction is in the region of *opinion* distinct from *Faith*. Nor[7] that it is speculative so much as Ethical.

Therefore my way from between your horns is this. Our Ecclesiastical, & social Church system has duration in it, but our theological & spiritual activities (as Garbett w[oul]d say[c]) are disengaging themselves rapidly.

Now as you are strong be merciful.

I could go on writing on a multitude of points theoretical & practical as of the See of Manchester,[d] & Hooks letter,[e] or of the Queens arrival today

---

ss. d. n. Pius papa IX apostolica benedictione erexit auspicante emo ac revmo dno S. R. E. cardinali Francisco Gaude. T. 5, A Eugenio IV (an. MCCCCXXXI) ad Leonem X (an. MDXXI) (Turin: S. Franco, H. Fory, & H. Dalmazzo, 1860), v. 149–50 (*Execrabilis*), 175 (Aeneam rejicite . . .). Note the discussion of *In melioribus agentes* in John Henry Newman, *Lectures on the Prophetical Office of the Church, Viewed Relatively to Romanism and Popular Protestantism* (London: J. G. & F. Rivington, 1837), 7, 14, and appendix to the chapter.

[c] The distinction between the theological and spiritual or religious dimensions of Tractarianism was made by Garbett as early as his Bampton lectures. See James Garbett, *Christ, as Prophet, Priest, and King: Being a Vindication of the Church of England from Theological Novelties, in Eight Lectures Preached before the University of Oxford, at Canon Bampton's Lecture, in the Year MDCCCXLII* (2 vols.; Oxford: Hatchard & Son, 1842), pp. xff. where he reverences Tractarians' 'piety' but notes their theological differences from the Church of England.

[d] See 'A Bill to enable Her Majesty to make certain Provisions for preventing the Union of the Sees of St. Asaph and Bangor, and for the Appointment of a Bishop of Manchester' (PP 1846 [522.] i. 25; 24 July 1846). On Gladstone's later comments on the issue see his letter to Graham, 21 July 1843 (Lathbury, i. 75–9).

[e] Walter Farquahar Hook, *On the Means of Rendering more Efficient the Education of the People: A Letter to the Lord Bishop of St. David's* (London: John Murray, 1846). See *Christian Rembrancer* 12 (Oct. 1846), 377, 411 (Gladstone was reading this on Sunday, 11 Oct. [*GD* iii. 576]) and a review of Hook in *English Review* 6 (Sept. 1846), 127. See reprint: *The English Review on Dr. Hook's Letter. An Article Reprinted from the English Review No. XI. On a Letter of the Rev. W. F. Hook, D.D. to the Lord Bishop of St. David's, 'On the Means of Rendering More Efficient the Education of the People'* (London: Francis & John Rivington, 1847), which Gladstone was reading on Sunday, 18 October (*GD* iii. 578). On 29 July 1846 a letter to *The Guardian* (217) expressed relief at recent comments by Lord John Russell which indicated the Government was moving away from Hook's proposal to move education more directly under secular control.

at Arundel,[f] & a Tithe Dinner which is routing my house out, but I will do no more than send my kindest regards to your wife, and my love to my Godson[g]—

When do you come to London?

Believe me,
Ever yours affec[tionate]ly
H. E. Manning

The Right Hon[oura]ble
W. E. Gladstone
[[Pitts; Chapeau, 133, 202–3]]

461207gm[a]

Fasque Fettercairn
Dec[ember] 7. 1846.

My dear Manning

The movement of our correspondence is so slow 'Che la memoria retro non può ire'.[b] Not that this is matter of blame to you or even to me, but it appertains to the nature of the thing itself, which is rather a continuous effort at shaping our thoughts upon subject matter itself[8] modified from day to day. But now in regard to the theological conflict in[9] the Church of England I surely have no difference of opinion from you, whether or not the quantity of misgiving in[10] your mind and in mine may or may not be exactly the same. I will however turn off into a new course of expression. It seems to me that there are two systems in the Church of England, which are vitally opposed, and which if equally developed could not subsist together in the same sphere. Were the puritanical doctrines the basis of our Episcopal and collegiate teaching generally, or (short of generally yet) extensively and habitually, the Church of England must either split or become heretical. But we have these two things 1. Episcopal Chairs, 2. Colleges, and also we have[11] 3. a Theology—whatever straightness or[12] ambiguity or other imperfection may attach to these, or any of them, the basis of them upon the whole is plainly antipuritanical and what we should call Catholic, and the puritanical or anticatholic ideas among us are

---

[f] On the visit see *The Times*, 30 November 1846, 5d, 1 December, 4f, 2 December, 5a, 3 December, 5b, 4 December, 5b, and 5 December, 5a.

[g] William Henry Gladstone (1840–91). See 400604gm.

[a] 'Wrote to Manning' (*GD* iii. 587).

[b] That the memory is not able to follow it (Dante, *Paradisio*, 1. 9).

generally[13] the ideas of individuals scarcely having a succession but reproduced here and there, not small in their aggregate but characteristically distinguished from the other system in this that not these but their opposite lie at the *root* of our known divinity, of our Episcopal teaching, and of our Colleges or normal schools of theology. Now it seems to me that if ever the doctrine of the 'Protestant declaration' should make good its ground among us in such a sense as that any man can colourably say this is the authoritative[14] system of the English Church—*then* we are at our crisis, and must either separate or sink. But the conflict may go on as now, and with a progressive advance of the good principle against the bad one—this, it is indisputable, has been on the whole the course of things during our lifetimes—and to judge from present signs it is the will of God that it should so continue.

The juxtaposition of Jansenism with the antagonist power in the Roman Church offers an analogy to the conflict among us: but a more true analogy I think may be found by taking on their side, as with ourselves, first the life of the Church, and then the disease which gnaws & corrodes it—with them this is the superstition and idolatry which I must say abide among them as puritanism abides among us, and with at the least as much of continence from authority. I take (*pace* Ward) the Psalter of Bonaventura to witness:[c] or my friend whom I heard at Naples: and of whose Sermon Dr. Döllinger[d] said to me, that on that side of the Alps he would have been suspended for it.—Now of course this is a mere *sbbozzo*,[e] which perhaps you may translate botch: but at least[15] I hope to profit, in the course of time, by your thoughts upon it: it must in some form be familiar to your mind.

[c] See Robert King, *The Psalter of the Blessed Virgin Mary Illustrated: or a Critical Disquisition and Enquiry Concerning the Genuineness of the Parody on the Psalms of David, Commonly Ascribed to St. Bonaventure* (Dublin: Grant & Bolton, 1840), which opposes Bonaventure's authorship of the work and the work itself as supporting idolatrous devotional practices, in contrast to Ward's praise of Roman Catholic books of devotion throughout the *Ideal*. Cf. his positive references to the meditations in *The Life of Jesus* by Bonaventure in the *Ideal*, 299, 393, and particularly, 455, and note Oakeley's edition and translation, *The Life of our Lord and Saviour Jesus Christ, from the Latin of St. Bonaventure Newly Translated for the Use of Members of the Church of England* (London, 1844), which Gladstone was reading on 16 June 1844 (*GD* iii. 382). Cf. Galloway (199), 143–6.

[d] On the conversation between the two men regarding the matter see Addenda to this Section. Note also that Gladstone began reading Döllinger's *Lehrbuch der Kirchengeschichte* (2nd edn.; 2 vols.; Regensburg: G. Joseph Manz, 1843) on 25 October 1846 and continued through 20 December of that year (*GD* iii. 579–89). Cf. 340505gm and Erb (1997).

[e] [*Sic*] sketch.

In October we visited Hope at his place (rented from his brother),[16] Rankeillour, in Fife: and he has lately been here[f]—he is going to build houses at St. Andrew's in conjunction with my Father.[g] His mind I think is quiet, and I look upon him as[17] practically fixed, *rebus sic stantibus*.[h] This is a great mercy: what there is still to pray for is that his ancient interest in the fortunes of the Church may be fully rekindled and his knowledge and ability applied to the task of working out and improving his system according to its best capacities.

My Father's Chapel was opened on the 18th of October,[i] and has been a great object of interest to us as well as we should hope something more. For a temporary pastor we have Mr. Teed from Lewes, your co-archdeaconry.[j]

---

[f] Gladstone and Catherine travelled to Rankeillour, near Cupar in Fife, on 30 September 1846. Hope rented the home from his brother, G. W. Hope, in 1845 and lived there with his sister, Frances, until 1847 (*GD* iii. 574). The Gladstones stayed for a week, to 7 October (ibid. 575). The Hopes visited the Gladstones at Fasque from 25 November to 1 December (ibid. 585–6).

[g] Gladstone discussed details related to the inheritance of the property on 2 November 1846 (ibid. 580–1; cf. Checkland, 342).

[h] Things standing as they are (Latin commonplace; as used in the 1580 *explanatio* of Pope Gregory XIII, suspending the earlier decree of excommunication against Elizabeth I and indicating that English Catholics were not required to act on the sentence of deposition against her 'as things now stand', the phrase came to be understood by English non-Catholics, particularly after the Gunpowder Plot of 1605, as marking Catholic duplicity. For details see Carrafiello [1994].) On 5 October 1846 Gladstone 'Rode to Falkland', some five miles from Rankeillour. There he held a conversation with Hope. 'C[atherine] had also a conversation with James Hope, wh[ich] with other symptoms, is very reassuring, & affords the liveliest cause for thankfulness to God' (ibid. 575). Note earlier references to Hope in 431028gm, 450118gm, 460419gm. On 23 April 1846 he spoke to Newman of 'desiring *some* termination to my present doubts; but whether in the direction you would think right, or by a return to Anglicanism, is the question'. Hope continued to fluctuate on the matter throughout the year and increasingly avoided discussion of the issue, even with his family (see Ornsby, ii. 84–5). See also 470514gm and 480120mg; see also the comment on Hope in 480312gm. On Hope's death (29 Apr. 1873) Gladstone wrote a memorial to his daughter on her father's life as Gladstone recalled it, forgetting it seems these indicators of Hope's concerns at the time and his future religious commitments (see Ornsby, ii. 284–98).

[i] The chapel was opened at 11.00 a.m. on 18 October 1846 (*GD* iii. 577–8).

[j] Frederick Teed (1810–63), was educated at Jesus College, Cambridge, ordained in 1839, and served as rector of St Michael's, Lewes, Sussex from 1841, before serving Fasque, 1846–7, and Broughty Ferry, 1849–51, returning to St Michael's in 1851 (Bertie, 459). Gladstone's father wished to keep the Chapel open longer than the initial three months intended, it seems (*GD* iii. 583 [16 Nov.1846]), but there were some troubles regarding this with Teed (ibid. 586 [3 Dec.]). The matter appears to have been settled on 5 December.

He is a very good man and good preacher. My Father wants him to print his Sermons.[k] Next June the Chapel is to be consecrated and a *Scottish* incumbent, not yet in orders is to have it.[l]

May every blessing of God attend you at this & all seasons.

Your aff[ectiona]te friend

W. E. Gladstone

My wife & children all well—we propose to stay here till Christmas, then to Yorkshire, headquarters Escrick, York.[m]

Ven[erable] Archdeacon Manning

[[BL Add. MS 44247, 316–19; Morley transcript; Lathbury, i. 353–5; cf. Morley, i. 325, Chapeau, 320]]

[[On Sunday, 7 March 1847 Gladstone read 'Manning's Tract on Lent to C[atherine]'[n] (*GD* iii. 605).]]

---

[k] On 6 December 1846, the day before Gladstone wrote this letter to Manning, he 'read one of Mr. Teed's Sermons to my Father, who was moved to tears' (ibid. 587; see also 27 December [ibid. 591]).

[l] Donald A. Irvine (d. 1852) was ordained in 1847 and served Fasque to his death (Bertie, 310). Gladstone engaged Irvine as a tutor for his son, William, on 24 August 1846 (*GD* iii. 567). On 5 December 1846, Gladstone wrote to Teed and the agreement for Irvine to serve as incumbent at the Fasque Chapel appears to have been made: 'All settled finally, by C[atherine], under God's assistance; for another quarter from Jan[uar]y, the voice of prayer is solemnly to ascend.... Conv[ersation] with Mr. Irvine' (ibid. 586). Gladstone did not arrive at Fasque until the following 7 July 1847 and immediately visited Irvine (8 July). On 11 July, his first Sunday at Fasque, he commented positively on Irvine's preaching (ibid. 633). On the consecration on 28 August see 470421gm.

[m] The Gladstones travelled to Escrick, 7 miles south-east of York on 29 and 30 December 1846. Escrick was the home of Beilby Richard Lawly (1818–80) and Elizabeth Grosvenor (1824–99), Lord and Lady Wenlock (see ibid. 49).

[n] That is, Manning's *What One Work of Mercy Shall I Do This Lent: A Letter to a Friend* (London: James Burns, 1847; preface dated 9 Feb. 1847) in which he commented on the 'well-spread boards' and extravagance of many households in which a single person eats the equivalent of one-half the cost of maintaining a poor family (9–10). Gladstone's annotated copy is preserved in SDL, F25Man2e (cf. also the unannotated copy among the Gladstone Tracts at NLW [SDL, GTM/ F 170/ 13]). Note that Gladstone's reflections on the Manning text are here framed by the General Fast called for 24 March 1847. Discussion of the matter had been taken up in the House of Commons on 25 February 1847 (*The Times*, 26 February, 3b), continued regularly thereafter (*The Times*, 2 Mar., 3b; 3 Mar., 3c; 6 Mar., 3f; 11 Mar., 3c) and a general proclamation was announced in *The Times*, 13 March, 6c, and reprinted regularly with readers' comments thereafter.

470309gm[a]

Hagley Stourbridge
March 9. 1847

My dear Manning

I heard with great grief from the Bishop of Oxford last week that you had been very unwell.[b] It did not indeed surprise me for from the little I have seen of your habits with regard to subsistence I do not understand how your physical strength has been so long upheld for your common & daily labours. However he told me also that you were under the coersion of medical care, and before we parted I had the comfort of hearing from him that you were better according to an account he had just received.

I suppose that there is a region between high health on the one side and ill health on the other, which is the region proper to the exercise of abstinence: & that deviation either way should at once be marked & corrected. I mean that as high animal health shows that there is not abstinence in the proper sense, so the first appearance of ill health shows that we are approaching danger and incapacity for duty, and that this *first* appearance should be cared for and removed that we may be put back into a condition for duty. Is this right?

Since I came back here I have received your tract for Lent, and I feel about it as everybody else does. But I wish it could have had your name as though the authorship is known it is not notorious, & it is not so known as to recommend the tract through as wide a circle as it would otherwise have ranged over.[c] There is another question important at the present time:

---

[a] 'Wrote to . . . Manning' (*GD* iii. 605).

[b] On 3 March 1847 Gladstone and his wife visited the Duke of Rutland (Lord John Manners [1818–1906]; *DNB*) at Belvoir, 12 miles south of Newark. They attended the consecration of a church in nearby Woolsthorpe the next day, 4 March, and listened to sermons by the Bishops of Lincoln and of Oxford. On the same day Gladstone met Mary Elizabeth Herbert (1822–1911; she married Sidney Herbert in 1846 and was received into the Roman Catholic Church in 1866; *DNB*): 'She seems very warm & artless & deeply interested in religion. I had a very interesting conversation with the B[isho]p of Oxford. He is most loyal to Manning: . . . He thinks Lady G. Fullerton is the writer of 'From Oxford to Rome'—I cannot think so but it is like a woman' (*GD* iii. 604–5). Lady Georgiana Charlotte Fullerton (1812–85: *DNB*), a well-known Catholic novelist, was received into the Roman Catholic Church in 1846, three years after her husband. She was born Leveson-Gower, the sister of Granville George Leveson-Gower, 2nd Earl Granville, Gladstone's Foreign Secretary (on Granville see 660822mg).

[c] Manning's tract supports fasting and is signed 'H.E.M.' without any other ascription as to the author.

I mean that relating to the use of animal food. Persons seem now to suppose that to economise flour and bread is everything. No doubt it is the first & most important: and for this reason I do not suppose it is desirable to keep Lent by total abstinence from animal food. Nor indeed do I think it is a good mode generally, at least for persons not living very privately: because it attracts attention: and it is quite plain to me that restriction of the total quantity of food may be made, and is likely to be made, more effectual in the way of abstinence than an abstinence from animal food as such, which at most is no better than a contraction of quantity. It is worth however reflecting now, that if the attention of all the consumers of meat should be concentrated only[18] on the notion of economising flour, this would cause a greatly increased consumption of meat: by raising the price of meat it would directly stimulate the breeding & feeding of cattle, and would thereby tend greatly to diminish the aggregate quantity of food available for man; because there is I believe no doubt that we might have a much larger *total* of subsistence from the earth if we consumed no animal food. These considerations seem to become important, when we reflect that the present scarcity cannot well be temporary. Even if we have abundant crops of all kinds the quantity one may fear of unsold land in Ireland, and the exhaustion of stocks through the present pressure will keep food more or less[19] high at least until after the harvest of 1848. But again it is fearful to remember that our harvests usually move in cycles—that from 1842 to 1846 inclusive we have had no *bad* harvest— and that these are due to us now according to the usual cycles, a majority of bad harvests in the next three or four years. So that if we look at natural circumstances only they show the likelihood to be that of severe & continued pressure.

But it will not do to look at such circumstances either as sole or as principal agents. Here is a calamity most legibly divine: there is a total absence of such second causes as might tempt us to explain it away: it is the greatest horror of modern times, that in the richest age of the world, and in the richest country of that age, the people should be dying of famine by hundreds: and we, the English community, have scarcely as yet got even the subtlest notion of this horror in its aspect to us. No mere giving of money will do: it can only be met by national & personal humiliation. To have balls and operas for the distressed is bad and rotten in principle at all times, but at this time it seems like a judicial blindness, a defiance of the Divine wrath, a looking up into the very face of God and saying 'thou hast called us to weep and lo we laugh.'[d] How can the handwriting be made clear against us if it is not clear now? To give money is very well, to economise flour is very well: because these go *to* diminish the quantity of actual suffering, the external range of the evil, but they do not touch its root; we want the heavy hand of God lifted from off the land: & so long as we ourselves personally continue in our usual tone of thoughtless joyous or ambitious life we cannot be in a tone to ask or in a state to receive the boon. But I find I am preaching to you, of which I had not the remotest intention when I sat down to write. The question however for us is what shall we do when at the end of this week we resume our household cares in London. As to my servants I have put them on board wages, making them a small allowance *over* an account of the clearness of provisions. I can now exhort them vigorously to save and spare, and I am political economist enough to believe that it is a sound & sure way of relief to increase the quantity of food in the market by lessening what is taken out. As to ourselves we have some difficulty from the circumstance that my mother in law[e] will be with us, and, as she is an invalid & nervously so, will prevent our being quite as thrifty as we could be for ourselves alone. But the most difficult question is as to entertainments. I feel that not only in Lent but during the continuance of this visitation people ought if possible to be set free from every entertainment which is either of a gay & austentatious kind, or which causes waste of food. But the degree and manner in which this principle can be worked out I am not as yet clear about. I shall be very glad if at any time you can give me your thoughts and advice. There will be time to think for I hope the question will not arise in any serious form before Easter. We[20] have not however thought it expedient to adopt any *rule* of refusing all invitations through Lent: although we do not give them.

There are an hundred more subjects on which I should like to communicate with you. But I will only say that we hope to be in town on Saturday[f] —& that I trust you have seen & been interested in 'From Oxford to Rome',[g]

---

[d] Cf. Luke 6: 21, 25.

[e] Mary (Neville) Glynne (d. 1854).

[f] Gladstone arrived in London on Saturday, 13 March 1847 (*GD* iii. 606).

[g] *From Oxford to Rome: And How it Fared with Some who Lately Made the Journey* (London: Longman, Brown, Green, & Longmans, 1847; preface dated Christmas 1846). The novel was written by Elizabeth Furlong Shipton Harris (1822–52), a former member of Oakeley's congregation at Margaret Chapel, whom Oakeley had counselled to enter the Roman Catholic Church (Boase, i. 1347). The novel appeared in April 1847, and contained clear references to Oakelely personally, who was charged with hypocrisy. He defended himself and received an apology from the 'unknown author' of the book, in the pages of the *Church*

further (just for the sake of breaking my word) I was much interested in the B[isho]p of Oxford's conversation at Belvoir[h]—

Your aff[ectiona]te friend,
W. E. Gladstone

Venerable
H. E. Manning
[[BL Add. MS 44247, 320–3; Morley transcript; Lathbury, ii. 274–6; cf. Chapeau, 320]]

470312mg

Lavington. March 12. 1847

My dear Gladstone,

Many thanks for your kind letter which reached me yesterday. As you begin with no better subject than myself, though you confess you have a hundred, I will do the same, & then go to worthier matters.

I cannot hide from myself that I have been ill. But, by Gods mercy, it may be rather called an escape from illness. The cold this winter had tried me unusually, & at last fell on my throat & lungs: In the throat with a little beginning of inflammation, & on the lungs with a bad cough. I fully believe there is no mischief: but I am still shut up, and when set loose must think rather of some idler sky than of work. I say this to you & your wife but I am anxious not to make much of a little, or to frighten my dear Mother who is absent & always nervous: so I have made as light of it as possible. Indeed I may do so with truth, for the most I think is that I have become susceptible where till now I have been free from affection.

As to diet I am satisfied that my usual quantity is sufficient for me. Sometimes I suffer by change of[21] hours or other hindrances: but I could not increase it & be well.

In this light illness I have felt uneasy & afraid at the boundless comforts & blessings around me with Ireland at our side, and our own poor at our doors lest I should grow delicate & thankless. I know you do not forget me in your prayers, but you do not & cannot know how much I need them or they would be tenfold.

---

and State Gazette and *The Tablet* between June and September 1847 (see Galloway [1999], 224–6). Gladstone began reading the work on 13 February 1847 and completed it 15 February (*GD* iii. 600–1). The following day, 16 February, he began another Tractarian novel, *Margaret Percival* (London: Longman, Brown, Green, & Longmans, 1847) by the Tractarian novelist, Elizabeth Missing Sewell (1815–1906; *DNB*) (*GD* iii. 601).

[h] See note b above.

So much for what ought to have been less.

And now for your 'century of invention'.

I read with great regret what you wrote about the probable price of flour, & the prospects of our harvests: the more so because the same opinion, & fears had already reached me through the City.

At this moment the poor of this neighbourhood (no bad example) have had three or four hard months. Flour has risen from 8s. 8d. a bushel to 12s. that is nearly as 3 to 2, & wages from 10s to 11s. or at most from 10s. to 12s. The average is 11s. And yet there are people, aye & clergymen, who wont see the hardship they endure. I find (though I am thankful to say that my brother Priests about here began to stir well as early as November) some benevolent people the blindest. They relieve a little world like the English Pale[a] in Ireland, round about them, and believe that Geography & creation go no further.

But if this is true here what is it in other places. It makes ones heart sick. Every word you wrote of the visibly divine character of this chastisement goes to my conscience. What is to be done?

I believe that with all our undeniable moral virtues we are as a people the least sympathising and the most isolated. In one sense we are not selfish, but in another we are fearfully so. We have no Power or Type out of ourselves, by which our individual & national self may be chastened and subdued. The State is an expression of our corporate self. We make it & not it us. The Church—and here is the sting & the quick—is no longer an objective ἰδέα[b] pouring forth influences with power upon the springs of the individual will, & the unity of the national life. We *praise* the Church. What more can we expect? The belief of its sanctity, supremacy, & divine inspiration has departed from us and we know ourselves to be naked. But this leads further than a chance letter ought to carry us. I will therefore only say that I have the deepest convictions that the very first principles of the doctrine of Christ are out of course among us, that they can only be restored by restoring the ascendency of a divine idea, and that the ethical, practical, & religious activities of this land, & time are predominantly on the side of retarding if not rendering for ever impossible the reascendency of that divine idea. You can read my riddle. I mean (as what else can I) the Church of Christ as an object of Faith, love, and veneration. Far be it from us to limit the power, or the Mercy of God. He might say 'let there be light'[c]

---

[a] The area in which English law held jurisdiction.

[b] Idea, form.   [c] Gen. 1: 3.

and make the whole Catholic world to be one. But you & I are speaking as men of action, and dealing with visible powers & facts. I have no thought that the Divine Character of the Church in England will reappear & be confessed upon the basis of the past. And for the future every distinct & successful advance towards it, narrows the sphere within which the intense & therefore true idea is recognized, & loved.

In all this I do not at all cross what you wrote to me some months ago. Our system in theory is, I believe, organically sound: functionally it is disturbed to a fearful extent.

But I must let you go—even though I have not so much as begun upon the other subjects of your letter I mean the perplexities of life & society & the like. Neither have I so much as mentioned other matters on which I have been much engaged since last August.

I will like you virtuously refrain from all other matters but two.

One is Thompsons answer to Allies.[d] I never before understood your high[22] estimate of Thompson, but this book worthily explains it.

The other is the book 'From Oxford to Rome'. In secrecy, even from your wife, I may say that I know its history. A greater bubble was never blown. I have not yet seen it: but I know all the writers case.

With my love to your wife & children, & my blessing to my Godson, believe me,

Ever yours affectionately,
H. E. Manning

The Right Hon[oura]ble
W. E. Gladstone
[[Pitts; Chapeau, 134, 203–6]]

---

[d] Edward Healy Thompson, *The Unity of the Episcopate Considered, in Reply to the Work of Rev. T. W. Allies . . . Entitled, 'The Church of England Cleansed from the Charge of Schism, upon Testimonies and Councils of Fathers of the First Three Centuries'* (London: Thomas Richardson, 1847). Thomas William Allies (1813–1903) was educated at Wadham College, Oxford, where he was a Fellow, 1833–41. Thereafter he served for several years as chaplain to the Bishop of London and then as vicar of Launton in Oxfordshire. He was received into the Roman Catholic Church in 1850. A prolific author, he served as secretary of the Catholic Poor Schools Committee, 1853–90. For details see *DNB*, Allies (1924), and McClelland in McClelland (1996). Thompson (d. 1848; *DNB*) was educated at Emmanuel College, Cambridge and served in a number of curacies to 1846, when he was received into the Catholic Church.

470315gm[a]

13 C[arlton] H[ouse] T[errace]
March 15. [18]47.

My dear Manning

Forgive me for writing to you again on the subject of the book 'From Oxford to Rome'[b]—particularly as I shall give you a laugh or at least a smile at my credulity before I have done. I want you to tell me more, but only so much more as I think you can without any license as to confidence. I ask then, is it the work of a person of reputable character—who has gone from us to the Church of Rome—and who laments having so gone?

For if it is not, it is necessary for me speedily to undo an engagement into which I have entered—to review the book for the Quarterly: this in my turn I must beg you to keep secret. But I mention it to show that I am not inquiring for the gratification of curiosity.

On perusing the book I thought (and still think) it a work which contains much true eloquence, much deep feeling, some strong nervous writing, and the evidences of a charitable temper and dispassionate mind: also that it presented strong internal presumptions of genuineness not as to its particular facts but as to its being a record at least with respect to the writer of real and deep experience. I do not attempt you see to soften the reproach which from your emphatic statement seems to lie against me as a pretender to the office of a critic—Mr. Lockhart I should add is proceeding upon trust in me[c]—& I on the other hand am pledged to him. I think I have now

---

[a] 'Wrote to Manning' (*GD* iii. 607).

[b] Gladstone's review, '*From Oxford to Rome*', appeared in *Quarterly Review* 81 (June 1847), 131–66. Gladstone first took up the novel on 13 February 1847 and completed it two days later on 15 February. The following day he wrote to Longmans, the publisher, seeking information regarding the author (*GD* iii. 600–1). He began to reread *From Oxford to Rome* on 4 March (see 470309gm), continuing with it to 7 March (ibid. 605). On 10 March he 'Just began [to write] something on "from Oxford to Rome"' (ibid. 606). See Gladstone's notes BL Add. MS 44684 and 470421gm.

[c] Gladstone offered Lockhart a review on *From Oxford to Rome* on 16 February 1847:

I cannot resist the impulse which I feel to call your attention to a little book, with a not very promising title' 'From Oxford to Rome'...which I happened to *open* from the circumstances of its having been sent to me and to which having opened it I found myself rivetted. It purports to be the work of one who has abandoned the Church of England for the Church of Rome and who has discovered and bitterly laments his error, and seeks earnestly to deter others from the like, but yet has not returned to his former position. I am far from thinking this position (whether it represents actual case or not) well founded in reason: but the book appears likely to me to do great good, and also to attract deep interest. I think it one of the most eloquent and touching works I have read,

told you all that you should know in order to form a judgment upon my predicament in regard to it—& I hope that under the circumstances you will not think my request immoderate—

As to your general views I will only say that they are darker than mine at least as to our own beleaguered, & bewildered Church. It may be that she is destined to become more contracted in persons as she grows more comprehensive in principles—but she has a very high mission before her: and I am convinced from my inmost soul that whatever her difficulties may be her members have a position, if they will use it or if they will not, far more according to the laws and will of God than is given to our brethren in the Church of Rome. She has aimed a deadly blow at man in his freedom the absolute tho[23] not sole condition of his wellbeing.

Your aff[ectiona]te friend
W.E.G.

[[BL Add. MS 44247, 324–5; Morley transcript; cf. Chapeau, 321]]

470316mg

Lavington. March 16. 1847.

Confidential

My dear Gladstone,

I have so strong a moral feeling against even such disclosures as may be made without positive breach of right, that I regret I said as much as I did. Not that the knowledge of it is confined to me, but my responsibility is.

All that I feel I can say is that the person is so far as I know, of a respectable character, understanding that to mean free from moral stain.

Your other question whether the writer has 'gone from us to the Church of Rome' & 'laments having so gone' I cannot answer without first seeing

---

and one of the most passionate and comprehensive in its view of the unhappy course of things which it principally describes. Your experience and penetration would probably enable you at once to see into the book so far as regards the personality and position of the author.

Thereafter Gladstone indicated his conviction that the author wrote from experience and requested an answer from Lockhart regarding a *review* of the book, 'that becoming extensively known it may operate widely and powerfully as a warning both against similar changes, and against contracting those predispositions of which the changes are simply the ripeness' (NLS MS 1556, 144–5).

what the writer has published. I would confirm or not as I am able what I saw to be 'publici juris'[a]—but your words involve what may not be stated. Under a limitation they are true.[24]

I can only repeat what I said that the case is a bubble—& that no good will be done by putting it forward.

It is no example for either the English or the Roman Church.

This will not comfort a Critic committed to the Quarterly. And all that I w[oul]d say is that I sh[oul]d be sorry to see you use anything in the book otherwise than as an enunciation of what you proceed to prove aliunde.[b]

One thing in the end of your letter connects itself with something you said to me in Jan[uar]y last year.[c]

Do you by 'the blow at mans freedom' refer to confession? If so, I trust, you will pause before you put anything forth.

I am at this time not quite so well able as when I wrote last to enter on any such subject: & I trust I may be only over anxious about your meaning. Believe me,

Always your attached friend—
H. E. Manning

The Right Hon[oura]ble
W. E. Gladstone
[[Pitts; Chapeau, 135, 206]]

---

[a] Open to public judgement.

[b] From another source, from elsewhere.

[c] See 460108gm. Note as well 451228gm and Manning's response, 460103mg. The letter referring to the 'blow at man's freedom' to which Manning here refers was written in March (470315gm). Issues related to confession became particularly acute with Pusey's sermons on 'The Entire Absolution of the Penitent' early in 1846 and their publication (Liddon, iii. 51–64; 94–111). See E. B. Pusey, *Entire Absolution of the Penitent. A Sermon [on John 20: 21–23] mostly preached before the University in the Cathedral Church of Christ, in Oxford, on the Fourth Sunday after Epiphany* (Oxford: John Henry Parker, 1846) and *Entire Absolution of the Penitent. Sermon II. Judge thyself, that thou be not judged. A Sermon Preached Before the University in the Cathedral Church of Christ, in Oxford, on the First Sunday in Advent, 1846* (Oxford: John Henry Parker, 1846). On Gladstone's ongoing concern with the issue of confession from the early 1840s, note his late autobiographical reflections on 17 December 1894 and 9 February 1897 (BL Add. MS 44790, 89–95; *Autobiographica*, i. 158–61, and cf. D'Haussy [1995]).

470317gm[a]

13 C[arlton] H[ouse] T[errace]

March 17. [18]47

My dear Manning

I think there is some confusion between us. I asked you whether the author of 'From O[xford] to R[ome]' were 1. respectable and 2. a person perverted to the Church of Rome who had repented—you answer the first question but say you cannot answer the second till you see the book—but I did not mean to make you responsible for the writer's sincerity—and it may simplify the matter if I withdraw 'who had repented' & only ask whether the writer is one who has[25] from having been one of our Church become a member of the Church of Rome?

By the 'blow at man's freedom' I mean compulsory confession,[26] confession[27] as the condition of admission of Sacraments, in part, but I mean more especially the development of that law into the system of 'direction' which goes much beyond it. It is one however of many counts in the indictment against the Church of Rome, which it has now, as it seems to me, become a most positive and pressing duty to keep alive—

I am grieved to see that you are not so well again—do not let writing to me sooner or later lay one grain's weight of additional thought upon you until you are fully & healthfully equal to it.[b]

Your aff[ectiona]te friend

W. E. Gladstone

[[BL Add. MS 44247, 326–7; Morley transcript]]

---

  [a] 'Wrote to . . . Manning' (*GD* iii. 607).
  [b] On Manning's health, note his letter of the day previous, 16 March, 1847:

Lavington. March 16. 1847

My dear Sir

A slight illness which has now for some weeks confined me to my house has made me delay to thank you for your kindness in sending me a copy of the new Edition of your work on the Human Mind.

The same cause has forbid, as yet my enjoying it: except in one way in which it has been at once of frequent and very pleasing thoughts, I mean as the token of kindly remembrance of an old friend: and of the undiminished esteem we have been to each other.

It is to me a subject of great gratification to remember that though we once crossed each other in opinion we left no wounds, & raised no warfare.

I trust you will oblige me by accepting a copy of some Sermons which the Publisher shall send you, and when you come to anything at variance with your opinion, believe that we are united in the desire to know His Truth, & to do His will who is our only hope.

470318mg

Lavington. March 18. 1847.

My dear Gladstone,

I fully understood your question. And my answer is pertinent & exact.

To you it must be unintelligible unless the Book has told you, what your not understanding my answer implies that it has not.

And in this I am confirmed by the present N[umber] of the[28] Guardian, which has this morning reached me. In it I find both the Editor & a correspondent at fault on the same point.[a]

This being so I must return you only the same answer & I do it with a feeling of pain, as it vexes me to seem ὀχληρὸς[b] to you in any thing. But my duty is clear.

Your explanation about compulsory confession, & direction does not relieve me of my fears. And I earnestly wish you would reconsider what you are about to do. I know your mind so well, its integrity, force of purpose, and practical character that I am not content to see you write in the Quarterly on subjects so holy. Remote & opposed οὐράνιον ὅσον[c] to Milman, & Michelet[d] it refers you to the same region, in which I do not believe you will either do, or derive good. Forgive me, my dear Gladstone, for taking on me to speak in this way. My reason is so properly convinced,

I trust your health is restored to you.
With my kind remembrances to Mrs. Davies.

Believe me,
My dear Sir
Yours faithfully.
H. E. Manning. (Pitts)

The volume was that of John Davies (1795–1861, an Evangelical, formerly of Chichester: *DNB* under son, John), *An Estimate of the Human Mind: A Philosophical Inquiry into the Legitimate Application and Extent of its Leading Faculties, as Connected with the Principles and Obligations of the Christian Religion* (new edn.; London: J. W. Parker, 1847).

[a] *The Guardian*, 17 March 1847, 167; the letter by Timidus commented on the Irvingite aspect of *From Oxford to Rome*, which the editor confirmed in part. The issue included in addition a review of *From Oxford to Rome*, Stephen Jenner, *Steepleton; or High Church and Low Church: Being the Present Tendency of Parties in the Church, Exhibited in the History of Frank Faithful* by a Clergyman (London: Longmans, 1847), as well as a review of *Trevor; or, the New Saint Francis: A Tale for the Times* (London: Longmans, 1847) (ibid. 173).

[b] Troublesome.

[c] As the heaven above; cf. Homer, *Iliad*, 8. 16 and Hesiod, *Theogony*, 700.

[d] Cf. H. H. Milman, 'Religious Controversy in France—Relation of the Clergy to the People', *Quarterly Review* 76 (Sept. 1845), 299–345. The article refers to Michelet's work.

& my spiritual instincts so intuitively confirm my conviction, of the sanctity, & blessedness of confession, & direction, that I cannot think even of the compulsory rule being discussed except under conditions of the greatest gravity of place, office, time, & necessity without fear.

May all blessings be with you, and always believe me,

Yours affectionately,

H. E. Manning.

Private

P.S. I have this moment looked at the Guardian again, & see a sketch of the Story of Oxford to Rome.[e]

I feel at liberty to say to you that the narrative sketched in it is so far as I know wholly fictitious both as to persons & events.

H.E.M.

[[Pitts; Chapeau, 136, 207]]

470320gm[a]

London March 20 [18]47

My dear Manning

I will endeavour to write so as not to disturb your sabbatical mood tomorrow,[b] and I would not have written at all but for the fear that silence might have an ungracious aspect.

This is not the first time that it has happened that we have approached questions from different sides and on that account, to say nothing of the other reason of my doing it much worse, have expressed ourselves very differently when our real meanings were not far apart. I hope and believe this must be the case in the present instance, though ever since a walk to St. Peters in Dec[embe]r 1838[c] we have had some shades of distinction in our views of the element of human freedom, its proper scope and action, in the Christian system. I have the belief that the earliest constitution of the Church was in its spirit singularly free and that it would be happy for us and would imply the real strengthening of the hands of authority if weight *could* again be given to it as was then given. In the case before us, I have

---

[e] That is, the review of *From Oxford to Rome*, and *Steepleton*.
[a] 'Wrote to ... Manning' (*GD* iii. 608).
[b] 21 March 1847 was a Sunday.
[c] On 12 or 13 December 1838; see 380809mg.

written under the belief that the twofold system of compulsory confession for retrospect, and direction for prospect not or scarcely less compulsory, do in practice so work as very frequently and extensively to take out of the hands of the individual Christian the chief care of and therewith the chief responsibility for his own conduct, and that *therefore* it is that in this country, notwithstanding our sins and miseries the moral sense upon the whole is at this moment more generally clear &[29] strong than in the lands where the Roman Church bears sway.

But I am sensible that I do not write on this subject with the weight[30] which is due to any dispassionate judgment concerning it: for my own convictions upon it are in an immature and half developed state, I mean in its relation to my own conduct. For I should reply much more aye than no upon the question whether my own conscience is not one of those to which the Church refers as having been[31] unable to bear the weight of its own government and as accordingly requiring not advice only but the aid which confession and the grace which absolution gives. The period of relief from distraction which I now enjoy I hope will as it certainly should enable me to shape definitely my own resolutions about it and to take them to a definite issue whatever that issue may be. But I must say that in all the reflections about it I have felt the pressure of the reasons in its favour had reference to my own peculiar case and by no means connected themselves with its appearing a general rule which ought to be obeyed by every normal mind.

Perhaps I am a little affected by having seen it, in a near and most unhappy instance, fail and not only fail but greatly (with the rest of the system to which it belongs) aggravate the existing evils. The blindness of one who confesses and yet remains blind must be the thickest of all blindnesses. I am aware that *this* is not a valid objection to the practice in its root: nor do I urge it as such.

I fear it is not in my power to satisfy the conditions which you lay down for the consideration of the compulsory rule: I mean as to the greatest gravity of *office*. But in strange times strange duties fall to men. Were a great opaque body between us and the Roman Church, the duty of silence might be as obvious as its delight: but considering the nearness and closeness of the aggression, the deep policy and the lax morality with which its schemes are often prosecuted, the fearful nature of the dangers into which the souls of men are led by its success, I feel, first that all those who are in any way over others ought according to their means to guard them, and secondly that upon all those who may even indirectly and unintentionally have been the instruments of bringing some within the reach of peril, are especially bound to do what they can in the way of warning. For instance all those who gave the vote that you and I gave in the case of Ward: a vote which to the public I think[32] might well bear a sinister construction.

Now let me comfort you by saying that I must have blundered some way in giving you the idea that I meant to write on this subject in the Quarterly. I never had considered particulars—my engagement was to review the book—

In that respect I remain wofully in the dark—you seem to hint at a plurality of authors: which also occurred to me in perusing it. The narrative I never took for true: I wished to know about the experiences, which I think if forged are wonderfully forged—if the writer, or a principal writer,[33] be a person who has joined the Roman Church, & who repents, & who may be believed upon his word, I must go on: if not, I must rescue Lockhart: but if I have neither aye or nay to say I know not what is my duty: I must hope for some solution, & in the meantime I promise not to worry you any more though my need as you see remains & ever waxes.

Your aff[ectiona]te friend
W.E.G.

[[BL Add. MS 44247, 328–31; Morley transcript; Lathbury, ii. 277–8; cf. Chapeau, 321]]

470322gm
My dear M[anning][a]

After all, the accompanying letter was delayed on Saturday[b] by an interruption. The postponement enables me by way of addition to assure you that I am deeply sensible of its one sidedness when considered with reference to the whole subject. No one can have such good cause as I even while exercising the function of rebuke or of protest, to remember possessing an unworthiness far beyond that which can be ascribed to any other persons, & to feel that any system, be it what it may, is too good for me to appreciate. But upon that subject I will not enter. I will only say further that I had not confession[34] & its appurtenances exclusively, though they were preeminently, in my view. Your aff[ectiona]te friend.

W.E.G.

L[ondo]n March 22 [1847]
[[BL Add. MS 44247, 332; Morley transcript]]

---

[a] 'Wrote to . . . Manning' (*GD* iii. 609).
[b] 20 March 1847. Note the comment on 'sabbatical mood' in preceding letter.

470323mg

Lavington. March 23. 1847.

My dear Gladstone,

Your very kind letter of this morning has relieved me of an anxiety I have felt ever since I wrote last. I feared that my letter would pain you, or cross your will in some way which would be most contrary to my desires.

It appears to me that you may very well review the Book with these precautions:

1. To treat it as it professes without any attempt to ascertain the historical or biographical Truth of its narrative.

2. To use it (as I said in my first letter) as an *enunciation* of views.

3. To draw your confirmation of those views aliunde[a]—from your own reasons & sources.

Without going through a long process of reference to persons I cannot ascertain how much more I am at liberty to say than I have said. And indeed, for a Reviewer it does not seem necessary that you should give to an anonymous book more than it gives itself. It is enough if a hint preserve us from resting upon its professions with confidence.

With these precautions I do not see any reason why you should not go on with your review.

Only insert clauses to save yourself from seeming to accept the *germ*, & *interior experience*[35] narrative as so much fact.

But your letter has relieved me still more on the main subject of importance.

I am conscious that we have had a shade hanging, almost *diaphanously*,[b] between our minds, on the subject of Infallibility—the office of the reason in relation to truth, & now (as a correlative) of the will in connection with probation. But I really trust it is as you say, because we approach from different sides.

And yet I think there is one central truth in which we can meet & harmonize our views.

What St. Leo says of the Grace of God seems to me to be equally true of confession & direction, rightly understood & used.

---

[a] From another source, from elsewhere.
[b] Transparent.

'Auxilio et munere Dei non *aufertur* liberum arbitrium sed *liberatur*'
Auctoritate de Gratia. IX.[c] And Bossuet says to Priests, 'Conduisez de
telle sorte qu'on puisse se passer de vous'.[d]

I do not say that the R[oman] Ch[urch] has not inverted this rule—or
that the 'sicut cadaver'[e] is not capable of being so used. But confession &
direction seem to me to be means divinely ordained to restore liberty to the
will, by freeing it from bondage to its own sin, and that the fruit of such
discipline is 'perfect freedom'.[f]

But the sanctity and blessedness of confession is in relation to the Keys of
the Church. Happy and blessed beyond words are they who have no
retrospect demanding shame, & absolution. And certainly I know of no
reasons but those of flesh & blood which keep us from accusing ourselves
before God in the hearing of a Pastor who holds the Keys. But all this goes
into an interior world of which though in illness we may better feel its
blessedness, it is less easy to write. This made me afraid of what you might say.

Whether the moral sense of England be clearer than in R[oman]
Cath[oli]c countries, & whether (if it be) the cause is to be found in the
abuse or the absence of confession is a large subject. I am doubtful of the
whole supposition, & need more facts. My own impression of our moral
state is full of fear & pain. The economical & political duties of man to his
neighbour are well kept: as in a country of commutative justice is likely
to be the case:[36] but how is personal sanctity, and the duty we owe to God
observed in secret? This is where confession penetrates. The other may be
inforced at Westminster Hall.[g]

---

[c] By the aid and gift of God free choice is not *removed*, but *liberated*. (Praeteritorum sedes
apostolicae Episcoporum auctoritates de gratia dei quas a sancto Leone Romanae Ecclesiae tunc Diacono collectas Quesnellus credidit, in *Sancti Leonis Magni ... Opera post Paschasii
Quesnelli recensionem ... curantibus Petro et Hieronymo Fratribus Ballerinus* [3 vols.; Venice: Simon
Occhi, 1753–8], ii. 258. [PL 51. 210; ascribed to Prosper of Aquitaine].)

[d] A commonly used admonition of Bossuet for priests: 'Conduct yourself in such a way
that you will soon not be needed.' See e.g. Ancien Curé de Saint-Roch. Morel, *Le Prédicateur,
ou examen, d'aprés l'Écriture, les conciles et les Saints Pères de ce qu'il doit être, et de ce qu'il doit dire*
(Paris: Poussielgue-Rusand, 1837), 394, and *Dictionnaire d'éloquence sacre: contenant ... les pré-
ceptes de l'éloquence chrétienne, et les règles spéciales que l'on doit observer dans les divers genres de
prédication, par M. l'abbé Nadal ... suivi de deux appendices contenant intégralement: 1. La Rhetorique
du prédicateur, par Augustin Valério ... 2. Le prédicateur, ou Examen ... de ce qu'il doit être et de ce qu'il
doit dire par M. l'abbé Morel* (Paris: J. P. Migne, 1851), 1297.

[e] As a corpse.

[f] Cf. Jas. 1: 25.

[g] On Westminster Hall and its historic role as the setting for coronations see Carpenter
(1966), 406–7, 413.

Believe me that not a word in my letter was intended to reflect on your *personal* fitness to touch any subject on which I can dare to think.

May all the good I daily desire, be with you.

Believe me,
Ever your affec[tiona]te friend,
H. E. Manning.

March 23. 1847.
[[Pitts; Chapeau, 137, 208–9]]

470421gm

13 C[arlton] H[ouse] Terrace
Ap[ril] 21.[37] 1847

My dear Manning

I write to you strange to say with an anxiety that you should not spend your strength in writing to me—but then this anxiety is contingent upon the supposition that you are still in a condition that makes rest desirable and I have the hope this may not be so. I have no definite news of you and I have comfort in thinking that it is a proof you are not worse for if you had fallen back materially it would have been sure to reach me.

My Father's Chapel is to be consecrated in the end of June—on Saturday the 26th.[a] You were under almost a promise to visit him, & us in his house, when that occasion should arise—but I fear you are now looking towards the south.

If you should happen to know any person of *note* in the English Church, whose appearance at our Consecration would be material as a mark of support to the Scottish Bishops in their conflict with the English Schism and who could be had[38] perhaps you will be so good as to let me know.

My working[39] upon 'From Oxford to Rome' has been torn into tatters by interruptions (I have been to Fasque since I last wrote to you[b]) and sorely beset with the phantoms of which since your oracular intimations I cannot clear my mind.[c] I have read the book again straining my eyes as it

---

[a] The consecration of St Andrew's Church, in fact, was to occur two months later on Saturday, 28 August 1847 (*GD* iii. 644–5, Bertie, 556).

[b] After a short stay in London, where he arrived on 13 March 1847 (*GD* iii. 606), and despite a 'Bad cough on my chest' Gladstone left for Fasque again because of his father's illness on 29 March where he remained until he left for London once more on 14 April (ibid. 613).

[c] On 9 April 1847 Gladstone began to read *From Oxford to Rome* once again 'with a view to writing, but singular as it may seem I could neither compose my mind nor command my

were to look through and into it. I come back to the old point—does it describe the real *experiences* of the *writer*? And I answer yes. I am pretty clear for its being by a woman. And I have had some intelligence which ought to be trustworthy that the person was in a dissenting body before coming to us, and went from us as the book describes.

We are all thank God well barring temporary colds. What a good article by H[enry] Wilberforce on animal magnetism in the Ch[ristia]n Remembrancer.[d]

Your aff[ectiona]te friend
W. E. Gladstone

Venerable
Archdeacon Manning

[[BL Add. MS 44247, 333–4; Morley transcript; cf. Chapeau, 322]]

470422mg

Lavington. April 22. 1847.

My dear Gladstone,

Many thanks for your kind letter received this morning, & as it begins about myself so shall this, & then something better.

By Gods goodness, I am, I trust, far on my way to health again. Last Monday made nine weeks in the house, & eleven of illness, so that I have nearly seen out a quarter of a year. My ailment, as I told you, has been in the throat & lungs. I did not when I last wrote to you, fully know its extent. By the mercy of God, I trust there is no organic mischief in the chest: but I was on a fine edge, & might have inclined either way. My Doctor is very absolute, & peremptory in forbidding me to stay[40] in England next winter, please God, we live. I am now so far restored that, I hope before long to get out & to season myself in fresh air: after that I may come to London &

---

time', and two days later on 10 April he 'worked on "Oxford to Rome" a little, but feebly' (ibid. 612). He continued the task to 13 April (ibid. 61), took it up again on 18 April (ibid. 614), and finished his manuscript on 23 April (ibid. 615). On 21 May he 'Adjusted MS on Oxford to Rome & sent it to the printers' (ibid. 622). He corrected the proofs on 27, 28, and 30 May (ibid. 623–4).

[d] [Henry Wilberforce,] 'Animal Magnetism', *Christian Rembrancer* 56 (Apr. 1847), 366–91, reviewed twelve books on animal magnetism and mesmerism. Cf. also Manning's letter to Wilberforce complimenting him on the piece: 'In two places you were secretly preaching for Pius the Ninth' (Ushaw College MS OS/P7).

hope to see you. This has been a new phase of existence of which I could say many things, & had rather say than write them. I hope I may never forget these months, or cease to be thankful for them.

Your journey to Fasque was, I fear, on account of your Father's illness. I hope he is better.

I am afraid my movements cannot be northward greatly (almost more than I can say) as I should enjoy seeing Scotland. And I need not say that the thought of Fasque & of your Chapel was peculiarly pleasant to me. 'Sed aliter visum'.[a]

The best person I can think of for the day of consecration is Robert Wilberforce. I do not know anyone in whom so many things, for this nonce, unite. He is able & learned: a dignitary: highly esteemed by the Church in England, & in thorough sympathy with the Church in Scotland. But I am sure you have thought of him already. After him I do not know whom to suggest, unless it be the Deans of Chichester & Salisbury:[b] but this is after a long interval.

As to the 'Oxford & Rome' business when it comes out, as I think it must, I feel that you will join with me in saying it is a bad affair doing Rome no harm & the English Church no good. If the writer had consulted me I should have had nothing to do with it. So I advised the Clergyman who was consulted. I think it will recoil upon us: but time will show & will tell you. There is another oracle for you.[41]

Farewell. With all kind words to your wife.

Ever yours affect[ionatel]y
H. E. Manning.

The Right Hon[oura]ble
W. E. Gladstone
[[Pitts; Chapeau, 138, 209–10]]

---

[a] But the view is otherwise. Cf. Virgil, *Aeneid*, 2. 428, dis aliter visum (the view of the gods is otherwise).

[b] George Chandler, Dean of Chichester, 1830–49, and Francis Lear, Dean of Salisbury, 1846–50. (*Fasti Ecclesiæ Anglicanæ: or, A Calendar of the Principal Dignitaries in England and Wales and of the Chief Officers in the Universities of Oxford and Cambridge . . . Compiled by John Le Neve. Corrected and continued . . . by T. Duffis Hardy* [3 vols.; Oxford: Oxford University Press, 1854], ii. 627.)

470514gm[a]

13 C[arlton] H[ouse] Terrace
May 14. [18]47.

My dear Manning

The time must now be that when you had intended to come up to London and I was going to write and to ask you whether you would dine with us on Monday to[42] meet the Dowager Duchess of Beaufort[b] when I heard yesterday through the Bishop of Oxford of the new affliction with which at this sacred season it has pleased God so suddenly to visit you.[c] I cannot avoid writing a line to assure you of our deep and unfeined sympathy—it would be presumptuous in me to say more than that I pray the abundance of Divine grace may ever overflow your need.

I am glad to hear from the Bishop of Oxford a favourable account of your health—and I had very much rather for the present continue to hear of than from you. Writing is fatiguing work, even when it is lightened by love—and I am sure that you will require to spare yourself in labour as well as to relax in regard to the supplies of food and I suspect also of rest necessary to carry you through it.—

We have great comfort in observing the course of Hopes mind. We not unfrequently see him even now at the high water of his work—and there seems to be a process of settling in regular advance: increasing interest in works within the Church, and a generally growing cheerfulness of tone—

He is warm about this anticipated Oxford vacancy:[d] I hope you may not be so far your strength cannot afford to be so spent. It is impossible I think to judge what form things will take—I am told 100 residents are in my favour: but there are three important questions to consider—

1. The academical objection to run as a member of Ch[rist] Ch[urch]— 2. The risk of a religious war, which, if such as well to deserve that name, would be an evil in no degree to be neutralised by success. 3. The question

---

[a] 'wrote to...Manning' (*GD* iii. 620).

[b] On 17 May 1847, Gladstone had the Duchess and five others to dinner (*GD* iii. 621). Charlotte Sophia, née Leveson-Gower (1771–1854) married Henry Charles, 6th Duke of Beaufort (1766–1835) on 16 May 1791 (*GD* ii. 340).

[c] Gladstone saw the Bishop of Oxford on the previous day, 13 May 1847, Ascension Day.

[d] As reported in *The Times*, 12 May 1847, 6e, Thomas Grimston Bucknell Estcourt declined re-election for Oxford University. In the ensuing election Hope worked energetically for Gladstone who had retired from public life with the defeat of Peel's Ministry in June 1846. On Hope's 'course of mind' see 461207gm. On Gladstone's securing of the seat in August 1847 see 470818mg.

whether I am stiff enough in[43] State & Church politics to be justified in assuming the position. But I can come to no decision until I know what amount of feeling may presumably exist for me outside Ch[rist] Ch[urch]. God bless you—

Ever aff[ectiona]tely yours
W.E.G.

Venerable
Archdeacon Manning
[[BL Add. MS 44247, 335–6; Morley transcript]]

470518mg

Lavington. May 18. 1847.

My dear Gladstone,

I could have wished to write to you of many things but this is a season which withdraws all active thoughts. I will, therefore, only thank you for your last affectionate letter, & will write again, please God, before long.

You probably cannot know that I have been all my life the youngest child in the sense of the proverb: and that my Mothers fondness was for its overflowing depth like the light I have lived upon all my life without knowing or thinking of it. Nothing that I can write will express it.[a] There is now in the world nothing in the same order and all the highest relations of love are now transferred into the presence of God. Pray for me that I may never rest till I rest there. I trust, I shall seek it more simply: for I begin to understand what it may mean to be in this world & not of it.[b]

To our common ways of feeling the end was what we do not desire for those we love. And yet I seem to see mercy within mercy, even in this: partly towards her, & partly towards myself: for I will say to you that a thought has for years given me the sharpest distress, I mean that of seeing my beloved Mother in pain, & dying. I have had her face, at times before me. And in compassion on my weakness God has seemed to spare me.

---

[a] Manning's mother died on 13 May 1847. See Bodl. MS Eng. lett. c. 652, 429–48 for a description of her final days, and 449; Purcell, i. 452 gives the date as 12 May but i. 454 notes the inscription on the tombstone as 13 May. The close attachment of Manning and his mother is evident in their correspondence between 1832 and her death. See Bodl. MS Eng. lett. c. 652, 450–531.

[b] Note the commonplace 'in the world but not of it', a compilation of John 17: 11 and 16.

Give my love to your wife, in whose sympathy I know I [44] share: & believe
me, Always your

affect[ionat]e friend.
H. E. Manning.

The Right Hon[oura]ble
W. E. Gladstone
[[Pitts; Chapeau, 139, 210–11]]

470521mg

Lavington. May 21. 1847.

After Post.

My dear Gladstone,

Need I say how earnestly I desire to see you sitting for Oxford? It is one
of those things which carries its own fitness on its face: & I have longed for
it. Not that I overlook future difficulties. I cannot but foresee that by 1849
you may be where Sir R[obert] Peel was in 1829. But I do not think this
need be entertained now. It will be time enough when the event comes.
There is, however, one point of practical moment I mean the possible
embarrassment to a man who must take your prominent position, in
having a constituency to think so much about. Your great difficulty will
be the Irish Church.

Now there is one point on which if you are free & willing to speak I
sh[oul]d like to have information. Cardwells being put forward looked at
in Oxford is intelligible: out of Oxford is a political mistake: with L[or]d
Villiers on his committee looks like something more.[a] People talk nonsense
at all times—& their use of Peels name may be such: but I can conceive
your relation to him to be changed & difficult. I am not asking questions
wh[ich] you know I never do: but if you have anything to say, it w[oul]d
interest me. Tho' truly nothing in public life except as affecting friends
interests me much. I seem to see that this way to serve the Church is aloof
from politics: & this has grown on me since we last met.

---

[a] Edward Cardwell (1813–86) initially stepped forward for the Parliamentary vacancy at
Oxford, but declined for want of support (Morley, i. 328–9; see Boase, i. 542). Cardwell's
candidacy was strengthened by the regard in which he was held by Robert Peel. Charles
Pelham Villiers (1802–98; *DNB*), served as MP for Wolverhampton, 1837 to his death.

Will you also tell me what are your thoughts about the pressure of food? Why is July named with special anxiety?

A thought struck me a day or two ago ab[ou]t Sicily, 'the Granary of Europe'. Why do not some people go & reclaim it from Malaria? It has 26 natural products including cotton & sugar. The king of Naples[b] w[oul]d be as glad of skill & Capital in this way as in making Marsala. I do not know what the Duke of Richmond[c] w[oul]d say—but it seems to me worth thinking of.

I have read the first 3 or 4 chapters of Bunsen's book:[d] & I have only one word for it: (abstracting the person) it is the most impudent production I ever read. I do believe that he & Hare sincerely think what they say: but it is to me a phenomenon. How the universal Priesthood of [Chris]t[ia]ns sh[oul]d exclude the real priesthood & the universal kingship not exclude all crowned Heads even to Frederick William,[e] I cannot tell except that the Church hangs nobody but Kings & Queens do. I call this imposture & fooldom. It throws me with all the weight of my soul upon the Catholic Church.

I do not as yet know when I shall get to London. But I am just returning into warm sun & fresh air which are blessings I never knew how to love before.

Ever your affect[ionat]e friend,
H. E. Manning.

The Right Hon[oura]ble
W. E. Gladstone
[[Pitts; Chapeau, 140, 211–12]]

---

[b] Ferdinand II (1810–59), King of the Two Sicilies from 1830.

[c] Charles Lennox (1791–1860; *DNB*), 5th Duke of Richmond and Lennox, and Lord Lieutenant of Sussex, was a Protectionist.

[d] Christian Charles Josias Bunsen, *The Constitution of the Church of the Future. A Practical Explanation of the Correspondence with the Right Honourable William Gladstone, on the German Church, Episcopacy, and Jerusalem. With a Preface, Notes, and Complete Correspondence*, translated 'under the supervision of, and with additions by, the author' (London: Longman, Brown, Green, & Longmans, 1847).

[e] Bunsen's *Constitution of the Church of the Future* emphasized both the universal priesthood of all believers and the rights of the state over the Church. See ibid. 14f., 31ff., and above all, 90–3.

470524gm[a]

13 C[arlton] H[ouse] Terrace
May 24. [18]47.

My dear Manning

I have not minute information of what passes in the committees for promoting my election: but the accounts which are given me have up to this time been very cheerful and sanguine. Among others, who do you think supports me but Garbett?[b] And not only so, but he writes a very sensible letter in announcing his intentions. Another week will probably let us know pretty clearly the feeling of the constituency as between us *three*. At present I think my friends view with most apprehension the possibility of the[45] retirement of Cardwell who is supposed to be the weaker of our two antagonists. The time has been a very anxious one and it is still so in a degree, for the dangers of evil are many; and had the seat for[46] the University been an object to be *actively* sought like other seats in Parliament I should not have put myself forward as matters now stand—Tyler,[c] Seymer,[d] & a few others wholly uncommitted, I think gave the turn to the thing, and carried the affirmative.

Should Cardwell retire the war might rage furiously upon religious and politico religious topics—At present there are cross ideas and arguments which blunt the edge of battle. But I feel that I am in[47] one great peril under that contingency, viz. the peril of either defeat or success (& I should not much care which it was) as the reputed representative of mere party. They *may* succeed in fastening that character upon me: and if they do it will incapacitate me, I fear, for serving the Church at any time in Parliament. Not that this is done yet, and I am on the whole hopeful about it, & most thankful to God for the degree in which virulence & calumny seem to have

[a] 'Wrote to...H. E. Manning' (*GD* iii. 622).

[b] Garbett's support at this time may have been oral (correspondence not located), but on 18 June 1847, he wrote to Gladstone: 'I shall heartily rejoice at your elevation to the academic position, the *idea* of which, you so fully apprehend and deserve the opportunity to carry out' (BL Add. MS 44365, 289–90).

[c] James Endell Tyler; no letter regarding his position located, but note his sharp and brief letter to Gladstone regarding the latter's position on the Welsh bishoprics on 24 June 1847 and Gladstone's lengthy reply the following day (BL Add. MS 44365, 312, 318).

[d] Henry Ker Seymer (1807–67), educated at Christ Church, Oxford, was a Fellow at All Soul's, Oxford, and MP for Dorsetshire, 1846–64 (Boase, iii. 501). No letter located, but note his later curt questioning of Gladstone, also regarding his actions on the Welsh Bishoprics (26 June 1847; BL Add. MS 44365, 319).

been laid or restrained in respect to me—but it all stands as it were upon the fineness of a razor's edge—

As respects future honour I think I am secure. I have given the Committee answers to two questions respecting Ireland. First I have told them that I do not object in principle to the payment of the R[oman] C[atholic] priests, but should treat it as a question of policy & detail; secondly, that *I do not foresee any circumstances* which would induce me to vote for the alienation of the Church property of Ireland. If a combination of contingencies, each somewhat remote, were to be realised, I might be compelled to resign my seat (you see I count my chickens before they are hatched) but not, I think, under the reproach of apostasy. This however I could more fully explain by speech.

I know no *facts* to substantiate the rumours about Peel: and probabilities are against them—I mean against his acting, not against his wishing which I think must be more or less for Cardwell, & this on diverse grounds, some of them friendly to me—

It is sad to be in a condition in which one's self is as it were the local centre of one's own anxieties, instead of having them projected upon the Church, or some other object, external to self—for all this the cure is in the grace of God, & in that gift of ready wisdom which He gave to Solomon for the asking,[e] & which, in such measure as I need it, I trust you implore of Him for me—

I wish I could discuss Sicily with you—the difficulty is I apprehend 1. religion and 2. monopoly in some form or other. You have hit Bunsen's theory a deadly blow in a single sentence. Thank God I have liberated my soul by writing to him sharply about the book on its very first appearance.[f] We rejoice in this warm weather for your sake and shall hear with delight of your further progress in recovery.

Your aff[ectiona]te friend
W. E. Gladstone

Venerable
Archdeacon Manning

[[BL Add. MS 44247, 337–40; Morley transcript]]

---

[e] 1 Kgs. 4: 29–30.

[f] See Gladstone to Bunsen, 13 October 1845, in which he indicates that he has completed reading the latter's *Die Verfassung der Kirche der Zukunft. Praktische Erläuterungen zu dem Briefwechsel über die deutsche Kirche, das Episkopat und Jerusalem* (Hamburg: Agentur des Rauhenhauses, 1845), and comments on it (BL Add. MS 44111, 288–90; *GD* iii. 487–8).

470604mg

44 Cadogan Place. June 4.
1847

My dear Gladstone,

I did not trouble you by writing to say that I am in London for I am not able to come & see you. But, I thank God, I feel much better. As to my plans I do not yet know anything: but shall, I hope, when I have had advice.

I do not ask you to come & see me because I suppose your time is more than full: but I shall have great pleasure in seeing you if you are able.

The surest time to find me is from 12 to 3—or after[48] ½p[as]t 6 in the evening.

I hope the promise of Oxford is good.

Believe me,
Yours affect[ionatel]y
H. E. Manning.

[[Pitts; Chapeau, 141, 212]]

[[Gladstone answered Manning's letter of 4 June 1847 on the following day (*GD* iii. 626; not located) and saw him on 17 and 19 June (ibid. 628–9).]]

470712gm[a]

Fasque Jul[y] 12. [18]47

My dear Manning

I should do you wrong if I suffered you to go abroad[b] without the letter to Dr. Döllinger. Although I am well assured that if you presented yourself

---

[a] 'Wrote to ... Manning' (*GD* iii. 634).

[b] Because of illness, Manning was, on doctor's advice, planning a trip to the Continent: 'I was ill in the spring of 1847, and in July went to Homburg. Dodsworth joined me, and we went on into Switzerland. I fell ill at Lucerne, and was obliged to come home. But in October started again with Colonel Austen and my sister Caroline, and stayed in Rome till May 1848, and reached home [Lavington] 18 July 1848' (Purcell, i. 348; cf. ibid. 547–8n.). See Thomas Allies' comments on a visit to Manning on 15 June 1847 (Allies [1924], 61). On 6 August 1847 he wrote to Mrs Lockhart from Homburg (Pitts). See also Manning's letters to Dodsworth, 8 and 14 August from Homburg, 24 September, 1 October 1847, and 28 January, 29 March, 18 July 1848 (Bodl. MS Eng. lett. c. 658, 83–94), Manning to NN, 16 July 1847, indicating plans to leave in second week in July (ibid. 662, 107–8).

unintroduced, after five minutes or less of embarrassment de part et d'autre,[c] it would be just the same thing.

You will find I think if he goes back to your book on Unity, that he will observe on its not containing any argument to show internal and moral unity in the Church of England. We had much talk upon this.[d] My view freely admitted this, that we have in the Church of England, and copiously, the loose and floating elements of that which if it become organised and systematic will either rend us in twain or else plunge us into heresy much more [49]virulent when so developed than the crude elements themselves albeit a heretical savour. But the Church of Rome has in her, not less copious, nor less poisonous materials, only wanting to become orderly, and to attain to the seat of the highest authority, where they would perform for her the same work, in a different direction. I remember also telling him of the Sermon I heard in Naples & which appeared then to be of an usual & an acceptable tone there.[e] He said that in Germany any man would be suspended for preaching such a Sermon. I asked how that bore upon the strict doctrine of internal unity—which he seemed to reserve for consideration.—This you will think little better than gossip or even egotism: your book served me for a pretence & perhaps misled me—

I expect to be in London not later than Tuesday or at farthest Wednesday of next week, perhaps earlier than either.[f] Our people continue to be most sanguine about the Election: but the case cannot be free from care,[50] by reason of the nature of the constituency, until it has passed out of the future tense into the past. I am thankful that the time approaches & though if I should be rejected my predicament will be an awkward one to all appearance, either way it will doubtless be for good, and such events would lose all their power for discipline, if we could see the issue by anticipation.

We earnestly hope that you are in constant[51] advance: and we wish that you had a friend who should also be a nurse engaged to bear you company. Believe me Aff[ectiona]tely yours

W. E. Gladstone

Venerable
H. E. Manning
[[BL Add. MS 44247, 341–2; Morley transcript]]

---

[c] Embarrassment on both sides.
[d] For details on this discussion and related topics see Erb (1997), 450–69.
[e] See 461207gm.
[f] Gladstone left on 18 July 1847 and arrived in London on the following day (*GD* iii. 635).

470818mg

Homburg. Aug[ust] 18. 1847.

My dear Gladstone,

The tidings of your success at Oxford[a] gave me the liveliest pleasure I have felt in any public event for a long time: and that it was by a majority so decisive of which I had not ventured to have a hope. You are where my thoughts and wishes have long placed you—from the time of our early correspondence & especially from the time of your first book when you & I were together in Rome—a time which comes back again to me now with a strange vividness as I am again on my way to the same place & for the same end. It w[oul]d have given me great joy to be at Oxford & to give my voice for you, but I must be content.

And now 'Saladin must die'![b] It is hard on you to tell you so on the morrow of your success. But so it is—unless a change greater than I can hope, be wrought in the minds of Convocation. I do not see how it is possible for questions of religious policy to be long postponed. Nevertheless your success is a great event for that form of belief & action which has reorganized the Church of England since 1835. It seems to show that the body of men combined on that principle are more or less prepared for the consideration of our real position and its necessities. May you have wisdom & strength for your task as I daily pray for you.

---

[a] Following the withdrawal of Cardwell and initial skirmishes related to a nomination supported by both Old High Churchmen (who opposed Gladstone's final stand on Maynooth) and Evangelicals, Gladstone's name was proposed in the Sheldonian on 29 July 1847. At the close of the voting on 3 August, Gladstone finished second as the junior member for Oxford behind the senior member, Robert Harry Inglis. On 5 August Gladstone was assured of the Oxford election (*GD* iii. 639). For details see *An Authentic Copy of the Poll for Two Burgesses to Serve in Parliament for the University of Oxford, taken on Thursday the 29th, Friday the 30th, Saturday the 31st of July, and on Monday the 2nd, and Tuesday the 3rd of August, MDCCCXLVII. Candidates: Sir Robert Harry Inglis... William Ewart Gladstone... Charles Gray Round* (Oxford: Oxford University Press, 1847), and note Morley, i. 327–36 and Liddon, iii. 173 ff. as well as comments in Roundell Palmer, *Memorials* (2 vols.; London: Macmillan & Co., 1896), ii. 453. Robert Harry Inglis (1786–1855; *DNB*, educated at Winchester and Christ Church, Oxford, MP for Dundalk, 1824–6, Ripon, 1828–9, Oxford University, 1829–54, was closely associated with the Clapham group, a strong defender of the Established Church and firmly opposed to Catholic Emancipation.

[b] Walter Scott, *The Talisman. A Tale of the Crusaders and the Chronicles of the Canongate* (London: Collins, 1832), ch. 28 describes the splendour of Saladin's tent in which he awaited the Christian princes. Amidst 'the trophies of battles won and kingdoms overthrown... and above them all, a long lance displayed a shroud, the banner of Death, with this impressive inscription,—SALADIN, KING OF KINGSSALADIN, VICTOR OF VICTORSSALADIN MUST DIE'.

Many thanks for your kind letter & for the letter to Dr. Döllinger.[c] I have been trying to make Munich fall into my course southwards, but in vain: & trust to take it, God willing, on my return.

My plans are to go by Basle Lucern and then St. Gothard to the Lakes & Milan. I hope to see Ravenna. My directions will be until the 1st of September Basle, until the 15 Como—until Oct[ober] 1. Milan. then Florence: and ab[ou]t the middle of Nov[em]b[e]r Rome, please God. I have been at this place nearly four weeks, drinking the water, and I trust & believe with real benefit. I feel both stronger & better: and some of the causes of an anxiety, which was not unreasonable, are certainly lessened. Tomorrow I hope to go to Frankfurt, and in a week to begin to move towards the South. It will be a great delight to me to hear from you.

Give my love to your Wife, with all my kindest wishes, & believe me,

Ever your affectionate friend,
H. E. Manning.

The Right Hon[oura]ble
W. E. Gladstone

P.S. I desired Barnes to send you a 3rd vol. of sermons.[d] H.E.M.

[[Pitts; Chapeau, 142, 213; cf. Leslie, 81]]

[[On a list dated 28 September 1847 and inserted after 13 April 1848, Gladstone tabulates all his relations and closest friends; among the latter is Manning (*GD* iv. 25). On 2 October 1847, following the near death of his daughter Agnes and difficulties again with his sister Helen, Gladstone wrote to Manning (*GD* iii. 658; not located). He was informed of Manning's departure on 16 October by Samuel Wilberforce who 'went on Thursday to spend yesterday with my family who are in Dover for sea air. Manning came yesterday to Dover on his way abroad embarking on Monday next with Col[onel] Austen & his sister. I was rejoiced to see him looking certainly better: & I think in better spirits about himself' (BL Add. MS 44343, 104–5).[e]]]

---

[c] Not located.

[d] William Barnes, publisher and bookseller, 44 Bridgehouse Place, Southwark, London, 1831–48. See Brown (1982). The volume was Henry Edward Manning, *Sermons. Volume Third* (London: James Burns, 1847*a*). Gladstone seems to have gained a copy of the sermons earlier. On 25 July 1847 he indicates he was reading them (*GD* iii. 636) and on 1 August he read Manning's 'Serm[on] IV aloud to C[atherine]', (ibid. 638), returning to the sermons on 12 August (ibid. 643) and consecutive Sundays, 12 (ibid. 648), 19 (ibid. 650), 26 September (ibid. 655), and 10 (ibid. 659) and 17 October (ibid. 661).]]

[e] Note also Manning to an unknown correspondent, 5 October 1847, indicating return because of illness in Switzerland and plans to leave once more (ibid. 109–10), Manning to NN, 4 October 1847, indicating that he is 'to leave London on Monday next [11 October] for Dover, and to cross over in a few days after' (Pitts), Manning to Priscilla Maurice, 3 October 1847, and 23 June 1848, indicating he was in London on those dates (Bodl. MS Eng. lett. c. 650, 63–4, 73–4).

2. Manning's Second Interlude in Rome:
January 1848–July 1849

480120mg

Rome. Jan[uar]y 20. 1848.

My dear Gladstone,

It is strangely & unusually long since we communicated last with each other—and yet it has not been from forgetfulness on either side.

You will have heard, I dare say, that I have been once more in England and again sent out to fare forth towards the South.[a] That I may have done with it I will say at once that I left England about October 19, went to Nice—stayed nearly 3 weeks, found the air sharp, & came on here where I have been about nine weeks. By God's blessing, I am greatly better & stronger, but my throat & chest are very sensitive; & I suppose will be for a long time.

I have been often reminded of you & of nine years ago as you may believe, seeing the same sights, & hearing the same Litanies we used to hear at S[t]. Luigi.[b] Outwardly Rome is unchanged, the streets, shops, pavements, heaps of dirt not yet taken away; & to sum up all I saw at S[t]. Peters the day before yesterday our friend Belliocchj.[c] But morally & inwardly there is a vast change: a very visible increase of intelligence & energy with free public expression in word & writing. When we were here last time there were three papers. There are[52] now (all included) 40: one or two daily—others several times a week. The political articles even after passing the Censura, & free spoken and all onward in their movement. Believing, as we do, that the unfolding of individual & national character & therefore of social forces & institutions is a divine law and blessing I cannot but hope more than fear for Italy. If only five years of mature & peaceful self organization can be secured—if not there is more to fear than to hope.[d]

---

[a] On Manning's travels and changing travel plans see 470712gm and 470818mg.

[b] See 390130mg. On Manning's activities in Rome note Gladstone's annotation of 'NB' to Purcell's later comment: 'Pope Pius, as far back as 1848, had noticed, as Mgr. Talbot, who was with him at the time, has recorded, how Archdeacon Manning knelt down in the Piazza di Spagna as the Papal carriage approached. The incident of a dignitary of the Anglican Church doing homage in public made a lasting impression on the susceptible mind of Pius IX' (PurGl ii. 546).

[c] Not identified.

[d] According to Purcell at this time 'Manning listened to the violent harangues of [Alessandro] Gavazzi [1809–89, Italian patriot, monk, professor, and later Protestant preacher], to the revolutionary theories of Padre Ventura, and to the propositions and plans of Ciceroaicchio [Angelo Brunetti, 1800–49, Italian patriot]'. Gladstone annotates this sentence with 'Trio?' (PurGl i. 345). On the revolution in Rome see Aubert (1952), 27–40, and Martina (1974), 197ff.

It seems to be a law that old countries if they destroy their organization cannot reform, & reconstruct themselves, at least not within a period shorter than a geological era; and I therefore, am afraid that anything which *upsets* an existing order instead of recalling it to its first idea only clears a field for confusion. But we have no need to go to Rome for a peg to hang this upon. If this upset is not preparing in England Lord John is at least blameless.

I do not say that I should like to know your mind about this miserable, ever, & thrice miserable Hampden affair[e] for where men have principles

---

[e] According to Leslie, 82, it was while at Nice that Manning heard of Hampden's confirmation as Bishop of Hereford on 11 January 1848. On the death of Edward Harcourt (1757–1847; *DNB*), Archbishop of York on 5 November 1847, and the transference of Thomas Musgrave (1788–1860), Bishop of Hereford, to York, the way was open for Hampden's appointment to a bishopric. *The Times* announced his selection by the Prime Minister on 15 November 1847, causing great consternation on the part of the Tractarian and High Church parties (see Liddon, iii. 158–66). For materials on the controversy over the appointment of Hampden as Bishop of Hereford, see *The Case of Dr. Hampden. The Official and Legal Proceedings Connected with the Appointment of Dr. Hampden to the See of Hereford, Including the Principal Documents Connected with the Important Controversy and a Translation of all the Extracts Collated by the Original Authorities. With Notes, and an Appendix* (London: George Bell, 1848). *The Times* printed a supportive 'Address', signed by 'between 600 and 700 of the clergy and laity' along with Hampden's reply on 28 December 1847 (5e). For a general review of the case see *DNB*, Chadwick, i. 232–50, and cf. Liddon, ii. 158–66.

A short time later, on 14 February 1848, Manning wrote to Herbert, commenting 'if the Church be a Divine polity, and if free institutions be divine blessings, I cannot see why they should not coexist'. Beside the sentence as quoted in his copy of Purcell's biography, Gladstone has written 'ma' (PurGl i. 377; for original see Bodl. MS Eng. lett. c. 657, 1–3). Gladstone also annotates ('Feb[ruary] 1848') a section in a Manning letter to Robert Wilberforce, dated 12 February 1848, reading 'And it is under this condition that I add, that I do not know how I can serve a body I cannot defend. I seem reduced to a choice between my faith and all its foundations on one side, and all that life has, which is dear to me, on the other' (PurGl i. 510). Note also that alongside Purcell's undated statement at the beginning of his chapter on Manning and Robert Wilberforce that 'Manning no longer believed in Anglicanism' Gladstone placed a '?' (ibid. 500). The remainder of the chapter includes two more Gladstone 'NB's: Purcell's statement, 'The condemnation which it expresses of Hampden as guilty of heresy could not have been clearer, or more emphatic or more complete, and offers a strange contrast to the way in which, on his return to England, he dealt in his Charge, July 1848, as Archdeacon of Chichester, with the Hampden case' (ibid. 510); Manning to Wilberforce, 15 February: 'God knows, my dear Robert, that every bond and tie of friendship and love, and a kindred higher than blood, to say nothing of every lower affection, which makes up home to me, bribe me into a state next to blindness, in the great issue between England and Rome' (ibid. 511). On Gladstone's own desire that the choice of bishops be fully in the hands of the Church and not at the discretion of the Prime Minister, see his earlier letter of 31 January 1848 to Blomfield (Lathbury, i. 79–81).

they understand each other without waste of breath or paper. To me it seems a crisis. I am deeply convinced that Dr. Hampdens B[ampton] Lectures[f] are Heterodox in substance: still more so that they lay down the science of heterodoxy. His Theological principle, if I can so call it, is an instrument for the proof of every heresy, as Catholic Tradition which he destroys is the sole external proof of the One Truth.

As an Academical Professor he committed an offence[53] within the jurisdiction of the University, & was censured. The Church left him in passive Communion. Let those who have compromised and condoned answer one by one. The Church of England only left him passively in Communion. He is now selected as for distinguished merit: as a martyr for Truth, & representative of the Reformation. He is to be—not discharged from censure—not absolved & restored—but actively received, invested with the highest functions, consecrated by the Church.

By the Canons of the Church Universal, a canonical number of Bishops, with the consent of the Metropolitan represent and bind the Province unless the other Bishops expressly dissent. Dissent in a matter of Truth requires Trial and either restoration of Communion or deposition. I see no course open for the Province of Canterbury but this: and as the Province of Canterbury acts, so will the Church of England be from the day of Dr. Hampden's consecration.

I put this out so that I may have your mind about it: if you can find time to write.

And now for yourself.—You are I see already in the Surf of Politics. I read your speeches about Mr. Ansteys bill,[g] & the admission of the Jews with great interest.[h] In the former I heartily agree, & rejoice that you

---

[f] See 360304gm.

[g] The second reading of the Roman Catholic Relief Bill ('For the further Repeal of Enactments imposing Pain and Penalties upon Her Majesty's Roman Catholic Subjects on Account of their Religion', PP 1847 [53.] iii. 623, 10 Feb. 1847 and PP 1847–8 [5.] vi. 239, 26 Nov. 1847) was moved by Thomas Chisholm Anstey (1816–73; *DNB*) on 8 December 1847 (Hansard, xcv. 800). On the same day Gladstone spoke in favour of the bill 'after a silence of nearly 2½ years' (*GD* iii. 674; Hansard, xcv. 840, 852). Note Anstey's earlier *Guide to the History of the Laws and Constitutions of England, Consisting of Six Lectures, Delivered at the College of SS Peter and Paul, Prior Park, Bath* (London: V. & R. Stevens, 1845). For Gladstone's response see Hansard, xcv. 840, *The Times* (9 Dec.), 3 f, and *The Guardian* (15 Dec.), 740, and his later comments on 16 February 1848 (Hansard, xcvi. 741; *The Times*, 17 Feb. 1848, 4).

[h] On 16 December 1847 Gladstone 'Spoke under an hour for L[or]d J[ohn] Russell's motion. It is a painful decision to come to. But the only substantive doubt it raises is about remaining in Parliament. And it is truly and only the Church that holds me in there though

declared openly against the deathly tradition of your Colleague and the old Oxford imbecility. As to the Jews I have doubts. It is a final abandonment of Christianity as a nation, which with you may perhaps weigh somewhat more than with me. A nation is represented by its organization. Denizens & sojourners unless they partake of that organization are in a nation but not of it.[i] This is a distinction, however, which I feel to be of little worth in this case as a Socinian is to me less of a [Chris]t[ia]n than a Jew, if possible. However the case is this—Civilized Europe was the fruit of [Chris]t[ianit]y. The Jews were in it but not of it—& ill enough they fared—now we have inverted the order and are thrusting away the [Chris]t[ianit]y which formed us, first by the civil equality of all [Chris]t[ia]n sects, & now by the equality of [Chris]t[ia]n & Jew. But 'non mea refert'![j] One thing I feel is that all legislation for the Church unless sanctioned by the Church in England is null & of no force to bind a [Chris]t[ia]n man. This you will not like I am afraid: but so it is in my hearts belief. The Ch[urch] must obey Parliament as she would Nero; for no other reasons, and no further, this is hastening on the period we used to write of, when a Member—a son of the Church can serve her no longer in Parliament. It remains only 'to let us go into the Wilderness to sacrifice to the Lord our God.'[k] And we must go with our substance at least, for I would neither ask nor accept any loans or spoil.

I could write of a thousand & one things if a sheet would carry them. As it is I can only send all kindness to Mrs. Gladstone. I heard with great concern of the illness of your little Agnes,[l] whose face is a blessed image to think of 'perla in bianca fronte'.[m] I trust she is well again. Believe me my dear Gladstone,

Ever yours affectionately,
H. E. Manning.

[[Pitts; Chapeau, 143, 214–16; cf. Leslie, 82]]

she may seem to some to draw me from it' (*GD* iii. 676; Hansard xcv. 282). For the Bill 'For the Relief of Her Majesty's Subjects Professing the Jewish Religion', see PP 1847–8 (49.) iii. 341, 20 Dec. 1847. Note as well *The Times*, 17 December, 4d, and compare Gladstone's earlier address on 31 March 1841 (Hansard, xlvii. 754; *The Times*, 1 Apr. 1841, 3f). On 4 April 1847 Gladstone 'Voted with a very clear conscience for the Jews in 234: 173' (*GD* iv. 33). Note as well his reflections on the matter to Lyttelton, 10 September 1847 (Lathbury, i. 79–80).

[i] Note the commonplace 'in the world but not of it', a compilation of John 17: 11 and 16.

[j] It does not concern me.

[k] Exod. 3: 18.

[l] Agnes Gladstone (1842–1931) suffered a serious illness from 19 September 1847 to the end of the month. She began to show signs of improvement on 1 October (*GD* iii. 650–7).

[m] A pearl on a white brow. Dante, *Paradisio*, 3. 14.

480312gm[a]

London
Sunday, March 12, 1848.

My dear Manning

At length I muster courage to take up my pen and reply to your kind letter. The first word I have addressed to you since the autumn when I dispatched to you—I think—at Milan a letter which you probably never got[b] for you had altered your plans & I had not heard of the alteration. It is always a pleasure to write to you, but it is an effort too because there is so much so very much—that I should like to pour out before you: and for a long time back I have had no energies to spare, nearly all my works have been works of anxiety, I have not had strength or elasticity to look any duties except those nearest hand in the face. Care has been very heavy upon me, and in some new and unaccustomed forms. You may remember one day, as we walked back from St. Marks, my telling you something as to my general views about the disposition of such property as I had or might have, and how they were qualified by my having become involved in a great iron mining and manufacturing concern which was opened many years ago by a reckless agent unduly trusted upon a property of his in Staffordshire & in which that harebrained schemer had involved him largely & even his sisters partially under the notion of turning the iron into gold for them.[c] The righteous retribution of Providence has in the late difficult times shattered that immoral undertaking: the catastrophe inflicts serious loss on Lyttelton and me but in our cases it is within bounds. In Stephen's it is far more extensive and combining with other circumstances which the same person had been chiefly instrumental in creating it has placed his whole property and the social position of his family ἐπὶ ξυροῦ ἀκμῆς:[d] has made it a question whether for pecuniary ease he should part with his estate and retain personal ease & independence or indeed

---

[a] 'Wrote to Manning' (*GD* iv. 17).

[b] Not located. Written 2 October 1847, following the near death of his daughter Agnes (*GD* iii. 658). Manning did receive the letter, referring to Agnes's illness in 480120mg, and noting its arrival in 480403mg.

[c] Stephen Glynne had early been involved in business interests at the brick and iron mining works, Oak Farm, near Stourbridge, and Gladstone, as an investor in the project (along with his bother-in-law, George Lyttelton), supported expansion under Boydell, the manager. When the company went into bankruptcy in 1847, the Hawarden Estate was threatened and saved only by heavy investments and great energy on Gladstone's part, eventually resulting in his full ownership of Hawarden. See 390718gm.

[d] On the razor's edge. Homer, *Iliad*, 10. 173.

wealth[54] which he would then amply command, or fight through the very severe conflict with his engagements. In the meantime good as he is accomplished as he is acute and sensible & prudent as in many ways he is he has not the smallest capacity for managing these affairs and the whole weight nearly of them comes on me in his stead not because I am competent to bear it but because I am in one degree less qualified—A concern in bankruptcy with £ 250,000 of liabilities, a vast and complex business to be recast, very heavy and early demands to be provided for, large sums of money to be borrowed and realised, and a constant uphill fight to be carried on against difficulties which are to all appearance all but and only not insurmountable, these are the additions now made by the dispensation of God to the usual engagements of my life, which have at all times for many years back seemed to be quite adequate to my very middling strength. How I get on with them I hardly know; they often make me faint & sick at heart, for there is something in having to deal with the case of another for whom you may not take the resolutions you would in your own case, that gives a peculiar form to the problem & the working of it. But do not suppose that I presume to talk of it as an affliction—it is a weight much more than a pain—on his account I might have much pain but that from the constitution of his mind he is able to throw it off in a great degree & betake himself to other pursuits. My recent experience of our little Agnes's struggle between life and death and my remembrance of the rebellious temper of my heart when I thought that God had evidently marked her for the world of spirits, and of the sharpness of that conviction, enables me if not to describe, at least acutely to feel the difference between the two. I cannot pray or wish that this should be removed: I have never seen the working of the prudential & moral laws of God's providence more signally exhibited, I fully own the signs of His Fatherly wisdom & love, were the task taken away from me I think it would leave me lightheaded such a difference would it make in the pressure on my daily existence and all I can presume to wish or pray is that it may please God to give me a little more strength to carry the charge so full of admonition. All this which as you will readily see is very private in its nature I have only been led to state in order to explain to you what really demanded explanation—namely, the reason why I have so often flagged and failed to discharge an office of friendship to you in your absence and in an absence from such a cause as yours by trying to bring[55] a little of the world in which we live and of its events and interests before you.

You have I see[56] heard about little Agnes how near she went to the very gates of death, and how she was wonderfully given back to us. It is like passing through a double Baptism, the obligations of the first covenant are multiplied in themselves when a child realises by this kind of experience[57] so much of death and of resurrection—God has given us also another infant & a yet more signal mercy was my wife's escape from the infection of Agnes' erysipelas.[e] Her state at the time & the subsequent confinement placed her in the most imminent risk: Lady Pakington[f] has just died in confinement of the same complaint: 'a thousand shall fall beside thee & ten thousand at thy right hand, but it shall not come nigh thee:'[g]—Another great domestic event with us is that we have got a governess for our children of whom we think most highly in all the weightiest points & indeed have seen no reason to think otherwise in any—

As to public and Church affairs there are so many & of so much interest that I scarcely know how to touch them in what remains to me of time & space. The course of things you see has brought me at once into collision with my constituents about the Jews and into a pretended collision about the R[oman] C[atholics]. As to the former, I agree with everything that you say; it is a decided *note* of retrogression in the matter of that text. The kingdoms of the world are become the kingdoms of the Lord & of his Christ;[h] but there is *a* point at which it becomes not politic only but obligatory to let down the theory of civil institutions, namely, when the discrepancy between them & their actual operation has become a hopeless falsehood and a mischievous & virulent imposture. It was time I think to unveil realities tho' in every case by unveiling you are apt, for the first effect, to confirm—but you open new sources of hope by throwing the minds of men into a more natural and genuine attitude, to think and to labour in fields that are not & cannot be exhausted. I have published my speech with a long Preface,[i] & I have the consolation of knowing that it has mitigated the displeasure of some excellent men, while in other cases I hope a form of thought has been suggested which will exercise hereafter an influence in modifying its course among the clergy. None of these things

---

[e] A disease causing inflammation of the skin, sometimes referred to as St Anthony's fire.

[f] Augusta Anne Pakington died 23 February 1848. The daughter of George Murray, Bishop of Rochester, she married John Somerset Pakington (1799–1880; MP for Droitwich, 1837–74 [*DNB*]) in 1844.

[g] Ps. 91: 7.

[h] Rev. 11: 15.

[i] William E. Gladstone, *Substance of a Speech on the Motion of Lord John Russell for a Committee of the Whole House, with a View to the Removal of the Remaining Jewish Disabilities; Delivered in the House of Commons, on Thursday, Dec[ember] 16, 1847. Together with a Preface* (London: John Murray, 1848).

can be done without a painful wrench. Though the National Club[j] tried to get up a requisition against me & failed, yet some weeks ago I was informed on good authority that if I vacated I should be opposed and beaten. It may still be so but that of course does not move me: I am deeply & energetically convinced that I have acted *for* the Church & that any other vote from me would have been decidedly injurious to her: and if Oxford should reject me on such a ground painful as the reverse would be I shall I trust take it cheerfully & believe that that too will work for good though in a way very different from the one imagined by those who might inflict the blow. Let me add that Hope, Lyttelton, R. Palmer,[k58] & some others to whose judgments I assign much weight had come separately to my conclusion.

As to the revived 'war of investitures' I think the remonstrant Bishops will be prepared to stickle for some provision which shall secure a power of equitable & canonical objection, when the question comes to be stirred. But it seems to be thought, & I for one undoubtedly think, that the Church has decidedly gained by the proceedings, except as to having Dr. Hampden for a Bishop which though serious is not *the* great question involved: so we are content to wait a while. Meantime the Gov[ernmen]t are in great difficulties & have blundered sorely with their finance—we are obliged (I mean the exofficial corps) to lend what help we can towards bringing them through. The case of Lord John & the Church is now I fear fixed for ever. To the Church as she is Apostolic, & as she is dogmatic, he will conscientiously do the very utmost of evil that he dare. And this I must say ought to have been foreseen by those who rushed into his train last summer & who (in my judgment) then and at other times have done Peel so much injustice.

Well here I am on my fourth page & not a word of you, not a word of Rome. I have been silent about you because I am told that there is actually flesh again on your bones: and this I take for the clearest & fullest confirmation of your own favourable accounts—Only I do hope that you will not any more trifle with yourself for the little I have seen of your

[j] The National Club was founded in 1846 in the aftermath of the Maynooth controversy 'in support of the Protestant principles of the Constitution, and for raising the moral and religious condition of the people'. Linked with Conservative, Protectionist, and High Church concerns, it had a substantial following in the House of Commons (less so in the Lords) and could therefore exert parliamentary influence. For details see Wolffe (1991), 210–27.

[k] Gladstone met with Hope on 9 March 1848 (*GD* iv. 16). There are no meetings listed with the other men in the *GD* and no correspondence located on this matter.

manner of subsistence & action goes far to convince me that the causes of your malady have all been put & kept in movement by yourself. Hope again is a metamorphosed man his mind seems composed again & his body thrives & I am again sanguine in the expectation that we may yet see him spend his energies in *the* cause for which I am insular enough to believe they were divinely designed.

As to Rome she wants no words from me. I am *always* there more or less & while you are there more &[59] not less. I take this offering as it is meant, not as it is done: & with kindest messages from my wife I remain your aff[ectiona]te friend

W. E. Gladstone.

Remember us most kindly to the Herberts & tell them we have now become their unworthy neighbours.[1]

[[BL Add. MS 44247, 343–4; Morley transcript; Lathbury, ii. 278–80; cf. Chapeau, 323–4]]

480403mg

Rome. April 3. 1848.

My dear Gladstone.

Your letter of March 12 reached me on the 31st having been delayed in the North of Italy.

The intelligence of Stephen Glynne's loss I had already heard, in a general way, from Lord Feilding: but no mention of any other member of his Family. I regret it very sincerely the more so now that I hear of your being a sharer in the misfortune. I do not say this as valuing money for you, because I have by large experience in my own Father's history learned how little happiness depends on the having or losing of fortune. But anything of anxiety and care on such subjects is wearing, and hinders the healthy exercise of life and its higher works. I trust, however, from what you say that it has not touched you enough to involve any serious inconvenience to you or your children. For Stephen Glynne I am very sorry: and shall much regret, though I could not doubt of the decision if you advise it, about Hawarden.

I very well remember the Sunday & the conversation you refer to in St. James's Park. Many things we then spoke of have since[60] come back to my memory, but never the subject of fortune till your letter recalled it.

---

[1] Note Gladstone's rental of 6 Carlton Gardens in May 1847. See 370220gm and 480807gm. The Herberts were in Italy late 1847 and early 1848. For their contact with Manning see Bodl. MS Eng. lett. c. 657, 4ff.

From your letter I see that you have been worn and tried: & though I could desire in one sense that my Friends might be free from such burdens & adversities, yet in another, and a higher I cannot wish them to lose their share in the best discipline of their life. I am sure that nothing short of what God, in His goodness, has appointed for me, could suffice for such a will as mine. Though my needs are no measure of yours, yet I must believe that the fears you have had to bear[61] for your dear Child with all the anxieties which follow on such an illness are full of beautiful & blessed chastisement. Without such things I never should have learned reality & sympathy: even in the little measure in which I know them. I hope your wife is restored to health & strength.

As to the general subjects which crowd upon me at the thought of having you for a reader, it is almost impossible to attempt them. The rapidity with which events have rushed onward since I came to Rome in November is out of all the proportions & analogies of my past recollection. When I came here the Romans were speaking of a Criminal & Civil Code, public trials, a moderately free press and a consulta nominated by the Pope as a sort of maximum with which they would be well contented. I may say that six weeks has revolutionized Italy & Europe. The Constitutions of Naples, Tuscany, Piedmont & Rome: the war of independence in Sicily, the Republic in France, the rising of[62] Lombardy, the constitution of Vienna, the Republic of Venice, the Revolution in Berlin, the rising in Hungary, and, if rumour be true in Cracow, & Poland, the expulsion of the Jesuits from Naples, Turin, Genoa, & the whole of Italy even from Rome—all these, to say nothing of lesser movements have thronged into, at the most, two months. What are we to read in this? Is it not the moral & popular development, the fruit of thirty years of peace demanding recognition, & social power? In this view I am inclined to look at it with hope, especially when I see what after all these sudden & violent movements in advance, England is in all popular freedom & power immeasurably ahead. When I think of our social state the only account I can give of it (as I often have to do to Italians) is that we are a republic under an hereditary President that the middle class which is two thirds of the Political force of[63] England is the Government of the Country, & that people do not make revolutions against themselves. It needed no great foresight to see that some such movement was preparing. All institutions have been evidently in solution, & the polarity of all Europe has been evidently shifted. It is wonderful to see the Catholic Church in America France & Italy distinctly of the progress and popular party: indeed in many ways at the head of it. My own impression is that in Italy there is a strong tendency to a Republic, &

nowhere more than here where the laity have no organization, no social order, a very small aristocracy, and an elective Ecclesiastical Sovereign. It needs but to take off the Pontificalia and the Sovereign is an elected chief whether for years or for life matters little, & may be determined hereafter.[a]

What the bearing of this may be on the Church is less easy to say. It falls in with an old belief of mine in which I think you share, I mean that the Church of the last ages will be as the Church of the first isolated & separate from the Civil Powers of the World. In the first ages the Church won them by making them Christians: in these days they are renouncing the Church by making themselves again merely secular & material. And in this has long been & is now my fear for the Church of England. I am afraid it will be deceived into trusting the State too long, and thereby secularising itself. I hope I may find some way of interpreting the 'insularity' you confess to. For myself I know no real sense in which I dare hold it. I never had much of it and feel that every year has convinced me more deeply that Protestantism is heretical, & Nationalism is Judaic. I remember you saying that the English Monarchy is an idea wh[ich] commands the veneration & affections of your mind in a way beyond what I am likely to feel. On the other hand 'Tu es Petrus',[b] & 'Credo in Unam C[a]th[olicam] Eccl[esia]m'[c] reveal to me a divine Monarchy claiming a sentiment of loyalty to a Person in Heaven before which all other kingdoms melt away. I trust that your insularity does not limit the full living practical realization of this transcendent[64] law of Faith and action. I do not think it does though your political life & sympathies give a tone to your mind which some who do not know you as I do might misinterpret.

Farewell my dear Friend: I begin to think of home, but the lines of confusion thus deep are drawn from Hungary to the Pyrenees and as yet

---

[a] Cf. Manning's comments on Easter Tuesday, 25 April 1848, to Henry Wilberforce: 'I am deeply convinced that the course taken by the Pope has been not only wise & good, but necessary. The unlooked for effects which have spread all up Europe even to England are his work, under God, so far as they are good, but he never dreamed of them, & so far as they are bad are no more his than sacrilege is the work of the Church. . . . I seem to see the beginning of a new order of international relations, and who can say that there will not be a new and a renewed system of relations between Christians? The opposition of the Civil Power everywhere is heaping up Church upon Church for mutual support and driving them into unity' (Ushaw College MS OS/P9). Note that Manning had an audience with Pius IX the following month on 11 May. For details on the state of Rome during the time see relevant sections in Luigi Carlo Farini, *The Roman State from 1815 to 1850*, trans. W. E. Gladstone (4 vols.; London: John Murray, 1851–4).

[b] 'You are Peter', Matt. 16: 18.

[c] 'I believe in One Catholic Church', Nicene Creed.

I have not fixed my route. If I can I hope to see Lombardy in its first days of freedom.

> With my kind regards to your wife.
> Ever yours affectionately,
> H. E. Manning

P.S. The Herberts were gone before your letter came. It was a great delight to me to see them so much and so long.

[[Pitts; Chapeau, 144, 216–18; cf. Leslie, 81, 83–4]]

480703mg

> Lav[ington] July 3. 1848.

My dear Gladstone,

I hope to be at 44 Cadogan Place on Thursday, & to stay till Monday. I am anxious to see you, & write to propose to come to you, *or you to me*, on Sunday at ½ p[as]t 2.[a] I wish much to talk with you, chiefly as in our last Sunday walk about yourself,[b] as you gave me leave. Thank God, I feel getting well enough to talk no more of myself, & hope soon to forget myself in working for others.

> With my love to your wife.
> Ever yours aff[ectionatel]y
> H. E. Manning.

The R[igh]t Hon[oura]ble W.E. Gladstone.

[[Pitts]]

[[Gladstone wrote to Manning on 4 July 1848 (*GD* iv. 47; not located). On the following Sunday, 9 July, Gladstone read Manning's sermons (ibid. 48) and held a conversation with him which he recorded on 10 July (ibid. 49).[c] On Sunday, 30 July Gladstone finished reading Manning's sermons (ibid. 58).]]

480806mg

> Wilton[a] Aug[ust] 6. 1848

My dear Gladstone,

In the hope of meeting you quietly at this place I brought the inclosed proof of my Charge[b] meaning to ask you to look at it, & give me your

---

[a] Sunday, 9 July 1848.   [b] 11 January 1846. See 460108gm.

[c] For details of the important meeting see discussion in Introduction. See also 501106gm.

[a] The Wiltshire country home of the Herberts.

[b] Henry Edward Manning, *A Charge Delivered at the Ordinary Visitation of the Archdeaconry of Chichester in July, 1848* (London: John Murray, 1848), was especially concerned with the appointment of Hampden as Bishop of Hereford and secular authority in religious matters. Manning delivered his *Charge* at Chichester on 18 July 1848 and received an address of the

judgment. And though I know how spare your time is I do so still. Nothing but the value I set on your advice and the fear I have of speaking rashly on the subjects I have touched would make me ask so great a favour. But if you would read it over you would confer on me a kindness, and an obligation of a high value. I am most anxious as to the effect of the Hereford case on many minds, and I should be greatly disturbed if I were to treat it either too rashly or too lightly.

I shall be at the Rev[eren]d W. Butler's, Wantage,[c] till Saturday: after that at Lavington. If you would cast your eye over it and give me a few lines I should be very grateful.

Ever yours affect[ionatel]y,

H. E. Manning

I cannot say how disappointed I am not to see you both here. Also the subjects[65] of Church & State are matters of anxiety now: & I should much desire your help.

[[Pitts; Chapeau, 145, 219]]

480807gm[a]

6 Carlton Gardens[b]

Aug[ust] 7. 1848

My dear Manning

Even with leisure I could have done poor justice to your request & as it is I am much pressed which I beg you to take as my excuse for slight & hasty handling—But indeed under any circumstances I find it difficult to provoke any critical faculty into activity in reading what you have written, so much more powerful is the appeal to other portions of our nature—

I inclose two leaves with marginal notes—also

p. 19.[66] I do not know with what strictness you mean to hold 1 Tim. iii and Tit. 1. applicable to a *Bishop*—except indeed a fortiori—[c]

Clergy welcoming him back after his long absence (*English Churchman* [20 July 1848], 484). An unannotated copy of the *Charge* is preserved at the National Library of Wales (SDL, GTM/ F 176/ 16).

  [c] William John Butler (1818–94), founder of the community of St Mary the Virgin, an Anglican sisterhood at Wantage. For details see *DNB*, William John Butler, *Life and Letters of William John Butler, Late Dean of Lincoln*, ed. Arthur John Butler (London: Macmillan & Co., 1897), and Anson (1955), 242–55.

  [a] 'Wrote to... Manning... Manning's Charge' (*GD* iv. 60).

  [b] Gladstone rented 6 Carlton Gardens from his father in May 1847 and received it in the partition of part of the elder Gladstone's estate in 1849. See 480403mg and 370220gm.

  [c] In the *Charge*, 19, Manning uses the biblical passages cited by Gladstone to define the act of confirmation of the Bishop.

p. 29. with us, a 'declaratory' law technically means a law which purports simply to 'declare' & does not 'enact'.[d]

p. 31. do not the Chapter properly represent the Clergy in the matter of election (l.4 from foot)[e]

p. 33.13. Again I observe that you do not ask for an absolute but only for a strictly judicial power of revue. (This distinction has been *most* brought out in the history of the Free Kirk and Veto questions in Scotland.)[f]

[p. 33.] l.1. From foot—'torture'—a malevolent critic will misapprehend this.[g]

37.7 from foot. 'refuse'. See on[67] sup. p. 14.[h]

44.8 & seqq. Doubtless there is great truth in this yet I would not have it said that the resistance of the Church to the State power was essentially the same as her resistance to the heretical principle. We must recollect the cases of Grosseteste Gerson[i] & some others the most admirable men which bear upon this question—I confess to strong sympathies with the (quasi)[68] anti-papal part of the Church of England before the Reformation.[j]

---

[d] Correction made by Manning; see *Charge*, 28 (pagination discrepancy here and later the result of other changes): 'the first Statute, which is the basis of all, is not an enacting but a declaratory law'.

[e] Change or adjustment made; there is no relation drawn between Clergy and the Chapter in the section cited.

[f] Cf. *Charge*, 32, and the use of the term 'judge': 'It is not more necessary that the Church should be ultimate judge as to truth of doctrine than that it should be the ultimate judge as to the fitness of those whom it ordains to preach that doctrine.' References to the Free Kirk and Veto are to the 'Disruption' in Scotland in 1843, when the Free Church of Scotland seceded from the Established Church of Scotland.

[g] *Charge*, 33: 'I must disbelieve that the laws of the realm of England can by any torture make persecution lawful, or sacrilege a duty.'

[h] Cf. *Charge*, 37: 'The only part hitherto borne by the Civil Power in this affair was to refuse to interfere: that is, to refuse to compel the Metropolitan to revoke his acts. The State, therefore, has hitherto been simply passive,' and *Charge*, 13, speaking of the consecration of Hampden: 'The only point of real importance in this part of the question I conceive to be the act of the Comissary of the Metropolitan in refusing to hear objectors whom he had duly cited, and in proceeding, nevertheless, to confirm the election presented to him.'

[i] Robert Grosseteste (1170–1253), Bishop of Lincoln, and Jean Gerson (1363–1429) both opposed papal incursions into religious matters for secular power.

[j] See *Charge*, 47: 'In the last eighteen years we have not indeed an enuciation of any such theory [of absorbing the Church into the State by denying its separate existence], but many facts which such theories would alone justify: as, for instance, the continued suspension of

p. 54. 'The Church of England' &c.—A most noble passage: only I wish
there were room in it for the Scriptures which of course are the highest
class of open 'spiritual decrees' but people will not all understand you so—[k]

I have only to add, God grant the Charge may have the composing effect
with respect to the Hampden question which you desire & which it seems
to me admirably calculated to produce—

It was not want of will that kept us from Wilton—My wife is gone to pay
a visit of more immediate duty instead and I am as yet tied by business in a
great degree—Next week I hope to go to Hagley[l]—and early in September
to Fasque, to remain there for the autumn with all my belongings

Believe me always
Aff[ectiona]tely yours
W. E. Gladstone

Venerable
Archdeacon Manning
[[BL Add. MS 44247, 345–6; Morley transcript]]

490109gm[a]

Fasque Jan[uary] 9. 1849.

My dear Manning
I have heard of you from time to time during the past autumn and have
cherished the hope that your remaining in England for the winter either
means that an increase of strength has led to the decision—or[69] at the least

---

provincial synods; the erection of civil commissions with ecclesiastical names and functions;
the initiation of ecclesiastical measures in Parliament, the sense of the Church not being
first taken upon them; the suppression and union of Sees,... attempts to secularise or
obtain control of the education of the people, projects respecting rules and judgments of
heresy...'

[k] See *Charge*, 53: 'The Church of England lives by lineal and unbroken continuity with its
past; it knows no founders but the Apostles; no doctrine but the Catholic Faith; no heresy
but what the Church condemns; no spiritual government but the one Episcopate; no
authority over the religious conscience but spiritual decrees...'

[l] Gladstone left for Hagley on 22 August and for Fasque on 13 September 1848. Note
that among the Gladstone Tracts at NLW is an unannotated copy (SDL, GTM/ F 182/14)
of Manning's *The Lost Sheep. A Sermon Preached on the Feast of St. Luke the Evangelist [October 18],
at the Opening of St. Paul's Church, Brighton* (Brighton: Henry King, 1848).

[a] 'Wrote to... Manning' (*GD* iv. 91).

& worst that it may not be attended with any ill effects. Two causes have kept me from writing to you, one that it can hardly be done without saying so very much: the other that my wearisome subjects of necessary correspondence yet continue and sorely indispose me, because of my own weakness (for it is no legitimate reason of necessity) for the *optional* correspondence which I should otherwise delight in. There is however yet a third reason: I know your fidelity in this character & I am very unwilling to draw upon it. Now therefore, while I write, I shall consider myself as saying something to you, but I look for no reply, until we meet please God in London. I expect to be there on the 25th for a night, then to go to Oxford until the 30th or 31st and then come back & be planted for the Session.

In the meantime please to look at the inclosed paper:[b] should you not have already seen it. The plan is a very favourite one with me: but I wrote to Mr. Palin[c] on getting his *first* circular to say it seemed to me that more command & discipline would be requisite, & that selfdenial should not be so studiously *minimised*.

What questions are in the perspective[70] of possibility! Heresy test[d]— Episcopal Elections—Education conflict[e]—the Jews, for love of whom I have been *fischiato*[f] (it sounds better than hissed) vanish into insignificance. Other great ones are the Eccl[esiastical] Courts—and the Eccl[esiastical] Commission & Chapters. Of these I think Education & the two last are the most likely to come on: & they make me least afraid. As to the heresy test, I see but one course to protest *ab initio*[g] against all mere statutes affecting the Faith: & not only the protest—(of which mode there are living examples—) but to follow up the protest & to signify beforehand the intention to follow it up by any & every means morally good that may tend to *realise* the protestation. On Episcopal nominations I think the course should be different. But there I think there should be without any *declinator* of the jurisdiction the very same stiffness to receive what is essential. When

---

[b] Not located.

[c] Gladstone wrote to William Palin (1803–82; *DNB*), Rector of Stifford, on 27 December 1848 (*GD* iv. 87; not located).

[d] On the appointment of Hampden as Bishop of Hereford in November 1847, legal procedures were initiated to prevent his confirmation because of earlier charges of heresy, but failed in January 1848. See Liddon, iii. 164–6 and Nikol (1974), 347.

[e] On education questions see 490112mg, 490705mg, and 490706gm.

[f] Whistled.

[g] From the beginning.

reflecting however on these matters I feel more & more that if the battle of the Church is to be fought successfully in England, the laity must be organized and enlisted in her regular army, and that too very promptly or the occasion will be gone.

My wife and I have had a great treat in a visit to Dalkeith. The Chapel there is worth a pilgrimage: and the example set by the Duke and Duchess another. There have been reports about her and Lady Lothian as unsettled: reports not less cruel than absurd.[h]

My wife is in London with two children. I remain here at present with three. God bless & prosper you, & give back your perfect strength—not for you but for us rather.

Your aff[ectiona]te friend
WEG.

Ven[erable]
Archd[eaco]n Manning
[[BL Add. MS 44248, 1–2; Morley transcript; cf. Chapeau, 325]]

490112mg

Lavington. Jan[uar]y 12. 1849.

My dear Gladstone,

As I have not yet bound myself by the 4th vow of cadaverous obedience, I begin by a direct breach of your injunction not to write to you. Why I have not done so before now[71] I cannot well say except for the reasons you give, according to my measure.

Certainly the feeling of unwillingness to write a little when I have much to say acts strongly to keep me quiet.

---

[h] The Gladstones visited Dalkeith from 30 December 1848 to 2 January 1849 when they returned to Fasque. While there they attended the Episcopal chapel, built by the Duke of Buccleuch between 1843 and 1847. Lady Cecil Chetwynd Kerr (1808–77), daughter of the 2nd Earl Talbot, married the 7th Marquis of Lothian in 1831. On her husband's death in 1841 she moved from the Church of Scotland to the Scottish Episcopal tradition, financed a church, built on Tractarian principles at Jedburgh, 1841–3, and after 1845 attended the Episcopal chapel at Dalkeith, the chaplain of which had been received as a Roman Catholic in 1847. She was received in 1851. See *DNB*, Nockles, 'Our Brethren' (1996), Ryrie (1994), Beard (1997), 81–6, and Yates (1999), 125.

My chief object in writing now is to say that I hope to be in London on Monday (15th) and to stay about three weeks; so that I hope to see you. (44 Cadogan Place) You do not speak of your health: which I hope is stronger than when I saw you:[a] and made up for the work which is plainly before you.

Before I go to better things I will say, as you kindly ask, that I am by Gods mercy, wonderfully well. I feel the cold at times, & take more care than I like: but I am at this moment in better health & strength than I have known for years: & letting me go my own way about it, that is wasting nothing on other matters. I feel able for any amount of work: so that my hands are full.

Now for the rest. I agree in every word you write about our probable future. And above all in what you say about the heresy Test. I am satisfied that the time is come for us to avert danger by moving first, & by moving onward. Our present position is one in which we cannot defend ourselves, & we must take higher ground. As to organizing the laity what you say is very true: but when I look at facts I see

1. That 'the Church of England Party', ie. 'the Aristocracy, Country Gentlemen &c.' are nine-tenths Erastian and opposed to such belief as you & I live by.
2. That the middle classes are against us.
3. That the[72] only laity we can depend on are (1) individuals from these two classes and (2) the poor.

But these last need no less than an Apostolic Mission to awaken and guide them.

And the Church has not one Missionary, she has a body of Pastors of whom individuals are awake and at work, but the mass are inert, timid, unpersuasive, & powerless. I am more & more deeply satisfied that the World will always be too strong for a Church which does not *honour* and *embody* the Counsels of Evangelical perfection. Let our clergy be as they are, but if so, & all the more for that reason, we need Collegiate Churches, & Confraternities on the one hand to raise the Parish Priests, & on the other to break the brunt of the Civil Power.

Now I am near the end of my paper and I will at least obey you so far as not to take a second sheet.

***

[a] 9 July 1848. See 480703mg.

As to Education,[b] I have great fears. My belief is that the Church has suffered the C[ommittee] of P[rivy] Council[c] to draw it into a net: & that we are already virtually secularized. But this I must justify when we meet. If you see the Report of a meeting of the Archd[eaconr]y of Chichester on this subject simply disbelieve what it makes me say.[d]

[b] The debate between the Privy Council Committee of Education and the National Society over the application of management clauses had been intense for well over six months. (Note the report on the meeting of the National Society on 7 June 1848 over this matter in *The Guardian* of the same day, 371–2, and *The Guardian*'s continuing coverage of the issue during that year (ibid., 21 June, 401–2 on the management clauses; 13 Sept., 50, editorial on the debate; 4 Oct., 626–8, correspondence between the National Society and the Committee of Education; 18 Oct., 654; 25 Oct., 665, 667; 1 Nov., 679; 8 Nov., 690–1; 15 Nov., 705–6; 6 Dec., 749–50; 13 Dec., 764–5) and the next (ibid., 3 Jan. 1849 suppl., 13; 21 Mar., 187; 4 Apr., 218, 221; 11 Apr., 237; 18 Apr., 251; 1 Aug., 503–4). Manning was deeply involved in these issues. On the meeting held in Chichester on 19 December 1848 see *The Guardian*, 20 December 1848, 780, and 3 January 1849, suppl., 16. On 1 February 1849 he wrote to Robert Wilberforce telling him of his committee activities: 'Matheson, Dodsworth, Gresley, Reg[inal]d Wood, Butler of Wantage met here on Tuesday and agreed to the inclosed resolutions [on education and the National Society]' (Bodl. MS Eng. lett. c. 655, 103). Note also that Manning's *Charge* of 1849 was directly affected by the issue. On it *The Guardian* of 22 August 1849 reported at length (548–52). For a full discussion see Burgess (1954) and (1958).

[c] Committee of Council on Education. For details on its activities in 1848 see 'Minutes of the Committee of Council on Education. Correspondence &c 1848–1849', PP 1849 (1090.) xlii. 83. See also PP 1849 (1111.) xlii. 243 and *Minutes of the Committee of Council on Education with Appendices. 1847-8-9. England and Wales. Schools of Parochial Unions* (London: W. Clowes & Sons, 1849).

[d] On 20 December 1848, 5f, *The Times* reported a meeting held the previous afternoon in the Cathedral Library at Chichester 'specially convened by the Archdeacon, in consequence of a numerously signed requisition presented to him . . . for the purpose of taking into consideration the correspondence which had recently taken place between the Committee of Privy Council on Education and the Archbishop of Canterbury on the part of the National Society'. The resolutions adopted emphasized that 'it is the duty of the clergy and laity to extend and improve by all means in their power the education of the people, and to render an actual and effectual co-operation to the state in all its measures relating to education, so far as they are consistent with the faith and principles of the Church. That this co-operation is at present time unhappily impeded, partly by general mistrust, arising from the want of clear and certain laws defining the character and powers of the Committee of Council in Education, and partly from the objectionable nature of objectionable plans, which from time to time have been proposed by that committee. . . . That the suspension of correspondence between the Committee of Privy Council and the National Society is to be lamented, especially as the cause of it is to be found in the Committee of Council. . . . That the clergy of this archdeaconry view with much alarum and mistrust the increased influence which the Government have acquired . . . in the system on which

Farewell. And may God richly bless you this & all years, both you, & yours.

Ever your affect[ionat]e friend

H. E. Manning.

[The] R[igh]t Hon[oura]ble
W. E. Gladstone

[[Pitts; Chapeau, 146, 220–2]]

[[Gladstone met Manning on 25 January 1849 (*GD* iv. 95) and on 2 February (ibid. 96). On 13 March 1849 he saw Manning 'on Church matters' and met with him again on the same subject on the day after the following letter, on 15 March (ibid. 107).]]

490316mg

44 Cadogan Place. March 16. 1849.

My dear Gladstone,

I return the inclosed letters[a] with many thanks. They are truly painful.

As to the alleged miracle I am convinced as you are, & as to the effect of such things. The case is too intimately painful for me to say more about. I am forced to write only a few words which is perhaps as well. May God bless you.

Ever yours aff[ectionatel]y.

H. E. Manning

[[BL Add. MS 44248, 3; Gladstone's annotation on margin: H.J.Gs recovery from neuralgia]]

[[On Sunday, 29 April 1849, Manning preached 'worthily of himself' at Margaret Chapel in London where Gladstone was in attendance (*GD* iv. 118). On 20 May he saw Manning (ibid. 123), on 24 May Gladstone had '10 to dinner (for Duchess of Buccleuch & Manning)' (ibid. 124), and he met with Manning again on 8 June (ibid. 127). He wrote to Manning on 12 June (ibid. 120; not located).]]

---

church schools are managed, especially as in its semi-official publication of the Committee of Council on Education, a preference is plainly declared for a foreign combined system of education, and a disinclination is plainly shown to relax the rule, by which all children in church schools are required to be learnt the church catechism . . . '

   [a] The specific letters have not been located but a collection of materials relating to Helen Gladstone's 'cure' is extant in SDL, Glynne–Gladstone MS 709, which includes a letter that Gladstone wrote on the subject of his sister's health and 'miracle' cure to James Hope (for text see Addenda to this Section), in all forty-two letters 'relating to the health and affairs of Helen J. Gladstone' with letters from Professor James Miller, Robert Ferguson, Charles Locock (doctors), Johanna Robertson, compeer, and Gladstone to Hope.

490705mg

Lavington. July 5. 1849.

My dear Gladstone,

I am anxious about the[73] negociation between the C[ommit]tee of Council & the N[ational] Soc[ie]ty and trust that if the subject comes up in the House of Commons you will be able to say nothing inconsistent with what passed[74] at the N[ational] S[ocie]ty meeting on the 6th of last month.[a]

The principle then accepted seems to me so fair & reasonable & so vital to our peace and order that I must follow it whithersoever it is driven.

You know that I am mistrusted & reproached for over anxiety not to break with the State: but I am prepared to break with Government if they refuse these terms of co-operation.

And what I am willing to do numbers are hardly to be restrained from doing with heat & haste.

I am anxious to say this to you because I see no one else has so much in his hands on this subject as yourself. We are in a reasonable & tenable position: one well formed for the H[ouse] of Commons. What we ask is to have our liberty as before, and liberty is energy from free trade upwards.

[a] On 6 June 1849 there was a meeting of the National Society for Promoting the Education of the Poor at the Society's Central Schoolrooms in Westminster from 12 noon to 8 in the evening (see *The Guardian*, 6 June, 381–4 [Manning's speech, 384], *The Times*, 7 June 1849, 8a; see also *Ecclesiastical Gazette* [12 June 1849], 273, and cf. *GD* iv. 127). The meeting resulted in a lengthy debate over specific amendments put forward by George Anthony Denison and Manning, the latter anxious to maintain some cooperation with the State in education. The Manning proposed amendment in part read: 'That while this Meeting desires fully to co-operate with the State in promoting the education of the people, it is under the necessity of declaring that no terms of co-operation can be satisfactory which shall not allow to the Clergy and Laity full freedom to constitute upon such principles and models as are both sanctioned and recommended by the order and the practice of the Church of England.' See also Purcell, i. 418–34. Denison (1805–96) was educated at Christ Church, Oxford, and elected a Fellow of Oriel, 1828. He was Vicar of Broadwinson, Dorset, 1838, of East Brent, Somerset, from 1845, and Archdeacon of Taunton from 1851. A strong defender of High Church views, particularly of the role of the Church in educational matters, he was prosecuted during 1854–8 in a series of highly publicized cases for his belief in the Real Presence in the Eucharist. For details see *DNB*, Denison's *Notes of my Life, 1805–1878* (2nd edn.; Oxford: James Parker & Co., 1878), and his *Fifty Years at East Brent: The Letters of George Anthony Denison 1845–1896*, ed. Louisa Evelyn Denison (London: John Murray, 1902), and Coombs (1984).

I should grieve if we were to be opposed in view about any thing, & for the first time, above all in a matter the sequelae of which will last the rest of our lives.

If you would take the lead of a liberty movement in this I believe it would draw to you numberless hearts, and open for the Church its path in all other things.

Only do not give up this principle & get into details which are as bad as the jungle at Chillian wallah.[b]

I hope your wife is quite recovered & well.[c]

Ever yours affect[ionatel]y

H. E. Manning.

The Right Hon[oura]ble
W. E. Gladstone
[[Pitts; Chapeau, 147, 222]]

490706gm[a]

6 C[arlton] G[ardens] July 6. [18]49.

My dear Manning

I do not see any immediate prospect of a discussion in Parliament about National Education. I am also far from desiring to hasten one for I know well by experience that whatever pleasure persons may have out of doors in reading speeches made in the House of Commons by those who sympathise with them, that a question touching spiritual or clerical power is never mooted there in opposition to the Executive Government without damage to the idea of such power and a diminished disposition to recognise it as the result. All *such* discussions should be contemplated as preludes to the severance of Church & state, remote perhaps but yet true & substantial preludes, and it is a misfortune that many persons regard them as mere flourishing of trumpets and sensible of the inspiriting effect on their own minds assume that they have no other or at least no different effect. But this is a lecture which you do not want & which those who do want it will miss. Therefore εἴρηται.[b]

---

[b] In the brushwood jungle near the Punjabi village of Chillianwalla in British India the English defeated a Sikh force at great cost on 13 January 1849. For reports on the battle see *The Times*, 30 March, 3c, and Roberts (1958), 342–3, 346.

[c] On 8 June 1849 Catherine Gladstone, 'with little Mary on her left arm slipped on the back steps, clung to the child with both arms to save her, fell *headlong* down a flight of 7 steep flag steps, then again five more' (*GD* iv. 127).

[a] 'Wrote to ... Manning' (ibid. 134).   [b] It is spoken.

I fear I cannot undertake by an engagement now to be formed to adhere in the House of Commons either to the principle that the whole extent of the prime liberty of the Church in constituting schools is to be preserved under the system of aid from the State, or to the particular application that it is necessary to retain a liberty of giving them a constitution by which all matters in dispute shall be referred to and settled by the Bishop. Indeed I would suggest to you to read the correspondence, which has just been published, between the Privy Council & the Roman Catholics[c] before *you* determine finally to insist on that liberty. I was before as you may remember not disposed to think it essential: I am even less disposed to stickle for it now. The Bishop has no strength to spare for purposes lying beyond his sphere: and a strict *bonâfide* definition of the spiritual sphere and restraint of his authority, as a general rule, within it in all new arrangements, I conscientiously think to be for his interests, since being already too weak for his spiritual & ecclesiastical work he has evidently no spare[75] force to spend upon other questions where he will be brought into collision with portions of the local communities interested in schools.

You will perceive that the concession to the N[ational] S[ociety] would at once be followed by a similar grant to the Vicars Apostolic.[d] The liberty thus given would be sometimes used among us, almost always among the Roman Catholics. I should be sorry to see that system at work in Roman Catholic schools aided by the State.

To obtain liberty for the Church is the object for which I should think it the highest, almost the only, honour and delight to spend and to[76] be spent. But by this I understand liberty in the English sense, liberty under rule, and the whole question is what such is admissible or desirable, what freedom will tend to or is required for the real development of your religious system.

My own opinion is that the N[ational] S[ociety] ought to have adhered to its first demand[77] for the moral & religious superintendence *of the school*: & ought now if possible to fall back upon it & allow them to push further[78] the question of Episcopal appeal. That further they should consider well *what* organ is to be empowered to draw the line between the two appellate jurisdictions[e] that of the Bishop and that of the mixed tribunal. According

---

[c] See 'Minutes of the Committee of Council on Education. Correspondence &c. 1848–49', PP 1849 (1090.) xlii. 83 (4 July 1849), 94–107 (PP pagination, 181–93) which treat the management of Roman Catholic Schools on a parallel with that of the National Society Schools.

[d] Titular bishops appointed by Rome to oversee Roman Catholics in England.

[e] 'Appellate jurisdiction', the power of a superior court to review the judgment of an inferior court.

to the P[rivy] C[ouncil] this is to be done by the mixed tribunal itself. This question I should push farther and it is I think the most vital one not yet explicitly discussed and settled. Assuming that no entirely satisfactory mode of settling it can be discovered, & that you ask for the universal appeal to the Bishop as a remedy, I would ask for it on that ground alone—and my mind leans to the belief that it would *not* be necessary in that point of view.

I shall be very glad to be corrected & further instructed by you: at the moment I have stated frankly my impressions. You may rely upon my taking no public step in the matter without very full consideration.

Should our views ultimately differ, the root of the difference may be in our several positions. I am doubtful whether two men having the most perfect unity of aim but so differently placed can in these times take it always as an evil sign that they have not the same practical view of the points to be finally insisted on in a delicate, perplexed & protracted negotiation.

Farewell—your aff[ectiona]te friend

W. E. Gladstone

Ven[erable]
Archdeacon Manning
My wife thank God is perfectly well & hearty.[79]
[[BL Add. MS 44248, 4–7; Morley transcript; Lathbury, ii. 281–2; cf. Chapeau, 325–6]]

3. The Lincoln Affair: July–October 1849

490707gm[a]
    Secret

6 Carlton Gardens
July 7. 1849.

My dear Manning

I am now going to put a question on my own responsibility alone which will surprise you but you will excuse it on account of my motive which is to be prepared as far as possible with the best advice in that most painful case

---

[a] On 7 July 1849 Gladstone notes: 'Wrote to Manning...Saw Lincoln & then Peel with him. We talked chiefly on the subject of a Mission. L[incoln] having said that the only persons whom he would like to send were in circumstances to render it impossible I told him he ought to let them judge of that. He there-upon named Manning & me, I undertook to write to M[anning] & said it might probably be practicable for me—which C[atherine] approved' (*GD* iv. 135). His Mission was to search out Lincoln's wife, Susan Harriet Catherine (1814–89; *DNB*; for later details see 891222mg), daughter of the 10th Duke of Hamilton and Brandon. She and Lincoln had married on 27 November 1832, but difficulties arose early in their relationship and by 1837 she was involved in an extramarital

of which you have heard from our friend most interested recently and from time to time.[b]

You know what has lately been heard of *her* equivocal & precarious condition, these epithets describing it under its best aspect. I am most deeply desirous that no other questions should be entertained at all until every means of stopping evil or averting danger by gentle influences shall have been exhausted. A personal mission from hence to Naples *now & with dispatch* is that which suggests itself if it can be arranged. I fear that you may have *more* than *one* insuperable impediment to undertaking alone or in company such a mission, still you are the judge of your own calling & comparative obligations and therefore I want to know from yourself, secretly & speedily, whether *such* impediments do or do not exist. I have in my mind 1. your health & the probable risk to it from a rapid & therefore laborious

---

affair. In 1848 she formed a liaison with Lord Walpole, son of the Earl of Orford, with whom she fled to the Continent and was later found to be pregnant. For general details see Munsell (1985), Gilliland (1994), 40–7, and above all Surtees (1977). Catherine Gladstone's approval was noted in a letter she sent to Lady Lincoln on 12 July 1849 telling her of Gladstone's forthcoming journey to Italy and commending him to her. Note also Catherine Gladstone's close attachment to Lady Lincoln, and the earlier correspondence between the two as well as from Lady Lincoln's sudden departure for the Continent on 2 August 1848 to the end of November of that year (see Eldridge [1967] for details and edition of the 12 July letter). The difficulties in the Lincolns' marriage parallelled Gladstone's general concern with marriage law at the time; a bill on the subject was passing through the Commons (see 'A Bill to amend and alter 5 & 6 William 4, so far as relates to marriage with certain of the prohibited degrees of affinity', PP 1849 [75.] iv. 167). On 22 April 1849, for example, he began to read the various publications on marriage law and continued to read regularly on the subject while the Bill was in the House and throughout the Lincoln affair (cf. *GD* iv. 116, 118, 119, 121, 122, 147; note Hansard, cvi. 616, 1318; *The Times*, 21 June 1849, 4 and 5 July 1849, 3). For Gladstone the two issues (the Marriage Bill and the Lincoln marriage) reached crisis points on the same day, 20 June: 'Saw Nicholl—Lincoln—The former disclosed to me new & very painful evidence raising for the first time in my mind the serious fear that Lady L[incoln] may have committed the last act of infidelity... H[ouse] of C[ommons] 12–6. Spoke 1½ hour on Wortley's Marriage Bill & voted in 143:177 ag[ains]t it' (*GD* iv. 131; cf. Hansard, cvi. 616). In addition Gladstone may have been troubled by the possibility of Lady Lincoln's conversion to Catholicism as suggested by Lincoln to Gladstone in a letter, 25 October 1848 (University of Nottingham MS NeC 11,695). On 7 February 1850 he abstained from voting on the Deceased Wife's Sister's Bill (*GD* iv. 183; Hansard, cviii. 524; see PP 1849 (250.) iv. 163 and 1849 (75.) iv. 171; for discussion see Liddon, iii. 177–85). For details on the Lincoln marriage, Gladstone's mission, and the eventual divorce in 1851, see Eldridge (1967) and Munsell (1985), 108–19.

  [b] For earlier correspondence between Lincoln and Manning on the matter see Addenda to this Section.

journey—2. your engagements in the Archdeaconry—the call on the other side being I must admit a forlorn hope or something near it. Want of will would of course be a third impediment that none would be entitled to challenge: but this in your case I do not suppose—as I know you would only entertain the question of duty & charity—

Now pray distinguish between this letter which I write of my own motion to obtain information, and a request to you—which may never be made & which of course I am not authorised to make—Nor have I written because I think it *probable* that you can be in a condition to undertake such a charge but at least to ascertain that you are not before turning to other quarters or committing myself finally by any particular advice—

I have proceeded on the belief that *notwithstanding* your not having (I apprehend) personal acquaintance in the case, our friend's confidence in you might probably lead him to turn to you: but I have said already 'alone or in company' because I think it might very probably be the latter, and also 'now & with dispatch' because I conclude that if done at all the thing cannot be done too quickly.[c]

I ought so far to define my own crude idea of such a mission as to say that I imagine it would have for its object inducing her to place herself in a position free humanly speaking from danger & affording reasonable guarantees for conduct whether by return to this country, joining friends abroad, or otherwise—

Believe me

Aff[ectiona]tely yours

W. E. Gladstone

An article in todays Daily News[d] strikes the chord I touched yesterday as to the relations of the P[rivy] C[ouncil] with other religious bodies & the tendencies of these discords to advance the cause of secular as opposed to religious Education.

Venerable

Archd[eacon] Manning

[[BL Add. MS 44248, 8–11; Morley transcript]]

---

[c] Cf. Shakespeare, *Macbeth*, i. vii. 1.

[d] The editorial in the *Daily News* of 7 July 1849, 5, opposed G. A. Denison's published comments that the Committee of Council on Education's insistence on the management clauses 'excludes absolutely the founders of this large class of Church Schools from a share in the education grant'.

490708mg

Lavington. July 8. 1849.

My dear Gladstone,

Your letter brings me to a question on which I have as you truly say a ready will.

My circumstances are these.

1. My visitations are not over until the 19th: and though[80] I could start immediately it would be difficult under some days.[a]

2. A rapid journey—such as you would make I am not able to bear without illness.

This I have found by long experience & no little travelling.

But I dare not say no to such a judgment as yours, & in such a case: especially as I said some time ago to our Friend that if she returned to any place nearer to England, I would gladly go if he desired it.

My chief fear is health. I am well, thank God, so long as I can avoid strain & derangement of habit but a slight thing produces general disturbance. But do not decide without letting me hear fully, what is needed for the carrying out of your view.

If it were possible for me, my whole heart & will would be ready. It would be hard to say how I have entered into their sorrow. Since he first wrote to me I have had it literally in my thoughts every day.[b]

All that I can say is that God is over all—& will rule all to His will. But these are strange exorbitancies, not to be reduced to any order or law till we are above all the courses[81] of heaven and earth.

The manly and great sorrow of our friend is an example, & makes me feel not only affection for him.

Let me hear from you again.

Ever yours affect[ionatel]y
H. E. Manning.

The Right Hon[oura]ble
W. E. Gladstone

[[Pitts; Chapeau, 148, 223]]

---

[a] See Manning's *A Charge Delivered at the Ordinary Visitation of the Archdeaconry of Chichester, in July, 1849* (London: John Murray; Chichester: W. H. Mason, 1849), almost twice the length of his earlier ones; it dealt primarily with educational matters and the problem of the separation of Church and State in regard to them. Gladstone's annotated copy is preserved in SDL, F25Man2e (cf. unannotated copy among the Gladstone Tracts at NLW [SDL, GTM/ F 177/ 18]).

[b] For Lincoln's letter to Manning of 24 November 1848 see Addenda to this Section.

490712mg

Lavington. July 12. 1849.

My dear Gladstone,

I send you Lord Lincolns letter and one from Mr. Henn.[a]

They will shew all that has passed to my knowledge.

The letters[82] of the former ought to touch any heart.

I need not say to you how I feel that you have advised & done the best thing & in the best of ways. May you have your fullest reward in restoring a wife to herself, & then to her home. I know no act of your life that would fill you with such joy at the last.

In what way can I join with you?

My visitation is a public obligation from which I could not withdraw myself without real failure of duty, and probable harm to others.

In this I am not free to choose. But after this is done I will hold myself ready to come & meet you or to assist in any way which will forward the object[83] of your mission.[b]

We cannot say beforehand whether this will be needful or not: but I wish you to know that I will answer your call, God willing.

May you be kept safely, & may your home be in peace till you come back.

Believe me,
Ever your affect[ionat]e friend,
H. E. Manning.

The Right Hon[oura]ble W. E. Gladstone.

[[Pitts; Chapeau, 149, 223–4]]

---

[a] The letter was destroyed; the one from Lincoln may have been as well. See 491020gm.

[b] On 8 July 1849, Gladstone 'Went with Lincoln to see Thesiger: who strongly agreed as to a private Mission. We discussed some particulars. Also with C[atherine]' (*GD* iv. 135). Sir Frederick Thesiger (1794–1878; *DNB*), 1st Baron Chelmsford, 1858, was an MP, 1841, Solicitor General, 1844–5, Attorney General, 1845–6, and Lord Chancellor, 1858–9, 1866–8.

490713gm[a]
Secret

6 Carlton Gardens
July 13. 1849

My dear Manning

I write in great haste on the point of starting by tonight's Mail Train.[b]
On Thursday next, or Friday at furthest I hope to find myself in Naples.[c]

My wife expects her confinement within five or six weeks:[d] indeed the period I have last named is an extreme one. This was the circumstance that made it absolutely necessary for me to go now and with the utmost speed if I were to go at all. I deeply feel how much better L[incoln] would have been served, and she also, had it been in your power to have gone at once or indeed to have gone with safety but I think Lincoln felt that so long a journey at the present season could not be warrantably undertaken by you under circumstances of any pressure.

It is more than I can hope that by an instrument so unworthy to be employed in any good work even the simplest, it should please God to accomplish any success however partial in one which is not simple—yet the shadow of hope which alone is upon me, is quite enough as I feel to justify & require the act[84]—it being of course taken into view that notwithstanding my wife's accident I have any reason to hope that things will go with her in the natural course—[e]

Should the message be so far prospered as to bring her within reach, morally & locally, I think L[incoln] will be very anxious to call your generous offer into life—You will be kept informed no doubt of what I may be able to write—You will not I am sure forget me on my way—Always

Believe me Aff[ectiona]tely yours
W. E. Gladstone

Thanks for Mr. H[enn]'s letter which it seemed needless to *keep*.
Ven[erable]
Archdeacon Manning

[[BL Add. MS 44248, 12–13; Morley transcript]]

---

[a] 'Wrote to H. E. Manning' (*GD* iv. 136).

[b] Gladstone left at 8.30 p.m. (ibid. 136).

[c] Gladstone was in Genoa on Friday, 20 July 1849 (ibid. 138). He did not arrive in Naples until Tuesday, 24 July (ibid. 140).

[d] See 490922gm.

[e] On the accident see 490705mg.

490810gm[a]
Secret

6 C[arlton] G[ardens] Aug[ust] 10. [18]49.

My dear Manning

I came home at eleven last night,[b] after a journey of which the labours, the interest, and the anxieties, all great, alike vanish into utter insignificance when compared with the afflicting weight of the circumstances it has revealed to me. I now write to you in the exercise of my own discretion alone, because matters have reached a point at which *I* want your aid and guidance, and at which the direct application of it to our friend will in all probability be requisite—

You will be shocked and stunned to learn that I can entertain no moral doubt whatever of the fact that the unhappy subject of our cares is within a few weeks, probably a few days of her delivery—this tells all.

I turned back upon her path at Lecco;[c] leaving her I may say, a few posts advanced, in full flight from me.

To overtake her would have been easy but she had (& alas one cannot condemn or even I would say disapprove) resolutely shut her door against me at Como:[d] and I was governed mainly by fear of consequences if I persevered and the almost impossibility of doing good under the circumstances by force.

But, as I have said, this case is beyond all reasonable doubt in my views: and I conceive it to be immoral in a husband to allow such matter to remain beyond the notice of the law. There will I cannot doubt be a suit of divorce.

But what divorce? a church divorce only? or a Parliamentary divorce or both? A Church divorce does not dissolve the vinculum matrimonii[e]—

---

[a] 'writing to . . . Manning' (*GD* iv. 147).

[b] From 6 to 10.15 p.m. Gladstone travelled from Folkstone to London on 9 August 1849 (ibid. 145–7).

[c] 1 August 1849 (ibid. 142–3).

[d] 2 August 1849 (ibid. 143).

[e] The bond of marriage. According to the Phillimore edition of Burn's *Ecclesiastical Law* (1842), there exist two types of divorce—*a vinculo matrimonii*, that is in the case where a marriage is void *ab initio*, from the beginning, in such cases as consanguinity, impuberty, malformation, or frigidity, and *separatio a thoro et mensa* in such cases as adultery. In the latter case the *vinculum matrimonii* remains. Manning's discussion in the following letter is consistent with the explication of the Church of England's matrimonial law as described in Burn/

does not (I suppose) touch in its essence the mystical union of man & wife. A Parliamentary divorce purports to do this inasmuch as it sets parties free to marry again.

Two things perplex me here—One, if the apparent sense of Scripture be the real one, I do not know why the law of the Church absolutely refuses divorce *a vinculo*. I rather conjecture the case to be, that this was reserved for dispensation in each particular case: That within the machinery of dispensation dropped: & that being with justice regarded as practically corrupt it has not been relieved. A secular agency has taken its place—and here arises my second difficulty. I cannot understand how all the acts of Parliament in the universe can *touch* the mystical union of one man to one woman. I know not *if* there be, according to the true will of God, a real dissolution of that union—and if there be, it seems as if there were no other real organ of the law in *that* respect than private conscience—

There is a great deal more that might be added, but I think applying what I have said to the facts (conjectures or suppositions they are in strictness but it would be hardly honest to call them so) you will fully comprehend the scope and purpose of my letter. L[incoln] does not yet know *all*—he is away & will not, *probably*, reach town for a day or two.

Aff[ectiona]tely yours

W. E. Gladstone

Ven[erable]
Archdeacon Manning
[[BL Add. MS 44248, 14–17; Morley transcript]]

Phillimore, ii. 499–500d. Note, as well, Canons 105–7 in *The Constitutions and Canons Ecclesiastical of the Church of England, Referred to their Original Sources, and Illustrated with Explanatory Notes*, ed. Mackenzie E. C. Walcott (Oxford: James Parker, 1874), 145–7.

Here and in the following letters see John Ayliffe, *Parergon Juris Canonici Anglicani: Or, a Commentary, by Way of Supplement to the Canons and Constitutions of the Church of England* (London: D. Leach, 1726) who discusses divorce in its twofold form, *a thoro* and *a vinculo* or *a foedere matrimoniali*: '*quoad thorum* happens when mutual Cohabitation or Conversation is forbidden to the Parties either with a Time, or without any Time prefix'd for their coming together again . . . *quoad vinculum* . . . the Marriage is entirely dissolv'd; and as to the Substance of it forever rescinded' (225). Some Canonists, according to Ayliffe treat divorce in a threefold way: (1) *quoad thorum*, 'with respect to carnal copulation', whereby a party may marry again; (2) separation *quoad thorum et mensam*, by which a wife for her safety is allowed to live separately from her husband, but cannot marry again; and (3) *a vinculo matrimonii* in which case the marriage is considered void *ab initio* (229).

490819mg

Inverness. Aug[ust] 19. 1849.

My dear Gladstone

I got your heavy letter late last night: & write at once!

Before any answer can reach me here I shall be, please God, on my way home. But I would ask for a line at the Post Office Edinburgh, if you desire to give me any instructions.

My return will be delayed by going to see a sick friend, until next week. I shall then trust to see you in London.[a]

The pressure of time prevents my writing more, & the deep heaviness of the subject will not let me touch it in haste.

May God as greatly reward our friend as He has afflicted him. And this I firmly believe He will do.

I trust you found your wife well.

May God ever bless you both.

Ever your aff[ectionat]e friend,
H. E. Manning.

I will write to Lord Lincoln tonight.
The Right Hon[oura]ble
W. E. Gladstone.

[[Pitts; Chapeau, 150, 224]]

490830mg

Matlock. Aug[ust] 30. 1849.

My dear Gladstone

I shall be in London, please God, on Saturday night;[aa] & will come to you between 2 & 3 ocl[ock] next day unless I find at 44 Cadogan Place a note to the contrary.[b] Ever yours affect[ionatel]y.

H. E. Manning.

[[Pitts; Chapeau, 151, 224–5]]

[a] See 490830mg.
[aa] 1 September 1849.
[b] The meeting did not take place. See 490903mg.

490903mg

London. Sept[ember] 3. 1849.

Private

My dear Gladstone,

I arrived in London on Saturday last;[a] and ascertained yesterday[85] that you were at Hawarden.[b]

The subject of your last letter has hardly been out of my mind since I received it. But so many points need to be considered that I have been unwilling to write, hoping to converse with you, & to correct misjudgments by discussion.

There is no doubt that the bond of matrimony is indissoluble by the law of England based upon the law of the Western Church.

The Parliamentary licence[86] to marry again are 'privilegia'[c] exempting individuals from the penalties of the general law.

I know that B[isho]p Cosin & men of high standing in his day, when the first privilegium was granted argued for the dissolubleness of marriage at least on one ground.[d] And the Greek Church seems to have permitted it.

But my inclinations are to abide by our law, & to wish that the privilegia were not granted or sought:

A Church divorce 'a mensa &c.' is obviously a duty in this most mournful case. The laws of right as you say require it.

Thus far there can be no question.

This letter is of course for your eye only.

If I were to say what I should most desire for one who has been afflicted as our Friend, it would be that he should take the release given by the Church, & seek no more.

Such a course seems to me more in proportion to the past, and more in harmony with what I could desire for the future.

But this must be determined by intimate personal, & private reasons, of which I am not in a position to judge. I do not wish to overstrain anything, &[87] am afraid of letting in anything which may tend that way.

---

[a] 1 September 1849.

[b] Gladstone had travelled to Hawarden on 23 August 1849 (*GD* iv. 149).

[c] That is, legally established dispositions.

[d] See John Cosin, 'Bishop Cosin's Argument Proving that Adultery Works a Dissolution of the Marriage: Being the Substance of Several of Bishop Cosin's Speeches in the House of Lords, upon the Debate of the Lord Ross's Case', in his *Works* (5 vols.; Oxford: John Henry Parker, 1843–55), iv. 489–502. Cosin was one among three bishops who had initially advocated divorce in the case of adultery.

But I can never clear my mind of the thought, that a wife may yet be saved by the[88] husband[e] (I mean for the World beyond the Grave—in this world all is dead & lost for ever) and that his power of saving her will be according to his state, & character of mind.

A second marriage would be a final act, not of separation only but of *opposition*. A woman ceases to feel that she has wronged a man who is again happier than herself.

It would seem to me as if all trials of life would be nothing to a man if he could pluck from the burning a wife who had lain in his bosom. Nothing can efface this fact of their mutual betrothing. I do not see how Sin can make a woman cease to be always a wife. The prodigal was still a son,[f] & would have been had he been lost eternally.

With this feeling I shrink from any thing which shall make still more absolute & active the repulsion of two such beings as Man & Wife. I say nothing of the effect of such an aim & prayers upon the husband: though I believe nothing would more deeply sanctify his own soul, or more powerfully intercede with God for the salvation of his unhappy wife. With these feelings you will easily see how the inclination I have to abide by the law & interpretation of the Western Church becomes strong enough for a practical conclusion.

But I say all this that your better judgment may correct me where you see need.

May God give you a right judgment for our friend relies on you as you deserve.

I trust your wife is well.

Ever yours affect[ionatel]y
H. E. Manning.

[[Pitts; Chapeau, 152, 225–6]]

490922gm[a]

London Sept[ember] 22. [18]49

My dear Manning

I have heard from Lincoln *since* he was with you and being in town until Monday I write a hurried line to say that if you think there would be advantage in my coming to see you *on that subject* I could do so on Monday

---

[e] 1 Cor. 7: 14.   [f] Luke 15: 11–32.

[a] '...inquiries about Manning....Wrote to Manning' (*GD* iv. 155).

afternoon or evening to return here on Tuesday.[b] If you write in the affirmative please to direct me as to the best route—I would on no account detain you at home[89] to see me & of course if you chanced to be passing through town that would answer the purpose. I would indeed be seeing Lavington & you there & so a great thing for me but I would rather do it with my wife.

I had some thoughts of coming down at a venture to-night but have thought it better to write.

My wife thank God is well again and baby was baptized last night[c]—In a week I hope we shall be in Scotland.[d]

Ever aff[ectiona]tely yours
W. E. Gladstone

Venerable
Archdeacon Manning—

[[BL Add. MS 44248, 18–19; Morley transcript]]

[[On 24 September 1849 Gladstone wrote to Catherine: 'Immediately after my arrival I wrote to Manning but I am in sore perplexity having no reply by the morning's post today, only the afternoon's for which I have waited. It therefore appears clear that he is not at Lavington, and I do not think it worth while to wait here for the chance of hearing from him' (SDL, Glynne–Gladstone MS 771, 181–2, 181). Catherine replied with a fanciful apostrophe: 'Oh, for a penitentary where for say a year she could be with a kind, judicious friend and under *good discipline*! Archdeacon Manning at the head—might she not come out a new woman?' (Battiscombe [1957], 75).]]

490924mg

Lavington. Sept[ember] 24. 1849.

My dear Gladstone,

My curate's[a] absence threw all the work of yesterday upon me so that I did not open your letter in time to write: for the Sunday Post goes immediately after Morning Service.

I cannot express how great is my regret, & my fear that I may lose one of the greatest pleasures I could receive.

Is it still[90] impossible for you to come to Lavington tomorrow. Nothing but an αἴδως[b] prevents my urging you to give me so great an enjoyment.

---

  [b] No meeting is indicated on either date in *GD*.

  [c] 21 September 1849 (*GD* iv. 155). Helen Gladstone (1849–1925) was born on 28 August (ibid. 150).

  [d] Gladstone left for Scotland on 2 October 1849 (ibid. 157).

  [a] Charles John Laprimaudaye.   [b] Sense of shame.

The only coach to this Place leaves London by the[91] 12 or 1.ocl[ock] train from Waterloo Station & gets in about[92] 6 or 7 oclock. It returns to London next morning by about 1.oclock.[93]

But the 10.30 train would bring you to Guildford by 11.30—& a gig would reach Lavington in about 2½ hours, or the 1 ocl[ock] train, and a gig would be here by 4.30 or thereabout.[94]

I say all this in the great hope & desire of having you under my roof, as a pledge of seeing you and your wife & my godson at a future day.

I would come up at once but that I am kept here by necessity: intending, please God, to be in London on Oct[ober] 4th.[c]

It was a great delight to me to receive our friend for his last Sunday. I can hardly say how I feel drawn to him. His sorrows,[95] & his manliness go to my heart.

I should greatly wish to speak on this most mournful subject: not that I venture to advise where you have advised: for I feel sure that all your judgments are so weighed that I should agree with them all.

The question he asked me was this:

Suppose that she should be awakened by this fact to a sense of the past & of the present, & should throw herself upon her brother,[d] would the likelihood of repentance be less *after* a prompt, & complete severance than it would be if the process were for a while hanging over her head, though with certainty at last.

I could not but say that I thought a complete severance promptly executed would destroy many of the moral conditions of a change: that the present dreadful exposure was a special and single event which could never occur again: (for a repetition would act in the contrary direction,) & that if the effects[96] & circumstances of this event & season could be seen & tried out before the final severance was completed the likelihood was greater than on this other supposition.

He then said he would write & desire the brother to communicate with you, that you might judge.

I should not have ventured, had he not asked in a pointed form, to give my opinion without hearing yours: As the whole has been so visibly [placed] by providence and by your generous friendship in your own hands.

---

[c] The two did not meet; Gladstone left for Scotland on 2 October 1849 (*GD* iv. 157).

[d] William Alexander Anthony Archibald Hamilton (1811–63; *DNB*), Marquess of Douglas and Clydesdale, 11th Duke of Hamilton and Brandon, and a close friend of Stephen Glynne, Catherine Gladstone's brother.

And apart from you I mistrust my own judgment: though I may say that I am convinced that what you have hitherto advised is sound & right, with the abatement of my last letter, so far as it is an abatement.

I shall not despair of seeing you tomorrow till tomorrow is gone, & will say no more. Believe me,

Ever yours affect[ionatel]y

H. E. Manning.

P.S. I must however send my love to Mrs Gladstone. I am truly thankful to hear she is so well: & cannot forget that Friday morning & the Stone Staircase.[e]

[[Pitts; Chapeau, 153, 226–7]]

490928gm[a]

Hawarden Sept[ember] 28 1849

My dear Manning

Unfortunately when I found Monday's post brought me no letter from you I concluded that you were not at Lavington and I came down here on Tuesday.[b] At the same time if a practical question of moment should arise, I shall be most ready to come from Scotland (we intend to go to Fasque on Monday morning[c]) to meet you.

I have now written to Lincoln and I inclose my letter to you for your perusal: Please to send it off unless you see cause to send it back to me.

I am happy to believe that you and I are practically at one in this most arduous question. But you give me as usual credit for much more than I deserve. All that I did was this. Lincoln and I had a walk when he was down here[d] and something that he said gave me such an opening that I then by word of mouth made known to him what I intended to convey at some time before the first Parliamentary step. It was only to point out that the present Ecclesiastical Divorce *plus* the Act of Parliament do not make up a divorce *a vinculo*: the former does not possess it—the latter is power-less—therefore *in foro conscientiae* the only authority for divorce is the private

---

[e] Reference to Catherine Gladstone's accident during her pregnancy; see 490705mg.

[a] 'Wrote to Lincoln (a difficult letter, even to do ill)—Manning (with the former enclosed)' (*GD* iv. 157).

[b] Tuesday, 25 September 1849 (*GD* iv. 156).

[c] Gladstone left for Scotland on Tuesday, 2 October 1849 (ibid. 157).

[d] Friday, 7 September 1849. 'Saw Lincoln. Walk with him & early dinner. We went through the various subjects standing for discussion, some of them of great interest: & an opening was given me to point out that the Eccl[esiastical] Court & Parl[iamen]t together do not really give a complete divorce' (ibid. 152).

persuasion acting upon a view of Scripture. I saw that this was very new to him: his idea had been that the two processes taken together made a full divorce the one integrating the other. We were just coming home, and I simply left the matter before him. It is evident that much has followed from his conversation with you: he has the soul of a hero. How small one feels in recommending fine things on paper to the man that has to *do* them—heavy burdens, but I do not touch them with any of my fingers. He has a very high vocation, written, by the hand of God, in the lineaments of his own character, its splendid integrity, its bravery, its manful will, and its deep affection. He must not shrink from it and he will not. If the steel could feel in the fire, it would writhe as he does. Believe me always

Your aff[ectiona]te friend
WEG

The letter I believe need not be postpaid and it is safer so.

Venerable

Archdeacon Manning[97]

[[BL Add. MS 44248, 20–1; Morley transcript]]

[Enclosure]

Hawarden Sept[ember] 28 1849[e]

My dear Lincoln

I received your letter written from Portsmouth on Saturday morning[f] as I was about to start for London. On arriving there I made inquiry about Manning, and learned that he was at Lavington, so far as was known. I wrote him offering to come down on Monday and postpone my return here until Tuesday. But when Monday came having no answer from him, and not considering that there was much to be done at present by conference I came down here to make ready for my journey to Scotland.

And now I must tell you, though I am not much given to the use of such language, that your letter is a piece of true Christian heroism, and it filled me, as well as my wife, with sentiments of admiration the deepest and most lively. As respects yourself it really is only another proof that the hand of God, while it seemed to be crushing, has only been training and ripening you for the work laid and to be laid upon you—And as respects the subject of it and its bearing upon me you may rely at least upon this that I am not

---

[e] 'Wrote to Lincoln' (ibid. 151).

[f] Not located. 'Received a letter from Lincoln which made me stagger with admiration' (*GD* iv. 155).

yet wearied of doing my limited and insignificant duty in the face of the noble example you set me and that if I mar your intuitions it will be through defects that I have not the power to countenance.

In the first place then be assured that there will be no difficulty about my meeting Manning whenever the time for any practical question may come. As to the abstract question, apart from the practical, I am in substance of this mind already. For myself individually I have always felt as if the link of marriage *could* not be broken: *and* as if our laws really afforded no process in the least amounting to the destruction of it: how I have also felt that this was strictly a private sentiment, and not one which I could so clearly found on the Scriptures or the law Christian as to be justified in urging it as obligatory upon others, and that this was one of the cases in which from the state of our law it was quite evident that each man must be his own, in the last resort, unaided, guide. As to the general effect of divorce and the question how far does repentance cancel the past, I fear Manning is right about the first and in regard to the last as between one human being and another I can place no limit to my creed: but then what a repentance it must be! so deep and solid, so grown into the habit and frame of the mind, as well as so vivid and sharp in its emotions. I never dared to raise this question feeling as if the time for it had not come, until we had some indication as to the fact which would justify making so great a demand upon your fortitude and longsuffering.

You will perceive therefore that presuming a given state of mind on the part of Lady L[incoln], I , like Manning, should be prepared to act, or to advise acting, in the sense, which you declare yourself still open to consider.

Nor, if we were to pursue the question further, can I think that there are any interests which require you to pursue, in the case of deep repentance, the way of penal justice. That God has given to a married person in the event of infidelity on the other side a *right* to be liberated from the contract I can conceive: but never that He has made it an obligation: the highest path I believe is that which without the dissolution of the contract aims at the conversion of the fallen. It is a path which very few have strength and grace to follow. It is a path so difficult and so much beyond the range of common appreciation, that much of the sounder part of public opinion, which generally is an aid to acts of virtue, here changes sides and discountenances the highest virtue. It is a path, the difference between recommending and treading which is so great, that I feel the greatest doubt as to the warrant to recommend it, except in one class of cases, namely that, when there are already indications of the capacity, which constitutes the Divine call to follow it. Those indications you have given. You have shown that though in agony you have a heart and a will to do *every* thing, without qualification or exception, that a regard to her interests would require even your own existence erased from the book of being. I cannot join with those who say 'you have done all that can be done, now consider yourself:' for I am deeply convinced that in your heroic resolution to keep yourself out of view you are somehow laying up and will hereafter reap an inconceivable harvest of reward.

The opinion of society deserves I think great respect in common cases: but that which it represents is too near the mere average of human nature to be a safe rule for solving those high problems, so rare in life, of which one has been presented to you.

Whether the interests of children may or may not be an[98] absolute bar to the restoration of *what was*, is a question only to be answered I think when in full view with all its particulars: at this time we are only on the point, do they unconditionally require the divorce of the offending parent? To me it appears that the reply is in the negative. The impunity of great sins and great errors is that which demoralises: but between the extremes of divorce and amnesty there is room enough to take such[99] security against this danger as may be needed.

As I have already said, my wish would be to reserve all this until the happy day, for happy in its ultimate promise it would indeed be, were we to know that it had pleased God to recall to Himself the heart of the wanderer. But it seems to have been ruled otherwise. It was the course of conversation, not my design, which led me then[100] to say at the close of our walk here so much as I did then[101] say about divorce: and your letter has drawn from me the rest. Nor can you ultimately be a loser by your inexaustible tenderness thus looking beforehand if it be possible for a way of escape, a way for 'truth and mercy to meet together,' for 'righteousness and peace to kiss each other.'[g]

Turning from this discussion I hope you will bear in mind that it rests with you the means of placing before Manning any facts of such a nature as might practically raise the question on which I have thus far written. At present so far as I know the suit would go forward in its regular course without our hearing of it unless Parkinson[h] should wish to take counsel on some difficulty.

---

[g] Cf. Ps. 85: 10.

[h] John Parkinson (1779–1855), the solicitor who handled the Lincoln divorce. See BL Add. MS 44368, 255–86, and Boase, ii. 1355.

I conclude also that it would be quite premature to open this subject to Thesiger, unless we have evidence of such a kind to induce a doubt whether the proceedings should be arrested. My impression is as to him, and still more as to Peel, that if there be any opening for it, they will lean on the side of mercy.

Manning after all is at Lavington but did not open my letter in time for his reply to find me.

Our journey to Scotland has been put off by letters from thence but we now intend to go on Monday.[i]

Your remaining children leave Hawarden tomorrow. I hope, that many years of consolation from them are yet in store for you: and I rejoice to think that you have friends whose affectionate care for them in the case of need would be worthier far than mine both of them and you. We shall look anxiously to hear of your progress and your health. I would strongly advise your seeing Rome if you go near it while the Cardinals the French and the people retain their present very singular positions: all that passes there is of such world-wide interest.[j] With my wifes kindest remembrances I remain

Always your affectionate friend
W. E. Gladstone

The Earl of Lincoln

[[University of Nottingham MS NeC 11,788]]

---

[i] They eventually left on Tuesday, 2 October 1849. See 490922gm.

[j] Giovanni Maria Mastai-Ferretti, Pius IX (1792–1878) was ordained a priest, 1819, served with the apostolic delegation to Chile, 1823, appointed Archbishop of Spoleto, 1827, Archbishop of Imola, 1840, and elected to the papacy, 16 June 1846. On his election he initiated a series of liberal reforms in Rome (note Manning's comments in his letter of 480120mg), but unrest continued and he fled the city, 24 November 1848, after which a republic (here referred to by Gladstone) was formed. (Note as well Gladstone's later interest in the history of the republic and his translation of Farini's history of the period; for details see 510621mg.) Pius returned to Rome under French protection, 12 April 1850. Thereafter, with the aid of Giacomo Antonelli, his Secretary of State, he endeavoured to maintain his temporal power in Italy against the growing unification movement, eventually losing the papal states following the defeat of the Austrian army at Magenta, 4 July 1859, and the papal forces at Ancona, 30 September 1860. Ten years later, the city of Rome was taken and established as the Italian capital. The pope was assigned rights under the Law of Guarantees, 15 May 1871. Pius was a focus for the growing ultramontanist movement, re-establishing the Roman Catholic hierarchy in England, 29 September 1850 (see 501220gm), defining the Immaculate Conception of the Blessed Virgin as a dogma of Catholic faith, 8 December 1854, issuing his Encyclical, 'Quanta Cura', with an attached 'Syllabus of Errors', 8 December 1864, and calling the First Vatican Council, opened 8 December 1869, at which the doctrine of papal infallibility was formally proclaimed, 18 July 1870. For details see Nielsen (1906), ii. 102ff., Hales (1954), Martina (1974, 1986, 1990), Chadwick (1998c), 61–272, Mattci (2004).

491006mg

Lavington. Oct 6. 1849.

My dear Gladstone,

I thank you much for letting me read your letter to Lincoln. It is every way most excellent: & I cannot say how much relief it is to me to see that you have, unknown to me, advised him so fully as I did.

I had been fearing that my line was too severe and at variance with the whole living counsel of those about him to do good, or even not to do harm.

I am firmly persuaded that the Church of England in the Marriage Service[a] teaches the indissolubility of marriage.

It contemplates death alone as dissolving it.

'As long as ye both shall live'.

It declares God to be the Ratifier.

'Those whom God hath joined together'.

It forbids all human powers to dissolve.

'Let no man put asunder'.

The law of the Church & of the land we know.

And my belief is that this is the revival in Christ of the original mystery.

'Sicut ab initio',[b] is the [Chris]t[ia]n law of marriage. & 'ab initio non fuit ita'[c] that a man should put away his wife.

Giacomo Antonelli (1806–76), educated at the Collegio Romano, the Roman Seminary, and La Sapienza, Rome, was ordained a deacon, 1840, having worked in the Vatican diplomatic service since 1830. He was appointed Substitute of the Secretariat of State for Internal Affairs, 1841, and was general treasurer, 1845–7, in which year he was created cardinal deacon, Pro-General Treasurer of the Apostolic Chamber, and President of the College of Consultors of the State, 1847, President Moderator of the Supreme Council of Public Affairs and President of the Supreme Council of External Affairs with the States, and Pro-Prefect of the Public Ecclesiastical Affairs,1848, in which latter office he was appointed Prefect, 1852, a position he held to his death. For details see Coppa (1990) and Weber (1978), 13 and *passim*.

[a] See 'The Form of Solemnization of Matrimony' in the Book of Common Prayer.

[b] 'As it was from the beginning'. Cf. Matt. 19: 4 (Vulgate): qui respondens ait eis non legistis quia qui fecit ab initio masculum et feminam fecit eos (answering he said to them: Have you not read that he who made them from the beginning made them male and female?).

[c] 'From the beginning it was not so.' Cf. Matt 19: 8 (Vulgate): ait illis quoniam Moses ad duritiam cordis vestri permisit vobis dimittere uxores vestras; ab initio autem non sic fuit (He said to them that Moses allowed you to put away your wives because of your hardness of heart; from the beginning it was not so).

But my present object in writing was not to open this subject, further than to say that your letter is a relief & a confirmation to me: And that when I saw Lincoln in London on Sept[ember] 8th I said all this in substance, little knowing, & he not implying, that you had spoken in the same sense.

I have not said that I posted your letter, the day I received it, for Malta. My object in writing now is this.

I believe (1) that the Hampden case has *materially* established the claim of the Civil power against the Archbishops power of judicially confirming the Election of Bishops. And (2) that this is a *vital* principle—sine qua non est Catholica[d]—(3) that if the next confirmation pass without undoing the precedent it will be *formally* established by the tacit reception of the Church of England: and (4) that, therefore, some step ought now to be taken.

My notion would be that certain persons (clergy & laity) sh[oul]d confer with the Archbishop and obtain his assent to the proceeding: that his Commissary[e] be directed to receive the objections & dispose of them judicially & that the advisers of Government should be left to find & take their remedy. Let me hear from you as speedily as convenient on this point.

There is a movement beginning against Dr. Hinds's Theology.[f] His book on the Three Temples, being decidedly unsound in the direction of Sabellianism.[g]

I feel these things to border upon 'the life'.

---

[d] 'Without which it is not catholic'. Cf. the final lines of the Athanasian Creed: Haec est fides catholica, quam nisi quisque fideliter firmiterque crediderit, salvus esse non poterit. (This is the catholic faith; unless one believes it faithfully and firmly, one cannot be saved.)

[e] An individual with ecclesiastical jurisdiction under and as limited by a bishop. See Ayliffe (1726), 160.

[f] On the death of Edward Stanley, *The Times* announced the vacancy of the Bishopric of Norwich on 12 September 1849, 5e. Cf. Manning to Mill, 12 October (Lambeth Palace MS 1491, 11) and Keble's letter to Manning a short time later, 19 October (Bodl. MS Eng. lett. c. 654, 152–3).

[g] Samuel Hinds, *The Three Temples of the One True God Contrasted* (London: B. Fellowes, 1830). Based on his University sermons at Oxford on the morning and afternoon of Whitsunday, 1829, the volume treats a 'progressive revelation', relating the three temples (tabernacle, temple of stone, and that of Christ, of 'immaterial realities') to the Trinity (ch. VII [124–43]). Hinds (1793–1872) was educated at Queen's College, Oxford, and served as Principal of Codrington College, Barbados, Vice-Principal of St Alban's Hall, 1827, domestic chaplain to Archbishop Whately of Dublin, 1831–3, and 1843, and Bishop of Norwich, 1849–57 (*DNB*, LD vii. 405). The charge of Sabellianism against Hinds was long-standing; Newman had noted it already in the 1830s. See Thomas (1991), 113–15.

I cannot put them by. They touch the Baptismal Faith & the foundation of the kingdom of our Lord Jesus Christ.

And my fear is that our position is changing if it be not already changed. May we do nothing rashly & nothing untruly or unfaithfully.

Believe me,

Ever yours affect[ionatel]y

H. E. Manning—

The Right Hon[oura]ble. W. E. Gladstone.

[[Pitts; Chapeau, 154, 228–9]]

491009gm[a]

Fasque Oct[ober] 9. 1849

My dear Manning

I wholly and cordially agree with you that the question as to the confirmation of Bishops goes to the very quick. My further statement would be this: that another appointment of an heterodox Bishop without protest, would be a strong indication and omen of total defeat in that question. But another such appointment with the Hampden issue over again would not I think in itself go far towards ruling the question against the Church: though a series of such cases, without any more ground made in them, would do so.

I am entirely ignorant of the nature of Dr. Hinds's doctrines unless from the very vaguest rumour: and I should hope they will receive every reasonable indulgence in the affair of construction: a principle which it seems to me necessary to apply even to the writings of so orthodox a person as Dr. Burton on that subject.

But if there be real heterodoxy in Dr. Hinds's works, or rather if there be what shall appear to competent persons as for instance to you, upon the best consideration that can be given short of the judicial, to be heterodoxy, I cannot but subscribe to the proposition that the work of the protestation and resistance ought to be undertaken anew: and that there could be no way of undertaking it so effective as a direct personal appeal to the Archbishop in the first instance, asking, we might almost say requiring from him an answer to the question whether canonical objections to a Bishop elect are to be treated by him and his Vicar General as triable or not?

---

[a] 'Wrote to Manning (2)' (*GD* iv. 159).

But I think the Bishop of London is too deep in this matter to be overlooked. You may remember that he is convinced of the necessity of giving some security to the Church & prepared on a fitting opportunity to make the needfull effort to obtain it. To move without him would be scarcely just to him, and would be full of danger. He probably with the B[isho]p of Winchester[b] would have the best chance of bringing the A[rch] b[isho]p to a right course, by making him feel how shameful & ruinous is the alternative.

When the matter comes to our sphere I feel persuaded that we shall be enabled to make at the least a stiff fight against this Jervisian doctrine.[c] I mean it so because he is the only man that has had either courage or impudence enough to undress it—

Any answer within three, or four, days after you get this had better be addressed to me at L[or]d Aberdeen's Haddo House Aberdeen.[d]

Your aff[ectiona]te friend
WEG

Venerable
Archdeacon Manning
[[BL Add. MS 44248, 22–3; Morley transcript; cf. Chapeau, 326–7]]

491017mg

Lavington. Oct[ober] 17. 1849.

My dear Gladstone
I send the inclosed without any comment:[102a] & ask you to advise me how to write.

---

  [b] Charles Richard Sumner.

  [c] An Arian or non-Trinitarian doctrine as held by the Unitarian preacher and writer, Thomas Jervis (1748–1833; *DNB*).

  [d] Gladstone travelled to Aberdeen's residence on 17 October 1849 and remained there until 20 October (*GD* iv. 160–2).

  [a] Not located. The letter was from C. Harris, an English resident in Naples, whom Gladstone met on 22 July 1849, while on his Lincoln mission (*GD* iv. 138). Gladstone's letter to Lincoln written from Fasque, 20 October is damaged, perhaps partially burned, and preserved in University of Nottingham MS NeC 11,789. The letter opens with Gladstone's reference to earlier letters he had sent (this letter is being sent to Lincoln at Malta) on the basis of which 'I could not doubt ... that the chain of evidence was complete and irrefragable' that Lady Lincoln was guilty. The relevant sections of the piece read thus:
[1v] ... With respect to your letter from Portsmouth I hope my last has explained at any rate the sense in which I took it and so given you the means of correcting me if need be.

I sent it through Manning in order to avoid misunderstanding and he signified to me by letter his [2r] approval. I have never supposed we were authorised to suspend any proceeding except upon given presumptions of a changed disposition. It never was my idea to recommend abandoning or delaying at all events the steps more immediately in prospect upon what I may term a speculation.

At the end of this letter I give you what has reached me from M[anning] today. I have replied to it by saying [th]at considering how far H[arris] is alread[y in] your confidence through us, it seems to me [that] it would be perilous and unjust to keep h[im] in the dark and that he should be succinctly informed that beyond all doubt the worst has happened and that sometime back—

H[arris]'s letter is a positive proof that up to a date within some three weeks the unhappy system of suppression and defiance was carried on—It is a great question whether this will last before the citation is served— ...

[2r; close of letter following Gladstone's signature]

Substance of a letter from Hon. & Rev. H[arris] to H.E.M. Florence October 1. 1849.

Reached Flo[rence] 25 Sept[ember] & found 26th that *she* was in same hotel, from the same day—came from Milan'. 27th sent up his card. 'She received me with much of her old cordiality. I thought her much altered since last year & very thin & pale. After a little ordinary talk I said I had not come as a mere caller but as an old friend & as a clergyman[.] she w[oul]d let me speak to her as such: she said [she] w[oul]d tho' she had not allowed others to do so.[' He wa]s not able to say much then being interrupt[ed by] the visit [of] a French gentleman. However [... 'a]fter morn[in]g service I went to see he[r.] She said she had not been well enough to come [to] Church. After a little while & after speaking of her future plans of going to Rome & perhaps Naples I spoke again of the deep pain it had given me to hear of her as I had done during the past year. She spoke of the world's ill nature upon which I briefly sketched all *I* had been able as a *friend* to learn of her history since Aug [ust] 48 & the almost impossibility of feeling any thing short of the greatest uneasiness // [*sic*] as to her life. After speaking as strongly as I could of the inevitable consequences of actual sin on her part I proposed taking the line of leaving such a view of her state to the judgment of God & assuming the perfect truth of her own statement that 'live with her husband she w[oul]d not, that her health precluded her from wintering in England, that she w[oul]d not submit to the irksomeness of attaching herself to any other lady while travelling & that therefore she must w[a]nder on as she does & ban the world. I de[al]t on the duty of not giving offence to others & ab[ove al]l when such offence must fall sooner or [later] upon her children. She seemed touched [when s]peaking of them but on the whole the impre[ssio]n she left on me was unfavourable..... [ellipses *sic*] [She] had not seen Gladstone but had heard of all his movements & was evidently disposed to look on him as L [incoln]'s agent & as having come out to collect evidence against her. I strove hard to combat this but do not think I succeeded.' He spoke plainly about sin ... [ellipsis *sic*] and expressed his 'utter disapprobation' of the present course on any supposition.—

My Communication with Harris was by L[incoln]'s sanction.

The effect of the inclosed letter on my mind is most painful.

May you be guided aright.

Ever your aff[ectionate] friend

H. E. Manning.

[[Pitts; Chapeau, 155, 229]]

491020gm[a]

Fasque Oct[ober] 20. 1849.

My dear Manning

I return Harris's letter of which I have sent the substance to Lincoln,[b] not taking thereby I hope an unwarranted freedom.

It appears to me pretty clear that Harris who already knows all that had taken place up to last July, at least all that we then knew, ought not to be left in the dark as to the subsequent mournful discoveries. It is revolting to write of them: —or I should have been more full in mind to you: nor is it necessary to enter upon any detail: one line alas is enough—You have I think only to say for His guidance that there can now be no doubt that the very worst has taken place and taken place too a considerable time ago. You will not attempt I know to turn him from thoughts of sympathy and mercy which this intelligence will not drive away but will only keep to their proper place.

I expect to hear in a day or two that the citation has been ordered unconditionally to be served. We I conceive had no authority to arrest that step except upon proof of presumption of penitence, or upon a decided lack of testimony. Neither plan is at this moment open.

I have a letter from him dated Sept[ember] 29 in the Tagus[c]—It contains evidence I think that his yachting administers relief though as it were surface—

Believe me Aff[ectiona]tely yours

W. E. Gladstone

P.S. I have heard nothing more about the case of Dr. Hinds: that I am thankful to think that your mind is fully applied to it.[d]

[a] 'Wrote to . . . Manning' (*GD* iv. 162).   [b] For text see 491017mg.

[c] Not located.

[d] Note the letter from Keble to Manning, 19 October 1849, indicating that extracts from Hinds's work were made up and signed by Mill, Keble, and others and sent to the Archbishop; although Keble did not think the presentation would yield results (Marriott had indicated to him that he did not think Hinds's book heretical), it would, he felt, strengthen their case with the public (Bodl. MS Eng. lett. c. 654, 152–3).

Since I wrote thus far I have seen a succinct intimation in the Guardian of Wed[nesda]y.[e]

[[BL Add. MS 44248, 24–5]]

ADDENDA TO SECTION VII

Gladstone and Döllinger on the Blessed Virgin and Purgatory: October 1845

[[On 3 October 1845 Gladstone conversed with Döllinger 'for one hour only but a good one' and wrote a full account of the meeting the day following (see *GD* iii. 486 and 451020gm):

Yesterday I had a conversation with Professor Döllinger on several questions of religion to the following effect, and I put it on record because of the pointedness of its results.

He spoke of the question of images as one on which there were great differences between the Church of Rome and that of England: I said not in regard to the formal and net doctrine, but to the practical system in the former Church; and then added that the points on which that system presented the greatest obstacles to communion were, I thought, the worship of images, the invocation of saints and particularly that of the Blessed Virgin, and the purgatorial indulgences.

He smiled, and said as to the last it was a subject scarcely existing or scarcely sensible for them in Germany. Then he stated the meaning of purgatorial indulgence to be this: that the Church offers her prayers for the deceased person in the belief that they are beneficial to him, but without defining the effect upon his state. I said: 'Then, I was right in supposing that yesterday you referred with reprobation to the preaching of Tetzel and his associates, because they told the people that their gifts were to be followed by the release of souls from Purgatory.' Yes, he said that was the case. 'Yet surely,' said I , 'indulgence is a judicial act, is it not?' 'As to the living, but not as to the dead,' he replied. 'The jurisdiction of the Church is over the living; it terminates with the grave. For the dead she can only pray, and she cannot measure the result of her prayer.' Upon this he expressed himself as most positive.

---

[e] On Wednesday, 17 October 1849, there was a mere postscript in *The Guardian* regarding the appointment of Dr. Hinds: 'We are informed that it is intended to offer an opposition to the confirmation of Dr Hinds, the bishop elect of Norwich' (682). Earlier editions of the paper also contained notices. On 26 September (638), the notice of Hinds's appointment appeared under 'Ecclesiastical Intelligence'. On 3 October there was an article on 'The New Bishop' (from the *Spectator*) on 646, and another on recent episcopal appointments (648–9). Finally there was an article on 10 October (663) and a letter (667).

I then asked: 'I conclude that with you all prayer for the dead is conditional upon the supposition that the person departed in a state of grace, although the condition may not be expressed?' 'Undoubtedly,' he said. 'We,' I replied, 'you see, who travel in Roman Catholic countries, do not see the signs of that condition, but everywhere see prayer absolute in appearance.' He said no Catholic can be misled upon that point.

To my inquiry (earlier in the conversation) what was the meaning of indulgence to the dead for so many days, or other periods of time, he answered it was still the application of the prayer of the Church for them for forty days.

(There are, indeed, difficulties left behind. Practically as they manage prayer for the dead, is not the result that all men are regarded as subjects of prayer under no condition at all, or one insensible—all who die ostensibly in the communion of the Church as no worse than in purgatory? And if so, must not the effect of this upon many living be immensely to diminish the force of the thought of death as the closing up of their moral account?

(And as to the indulgences, an indulgence is taken from some proclaimed paper of terms by someone living on behalf of a dead person. There is no act of the Church subsequent to, it may be, the printing of the paper with the conditions. Is it, then, meant that the force of the petitions of the Church for the peace of the departed is, unconsciously to those who offer them, distributed according to indulgences which have been obtained by other parties, so that the effect of the prayer is thus separated, systematically and by anticipation, from the consciousness of those who offer it? There is something slippery in this, yet it seems capable of an explanation.)

I said to him: 'I wish you could have heard sermons which I have heard, particularly two to which I have adverted, in Italy and Sicily; and to know what your view of them would be. In a sermon at Naples I heard the preacher found himself on these two main propositions: (I) That the Blessed Virgin differed essentially from all created beings whatever in that their gifts and graces were finite, whereas hers bordered upon the infinite; the words used were 'Toccano a'cancelli del infinito.' [Touch the gates of the infinite.] I know it is difficult to give a metaphysical meaning to this sort of medium between finity and infinity; but the practical force of the sentiment is clear and positive enough. The second was that the Blessed Virgin Mary was invested extrinsically with all the attributes of the adorable Trinity—infinite power, infinite wisdom, infinite love.' He replied, with a little straining—then corrected himself, and said with a great deal of straining—'the words might be made to bear a tolerable sense; but taking them as they stand, I should say they border upon blasphemy.' I said: 'Toccano a'cancelli della blasfemia' [touch the gates of blasphemy]. He replied yes; that no such thing would be tolerated here. I answered: 'Then, you see, this has some bearing upon that matter on which you press us so much, the unity of doctrine.' He seemed a little touched and made no reply, but that it must be the neglect of the Bishops. I answered I hoped it might be so (meaning, I feared they either did not wish or, *more* probably, did not dare to disturb such teaching). (Lathbury, ii. 383–6; *Autobiographica*, iii. 1–2)

Cf. his *Church Principles*, 350–2, where he described a sermon on purgatory in detail:

I have heard many sermons in Italy and Sicily, of which the great majority have been such as would have commanded, at least with reference to their general tenor, the respect and assent of every tolerably candid member of the principal reformed communions. But, upon the other hand, my own ears have listened to sounds, accepted with intense admiration by crowded congregations, so fearful and appalling, that I do not dare to give them the names which they seemed to me to merit, and that I am convinced the high and pure minds of many persons included within the pale of the Roman Catholic Church, and devotedly attached to it, would regard with the same horror which they painfully awakened in myself. And this not in distant and obscure places, but in churches, for example, in the very centres of Naples and Messina. And not from obscure or ill informed men, but from preachers of evidently considerable accomplishment, and conspicuous popularity. Once in particular, on the anniversary of the *Anime del Purgatorio*; and once on the dignity and attributes of the Virgin. Both were addressed to very crowded audiences. I subjoin at once the painful details, which a regard to truth forbids me to suppress.

The first named of these discourses was preached on the 2nd of November, 1838, in the Church of the Anime del Purgatorio, at Messina, by the Padre Cavallari. The preacher alluded to the gloom with which the day was invested by the Church, and said that he however would console his hearers by setting before them their great privilege in being allowed to succour those souls of the just, which though they had died in faith and merits, had not yet sufficiently expiated their sins, so that while the love of God yearned towards them, it could not take effect, inasmuch as his justice on the other hand bore them away to inflict the awful pains which they were at the moment enduring. To the faithful on earth it is given to procure their release, which they are to do by means of prayers—of alms—and of masses: through these last there comes to the sufferers great relief during the time which they are said. According (as he stated) to Saint Jerome, at the moment when the Host is elevated, there is even an entire suspension of the pains of those on whose behalf the sacrifice is offered. Without any doubt or scruple, therefore, he would affirm, that the zeal of the Apostles of Christ, which was so much commended in the Church, and by which they preached the Gospel to the world, was a zeal far inferior to that of those who by such masses should procure the release of souls from purgatory. For those, to whom the Apostles preached, were men yet in their sins, of whom it was quite uncertain whether they could ultimately profit by the grace tendered them or not, or whether they were objects of the effectual and permanent love of God or not: but these are souls everlastingly redeemed and already holy, only waiting for the consummation of their holiness: as they then are infinitely more dear to God, so is it a far higher work to be concerned in their relief. And they, when liberated from torture and received by Christ into heaven, will retain especially, and first of all, their gratitude to those on earth who have been the means of their release, and will powerfully intercede for them, as he instanced by a number of temporal deliverances. By these reciprocal good offices the present is bound to the future, and life to death. Both then to testify against the blasphemies of those who deny the purgatorial pains of the dead, and by their own most sacred interests, he conjured his hearers to avail themselves of the means in their hands. For his own part he would esteem the sharing in the liberation of a soul from purgatory his best assurance of his own eternal salvation. And he concluded with an invocation to these departed spirits to remember in their prayers the preacher Cavallari, who had on that day feebly endeavoured to plead their cause, as well as to care for the city of Messina. He had preached for some time with great vehemence and considerable power. A deep and half articulate amen broke from many of the auditory as he concluded: he descended from the pulpit in a state of exhaustion, and as he left its steps one of the congregation fell on his neck and kissed him with enthusiasm.

The second of the two sermons to which I have alluded, was preached in the church of San Ferdinando, at Naples, on Sunday afternoon, December the 2nd, 1838. The preacher who in this case also appeared to be a man of ability and popularity and (I think) a Franciscan Monk, chose for his subject the Divine Maternity of the Virgin. He described it as being morally of a highly mysterious character, and appeared obliquely to assimilate it to the Divine Paternity. This wonderful creature, he said, triumphed over the general laws of human nature as an exception from the taint of original sin: she was formed by the selection, as it were (like that of the painter of Agrigentum in an old tale) from all quarters of all the choicest elements of excellence; she is *regina de' cieli* [queen of the skies], and *imperatrice del mondo* [empress of the world]: her virtue and glory differ, in this essential respect, from those of the angels and archangels, that their gifts are restrained within the bounds of what is finite, *i cancelli del finito*, while hers *toccano ai cancelli del infinito* [touch the bounds of the infinite], so that there can properly be no relation or comparison between them. In her are exhibited the several distinctive virtues of apostles, doctors, martyrs, virgins: in her are represented also those, which belong to the heavenly circles of cherubim and seraphim, of angels and archangels: nay more, and most of all, she is invested with the extrinsic attributes of the blessed Trinity, namely Infinite Power, Infinite Wisdom, and Infinite Love. Saint John in the Spirit saw our Lord on His throne, calling up His spouse to her throne by His side; this was the Virgin: and He set upon her head a crown adorned with lions, bears, and leopards, beasts emblematically representing the sinners whom she had saved. Her part in the redemption of the world was analogous to that of Eve in its destruction. Accordingly, he proceeded, let us go with confidence to her feet, and he was about to offer to her his concluding address, when with my companions I quitted the scene.]]

Lincoln to Manning: November 1848

481124 lm

Wilton House
24 Nov[embe]r 1848.

My dear Archdeacon Manning

It is most kind and friendly of you to have bestowed so much time upon me in your last letter[a] and to assure me that I may continue to write to you without annoying you.—I was gratified at the interpretation you put upon my letter for it was written freely and as the sentiments of the heart occurred to me—and therefore it had I believe the merit of sincerity,—but I still fear you overrate the effect which deep and constant and long continued through often varying sorrow has yet had upon my mind. You speak I fear more of yourself than of me when you say that suffering in silence & solitude makes us leave off resting on anything which can change and seeking our happiness in anything which is not eternal. Were it so, I should cease to mourn for my blighted hopes of domestic happiness—my heart would yearn less after her who has offended me and more after God whom I have offended. I pray however that his chastening hand which I feel heavy upon me may more & more produce this result and may eventually subdue the rebellion of the spirit which has hardly yet resigned itself to an earthly lot which seems so hard to bear—

In one thing I do feel that the *long continuance* of my sorrow has improved the temper of my mind. Formerly I may have felt heated in spirit and resentful when my Wife's conduct brought grief and shame upon me—Now I hope and believe it is far otherwise—and yet strange it is that I never suffered in spirit so much as now—on no former occasion have I felt so sick at heart or so incapable of comfort. I think, as well as hope, I mourn for her even more than for myself—I know I am indifferent to the scoffs of men and the rebuke of friends when they see that I care for her still—and in one sense at least, that in which I believe forgiveness is enjoined, I have forgiven her already.—Why then do I feel a deeper grief now than when sorrow of this deep dye was yet young? I hope it is because on former occasions I buoyed myself with a hope to restore a Mother to my Children—now I despair.

You will not be surprised that the people who are endeavouring to assist me in saving my unhappy Wife from utter destruction if it is yet possible are William Gladstone and his admirable Wife. Of course I cannot appear to be a party to anything that is done but Mrs. Gladstone is most kindly and

---

[a] Not located.

judiciously making a last effort for what alone can now be hoped. God grant that contrary to all human probabilities it may be successful.—

When do you go to London and where shall you be found?—I am sure you will let me call upon you.

The Herberts hope to leave Scotland today and to be here in about ten days.[b] I am sure you will rejoice with him in the cause which has hitherto prevented their journey.

Believe me to be ever,

Yours sincerely and aff[ectionate]ly,

Lincoln.

[[Pitts; Chapeau, 145a]]

Gladstone to Hope on Helen Gladstone: November 1848

481127gh

Private[a]

Fasque Nov[ember] 27. [18]48.

My dear Hope,

Under the appeal w[hi]ch you have made to me I must not delay a moment my answer to you respecting my sisters case. She has had an attack of neuralgia brought on by causes to which it is needless to refer particularly. About the end of Sep[tember] she went to Edinburgh when this was aggravated. She was under the care principally of Professor Miller,[b] in whom we repose much confidence: his attendance on her was partially interrupted by ill health, & was for a time rendered less effective by his ignorance of the antecedents of her case. However she improved under his hands, the stomach & diet being rectified: but not without some checks by the incautious use of remedies in his absence or from other incidental causes. On Oct[ober] 27 Prof[essor] Miller wrote that her jaw had been locked—a circumstance by no means new with her: but he intimated to me, in terms which I cannot repeat, that this phenomenon was under the control of the will: he afterwards stated that he knew this at the time from particular

---

[b] Note the letter of Herbert to Manning, 23 January 1849, indicating that Lincoln had left (Bodl. MS Eng. lett. c. 657, 25).

[a] 'Wrote to...J. R. Hope (2) & copy: this being an account of Helen's case on which I examined the correspondence, & stated in my letter the result' (*GD* iv. 80).

[b] James Miller (1812–64; *DNB*), educated at St Andrew's and Edinburgh, Professor of Surgery at Edinburgh University from 1842, and Surgeon-in-Ordinary to Queen Victoria, 1848.

circumstances which he mentioned & w[hi]ch are beyond all question demonstrative. What he said of the jaw, he also said of the hands which were clenched, & he gave a proof equally clear about them. He also told me on the 27th. Oct[ober] that since the 25th scarcely any pain had been complained of—& that notwithstanding her being weak & thin she was freer from the neuralgic ailment on the whole than she had been at anytime during the period of the attack.

His reports were confirmed by constant *bulletins* from my Aunt Miss Robertson who was with my sister & has her confidence.[c] My Aunt writes as follows, being as I should tell you not of any medical discrimination & you will know how much more formidable such complaints are in the eyes of those who judge only by the present suffering. Prof[essor] Miller I must add at no one moment allowed that the case was one for the slightest anxiety as to its issue. To return[:] My aunt writes Oct[ober] 21. she is a 'little better.' Oct[ober] 25 a more favourable report 'the pains more bearable'—'the Doctor has pronounced her to be much better'—[']in a few days we may hope for her being able to leave her bed'—That night came the lockjaw of which I have already given you the account. But on the 27th my Aunt agreeing with the Doctor wrote 'she lies quiet & still w[hi]ch is a blessing compared to the painful state she was in'—she had also had brandy & water, wine & water, & milk, by spoonfuls w[hi]ch showed that the great evil, the irritation of the stomach was overcome (see A). Again the 30th she 'continues a little better, not withstanding her sufferings are very severe, but it could not be expected they should all at once subside'—The Priest had just been 'quite pleased with the improvement he saw' & she was taking food frequently—My Father had talked of going there & she begged *most particularly that he would not* because such was her message 'though better than when he was last there (24 & 25 Oct[ober]) she was not able to speak' but that you may not overestimate this I must tell you that during the lockjaw *she had spoken*. Of course in a state of weakness she could not speak to my Father.

Such were the circumstances of the ten days from Oct[ober] 21 to Oct[ober] 30. I have only to add that Dr. Miller on Oct[ober] 24 or 25 told my Wife that the pain would in all probability having been got down gradually for a certain time, at last *cease* suddenly.

Thus there the stomach had began to receive & to retain nourishment— the pain had been very greatly reduced—the lockjaw was known to the

---

[c] Joanna Robertson (1776–1867), Gladstone's mother's sister, appears to have always been close to Helen, who called Gladstone to his aunt's deathbed (*GD* vi. 528).

doctor to be under command of the will, both before & *after* the check of her 25th steady improvement had been announced—on the 20th the D[octo]r had declared that only care & nourishment for the restoration of strength were required: *danger never* having been dreamt of.

Later on the night of the 30th Dr. Wiseman arrived.[d] On the 3d of Nov[embe]r my poor sister wrote the narrative of the supposed wonder. She stated that on the 25th she had been at the point of death (I do not use her words but the effect of them) & received the last sacraments: the next day somewhat better—but in excessive exhaustion—with 'constant & severe pain'—then she passes over the time (of which obscure the reports) until the morning of the 31st where she says through the Bishop & by the relic her speech in a moment was restored hands opened & pain removed 'or at least reduced to a shadow of what it was'—& a degree of strength quite extraordinary given to her—Dr. Miller's amazement indescribable—& that he said he & his medicines had nothing to do with it. Then she adds that she has been at once freed from suffering so heavy, & for which the doctors acknowledged [']all their medicines to have failed.' On the 2nd Nov[ember] she was out of bed & lay on the sofa 'seven hours'. On the 3d she 'hoped soon to be able to use her feet'—but she would still require 'very great care'.[e] On the 10th, the 12th day from the use of the relic, she writes that she is regaining health & strength with 'wonderful' rapidity—but it is almost an impossibility 'for her to get up stairs' even with the help of two nurses.

I think I need scarcely go farther but I will observe first that she had the same impressions about death in 1845 when she had a much worse lockjaw but was not in danger.

2. She then got her speech quite suddenly.—

3. She makes a reference in her narrative to her illness of last year which to us who knew its history shows her total incapacity to form a trustworthy judgement on the evidence attending such a case as this.

In that she is as on some former occasions the victim of a deplorable delusion, of one of those delusions which seduce some minds into superstition, but in the long run react and far more powerfully towards unbelief.

[d] Arrival not noted in *GD*.

[e] On Saturday, 4 November 1848, Gladstone discussed Helen's narrative with his father: 'I advised him to send it to Miller—which he did, by me—to answer it without disputing but particularly without recognising the reality of her impressions—& to have the written evidence put together which shows that they are in short fanatical. It is dismal that true miracle should be brought into discredit by these notions sheer products of a heated imagination' (*GD* iv. 76).

It is true and has been abated by Dr. Miller that she was much better after Dr. W[iseman]'s visit. The question is as to the kind or the defence of the improvement: & when that has been fairly ascertained & measured it must be dispassionately compared with the known power of the will in nervous complaints. I knew of one 17 years ago which appeared & still appears to me much more remarkable & it decidedly within those bounds beyond which only lies the region of miracles.

It is scarcely with notice that upon crossexamining the testimonies I find a strange difficulty as to the day of this occurrence. My sister writes distinctly that it was on Tuesday morning the 31st that it took place & that Dr. Miller recognised the change. But 1. Dr. M[iller] who was most careful in keeping us informed of what was material did not write to mention improvement till the latter part of Wednesday after the post of that day. 2. He declares that on the afternoon of the first day (Tuesday the 31st) on which Dr. W[iseman] saw her, but saw Dr. W[iseman] and explained to him the case in the general sense he had explained to me & that it was the next day when he saw her & found the lockjaw gone. 3. my Aunt writes a letter from which it is quite clear that Dr W[iseman] was with her most of the 31st, but that the great improvement was on the subsequent day. My own impression is, that my sister was mistaken as to the day (a singular & significant circumstance) & that it was really the Wednesday (unless which I seriously think probable it happened *twice over*—) indeed we have found that preparations had been made for it some time before.

Lastly, for myself, in considering this question I have looked at it simply as a matter of fact & of evidence, like any other within the range of our experience. I have not applied to it any abstract opinion or prepossession. I have made a long but yet an incomplete statement: yet I think its effect is clear: but for one who knows the case from the experience of many years it does not admit of the veriest shadow of a shade of doubt.

You will see that this letter is for very guarded use: but the general result of it we wish to be spoken out freely.

Your aff[ectiona]te friend
(S.) W E Gladstone

J. R. Hope Esq.
(A.) On the 29th, she is 'very thankful to be able to continue a better account.' 'She lies still & quiet without being in racking pain. Dr. M[iller] was here last night, & early this morning, both times pronouncing that the dear soul is better, & that *care with nourishment, to regain strength (but) little else is required.*'

[[SDL, Glynne–Gladstone MS 709 (copy)]]

ENDNOTES TO SECTION VII

1. troubles] inserted, replacing overscored: thoughts
2. Pray...Father] on first page
3. The...Gladstone] on first page
4. differences] inserted
5. we trust] inserted
6. I...offer] Chapeau omits
7. Nor] Chapeau: Not
8. itself] inserted, replacing overscored: which is
9. in] written over: of
10. in] written over: of
11. also we have] inserted
12. other] overscored
13. i.e.] overscored
14. authoritative] corrected from: authority
15. as] overscored
16. (rented...brother)] inserted
17. given up] overscored
18. only] inserted
19. more or less] inserted
20. We] corrected from: I
21. change of] Chapeau: changing
22. high] Chapeau: highest
23. tho] inserted
24. they are true] inserted
25. illegible word overscored
26. confession] Morley: confusion
27. confession] Morley: confusion
28. present...the] inserted
29. clear &] inserted
30. with the weight] inserted
31. having been] inserted
32. think] corrected from: think
33. were] overscored
34. confession] Morley: confusion
35. *germ* & *interior experience*] inserted
36. to be the case] inserted
37. 21] Morley: 22
38. and...had] inserted
39. working] corrected from: work
40. stay] inserted, replacing overscored: winter
41. There...you] Chapeau omits

42. to] written over illegible word
43. its] overscored
44. Chapeau adds: shall
45. possibility of the] inserted
46. for] inserted, replacing overscored: of
47. in] inserted
48. after] inserted, replacing overscored: from
49. I] overscored
50. fr] overscored
51. constant] corrected from: constantly
52.)] overscored
53. offence] written over illegible word
54. or indeed wealth] inserted
55. you] overscored
56. I see] inserted, replacing overscored: possibly
57. of] overscored
58. R. Palmer] inserted
59. &] Morley omits
60. since] Chapeau omits
61. to bear] Chapeau omits
62. of] Chapeau: in
63. of] Chapeau: in
64. transcendent] Chapeau: tremendous
65. subjects] Chapeau: subject
66. 2] overscored
67. on] inserted
68. (quasi)] inserted
69. that overscored
70. perspective] written over illegible word
71. before now] inserted
72. the] inserted
73. the] Chapeau omits
74. passed] Chapeau: happened
75. spare] inserted
76. to] Morley omits
77. of] overscored
78. further] inserted
79. My wife...hearty] at top of letter
80. though] Chapeau: although
81. courses] Chapeau: course
82. letter] Chapeau: letters
83. object] Chapeau: objects
84. ten] overscored

85. yesterday] Chapeau omits
86. licence] Chapeau: licences
87. &] Chapeau: I
88. the] Chapeau: a
89. at home] written over illegible words
90. still] Chapeau omits
91. the] Chapeau omits
92. about] written over illegible word
93. next ... oclock] inserted
94. thereabout] Chapeau: thereabouts
95. sorrows] Chapeau: sorrow
96. effects] Chapeau: effect
97. Venerable ... Manning] on first page
98. an] inserted
99. such] inserted
100. then] inserted and overscored
101. then] inserted
102. comment] Chapeau: comments

SECTION VIII

The Gorham Crisis

1. The Problem of Response: November 1849–April 1850

491111mg

Lavington. Nov[ember] 11. 1849.

My dear Gladstone,

I have taken the liberty to desire my Printer to send to you a proof of a Sermon on which I would ask you kindly to read & give me your judgment.[a] I could not ask it if I did not wish it: nor if it would inflict on you any labour except that of reading one of my lucubrations.[b]

If you would kindly send it to me & as soon as you conveniently can I should be much obliged. With proof as with all other bis dat &c.[c]

Ever yours affect[ionatel]y

H. E. Manning.

[[BL Add. MS 44248, 26–7]]

491114gm[a]

Private

Fasque Nov[ember] 14. [18]49

My dear Manning

Your letter & proof[1] has found me but has found me in a state of real and entire incapacity to do justice to the[2] subject. Besides which I am very angry & indeed indignant at your 'taking a liberty'! You could not possibly take any liberty with me so great as to tell me that your writing asking saying or sending any thing to me was to take a liberty. However I do

---

[a] Henry Edward Manning, Sermon IX, 'The Analogy of Nature', *Sermons. Volume the Fourth* (London: William Pickering, 1850*b*), 152–75. See 491114gm. On the issue see also 640801gm and the broader perspective of Pereiro in McClelland (1996).

[b] Work carried out by artificial light, that is by night; therefore: laborious study.

[c] Bis dat qui dat celeriter (he gives twice who gives quickly). Pubilius Syrus, *Sententiae*, 1. 6.

[a] 'Wrote to ... Manning. ... Manning's Sermon on Analogy, in proof, on wh[ich] I had to comment' (*GD* iv. 166).

believe it was a lapse of the mind and so[3] I will come down from the clouds and say that matters of business and correspondence have stuffed my head so full of the most uncongenial matter that I cannot lift or screw myself to the point of fairly criticising your argument against *Toland*[b] *& me*: I have read it with all the attention I can: & I would postpone my answer but for my one great doubt whether it would be improved thereby.

My doctrine would be this that the argument from analogy is good in homogeneous subject matter: but then this is where we speak of analogy in its higher forms and not as the mere comparison of ratios which is independent of homogeneity.[4] Then I should say that the whole moral training of man is essentially on subject matter so far that a law traceable & dominant in that which is called natural is likely also to prevail in that which he receives under revelation. I think that instead of quoting the sacraments as a proof of the contrast, I should rather quote the principles on which they are constructed as illustrating the doctrine of analogy. Not denying the certainty of some truth in the Church, I should also here find a parallel in the certainty of those principles of natural religion to which St Paul appeals. It is against the formalised and technically defined infallibility of Roman theology—in most of, if not in all its varied shapes—that I think the argument from the analogy of God's teaching as a moral Governor tells with great force. I would not use the argument you deprecate from the earth to the planets p. 162[c] because I don't think the several

---

[b] John Toland (1670–1722; *DNB*), Irish Roman Catholic convert to Protestantism and well-known Deist writer, particularly for his *Christianity Not Mysterious: Or, a Treatise Shewing, That There is Nothing in the Gospel Contrary to Reason, Nor Above It: And That No Christian Doctrine Can be Properly Call'd a Mystery* (London, 1696). Gladstone seems here to have mistaken the allusion in Manning's sermon ('Christianity as old as creation') to the Deist Matthew Tindal (bap. 1657–1733; *DNB*), *Christianity as Old as the Creation: Or, The Gospel, A Republication of the Religion of Nature* (London: n.p., 1731). On Manning's use of the adage see Sermon IX, 158, 162.

[c] Note Manning's comment: 'The force of analogy is here assumed to be positive and constructive, and that too in matters beyond its sphere. It is as if we should argue, that because the earth is a planet, describes an elliptical orbit round the sun, is spherical in form, and revolves on an axis, therefore the other planets, in which all these conditions are equally fulfilled, are in all other conditions like the earth; for instance, inhabited, and by a fallen race, and endowed with no higher functions or conditions; that, in a word, they are as our earth is, and transcend it in no-thing. Now it is scientifically true that this analogy raises a high amount of probability; and until the positive and proper evidence can be brought to shew that it has pleased God to endow other worlds more highly than our own, this analogy is master of the field. It has no antagonist: high probability is, in this case, our highest proof, and, as a presumption, no one can gainsay it. But here is exactly the point where false analogies fail. The planets can put in no proper evidence for them selves, but revelation can and does' (Manning, 'The Analogy of Nature', 162–3).

conditions there described as attaching to the earth are bound together by any such chain of similitude or relation as to make it warrantable to treat their co-existence as having a ground in general laws, so that there is no middle term by which to draw the argument. But when I look at the divine teaching in Providence I trace its profound adaptation to the structure of men's nature so that I find analogy violated when some one tells me of a system of discipline framed for him[5] upon quite other principles.

Of the sharp contrasts drawn in p. 166[d] I should only say I regard them with some fear & should like to know what I am affirming by them. You ask whether though natural truth be an uncertain light the light of Christ may not be infallibly clear? I answer you must shew me that the 'uncertain' of natural truth pertains to what is weak and defective in nature—then I grant your argument, but at present I contend that much of the uncertainty on the contrary is among the proofs of Divine wisdom & the effective means of our training. And further without an use of their doctrines as broad as mine I do not see how you are to sustain the principle on which the evidences of Christianity are constructed. But I do not give up *certainty*, nor should I perhaps shrink from your statements about that: only I do not think it is measured out in gallons quarts and pints but that it comes to us like the dews of heaven and the vital forces of the atmosphere.

The self-proving power I have always presumed to be *to persons as such*[6] an advanced gift, vouchsafed to those who have made full use of all the ordinary machinery of divine teaching, but not the wholesale possession of common and mixed professors of Christianity irrespectively of their personal state. It is, by *analogy*, like σοφιά[e] into which the φρόνιμος[f] by using his φρόνησις[g] arrives, a divine element of course working throughout the ascending scale from below[7] & from[8] the rudest faith to the most ripened and heavenly.

---

[d] 'Because our human personality divides the unity of substance, must, therefore, the divine? Because our personality can unite no more intimately than by a moral union, can there be no consubstantial unity in God? Because among men the father is before the son, cannot the ever lasting Son be co-eternal with the Father? Because the old creation is fallen and divided, may not the new have an unity derived from heaven? Because sense rules in the world, may there not be sacraments in the Church? Because human traditions grow corrupt, may not divine traditions be kept pure? Because keen intellects rule among human reasoners, are they to be instructors of the Saints? Because natural truth is an uncertain light, may not the light of Christ be sustained by Himself infallible and clear? Surely all this is nothing less than to take nature without revelation as the measure and limit of Christ's presence and office in the Church' (ibid. 166).

[e] Wisdom.   [f] Person with practical wisdom.   [g] Practical thought.

I am persuaded there is not much between what you mean & what I mean but I come rudely to the question & am aware that at best I am but feeling along the surface of something in the dark.

Am I to understand in p. 172 that the original inspiration and the perpetual illumination are the same thing in their degree?[h] If not in their degree then there is room for those who admit both to object to the Roman doctrine of infallibility.

I have a letter from Lincoln Oct 31 at Malta.[i] From the other *side* it appears, that the suit will be facilitated. This may be a sign of penitence or may not. My wife has written,[j] assuming that it *is*, to urge full clear & immediate acting in that sense—a forlorn hope. But without this we have no authority to suspend what is going on. I may add for your guidance that S[idney] Herbert—now knows the substance, & that my conclusions at Como were but too correct.[k]

If you have any thing more to say about Bishop elect H[ampden] it will perhaps appear in your next[l]—our headquarters will be here I think till after [Christ]mas.[m]

---

[h] 'Now it is no answer to this to ask, But how many attain to this certainty? This is only the objection urged against the Gospel by free-thinkers from without the Church, namely, its want of universality. It is no objection against either the universality of redemption, or the infallibility of the Church. What has been said amounts to this: that the doctrines of the faith, fully and clearly revealed by inspiration in the beginning, were fully and clearly apprehended by the Church; that the original inspiration has descended in a perpetual illumination; that this divine gift, as it was, at the first, not discovered but received, so it has been, not critically proved, from age to age, by intellect, not gathered by inductions or by the instruments of moral reasoning, but preserved and handed on by faith; that the office of reason is, not to discover and attain, but to illustrate, demonstrate, and expound; that the perpetual preservation of truth is a part of the divine office of the Holy Ghost, ever present in the mystical body of Christ; and that the presence of an infallible Teacher is as necessary to the infirmities of the human reason, as the presence of an omnipotent Comforter is necessary to the infirmities of the human will; that both the will and the reason, without such a presence, omnipotent and infallible, would be in a bondage to evil and to falsehood' (Manning, 'The Analogy of Nature', 172).

[i] Not located.

[j] Not located; see 491017mg, note a.

[k] See 490810gm.

[l] Reference perhaps to a *Charge* in 1849. Manning's 1848 *Charge*, which Gladstone read in proof, commented on the Hampden selection as Bishop of Hereford. See 480806mg to 491009gm inclusive.

[m] Leaving Fasque on 28 January 1850, the Gladstones returned to London on 30 January (*GD* iv. 181).

Believe me always aff[ectiona]tely yours
W. E. Gladstone

Ven[erable]
Archdeacon Manning
[[BL Add. MS 44248, 28–31; Morley transcript; cf. Chapeau, 327]]

491230gm

Fasque Dec[ember] 30. [18]49.

My dear Manning

I am reading your noble and beautiful Sermons,[a] which you have been so kind as to send after me, upon the wings of the post, into this remote quarter. It is dangerous to begin admiring (besides that I am never quite at my ease in dealing with Sermons as a product of the press subject to criticism, but it cannot wholly be avoided;) I will however confine myself to a single instance about which I cannot be silent namely the Fourth—in which you have gone so boldly and so far in expounding that great truth that it is only the positive and Catholic belief which leaves room for a genial view of the condition of great multitudes of men not within the full light of truth. I well remember the distress with which, bred in the extreme narrowness of the so-called evangelical opinions, I used to puzzle myself about the condition of persons apparently obedient and contemplate the two great horrors on either side, one of saying the appearance was all false and the other of saying that it must be followed by eternal misery. However it is not there only that narrowness is to be found—every fervent religious movement particularly among Englishmen will partake of it: I remember a Sermon of Newman's which was a valuable corrective—perhaps he would

---

[a] Manning, *Sermons. Volume the Fourth.* Gladstone began to read the Sermons in proof on Christmas Day 1849 and continued with it on 26 December (*GD* iv. 174), as well as on the day he wrote the letter, Sunday, 30 December (ibid. 175). He returned to the sermons on the first three Sundays of 1850, 6 and 13 January, completing them on 20 January (ibid. 176–9). Gladstone had also expressed his appreciation for the sermons to Lord Richard Cavendish (1812–73; *DNB*), brother of the 7th Duke of Devonshire. On 15 January 1850 the latter responded to a letter by Gladstone: 'I most entirely share in the admiration, you assess of Manning's last volume. One cannot be too thankful for such a gift at such a time—It seems to me far superior to anything which he had yet published' (BL Add. MS 44124, 253–6, 255).

unsay it now—& surely yours must under God operate powerfully in the same way[b]—

I have not yet reperused the Butlerian Sermon.[c]

In the new Quarterly you will see an article of mine on the Clergy Relief Bill.[d]

---

[b] Gladstone's reference appears to be to John Henry Newman, 'The Influence of Natural and Revealed Religion Respectively', Sermon 2 in *Sermons Chiefly on the Theory of Religious Belief. Preached before the University of Oxford* (J. G. F. & J. Rivington, 1843), sect. 28 (4): 'And hence, at the same time, may be learned the real religious position of the heathen, who, we have reason to trust, are not in danger of perishing, except so far as all are in such danger, whether in heathen or Christian countries, who do not follow the secret voice of conscience, leading them on by faith to their true but unseen good. For the prerogative of Christians consists in the possession, not of exclusive knowledge and spiritual aid, but of gifts high and peculiar; and though the manifestation of the Divine character in the Incarnation is a singular and inestimable benefit, yet its absence is supplied in a degree, not only in the inspired record of Moses, but even, with more or less strength, as the case may be, in those various traditions concerning Divine Providences and Dispensations which are scattered through the heathen mythologies.'

[c] Manning, 'The Analogy of Nature', 152–75.

[d] W. E. Gladstone, 'Clergy Relief Bill', *Quarterly Review* 86 (Dec. 1849), 40–78. Shortly after he was beaten on the Bill on 2 May 1849 (*GD* iv. 119; Hansard, civ. 1127, 1131), Gladstone discussed the issue with the Bishop of London and wrote a memorandum for him on it (cf. 5, 6 May; *GD* iv. 120). He seems to have considered the matter only sporadically for some time thereafter (13 June, ibid. 129, and 25 June, ibid. 132, and Hansard, cvi. 830) during which his concern was primarily given to Lincoln's marriage. After his return from the Continent on 22 August (*GD* iv. 149) he began to write on the Clergy Relief Bill, continuing through 21 September (ibid. 154–5), revising the paper on 23 September after which he appears to have sent it to the Bishop of Exeter who returned it by 20 October when Gladstone 'corrected a portion' of it, and the following day 'Finished correcting (anew) C[lergy] R[elief] paper & dispatched it' (ibid. 162). The corrections were done on 15 and 16 November (ibid. 166). 'A Bill for the Relief of Persons in Holy Orders of the United Church of England and Ireland, declaring their Dissent therefrom' (PP 1849 (95.) (207.) (319.) ii. 61 (5 Mar.), 65 (3 Apr.), 71 (31 May), was never enacted. It was initiated primarily as a result of the case of Revd James Shore (1795–1874). Shore was an Anglican priest at Bridgetown in the Diocese of Exeter and his Evangelical preaching and activities were opposed by Bishop Henry Phillpotts in 1844. Having seceded from the Church of England, he was nevertheless prosecuted in the Courts for publicly continuing to read prayers according to the prescriptions of the Book of Common Prayer and for preaching without a licence in an unconsecrated chapel. Shore appealed to the Judicial Committee of the Privy Council in August 1848, which found against him, judging that Anglican clergymen could not voluntarily relinquish their orders or officiate as a Dissenting pastor. Refusing to cease his activities Shore was arrested on 9 March 1849 as he descended from the pulpit. For details see Carter (2001), 356–90.

Were we together I should wish to converse with you from sunrise to sunset on the Gorham case.[e] It is a stupendous issue. Perhaps they will evade it. On abstract grounds this would be still more distasteful, than a decision of the State against a Catholic doctrine. But what I feel is that as a body we are not ready yet for the last alternatives. More years must elapse from the secession of Newman & the group of secessions which following or preceding belonged to it—A more composed & settled state of the public mind in regard to our relations with the Church of Rome must supervene—there must be[9] more years of faithful *work* for the Church to point to an argument, and to grow into her habits—and besides all these very needful conditions of preparation for a crisis, I want to see the question more fully answered, what will the State of its own free and good will do or allow to be done for the Church while yet in alliance with it? There are some questions of which I can conceive, & imagine practicable, a Parliamentary settlement that would be of immense value. The Colonial Church for instance and the Church Rate. Of course I mean in the way of liberty, to be bought with gold. But I also fear and feel that we are not yet prepared for the temporal sacrifices that are indispensable to a prosperous issue.

Many things look as if it were the purpose of God that the crisis of the Church quoad[f] her nationality should be delayed. Upon the other hand no more signal Providence has ever attended her destinies, than that which has now placed Baptismal regeneration in the front of the battle: first because it really lies at the root—second because also visibly—thirdly because the sense of the Church, as written, is so plain, that an opposite decision would be non-natural to the very last degree, & would even shake the credit of the judicial character among us. As to the Real Presence and some other doctrines one can understand how their opponents lay claim at least to a *locus standi*:[g] but if Mr. Gorham be carried through & that *upon the merits*, I say not only is there no doctrine of baptismal regeneration in the Church of England as State-interpreted, but there is no doctrine at all—and Arians or anybody else may abide in it with equal propriety. So that this would be a *reductio ad absurdum*[h] of the present position—and there would stand forth clear as day to all who did not shut their eyes the absolute necessity of the living voice of the Church to guard her mute witness against profanation.

---

[e] For details on the Gorham Case see Introduction. Gladstone's first explicit Diary note on the Gorham issue occured on 11 January 1850 and the following two days when he spoke at length with Hope on the 'crisis of the Church of England' (*GD* iv. 178).

[f] As to.   [g] Place to stand.   [h] Reduction to the absurd.

But are we ready for this? Of what I am—since each must in the first place answer for himself—practically, I know nothing: but in the reflective man I am ready for the worst; though not having lost hope in what is[10] better: On the contrary as to this particular judgment I cannot but think the question is will they sustain the Bishop—or will they evade the point. But the matter will not end here.

Badeley seems to have made another great and noble effort for the Church.[i] I fear however he committed a great mistake about the A[rch]b[isho]p of Canterbury. It seems to me that the more direct as

---

[i] Badeley defended Phillpotts against Gorham, 17 and 18 December 1849. He published a lengthy transcript of the proceedings touching his own presentations (*Gorham, Clerk, against the Bishop of Exeter. Substance of the Speech of Mr. Badeley on the Part of the Respondent, In the Privy Council. Whitehall 17th December, 1849*), and following the decision against him on 8 March 1850, a shorter work, *Substance of a Speech Delivered Before the Judicial Committee of the Privy Council, On Monday the 17th and Tuesday the 18th of December, A. D. 1849, Upon an Appeal in a Cause of Duplex Querela, Between the Rev. George Cornelius Gorham, Clerk, Appellant, and the Right Rev. Henry, Lord Bishop of Exeter, Respondent. With an Introduction* (London: John Murray, 1850; preface dated 3 April 1850). 'Duplex querela' refers to the suit which can be brought against a bishop if he refuses to institute or admit a candidate on doctrinal or liturgical grounds.

Reports of the proceedings were also published in *The Times*, 18 December 1849, 6a, and 19 December, 6d, and *The Guardian*, suppl. 19 December. Both noted the exchange between the Archbishop and Badeley. Near the end of the hearing on 18 December, Badeley commented that two prelates before him had already committed themselves on the issue. The Archbishop of Canterbury immediately responded ('with some emotion' according to the transcript *Gorham v. the Bishop of Exeter. A Full Report of the Arguments of Counsel, in this Important Case, before the Judicial Committee of the Privy Council, to Which is Added the Judgment* [2nd edn.; London: William Edward Painter, 1850], 126) that Badeley meant him. Badeley replied by noting that the Archbishop had preferred an individual (William Goode) who supported the Gorham view of baptism and the Archbishop countered by pointing out that the preferment had been made on the basis of his book, *The Rule of Faith and Practice*, some five or six years earlier (William Goode, *The Divine Rule of Faith and Practice; or, A Defence of Catholic Doctrine that Holy Scripture has Been Since the Times of the Apostles the Sole Divine Rule of Faith and Practice to the Church, Against the Dangerous Errors of the Authors of the Tracts for the Times, and the Romanists*... [2 vols.; London: J. Hatchard & Sons, 1842; preface dated 20 Nov. 1843, postscript to preface dated 3 Dec. 1843]). Badeley's later editorial comment in his edition of the transcript states that the Archbishop was mistaken on this matter as he (Badeley) discovered after the hearing (footnote in *Gorham, Clerk... Substance of a Speech*, 212–15). William Goode (1801–68; *DNB*) was educated at Trinity College, Cambridge. A clergyman, active in defence of Evangelical causes, he served as editor of the *Christian Observer*, and wrote extensively against Tractarian positions. Note above all his *Review of the Judgment of Sir H. J. Fust, Kt, in the Case of Gorham v. The Bishop of Exeter. By the Late Editor of the Christian Observer* (London: Hatchards, 1850), *A Letter to the Bishop of Exeter* (London: Hatchards, 1850), and his earlier *A Vindication of the Defence of the XXXIX Articles* (London: Hatchards, 1848).

well as the more politic course would have been to have quoted the Apostolic Preaching (e.g. page 165 of the 6th Ed.) in support of his case—and thus to have visibly isolated him of York.[j]

But I must have done—& will only give you our best wishes for the time, and add that Lincoln writes from the Piraeus all well on the 2d. Dec[embe]r. From the other quarter all we hear is bad.[k]

Believe me aff[ectiona]tely yours
W. E. Gladstone

Ven[erable]
Archdeacon Manning
I remain here probably till Parl[iament] meets.[l]

[[BL Add. MS 44248, 32–5; Morley transcript; cf Chapeau, 327–9; Lathbury, i. 95–6; Butler, 209–10]]

491231mg

Lavington. Dec 31. 1849.

Private

My dear Gladstone,

Let me before I go to the subject of this letter thank you for your last,[11] & tell you that the word liberty was an archaism & meant nothing,[a] except that to trouble a friend with a sermon in proof is a proverbial[12] torture. Forgive me this wrong, the worst I hope I ever did you, &, with my will, ever shall.

---

[j] On the page to which Gladstone refers Sumner writes: 'On the authority of this [Paul's] example, and of the undeniable practice of the first ages of Christianity, our Church considers baptism as conveying regeneration, instructing us to pray, before baptism, that the infant "may be *born again*, and made an heir of everlasting salvation;" and to return thanks, after baptism, "that it *hath* pleased God to *regenerate* the infant with his Holy Spirit, and receive him for his own Child by adoption" ' (John Bird Sumner, *Apostolical Preaching Considered, in Examination of St. Paul's Epistles* [6th edn.; London: J. Hatchard & Son, 1826], 165. Gladstone's annotated copy [SDL, Glynne F/221] is marked on p. 166, on which Sumner's point is continued). Note Sumner's concern with the use of his early work by High Church interpretations of baptismal regeneration such as that of Gladstone, and his resulting new edition (the ninth) and preface to the work in 1850. On Sumner's Evangelical approach to baptism see Scotland (1995), 87–8, 118–19, and notes 15–18, as well as Carter (2001), 347. The Archbishop of York, Thomas Musgrave (1788–1860; *DNB*) was educated at Trinity College, Cambridge, elected a Fellow, 1812, consecrated Bishop of Hereford, 1837, and Archbishop of York, 1847. Decidedly liberal in his political views, he was generally associated with the Evangelical party, but demonstrated a marked dislike of change.

[k] That is, regarding Lincoln's wife. Correspondence from the Piraeus not located; see 491017mg, note a.

[l] On Gladstone's movements see 491114gm.

[a] Reference to Gladstone's comment on Manning's 'taking a liberty', 491114gm.

And now let me ask of you a more important service. It is to read & give me your judgment on the inclosed point of conscience.

You have known me too long & too well to think that 'I use lightness' in such matters. The whole weight of my life is in the scale, & this makes it a matter which meets me at the Altar and must decide all my future.

I will not trouble you with more than my love for yourself[13] & for your wife, & such a blessing as a Priest may give to others better than himself. All Grace & Peace of Christmas be with you.

Believe me,

Ever your affect[ionat]e friend

H. E. Manning.

The Right Hon[oura]ble
W. E. Gladstone

[Enclosure[b]]

My submission to the Church of England, & the service I have endeavoured to fulfil has been rendered on the following principles.

1. That the Church of Christ is a divine kingdom invested by its divine Head with the custody of doctrine, & with the power of discipline, & that in the discharge of this custody & power it is sole, supreme & absolute under the guidance of Christ by His Providence, & His Presence through the Holy Spirit.

2. That the Church in[14] England being a member of this Divine Kingdom possesses 'in solidum'[c] by inherence in the whole Church this full & supreme custody of doctrine, & power of discipline, under the same guarantees & guidance with the whole Church at large.

3. That the Church in England being thus an integral whole has the fountain of doctrine & discipline within itself, & has no need to go beyond itself for succession, orders, mission,[15] jurisdiction, & the Custody of Catholic Tradition.

4. That on this ground alone our present relation to the Church at large can be justified.

---

[b] The Enclosure which follows was also sent to Hope on the same day. For details of the Hope reaction see Addenda to this Section. Note also Manning's active work in repairing and building churches in his parish. For details see his letter in reponse to a request from an unidentified priest for funds on 17 November, 1849: 'I have work going on in both of my own churches, and a new Church building in the Parish for the endowment of which I am solely responsible' (Pitts). On the planning for the new church building see Manning to NN, 26 April 1849 (Pitts).

[c] Reference is to Cyprian, *On the Unity of the Church*, 5 (PL 4. 501): 'Episcopatus unus est cuius a singulis *in solidum* pars tenetur (the Episcopate is one, each one of which is held *by the whole*)'. Cf. Newman, *Apologia* (Svaglic edn.), 72.

5. That the Office & relation of the Civil Power towards the Church in England is to protect, uphold, affirm, & further this its[16] sole, supreme, & absolute character & office in all matters of doctrine & of discipline.

In this sense I have accepted & interpreted expressly or implicitly our whole Ecclesiastical law: & I can accept it in no other sense, either expressly or by silence.

6. That the Royal Supremacy is therefore strictly & simply *civil*: & in no sense Spiritual, or Ecclesiastical understanding that word to mean concurrent or mixed *spiritual* jurisdiction.

It seems to me

1. That the claim of the Crown in the confirmation of Dr Hampden to the See of Hereford is a violation of the Divine office of the Church in respect to its discipline.

2. That the pending[17] appeal to the Judicial Committee of the Privy Council is a violation of the Divine office of the Church in respect to its doctrine.

I say the *appeal*, because it is indifferent which way the judgment may go.

Indeed a decision in favour of the true doctrine of Baptism would mislead many.

A judgment, right in matter, cannot heal a wrong in the principle of the Appeal.

And the wrong is this.

'The Appeal removes the final decision of a question involving both[18] doctrine & discipline out of the Church to another centre and that a Civil Court.'

It is not enough to say—

1. That the Appeal is only for a review of facts: or

2. That it is only for a review of the application of law.

Because the Judicial Committee may decide—

1. Either that the formularies of the Church admit this or that interpretation, which is a violation of the Custody of doctrine in its written definition.

2. Or that Mr. Gorham is qualified to receive institution which is to do two things at once (1) to violate the custody of doctrine in its oral proposition to the Church & (2) to deprive the Bishop of his power to try[19] judicially the fitness of a Priest, as the Archbishop has been denied the power to try judicially the fitness of a Bishop elect.

Now for these reasons, supposed to be undenied, I am unable to obey the existing Law.

But at my ordination institution, & collation I took oath to recognize the Ecclesiastical Supremacy of the Crown: of which this Appeal is an exercise & application.

I desire, therefore, to be advised on two points.

1. Whether these premisses can be denied?

2. Whether, granting these premisses, I can with a just conscience towards God hold offices of which that Oath of submission to the existing Ecclesiastical Law is a condition?

[[Pitts; Chapeau, 156 and 156a, 229–31]]

500105gm[a]

Fasque Jan[uary] 5. 1850

My dear Manning

You may think it strange that in reply to so grave a question only this short and insignificant note should make its appearance. But I am resolved to be very brief because I feel that to attempt a discussion of a subject so immense from my own unaided resources & in the midst of *more* distractions (—you may remember my Father's age[b]—) than in my usual London life—would be a mockery. Besides I feel another thing yet more deeply and I hope that you also will feel it. The feelings that now agitate your breast are the feelings of thousands: of many whom you know and love: of many men with whom you sympathise. That which most deeply impresses me is the duty of large counsel;[20] that those who agree together should in these awful seasons act together; & that the amplest time should be given, all means employed, minds brought into free contact, to ascertain who they are that do agree together. Be assured for me that while there is no man on this broad earth less worthy morally of the Christian calling, there is no man more entirely and steadily resolved with God's help to hold by the Catholic Church and if which may He forbid the ark drifts from the place of its mooring, to leave the mooring place and to follow the ark. Except in such writing to you, it would be more than idle—to say this.

Now I put forth these fragments.

1. In the case of B[isho]p Hampden, it was the Church, it was the A[rch]b[isho]ps legal organ, where the failure lay. Had the Eccles[i astical] Judge done his duty, then we should have seen what mind was in the State. But now we have not the means of judging.

---

[a] 'Wrote to … Archd[eacon] Manning' (*GD* iv. 176).

[b] Note Gladstone's comment on 11 December 1849: 'Worked & wrote for my Father most of the day. He is now 85. His prospects of life might be & may be excellent: but from particular causes they are more precarious' (ibid. 171).

2. The Judicial Committee of P[rivy] C[ouncil] is & can be never other than the exponent of the construction on which alone the State will permit the Church to hold her civil station.

3. The necessity that the Church should have her own organs to guard & construe doctrine is palpable. The *Daily News*!! of last Wednesday urges it.[c]

4. But as to the incidence of this necessity on a given point of view I hold it of material & even vital importance that the P[rivy] C[ouncil] should decide in favour of the true doctrine.

5. *Doctrine has been* interpreted in the Church of England, in practice, by the proper parties: not by Civil Courts: not even by the mixed Court of Delegates.—That was the real ecclesiastical law when you took your oaths.

6. The recent phase of the question I admit to be wholly new—& to require deep & patient consideration: but a consideration which *cannot* be perfect, till we know the issues of the appeal.

Farewell. I expect to be here till the 28th—in London on the 31st.[d]

Your aff[ectiona]te friend,
W.E.G.

Archdeacon Manning
I concluded you wished me to return the memorandum.[21]
[[Pitts; Chapeau, 156b, 232]]

500122mg

44 Cadogan Place
Jan[uary] 22. 1850.

My dear Gladstone,

Although I am hoping to see you next week I write partly because I must thank you for your last letter, & partly because some things are more clearly written than said.

It was curious that my last letter, & your last but one[a] should have crossed, & I believe we must have been reading them almost on the same day.

Since I came to London I have conferred with several persons of weight with us both—and my difficulties do not lessen.

---

[c] The case was made in the editorial of the *Daily News*, 2 January 1850, 4a.
[d] See 491114gm.   [a] See 491230gm.

I find by high legal opinion that the Royal Supremacy carries the full power to reverse the interpretations of Church courts in matter of doctrine: & that the oath of Supremacy binds me to accept that sense of this Supremacy.[b]

The acceptance & recognition made by the oath is not of a mere legal *fact* but of an abstract *right*. On examining the Statutes of Henry VIII. Edw[ard] VI. Eliz[abeth] & W[illia]m IV. I am satisfied that this Judicial Committee is a legitimate exercise of the Royal Supremacy as originally founded in 25 [*sic*] Henry VIII.[c]

---

[b] The response to Manning on his legal inquiries reads:

Case

1. Does the Supremacy of the Crown in Ecclesiastical causes carry with it a claim to confirm or reverse in appeal the declarations or interpretations of the Courts of the Church in matters of Doctrine.

I am of opinion that all causes which by the Laws, Customs and Constitutions of this Realm are properly cognizable in the Ecclesiastical Courts whether they involve matters of Doctrine or not, might before the passing of the Statutes 2 & 3 Will[ia]m 4 C. 92 ['The Privy Council Appeals Act', 1832], & 3 & 4 Will[ia]m 4. C. 41 ['The Judicial Committee Act', 1833]—have been appealed to the King as the Dernier Resort [final resort], and that the Sentences pronounced by the Ecclesiastical Courts in such cases might have been confirmed, reversed, or varied by the Decision of a Court of Delegates, duly appointed under the Great Seal; and I am further of opinion that since the passing of the above-mentioned Statutes, the same causes may now be appealed to the Queen in Council, & that the Sentences of the Ecclesiastical Court, may be confirmed, reversed or varied by Her Majesty at the Recommendation of the Judicial Committee of the Privy Council.

2. Does the Oath of Supremacy in your opinion bind those who take it to recognize, and accept the Supremacy in the sense of that claim.

I am of opinion that the Oath of Supremacy binds those who take it to recognize and accept the Supremacy of the Crown in Cases of Appeal from the Ecclesiastical Courts, in the sense, and to the extent stated in my answer to the former Query.

(signed) John Dodson

Doctors Commons
January 16th 1850. (Bodl. MS Eng. lett. c. 664, 35–6)

John Dodson (1780–1858; *DNB*) was educated at Oriel College, Oxford, and had a distinguished career in law, appointed Vicar General to the Lord Primate, 1849, Judge of the Prerogative Court of Canterbury, and Dean of the Arches Court, 1852. Manning appears to have sent the opinion out for review immediately on receiving it, the reply of 25 January 1850 indicating that he 'ought to be under no embarrassment from the oath of supremacy properly understood and weighed', although the reviewer insists that he must have more time to weigh the evidence properly (ibid. 37–8).

[c] 25 Henry VIII c. 19 ('Submission of the Clergy'). On Manning's understanding of the Act as linked to 26 Henry VIII c. 1 ('The Act of Supremacy') see Henry Edward Manning, *The Appellate Jurisdiction of the Crown in Matters Spiritual. A Letter to the Right Reverend Ashhurst-Turner, Lord Bishop of Chichester* (London: John Murray, 1850), 13.

Now I believe as a matter of Christian Faith, that the ultimate interpretation of doctrine both legislatively & judicially is by Divine commission, & command in the Church alone: in the Church Catholic acting by way of definition: in every particular church acting under the Catholic Church by way of judgment.

You will see therefore that I find myself in the presence of a contradiction.

And if that contradiction be established as the law of the Church of England I must leave to the advice of others & to the guidance of God the course before me.

I write this that you may turn it over in your mind: and I will, come to you please God the morning after your arrival in London, or any other time more convenient.

Give my love to your wife & thank her for her little note,[d] which I received with great pleasure at that time. Tell her that Miss Lockhart begins her work on the Feast of the Purification: on which day the Holy Sacrament will be first celebrated in the Chapel of the Penitents Home.[e]

God be with you & bring you safe home.

Ever yours affect[ionatel]y
H. E. Manning.

The Right Hon[ourable] W. E. Gladstone.[f]

[[Pitts; Chapeau, 157, 233]]

[[Manning met with Gladstone on 31 January 1850 (*GD* iv. 181).]]

500203gm[a]

6 C[arlton] G[ardens] Feb[ruary] 3. [18]50.

My dear Manning

A particular call upon me tomorrow[22] may keep me out till halfpast twelve or so.[b]

---

[d] Not located.

[e] Elizabeth Lockhart officially established her work with 'fallen women' at Wantage on 2 February 1850, The Feast of the Presentation of Christ in the Temple and the Purification of the Blessed Virgin Mary. See *Life and Letters of William John Butler*, 135.

[f] On the day following, 23 January 1850, Manning expressed equal concerns to Hope, noting his earlier reservations to Gladstone. See Addenda to this Section for related correspondence.

[a] 'Wrote to . . . Manning' (*GD* iv. 182).

[b] Gladstone was engaged with the 'Clydesdale Junction Meeting (Temple)' from 11.30 a.m.–2.30 p.m.; the shareholders had been called to a special meeting because of difficulties in the company (*GD* iv. 183).

In the meantime perhaps you will think of one among many contingencies—I yet hope an unlikely one—to which your mind may have been less turned than to others.

Suppose a judgment flagrantly at variance with the common sense, plain meaning, & known & clear law of the Church of England.

I hold that no clergyman is bound by his oath to obey or regard such a judgment until it becomes the definitive act of the State by the assent of Parliament.

Until then it would be no better than the judgment of the twelve Judges in the case of ship-money: which the subject was not bound to obey, but rather was bound according to the doctrines long since embodied in our law to disobey.[c]

No doubt a great responsibility is incurred in pronouncing with a private voice that a given judgment is of such a nature: but this is quite a different matter & with a different issue.

Affect[ionate]ly yours,
W.E.G.

You may perhaps read with some interest the accompanying letter which with the map will partly explain itself.[d]

[[Pitts; Chapeau, 157a, 234]]

[[On 4 February 1850, after the shareholders' meeting Gladstone met 'with Manning till 5 on the Gorham case & its consequences' (*GD* iv. 183). The two met again on 8 February (ibid. 184). On 22 February he met with Manning[e] after which he wrote to Catherine:

[c] The case of John Hampden (1595–1643; *DNB*) who refused to pay the amount of ship-money assessed to him was heard by twelve judges in the Exchequer Court in 1637. Hampden was defended on the principle that when the normal means of finance available to the king were expended, no additional tax could be levied without the consent of Parliament. Although the judgment was initially against Hampden by a division of 7 to 5, the case was overturned by the Long Parliament in 1641 (16 Charles I, c. 14). For details see Sharpe (1992), 545–600.

[d] Not located. John Powell suggests that the map referred to may be the one printed in the *Quarterly Paper* of the Church Missionary Society for Christmas 1848, dividing the world into separate categories according to the degree in which the Bible was 'withheld or used only in an unknown tongue'. Gladstone objected to the assumption of spiritual judgement, and to the suggestion that the Bible was less available in Orthodox countries than in Protestant ones, leading to his resignation from the Church Missionary Society. See BL Add. MSS 44368, 145, 290; 44369, 14. Cf. his favour for a 'Catholic belief which leaves room for a genial view of the condition of the great multitudes of men not within the full light of truth' (491230gm).

[e] Note as well Manning's comments to William Maskell the day earlier (21 Feb. 1850), thanking him for his book, *A First Letter on the Present Position of the High Church Party in the Church of England... The Royal Supremacy and the Authority of the Judicial Committee of the Privy*

I cannot form to myself any other conception of my duty in Parliament except the simple one of acting independently, without faction, & without subserviency, on all questions as they arise. To the formation of a party or even the nucleus of a party, there are in my circumstances many obstacles. I have been talking over these matters with Manning this morning and I found him to be of the opinion which is deliberately mine, namely that it is better that I should not be the head or leader even of my own contemporaries. (SDL, Glynne–Gladstone MS 771, 200–2, 200; Bassett (1936), 80; Morley, i. 355–6)

On 25 February he wrote to Catherine again:

As to my political lucubrations it has struck me as odd that Manning and I should have entered at so much length into speculative conversation of that kind at a time like this when my political future at any rate is made so peculiarly uncertain on account of the uncertainties overhanging the Church. It is quite possible that the judgment about Mr. Gorham may impose duties upon me which will separate for ever between my path of life public or private and that of all political parties. The issue is one going to the very root of all teaching and all life in the Church of England: but no judgment can be formed on the matter until we see what really is done. (SDL, Glynne–Gladstone MS 771, 205–6, 205)

Gladstone met with Manning and Wilberforce on 7 March[f] and again on 8 March, the day on which the decision on Gorham was handed down at the Court of Arches.

Council (London: W. Pickering, 1850; dated: 9 Feb. 1850): 'It seems to me very well & ably argued: and the conclusions respecting the existing law are as far as I can see or say, undoubtedly true. I have always lived in a vague belief that the civil power had no cognizance of matter purely spiritual: & I have so written & printed again & again. . . . The crisis is so full of unknown effects: perhaps on the faith of England and generations to come' (BL Add. MS 37824, 116–17). Shortly thereafter on 26 February, in a letter to an unknown correspondent, Manning noted: '? The Saxon race is great but the Catholic Church was the Mother & must be the upholder of its greatness' (Pitts). Maskell (1840–90; *DNB*) was educated at University College, Oxford, Rector of Corscombe, Dorset, 1842–7, the Examining Chaplain of Bishop Phillpotts at Gorham's initial interrogation. He was received into the Roman Catholic Church on 22 June 1850, and as an inopportunist entered into controversy with Manning over the Vatican I dogmatic definition of Papal Infallibility.

[f] Note Manning's letter to Maskell the same day:

44, Cadogan Place
March 7. 1850

My dear Maskell,
  Henry Wilberforce will come to you between 10 & 10½ tomorrow morning: or failing this at half past one & to go down with you to the Council Office.
  Since we parted I have thought over the question for tomorrow more fully, & though I feel that in my own case I would not raise the objection, yet for others, & to avert a mischief it may lawfully & fairly be done.

He 'Spent the morning in conference with Hope—Manning—& Archd[eaco]n & H. Wilberforce, on the Gorham case & its probable consequences.'[g] He met with Hope, Manning, and others again on Saturday, 9 March and on Sunday, 10 March, he 'Spent the aft[ernoo]n in conversation with Manning & we found ourselves still in substantial agreement.' On Monday, 11 March, he met again with Hope, Manning, and others in his bedroom, 'Laid up with cold,' as he was at the time (*GD* iv. 191–2). On a letter, written by the Bishop of London on 11 March to Gladstone and telling him that the Bishop could not concur with Gorham at the Court of Appeal, Gladstone notes: 'See also . . . Hope, Manning, R. Wilberforce . . .' (BL Add. MS 44369, 60–1, 61).]]

500312mg

March 12. 1850

My dear Gladstone,

Trusting to your offer about last night we have ventured to agree to come & ask the use of a room in your house tonight in the hope of having your help if you can gain time from the House of Commons.

I will be here a little before eight to make another arrangement if it should be inconvenient to you.

This morning I was unable to come to give earlier notice.

Ever yours aff[ectionate]ly
H.E.M.

[[Pitts; Chapeau, 158, 234]]

[[On the evening of Manning's letter, Tuesday, 12 March 1850, 'Before 8 P.M. Manning came & a party followed him. They went at 12 but Badeley stayed until after one explaining to me the position of the question as to the prohibition in the Gorham Case' (*GD* iv. 192). Gladstone kept a copy of the 'Resolutions Agreed to at a meeting held on Tuesday, March the 12th, 1850' (BL Add. MS 44566, 94).[a]

Manning in his later reminiscences described the meeting thus:

One doubt however crosses me. How far will this prejudice the Bishops Address to the Crown? It will raise bad blood: & tend to make his petition seem like importunity.

Believe me,
Yours very sincerely,
H. E. Manning (BL Add. MS 37824, 154)

[g] *The Times* reported the decision the following day, 9 March 1850, 5e, as did *The Guardian*, 'Judgment in the "Gorham Case" ' (172–4, 183–4).

[a] For details on the development of the 'Resolutions' to their final form on 18 March 1850, see Addenda to this Section.

In the course of that year came the Gorham Judgment. I remember that I was in London when it was given. I went at once to Gladstone who then lived in Carlton Terrace. He was ill with influenza & in bed. I sat by his bed & told him of the judgment. He sat up & said: 'the Church of England is gone unless it releases itself by some authoritative act.'[b] We then agreed to draw up a declaration & to get it signed. For this purpose we met in the Vestry of S[t]. Pauls Knightsbridge. There were present Bennett, Hope, R[ichar]d Cavendish, Gladstone, Dr Mill[c] I think & some others. They made me preside. We agreed to a string of propositions declaring that by the Gorham judgment the Church of England had forfeited its authority as a Divine Teacher.[d] The next time we met Pusey & Keble I think

---

[b] Note the words indicated by Purcell (1892), 426, as told him by Manning in 1887: 'Then the Church of England is ruined, irretrievably ruined.' Cf. Francis de Pressensé, *Cardinal Manning*, trans. E. Ingall (London: William Heinemann, 1897), 135: 'Mr. Gladstone rose from a sick-bed to tell Manning: "The English Church is lost if she does not save herself by an act of courage." '

[c] William James Early Bennett (1804–86) was educated at Christ Church, Oxford, and after serving in London parishes was appointed Priest-in-Charge of St Paul's, Knightsbridge, 1840, where he actively supported the building of St Barnabas, Pimlico (dedicated 11 June 1850, at which ceremony Manning preached) and ritualist practices, which raised strong opposition and some rioting and resulted eventually in Bennett's forced resignation in December 1850. Throughout the rest of his life he continued to write in support of ritualist activities. For details see *DNB* and Bennett (1909). William Hodge Mill (1792–1853; *DNB*) was educated at Trinity College, Cambridge, elected a Fellow, 1814, and served as Principal of Bishop's College, Calcutta, 1820–38, before returning to England because of health problems to serve as Chaplain to the Archbishop. A fine student of Semitic languages, he was appointed Regius Professor of Hebrew at Cambridge, 1848.

[d] See also Manning to Maskell:

44, Cadogan Place,
March 12. 1850

My dear Maskell,

Many thanks for your letter. Sunday must have been a hard day for you: but I trust that the kindness of your people has helped you on.

I have little to report of a final sort.

The Church Union is at work under the guidance of John Talbot [John Chetwynd Talbot (1806–52)]: and as far as I hear has done well. I have not attended because we have had other meetings of perhaps a more satisfactory kind.

Last night Dr. Mill, Mr. Keble, Dodsworth, Bennett, Denison, H. Wilberforce, Arch d[eaco]n. Thorpe, Talbot, James Hope & Cavendish met at the Vestry of St. Pauls. W[ilton] Place. We got some resolutions of a direct & sufficient sort, and are to meet again tonight with R. Wilberforce & I hope Gladstone. The resolutions are in effect

1. That the Church will be bound if the Sentence be not rejected. (if not already bound some so[illegible word])
2. That the Sentence sanctions contradictory doctrines [therefore]
3. That it denies the whole doctrine of Baptism [therefore]
4. That it destroys the rule & authority of Faith.

were there. They refused this: & got it changed to 'if the Church of England shall accept this judgment it would forfeit.' This was accepted because it did not say whether the Ch[urch] of England had or had not *de facto* accepted the judgment. Hope said 'I suppose we are all agreed that if the Ch[urch] of England does not undo this we must join the Church of Rome.' This made an outcry. And I think it was then that Keble said 'If the Church of England were to fail it should be found in my Parish.' We met for the last time in Gladstones house. There were thirteen present. We agreed to the Declaration: & then came the signing. They called on me to sign first. I did so then Robert (Archdeacon) Wilberforce. I cannot certainly remember the others, but the list is printed. [Marginal note: see Weekly Register, 1881.] Then they called on Gladstone to sign. He was standing with his back to the fire. He began to demur: after a while I went to him & pressed him to sign. He said in a low voice to me 'do you think that I as a Privy Councillor could sign that declaration'. I knowing the pertinacity of his character turned & said: 'We will not press him further.'

This was the first divergence between him & Hope & myself. (Manning, 'Later Reminiscences', i. 34–5 [CP]. See also Purcell, i. 530)

Gladstone later disavowed this. See above all his comments on the event in his 14 January 1896 letter to Purcell, printed in the closing annotation to Section Twelve, and his annotation in PurGl i. 530, beside Purcell's quotation of the section: 'after 35 years' and his underscoring of the word 'Privy'. Cf. Lathbury, ii. 338, Leslie, 90, and Morley, i. 379–81, and note Gladstone's ongoing concern throughout his political career thereafter to remove bishops from the Judicial Committee and to restrict the Committee from deciding on doctrinal matters (Stephen [1966] and [1989]).[e]

5. That a Church acquiescing in this forfeits authority to teach as a member of the Universal body.
6. That it also forfeits its office to assure men of the grace of Sacraments, & remission of Sins.

There follow certain suggestions as to the mode of rejecting the Sentence.

If this paper should be adopted it may possibly be published at once, & throw up a light. I shall know more tomorrow.

The bishop I have seen but I do not know of any final resolve as to his course.

The depth to which people are stirred by this increases, and I trust that good, though as yet little peace must come.

On Thursday night I hope to be at Lavington: direct to me there.

I shall be glad to go home & spend the rest of this season in retreat, for the last two months have much disturbed & hindered me: and I always mistrust myself when I find certain habits weakened, and certain others in greater activity. Remember me at the altar, & believe me,

My dear Maskell,
Always very faithfully yours
H. E. Manning (BL Add. MS 37824, 170–2)

[e] Wilfrid Meynell in his *Memorials of Cardinal Manning* (London: Burns & Oates, 1892) outlines the meeting thus:

The following day, Wednesday, 13 March, Gladstone met with Hope, Manning, and others on the matter (*GD* iv. 192). The meeting disturbed Manning and he wrote to Hope on 14 March from Brighton: 'I found yesterday that Gladstone's objections had increased. Anything coming from him is so much to be weighed that I could much wish that you would see him, & judge of the whole question on to the time of publishing' (NLS MS 3675, 68).

Hope answered immediately: 'Y[ou]rs from Brighton has just reached me— I will see Gladstone & talk matters out with him.—but there are worse hindrances than he is likely to prove.—Pusey came here with Keble yesterday, and remained some hours criticising our "Resolutions." Hoping to get matters adjusted, I proposed a meeting of all who could be got together at Gladstone's this morning. I think all but Gladstone are for Resolutions to be immediately put forth. There are several, however, who are alarmed at the thoroughgoing tone of those we have adopted, and fear the recoil. Horror of Rome seems to be at the bottom of these minds; and some spoke even of a generation passing away before the Church be deemed unsafe, which translated seems to mean that, happen what may, it will do for their time.' (Bodl. MS Eng. lett. c. 657, 66–8; cf. Purcell, i. 529)

The meeting proposed by Hope occurred. On Thursday, 14 March Gladstone writes: 'Hope, Badeley, Talbot, Cavendish, Messrs. Keble, Denison, and Bennett here from 9¾ to 12 on the draft of the Resolutions.[f]— Badeley again in the ev[enin]g. also saw Prosser & L[or]d Powis: on the

'The Gorham Case came as a crisis.... A meeting of earnest Anglicans was held in Mr. Hope-Scott's house in Curzon Street, and a protest was drawn up which Archdeacon Manning was the first to sign. Mr. Gladstone, who stood and warmed himself by the fire, was the first layman who was asked to sign. But he refused. The Archdeacon took him aside. "How can I, consistently with my oath as a Privy Councillor?" he asked. The Archdeacon then announced that Mr. Gladstone's reason for refusal affected no one but himself, and passed to the next name. Father Morris, who says that the Archdeacon believed then as always in "Mr. Gladstone's perfect sincerity and complete good faith of many years." '

[f] Three drafts of the Address by Gladstone and a printed copy, annotated by him and dated 15 March 1850, are preserved in BL Add. MS 44738, 118–21. Note Gladstone's letters to Sidney Herbert encouraging him to sign the Address on 19 March and again on 20 March. In the latter letter he comments (perhaps alluding to Manning and Hope) on 'what seems to be a misapprehension & if so it is a serious one—surely secession is a terrible event: but 1. if nothing be done it is absolutely certain—2. if it take place *with nothing done* it will be the very worst kind of secession (as I think) viz. in the main a despairing self-abandonment to the Church of Rome, which will certainly destroy the Church of England by leaving it a prey to further innovations: but on the other hand the secession of the

whole I resolved to try some immediate effort' (*GD* iv. 192). Manning, in Brighton, was not present, but by the next day, 15 March, he was back again at Lavington and still concerned with Gladstone's full participation (as was Hope) and Pusey's proposed changes:

Denison tells me that Pusey proposes changes in the resolutions.[g] It is impossible for me to come to London. The meeting of the Archdeaconry on Tuesday makes my being here altogether necessary. . . . [h] If Pusey amends I assume that he will sign. If he signs we open the door for other names such as R. Palmer &c. . . .

Nonjurors though bad on its own ground yet saved the Church of England at the epoch of the Revolution—3. the specific object of the Address is to promote such measures as may avert disruption . . . —the persons who have realised most to themselves the alternatives that would drive them from the Church of England, have been the two or perhaps three most reluctant to subscribe' (Wiltshire Country Archives, Wilton Papers, 2507 F4/60).

[g] In the Gladstone Papers (BL Add. MS 44566, 99–100) there is a note in Pusey's handwriting dated 16 March 1850. See Addenda to this Section for text.

[h] Manning was present at a meeting of the clergy of his archdeaconry in the Cathedral Library on Tuesday, 19 March 1850, where resolutions were adopted and forwarded to the Bishop who acknowledged receipt on 21 March and indicated in his acknowledgement that he understood from Manning's letter that an Address would shortly be forthcoming which is 'likely to touch upon an important doctrine which was excluded from discussion while the Resolutions were under consideration' (Bodl. MS Eng. lett. c. 653, 659–60). The Bishop did not yet have the Address on 26 July 1850 [see ibid. 661–2]).

In a later note Manning recorded: 'I convened the clergy of the Archdeaconry of Chichester in the Cathedral Library, and we unanimously voted (8 only excepted out of 100) a protest against the Gorham Judgment and the interference of civil authority in questions of doctrine' (Purcell, i. 533). A full description of the meeting and of Manning's speech was published in the *English Churchman*, 4 April 1850, 210–12, and *The Guardian*, 4 April 1850, 232–4; see also ibid. 22.

The Resolutions read thus:

19th March 1850.
We, the Archdeacon and clergy of the archdeaconry of Chichester, desire to lay before your Lordship, as our Bishop, the deep anxiety awakened in us by the decision lately given in the case of *Gorham v. the Bishop of Exeter*.

Believing as a fundamental article of the Catholic faith, that all infants baptized, according to the institution of Christ, with water in name of the Father, and of the Son, and of the Holy Ghost are regenerate by the Holy Spirit, we are convinced that the Church cannot, without betraying her highest trust, permit that doctrine to be denied.

We therefore urgently pray that your Lordship will take such steps as shall seem most effectual for the declaration and maintenance of the doctrine of holy baptism, and for relieving those who feel grieved in conscience by the legal sanction given by the late sentence to the denial of that article of faith. (Purcell, i. 535)

His name will give an entirely new face to all the rest.... His name demands Gladstone's—or five officers at least. *I say this only for you.* (NLS MS 3675, 72–3)

He makes the same point again in letters to Hope on the following two days. On 16 March he wrote:

It is impossible for me to be with you: but we so clearly think alike that I believe I can take any line you advise. I will therefore say a few things which strike me.

1. The object & affect of the changes appear at once to be indecisiveness & delay.

But we have pitched the note too high as to be able to afford something to obtain an act which shall include Gladstone, Keble, & Pusey, with others.

2. If Gladstone will join in the resolutions & sign. I s[houl]d prefer embodying them in an address to be presented *at once* [double underlining], say to the Bishop of London in reference to his dissent & communicated by authority of the subscriber to the rest of the Bishops.

I prefer acts which terminate in a person—not in the air. The only danger is that the Bishop may neutralize by some public reply.

But this is not a sufficient reason against the cause if Gladstone will join.

3. As to the Resolutions

(1) The first is inspired excellently by the word 'essentially'.

The first amendment carries no meaning to my mind. The Ch[urch] of E[ngland] will be bound or not bound. A church cannot be partially heretical, or partially schimaticized. 'Formally' & 'intentionally' I understand, but not partially! i.e. 'in so far as.'

The second amendment w[oul]d do if the meaning of accept were defined, & as to include [illegible word] in action, and execution of the sentence by Courts & Bishops: do without these, it is as you say inadmissible altogether.

(2). by inserting after sin 'by the exact organization' & striking out the parenthesis which weakens it, I think the amendment in some ways an improvement. As it stands it will not include 'the infusion of grace' which is the point chiefly at issue.

(4)(5)(6) The inserted words seem to me so many loopholes for the future: and to raise a cloud of uncertainty.

I could not sign them if by so doing I laid myself under any obligation to receive the interpretation which A and B may hereafter put upon them.

But with the full & clear understanding that these are only as guaranties against hasty and premature judgement I would not refuse to sign.

My object is.

1. To set a prompt, & clear declaration of the truths & laws which must govern our conscience & conduct.

2. To unite those who will hold them sacred.

3. To leave freedom for every one hereafter without [illegible word] bound from this united act to do what he believes to be his duty towards God.

I shall be most anxious to hear the result of Monday night, unless something intolerable be annexed as a condition, I would fall in with Gladstone's proposal.

If we cannot strike 12 let us strike 9: this would be intelligible & positive and it is easier to advance than go back.

Believe me,

Always most truly yours

H.E.M.

The B[isho]p of Glasgow is strongly with us & is moving not so Edinburgh. (NLS MS 3675, 74–7)

And on 17 March: 'My letter of yesterday will I think convey all I have to say about the amendments. I am still convinced that some such declaration of principles is necessary. And if it could satisfy Gladstone to frame them into an address to the Bishop of London as I suggested yesterday I should prefer it to any other form' (NLS MS 3675, 78–9).

During the same period, Gladstone too continued to be concerned with the issue as his Diaries and correspondence make evident (*GD* iv. 192–3). On 18 March, Gladstone spoke on the Gorham case in the House of Commons (Hansard, cix. 1050, 1054) and noted another meeting on the matter: 'Drs. Mill, Pusey &c. met here in the ev[enin]g. I was not with them' (ibid. 194). Manning continued to be concerned about Gladstone's participation as his letter to Mill on 19 March, asking him to sign the resolutions, indicates, stating: 'We propose to publish it in the Times on Monday next. And we hope by that time to obtain Mr. Gladstone's name. He entirely concurred but strong and special reasons delay him attaching his name' (Lambeth Palace MS 1491, 33–4, 33). The following day, the 'Nine Resolutions' were published in *The Times*.[i]

---

[i] They also appeared in *The Guardian* (206) on the same day and in the *English Churchman* on 21 March 1850 (185) with slight variants in capitalization. For the text as it appeared in *The Times*, 5b, see Addenda to this Section.

The Gorham issue remained continually with Gladstone throughout March. On 20 March it was central topic at a dinner at Peel's (*GD* iv. 195). On the same day Manning wrote again to Hope:

Lavington. March 20, 1850

My dear Hope,

Many thanks to you for subscribing my name to the Resolutions. Though somewhat loaded they are enough to break this ground. And the getting of so many, & such as some of the names is not unimportant.

Now I feel that we have cleared our positions & measured our range. It remains to be seen what resistance & what response we shall meet, & then we shall be able to judge of the future more clearly.

Yesterday we met to the number of about 90 at least. We passed resolutions in substance identical with those published by the Church Union. There were 8 objectors—weaker than can be conceived. The rest voted as one—of course with no such view as you and I take. But sincerely up to the high Anglican ground.

Afterwards we signed an address to our Bishop on the subject of the Doctrine. I expect a vast majority of the Archdeaconry to sign it.

I think you have done well to join with Gladstone. Do not let his mind disengage itself from yours.

Let me have a word if anything of moment turns ups.

May we be guided to do nothing, & to leave nothing undone, which may hereafter give no cause of self accusation.

Believe me,
Ever yours affec[tionate]ly
H. E. Manning.

The Bishop of Glasgow is acting stoutly & has convened his squad. Can you direct copies of the resolutions to be sent to me. (NLS MS 3765, 80–1).]]

500404gm[a]

6 C[arlton] G[ardens] Ap[ril] 4. 1850.

My dear Manning

I have been desirous every day of writing to you: but other cares have intervened. Our little Jessy has within these few days been very near indeed

---

[a] 'Wrote to Manning' (*GD* iv. 194).

to the doors of the grave:[b] and she still lies in a state requiring the upmost care. She cannot I fear be considered by any means out of danger but hope decidedly predominates, which is indeed very different from what I would have said 48 hours ago. The brain is the seat of the disease and it is of her subtlest character. Under God we seem to owe much to the extraordinary skill and delicacy of Dr. Locock's[c] treatment. In the country I think we should before this time have been mourning our little sufferer's departure. My wife has borne up, or rather has been borne up wonderfully: riding as usual with the emergency.

I was very anxious to have employed all the[23] quiet of this week in arranging my views about the Gorham question so as be ready to cut promptly whenever the time comes. But of course under the circumstances I have not only made no progress but am dissipated and unmanned. I shall therefore write you a less selfish letter than would otherwise have been the case. I am most anxious for advice and guidance being placed between a variety of distinct obligations the harmony of which it is not easy to discern at certain given points. The main question is, should one try to act for the Church *in* the State or *on* the State: you will comprehend all that the change of the single letter implies. Sidney Herbert's declining to sign the address to the Bishop of London seems to come to me as a sign to prepare for making that change soon:[d] for the reluctance of other men in politics to commit themselves in any degree of course must tend to drive me forward, as the keeping in company with them would tend to hold me back. Do not understand me to be blaming him: doubtless he has his work and is doing it—

I have written strongly to Lincoln[e] but have had no time for a reply.

---

[b] Catherine Jesse Gladstone (b. 27 July 1845) was dying of meningitis; the disease took a marked turn for the worse on Good Friday, 29 March 1850, was much worse, Tuesday, 2 April, and seemed to be improving by 3 and 4 April (*GD* iv. 196–8), but the child died in the morning of Tuesday, 9 April (ibid. 200). For Gladstone's reflections see his 'Some Account of our second daughter Catherine Jessy Gladstone', BL Add. MS 44738, 122–46 (*Autobiographica*, ii. 50–66).

[c] Sir Charles Locock (1799–1875; *DNB*) MD Edinburgh, 1821, FRCP, 1836 Physician at the Westminster Lying-in Hospital and First Physician-Accoucheur to Queen Victoria, 1840.

[d] See Lord Stanmore, *Sidney Herbert Lord Herbert of Lea: A Memoir* (2 vols.; London: John Murray, 1906), i. 128–9, for discussion between Gladstone and Herbert on the matter.

[e] Not located; on 1 April 1850 Gladstone was 'Examined 3½ hours (by a most tedious process) on Lady Lincoln's wretched case', the private examination before the hearing of the case in the House of Lords (*GD* iv. 197). See 500523gm.

In the meantime all the essential points of the case stand out more & more as one ruminates upon them in characters of light. It is for ever, and for all, that this battle is to be fought in the Church of England. I am more and more consoled in reviewing the historical part of his case. The article in the Christian Remembrancer was very welcome to me.[f] But I promised to spare you egoism: & I go on to say I have read your Speech in the Guardian[g] as well as the type & my eyes (rather put out by irregular hours) would allow & trust it will do great and extensive good.

The Bishop of Glasgow has requested me to send you the inclosed paper[h] & letter for your opinion which you will doubtless send him: and perhaps you will return me his letter. I write to him to say that it appears to me the objection to B[isho]p Terrott's words are that as they stand: they may be held to reach too far over unseen contingencies on account of the 'will', and I venture to suggest '*we see no cause for*' in the present tense. It seems to me that we ought all to maintain to the uttermost the clearness & abundance of the present declarations of the doctrine: & further that B[isho]p Terrott has now been acting *well* & ought as far as possible to be met and encouraged.

Secondly. Redesdale, who is thoroughly in earnest, doubts the Upper House of Convocation as a Court and suggests by way of sketch two persons chosen by each House, and a legal assessor appointed by the Crown.[i] I have been thinking whether a limited number of Bishops, or Bishops & Divines, representing the Upper House (therefore[24] *chosen by it*) might not be more attainable than the Upper House and as desirable. It is certainly large for a Court especially if as I presume is the case the Colonial

---

[f] See 'Church and State', *Christian Rembrancer* 68 (Apr. 1850), 471–516, a review of John Keble, *Church Matters in MDCCCL. No. 1—Trial of Doctrine* (London: J. H. Parker, 1850). Cf. John Keble, *Church Matters in MDCCCL. No. II—A Call to Speak Out* (London: J. H. Parker, 1850; preface dated 20 July), W. J. Irons, *The Present Crisis in the Church of England* (London: Masters, n.d.), William Mayow, *A Letter to the Rev. W. Maskell* (London: Pickering, 1850), W. J. E. Bennett, *The Crown, the Church, and the State* (London: Cleaver, 1850), and J. M. Neile, *A Few Words of Hope on the Present Crisis of the English Church* (London: Masters, n.d.).

[g] The speech Manning delivered on 19 March 1850 in the Cathedral Library, Chichester, was printed in *The Guardian* of 4 April, 232–4.

[h] Not located; possibly a draft for the eventual resolutions of the Scottish bishops on Gorham, for which see Addenda to this Section.

[i] Perhaps by personal comment to Gladstone; the suggestion is not in Lord Redesdale, *Observations on the Judgment in the Gorham Case: and the Way to Unity* (London: Francis & John Rivington, 1850). John Thomas Freeman-Mitford (1805–86; *DNB*), 2nd Baron of Redesdale, 1830, 1st Earl of Redesdale, 1877.

Bishops are members of it. I am unfeignedly desirous of asking the very least that will rescue and defend the conscience of the Church from the present hideous system. For upon that minimum must be made a stand involving certainly tremendous issues.

I think the Bishop of London is in deep earnest.[j] He has broached his Upper House plan through the A[rch]b[isho]p to the Government—and I apprehend he is also in communication with other B[isho]ps about the declaration by them which would be a very good measure if sufficiently signed.

I remain always

Aff[ectiona]tely yours

W. E. Gladstone

Venerable

Archdeacon Manning

[[BL Add. MS 44248, 36–8; Morley transcript; Purcell, i. 536; cf. Chapeau, 338; Butler, 214]]

[Enclosure]

Moray Place. April 3. 1850. *Confidential*

Dear Mr. Gladstone

Thank you for your kind contribution to Hawick School. It is one of the most promising missions in my Diocese. The D[uke] of B[uccleuch][k] is building a schoolhouse, & tho' I did not know that the Clergyman was collecting subscriptions, I dare say that he has but too much occasion for them.

The result of our address to B[ishop] of London was, I think, satisfactory. His reply was in so different a tone from what I sh[oul]d have expected from his answers to B[ishop] of Edin[burgh] that I think he must have been led by some influences to change his view.

The B[ishop] of Edin[burgh] is now willing to agree to a Syn[od] declaration from the Epis[copal] Coll[ege]—and has drawn up the inclosed papers, which in many respects is far more satisfactory than I should have expected or thought possible from his first[25] expressions on the subject.

---

[j] On the eventual form of the Bishop of London's bill see 500520gm and note Johnson (2001), 137–41.

[k] Walter Francis Montagu-Douglas Scott (1806–84; *DNB*), 5th Duke of Buccleuch and 7th Duke of Queensberry.

At the same time you will see that he would pledge the Epis[copal] Col l[ege] not to *admit at any future time*[26] *any further definition* (i.e. by a General Synod, binding the whole Church) and this he makes a sine quâ non in agreeing to the declaration that goes before it.—Now I am disposed to be satisfied with the doctrinal part of this paper: but, as at present advised, no earthly consideration would induce me to commit myself to such a pledge. I am indeed *for the present* satisfied with what has been done and with a Synodical declaration of the Bishops, and am *content to wait* & see whether the Eng[lish] Church rights itself or not:—But if such a pledge were to pass the Episc[opal] Coll[ege] I believe that I should feel myself bound at once[27] formally to protest against it, and appeal to a General Synod.

Bishop of Brechin[1] and I have been with B[ishop] of E[dinburgh] this morning:—and he says nothing will induce him to consent to anything so definite in doctrine as the first part of this paper, unless the pledge in the latter part is given. He would consent to a paper, declaring on general terms

1. That the decision has no authority here.

2. That the Bishops repudiate the *doctrine of the decision*, & the reasons on which it is founded.

3. That as the Church of Eng[land] is primarily affected by the decision, the Bishops think that the Church should wait and see what line is taken in England, and be content with what has been done here in the way of declaration.

Now the concluding part of this scheme I should be satisfied with:—but the expression 'the doctrine of the decision' is (I think) too vague. Qu[estion:] What doctrine? The Doctrine that the subject of Bap[tismal] Regen[eration] is an open question?—or the Doctrine that the words are a charitable hypothesis? &c. &c.

Will you tell me how this appears to you, & will you forward this to A[rc]hd[eaco]n Manning:—to whom I intended to address it,—but having to acknowledge your cheque, I venture to ask also the benefit of your opinion. I should be glad to have the Bishops paper again and as the Synod is this day fortnight (17th) at Aberdeen, there is not much time.

---

[1] The Bishop of Brechin had sent his manuscript circular of protest to Gladstone on 16 March 185 (BL Add. MS 44566, 106–7). Alexander Penrose Forbes (1817–75) was educated at Brasenose College, Oxford, and appointed Vicar of St Saviour's, Leeds, in 1847, but immediately thereafter elected Bishop of Brechin. For details see *DNB*, Bertie, 258–9, Lochhead (1966), 106–38, and Strong (1995).

I should observe that the Primus seems quite satisfied with B[ishop] of Edin[burgh]s paper. Now the two elder Bishops will not be present:—and as the B[ishop] of Argyll[m] will vote with B[ishop] of E[dinburgh] the *probability* is that there will be three Bishops against the Bishop of Brechin and myself.

You may suppose that this makes me very anxious:—With my deep persuasion that this question is *vital*, & that if the English Church should not right herself, a Synodical act on the part of this Church will be absolutely necessary, I see no possibility (as I said before) of my[28] assenting to a pledge to admit no new Definition on the subject. A formal appeal to a General Synod seems the only course left; if the Episc[opal] Coll[ege] thus commits itself. The Primus *may* be influenced to assent to a paper *with no pledge* (one way or other) as to anything ulterior. This I could agree to:—but I fear.

Yours very truly

W. T. Episc[opus] Glascu[ensis]

Rt Hon W. E. Gladstone

[[BL Add. MS 44369, 126–7]]

500406mg

Lavington. April 6. 1850.

My dear Gladstone,

I am truly grieved to hear of your anxiety about your child: & trust she may be spared to you: & that your wife will not suffer from care & fatigue. You have had many intimations that such fair gifts are held on frail tenures,[29] & full of change. May they be long spared to you with the living consciousness of Gods love of whom you hold them.

We too have been in sorrow. Five hours of most sudden and inexplicable illness has taken away my dear Sister Sophia Ryder. Now only one remains to her Mother: only two of all the home I entered seventeen years ago.[a]

---

[m] Alexander Ewing (1814–73), Bishop of Argyll and the Isles, 1847–73 (*DNB*; Bertie).

[a] Sargent's wife, Mary, lived until 1861, her daughter Mary, the wife of Henry Wilberforce, to 1878. They were predeceased by Mary Sargent's children: Charlotte in 1818; John (b. 1808) in 1829; and Henry Martyn (b. 1816) in 1836; Manning's wife, Caroline, died in 1837; Emily, the wife of Samuel Wilberforce, in 1841, and Sophia (married to George Dudley Ryder) in 1850. On the death of Sophia, note Manning's brief Palm Sunday letter, 1850, to her husband, as well as his letter on Tuesday in Holy Week (copies in CP).

Since that time I have hardly been for one year out of mourning. But it is a blessing second only to the light of Faith, & the grace of the Sacraments.

I will now come to your letter, and to matters less peacefully sad. By this post I have written to the B[isho]p of Glasgow.[b] They ought to have no difficulty in agreeing. To bind themselves to do nothing hereafter would be a sin, if it were not impossible: & to do anything in the way of touching definitions of faith until forced by a necessity within their own sphere would be most rash. Between these two I think they may word their answer, or omit their point wholly.

Your letter deeply interested[30] me: & I will try to think it over more fully: & if it will suit you I will, please God spend Sunday afternoon with you as before.[c]

Meanwhile I will say:

First that I feel as you do about Sidney Herbert. I did not expect his signature. I observed that it was not there: but at once thought I could see how to explain it. His life & convictions which are the sum of a man's life are not up to the point of so decisive a step in a matter of the Faith: also his environments in politics & in the World hamper him. He has his work as you say.

Next for yourself. I am well satisfied much as it cost me, that you did not sign our paper. Your address was very valuable and was a second witness: and it leaves you freer.

Not that freedom can long remain to us. In the last fortnight of quiet my thoughts have been settling calmly down into a conviction which is part of my consciousness that this question is vital:

1. As an article of necessary Faith.
2. As involving the Divine authority of the Church both in dogma & in Mission.

The least part of this contest involves the whole debate about investitures.

Now I feel finally convinced that neither of these two points can be yielded, even to preserve the whole legal Status of the Church.

You could not be slower than I to come to this point. But it is a question of gold or life.

---

[b] Not located; Manning received two letters from Trower at this time, one undated, the other dated 7 May 1850, indicating the Bishop's general agreement with him. See Bodl. MS Eng. lett. c. 653, 780–4.

[c] The meeting was not held, Gladstone having left on 12 April 1850, for Fasque for the burial of his daughter (*GD* iv. 201).

The following thoughts have struck me.

1. That if we do not loosen ourselves from the State now for our own safety, the State in a few years will either sink us, or reject us to our greater hurt.

2. That the change of Polity in 1828–1829 has only begun to unfold its full tendency to comprehension, & religious indifference, & that it is impossible to stay that tendency, unless you repeal these statutes: neither w[oul]d that suffice.[31]

3. That the time of doing any thing for the Church in Parliament (except as a Government measure) is past. The sooner we can get an amicable settlement the more favourable it will be.

4. That this internal split in the Church makes the obtaining of any such settlement, except upon Gorham terms next to impossible.

5. That in a country with an income of £500,000,000 a year the Church must be dead already if it would starve—forgive me.

6. That we are really dying under[32] uncertainty, contradiction, indifference, & consequent inertness & unbelief. We want Truths[33] & Principles to which the reason & heart, the whole soul in man can respond.

These have no voice or life in Anglicanism.

Where is the man who does not say & unsay in one breath, We are Catholic but communicate with no part of the universal Church: hold all primitive doctrine but dare not preach it: claim Divine authority to teach and argue from texts. The Soul of this people is weary of it.

But in the English race there is a manhood, & in the English Church there is a devotion of will which needs nothing but Faith in the Presence and authority of Christ dwelling in His Church One, Visible and Unerring to gather millions within its Fold. May our eyes see this salvation.

Ever yours affect[ionatel]y,
H. E. Manning.

P.S. Since writing this I have been reading the last article in the Westminster Rev[iew]. See pp. 180 &c.[d]

---

[d] 'The Church of England', *Westminster and Foreign Quarterly Review*, 104 (Apr. 1840), 165–218, reviewed Bennett (1850), J. H. Newman, *Lives of the English Saints* (London: James Toovey, 1844–5), William Beeston, *The Temporalities of the Established Church* (London: John Chapman, 1850), and J. Hamilton Thom, *Religion, the Church, and the People* (London: John Chapman, 1849). Page 180 of the review speaks of 'the antiquation of the Church. . . . Recent events, we believe, have awakened thousands to the consciousness of an alarming interval between the

My direction for the 9th, 10th, 11th will be East Farleigh, Maidstone.[c34]
The Right Hon[oura]ble. W. E. Gladstone
[[Pitts; Chapeau, 159, 235–6; Leslie, 90–1]]

2. *The Royal Supremacy* and a Proposed Engagement: April–June 1850

[[On 23 and 24 April 1850 Gladstone met with Manning (*GD* iv. 204), meeting with Badeley and Wilberforce on Gorham on 25 April, writing on Gorham on 27 April, and on the Royal Supremacy on 28 April (see BL Add. MS 44684, 203–8) (*GD* iv. 205).]]

500429gm[a]

Brighton Ap[ril] 29. 1850.

My dear Manning

From the great addition to the ordinary cares of this busy period of the year which the troubles of the Church had made, and now again from the arrear and confusion into which circumstances purely private have thrown my business, my brain has been swimming for weeks past,[b] and I failed to turn to the desired account the scanty opportunities of conference with you which I have enjoyed: and mutual counsel is it seems to me even more the duty than the consolation of this trying period.

I do not think I said to you how thoroughly I entered into your last letter: which I ought to have done, and I now though late supply the omission.

I have been putting down some thoughts as to the supremacy.[c] After the ordeal of this particular time, and after pursuing Cawdrey's case which

dogmatic system of the Church and the living spirit of the time. . . . The patience of the English race, the endowments of the English Church, and the respectable character of the English clergy, only mask for awhile the fact, conspicuous in the rest of Europe, that the Protestantism of the sixteenth century has worn itself out, and gives no adequate voice to the faith and piety of the present age.'

[e] The home of Henry Wilberforce.

[a] 'Wrote to Manning' (*GD* iv. 206).

[b] Gladstone had travelled to Brighton on 27 April 1850 to be with his family where they had gone for the health of his daughter Mary. At the same time he had received a letter from his father, whose mental and physical health was deteriorating, 'calling him to Fasque' (ibid. 205).

[c] The treatise eventually to appear as William E. Gladstone, *Remarks on the Royal Supremacy as it is Defined by Reason, History, and the Constitution: A Letter to the Lord Bishop of London* (London: John Murray, 1850; preface dated 4 June 1850). Gladstone appears to have begun

contains Lord Coke's view of the law,[d] I feel better pleased with the Reformation in regard to the Supremacy than at former times: but also much more sensible of the drifting of the Church since, away from the range of her constitutional securities: and more than ever convinced how thoroughly false is the present position.

Whether they will ever be made use of, depends on other considerations. You will I am sure bear in mind, even amidst the pressure of more important thoughts, that I am looking individually, at the proper time, for your advice. When you think I ought to take any more prominent step than I seem to be taking, I trust to your saying so. I have two characters to fulfil, that of a lay member of the Church, and that of a member of a sort of wreck of a political party. I must not break my understood compact with the last and forswear my profession, unless and until the necessity has

to write on 27 and 30 April (see BL Add. MS 44684ff.), on which days he was also studying Cawdrey's Case (*GD* iv. 205). Note Manning's later comment to Robert Wilberforce (22 Oct. 1850): 'For this Royal Supremacy is in principle as old as Henry the VIII. Gladstone's view is to me a clever theory. But all facts and histories are against it. Goode is right, I believe, to the letter. The Crown is supreme judge' (Purcell, i. 565).

[d] 'It was decided in the well-known case of Cawdrey, that the Act of Supremacy (1 Elizabeth I c. 1) "was not a statute introductory of a new law, but declaratory of the old;" and that if it had never been enacted "the king or queen of England might make such a provision as is there provided, by the ancient prerogative and law of England" so that independently of the powers acknowledged in the statute, there was yet in reserve within the capacious bosom of the common law an undefined authority, which, being similar in its character, might also be equal in its amount, to the omnipotence of Rome.' Edward Cardwell (ed.), *Documentary Annals of the Reformed Church of England; Being A Collection of Injunctions, Declarations, Orders, Articles of Inquiry, &c. from the Year 1546 to the Year 1716* (2 vols.; Oxford: Oxford University Press, 1839), pp. xi–xii, quoting Coke's *Fifth Report*, 8. See *Les Reports de Edvvard Coke...Londini in aedibus Thomae Wright. Qvinta Pars Relationem Edwardi Coke... The Fifth Part of the Reports...* (London: Printed for the Companie of Stationers, 1605), 'Of the King's Ecclesiastical Law', 1–40. Manning takes up the question at several points in his *The Appellate Jurisdiction*. See Henry Edward Manning, *The Appellate Jurisdiction of the Crown in Matters Spiritual: A Letter to the Right Reverend Ashhurst-Turner, Lord Bishop of Chichester* (London: John Murray, 1850), 9: 'And we will here take up the well-known Cawdrey case. The object of Lord Coke's argument was to show, "That our ancient law doth give to the king a power, by virtue of his Ecclesiastical Jurisdiction, to appoint Commissioners by the extraordinary way of jurisdiction, to proceed, *in primâ instantiâ* [in the first instance], against persons by Ecclesiastical censures",' citing Edward Stillingfleet's *Ecclesiastical Cases Relating to the Duties and Rights of the Parochial Clergy, Stated and Resolved According to the Principles of Conscience and Law: and, A Discourse Concerning Bonds or Resignation of Benefices, in Point of Law and Conscience* (2nd edn.; London: n. publ., 1704), ii. 85, and Gibson, i. 44, note k. Cf. also Manning's reference to Coke's adage, 19: 'that the 1st Statute of Queen Elizabeth "was not introductory of a new law, but declaratory of the old".'

arisen. That necessity will plainly have arisen for me, when it shall have become evident that justice cannot, i.e. will not be done by the State to the Church. But it may arise as truly though less plainly: for I am not to *assume* that if there be a hope of justice from the State my continuance in political life is necessarily right in order to do what I can towards improving that prospect. The one thing I hope you understand clearly is that the political life is simply a means to an end, and is to be considered in no other light whatever: and that the abandonment of it may be the best mode of using it.

Another point. Let us look at the very blackest side of affairs: and assume that the majority of the Bishops do nothing except to ask for & obtain a *cobbled* amendment of the Constitution of the Court not recognising any principle nor giving any guarantee to the Faith. Still I suppose that it would be a first duty, upon the adoption by law of any such proposal, to take steps for bringing Gorham's book, or the doctrine in some other form, before such a Court, and to obtain its judgment—if the judgment were really right, it would give relief to the urgency of the pressure. If it were palpably wrong and the Bishops still acquiesced, the matter would be bolted[e] to the bran so far as concerns them. Then might come a middle kind of judgment not clearing up the case either way: but I suppose it would rest with those who carried on the suit to prevent any evasive issue, and keep the head straight to the wind.

Again. It occurs to me & I suggest it for your consideration that a strong reason for Pusey's phraseology,[f] making all turn upon the remission of original sin, is to be found in the language of the Nicene Creed which stamps Baptism as the Sacrament of remission:[g] and that this makes it the most regular and most strictly legitimate phraseology apart from any question of policy though they happen[35] to coincide.

From what I have seen of the Bishop of Oxford I am in hopes that he will do his best among his brethren to induce them to demand[36] some real amendment of the law which of course means our not merely amending its machinery. There has been on the whole I think considerable patience in waiting till this time for any manifestation from the Episcopal body: but a wise patience, & therefore a patience of that kind which acquires strength instead of becoming exhausted with the lapse of time.

---

[e] Sifted (archaic).
[f] See 500404gm and Addenda to this Section.
[g] That is, 'I acknowledge one Baptism for the remission of sins', in the Nicene Creed.

I suggested to Archdeacon Wilberforce the other day[h] a point which has occurred to me, namely whether at this time it would be possible, & advisable, to combine men together under some engagement to one another, of which the general effect should be to bind them to consult one another before taking any step of a decisive character such as either quitting the communion of the Church, or even announcing e.g. publishing any new principle or mode of action. I think that the subject is well worth *considering.* The objections which apply to & combinations for a narrower purpose do not apply to one of which the sole purpose is the maintenance and enforcement of an article of the Faith.

Another point which occurs to me is this: that next to the Bishops of the English Church the parties most responsible in this matter are not its other members lay or even clerical, but the Bishops in communion with it, especially those of Scotland and the Colonies: and if so that no far reaching view can be taken of the future, even irrespective of all other difficulties, without knowing what they are to do. The Scotch Bishops have given a clear indication:[i] but we must have some time to know anything of the Colonial.

I am just going back to town[j]—where my wife will I hope rejoin me in a few days: but not with all the children so much restored as I am tempted to desire.

I hope you are taking some little care of your health and am always

Your aff[ectiona]te friend

W. E. Gladstone

A letter detestably written but with a fuse only two inches long.

Ven[erable]

Archdeacon Manning.

[[BL Add. MS 44248, 39–42; Morley transcript; Lathbury, i. 100–2; cf. Leslie, 91; Chapeau, 331–2; Morley, i. 381–2]]

[[On 2 May 1850, Gladstone met with Manning on the Gorham controversy and he breakfasted with him on the same issue the following morning, 3 May. Following the 3 May breakfast Gladstone wrote to Catherine:

---

[h] On 26 April 1850, Gladstone 'Breakfasted with B[isho]p of Oxford & Archd[eaco]n W[ilberforce], when we discussed the Court of Appeal at much length . . . then from 5 P.M. to 7¼ was with . . . Archdeacon W[ilberforce and others] . . . on a Plan which seems very good for the Court of Appeal' (*GD* iv. 205). For details of the Plan see 500520gm.

[i] See 500404gm. The Declaration by the Bishops of the Church of Scotland, supporting the doctrine of baptismal regeneration was made at Aberdeen on 19 April 1850. See Addenda to this Section.

[j] After writing to Manning, Gladstone 'returned to London by the train at 6:30'. His wife remained with Mary, who was suffering from whooping cough (*GD* iv. 206).

Manning breakfasted with me today—he is decidedly better I think, & even much better, both in spirit & in tone—and seemed to assent to the broad proposition that the thing to be done now was to organise and marshall the right sentiment in the Church (SDL, Glynne–Gladstone MS 771, 227–8, 227).]]

500509gm[a]

6 Carlton Gardens
May 9. 1850

My dear Manning

All that passed on Monday night did but the more convince me of the security & strength of the ground taken in my motion.[b] Tufnell[c] told me after the division that R. Palmer's Speech gave them their majority. He by some fatality was led to make a regular argument for Convocation in England. For such an argument it could not have been more temperately and sensibly done:[d] and I daresay it will please out of doors: but it was the very thing to cause ruin within—the Gov[ernmen]t however do not like the affair at all: I have asked them whether they are prepared to accede to my principle guarding it with words they may think sufficient and I hope if it please God to push the matter in one form or another. They seem to *feel* that something should be done.

The tone of the House therefore on the whole did not discourage me as to the Colonial Church: which as you may know is wholly emancipated already in the matter of appeals from royal authority.[e]

[a] 'Wrote to . . . Manning' (*GD* iv. 209).

[b] On Monday evening, 6 May 1850, Gladstone was in the House of Commons where he 'Spoke briefly on Molesworth's motion and at length on the *just* claim for the freedom of the Church in the Colonies' (*GD* iv. 208; cf. Hansard, cx. 1232; *The Times*, 7 May, 3). Gladstone moved a new clause to the 'Bill for the better Government of Her Majesties Australian Colonies' (PP 1850 [306.] i. 113, introduced 6 May; original bill introduced 11 June 1849 [PP 1849 (375.) i. 107]; see also PP 1849 [429.] i. 137, 26 June 1849; PP 1850 [36.] i. 83, 11 Feb. 1850). All that he 'designed by the clause in question was to give the Church of England in the Colonies the very same power . . . which [was] at present moment possessed and exercised by every other religious body in the colonies'. The measure lost (Hansard, cx. 1232). Note Gladstone's comments on 13 May 1850 (ibid. 1384; *The Times*, 14 May, 3). The bill went through one more printing (PP 1850 [533.] i. 143, 9 July) and passed. (See Gladstone on 1 Aug. 1850 [Hansard, cxiii. 626; *The Times*, 2 Aug., 2].)

[c] Henry Tufnell (1805–54), son of Colonel George Foster Tufnell of Chichester, educated at Christ Church, Oxford, served as MP for Devonport from 1840 to his death (*DNB*, Stirling [1913], ii. 213).

[d] For Palmer's speech and his conclusions regarding Convocation see Hansard, cx. 1222.

[e] On Gladstone's ongoing correspondence with Australian and New Zealand bishops with respect to the Gorham decision see Cooper (2005).

An allusion of Grey's to the Gorham business drew forth cheers from his people, which was not surprising:[f] any question of the same kind for *England* is of extreme difficulty as we know from experience in the H[ouse] of Commons. Still I think the new Bill by no means a desperate case.

I have begun Pusey[g] but he is never very easy reading and somehow or other one hardly ever finds the facts of Church history put into even a tolerably attractive form. But I am exceedingly disappointed and dismayed at your questioning his precedents. I had supposed him with regard to the accuracy of the facts all but infallible: how am I to verify them? Should you not put somebody to let us know what they really are? It is most important that they should be brought out without fear or favour and we should get at them without a predetermination to bend and fit them to our wisdom. I feel deeply the mischief that Messrs. Allies[h37]

---

[f] Grey responded directly to Gladstone on this issue (Hansard, cx. 1226). George Grey (1799–1882; 2nd Baronet, 1828; *DNB*), educated Oriel College, Oxford, and called to the bar at Lincoln's Inn, 1826, was a strong supporter of Evangelical causes, MP for Devonport, 1832–47, Northumberland, 1847–52, Morpeth, 1853–74, Under-Secretary for the Colonies, 1834, 1835–9, Judge Advocate General, 1839–41, Chancellor of the Duchy of Lancaster, 1841, 1859–61, Secretary of State for the Home Department, 1846–52, 1855–8, 1866, and Secretary of State for the Colonies, 1854–5. The reform of prisoners, particularly their religious instruction, was one of his many principal interests when he served in the Home Department.

[g] On 4 March 1850 Gladstone noted that he was reading E. B. Pusey, *The Royal Supremacy not an Arbitrary Authority but Limited by the Laws of the Church of which Kings are Members* (Oxford: John Henry Parker, 1850) (*GD* iv. 207–8; for a discussion of Pusey's position and a reflection on the 'unfinished' nature of his book see Liddon, iii. 257–89; on Pusey's views regarding Church–state issues see Nockles [1983]). On 3 March he read Wiseman's article in the *Dublin Review* on the Gorham Case (27 [Mar. 1850], 234), which struck him as 'astounding', and other pieces on the topic (*GD* iv. 207–8). Note Wiseman's continuing interest in the case as evidenced by his *Gorham vs. Bishop of Exeter: Final Appeal in Matters of Faith; Being a Lecture Delivered at St. George's Cathedral, Lambeth . . . on Sunday Evening, March 17, 1850* (London: Strange, [1850]), *A Discourse Delivered at St. John's, Catholic Church, Salford, on Sunday July 28th., 1850 . . . on the Gorham Controversy* (Manchester: Abel Heywood, [1850]), and the reply, *The Providential Effects of the Late Gorham Controversy; A Sermon In Reply to that Delivered in the Roman Catholic Church of St. John, Salford, by the Right Rev. Dr. Wiseman, now Cardinal Wiseman Entitled The Permanent Effects to the Church of England of the Late Gorham Controversy by The Rev. William Verdon, B.A., Curate of Trinity Church, Salford, 'Wherein also Dr. Wiseman's Assertions are Fairly Answered and Fully Refuted; Wherein the Complaints of the Dissatisfied Party in the Church of England are Proved to Be Frivolous and Vexatious; and it is Further Shown that the Assembling of a Synod or Convocation in the Present Crisis is Neither Necessary or Expedient'* (London: Seeleys, Hamilton, Adams & Co.).

[h] T. W. Allies, *The Royal Supremacy Viewed in Reference to the Two Spiritual Powers of Order and Jurisdiction* (London: William Pickering, 1850).

and Maskell[i] have done by their entire ignorance of *one side* of their question: but I am far from thinking that that mischief can be cured by a counter onesidedness in another region—

I have no Church news.

Believe me always
Aff[ectiona]tely yours
W. E. Gladstone

You would see Lady L[incoln]'s divorce in the papers.[j]
Venerable
Archdeacon Manning
[[BL Add. MS 44248, 43–5; Morley transcript]]

500520gm[a]

6 C[arlton] G[ardens] Whitmonday
May 20. [18]50

My dear Manning

The Bishops' Bill stands for next Tuesday[b] and I suppose we must prepare to see it rejected by the Lords. The question really is what will the Bishops *then* do. But I have a fear lest men should scatter under that

---

[i] William Maskell, *A First Letter on the Present Position of the High Church Party in the Church of England . . . The Royal Supremacy and the Authority of the Judicial Committee of the Privy Council* (London: W. Pickering, 1850; dated 9 Feb. 1850). Note also his *A Second Letter on the Present Position of the High Church Party in the Church of England . . . The Want of Dogmatic Teaching in the Reformed English Church* (London: W. Pickering, 1850; dated 8 Apr. 1850). Gladstone stated his differences with Maskell in a letter to the latter, 23 February 1850, arguing for a less extreme view of the place 'of the royal supremacy as established at the Reformation', and a emphasizing its 'limited' function (Lathbury, i. 97–9).

[j] The divorce was finalized in 13 & 14 Victoria Private Act (unprinted), 24 (1850). See *The Times*, 15 May 1850, 7b.

[a] No reference to letter in *GD*.

[b] Tuesday, 28 May 1850. 'A Bill to amend the Law with reference to the Administration of Justice in Her Majesty's Privy Council on Appeal from the Ecclesiastical Courts', *Sessional Papers of the House of Lords* 1850 (134.) iii. 51 (6 May 1850). Section 1 of the Bill stated that if an appeal was made 'to Her Majesty in Council from any Ecclesiastical Court of England, if and so often as it shall be necessary to determine any question of the Doctrine or Tenets of the Church of this Realm, arising either in a Criminal or Civil Suit, it shall be lawful for the Judicial Committee of Her Majesty's Privy Council, and they are hereby required, to refer such Question of Doctrine to the Archbishops and Bishops of the Province of Canterbury and York', and that their opinion 'when duly certified to the said Judicial Committee . . . shall be binding'. *De jure* final authority remained with the Crown.

defeat: and I want *now* to see whether it is not possible to insure *deliberate* action, & cooperation *within the limits of* their convictions, among those who are agreed fundamentally about the Gorham case.

Please then to read the inclosed & to judge it *not in its details* which may be too stringent, or otherwise faulty, but by way of finding an answer to the question whether by this or any like or unlike means we can obtain[38] guarantees for[39] joint action as far as joint action is a legitimate object of desire i.e. while it continues to be grounded on union of conviction: & shall prevent dispersion under rash & momentary impulses.

I have named it (I think) to Archd[eaco]n Wilberforce,[c] Lyttelton,[d] Simeon,[e] R. Cavendish,[f] Wegg-Prosser,[g] Monsell,[h] all[40] but the latter (who wholly reserved himself for conv[ersatio]n & to hear what you thought) like it[i]—

The men for the Delegation as far as I can see would be you Dr Mill & Judge Coleridge: another Judge, or London man might be desirable.

I remain Ever aff[ectiona]tely yours

WEG

[[BL Add. MS 44248, 46; Morley transcript; Leslie transcript; addressed: Archdeacon Manning Lavington Petworth; Postmarked: MY 20 1850]]

[Enclosure: Gladstone Proposal[j]]

[c] Perhaps following a visit from Robert Wilberforce to London. See Wilberforce to Gladstone, 20 April 1850 (BL Add. MS 44369, 166–7) in which he plans to meet with Gladstone and thinks that something must be done: 'I know no one with whom I accord as well as yourself, & I wish to consult you as to the steps, w[hic]h I think of taking. My own feeling is that the time is come when the State should be called upon to take back those treacherous gifts w[hic]h it has bestowed upon us.'

[d] No correspondence located.

[e] No correspondence located. Sir John Simeon (1815–70), 3rd Bart., 1854, was educated at Christ Church, Oxford, and served as MP for the Isle of Wight, 1847–51, 1865–70; he was received as a Roman Catholic in 1851 (Boase, iii. 575; Gordon-Gorman (1910), 251). Manning's later correspondence with him (from the 1850s) is preserved at Syracuse University Library, Syracuse, New York.

[f] No correspondence located.

[g] No correspondence located. Francis Richard Wegg-Prosser (d. 1911), was educated at Eton and Balliol College, Oxford, served as MP for Herefordshire, 1847–52; he was received as a Roman Catholic in 1852 (Gordon-Gorman (1910), 289).

[h] William Monsell, 1st Baron Emly (1812–94; *DNB*) was educated at Winchester and Oriel College, Oxford, and served as MP for Limerick, 1847–74.

[i] Cf. Purcell, i. 538: 'In a letter to Archdeacon Manning, Mr. Gladstone said, "Among others I have consulted Robert Wilberforce and Wegg-Prosser and they seemed inclined to favour my proposal. It might perhaps have kept back Lord Feilding. But he is like a cork."'.

[j] On 20 May 1850, amidst work on the Colonial Bishops Bill and a proposed amendment for it, Gladstone 'Wrote . . . Draft of proposed engagement' among the Tractarians to delay action on the Gorham decision for two months (*GD* iv. 4211).

Private

We the undersigned being members of the Church of England, agreed in the conviction that[41] acquiescence in the principles of the Report in the Gorham Case would be fatal to her life and authority as a Branch of the Catholic Church,[42] and deeply anxious to aid in averting so great a calamity, do hereby, as in the presence of Almighty God, for mutual counsel and support, and for the better discharge of our duties to the Faith and to the Church, solemnly engage ourselves one to another as follows:

1. That the first twenty-five persons subscribing this Engagement will appoint from among themselves a Delegation of four[43] viz two[44] Clergymen and two[45] laymen.

2. And that the Delegation shall have power to fill up any vacancy occurring in its own body.

3. And that in or before the month of May 1851 the Delegation will summon a meeting of the persons engaged in London to report to them the state of this Engagement, and to lay down their trust that it may be received or that successors may be appointed.[46]

4. And that person chosen to be the said Delegation will appoint one of their own body to be a Secretary, to whom all notices herein provided for shall be sent and will give information and advice to all who may apply to them[47] and will make and receive as in confidence all communications relating to the objects of this engagement and in selecting any[48] persons[49] under this trust committed to them, will have careful regard to the individual circumstances and relations.[50] And will discharge all the duties appertaining to them under this Engagement, to the best of their power, for the purposes and in the spirit which it requires.

5. And each of us including those who may be chosen to the said Delegation[51] for himself engages:

That if during the continuance of this Engagement, he shall form the intention of taking any step which could imply finally and irrevocably an adverse judgement upon the position of the Church of England in reference to the Gorham case, or would otherwise commit him to any grave alteration in his[52] course of action, he will give notice of this his intention to the Secretary: & will, at any time during the space of [one calender month thereafter][53] which the Delegation may appoint, meet the members thereof personally if they shall require it, & do all in his power to facilitate such meeting: & will likewise, during the same period at the least, hold himself prepared to receive from them, & duly to consider, all such communications as they may think fit to make to him[54] touching[55] his said intention.

6. And that if within the said space of one month he shall be apprised or the part of the members of the said Delegation or the majority of them that in their judgement it is requisite that he give the like opportunity of communication, if a clergyman to the clergymen engaged or any portion of them, or if a layman to the clergymen & laymen engaged or any portion of them, where the said Delegation may then point out, in such case the promise set forth in the last Section shall extend & have full force with respect to all such persons engaged as the said Delegation shall have so pointed out, & until the full period of two calendar months from the notice originally given by him shall have expired.

[[56]It being clearly understood that if after having given such notice, and then having[57] for the times herein before specified held himself open and given every facility in his power to the receipt of such communications, and having, according to his own best judgment, as in the sight of Almighty God, fully weighed them with himself, he shall finally determine to act, & shall at the expiration of the period above named act in opposition to the tenor of any or all the representations which may have been laid before him, he will then have fulfilled in letter & in spirit this engagement, & will be free to take his own course with a conscience so far clear.][58]

7. And that every person engaged may admit to the Engagement other persons as he shall think fit, giving notice thereof forthwith[59] to the Secretary.

8. And that every person engaged may have access upon demand to a list of all the persons engaged which shall be kept by the Secretary.[60]

5. [*sic*] And lastly, that he will not withdraw from this present Engagement without a notice of [two][61] months.

London May 1850
Signed

[[BL Add. MS 44738, 173–4 (Gladstone's second draft of the proposal; the first preserved, 170–2)]]

500522mg

Lavington. May 22. 1850.

My dear Gladstone

A wish of yours, if there were no other reason, would be enough in all things of a normal kind to ensure my consent. And the desire I felt to do as you proposed[62] in your letter of Monday[a] has made me take a day & a night to consider it.

But I am compelled by reasons, which with me are final, to say that so[63] far as my own duty is involved I feel obliged to decline any engagement of the kind proposed.

When I was last in London one of my oldest & nearest friends desired that a similar engagement should be made with an opposite view, namely that unless certain events should take place a number of persons should take definite steps within a given period.

I refused altogether to join in such a proposal for reasons which in principle apply to the[64] subject of your letter.

In such a moral probation as is now upon us I conceive that time is not to be measured by the dial but by events—that it is not chronological but moral: and therefore I cannot lay myself under any obligations which shall in the least fetter my fullest freedom of action. To be too hasty or to be too slow may produce under given circumstances, effects which are injurious & immoral. This applies with a force & a point perhaps beyond anything I can convey to you, in the present case, and in the trial of those who bear the most responsible of all trusts, I mean the spiritual care of souls.

But perhaps, your view may be chiefly to obtain a security against precipitate acts. This may be needful for myself, & for others.

As for others, all the help I can give shall be given, as it has been for years past, as it is now with a painful increase of work, but I cannot undertake any office by delegation, I am employed up to the last point at which I can hope to do any real service already, and even for this reason can undertake no more. But I feel other reasons why I could not accept such a delegation.

As for myself, the engagement would add nothing to the responsibilities or the bonds which already bind me.

Moreover it has long been my practice in all questions of moment to ask counsel of 3, 5, or 7 persons according to the importance of the matter.

My letters to you & Hope on Dec[ember] 31, 1849[b] were in obedience to that rule.

I shall with thankfulness weigh all advice sought or unsought which may be given to me, but I cannot combine in an engagement which so far as it is right ought to be fulfilled by reference to those whom God has placed over me in either Ecclesiastical or Spiritual guidance.

[a] Monday, 5 May 1850.
[b] For correspondence see 491231mg and Addenda to this Section.

I will add only one word more, which I do not apply to any of the names you have mentioned—far from it—I fear human engagements in matters of conscience. And I am afraid that the effect of such a system will be to entangle, hamper, &[65] embarrass, and in the end to stifle convictions by delay, discussions,[66] and material agreement. I see some minds so visibly changed not for the better that I am constrained by self mistrust to with-draw from the path in which they seem to me to have lost their former selves.

I could not write less than this to you. But do not put upon it more meaning than it demands. I have no thought or temptation to hasty acts. My whole heart is too much drawn the other way.[c]

May our guidance like every good & perfect gift come from above:[d] & may God be with you.

Believe me,
Always affect[ionatel]y yours
H. E. Manning.

The Right Hon[our]able
W. E. Gladstone
P.S. Tell me by what *acts*, & by what declaration of *intention*, the Protest against the Heresy affair could be followed up?

H.E.M.

[[Pitts; Chapeau, 160, 237–8; Leslie, 91; Gladstone's note: a. By repeated movements for repealing this enactment—b. On[67] the failure of those movements when proved by laboring at all costs for the release of the Church.]]

500523gm[a]

6 Carlton G[ardens] May 23.1850

My dear Manning

It is very like if not more than very like presumption in me to reason with you, nor do I look to drawing you into further discussion, yet I think it right to make the very succinct replies for which your arguments appear to me to call—I ought to ask your pardon for having omitted to send proper explanations before.

---

[c] On 22 May 1850 Manning wrote to Wilberforce as well concerning Gladstone's plan and continued the correspondence thereafter. For details see Addenda to this Section.

[d] Cf. Jas. 1: 17.

[a] 'Wrote to Manning' (*GD* iv. 212).

1. Though time is measured at these periods by events yet there are certain proceedings of such gravity as by our feeble minds should never be taken without the lapse of a certain amount of dial-time—it is the intervention of that amount that I want to secure.

2. If the space of time be rightly chosen, no one will be 'too slow': or can therefore produce the 'injurious & immoral' fruits which I should quite agree in apprehending.

3. You promise to give all the help you can against precipitate acts by others—that means by certain instruments, which you are now using. But I ask you to adopt a new instrument that of the authority of your name joined with that of others.

4. You are now fully occupied in the use of those instruments: but the new one I suggest would work powerfully independent of any additional demand on your time—what I look to[68] mainly is not dissuasion after intentions are announced, but preventing their hasty formation and announcement.

5. That you could not accept of the Delegation may be true but does not imply the rejection of the plan.

6. That you take counsel in grave cases already is really irrelevant to my purpose which was not to ask *you* to impose a new check upon yourself but to beg you to become the means, by a fresh and additional mode, of inducing other very different men, who *may* be tempted to precipitancy, the very last thing to be dreamt of in your case, to put a check upon themselves—that is the whole idea and purpose of the scheme—

7. And again I would say distinguish between the idea, & the particular form—it may for instance be a question even with those who approve the former, whether the latter might not well be changed for one contemplating only very small unions of men already personal friends—

8. As to entangling I observe that nothing more is or need be[69] promised than 1. the lapse of a certain time—2. the *reception* of communications: not replying to them—

9. And if the time be well chosen it will not stifle conviction by delay—if ill let it be amended—

10. You speak of the alteration of some minds & their path—but the only path in which I seek to induce mine to go is that of adequate deliberation—convinced as I am that there are so many who have nothing like a proportionate idea of the great Christian interests placed in their hands. Have these altered persons been altered in consequence of any such measure: & if not, is the practical[70] conclusion drawn a just one.—

Pray do not for a moment suppose that I shall ascribe a hidden meaning to your words. I am fixed in the belief that after so many years you would not use any words to me without endeavouring to make them convey all their meaning—as far as the defects of the recipient would permit.

My only difficulty is this—I do not think I shall proceed, on my own responsibility, or without you: but after what I have said to others I perhaps ought to assign your feeling as my reason for withdrawing, & to show your reasons if they were not likely to be misapprehended, and over interpreted, by them—

If I have time I may work through with something on the supremacy: but I am so pressed as to be very uncertain indeed of effecting anything.

When you write pray to be so kind as to tell me whether you see any thing improper in my placing the Verse Rev. XIV. 5 over my child Jessy?[b] She was four years & 8 months old: and as good and full of love, as our fondest wishes could desire.

We are thank God more easy about our little Mary who has been a good deal shaken, and have also satisfaction in looking to a close of the Session rather earlier than usual.

I remain always
Your aff[ectiona]te friend
W. E. Gladstone

Lincoln's Divorce Bill is to be read a second time on Tuesday.[c]
Venerable
Archdeacon Manning

[[BL Add. MS 44248, 47–50; Morley transcript; Leslie transcript; cf. Chapeau, 332]]

[b] 'And in their mouth was found no guile: for they were without fault before the throne of God' (Rev. 14: 5). The inscription was written on 10 April 1850, the day following the child's death:

> Underneath
> Sleep the mortal remains of
> Catherine Jesse Gladstone
> Born July 27, 1845
> Died April 9, 1850
> 'And in their mouth was
> found no guile: for they
> are without fault before
> the throne of God.'
> Rev. XIV. 5. (*GD* iv. 201)

[c] Gladstone was 'examined on Poor Lincoln's Divorce Bill' in the House of Lords on Tuesday, 28 May 1850 (*GD* iv. 214).

500524mg

Lavington. May 24. 1850.

My dear Gladstone

You 'chode' me for using the word 'freedom' to you,[a] & I now chide you for using the word presumption to me. You know as I have told you that I have no friend to whose counsel I so turn: nor any whose counsel has such abiding weight with me.

My feeling is that the 'instrument' is not so good.

1. I feel that the effect of collecting a number of minds round such an idea, would precipitate the evil when it is already at work, by publishing it so far, and making it a subject of discussion.

2. In a matter so intimate & personal, I fear that the effect of any communications with or from persons so various, & so remote from each other in disposition and convictions would have a disturbing and driving effect on those for whose sake you specially desire a restraint. This I say from long observation of particulars.

3. I have great faith in counsel & guidance of a private & religious[71] kind, but, in such a question as that before us, very little in engagements or communications arising out of an assemblage[72] of minds having no relations higher than their own compact.

4. Since the beginning of this year I have seen (1) an attempt by Dodsworth, Pusey, Keble etc., to act together,[b] (2) a second on a larger basis, your house being the scene,[c] (3) a third in the[73] Church Union discussions,[d] & the result of all has been to convince me that instead

---

[a] See 450418mg.

[b] On Manning's role in Pusey–Dodsworth differences over the issue, see his letters to Dodsworth in first five months of 1850 (Bodl. MS Eng. lett. c. 654, 125–39, *passim*) and to Pusey in May 1850, ibid. 324–33). Dodsworth increasingly found his views close to those of Maskell, who insisted that spiritual authority rested in the Episcopate alone, whereas Pusey held 'that every bishop derives spiritual jurisdiction, not from the Crown, or from any superior or independent source, but from his See; he therefore maintained that the Crown, in moving bishops to decide spiritual cases, was not the source of jurisdiction, but only the power which put into motion a jurisdiction existing independently of itself' (Liddon, iii. 259; for full discussion on the debate with Dodsworth see ibid. 261–6).

[c] See 500312mg.

[d] Note the actions of the London Church Union on 4 February 1850 (*English Churchman*, 7 Feb., 90), the Union's Petition to the Queen on the matter (ibid. 14 Feb., 106), extracts from the Quarterly report of the Metropolitan Church Union (ibid. 28 Feb., 141), and note

of mutual attraction &[74] reciprocal repulsion has been awakened and increased in every instance.

Also I have seen or[75] I think a real deterioration in some of the religious qualities of the character under the effect of contact with ill-sorted and inharmonious minds.

My feeling, therefore, that the instrument is not good is very strong.

This is confirmed by my having already made trial of some who would be in such an engagement.

Now I am even going so far as to ask you to reconsider the whole subject for your own decision.

I referred to myself because I felt that it would be unseemly to give any answer which should not assume the need I have of counsels & restraints.[76]

In what I said of attaching meaning to my words I referred only to what I had said of myself. I did not wish my letter[77] to convey the idea that I am preparing to take any step which must anticipate your engagement.

My own thoughts I have spoken to no one—I mean as to the steps I may feel forced to take. And if you will hear them you shall be the first, when they are defined to my own mind, to hear them.

And now for sad but more soothing thoughts—

Rev. XIV. 5. seems to me very fit for such a grave—Saints & Children are the chief friends of God—and Children are the types of Saints. You have a share in the Heavenly Court now beyond all you had before. And she intercedes for you with a fuller knowledge of this world & of its perils than you have. I am thankful to hear that little Mary is gaining strength. And I trust your wife is well. I have not seen her since her sorrow—her first own sorrow I believe. My love to her. Believe me,

Always affect[ionatel]y yours,
H. E. Manning.

The Right Hon[oura]ble
W. E. Gladstone
[[Pitts; Chapeau, 161, 238–9]]

Dodsworth's letter of resignation from the London Church Union of 19 April, following the rejection of his motion for action on the Gorham judgment at a general meeting of the Union on 9 April (letter and motion printed in *English Churchman*, 2 May, 283).

500527mg

Lavington. May 27. 1850.

Private

My dear Gladstone,

Will you kindly read the inclosed[a] & tell me in what way you would answer the points raised in it.

I am to see the Writer for that purpose next week. And you will feel that she is worthy of help, when I tell you that after a long & painful trial she broke off a marriage with a person to whom she was engaged, because he went to the Roman Church. After a while he was induced to return to the Church of England.

The engagement was renewed.

This Gorham case has decided him on finally submitting to the Church of Rome.

And the engagement is again broken off.

She is prepared again to be guided by my advice as before.

I have never seen her. I acknowledge that I feel great embarrassment in advising and as it is a question in which a layman may use his 'clavis discretionis,'[b] I should be greatly obliged to you for a few words, which (though I am not wise) will suffice.

Believe me,
Ever affect[ionatel]y yours,
H. E. Manning.

[[Pitts; Chapeau, 162, 240]]

[[Gladstone continued to work on his treatise on Supremacy from 25 May until 2 June 1850, when he finished it (*GD* iv. 213–16).]]

500601gm[a]

6 Carlton Gardens
1 June 1850.

My dear Manning

You may justly, or [78]fairly, have presumed from my silence, that I had been endeavouring to write a careful answer to the points raised in the very interesting inclosure to your letter. And so it would have been, had I had the power. But in truth I have been utterly disqualified. Nothing but shreds

---

[a] Not located.   [b] Key of discretion.
[a] 'Wrote to . . . H. E. Manning' (*GD* iv. 216).

and patches of time have been at my command, so heavy at the present time of year is the mass of ordinary business & correspondence, and there I have been devoting to the accomplishment of my endeavour in which after all I may very possibly fail, to write something for publication on the subject of the Royal Supremacy.

If I were obliged to make an answer to a person putting to me what appears to be the essential point in this letter—that the Church of England must be understood really to deny that the Church of Rome is a true Church, because they differ 'on essential points' I should answer that I know of no such points. On the point of Transubstantiation, accepting from and with the Church of England the truth and reality of the visible elements in the Holy Eucharist, I have not the misery of thinking that the Church of Rome, in her denial of that reality, within the limits to which she has confined it, constitutes a difference on an essential point—We have with us I fear those who do not believe that 'whole and entire Christ' is received in that sacred ordinance by the faithful: and they have those I likewise fear who pay worship to that which they see, and who if judged severely in the abstract (as God will not judge them) do evacuate and destroy the realness of a sacrament. But I do not think it lawful to[79] hold either the one or the other fully responsible for error that has crept into and kept a place within its borders: and I have always remembered with much comfort a passage quoted by Newman, in his former self, from B[isho]p van Mildert, setting forth the outlines of that one faith which always has been & now is professed by the Church.[b] Much less am I aware that as to Penance any essential difference, upon matter of faith, is alleged, much less can be proved, to exist between the Churches.

The rejection from the fellowship of the Christian covenant of all who do not receive the authority of the See of Rome is to me an awful innovation on the faith and a dark sign of the future for the[80] large part of Christendom which is in Communion with that See, and with which we have so deep a common interest in the maintenance of the Faith.

---

[b] In his *On the Prophetical Office of the Church, Viewed Relatively to Romanism and Popular Protestantism* (2nd edn.; London: J. G. & F. Rivington, 1838), lecture VIII, sect. 18, Newman quotes a lengthy section from William van Mildert, *An Inquiry into the General Principles of Scripture Interpretation in Eight Sermons Preached before the University of Oxford in the Year MDCCCXIV at the Lecture founded by the late Rev. John Bampton* (3rd edn.; Oxford: Samuel Collingwood, 1832), 225–6, on the indefectibility of the Church Universal: 'at no point in its history has any fundamental of essential truth of the Gospel been authoritatively disowned'.

I will not refer to any other point: the[81] details to some of which she refers are details upon which you doubtless[82] will give this lady to understand that the matter does not & cannot[83] turn—

But independently of my own inability duly to handle those details, I must own there never was a time where I should have felt so much disposed to strive earnestly to draw off a disturbed and unsettled mind from their contemplation, and to fix it on the great and noble work which God has now given to the children of the Church in England amid trouble, suspense, and it may be agony, to perform. I do not believe that a more arduous, a more exalted or a more exalting task ever was committed to men. They are called and charged to do battle for the Faith in the very point now plainly selected for[84] the great battle field of modern infidelity: and with the consolation of being sustained by declarations of the local Church not sufficient only but redundant, and not clear only but of overpowering clearness. I hope you will induce this interesting pupil to take her part in the battle and her share of the prize.

I hardly know whether any thing will be done in the matter of the covenant about which I wrote to you: when we meet if I have not time before I will detail what has taken place—

I remain always
Your Aff[ectiona]te friend
W. E. Gladstone

Venerable
Archdeacon Manning
[[BL Add. MS 44248, 51–3; Lathbury, ii. 26–7; cf. Leslie, 92]]
[[Gladstone saw Manning 2 June 1850 (*GD* iv. 216).]]

500606mcg

61 Eaton Place.[a]
June 6. 1850

My dear Mrs. Gladstone,

I came back from Hams Weald today & found your kind note. It would give me much pleasure to come on Saturday[b] but I am sorry to say that I am engaged.

But tomorrow morning I hope to see you & I will try to call by 9½. I much wish to see William.[c]

---

[a] The home of Samuel Wilberforce.　　[b] 8 June 1850.

[c] William Henry Gladstone, Manning's godson.

The Bishop of Oxford will not be in London till Monday next,[d] so that I fear I may also answer in his name.

Believe me,
Always affec[tionate]ly yours
H. E. Manning

[[BL Add. MS 46227, 53–4]]

[[Gladstone saw Manning on the following day, 7 June 1850 (*GD* iv. 217) and again on 9 June (ibid. 218). On 11 June, he met with Samuel Wilberforce, the Bishop of Oxford, who wrote to him the same day telling him that he would be at Eaton Place on 12 June at 1.45 p.m., and that he hoped Manning and Gladstone would be available, but Gladstone does not record a meeting with either on that day (BL Add. MS 44343, 118). Manning preached at the consecration of St Barnabas, Pimlico, 11 June 1850.[e]]]

500612gm[a]

6 C[arlton] G[ardens] June 12 [18]50

My dear Manning

So many are the points from which the present crisis of the Church may be regarded that I always find after the opportunity of a conversation with you that I have forgotten something that was material, and on Sunday last[b] there was an especial omission which I now want to repair. I am not indeed certain whether I wholly failed to mention the particular subject I refer to but I certainly did not do it in the pointed manner which it seems to me to require.

The argument of Baron A[lderson][c] that the propositions affirmed are not formally heretical led us into a conversation upon the accuracy of

---

   [d] 10 June 1850.

   [e] See Bennett (1909), 61ff.

   [a] 'Wrote to Archd[eaco]n Manning' (*GD* iv. 218).

   [b] 9 June 1850.

   [c] [Edmund Hall Alderson,] *A Letter to the Bishop of Exeter by a Layman. For Private Circulation only* (London: Joseph Masters, 1850); the treatise states that 'a decision is not properly to be treated as a law' (3), that a future committee can overrule a decision, (4) and points out that a decision can be appealed, while admitting 'the evil of a clerk of heretical opinions admitted into the Church' (5). Alderson then discusses the main points of Gorham's position as decided by the Court and concludes that none of these 'propositions taken to the letter necessarily and clearly militates against any known rule or doctrine of the Church of England' (8). Cf. [E. H. Alderson,] *A Second Letter to the Bishop of Exeter by a Layman* (London: Joseph Masters, 1851). Edward Hall Alderson (1787–1857; *DNB*) was educated at Caius College, Cambridge, called to the bar in 1811, appointed a judge in the Court of Common Pleas, 1830, and Baron of the Exchequer, 1834.

that allegation and drew me off the scent. What I wish to put to you is this. The fact that such a man can so allege at once reminds me of the ambiguity in which the Judges have contrived to shroud if not the whole yet a great part of the question. For myself indeed I feel that the Church is bound to reject propositions manifestly leading towards and terminating in heresy, & having an heretical *animus*,[d] as much as if their spirit were fully expressed in their letter. But this ambiguity is for many an effectual blind. Many will say this Judgment does not really affect the teaching office of the Church except by departure from her rule;[85] and it is doubtful whether there has been such a departure. Towards[86] all such persons, honest in mind, it seems to be a duty, and towards the Church of England still more a duty, to have that ambiguity cleared up.

The question therefore arises, is it not [an] essential part of our obligations at the present time with a view to a fair full and clear issue upon a matter so vital to take measures for obtaining a judgment upon not the falsified and reduced statements of the Gorham opinions which the Judges have given but upon his real doctrine extracted in the form of precise propositions and submitted to them for an aye or no in such a way that they could not be ended.

I should be unwilling I confess to be an active party in taking any new matter into the Court of Privy Council. But this would be not a new matter; it would be a *bonâ fide* attempt to rectify the error and defect of a judgment already given, as far as that error and defect is connected with a misstatement of the matter put in evidence.

Supposing this opinion to be sound and to be acted upon accordingly: the Judicial Committee might condemn the propositions—and in that case they would have made a material step towards the rectification of the present state of things—or they would acquit them, and in that case also a light would be thrown upon the path where true light is I may say all that we have to desire.

I wish you would consider this and blame myself for not having been distinct and full upon it when we were together.

If you are inclined to think there ought to be a movement such as I have suggested[e] I wish you would write to Hope sending him this letter or as you please—And he could probably communicate with me.

---

[d] Intention.   [e] See 500615mg.

In such case you probably could look at Gorham's book[f] or ask someone else to do so to extract propositions from it on which to present to the Office of the Judges—or it might deserve consideration whether Mr. Goode would be the more proper person against whom to proceed. The suit however if ag[ains]t Gorham should be on the propositions only, if possible, so as to divest the case of its more insidious and personal aspect.

It would not be difficult I apprehend to raise the necessary funds.

You will I am sure appreciate my object namely to assist men in acting with a clear conscience whatever you may think of the particular means I have proposed.

I remain

Your aff[ectiona]te friend

W.E. Gladstone

Archdeacon Manning

H[enry] Wilberforce told me in confidence your decision to write & publish; at which I am greatly pleased.[g]

[[NLS MS 3679, 44–7]]

500615mg

Lavington. June 15. 1850.

My dear Gladstone,

I have given the best thoughts I can to the subject of your letter and it seems to me to be desirable:—

1. That a fuller & directer trial of the doctrine of Baptism should be made.

2. That it should be taken in the person of Mr. Goode. Because to take Gorham w[oul]d seem vindictive. It would be also an *abnormal* case,

---

[f] See George Cornelius Gorham, *Examination before Admission to a Benefice by the Bishop of Exeter: Followed by Refusal to Institute on the Allegation of Unsound Doctrine, Respecting the Efficacy of Baptism, Edited by the Clerk Examined, George Cornelius Gorham* (London: Hatchard, 1848) and cf. *Extracts from the Writings of Martyr and Bullinger on the Effects of Baptism: In Illustration of the Doctrine held by the Reformers of the Church of England, with some Preliminary Remarks by George Cornelius Gorham* (London: Hatchard & Son, 1849), and George Cornelius Gorham, *A Brief Vindication of Jewel, Hooker, Ussher, Taylor and Pearson, from Misrepresentations in the Recent Baptismal Judgment* (Cambridge: John Deighton, 1850).

[g] Reference to *Appellate Jurisdiction*. No correspondence located. See Robert Wilberforce's letter to Gladstone on 13 June 1850 with which he sends papers, containing his *Charge*, and asks that they be sent 'on to Manning, who I think will like to see what has past [*sic*]' (BL Add. MS 44369, 256–7).

> his heresy being as solitary as it is stolid, and because Goode has invoked it by his prominence.

The mode would be to promote the office of the Bishop in the Court of Arches at once.

And Robert Wilberforce will know what to supply as raw material for Articles.

But to make the attempt worth attempting care must be taken to define the heterodoxy so as to leave no room for such a pamphlet as Alderson's.

I will send your letter on to Hope.[a]

Now for your Pamphlet.

I conceive your object was:

(1) to make out your position without exposing yourself too soon by advanced statements and (2) to give scope for any line you may[87] hereafter be compelled to take.

Also I suppose that as a statesman who has held high trust, and still holds high position it was necessary to unite yourself with the *actual* of our English law and to show a thorough mastery of it and desire to defend it, if possible.

All this explains to me why you have taken so 'insular' a tone, and satisfies me that you do not accept it as a 'bonum in se'.[b]

It seems to me very ably done.

[a] Manning sent the letter with the attached covering letter:

Lavington. June 15, 1850.

My dear Hope,

The inclosed letter from Gladstone will explain itself and when you have read it you will understand my answer which was

1. That it seems desirable to try the question in a direct form. &
2. That not Gorham but Goode ought to be the subject of it.

The course of the Judicial Committee was so evasive that I should feel glad of a full and direct force if only as one more fact added to the foundation of so great a personal act as we have spoken of.

Would you kindly refer me to any *ante* reformation authority on the Regale in this country. And if the books are in your possession might I further ask the kindness of your directing them to me in a parcel by the Petworth Coach from the Old White Horse cellar. I will tender them well.

I hope your chest is strong again. You must take care of yourself.

Ever yours affect[ionate]ly,
H. E. Manning (NLS MS 3675, 82–3)

[b] Good in itself.

The line, as it seems to me, most fair, peaceful & conservative is to contend for these two points.

1. The full & sole authority of the Church of E[ngland][88] in matters purely spiritual, by virtue of the authority of the universal Church flowing into & residing in it.

2. The Supremacy as known to the Common Law, which the Tudor Statutes profess only to declare.

My deep conviction is that they went beyond the Common Law in the vital point; & that Sir Thomas More[c] lost his head between the edges of the old & new Supremacy.

But the lapse of time seems to give us great popular advantage for restoring this Common law supremacy—to which I believe P[ius] IX would make as little objection as Pius II.

I will not add more to this. May God guide us to serve Him & His kingdom.

Ever yours affect[ionatel]y,
H. E. Manning.

[[Pitts; Chapeau, 163, 240–1; cf. Leslie, 92]]

500617mg

Lavington. June 17. 1850.

My dear Gladstone,

Would you send me a few words—aye or no—to this point.[a]

I have been again & again urged to take part in the public meeting of the 27th & have refused.[b]

---

[c] Thomas More (1478–1535; *DNB*), Lord Chancellor of England under Henry VIII, was executed for refusal to take the oath to the Act of Supremacy, 26 Henry VIII, c. 1, declaring Henry as the 'supreme head of the Church of England'.

[a] Manning made the same request of Hope on 17 June 1850:

Lavington. June 17, 1850.

My dear Hope,

I am so much urged to be at the Public Meeting on the 27th that most reluctantly I have consented to reconsider my repeated refusal.

I have asked Gladstone, & I ask you to tell me aye or no. One word will suffice.

Every yours aff[ectionatel]y,
H. E. Manning. (NLS MS 3675, 84–5)

[b] Cf. Hubbard to Manning, 16 June 1850 (Bodl. MS Eng. lett. c. 664, 79–80) asking advice regarding the meeting.

(1) Because I am anxious to maintain quiet and the retirement due to such a trial as is on me & perhaps before me.

(2) Because I could not join in asking convocation.

(3) Because I feel unable to engage in any movement such as the Church Union People aim at. I go beyond them: & may harm them.[89]

(4) Because all my strongest personal feelings recoil from it and nothing short of duty would make me consent.

Let me have in fewest words your mind.

Ever yours affect[ionatel]y,

H.E.M.

[[Pitts; Chapeau, 164, 241–2]]

500618gm[a]

6 Carlton Gardens
June 18. 1850

My dear Manning

I had the idea that you had at an early stage taken part in the preliminary discussions about the public meeting and had been understood to be a consenting party.

I cannot think the desire to remain quiet which is your first reason *and your fourth* is a reason of itself sufficient.

You have though it may be involuntarily acquired a position in the Church which I think gives her members[90] a right to look to you for *public* advice and guidance. Such advice and guidance they have not yet had from you and in that respect I am persuaded you have a debt to pay. Hence my satisfaction on learning you were likely to publish—To remain in the conflict is not all which we expect of you but to take a large share in its direction—

Now having said so much which looks *towards* the affirmation of[91] the question you put to me, I must add that if you do not think it right, or do not think it wise, that you should ask for a restoration of the Synodical action of the Church that is a great objection to your taking part in the proceedings of the meeting.

Something depends upon your antecedents: if you have taken part at former meetings for public objects more or less polemical as between the Church and State, that would render it more difficult for you to hold back on this occasion, and would give a dangerous plausibility to the misconstructions which must arise.

---

[a] 'Wrote to ... Manning' (*GD* iv. 220).

Upon the whole I confess I have the strongest feeling that your place and your gifts endow us with a strong and valid title to call upon you for public counsel & guidance.

I cannot say that it appears to me *equally* clear whether you should take part at this meeting. That really must depend upon weighing circumstances with care of the details of which I am not fully informed. It is a question as to the particular form in which a genial duty should clothe itself for a given occasion.

For one reason I should be most glad to see you find yourself able in honour to refrain—it is that you might *husband* yourself for the most disguised and unimpeachable course of action, viz.[92] in your own personal capacity. Valuable as your authority would be to the meeting, it would rather suffer than gain with the world at large by attending it and that loss is one which I would fain avoid for the sake of the Church whose servant you are. Not that it could suffer in substance but these meetings always give more or less occasion to cavil and the temper of the violent who go to them is imputed to the soberminded.

I have referred to the points which seem to me to bear on the question. If you ask me what I would do myself in your circumstances, certainly I would go if I felt that I had even seemed to be a concurring party at first: otherwise I would not go but would through the press constitute all that my mind could supply of direction for my brethren in the great difficulties of the crisis.

To tell out finally all that remains upon my mind what I desiderate in your letter is the evidence of the intention to exert yourself up to the top of your bent not on the 27th in particular but generally, at a time which demands and which will repay your utmost labours.

I thank you much for your comment on my pamphlet. It is indeed exceedingly insular, partly from intention, partly from circumstances: as I wrote every line of it I had in my mind the idea of obtaining a remedy from the State which seemed to me the duty first in time. I shall try to pursue further the question about a new & unambiguous trial. Your aff[ectiona]te friend,

W. E. Gladstone

Ven[erable]
Archdeacon Manning

Up to 6 P.M. we don't know what the Gov[ernmen]t will do. Something they must.[b]

[[BL Add. MS 44248, 54–7; Morley transcript; cf. Chapeau, 333]]

---

[b] In the face of a censure in the House of Lords over the handling of foreign affairs in Greece (see debate in the Lords on 17 June 1850: Hansard, cxi. 1293), the Government ministers were faced with a defence of their policy in the House or resignation. See Prest (1972), 316 and 500626gm.

500619mg

Lavington. June 19. 1850.

Night.

My dear Gladstone,

Your letter has brought me to decide on taking part in the meeting of the 27th, unless my letters tomorrow morning contain anything to over-rule it.

Some time ago it might have been worth while to keep aloof, & to take a calmer line: but many things put me beyond that point now.

You will let me trespass on you once more for my own sake: and say a few things on which at your leisure you will give me counsel.

1. My name is so deeply compromised by rumours of Rome, by relation to some who are gone, & some who are going: I am so unable to purge myself by declarations that I feel it to be a fact not to waste time over in lamenting, but to calculate & work from.

2. The question then is what can I do to serve the Church of England?

3. It seems to me that I can no longer serve it in the way I have until now I mean upon its old basis partly because I am marked, but chiefly because that basis is passing away.

4. I have long believed that as the French Revolution of 1830 extinguished Gallicanism, & threw the F[rench] C[hurch] on Rome as its centre—so the stream of public events & policy before[93] & since 1828.1829, have been extinguishing our Erastianism & throwing all the Catholic elements of the Church of E[ngland] first upon our spiritual order & principle, & next upon this universal Church.

5. There must be among the clergy & laity a large body—more or less anti Roman—but still more anti Protestant, & anti erastian. On these the hope of doing any thing for the Church of E[ngland] in the way of freedom must rest.

6. Can I serve them? Is it within the sphere of reason, Christian prudence, & integrity as tried by my oath & subscription to labour for these two points.

    (1) The reducing of the Supremacy to that known to Common law before 1530[a]

---

[a] That is before the various acts of Henry VIII, above all 'The Act of Supremacy', 1534, 26 Henry VIII, c. 1.

(2) The re-admission of the Catholic authority, purely spiritual, in doctrine & discipline as an active & sustaining principle of the Church of England.

This is in effect the clearing away of the secular barriers, & the promoting a tendency and desire towards re-union—I will not say with Rome— because that is not the feature which arrests my conscience, but with the Church throughout the World.

If this be a feasible course, or a course which in prudence & conscience may be attempted, I would with joy give my life to it.

The dream of my life has been unity, unity among ourselves, & unity with the Church universal.

At this moment I am freer than ever I was to give myself to any course. Events are dissolving relations which bound me hitherto and I could act with ease & alone.

The persons who would determine me would be above all yourself, Hope & Robert Wilberforce.

In some such way as this I cheerfully accept the demand your last letter makes, little as it must be that I can ever do.

If I have seemed to write of myself as if any line or work of mine were of any worth it is not my meaning, but to get your counsel I must ask it & in asking it speak of myself.

And I must add that I can do nothing but as seconding you. Although your Pamphlet is insular it gives scope & play[94] for all I have written.

May we be guided in this vast crisis & may we begin by realizing its vastness—I am under an illusion if it is not the spring tide[95] of a new & broader movement, in which Anglicanism will survive only by rising into a higher form & spirit.

But this at what cost of public & private changes?

Believe me, my dear Gladstone
Always yours affect[ionatel]y
H. E. Manning

The Right Hon[oura]ble.
W. E. Gladstone
[[BL Add. MS 44248, 58–60; Pitts (copy)]]

500619mcg

Lavington. June 19. 1850.

My dear Mrs. Gladstone,

Many & grateful thanks for your kind note.[a] Alas alas, I have no need of unwise friends to put such things about. They are too rife already: chiefly I believe without cause from me. I am sure that the thought of being anywhere but where I am is to me like the thought of death. To lay my bones under the sod in Lavington Church yard is all my desire. But the stream of evils is carrying us with fearful speed. Let me say to you that one of my truest comforts is the stay of your husbands mind. I so thoroughly trust him from long experience, that no one helps me as he does and we are one in love. These things make us long for the rest, & home where all will be united for ever.

Believe me,
Always affect[ionatel]y yours
H. E. Manning

[[BL Add. MS 46227, 55–6]]

500619mcg

Lavington June 19. 1850

My dear Mrs. Gladstone,

I forgot today to say a word to you about the alms you spoke of for the Wantage Penitentiary. It is now in the Bishop of Oxfords hands who will carry it on.[aa] William will tell you what has transferred it from my hands to his. I scrupled to receive any alms from you: but I have now no scruple in saying that the Bishop of Oxford will be in need of help and I should rejoice to get for him all I can.

Ever yours very affect[ionatel]y
H.E.M.

[[BL Add. MS 46227, 57]]

---

[a] Not located.

[aa] On the foundation of the Penitentiary see Reginald G. Wilberforce, *Life of the Right Reverend Samuel Wilberforce, D.D., Lord Bishop of Oxford and afterwards of Winchester with Selections from his Diaries and Correspondence* (3 vols.; London: John Murray, 1882), iii. 322–3, where a letter of Wilberforce to Butler (29 Dec. 1849) indicates that Miss Lockhart had settled in Wantage with two friends as Sisters of Mercy and were working with 'fallen women'.

3. *The Appellate Jurisdiction*:
June–September 1850

500621gm[a]

6 Carlton Gardens
June 21. 1850.

My dear Manning

I am very glad that the meeting is postponed from the 27th[b] so far as relates to its liberating you from the Resolution[96] you had generously taken. In other respects one hardly knows what to say—the measure was questionable, recession from it had disadvantages of another order—

But my main object in this hasty line is to say that I have read with very deep interest your letter of yesterday,[c] and although I am in a tumult of business, (everything being agog with the question now announced for next week,) I cannot postpone replying to it without at least writing to assure you that the postponement is not the result of anything less than necessity.

I have heard with some indignation reports about you but when I have come across them I have dealt with them summarily.

I hope to write on Sunday.[d]

Your note is gone to my wife—she has been obliged to repair to Hagley to see her Mother[e] who is not so well as usual.

I remain
Your aff[ectiona]te friend
W. E. Gladstone

Venerable
Archdeacon of Chichester
[[BL Add. MS 44248, 66–7; Morley transcript]]

---

[a] 'Wrote to Manning' (*GD* iv. 220). On the same day Gladstone wrote to his wife: 'I have a letter from Manning which has given me the greatest pleasure' (BL Add. MS 46221, 2–3).

[b] The meeting, initially intended for 27 June for the Churchmen of London to protest the Gorham decision (see *The Guardian*, 12 June, 453), was put off until the decision of the Exchequer was announced on the Bishop of Exeter's appeal (ibid. 26 June, 456) and was eventually held at St Martin's Hall, 23 July (see ibid. 17 July, 513). Manning was in attendance and moved a final thank you to the organizers. (See the full report of the meeting ibid. 24 July, 533–8, cf. Liddon, iii. 241–56, Purcell, i. 543–5, and see 500719mg.)

[c] That is, of 19 June, 'Night'.

[d] Sunday, 23 June 1850. See 500623gm.

[e] On 20 June 1850 'C[atherine] G[ladstone] went off unexpectedly to Hagley to nurse Lady G[lynne]' (*GD* iv. 220). Mary (Neville) Glynne was residing at the home of her daughter, Mary (Glynne) Lyttelton (1813–57), where she died in 1854 (Fletcher [1997], 17).

500621mg

Lavington. June 21. 1850

My dear Gladstone,

I know you never rack men's words to their utmost sense, nevertheless I must add to my letter of yesterday one sentence.

My letter amounts to this—

If the Church of England can be served on the laws which bind the Universal Church, & if I can serve it on those laws I am more than willing to make the trial—

If not, those laws have jurisdiction over conscience, & the individual must obey if the body in which he is refuses—

I say this, not that you need it, but for the peace of my own conscience.

Ever Your affect[ionat]e friend
H. E. Manning

The Right Hon[oura]ble W. E. Gladstone
[[Pitts; Chapeau, 166, 243–4; BL Add. MS 44248, 61 (copy)]]

500623gm[a]

6 Carlton Gardens
June 23. 1850

My dear Manning

I tremble to think of any effort however slight at complying with your request and fulfilling my own promise. It was so easy at a distance and looks so formidable when the pen is actually in hand: such vast interests are at stake, such unbounded prospects open before us, and the tone of my life is so out of harmony with that tone which detects and assimilates truth.

If there be a real standing ground within the Church of England for the principles of the Church Universal, then indeed this controversy with its disastrous incidents has for its evident purpose to lift her up to a higher vocation and destiny than she has ever reached before: of course with the correlative of ruin and shame proportionally deep. As to the reality of that standing ground, my mind has no misgiving. This is indeed a judgment of trivial weight, founded upon very narrow knowledge; but it is deliberate, and is formed after trying to appreciate arguments the other way.

The truth seems to me more and more to be, that a *Church* takes a great deal of killing. It is an historical reality: of a continuous and immensely

---

[a] 'Wrote to Manning' (*GD* iv. 221).

prolonged existence with all the incidents that attach to long duration combined with a fluctuating indeed but never ceasing activity. No institution even human that can be thus described, easily dies, disappears, or passes out of its own essence: much more is this the case when, for the particular instance, the historical element reaches back to, is founded in & coincident with the Divine. I mean the Divine not merely in the deep and real sense of the abiding Presence, but in the sharply defined sense of the Apostolic Charter and words from our Saviour's lips.

My mind I confess recoiled from Sewell's doctrine as an outrageous paradox when in a recent Sermon he spoke of the forfeiture of her independence by the Church as a thing impossible:[b] andI still feel it to be indubitable that under a certain amount of pressure the soul is pressed out from the body: but that operation is no slight matter—

Although there is certainly another side to the question, yet in part also it seems to me as if it were want of strong habitual faith which made the mind sometimes incline to estimate lightly the relation of duty and substance between itself and the Church: even when in point of affection and delight that relation is all absorbing. If it has the reality and solidity of a Divine ordinance, as we believe in the letter, it is indestructible until the Divine Spirit shall have passed from the vacant shrine—and then it is not destructible only but destroyed.

But what an event is the passing of that spirit! I have seen twice in my life a[97] very fearful conflict between life and death for the possession of a human form:[c] it seems but a weak type of the mortal agony of an ancient and Apostolic Church: when the strong man armed keeps his house and the[98] stronger man comes to dislodge him.[d] But the parallel fails: the defender is stronger than the invader: there cannot be death by violence from without, only by treachery from within. If the Episcopate, in which the Church is founded, fall bodily away, then indeed the sheep are scattered upon the hills:[e] but if a portion of that body[99] be faithful, must not the authority of God remain, and remain entire, with them?

In this rambling way, I get at a conclusion nearly this: that, assuming we have now a basis in the Church of England on & from which to contend for

---

[b] See the High Churchman, William Sewell (1804–74; *DNB*), *Westminster Churches. A Sermon Preached in the Royal Chapel, Whitehall, on the Fourth Sunday after Easter, 1850* (Oxford: John Henry Parker, 1850). The sermon was highly pessimistic, describing a deep division between rich and poor, and offering no hope of its being overcome (p. 13 in particular).

[c] The cases of his daughters Agnes and Jesse. See 480120mgff. and 500404gmff.

[d] Cf. Luke 11: 21.

[e] Cf. Zech. 13: 7.

ever, then, in the event of an issue to the contest unfavourable so far as the public establishment of religion is concerned, the first and greatest question of duty arising after that issue must in the first instance be solved not *by*, but *for*, us who are layman, and even you who are clergymen: for us, and the Episcopate, which term must mean in the last resort those members of it who adhere to the Catholic faith, not merely to opinion coincident with it in the matter *immediately* at stake.

I entirely enter into your feeling, if I rightly apprehend it to be that you can now no longer assume the basis of the Church of England and simply work for her upon it, but the basis itself requires to be vindicated and cleared against the encroachments which it has suffered.

Yet I do not accept even partly your final reason 'partly because I am marked'—I do not believe you are in that sense marked either by the wise, or by the many;[100] but only by a few of those who merely gape for rumours from morning to night and whose gossip you will very soon live down—

You are indeed the man among the clergy whom I should have most desired to see in *perfect* harmony with the State: but that *now* means something very like treason to the faith. Yet I am sure you will still find it[101] a duty, nay it is almost a necessity of your nature, to be measured in your march, and not to anticipate stages in hostility that (I fear) are yet to come.

Leaving out of view for the time the question whether the appellate jurisdiction is not when rightly understood compatible with the perfect health and rectitude of the Church, I cannot doubt that you may 'in reason Christian prudence & integrity, as tried by your oath & subscription labour' 'to reduce the Supremacy to that known to common law before 1530', & to bring in 'the Catholic authority purely spiritual in doctrine & discipline to direct the Church'.

How far the appellate jurisdiction belongs to the distinctive[102] Reformation idea of the Supremacy I am not quite certain: but I would have you observe that in many Colonial Dioceses the Supremacy has ceased to exist, for the appellate power is gone, and it existed in no other shape. There is indeed the nomination of Bishops—without any power to compel their consecration: but I really think that nothing is required beyond such Clauses as we have tried this year & shall soon get for Australia[f] to settle the whole question for the Colonies, which is a great step gained.

---

[f] See bills noted in 500509gm and the resultant 'Act for the better Government of Her Majesty's Australian Colonies', 5 August 1850, 13 & 14 Victoria c. 59, by which partial self-government came to the colonies.

I wholly agree that the attainment of your two objects would prepare the way for reunion with the universal Church, and your words quite express my feeling as to the sense in which reunion with Rome enters into that expression. Indeed it is an inexpressible comfort and joy to me that as you open out your thoughts in your letter I seem to follow them with full harmony throughout.

If it be the will of God that we reach the point of disruption in the Church of England, I suppose it should be the first thought in the mind of those whom she may expel how they can glorify God by devoting their feeble instrumentality to the purpose of the reunion of Christendom: which the Christian destinies of England will still have a large share in their heart and work.

One main reason why I have never ceased to deplore the continual raindropping of proselytes into the Church of Rome is, because it seems to me that this process is one essentially retrogressive with reference to that great subject of reunion: & one that, sufficiently widened & continued, would place an impassable chasm between this noble English people, and the Catholic Church.

My hopes and convictions for the English nation are only second to my faith in the Church. Yet, while I do not presume to say[103] how far (for instance)[104] the Church of France may be necessary *for France*, with my whole soul I am convinced that if the Roman system is incapable of being powerfully modified in spirit it never can be the instrument of the work of God among us, the faults and the virtues of England are alike against it, and the English nation must be reprobate.

When I say against it, pray understand that I mean against those elements of it which have of late been acquiring greater prominence: those elements of it which strange to say are represented in their highest intensity by the English proselytes.

But this is digression: the principal present duties seem to be: to watch and promote the carrying of this great controversy steadily to definite legal and constitutional issues—in the mean time[105] to marshal, by all such means as men like you can employ, all that mass of feeling & principle lay as well as clerical in England which you describe as antiroman & also antiprotestant—and to prepare men of right intentions but less defined ideas lying outside that circle, to recognise and act upon this principle, that the faith of the Church is her first concern, her position relatively to the State and even to the people, her second.

And now my dear Manning I have tried you with many words signifying little & I must bid goodnight—only, as far as I may, re-echoing your prayer.

I remain always

Your aff[ectiona]te friend

W. E. Gladstone

Venerable

Archdeacon Manning

[[BL Add. MS 44248, 68–73; Morley transcript; Leslie transcript; Lathbury, i. 102–4; cf. Leslie, 92, Chapeau, 334–5]]

500625mg

Lavington. June 25. 1850.

My dear Gladstone,

I do not write in answer to your kind letter of this morning, for it demands fuller consideration. But I must send you my best thanks and a few words to clear my own meaning.

Last night I finished the first draft of what I think of printing on the Oath of Supremacy:[a] and I cannot conceal from myself two facts. 1 that the Royal Supremacy since H[enry] VIII. is not the Royal Supremacy before. and 2. that the later R[oyal] S[upremacy] is a violation of the Divine Office of the Church: and both a cause and a perpetrator of Schism.

I do not know how to elude or avert this conclusion.

Let me send you my proofs when ready. They will not be long and will take no time or labour to read.

Your generous & friendly affection made you deny rumours affecting me, as you say, with indignation. But I do not deserve that: for though I am neither unstable nor hankering, but slow to obstinacy, & suffering day & night I dare not say that my conscience will not submit itself as the last & long delayed dictate of my duty towards the Person & Kingdom of Our Lord, to the Church which has its circuits throughout the world, and its centre by accident in Rome.

It is in this sense I mean that Rome does not arrest my conscience. It is the consequent not the antecedent of the question.

But this is a result not as yet within the sphere of action or even of intention.

---

[a] That is, *The Appellate Jurisdiction of the Crown in Matters Spiritual.*

For the present two works are to be done.

The one to ascertain & openly to lay down the broad principles of this great controversy.

The other to disentangle and ascertain the facts of our state by their conformity or variance with those principles.

The former work I think is nearly concluded, & the latter is advancing more by its own revelations.

> But I have written too much.
> Once more with my thanks. Always affect[ionatel]y yours,
> H. E. Manning

[[Pitts; Chapeau, 167, 244–5; cf. Leslie, 92–3]]

500626gm[a]

> 6 Carlton Gardens
> June 26. 1850

My dear Manning

I need hardly write to say that your proofsheets will have my best attention. The point to which I shall look in a critical and rather jealous temper will be your *historical* proofs: because I do not recollect that heretofore you have busied[106] yourself with proof of that kind in the same subject matter[107] and because it must be made[108] in *most* cases not wholesale but by careful and systematic pondering of details. Now, you are going about to prove that the Reformation Supremacy differs essentially from that not indeed[109] of the immediate but of the remote[110] Pre-Reformation period: i.e. to deny the sense which not only the formularies of the Church but the texts of the law books give to certain *legal* declarations.

This upon the face of it is a bold undertaking; and surely every principle of duty will bind you to the strictest examination and proof and to ruling real doubts, otherwise insoluble, not for but against your conclusion.

The indignation with which I denied rumours respecting you had reference simply to this: that *they* implied precipitancy and lightmindedness and[111] I knew not only that you would not be guilty of either[112] but that it would be monstrous to presume them. I did not mean to fix your ultimate course in unforseen contingencies. Nay I could not even for myself sub-scribe the promise of renunciation which you declare your inability to make: strong as are my feelings with respect to the anathemas of the

---

[a] 'Wrote to Manning' (*GD* iv. 221).

Church of Rome enforced upon proselytes, (most of all as[113] considered in reference to the Eastern Churches), with respect[114] to the corruptions which she more than allows within herself,[115] with respect to the impossibility of her recovering England until she has herself come to a wiser mind, according to those very pregnant words[116] ascribed to Laud;[b] and generally, to her incapacity as she is now worked of satisfying the rational (and therefore in my view sacred) needs of the human mind and the demands of such freedom as is essential in the long run to spiritual moral and mental, as much as to corporal, health.

It is I feel a tremendous thing to err in our historical bases when they are likely to be the ground of great measures affecting the whole life and conscience. These words hit myself, and they are meant to do so. I hope that the matter of the Supremacy will now be bolted[c] to the very bran. I am sure the time has come which renders it matter of vital necessity. And do[117] not think that what I have said of jealous criticism implies forgone conclusion or conscious bias. I rejoice from my heart that you are going to work in the mine. In my view the Reformation scheme of Church & State is essentially shifted from its centre of gravity. You incline to think it never had one. Our practical results may nevertheless coincide.

This letter like yours of yesterday is interlocutory. In the course of time I shall long to know in what way those points appear to you which my last letter was meant to raise.

I remain always
Your aff[ectiona]te friend
W. E. Gladstone

Ven[erable]
Archdeacon Manning

We had last night an astonishing effort of mind and body from Lord Palmerston. He spoke at 66 with the highest energy from dusk to dawn![d]

---

[b] 'At last came in the last charge of this day. That a cardinal's hat was offered unto me.... My answer was, that somewhat dwelt in me, which could not suffer me to accept that, till Rome were other than now it is' [Frederick W. Faber (ed.),] *The Autobiography of Dr. William Laud, Archbishop of Canterbury, and Martyr. Collected from his Remains* (Oxford: John Henry Parker, 1839), 376–7. Cf. John Henry Newman, 'The Catholicity of the Anglican Church', 88, *A Letter Addressed to the Right Reverend Father in God, Richard, Lord Bishop of Oxford, on the Occasion of the Ninetieth Tract in the Series called The Tracts for the Times* (Oxford: John Henry Parker, 1841), sect. 9, and *An Essay in Aid of A Grammar of Assent* (Ker edn.), 232.

[c] Sifted (archaic).

[d] On 25 June 1850 Palmerston spoke at length on the Pacifico affair, 'an extraordinary & masterly effort' (*GD* iv. 221; cf. Hansard, cxii. 380), defending the British blockade of the

[[BL Add. MS 44248, 74–6; Morley transcript; Lathbury, i. 104–5; Purcell, i. 545–6]]

[[According to a Manning letter of 30 June 1850, quoted by Purcell (1892), 429, Manning was to meet with Harrison the following day, 1 July, regarding his letter to the Bishop of Chichester, that is *The Appellate Jurisdiction of the Crown in Matters Spiritual*, and following that meeting 'then with Gladstone and Hope'.[c]]]

500704mg

Lavington. July 4. 1850.

My dear Gladstone,

This morning brings me the tidings you have known for more than twenty four hours.[a] I cannot refrain from writing a few words—for I feel this event chiefly as it reaches me through you. I did not personally know Sir Robert Peel: but your relation to him always made me feel to know him.

Apart from this I have always believed him to be, almost more than any public man I know, worthy of the names good and great. When I have said this I have said all that I can find to say of men. He was both: and his sway & power over men was not more from capacity of intellect than from the command of moral integrity. As a public man he seems to me on a level of greatness above all but our greatest names. As a private friend he must be a loss indeed: for we love not simply by affection but by reverence, by admiration, & by the homage of our moral sense.

And it seems to me as if this end were measured upon an idea of greatness having a singularity in its time & kind which takes him & his memory and his last mature presence out of the record and sphere of common histories.

Piraeus and requiring compensation from the Greek government for damages to the home of a British subject, a Portuguese Jew, Don Pacifico. Gladstone responded on 27 June, speaking for 2½ hours (*GD* iv. 222; Hansard, cxii. 543–90). See Morley, i. 368ff.

[c] *GD* does not record a meeting.

[a] Sir Robert Peel was thrown from his horse on 29 June 1850 and died on 2 July (*GD* iv. 223; see Parker (1891–9), iii. 544–6). For Gladstone's eulogy on Peel in the House of Commons on 3 July, see Hansard, cxii. 855, and *The Times*, 4 July, 3j. Note Manning's reflection to Herbert on 5 July: 'It is a deep sorrow public and private. I did not know him; but through you and Gladstone I have learned to feel for him more than the admiration which his public life commanded' (Purcell i. 456). Herbert had written to Manning on 4 July. See Bodl. MS Eng. lett. c. 657, 46–7.

I could not restrain the inclination to write this for I share your sorrow with a very deep and humbling sense of this great warning: and a heartfelt admiration for the greatness & goodness which has so suddenly passed from the midst of us.

Believe me, my dear Gladstone,
Always affect[ionatel]y yours,
H. E. Manning

The Right Hon[oura]ble
W. E. Gladstone
[[Pitts; Chapeau, 168, 243]]

500708gm^{aa}

6 Carlton Gardens
July 8. 1850

My dear Manning

You have made a very just and feeling estimate of the character of Sir Robert Peel. He was a good[118] man as well as a great one: always working according to conscience and duty as he saw them before him. And I felt very much the kindness of your letter. Silence for some days after receiving it may have looked like indifference: but it was only the pressure of business which prevented me.

The melancholy end of Sir R[obert] Peel's Life will produce of necessity great effects in public affairs, which it is not easy at this moment to forecast, but the loss of him is one immense one & will be more & more, not less & less, felt for some time to come. But an event in proportion as it externally appears accidental is really Providential, and I never recollect one which more impressed me with the belief that God had taken the matter into His own hands and had a special meaning in the occurrence, a meaning we must trust of mercy, though we know not how.

The case of the Bishop of Exeter has been finally lost[b]—this morning the Court of Exchequer having discharged the rule—and now is the time to consider whether a further suit ought not to take place.—

---

^{aa} 'Wrote to H. E. Manning' (*GD* iv. 224).
^b *The Guardian* of 8 July 1850, 481–4, announced in a lengthy lead article that the Court of the Exchequer had turned down the Bishop's appeal concerning the Gorham decision on the previous Saturday, 6 July.

Dr. Mill is clear in the opinion that Goode is too ambiguous & shifty in his language to be caught.[c]

I remain

Your aff[ectiona]te friend

W. E. Gladstone

Venerable

Archdeacon Manning

[[BL Add. MS 44248, 77–9; Morley transcript; Leslie transcript]]

500709gm[a]

6 C[arlton] G[ardens]. July 9. [18]50

My dear Manning

I have to-day received and read the proofs of your letter to the B[isho]p of Chichester[b] & with the same feelings as usual.

The only use however of my writing is not to refer to the principles and results in which I agree but to any point in which I do not follow you—

The main one is your view of the right of appeal as settled under Henry VIII (NB error on p.47 first of Q[ueen] Elizabeth[c]). I am at issue with your constitutional doctrine. The King is not the will that governs the land: but the symbol of supreme power. Even then he was so, for judicial purposes: and it was not long after that he was declared incapable of sitting in his own Courts. The power, of which the Crown was the symbol, was that power in which Church decrees were to be clothed. The mind which was to wield that power was in the case of temporal law the mind of the legal profession, in the case of the Church the mind of the Spiritualty. If you say

---

[c] On 5 July 1850 Mill returned Goode's book to Gladstone and commented on Goode's shiftiness (BL Add. MS 44369, 312–13). Robert Wilberforce also saw Mill's letter and agreed (ibid. 339–40). Cf, also Goode's later response to the Manning, Wilberforce, and Mill declaration of 21 August 1850 (see Addenda to this Section) in his *Reply to the Letter and Declaration Respecting the Royal Supremacy Received from Archdeacons Manning and Wilberforce and Professor Mill* (London: Thomas Hatchard, 1850).

[a] 'Wrote to…Manning…read Manning's Letter [*The Appellate Jurisdiction*] in proof' (*GD* iv. 224). The preface to Manning's *The Appellate Jurisdiction is* dated 2 July 1850. Gladstone's annotated copy is preserved in SDL, N 62/9.

[b] On 6 July 1850 a set of proofs of *The Appellate Jurisdiction* was also sent to Hope (NLS MS 3675, 88–9).

[c] Correction made by Manning.

the Appellate jurisdiction committed to the King the choice of persons in a manner quite outside the law of the Church's order, I will not stop to dwell on the case of Constantine and the Donatist appeal,[d] but I say this: de facto the Delegates did never as far as we know till 1½ century later sit on a case of heresy—the question therefore is how was it *intended* to deal with such cases? and this it appears to me is most rationally answered by the passage in the Reformatio Legum *si gravis sit causa* &c.[e]

Of course it is essential to estimate aright the *animus*[f] of the State in those Statutes before you can measure the bearings of theological principles on the Case: for that *animus* rules the fact with which you have to deal.

I should be little vexed at a variance between us on a point of historical or constitutional doctrine were it not that it appears to me your account of the Statutes of Henry VIII greatly weakens the authority which your Tract is in other respects so well fitted to carry.

I have said this without going at all into the *nature* of the appeal which I am quite convinced partook, at least, of the character of the *tamquam ex abusu*:[g] and before you decide to the contrary look back to the Constitutions of Clarendon (I believe I have quoted the passage) & note the significant similarity of language. I am clear of this from the Statute itself

---

[d] See 371027gm.

[e] 'Quo cum fuerit causa devoluta, eam vel concilio provinciali definiri volumus, si gravis sit causa, vel a tribus quatuorve episcopis, a nobis ad id constituendis' (A particularly serious case is to be treated by a provincial council or by three or four appointed bishops). *The Reformation of the Ecclesiastical Laws as Attempted in the Reigns of King Henry VIII, King Edward VI, and Queen Elizabeth*, ed. Edward Cardwell [from the *Reformatio legum ecclesiasticarum* 1571] (Oxford: Oxford University Press, 1850), 302; De Appelationibus, 11. See 500711mg, 500712gm, 501006gm.

[f] Intention.

[g] See Manning, *Appellate Jurisdiction* (1850*b*), 29–30: 'This is a security known and exercised, as we have already seen, in all Christian kingdoms, by the process known in the canon law as the *Appellatio tanquam ab abusu*, by which right of receiving appeals the Civil State has the power of reviewing the acts and proceedings of all Ecclesiastical Judges, and of keeping them within the bonds of their own rules and jurisdictions. But there is no parallel between this appeal in the case of abuse, and the appeal to the Crown in Council.' The *tam quam* is a prosecution undertaken for the person prosecuted as well as for the Crown; see Jacob Giles, *A New Law Dictionary*, corrected and enlarged by J. Morgan (London: W. Stahan & W. Woodfall, 1782). On appeals in general see Gibson, Tit. xlv Cap. vi, and Henry Charles Coote, *The Practice of Ecclesiastical Courts with Forms and Tables of Costs* (London: Henry Butterworth, 1847), 860ff.

that the appeal to the Crown was not intended to be the addition of another term to the series, but something specifically distinct.[h]

Query the word *overruled* in p.34. (Holy Scripture being among the objects of it.)[i]

I wish you had space for a few words on another point besides all you have so admirably handled—viz. the immorality of the mode of subscription which has now received legal sanction.

Mrs Herbert goes on as well as possible. We are advised to take our little Mary to the South of Europe for the winter[j]—

I remain your aff[ectiona]te friend
W.E.G.

Venerable
Archdeacon Manning
I have seen Hook,[k] he *drivels*: nothing more: nothing less.

[[BL Add. MS 44248, 79–82; Morley transcript; Lathbury, i. 111–12]]

---

[h] Gladstone (1850) argues the issue with quotations from and a discussion of 25 Henry VIII c. 21 (The Ecclesiastical Licences Act, 1533), preamble and sect. 19 in his *Remarks*, 357. Following this section he discusses Coke's commentary, summarizing among other maxims:

That the 24 Henry VIII c. 12 [An Act in restraint of Appeals] is a great constitutional statute, distinctly marking out a province of ecclesiastical, and another province of civil, causes.

That the laws ecclesiastical are for the settlement of 'causes of the law divine, or of spiritual learning'.

That the laws temporal are 'for trial of property of lands and goods, and for the conservation of the people of this realm in unity and peace...' (*Remarks* [1850], 39).

His reference to the 'Constitutions of Clarendon' appears to be to sect. 7 in which it is stated 'that what shall appertain to the royal court shall be concluded there, and that what shall belong to the church court shall be sent to the same to be treated there', immediately prior to sect. 8 on appeals, which reads: 'In regard to appeals, if they shall occur, they must proceed from the archdeacon to the bishop, and from the bishop to the archbishop. And if the archbishop fail in showing justice, they must come at last to the lord the king, that by his command the dispute be concluded in the archbishop's court, so that it must not go further without the assent of the lord the king' (trans. from Bettenson, 1963], 157ff. For text see William Stubbs, *Select Charters and other Illustrations of English Constitutional History from the Earliest Times to the Reign of Edward the First* [Oxford: Clarendon,1888], 135ff.).

[i] Correction made by Manning: Sentence reads: 'The known intention of our Lord and of his inspired servants is the rule of interpretation: all the records and documents, the formularies and definitions of the faith are subject to that known intention, and ruled by it.'

[j] See 501106gm.   [k] Gladstone saw Hook on 6 July 1850 (*GD* iv. 224).

500711mg

Lavington. July 11. 1850.

My dear Gladstone,

Many thanks to you for your letter & the valuable remarks on my proofs. I trust that I can reduce our apparent difference to a very small amount.

1. And first, I altogether hold your constitutional view of the Crown, & intended to express it in p. 6. 'The King expressing & exercising the sum of the Civil Power &c.'[a] This is manifestly seen in the Saxon times[b]—also in Lord Cokes precedents which I have so analysed as to say nearly every where the King 'in Parliament'.[c]

So far we are wholly agreed.

2. Also I agree that it was intended that the 'mind of the Spiritualty' sh[oul]d be applied to Eccl[esiastical] causes by the 24 Hen[ry] VIII.[d]

But as a *fact* we know that it was not so *prescribed* by the constitution of the Court of delegates.

Neither was it so practised. And be this as it may, the *King* had the powers of selecting the persons & thereby of *creating a tribunal superior to the Primate* for the trial of a matter howsoever spiritual.

This I believe to be a principle in violation of the whole spiritual order of the Church—& unknown till then.

As to the intention, implied by the Reformatio L[egum] E[cclesiasticum] I feel that it is not without weight[e] —but I am dealing with *facts* & with *law*, not with intentions which if not expressed by the law are out of court.

***

[a] See Manning, *Appellate Jurisdiction* (1850*b*), 6: 'The joint but independent action of the spiritual and civil powers from our earliest history may be traced through the succession of our Councils and Parliaments—the King expressing and exercising the sum of the Civil power, the Archbishop of the Spiritual; of which joint action the celebrated preamble of the 24th of Henry VIII., 12 [The Ecclesiastical Appeals Act, 1532], is a recital and proof.'

[b] Ibid. 9–10 and notes.

[c] For examples, ibid. 11–12.

[d] See Gladstone, *Remarks* (1850), 75: 'the Crown possesses the appellate jurisdiction, if we construe the two statutes 24 and 25 Henry VIII. together, under the express cover of the remarkable preamble that assigns to the spiritualty the administration of ecclesiastical laws'. Cf. also Gladstone's comment, ibid. 39, concerning 24 Henry VIII c. 12.

[e] *Reformatio Legum* ('De Appelationibus', 11), 302; See 500709gm.

3. As to the Donatist case I will not attempt it in this letter. I will only ask leave at present to[119] say that I believe its irrelevancy to be complete.

4. But the Constitutions of Clarendon come nearer home & I ought to say a word.

I believe that the following points may be made clear beyond doubt:

1. That they existed for two years—& that *in the point we are discussing*, they had no warrant in any period before that date, nor afterwards.

2. That the appeals then spoken of were *to be terminated in the Court of* the Archbishop: not before the Crown in a court of its own.[f]

3. That if not *capable* of being then terminated they might still be carried to Rome.

4. That they had, avowedly, reference only to the *civil* correction & discipline of the Church 'ob civilem causam'.[g] It was absolutely impossible for such a case as Gorhams or any cause of doctrine to be touched by the King.

But I feel that I am bound to make all this good and will endeavour so to do. Meanwhile I will only say that I feel the constitutions of Clarendon to be no bar in the matter.

The only point where I conceive we do at present slightly differ is that you think the Tudor statutes more defensible than I do. And yet I may reduce their difference by saying that I think them defensible (more or less) in every thing but this one point, namely that they have made possible & legal such a case as the Gorham appeal.

---

[f] 'Constitutions of Clarendon', sect. 8. For text see 500709gm, note.

[g] 'Because of a civil cause'. Compare the argument of Maskell: '[T]here is an epistle of Gilbert Foliot, at that time bishop of London, and of the king's party against the archbishop of Canterbury, which explains to us in what sense we are to understand the word 'appeals,' as meant and intended by the king. The bishop is writing to the pope, Alexander the third. "In appellationibus ex antiqua regni sui constitutione id sibi vindicat honoris et oneris, ut ob civilem causam nullus clericorum regni sui ejusdem regni fines exeat, nisi an ipsius authoritate et mandate jus suum obtinere queat, experiendo cognoscat . . . " So that the causes which are spoken of in the constitutions of Clarendon, according to the intention of Henry the second himself, are civil causes, and not ecclesiastical; a distinction which, as most people will agree, carries with it a difference' (William Maskell, *A Second Letter on the Present Position of the High Church Party in the Church of England. The Want of Dogmatic Teaching in the Reformed English Church* (London: William Pickering, 1850), 87–8.

If I understand your views it is that they intended to give the final discretion to the Spiritualty Rege *advocante*.[h]

It seems to me that to give to the King this choice of Judges *in matters of Faith*, is indefensible; at least in the absence of a Superior & independent correcting[120] power. To put the last judicial power and the Synods of the Church into the control of the same hand is to make the Crown final in a sense not to be defended.

There is no doubt that your Pamphlet upholds the Tudor Statutes: and mine censures them in this point.

You censure the present application of them: to me they seem originally in fault.

But I am doing no more on the appellate branch than our forefathers did on the Visitatorial in Charles 1st time.[i] And surely this is all the more necessary now that the Crown is more than ever the symbol of the Legislative will and that will has departed from the Church.

Now Hope tells me that before H[enry] VIII. there was no such process as an 'appellatio tanquam ab abusu' in England.[j]

Also Badeley (this morning) says that he thinks my law right, & that the Year Books would give examples[121] in point.[k]

I did not mean to write so much: but my anxiety to be right and safe & to keep pace & pace with you has drawn me on.

There are other matters on which I meant to write: & will: such as your long & valuable letter[l] in answer to my question of conscience on which I have much to say: and also the bearing of this mournful public loss on our own work and duty. I kept this out of my last letter: for it was too soon to write of it, with such a blow still ringing. But it seems to me that it has struck out a keystone & I do not see what is to avert many changes, & some so rapid as to be dangerous.

---

[h] With the King's advocacy.

[i] The visitatorial powers over ecclesiastical bodies assigned to the Crown under 1 Elizabeth I c. 1, art. 8, were used by Charles I over laity as well and were repealed by 16 Charles I c. 11, s. 1 (1640).

[j] Hope wrote to Manning on the subject (see 500709gm) on 29 June 1850 (Bodl. MS Eng. lett. c. 657, 77–80) in response to a query by Manning the day before (NLS MS 3765, 86–7). Manning had sent proof sheets of his *Appellate Jurisdiction* to Hope on 6 July 1850 (NLS MS 3765, 88–9).

[k] See Badeley to Manning, 10 July 1850 (Bodl. MS Eng. lett. c. 664, 87–8).

[l] 500625mg.

I trust your child is not less well again. Your talk of the South reminds me of the days when I chode with you for buying apples on Sunday Evening after sermon at the Caravita.[m]

> Believe me, my dear Gladstone,
> Ever yours affect[ionatel]y,
> H. E. Manning

The Right Hon[oura]ble W. E. Gladstone
[[Pitts; Chapeau, 169, 243–7; BL Add. MS 44248, 61–5 (copy)]]

500712gm[a]

> 6 Carlton Gardens
> July 12. 1850.

My dear Manning

I still think that such difference as exists between us is upon the Constitutional point, & lies farther inwards in that part of the question than the idea in which you justly state that we concur as to the royal power. My feeling is this: that the Crown had an autocracy given at the Reformation, or at least then determinantly given & secured to it, which when regarded strictly amounts to a power of superseding the regular order of the Church in her judicial functions. But then when I turn to the law and find that the Crown had the same autocracy in regard to the administration of it, I am struck by this fact that notwithstanding such nominal absolutism in regard to the choice of instruments these facts are incontestable.

1. That the King has felt it a duty to choose the most competent lawyers speaking generally to be judges: to give effect to the mind of the legal profession in the appointment of Judges and therefore in their sentences.

2. That if he had done otherwise he would have offended grossly against the spirit of the constitution & would have abused his trust.

Now in considering the relation of the case of the Church to that of the law I at once admit that the King would not have satisfied the former case as he

---

[m] While in Rome in December and January 1838 Gladstone was in regular attendance at the night oratory, the Caravita (named after its founder Pietro Caravita, SJ, in 1711) on the Via del Seminario where services were held after sunset (*GD* ii. 530). Manning may here have reference to Sunday, 23 December, when he was present with Gladstone at a morning service (ibid. 538). On Epiphany, 1839, Manning noted in his diary: 'The Caravita. Christ suffered for us. If Christ is our Saviour, then our Example. Patience in duty. Purity in tongue, eyes, ears. Very good' (Leslie, 56).

[a] 'Wrote to . . . Manning' (*GD* iv. 225).

did the latter by the mere choice of eligible persons. The Church had a fixed constitution, the law had not—In order to make the analogy hold strictly we ought to be able to shew how the Reformation Statutes intended that all Church questions should be decided according to the Constitution of the Church though by the authority of her[122] Crown—

Now I will not say this was their intention because plainly many questions were decided, & probably were always meant to be decided by mixed Commissions of Delegates.

These mixed Commissions I think had reference to the mixed nature of the immense preponderance of mixed cases in the Ecclesiastical Courts.

But when we come to the highest & most purely ecclesiastical question, a case of the definition of doctrine, then I think it is very fair to question whether the Statute of appeal did intend that to be decided by such mixed Commission: it does not express the contrary: but we have no facts of[123] decisions made by such commissions—and we have the passage in the Reformatio Legum shewing what the intention was.[b]

If indeed and so far as the appeal under Henry VIII partook of the tamquam ex abusu[c] we could not expect to find any words in the Statute linking the Crown to the choice of ecclesiastical judges.

I observe your[124] reference to Hope about the *tamquam ex abusu*: but pray look whether as a regular legal *form* it did not take its starts from about that same period in other countries?

As to the Const[itutions of] Clarendon the ending in the A[rch]b[ish o]ps Court seems to me very much as if it meant that the archbishop's Court was to settle the matter according to the King's orders—

Pray consider whether the principle of appeals to Rome in ecclesiastical causes was I do not say tolerated by but regularly and firmly fixed in our common *law* or statute law before the Reformation—

I think you will greatly clear & strengthen your position by placing yourself on the ground, indicated in a part of your letter, that where you say you are now doing by the appellate jurisdiction what was done[125] under Charles I[126] in respect to Visitatorial power.

I am obliged to write in much haste & am ever

Your aff[ectiona]te friend

W. E. Gladstone

Ven[erable]
Archdeacon Manning

[[BL Add. MS 44248, 83–6; Morley transcript; Leslie transcript]]

---

[b] *Reformatio Legum* ('De Appelationibus', 11), 302. See 500709gm.   [c] See 500709gm.

500715mg

Lavington. July 15. 1850.

My dear Gladstone,

I write a line to say that I hope to be in Cadogan Place on Thursday.[a]

If your Sunday afternoon[b] is not already bespoken, I shall be rejoiced to claim it as usual. But I shall hope to see you even sooner.

Many thanks for your last letter. I hope I have left room for our Pamphlets to unite in the 'Spiritual causes by Spiritual Courts.'

I have more to say than I can attempt to write.

Believe me, Always your
affect[ionat]e friend,
H. E. Manning

The Right Hon[oura]ble W. E. Gladstone[127]

[[Pitts; Chapeau, 170, 248]]

[[On 16 July 1850 Gladstone completed a draft of his letter on Gorham and sent it to the Bishop of London (*GD* iv. 226; cf. Lathbury, i. 105–8 and BL Add. MS 44369, 335). He saw Manning again on Friday, 19 July[c] (*GD* iv. 227).]]

500719mg

61. Eaton Place. July 19. 1850.

My dear Gladstone,

After I have seen Hope tomorrow I must return home—& then go to Bennett[a] by engagement made before I saw you today so that I shall not see you until Sunday[b]—& therefore send the enclosed.[c] Many thanks for sending it to me. It seems to me most seasonable & valuable: and when we meet I will say more. I am sorry to lose coming to you—but I could n[o]t without failing in engagements made before.

Believe me, Ever affect[ionatel]y yours,
H. E. Manning

[[Pitts; Chapeau, 171, 248]]

[[On 20 July 1850 Catherine Gladstone added in a postscript to a letter to Gladstone: 'I long to see A[rchdeacon] Mannings note to you' (SDL, Glynne–Gladstone MS 612).]]

---

[a] 18 July 1850.   [b] 21 July 1850.

[c] See 500825gm. A full text of the letter is provided in Addenda to this Section.

[a] Gladstone met with Hope on Saturday, 20 July 1850 (*GD* iv. 227).

[b] 21 July 1850.

[c] Not located; possibly a draft of Gladstone's letter to the Bishop of London. (See comment in 500825gm and Addenda to this Section.)

The following day, 21 July, Gladstone 'Saw Archd[eaco]n Wilberforce—& Manning for a good long while' (*GD* iv. 228) and commented on the meeting at some length in a letter to Catherine:

Manning has been with me today: looking better, and talking with much interest about our intentions & plans of travel and my position in politics. As to the former he is against Naples which he says is liable to sudden changes of temperature, and favourable to Rome—but I can hardly think he can be right for *us*; it was in April too that he had his experience of Naples.

As to Church matters I am not less well pleased with his present frame than I was. His letter to the Bishop of Chichester is out and is very *strong* but has none of the aspect of an intention to move. (SDL, Glynne–Gladstone MS 771, 249–54, 251–2)

On 23 July the London and the Metropolitan Church Unions organized a large protest against the Gorham decision at St Martin's Hall, Longacre, at 12 noon.[d] Gladstone did not attend, but Manning did, proposing a vote of thanks to the chair of the meeting and using the opportunity to express his hope that the meeting would result in an action of the whole Church to respond to the decision.[e] Manning visited Gladstone on the following day, 24 July (*GD* iv. 228).]]

500725mg

Lavington. Feast of S[t]. James.
1850.

My dear Gladstone,

When I said yesterday that the Bishop of Londons Bill did not satisfy me I meant that it recognizes the Crown as an *Ecclesiastical Ordinary* Judge[a] with discretion to decide the whole matter external & internal of all spiritual appeals.

Lord Stanleys proposal makes this even worse.[b]

---

[d] See Gladstone's printed letter of invitation from B. Hughes, G. J. Ottaway, and R. N. Wood (BL Add. MS 44566, 205–8).

[e] *The Guardian*, 24 July 1850 (Extra Number), 337–8.

[a] On the definition of Ordinary see 500819mg.

[b] *The Guardian* of 5 June 1850 reported on the second reading of the Bishop of London's bill in the House of Lords on 3 June and noted that Stanley 'confessed . . . that he would see with satisfaction, not for his own sake but for the sake of many others, whom a modification

I believe the sound & true course w[oul]d be—

1. That all cases heard by a Bishop & the Archbishop, if these shall agree in their sentence, shall proceed no further.

2. That if they differ, or if the case begin with the Archbishop either party may pray the Crown to order it to be reheard by the Provincial Council which shall judge of its gravity and either hear it in Council or by some of its own members appointed by its own authority.

3. That if the Provincial Council shall judge or so many Bishops of the Province that the concurrent sentence of the Bishop & Archbishop as under No. 1. is at variance with Faith, they may review the Sentence. This I conceive w[oul]d be only an ultimate security rarely to be invoked.

If there be any alleged wrong in the *form* or *process*, the extraordinary appeal tanquam ab abusu might be to the Crown from all courts, & be heard as now by the Crown in Council. This with the remedy of Quare impedit[c] is abundant security for the Beneficiary pact.[128]

All schemes for keeping up an insular & final Tribunal must be open to objection: & I can think of no scheme open to fewer than the above.

Believe me,
Ever yours affect[ionate]ly,
H. E. Manning

[[Pitts; Chapeau, 172, 248–9]]
[[On 30 July 1850 Gladstone wrote to Catherine:

of the Bill might reconcile to its passing, such an alteration as would not withdraw from the Judicial Committee the power of passing the sentence.... [I]n ninety-nine cases out of a hundred the Judicial Committee would be guided by the Bishops, if such a reference were made to them on questions of doctrine' (406). Hansard, cxi. 653 reads: 'He [Lord Stanley] believed the Bill had received the assent of the majority of the members of the Episcopal Bench, and he knew it was supported by a large body of clergymen of various shades of opinion, and by many of the laity.' See also the *Speech of the Bishop of London in the House of Lords, on moving the Second Reading of the Bill relating to Appeals from the Ecclesiastical Courts, on Monday, June 3, 1850* (London: B. Fellowes, 1850). On the rejection of the bill in the Lords on 3 June note Gladstone's diary comment: 'heard the disastrous news of the division in the Lords 84:51. I heard the most important parts of the debate: greatly pleased and not less shocked' (*GD* iv. 216).

    [c] A writ issued in the case of a disputed benefice by which the defendant is required to state 'wherefore' (*quare*) the plaintiff 'is impeded' (*impedit*) from the presentation.

I forgot to tell you several days ago that I had seen Manning and talked fully to him about the Penitentiary[d]—He considers it quite reasonable that we should act in the matter as we pleased: and will be gratified by any thing you give to Wantage but quite recognised that as matters now stand Windsor has a nearer claim upon us. (SDL, Glynne–Gladstone MS 771, 265–8, 266–7)]]

500730gm[a]

6 Carlton Gardens
July 30. 1850

My dear Manning

I at once admit that the Bishop of London's Bill as amended by Lord Stanley would do little towards settling[129] the discharge of the duty of the State to the Church: but I cannot feel strongly the objection which lies against it either in that or in its present form on the ground[130] that it admits the Crown as an Ecclesiastical Ordinary[b] in matters spiritual— there again I think we strike on the old rock of the constitutional doctrine concerning the position of the Crown: which I take to be the mere symbol of the attribute of power, given to civil society that it may work out its purposes, and represented, by tradition consent and moral fitness, in that symbol.

I must confess that I should not only be satisfied to accept a measure which would give the Church forthwith a voice for judicial purposes in[131] the public solemn & collective sense of the Episcopate but sh[oul]d be better content with it,[132] than with the immediate restoration of Synodical action.

Before you put wholly out of your mind the question, what is the effect upon a Church of conceding to the Prince a power of selecting Ecclesiastical Judges from among the Bishops—which certainly involves in *posse*[c] a departure from her regular organisation—I should be glad[133] to know that you had considered fully the bearing of the principle upon the case of the Church in Russia: where if I understand right its government is in the

---

[d] The Gladstones were at the time active in the new foundation for 'fallen women', the Clewer House of Mercy, inspired by Manning's 1844 sermon, *Saints and Penitents*, after the preaching of which the Revd John Armstrong, Vicar of Tidenham, began to plan for such a house, publishing *An Appeal for the Foundation of a Church Penitentiary* (London: John Henry Parker) in February of 1849. The parish of Clewer reached as far as Windsor at the time. For details see Bonham (1989, 1992).

[a] 'Wrote to . . . Manning' (*GD* iv. 230).

[b] On the definition of 'Ordinary' see 500819mg.

[c] As a possibility.

hands of the most Holy Synod and this is not only subject externally to restraint but is also composed of persons nominated from among the Prelacy by the Emperor, with a lay supervisor or Commissioner.

A principle ought indeed to be stronger than a fact. But yet before fully committing myself to the consequences of any abstract proposition which purports to apply general truth to the course of human affairs I should always wish to have the general & broader results of it before me as they not unfrequently lead to useful re-examinations.

I cannot dismiss from my mind the doubt whether you do not give a little more stringency to the obligations *per se*[134] of the provincial organisation of the Church (so to speak) than it is in rigour entitled to—It is after all I apprehend in the Episcopate that the sum of the Divine Charter lies— the provincial organisation is the regular means of ascertaining & giving effect to the sense of the Episcopate—any supercession of it involves danger, but I do not see that so long as it is danger only vitality need be touched—

On these matters at any rate I think we want instructions long & large.

I go to Hagley please God on Friday & much rejoice in the prospect of getting away as I have a tearing cough & much headache & am very ill fit for work.[d]

I find Clark on climate recommends the Naples winter and the Roman spring. Naples according to him is a mild form of Nice: and both are bad for pulmonary patients especially in spring but good to give tone.[e]

In haste
Your aff[ectiona]te friend
W. E. Gladstone

Ven[erable] Archdeacon Manning

[[BL Add. MS 44248, 87–90; Morley transcript; Lathbury, i. 112–13; cf. Chapeau, 337]]

[[In a letter to Gladstone of 31 July 1850 Catherine Gladstone commented: 'Im glad you talked to A[rchdeacon] Manning about our [Wantage] P[enitentiary] money' (SDL, Glynne–Gladstone MS 612). During the night following the London meeting of

---

[d] Gladstone arrived at Hagley on 2 August 1850 (*GD* iv. 230). Three days earlier, on Saturday, 27 July 1850 his cough was 'very bad & headache almost unmanageable' (ibid. 229).

[e] Sir James Clark, *The Sanative Influence of Climate: with an Account of the Best Places of Resort for Invalids in England, the South of Europe, &c.* (3rd edn.; London: John Murray, 1841), advises arrival in Rome in October and departure at the beginning of May at the earliest (237), indicates that Naples and Nice have similar climates (238), and points out that no consumptive patients should be sent to Naples (239).

23 July 1850 Manning drew up a 'Declaration' against the Royal Supremacy together with Robert Wilberforce.[f] They invited Dr Mill to attach his name to it, purposely ignoring all others. By 17 August they had sent their paper to all clergymen and laymen who had taken the Oath, inviting signatures. The Declaration was printed in *The Guardian* on 21 August (p. 602).[g]]]

500819mg

Lavington. Aug[ust] 19. 1850.

My dear Gladstone,

I have been day by day intending to write, but always obliged to delay.

Before I say any thing on the subject of our last letter let me hope that your child is gaining health & strength, and your anxiety lessened about her.[a] I hope also that your wife is well.

To go back to our old matter.[b]

The[135] objection to recognizing the Crown as an *Ordinary* Judge seems to my mind unanswerable. The definition of an ordinary judge is in the Canon Law—Ordinarius[136] ille, qui potestatem judicandi habet *jure proprio*, seu[137] ratione *officii* aut *dignitatis suae* ac *eo ipso quod est talis* ut Episcopus.[c]

---

[f] It appears to be this to which Manning was referring in later life when he recalled: 'In the month of May or June in 1850 [6 June], I was staying at B[isho]p Wilberforce's house in Eaton Place. Robert Wilberforce was there. We were both trying to find some way of acting against the Gorham Judgment. I remember one night I woke about 4 o'cl[ock] and lay awake long. I then worked out the Declaration against the Royal Supremacy; admitting it in all Civil matter, but rejecting it in all spiritual and mixed matters. I then went & woke Robert Wilberforce & put it before him. He accepted it at once. We then got it into writing & invited Dr. Mill to sign it with us. We then sent it to every Clergyman & Layman who had signed the Oath of Supremacy, and to all Colleges and newspapers, inviting signatures. About 1800 Clergymen signed it out of 20,000; and I saw that the game was up. It was fair test fully applied; & it received next to no response' ('Later Reminiscences', i. 36 (CP); Purcell, i. 543).

[g] For a copy of the Declaration see Addenda to this Section. Cf. Purcell, i. 540–1; see also letter of Walter K. Hamilton to Manning on 19 August 1850 (Bodl. MS Eng. lett. c. 664, 121–2; Purcell, i. 531). The former had received a request to sign the declaration and felt that rather than signing (and therefore declaring 'that I will not acknowledge the law') he was duty-bound to resign his position.

[a] On Gladstone's concern over his daughter's (Mary's) health see 500709gm and 500825gm.

[b] On Manning's view of the Gorham decision at the time, compare his short treatise on the matter, sent to Priscilla Maurice the following day. For text of letter see Addenda to this Section.

[c] 'An Ordinary is that person who has the power of delivering judgments by his own proper jurisdiction or by reason of his office or his dignity and therefore is as such a bishop.'

It is manifestly impossible to acknowledge the Crown as an Ecclesiastical Ordinary in any such sense.

But such I believe to be the effect (I say nothing for your sake of the instruction) of the Tudor Statutes.

It will not relieve this difficulty to regard the Crown as the symbol of the supreme power of the State: for the State cannot receive appeals from the Church as such an Ordinary.

Do you feel the practice of the Church in Russia a commendation of anything? My own disposition is to regard it with extreme mistrust,[138] or rather with a strong sense of its debased and indefensible state.

The Holy Ecclesiastical Synod is the Patriarch of Moscow in Commission, & practically is the Registry of the will of the Czar.

But your third point I admit to be graver, I mean the stringency of my view respecting the Provincial organization. Here[139] I confess[140] you have me at a disadvantage: for the Divine Office of the Church is[141] in the 'Episcopatus undique diffusus',[d] and a[142] province, or two provinces are a very uncertain exponent of its judgment.[143]

But the difficulty is not of my making. There is a saying about the bed as we make it.[144]

See the definition of Lucius Ferraris, 'Ordinaria (jurisdictio) est illa quae cuipiam, jure proprio, seu ratione officii, aut dignitatis suae, ex lege, canone, vel consuetudine competit', in *Promta bibliotheca canonica, juridica, moralis, theologica: necnon ascetica, polemica, rubricistica, historica (juris Hispanici hodie etiam vocabitur) de principalioribus, et fere omnibus, quae in dies occurrunt, nec penes omnes facile, ac promte reperiri possunt, ex utroque jure, pontificiis constitutionibus, conciliis, sacr. congregationum decretis, sacrae Romanae Rotae decisionibus, ac probatissimis et selectissimis auctoribus. Accurate collecta, adaucta, in unum redacta, et ordine alphabetico congesta, ac in decem tomos distributa. In hac editione, secunda Hispana non solum additiones legales, jam antea publicatae, accedunt, sicut in prima, verum etiam leges, auctoris doctrinam astruentes, permultaeque aliae adnotationes, eisdem decisionibus insistentes, numquam antea aditae | opera ac studio id totum elaboratum . . . Francisci Mariae Vallarna* (10 vols.; Madrid: Typis et sumptibus Regiæ typographorum et bibliopolarum societatis, 1795), V. Jurisdictio, n. 6. Cf. Ayliffe (1726), 319: 'Now ordinary Jurisdiction, is that which arises to anyone, either by means of some Written-Law, or Hereditary-Right, or else by the way of Custom or Privilege; or, thirdly, is that which is conferred on anyone by the Grace and Favour of the Prince or State whereunto he belongs. [marg.] Bart. in L. 5. D. 2.1. N.9; Lyndewood Lib 5, Tit. 5, Cap 2.' Cf. also William Lyndewood, *Constitutiones Angliae Provinciales ex diversis Cantuariensium Archiepiscopum Synodalibus decretis* . . . (London: Thomas Marbst, 1557), Bk. 1 Tit. 3.

[d] The episcopate, everywhere diffused; 'episcopatus unus episcoporum multorum concordi numerositate diffusus' (Cyprian, *Letters*, 55. 24. 2). Cf. 400805mg, Cyprian, *On the Unity of the Church*, 5: 'Episcopatus unus est cuius a singulis in solidum pars tenetur. Ecclesia una est quae in multitudinem latius incremento fecunditatis extenditur' (PL 4. 501).

A provincial Synod is the maximum of evidence or judgment[145] we[146] possess, and I feel[147] little difficulty in maintaining its supremacy[148] within the four seas.[e] But I confess I can say little when the challenge[149] comes from over the water. And here I feel the real flaw in your Pamphlet & in my own. Both are insular and I am without any adequate defence for our separation from the Universal Church, whose authority & tradition we claim to hold.

The more I look into it, the less I can uphold or palliate it, by any real proofs.

Your ὑποκόρισμος[f] about 'reattaching' the Church of England to the 'Roman obedience' I find hard to reconcile with the article of the Creed, which says the Church is One.[150]

In truth can a divided Church speak with authority?[151] If local Churches may err how do I know that the Church of England has not erred for 300 years?

And what security is there for its judgments in appeal: the water cannot rise above its source!

I wish you would tell me how these last points are solved in your mind. At all events let me hear of you and yours.[152]

Ever your affect[ionat]e friend,
H. E. Manning

The Right Hon[oura]ble
W. E. Gladstone
[[Pitts; Chapeau, 173, 249–50 (original and copy)]]

500825gm[a]
Private

Hawarden Aug[ust] 25.[18]50

My dear Manning

We have now got little Mary at the sea and we hope that she has derived some benefit from it:[b] but nothing has occurred to remove or lighten the obvious necessity for our taking her abroad. We expect to go about

---

[e] That is, in Great Britain.   [f] Use of diminutives.

[a] 'Wrote to Manning' (*GD* iv. 234).

[b] On 21 August 1850 Gladstone went with his wife and daughter, Mary, to Rhyl, and the following day moved her to a 'sea-lodging' there (ibid. 234).

the 8th or 10th of October, and to be a week in London before setting out. The month of September I am to spend at Fasque.[c] My wife will be chiefly here or at Hagley for the next five weeks.

I don't know whether it is worth while at present to pursue the discussion about the Judicial Supremacy of the Crown for at the present time our difference I think[153] is not practical: & the juncture in which it could become so would be one greatly advanced and improved in comparison with this. Of course however I admit, the Crown cannot be an Ordinary in the proper sense. When I urged it being the symbol of the Supreme *Power*, I meant to lay the stress wholly on the last word: on an idea which does not belong to Church Authority at all: but is conferred by the State & is distinct from the guiding mind & from authority.[154] There is a dilemma involved in the very foundation of a national establishment of religion: and I have some doubt whether your present form of reasoning is not too strait for its solution: but I have no heart to contest that matter, at a time when I sadly feel that it is now become or fast becoming one practically insoluble.

I do not think so badly of the Church in Russia as you do. I could assent indeed to the terms 'debased and indefensible' for it: but on principles which would certainly insure their application &, though in[155] different senses, with equal force, to the Church of England and the Church of Rome. I don't believe the Synod is practically the registry of the will of the Czar: you might I think have said with more justice it was so theoretically. I find in that Church a strict and unbroken custody of the faith, much more than in the Church of Rome: art, literature, civilisation, I can hardly look for in a people so late and recent in European society: my mind revolts from its exclusive and anathematising spirit but in this unhappily it only imitates &[156] retaliates upon the Church of the West.

My third point you have turned round upon me, and given it a sense different from my idea, but one no doubt of infinite importance. My answer will be clear. I find the Church in fractions. One of these pretends to be the whole Church but palpably is not for there are other vast bodies which even *its* own voice admits to hold the faith while it condemns them as in schism. *As* to *us*, I entirely feel with you 1. that our Provincial Synod is the Judge of Faith within the four seas 2. that it is after all an insular authority. I might feel the force of the 'challenge that comes over the water'

---

[c] Gladstone left for Fasque on 30 August 1850 (ibid. 235), and returned to Hawarden on 24 September (ibid. 240). He was in London again on 14 October, and on 18 October left for the Continental trip (ibid. 244–5).

if it came from *one*: but it does not. I *may* feel it, if present fears grow into reality, and the Church of England ceases to teach the Faith with authority and in its oneness—you ask[157] is it possible to defend our separation from the Universal Church? I reply it is impossible, by any act in the power of man, to rejoin the Universal Church; for in rejoining one part you must anathematise another. There is no act or form of duty that seems so high in these days (if in any days)[158] as to strive for[159] 'reconciling the members of Christ's body in the Unity of the Divine Kingdom': if I desire *anything* with sincerity, with my whole soul I desire that: the Church of Rome of necessity enters largely into any such conception but in my conscience I believe that no living men have done so much to prevent the reunion of England with the Western Church as those who by seceding to it have brought our communion to the verge of disorganisation, and given to the popular heresy, which was fast sinking into annihilation, a strong, perhaps it may prove a triumphant position. True you do not speak of reuniting individuals, but the *Church* of England. That is a very different matter. Still, how can I desire that the Church of England should become party to an anathema upon other portions of the household of Christ?

It may seem chimerical to say, would to God that the See of Rome would be content with having its own abuses and corruptions endured, and would be more enduring towards others, and fling away the curse that it deals except where they are uttered in vindication of the Faith of Christ. Perhaps it is so: perhaps she has bound herself too fast to what in brevity but not in jest I will call the neck or nothing policy: further, perhaps, even being such as she is, she nevertheless may be the last compulsory home of all who, in the[160] West at least, intend with God's help to hold by a definite revealed truth: but if it be so, a long and loud alas! for Christendom.

It seems to me, I confess, that what[161] we want is the divine art to draw from the present terrible calamities and appalling prospects the conquering secret which doubtless they contain, the secret which shall realise the object you yourself have clearly and recently set upon me: namely to rise through this struggle into something better than historical Anglicanism, which essentially depended upon conditions that have now passed away: to struggle to turn the present position to account for Christendom, which those now engaged in resisting the Committee and its Judgment may do, if God shall so turn their hearts.

I rejoice to see that you are at work bringing this resistance into form. We see no new sign of hope from the Bishops. He of Exeter seems to me to have befooled himself—I hope but know not that the word is too strong—

by his letter to the Churchwardens.[d] Under these circumstances much passes through the mind, such is my experience, which for the present defies verbal expression: and I feel that I cannot write a letter, even to you without misrepresenting myself, and the more so in proportion as I try to write seriously and plainly. Nor perhaps is this unnatural: events are in germ, so should not thought be?

But from month to month the germ unfolds: and I find in myself a growing sense of two things: first the duty to make a fight in and for the actual Church of England. On which I propound this question: whether any man ought to *resign* a charge or post of trust in her until she has herself either by Convocation or by the Episcopate accepted the Judgment itself (as some Bishops certainly have), or the authority of the Committee (as others have). At first it seemed to me that supposing the B[isho]p of E[xeter] to renounce obedience to his metropolitan & to be deprived, that then others should resign & not prolong the contest: but now I ask myself whether they can lawfully give up a cure of souls (say) which they have lawfully had laid upon them, unless either in one of the cases I have already named, or in the case that the Judgment shall have grown by use into clear law.

The other point I have to name is one which perhaps drew your notice in my draft[162] letter to the B[isho]p of London.[e] Will not many remain in the Church of England avowedly for the purpose of effecting a change in her position? If the State will not allow her to construe her own laws, and itself plainly & wilfully misconstrues them, will they not perhaps say *summa res agitur*,[f] you must not speak to me of this or that detail, you want to destroy the life of the Church, I must struggle to save it? Is it among the possibilities of this strange time that we should see men, clerical and lay, in the Church of England, avowedly endeavouring to *negotiate* with the See of Rome? I do not much like the word which I have used: but as to the thing I can conceive of postures of affairs in which it might be warrantable or even[163] laudable. Thus much I strongly feel that whatever sense of *duty* may remain, or whatever love, towards that ancient & venerable branch of the Catholic Church under whose shadow we have grown up, a great & rapid change is passing upon my feelings towards its rulers & representatives

[d] Henry [Phillpotts] Lord Bishop of Exeter, *A Letter to the Churchwardens of the Parish of Brampford Speke* (London: John Murray, 1850; preface dated 16 Aug. 1850).

[e] On the draft see 500719mg.

[f] The highest matter is at stake. Cf. Horace, *Epistles*, 1. 18. 84: nam tua res agitur, paries cum proximus ardet (for your situation is at stake, when your neighbour's wall is burning).

as such: or at the least, it now becomes a question in each case what sentiments are due to this or that priest or Bishop, according as he has shown his intention to cast his lot this way or that in the great agony that has begun.

A month in freer Scotland will be some relief[g]—I never wrote a letter which had so much need of your pardon. While[164] laying down principles on which I ought not to have written anything, I have filled three sheets: and that with matters which if touched at all should have spread over 30 or 300. It is one added to those trials of your patience, of which the catalogue is long already.

My address is Fasque

Believe me always
Your aff[ectiona]te friend
W. E. Gladstone

Venerable
Archdeacon Manning

[[BL Add. MS 44248, 91–6; Morley transcript; Lathbury, i. 113–17; cf. Leslie, 92–3, Chapeau, 338]]

500827mg

Lavington. Aug[ust] 27. 1850.

Private

My dear Gladstone,

A friend of W[illia]m Monsell, the Rev[eren]d W[illiam] Todd—brother of Dr. Todd of T[rinity] C[ollege] Dublin,[a] & a very able & excellent man is like many more in extreme perplexity. He has resigned his curacy that he may give himself to make up his mind—thereby he has given up all his means—& is very poor.

He has been with me ten days & I am much impressed by his acuteness, goodness & devotion. He is most willing to be advised and to listen & read. But he shrinks from the oaths & subscriptions.

---

[g] Gladstone left for Scotland on 30 August 1850 (*GD* iv. 235), staying this time only for a few weeks and returning on 23 September (ibid. iv. 240).

[a] William George Todd (1829–77; *DNB*), MA Trinity College, Dublin, curate of St James, Bristol, was received into the Roman Catholic Church in 1851. On 9 January 1841 James Henthorn Todd (1805–69) of Trinity College, Dublin (Professor of Hebrew, 1849) was part of a group who approached Gladstone, informing him of the work of the College and of the group there working with converts from Catholicism (BL Add. MS 44357, 253–7).

His desire is to employ himself in tending sick, or teaching. What he would most desire is to be as Tutor for a time, above all abroad. And this brought your name across my mind.

I do not know whether you have seen his book on the Church of St. Patrick.[b]

Having said thus much I will say no more than that if such a thought be within your consideration he is a very fit man to undertake such a charge.

Let me know when you come to London that I may not fail to see you.

Believe me,

Ever affect[ionatel]y yours,

H. E. Manning

The Right Hon[oura]ble
W. E. Gladstone
[[Pitts; Chapeau, 174, 251]]

500830gm[a]

Hawarden Chester

Aug[ust] 30. 1850.

My dear Manning

I have just got your note about Mr. Todd. I know his book[b] & even without, much more than with, your account of him, I should be delighted if I knew of a suitable opening for such a man. But I think you are under a misapprehension about me. I do not take Willy abroad. Indeed I might add that if I did I could not well afford at present to add a Tutor & must try myself to discharge that function.

A good[165] man & churchman[166] but one perhaps apt to take up rumours, writes to me that he fears the Feildings[c] are about to join the

---

[b] William G. Todd, *The Church of St. Patrick: An Historical Inquiry into the Independence of the Ancient Church of Ireland* (London: John W. Parker, 1844).

[a] 'Wrote to . . . Manning' (*GD* iv. 235).

[b] Gladstone read Todd's *Church of St. Patrick* on 11 June 1844 (*GD* iii. 381).

[c] Not located. What was striking was the speed with which the Feildings moved; Feilding had chaired the 23 July 1850 meeting on the Gorham Decision and was received into the Catholic Church one month later, on 28 August (see *The Guardian*, 11 Sept. 1850, 647–8). The same issue of *The Guardian* reprinted Feilding's letter to *The Times*, dated 3 September (*The Times*, 6 Sept. 1850, 4f; *The Guardian*, 11 Sept., 650). Note Hope's letter to Gladstone a few days later on 6 September: 'I have heard a good deal on the Feilding's change: it is attributed more immediately to her—but however brought about I cannot think hardly of it. Rather I feel as if those were to be congratulated who have already done that wh[ic]h *intellectually*, & to a great extent *morally*, I feel persuaded should be done' (BL

Ch[urch] of Rome immediately and wishes I could write to you or some one in whom they have confidence to check them. You probably know the case whatever it may be; but[167] if you do not happen to be in possession of the actual state of things, it may be well that this should come to you—My correspondent wishes me not to name him, which I think foolish: but I have described him. If there be trouble in the account, I apprehend it must be on the specific ground of the Gorham Judgment: & for all such persons it is as plainly right, as obviously in the highest sense prudent, that they should not at such a crisis act individually without having at least consulted others having a common interest & feeling. L[or]d F[eilding] seems to me very good but rather too like a cork: & he is the kind of man who some months ago might I think have in some degree profited by the scheme which miscarried[d]—

I am on the point of starting for Fasque—

I should have thought it likely that Mr. Todd might have found something to his mind in Scotland, where though at this moment there is strife, there is freedom; & the strife is on a much higher ground than ours, for it is about particulars among those who are entirely brethren, as I believe, in the principles both of authority & of sacramental grace.

I remain
Ever aff[ectiona]tely yours
W.E.G.

Ven[erable]
H. E. Manning
[[BL Add. MS 44248, 97–8; Morley transcript; Leslie transcript]]

500901mg

Lavington. Sept[ember] 1. 1850.

My dear Gladstone,

I have to thank you for two letters: especially for the former of Aug[ust] 25. There was only one sentence to quarrel with, where you apologized for writing it.

Add. MS 44214, 345–6, 346). Manning had preached at the laying of the foundation stone of Feilding's church in Wales in the autumn of 1849 (Leslie, 86–7, and Elwes (1950), 43. See also Edward George Kirwan Browne, *Annals of the Tractarian Movement, from 1842 to 1860* [London: The author, 1861], 210, 605.)

[d] See 500520gmff.

Today is Sunday, & the work of the day is over. I am more disposed to 'go into the fields to meditate at eventide'[a] than to enter upon the subjects on which we have lately written. If I touch on them it shall only be upon the more personal & passive side.

But first I must say that what you have heard of the Feildings will certainly come true. I have heard from them. At Edinburgh they have become known to Bishop Gillies:[b] and he has decided them. I wrote praying them to do nothing till I could see them: but they answered that their decision was made.

I did not know whether you have heard that the same event has befallen Henry Wilberforce's wife. He has not moved: but I cannot look for any other event.[c]

Now in all these questions I distinguish between the intellectual & the spiritual discernment. The intellectual I feel better able to apply: and if I went by this alone I should feel that the Anglican system has little it can maintain against the Roman Church. But I misgive my own spiritual discernment and fear to go by intellect alone lest truths should be hid from me which are revealed unto babes. Such instances as my two Sisters in law—Sophia Ryder & Mary Wilberforce[d] weigh much with me in this point. I have known them long, intimately, and thoroughly. Two more devout, devoted, spotless, chastened spirits, I have never known. If a knowledge of Gods truth came by doing & learning His will I feel that they may be guides to me.

[a] Gen. 24: 63.

[b] Prior to their reception into the Roman Catholic Church by James Gillies on 28 August 1850, Rudolph and Louisa Feilding wrote to Manning to inform him of their decision. He replied on 22 August (Elwes [1950], 49–50). James Gillies (1802–64) was educated in Montreal and Paris and in 1837 was appointed coadjutor to Bishop Andrew Carruthers, Vicar Apostolic of the Eastern District of Scotland. In 1838 he was consecrated Bishop of Limyra in partibus and in 1852 succeeded Carruthers as Vicar Apostolic. Note in particular James Gillis, *Facts and Correspondence Relating to the Admission into the Catholic Church of Viscount and Viscountess Feilding* (Edinburgh: Ch. Dolman, 1850).

[c] Mary Wilberforce was received into the Roman Catholic Church at her residence in London on 22 June 1850 (*LD* xiii. 455; on the importance of his sister-in-law, Mary Wilberforce, in Manning's own life see as well Eastwood [2006]). Henry Wilberforce was received several months later, on 15 September 1850. On Wilberforce's theological reasons for the action see his *Reasons for Submitting to the Catholic Church: A Farewell Letter to the Parishioners of East Farleigh, Kent* (4th edn. with postscript, 1854; 1st edn. dated 10 Jan. 1851).

[d] Sophia Ryder's husband, George Dudley Ryder, was received on 5 May 1846, she herself several days later. See *LD* xii. 162–8, Adams (1977), 1–5, and Newsome (1966), 310–11.

What will you say to me if I reverse your view about them who leave us: & say that such losses are necessary: that they are the conditions of re-uniting: the only effectual rebukes, warnings, and rods to waken us and teach us self knowledge & humiliation. Our compact, unassailed, unhumbled Anglicanism was our sin and our bondage. It must be broken at any cost. All this, taking the highest view of our claims. We have been too worldly, self approving and self confident. My belief is that all we have lost has been for our sure gain at last: & that if we had not lost we should have dissembled & prospered in this world. There are fearful signs about us: Insensibility to the World unseen, shallow perceptions both of sin & of sanctity, low ideals: torpor of conscience: indifference to objects of Faith & Worship. The evils of the R[oman] C[hurch] are more external & mater-ial: we see and note them: but ours are inward spiritual and of exceeding subtlety. Such are my thoughts. So much for Sunday. Before long I may trouble you again not on the Supremacy any more but on a deeper matter. May God bless and guide you always.

Ever your affect[ionat]e friend,
H. E. Manning

The Right Hon[oura]ble
W. E. Gladstone

[[Pitts; Chapeau, 175, 251–2]]

[[On 5 September 1850 Gladstone wrote to Catherine and in a postscript noted: 'I advise Henry to sign Manning's declaration about the Supremacy if he agrees with it' (SDL, Glynne–Gladstone MS 771, 281, 281–2). Gladstone had heard word concerning Manning three days earlier from Richard Cavendish who, after a visit to Laving-ton, wrote to Gladstone on 3 September:

I paid Manning a visit last week at Lavington. Though he is the last man in the world to take any hasty or ill considered step, & though he is so deeply impressed with a sense of the great responsibility which attaches to every step which he takes, still I fear he is more than ever likely to come to the conclusion that there is but *one* alternative & that, the one that you & I would be most sorry to see acted upon by him. He seems fully persuaded that the great bulk of the clergy & laity of the English Church will acquiesce in the present state of things—that then, she will cease to have any claims to be considered as a true branch of the Church Catholic. Should such prove to be the case, he would then feel that it would no longer be a question about Rome or England but about the universal Church, & he could not safely remain where he is—Of course you who have known him so well are aware that such are his views & expectations, but I am anxious to impress on you the necessity of doing what you can to encourage him to take a more hopeful view of our position & prospects. I believe no one has such influence over him as you have, or is so likely to retain him—

About 1500 Clergy had then signed the declaration regarding the oath of Supremacy put forth by him, R[obert] Wilberforce & Dr. Mill. The Bishop of Oxford was at Lavington, & he was also of opinion that Manning took if possible a more gloomy view of things than he had previously done. (BL Add. MS 44124, 259–61, 261–2).

According to Purcell (1892), 431 Gladstone wrote to Wilberforce on the same day, 5 September,[e] stating 'that from the conversations that had taken place and the letters that had passed between Archdeacon Manning and himself, an impression was created in his mind, that though the Archdeacon was convinced of the authority of the Church of England, and believed in her mission, yet he could not disguise from himself, that there were things in the Roman Church that he preferred. Mr Gladstone, therefore, attributed the decided attitude of Archdeacon Manning to the result of the refusal of the Bishops to propagate a declaration that the Gorham Judgment was neither the law nor the faith of the Church of England.']]

4. The Growth of Separation: September–October 1850

500905mg

Lavington. Sept[ember] 5. 1850.

My dear Gladstone,

Before I say anything else I must tell you, as Mrs. Herbert desired not knowing whence to direct, that they have moved to the Caledonian Hotel, Inverness, to obtain hourly medical attendance for their little girl. She has I fear water on the head. Her poor Mother writes in great distress & asks all our prayers. She says of you—'They will know how to feel for us'.[a]

It seems strange to see you, Herbert, & Lincoln so united in public & private life and all three sharing the discipline. It is all good as they who have well used it, & even they who have used it as ill as others,[168] bear witness. And it brings 'peace at the last.'[b]

[e] There is no reference to the writing of such a letter in *GD* on or shortly after that date.

[a] See the Herberts' letter to Manning, 2 September 1850, regarding their child's health and asking Manning to inform the Gladstones (Bodl. MS Eng. lett. c. 657, 51–2). On the health of their child note also their letters to Manning of 19 August (ibid. 48–50) and 8 September (ibid. 53–5).

[b] Ps. 37: 38 (Book of Common Prayer).

I said on Sunday[c] that I should write to you again. Your letters have given me so many points that I have seemed to pass them by. And now I cannot retrace them for fear of laying a penance on you in a heap of paper.

I will therefore only say a single word in passing on two points.

One was what you said of a Church taking much killing[d] & the inferences.

Life does not seem to me to prove a body to be a Church nor long life a Catholic Church. The Kirk and the Nestorians seem to be a full reply. Nevertheless a living much more a long lived body may be *materially* tho' not *formally* a Church. It may be as the Nestorians are a Church needing only restoration to Catholic Unity in certain points.

This seems to me to make a large & good plea for the Church of England in posse.[e] But to fail in the very crisis.

It leaves us under sentence. The other point is the view you use, as we all did of old, respecting the manifold portions of the now divided visible Church.

This brings me to what I intended to write.

I have been using the best inquiry I can into the nature of the Church as revealed in Holy Scripture: and examining the interpretations of the first ages.

It seems to me that indivisibleness of communion was held to be by a Divine necessity, so that any person or portion falling off, or being in fact separate ceased to be of the Church; & yet the indivisible remainder was the Church as fully as before. Ephes. IV. 1–16. especially vv.13. & 16. appear to me to be decisive, speaking popularly. In the whole passage I see[169] that the Church is:[170]—

1. One. v.4. A Body Visible.

2. Living by the Life of the Head.

3. Organized by unity of members.

4. Self edifying by Pastors of itself.

5. Successive in all time.

6. Self contained by harmony of parts.

7. Conscious of its own intelligence & charity.

8. Divinely guided for the sake of its members.

9. Perpetual & self edifying until its work shall be complete—the number and perfection of the elect—'the Christ Mystical'.

---

[c] Sunday, 1 September 1850. See 500901mg.
[d] See 500623gm.   [e] In possibility.

All this appears to me to show *that indivisibleness is of the essence of indefect-ibility*—except so far as a living body may lose members. But they are no longer of the body. They *were*, but *are* not.

And also it shows *that indivisible unity is essential to the functions of life intelligence, & love.*

I have no doubt that you know Möhlers book on the Unity of the Church.[f] It is a small work[171] written when he was young but very able.

Now I confess it is no argument to me to say 'This is ideal. Look at the history and the face ['; manuscript torn]. The same answer [manuscript torn] threw the unity of the Person of our Lord, and the unity of the B[lessed] Trinity. Against these three unities the world has striven with a running series of contradictions. The Branch Church Theory is the Arianism of Indivisible unity.

With this view I find the whole Church East and West for 600 years pervaded: e.g. S[t]. Cyprian De Unitate & S[t]. Chrys[ostom] on Ephes. IV.1–16.[172][g] At [manuscript torn]t East & [manuscript torn] & continued it [manuscript torn]nd on each side to itself exclusively.[173]

Neither ever dreamed of a *divisible* unity.

I can find no trace of it till I find also presbyterian orders, & lay elders. It is a theory peculiarly Anglican that is of a school in the English Church.

All this I state in the fewest words. To write[174] all I could would be endless. I feel it very deeply as bearing on our present stranded state: and on the 'insular' position.

On no side is there Bishop or Priest able to steer. For we have no helm, and if we had the ship will no longer answer.

The letters which pour in on me (these three weeks) are beyond belief. If the idea of number had been effaced from the English mind the arithmetical chaos would give some notion of our Eccles[iastical] theories:

---

[f]   See Johann Adam Möhler, *De l'unité de l'église, ou du principe du catholicisme d'après l'esprit des pères des trois premiers siècles*, trans. from German by Philippe Bernard (Tournai: Castermann, 1835). Manning's annotated version of the work is preserved in Pitts Theology Library, Emory University, Atlanta, Ga. (signature: 1834 Möhl). The translation was reprinted in Brussels by H. Remy in 1839 and again in the same year in Paris by Sagnier et Bray. It first appeared as *Die Einheit in der Kirche oder das Prinzip des Katholizismus dargestellt im Geiste der Kirchenväter der ersten drei Jahrhunderte* (Tübingen: Heinrich Laupp, 1825). For details see the introduction to Möhler (1996).

[g]   Note particularly homilies 10 and 11 on Eph. 4: 4 and 4: 4–7 in John Chrysostom, *Commentary on the Epistle to the Galatians and, Homilies on the Epistle to the Ephesians*, trans. with notes and indices; Library of Fathers of the Holy Catholic Church, 5 (Oxford : J. H. Parker, 1840). Note also PG 61. 611ff. and 62. 5ff.

for the *idea* of the Church Teaching & Ruling for Christ: & of Christ in it, & through it has been effaced. And I must believe that the separation effaced it.

I have therefore no longer power or faith to work on a basis of separation.

Do not *force* yourself to write or lose your rest & holidays on me. When we meet in London, God willing, we may talk of this. But it is as I said in my last a deep matter and all depends on it.

And now I will only add my hope that Mary is not adding to your anxieties about her.[175]

> With all kind words & my love to your wife, believe me, always,
> affect[ionatel]y yours,
> H. E. Manning

The Right Hon[oura]ble
W. E. Gladstone
[[Pitts; Chapeau, 176, 252–5]]

500908gm[a]

Fasque Sept[ember] 8. 1850.

My dear Manning

I deeply grieve over the intelligence you send me about Mrs. Herbert's baby. I fear they too are to endure the sharp pain of the severance of that heartstring with which Nature binds the parent to the child. I shall write to my wife, but there is no post till tomorrow:[b] her prayers when she hears from me will not be wanting.

But the pains which come in the way of God's ordinary dispensations are light compared with those which belong to the religious convulsion of the present time. If flesh writhes under the former, at least Faith is not perplexed but feels that her appointed work is passing and taking effect upon her. But in the changes which I see taking place on every side of me, both in the Church of England, and in those who deplore her changes, there is no such consolation. The grief for the loss of children has a natural

---

[a] 'Wrote to Manning' (*GD* iv. 237).

[b] Gladstone did not report the matter to Catherine until 14 September 1850 when he wrote to her: 'I heard about the Herberts on Sunday from Manning, in terms which ought to have made it impossible for me to forget to name it to you on Monday, for they were these, that you should pray for them. It was a shameful omission—not the less so because some other person has supplied it' (SDL, Glynne–Gladstone MS 771, 297–8, 298).

vent in tears: but tears do not come, and would not be adequate if they did, for the laying waste of the heritage of God. The promise indeed stands sure to the Church and to the elect. In the farthest distance there is peace, truth, glory: but what a leap to it, over what a gulf. You see nearer comfort: you have the advantage of me, if you are right & see truly.

In the grounds and materials of judgment neither intellectually nor morally can I compete with you. As to the last let me not go beyond those words of to-day's Psalms, which are given for our use and may be used therefore without affectation. 'My wickednesses are gone over my head and are like a sore burden too heavy for me to bear!'[c] As to the first I follow you from letter to letter with amazement. I know not indeed how far your thoughts are tentative, how far they are entire expressions of your mind: but while each letter is in itself a polished whole, & would defy greater skill than mine to undo, taken as a series they are not fixed, nor consistent, nor consecutive. Your last especially passes quite beyond my power to follow. I am wholly unable to conceive how the theory of the Church and its unity that is now before you can stand application to the times of schism in the Roman Church itself when both parties had the intention of union with the Chair of St. Peter but were in fact divided & one of them therefore is smitten by your doctrine though both are recognised as Catholic by the Roman Church. The Branch Church theory is hers: only she makes a more limited application of it. To my eye the reasoning of your letter seems so far from your former self, to say no more, that it leaves me in doubt and perplexity as to its real purport, and extorts from me by force the question whether your intellect is for the moment in the class of those of which the extreme power and facility, and their[176] satisfaction, unconscious often yet a great reality, in their own vivid play, become snares to the possessor and seduce him from fixity by the smoothness and ease they shew in movement. But if you are deceived you will need some other and worthier one to undeceive you. I am suspicious and afraid of the disposition you state to follow in the path of relatives whose sanctity you venerate for surely though personal sanctity may give us every comfort respecting the person so blessed, it does not make such person a guide for others in the changes they may make, and to view them so is unsafe & in principle: but I would readily admit and feel, that modesty at least should be with those who have no such title written upon them, that the freedom I use as friend with friend ill suits me, (it is really so: te

---

[c] Cf. Ps. 38: 4.

propter eundem. Amissus pudor;[d])[177] and that I am fitter to be mute at last for a time in the presence of such deep problems and such crushing sorrows as seem to be coming upon us.

Ever your aff[ectiona]te friend
W. E. Gladstone

The first days of October will I think see us in London.[e] We have no change to report.

Venerable

Archd[eaco]n Manning.

[[BL Add. MS 44248, 99–101; Morley transcript; Leslie transcript; Lathbury, i. 355–6 (merged with BL Add. MS 44248, 102–5); Purcell, i. 570–2]]

[[On 8 September 1850, the same day as his earlier letter to Manning, Gladstone wrote to Hawkins at Oriel, commenting:

I lament to say that my own views are still dark and gloomy with respect to the Gorham Judgment and its consequences, and to the appellate jurisdiction of the Church. No former struggle has made me doubt the strength of the Church of England to bear, and even to derive new force from, the trial. The features of this seem to me new and very formidable. In the present opinions or impressions of such a man as Manning, though I may not follow them, I read new evidence of the power of the shock which has shaken him on his ground. With Dr. Pusey and Mr. Keble I have had little intercourse of any kind: but with Manning for many years, the closest and most constant, & for a large proportion of these years the most *cordial* union in all *practical* convictions. To feel that a space is interposing itself between us is to me little short of agony: and, if you knew him as I have done, I am sure you would share my sentiments of unbounded admiration and affection for him. But I am wandering into impertinences. My desire was to convey my thanks. (Oriel College Library MS Gladstone–Hawkins Correspondence, GL7)

On 8 September, as well, he wrote to Samuel Wilberforce, transferring some moneys collected for the Wantage Penitentiary,[f] and noted:

Possibly you may remember a conversation in a Committee Room of the House of Lords in which I expressed my belief that Manning might be saved to the Church of England. I am still convinced that that belief was then correct. I dare not say the same as to the present time. It seems to me likely that if he shall go, he will do it upon broad ground reaching far back into history as well as forward into

---

[d] Cf. Virgil, *Aeneid*, 4. 321–2: te propter eundem | exstinctus pudor (for you also my honour is lost).

[e] Gladstone was in London 2–5 October 1850 and again 14–18 October (*GD* iv. 241–2, 244–5).

[f] See 500619mcg.

the future: upon these grounds avowedly, not really, though less consciously, in consequence of the equivocal and hesitating attitude of the Church of England during the past months of crisis with respect to the maintenance of the faith. If you yourself, if a few other Bishops have declared that the doctrine of Baptism will be by them maintained as the doctrine of the Church, such has not been the voice of the English Episcopate at large.

I write this not as apprising Manning's state of mind, which you probably have had the best opportunities of judging: but because I feel the responsibility of what I said, and the duty of modifying it when the grounds of it appear to be impaired.

Not that I at all despair. His mind has it seems to me fluctuated much: his almost unrivalled intellect giving to each momentary phase all the semblance of completeness and solidity. Even now I believe he would be secure—and with him many more, of such men as are not to be numbered but weighed—were there a hope of a resolute movement, if not corporate, yet at least combined.

Perhaps I need hardly add, he has not led me to the point at which he stands. (Bodl. MS Wilberforce d. 35, 80–1)

Two days later, on 10 September, Catherine informed Gladstone that 'Henry [Glynne] *did* sign the Manning paper. I was rather amazed to see Ffloukes ½ frightened at doing so. I think he is one who easily believes what he hears & idle reports are ripe. Can I say anything to back him?' (SDL, Glynne–Gladstone MS 612).[g]

[g] Gladstone was also continuing to receive correspondence at the time from Cavendish concerning Manning. Cavendish had written on 15 September 1850:

I was present at the meeting of our diocesan association on Thursday last. Manning came & spoke, shortly, but, if possible, more beautifully than even he usually does. I had a long talk with him afterwards & I grieve to say that he is deliberating whether or no he shall resign his preferments. He spoke of the great importance which he attached to *public honour*, & seemed to doubt whether he should be acting consistently with his sense of it in retaining his present position—You know so well his whole mind respecting the actual position of our Church that I need not repeat what he said on this subject. I said what I could to dissuade him from taking a step which I fear would only be a prelude to a still more lamentable one. I told him that as long as he felt that he could fight for the Church of England with a sincere desire that she should come victorious out of the struggle in which she is now engaged, whatever his anticipations may be as to the possible result, his continuance in his present position seemed to me compatible with the most scrupulous & refined sense of honour. He did not dissent altogether from this & ended by saying that as soon as the Bishop's confirmations & visitation should be over he would open his whole mind to him.

I fear that the way in which his & R[obert] Wilberforce's & Mill's declaration on the subject of the Supremacy has been received, has made him more desponding than ever before. Barter's letter which doubtless you saw in the last week's Guardian is a sad sign of the degree of mistrust felt now with regard to him. He seems to think that being an object of suspicion as he now is, he can only do harm to the cause by attempting anything more.

On 17 September, Gladstone again wrote to Wilberforce in response to a letter from him on the same day:[h]

With regard to any anti-Roman appendix to his declaration, it is of course out of the question as regards him. He said emphatically, 'Whatever I do, I will not dissemble.'

I have thought it desirable that you should be in possession of what I have told you, in order that it may not come upon you unprepared when you meet in October. I feel that I may tell *you* what I could not tell anyone else without a breach of confidence towards Manning (BL Add. MS 44124, 263–6; On 11 September, 1850 William Brudenell Barter, rector of Burgchlere and Highclere, republished a letter in the *Guardian*, 651, stating that he would not sign the Manning, Wilberforce, Mill declaration in any case, but particularly since 'we are left in doubt by its promoters whether, if such and such things take place or are remedied, a secession may not be contemplated to the Church of Rome.' Then follows an attack on the Roman Church, quoted from the Barter's earlier, *The English Church not in Schism* [London: F. & J. Rivington and James Burns, 1845]. The letter was responded to by Mill in the next issue of the *Guardian*, 18 September 1850, 668. In response on the Barter matter, Manning wrote to an Arthur Barter on 6 September 1850, regretting that William Barter had not written to him privately and noting among other things: 'I believe the Royal Supremacy as by Statute, & the late Judgment to be at variance with the Will or the Truth of our Blessed Lord. And I hold myself bound to resign my charge if the Church of England shall acquiesce in them. I shall then feel that the Church of England has put me from her' [Pitts]).

Again, two days later, on 17 September, Cavendish wrote:

. . . that very great good might be done if Manning would put forth an appeal to the Bishops, Clergy & laity of the English Church, on the subject of the Supremacy & the present state of the Church in general—His letter to the B[isho]p of Chichester is hardly popular enough for the purpose, & it would perhaps be possible for him to state the matter in a way more likely to arouse the popular mind. In addition to this he might append a few words of earnest exhortation to English Churchmen to bestir themselves with all their might in order to place the Church in a more favourable position. Such an appeal from him would, I am sure have an immense effect, & I cannot see that there is anything in his way of viewing the whole matter to prevent his making it. If you are of the same opinion, no one could propose such a step to him with at all the same hope of success as yourself.

I cannot but think that it would also be good for M[anning] himself to put forth something of the kind. He is disposed to think that he has done all he can do, & of course is all the more prone to despond from thinking so. (BL Add. MS 44124, 267–70)

[h] Samuel Wilberforce's letter was written from Lavington:

My dear Gladstone,

I have received your kind letter here where I have been spending a month of my boy's holidays at my own House. Thank you very sincerely for your and Mrs Gladstone's Contribution to the Wantage House. I trust we shall weather the great difficulties in which poor Miss Lockhart's defection has for the present involved us. My stay here has let me see much of Manning. Never has he been so affectionate, so open, so fully trusting

As to our dear friend, I quite perceive that he had attuned his mind to all the principles of the Roman system, in a more or less developed form, so far at least that all active repugnance was subdued while in most he had an active sympathy, before the Gorham Judgment. At the same time I am *sure* that before that judgment he might have been kept, had the Church of England, had her Bishops as a body, declared themselves plainly and manfully for the faith. His letters and his conversations since that date have not indeed been uniform or consistent (as I have plainly told him): but I have letters of his, written within this dark period, which I think demonstrate that he might have been held, & that not by constraint but with all his heart. I grant that even some time ago[178] he saw in the Church of Rome many things holier and more Catholic than with us: but that I think he was willing to accept as the dispensation of Providence: I do not think he had allowed his affections to become estranged. I do not think he was in the state, or anything like it, in which Newman passed his last years of Anglican profession. He had a firm faith in the mission & authority of the Church of England, because in her law she taught the faith, taught it as the faith.[179] But now comes a judgment, claiming to be her law, which denies it as faith: and the Church of England has not plainly said, whether she will endure such a law or not: and her highest Bishops join in the claim that this shall be law: and many other Bishops some actively some passively back them. This if I may work outwards from your language has not simply made practical what was in Manning's mind before, but it has thrown his convictions on the side where a larger part of his sympathies stood indeed[180] already, but were effectually neutralised by a sense of duty, not abstract and cold, but strong, commanding, & warm with life and action.

with me. We have been together through all his difficulties. But Alas! it has left on my mind the full conviction that he *is* lost to us. It is as you say the broad ground of historical enquiry where our paths part.

He seems to me to have followed singly, exactly the course which the Roman Church has followed as a body. He has gone back into those early times when, what afterwards became their corruptions were only the germ buds of Catholic usages: he has fully accustomed his mind to them: until a system which wants them seems to him incomplete & uncatholic: & one which has them is the wiser & holier & more Catholic for having them: until he can excuse to a great degree their practical corruptions; & justify altogether their doctrinal rightness. All this has been stirred up and rendered practical in his mind by our own troubles but the result of all leaves me very hopeless of the issue. Few can at all understand what *his*, & my brother's present state are to me. I believe you can: the broken sleep, the heavy waking before the sorrow has shaped itself with returning consciousness into a definite form, the vast & spreading dimensions of the Fear for others which it excites, the clouding over of the Future. It has quite pressed upon me, & I owe I believe to it as much as to anything else a sharp attack of fever which has pulled me down a good deal. (BL Add. MS 44343, 119; A. R. Ashwell, *Life of the Right Reverend Samuel Wilberforce, D.D.* [3 vols.; London: John Murray, 1880], ii. 47–8).

Now as I referred to the state of my own mind, I find myself constrained to be more full. My difficulties with Manning (I speak God knows only of those which have their seat in the speculative mind) are mainly these two: repugnance to many things tolerated and encouraged in the Church of Rome, perhaps even to some enforced, is with me still awake and energetic (without going into matters social ethical or practical more than directly religious)[181]: and secondly I think strongly, that his reason has been pushed on by the state of his sympathies and that he has judged too hastily of the Church of England. He had now indeed taken up with theories, which if he acts will probably appear to himself the ground of his actions, & will be so declared to the world: but I do not believe they will be the real and formal ground of it. But I cannot deny that, while the hesitation of the Church of England concerning the faith continues, a change comes slowly over my feeling and the whole attitude of my mind towards her. The meanest individual, holding the faith, owes no allegiance to a body which has ceased to hold it, and none other than provisional allegiance to a body which doubts whether to hold it or not. This last appears to me the predicament of the Church of England. All should feel & make allowance for the predicament in which she is placed from the want of collective organs: but that want would not have prevented her from finding a voice to make heaven and earth ring again, had the Judicial Committee, instead of denying the obligation of the Baptismal doctrine, affirmed the supremacy of the Pope. Pray interpret indulgently what I have said: for in circumstances like these the very effort to be distinct often gives cause for misapprehension. (Bodl. MS Wilberforce d. 35, 82–5; cf. Purcell, i. 568)

On the same day Gladstone informed Catherine about the correspondence:

I have been writing to the B[ish]op of Oxford who is very apprehensive about Manning—And indeed I must be apprehensive about him & many more if the Church of England quietly sets down under the abominations that have been practised. While we feel for the Feildings, and feel also the evil they have done, we must not forget what was the occasion of it, & that if they are to blame, so & much more are the perpetrators and abettors of that mischief which has been the occasion of their error, from the Archbishop !! of Canterbury downwards. Manning writes & asks when we shall be in London that he may be there. I shall not now stay to see Hope here, indeed I think John shall stop his coming as it shall be of no use. (SDL, Glynne–Gladstone MS 771, 301)[i]

---

[i] According to Arthur Wollston Hutton, *Cardinal Manning* (London: Methuen, 1892), 73–4, Gladstone responded to Wordsworth's letter, 'so admirable in its tone and thus contrasting sharply with later letters from the same hand, wherein Manning's "subtleties"

In a letter to Catherine on the following day, 18 September, Gladstone discusses the matter of appointing a chaplain, turning down one because he is not 'stiff enough about Gorham,' and then continues, 'But Manning knows a Mr. Todd who I think might be found to suit' (ibid. 303).[j]]]

and "denunciations" were bitterly referred to, as accounting for other secessions from the Church of England. Mr. Gladstone replied to the effect that from his own personal knowledge he had concluded that even before the Gorham judgment the Archdeacon's mind had become imbued with Roman Catholic ideas. He had not before that date ceased to believe in the authority and mission of the Church of England, but he had recognized behind that Church the presence of a communion more august, more venerable, more commanding. He had dwelt for near upon ten years on the vital importance of the unity of the Church. Of the three centuries of the Church of England's separate life, the seventeenth was the only one in which he could find a congenial refuge; and the more he scrutinized the doctrine of the Jacobite divines, the more he saw it was based on political expediency, without foundation in the Reformation period, and that it crumbled to nothing on the accession of William III. The demonstration that a civil court could without remedy, decide for the Church of England a point of doctrine, could hardly fail to shake an allegiance which such considerations had already effectively undermined.'

[j] Note Gladstone's annotation to his copy of Purcell's biography, marking in particular pt. 1, ch. 22 in the Index with 'NB' (PurGl i. p. xviii), and places the same annotation beside a sentence by Purcell in that chapter: 'What, I grant, is a curious difficulty, almost startling at first, is to find Manning speaking concurrently for years with a double voice' (ibid. 463). Shortly after this section, Gladstone annotates 'ma' beside each of the following sections:

To see things in one light to-day, in another to-morrow, is but natural in such a transition-state of mind. To make statements on grave matters of faith to one person or set of persons in contradiction of statements made to others, is only a still stronger proof of a sensitive mind, perplexed by doubt, losing for the time being its balance.

In Manning's mind there was a superadded difficulty: he was by nature, if not absolutely incapable, unwilling in the extreme to confess his inability to answer a question or solve a difficulty or doubt. As an accepted teacher in religion, the habit had grown upon him of speaking always on all points of faith with an absolute assurance of certitude. (Purcell, i. 464)

On the inner margin of the first of these passages, Gladstone writes: 'and to conceal from each!' (PurGl i. 463). Likewise he notes with 'NB' Purcell's comment: 'Manning had . . . two sets of people to deal with: the one set those who put their trust in him . . . ; the other set, those in whom he put his trust—his intimate friends and confessors' (ibid. 465). Gladstone marks with double bars a passage from a Manning letter of 6 May 1850, reading: 'I have not yet heard Him in my conscience saying, "Flee for thy life." Till then, I will die rather than run the risk of crossing His will' (ibid. 474). In the same way he annotates an 1846 journal entry: 'May not this be a feint of the tempter? I fearfully mistrust myself, especially when I see that those who stay seem humbler than those who have left us' (ibid.486), writing his 'ma' alongside a Manning reflection on the Assumption of the Blessed Virgin ('If Enoch and Elijah were exempted from death, why not the B. V. from sin?' [ibid. 484]), and 'NB' alongside Purcell's comment: 'It is curious to note from these entries that the break down of Manning's belief in the English Church took place so early as 1846, two years before Hampden's appointment and four years before the Gorham Judgment' (ibid. 487).

500919mg

Kippington. Sept[ember] 19. 1850.

My dear Gladstone,

I do not write to pursue further the subject of my last letter fearing that I have done so too closely already: but to ask you to oblige me by bringing with you to London, if you have not destroyed them, the letters you have received from me.

You are so grave & deliberate in word that I cannot but feel bound to suppose that you have some good ground for saying that they are neither fixed nor consistent nor consecutive. And I shall with real mistrust desire to ascertain the correctness of your judgment.

Although no infirmity of mine can affect such questions of fact as I wrote of it must deeply affect my competence to treat them. It would be unseemly for me to speak on this point further than to say that I have for long years, & never so much as now, sought the guidance of others: and have only gone alone when the manifest shrinking of others from painful or difficult duties towards the Truth has thrown me upon myself.

I was glad to hear from the Bishop of Oxford that you wrote more hopefully about your child.[a]

Believe me,
Ever your affect[ionat]e friend,
H. E. Manning

The Right Hon[oura]ble
W. E. Gladstone

[[Pitts; Chapeau, 177, 255]]

[[The growth of division between himself and Gladstone, Manning noted in a letter to Hope on 20 September 1850:

Kippington, Sevenoaks.
Sept[ember] 20, 1850.

Private

My dear Hope,

Tomorrow I trust to be in London for four or five days, & write in the chance of your being there, or if not to obtain a line from you.

I wish I could see you: & know your personal mind. For myself difficulties have thronged upon me and I begin to feel as if there can be but one

---

[a] Not located; possibly Manning heard directly on one of his visits to London.

end, & that not far off. I have been trying to get Gladstone's mind but he dwells fixedly in the view of his pamphlet. And his caution depresses me of help in my doubts.

> Let me hear from you.
> Ever affect[ionatel]y yours,
> H.E.M. (NLS MS 3675, 90–1)]]

500922gm[aa]

> Fasque Sept[ember] 22. 1850.

My dear Manning

Your letters are all safe, and accessible. I am a great letter-keeper, but however eclectic I might be, yours would have escaped the fire.

I am *not* 'grave and deliberate' in word, and there is a proof of it in the terms you quote: it was enough for me to say 'neither fixed nor consecutive' and 'nor consistent' is surplusage, but surplusage in such matter shews the want of gravity. It will probably prove that the want of consistency which there must[182] be in what is neither fixed nor consecutive,[183] lies in my inferences and constructions of your letters. I will at any rate explain what I meant: the explanation cannot make it more harsh or presumptuous, & may make it less.

I had letters from you in London, one in particular,[b] which seemed to demonstrate your conviction that if there were a body open within the pale of the Church of England ready to fight there the great battle now beginning for the Faith of Christendom & its reunion in the profession of that Faith, your lot would be cast with them: and all you might do or project would be upon & from that basis.

But the letter to which in my last I was replying[c] would have given, I thought, the impression, that you had come to the negative of the great practical proposition which you had before affirmed—

Not because of its mere words in their positive sense: for I can understand its being said 'I have no longer power or faith to work on a basis of separation' by men convinced under the teaching of the present circumstances that the unity of the visible Church ought henceforward to be the all absorbing aim of their labours, and yet having the same conviction as to the sense of those labours appointed them by the will of God that you had expressed in the former letters. But it was by putting together the general tone of the letter with its affirmations, & with the thought of what it did not

---

[aa] 'Wrote to Manning' (*GD* iv. 239).   [b] See 500619mg.   [c] That is, 500905.

affirm, that I came to read it as an undoing and breaking up of your former ground of life and action—

Nothing more easily than grief makes a disposition, neither chastened nor balanced as it should be, fly out and become utterly unreasonable. I dare say that was my case.

Only one consideration led me to write as I did—the consideration namely of one point in the discipline life has given me, and one only, that can ever be of use to you. My life has, I know and feel, had this tendency, to lay a heavy weight upon the movement of the understanding when solicited to depart from the main practical principles by which it has been anchored, and to make the movements of all such processes exceeding slow. I mean the common discipline of my life: that which has come upon my understanding only, and affects only *its* habits—and which comes in through common acts, apart from disturbing causes such as those that join themselves to all questions deeply piercing into our moral being.

Lagging behind you as, whenever I read your letters, I always feel myself to do, on this occasion for the first time it occurred to me not because of the[184] apparent interval between you & me, but between you and your former yet recent self. Can it be that, the shock of these awful times having driven him upon the problems that oppress other men, his trenchant intellect has found for him too sharp and short a way through them?

The vice I meant to suggest was strictly and wholly in *that* region: and what it was I hope I have now made clearer. I am anxious to purge the offence away, not from your mind, for I am certain it did not arrive there, but as it is in itself.

At any time in the *next* week after Monday[d] you would find me in town—perhaps you would take a bed at our house. If so, a few hours notice will amply suffice. Hope is here and I have felt the privilege of talking with him but only to lament the more that my departure to-morrow[e] cuts me off from the means of talking through, instead of merely upon, the great subject. I look forward anxiously to seeing you but with a similar anticipation. Weeks at least of continuous exercise seem necessary, besides every else [*sic*] of a higher nature that is more necessary, to give the

---

[d] That is, Monday, 30 September 1850.

[e] On the same day as he wrote to Manning Gladstone commented: 'Walk with Hope and conversation on the case of the Church. All his old doubts and dispositions have revived; but he seems disposed to think and act steadily' (*GD* iv. 239). Gladstone left Fasque the following morning, 23 September 1850 (ibid. 240).

least hope of a conscious grasp either of the true idea or of the right course, nor do I believe that events are yet ripe for more than to give light a little beyond the actual point at which we stand. But to the questions—first, can peace be permanently kept with the now dominant system in the Ch[urch] of E[ngland]—namely, will that system be cured by remedies such as any of its Bishops may devise, *and* such as the State will permit to be administered?—I fail to find any answer but in the negative.

Thank God, Mary improves.—the last accounts I had, very indirectly, of the Herbert child were better.

I remain always
Your aff[ectiona]te friend
W. E. Gladstone

Ven[erable] Archdeacon Manning

You do not require to give me assurances of your self-interest. By the way in which you can bear with me, I can well judge what it must be towards others & in itself generally.

[[BL Add. MS 44248, 102–5; Morley transcript; Leslie transcript; Purcell, i. 572–4; Lathbury, i. 356–7 (printed consecutively with BL Add. MS 44248, 99–100); cf. Chapeau, n. 178]]

500927mg

44. Cadogan Place
Sept[ember] 27. 1850.

My dear Gladstone,

I cannot thank you as I ought for your last letter, except by saying that I trust there is nothing wrong in mine to you that you should write with such undeserved kindness.

But my present purpose is not to write on these matters.

My object is to make sure of our meeting. In your letter dated 22d, Sunday last, you say 'the next week after Monday'. I assume this to be Monday 23d., so as to bring your arrival in London to Monday next Sept[ember] 30.

I will therefore be in London, please God, on Wednesday, *unless I have a line to the contrary.*

Many thanks for your kind offer of hospitality, but I shall see no less of you by continuing at my sisters. My time[185] shall be at your disposal.

If you have not engaged a travelling Servant, I may mention that Fedale Ricci who has twice travelled with me is here. He is honest, quiet, & good in every sense. I would confide the care of anyone to him in my absence.

I cannot end this without one word to say how great solace & thought I feel to owe through many years to you: & how much the habit of mind you speak of has taught me in the way of example & reproof. May God ever bless you. Ever your aff[ectiona]te friend,

H. E. Manning

The Right Hon[oura]ble
W. E. Gladstone[186]

[[Pitts; Chapeau, 178, 255–6]]

[[The meeting Manning proposed occurred on Wednesday, 3 October 1850 ('Manning with me 7–11 [*GD* iv. 241])[a] and again on 4 October: 'Manning came to dine & staid 7–11. . . . His conversation with me on these two evenings opens to me a still darkening prospect. Alas for what lies before us: for my deserts it cannot be gloomy enough: but for the sheep & lambs of Christ!' (ibid. 242; cf. 501117mg).]]

501006gm[aa]

6 C[arlton] G[ardens] Oct[obe]r 6.
1850.

My dear Manning

Mrs. Glynne is dead[b]—As nearly as possible at the moment when we parted she was called from a dark world, perhaps never darker than now in its prospects, to the rest and felicity into which few indeed could make an easier passage.

I go down probably tomorrow night.[c] Our journey must now stand over for a week: but this I fear can hardly bring us within reach of you.

When you were here, I had not brought my letters into order: & and I am sorry to find that I failed to place some of yours in your hands, I am not sure which; but I think they may have been those which[187] related to your letter to the B[isho]p of Chichester.

In looking back upon our conversation, much occurs & recurs: it is not now as it was: a jar ran through it, the latent idea on my part that you were

---

[a] On the same day Cavendish wrote to Gladstone: 'I rejoice in the thought that Manning is to meet you & that you will have an opportunity of encouraging him to work for the liberation of the English Church' (BL Add. MS 44124, 274–7, 276).

[aa] 'Wrote to Manning' (*GD* iv. 243).

[b] Gladstone was informed of the death of Lavinia (Lyttelton) Glynne (b. 1821; the wife of his brother-in-law, Henry Glynne) by her brothers, George (1817–76) and William (1820–84; Rector of Hagley [*DNB*]) Lyttelton on 4 October 1850 (*GD* iv. 242; Fletcher [1997], 17).

[c] He went on the evening of 7 October 1850 (*GD* iv. 243).

unjust in your modes of judgment to the Church of England, & on yours, perhaps, that I am lagging behind the Truth. There is however only one point on which I wish to say a word—for it is practically I think very important: and shall be briefly handled—

I said the 'Church and realm' was not bound to the Judicial Committee and the Gorham Judgment: that the Church had not 'received the same,' you said, yet it had accepted the 'discipline', the judicial system[188] established by the Statute of Appeals. The point therefore is this: whether the Judicial Committee be within the Statute of Appeals. But which of the two, its letter or its spirit? I say that within the letter of our statutes, & of our Constitution every fraud, every falsehood, every absurdity, may be found to lie. That it is in the spirit, the constitutional intent of that Statute, I emphatically deny. If you ask me for proof, I cannot find it in the *practice* under it: since no case of heresy has every been tried through, under its provisions. But surely nothing can be more complete as a proof of its *spirit* than the contemporaneous provision of the *Reformatio Legum* which said if a grave cause arose, it was to be tried by a provincial Council.[d] Therefore the Judicial Committee being a secular tribunal, wholly foreign to the order of the Church, is at variance with the spirit of the Statute, and the Church which has accepted the Statute has not accepted the Judicial Committee. The Acts of the 3d and 4th William are no more morally than they are chronologically within reach of the canon of submission.[e] That they stand in a certain relation to the Statute, I grant: but it is the relation in which the $\phi\theta o\rho\acute{a}$[f] of a thing always stands to the thing, beginning from the nature of the thing itself, and by an undue preponderance commonly of *some* among its elements.

This is to supply a gap which I ought to have filled when we were together. Pray remember the other matter which was named as we were going to part—

> & believe me always
> Your aff[ectiona]te friend
> W. E. Gladstone

---

[d] *Reformatio Legum* ('De Appelationibus, 11'), 302. See 500709gm.

[e] The Judicial Committee of the Privy Council was established in 1833 by 3 & 4 William IV, c. 41 By this Act and the earlier 2 & 3 William IV, c. 92 (1832) the Delegate for Appeals (25 Henry VIII, c. 19) was superseded as the final court for ecclesiastical appeals.

[f] Destruction. On the subject see Plato, *Republic*, 485b: 'between generation and destruction', and Aristotle, *Metaphysics*, 994a6, 1000a27, 1067b24, 1069b11, and 1070a15.

Venerable
H. E. Manning
From what I hear I suppose Rev Dan[iel] Wilson[g] is *worth reading.*
[[BL Add. MS 44248, 106–8; Morley transcript; Leslie transcript; Lathbury, i. 117–18; Purcell, i. 574–5; cf. Chapeau, n. 179]]

501010mg

Lavington. Oct[ober] 10. 1850.

My dear Gladstone,

Yours are sad tidings. This is the third young Mother taken in six months with short if any warning: two in my kindred, one in yours.[a] And so it must be if 'He is to make up His Jewels'.[b] We call it parting, He uniting, & our contradictions make our sorrows.

Many thanks for your kind words about our conversations. They saddened me: but chiefly because I feared that some impatience of mine was in fault.

They forced on me the conviction that our diversity of view, for I would fain call it no more, is not verbal. Perhaps no two men have written &[189]spoken so much on Ecclesiastical matters, & so little on Theology: & it is in that region I think I see our present difference to lie.

If I am unjust to the Church of England it is unconsciously: perhaps it may be as sons are sometimes for very grief more plain to their parents than strangers. But I did not know it. With me as I tried to express, the question has assumed a deeper & greater form. I am thrown by the signs of the times upon the first principles of the doctrine of Christ and of the Church of God. And I am unable to find a harmony between them and the principles on which we stand at this time.

Those principles also seem to me identical with the principles of the Reformation. I am not ashamed of saying that the events of this year have in my mind[190] fixed an interpretation on the position of the Church of England, which overthrows what I have hitherto believed.

---

[g] Daniel Wilson (1805–86; Vicar of St Mary's, Islington [Boase, iii. 1406]), *Our Protestant Faith in Danger: An Appeal to the Evangelical Members of the Church of England, in Reference to the Present Crisis* (London: Thomas Hatchard, 1850). Note that the piece is fiercely anti-Tractarian and calls on Evangelicals to unite against 'Romanizers'.

[a] Sophia Dudley Ryder, Manning's sister-in-law, died in Holy Week, 1850.

[b] Mal. 3: 17.

As to my letters. I saw all I wished. Being unwilling to prolong that part of the subject I said no more. I chiefly wished to see the letter written by the next or 2d[191] post after the one you referred to guarding against an overstrain of my meaning. I think it is June 19. or 23 & very short.[c] But of this too much.

And now for foreign travel. I fear that even your delay will not reach me: much as I should enjoy it: but my mind seems nearly at the decision to go about the end of next month. As to destination I can hardly say but I have for years longed and almost resolved to go to Jerusalem.

My thoughts at our parting were so full of our conversation that I do not clearly remember the other matter you remind me of. Farewell, and believe me,

Always your affectionate friend,
H. E. Manning

The Right Hon[oura]ble
W. E. Gladstone
[[Pitts; Chapeau, 179, 256–7]]

501013gm[a]

Hawarden Oct[ober] 13
1850.

My dear Manning

The word at parting to which I made in my last letter an indistinct allusion, was my request to you that you would carefully consider & let me know in course of time your thoughts upon the question, what are the obligations of the individual priest or layman, in the Church of England, to any such Bishops of the Commission as may set themselves resolutely to contend for the Catholic Faith in the article in which it is now assailed and in that principle of its delivery, in which all its articles alike are struck at with one blow.

The only importance that I recollect in our conversation was that of mine, which led me in a particular point to mistake your[192] course of reasoning & for which I expressed my regret—but on your side there was nothing. And of course if I speak of injustice to the Church of England

---

[c] See 500621mg.   [a] 'Wrote to Manning' (*GD* iv. 244).

I do not mean intended injustice, but we have no word for that kind of act between bare[193] injury and injustice which is hurt done that ought not to be done, yet without the thought of doing anything but right. That is the question I raised, & that is what seems to me to be done when a surrender of power which I know to have a certain sense in the political sphere is interpreted, in its relation to the Church of England & her dealings within that sphere, in a sense quite different—through which sense I think it is that you get at a condemnation so broad as yours, of the Tudor clergy. But if you tell me 'it may be as sons are sometimes for very grief more plain to their parents than strangers' you stop my mouth & take away my will to push the subject: your recognition of that relation answers me: I cannot take you to task about what you may do in it, for indeed it is little short of ludicrous to see me schooling you on such a matter.

We mean to start on Tuesday morning.[b] We have reluctantly given up the German route: and intend to go direct to Naples, reaching it probably about the 1st of Nov[embe]r unless we find there is quarantine in which case we shall probably turn off to Hyères[c] on our way.

Ever aff[ectiona]tely yours
W. E. Gladstone

Venerable
Archdeacon Manning
[[BL Add. MS 44248, 109–10; Morley transcript; Leslie transcript; Purcell, i. 575; cf. Chapeau, n. 180]]
[[On 14 October 1850 Lincoln wrote to Gladstone concerning Manning:

Now for that all important question of this moment—the state of the Church and the danger of far more secessions from her fold than poor Feilding unless some effort be made to rally their hopes and without taking any violent or hasty steps shewing them that there are men in higher quarters upon whose cooperation they may rely and upon whose zeal as fellow-labourers they may count if they will only cling to the ship & not desert her at this the hour of need. You may be sure when I write this I have first & foremost in my mind our good friend Manning whom I have been greatly grieved to hear from many quarters is at this moment on the edge of the precipice and may any day take the fatal leap.—Now *I* avow that I can easily contemplate the possibility of a secession—like the non-jurors of old—with the *doctrines* of our Church intact but I cannot understand the views of those who in their longings for a Church which shall be free from secular interference in her doctrines are willing to flee to a Church whose

---

[b] Because of 'new inflammation in Mary's eye', on 15 October 1850, they were not able to set out until 18 October (*GD* iv. 244–5).
[c] Hope's residence in France.

doctrines are at variance with those which they profess—Such however is now the tendency of mens minds and it is the prospects of those secessions which makes me so anxious to see some calm and well-regulated movement commenced. We should not obtain our object at first, but the freedom of the Church (to the extent to which I and I believe you desire to see that freedom given for I am no 'separatist' unless as a measure of *last* necessity and after every effort has failed) is a demand so moderate so palpably just and so sure when understood to make way in the minds of thinking men that I have no doubt we should eventually succeed if the public alarm is not raised by these— as I must ever consider them—*petulant* desertions.—I would gladly devote myself to this movement if I had the cooperation of yourself & such men as James Hope Dr Hook and 4 or 5 more,—but I am not in a position to *originate* anything.—(University of Nottingham MS NeC 11,698, 2).]]

501016mg

Lavington. Oct[ober] 16. 1850.

My dear Gladstone,

In the event of your going to Hyères will you let me have one word to Cadogan Place; as it would draw me that way if indeed I launch for the winter: which I still am weighing.[a]

As to the question you ask me, I will try to consider it. But I have this difficulty. If the position of the Church of England as a whole be untenable no question survives. All obligations bind us to the Church universal. If it be tenable our continuance in the Church of England would rest not upon those obligations, but on the basis on which they rest.

The real question is the position. Is not this so?

But I will write no more than God speed you & yours, in going out & in coming in.[b]

Ever yours affect[ionatel]y,
H. E. Manning

[a] Also on 16 October 1850 Manning received a letter from Robert Wilberforce, who asked him in a postscript: 'Is your idea to go to Italy? Does Gladstone go there?' (Bodl. MS Eng. lett. c. 656, 53) in response to an earlier letter of his in which Manning told him he was planning to go abroad (ibid. 50–1; Purcell, i. 561). On 22 October in a letter to Wilberforce, Purcell comments, 'nearly eight months after the Gorham Judgment, Manning makes an explicit profession of faith in the Church of Rome as infallible through the guidance of the Holy Spirit, and expresses his deep conviction that the Church of England is not under that guidance' (Purcell, i. 564). Gladstone annotates the passage with 'NB' (PurGl, ibid.).

[b] Deut. 28: 6.

The Right Hon[oura]ble
W. E. Gladstone

[[Pitts; Chapeau, 180, 257]]

[[*Butler* v. *Purcell* Trial records Schema B indicate that Gladstone wrote to Manning on 5 November 1850 (not located).]]

5. Gladstone to Italy and Manning's Resignation: November 1850–April 1851

501106gm[a]

Genoa. Nov[ember] 6. 1850.

My dear Manning

My time has nearly arrived when you are likely to be quitting England and in the hope of our meeting I write to give you this indication of my course. The prospect of quarantine at Naples, and the cold weather in France have been much in our way: but we hope to reach our destination sometime next week, and thank God we have every reason thus far to be satisfied as to the main purpose of our journey, for the effect of the mild climate upon our little Mary is strongly favourable.

Now, my dear Manning, I will make another appeal,[194] within the few lines which this bit of paper will contain, to you from yourself, and from you to yourself. I reflect with undiminished surprise upon the undermining of those historical and theological foundations in your mind, upon which you were so firmly established in allegiance to the Church of England. Speaking thus, of course I set aside the Gorham Case, which to you I know[195] has only seemed to be[196] the candle that dispelled the darkness. My feelings came upon me in a mass, and I could not at once analyse or understand them; but I seem to do so now when I reflect that you seemed to be placed upon the rock not only of convictions, but of the most awful experience a man can undergo, namely that which comes to him on the brink of the other world. I do not know whether you have forgotten, I am certain that I never shall forget, a conversation in which after your return from the Continent[b] you detailed to me (between the Pimlico quarter & my house)[197] what in communion with Death & the region beyond death, you

---

[a] 'Wrote to Manning' (*GD* iv. 264).

[b] Manning returned from Rome in June 1848. The meeting referred to was on 9 July 1848. See 480703mg.

had not newly but freshly learned. It was in conjunction with an increased disinclination to dwell on corruptions in the Church of Rome, an increased aversion to mere nationality in the Church of England that you most fervently declared to me how beyond expression solemn & firm was your assurance, brought from the region you had then been treading, not of the mercy of God to those in invincible ignorance, a mercy reaching to every religious profession, and to none, but of the unmoved and immovable title of the Church of England to her share in the one divine and Catholic inheritance. Have you *really* unlearned those lessons? It cannot be: and if it were, I for one should have this mournful idea driven home upon me, as I have long felt it of Newman, the destiny of that man has been to do little comparatively for the Church of Rome, much against the whole ethical grounds and structure of belief in Divine Revelation. But I have touched my limit & must end, remaining always as I trust

Your affectionate friend,
W. E. Gladstone.

Ven[erable]
Archdeacon Manning
[[BL Add. MS 44148, 111–12; Pitts (Chapeau, copy); Purcell, i. 580–1; cf. Chapeau]]

501117mg

Lavington. Nov[ember] 17. 1850.

My dear Gladstone,

I had been looking out for some tidings of you: & received your letter this morning with much pleasure: especially as it gives a good account of your child. I trust your anxiety is reasonably decreasing.

For my own plans I think I have made up my mind to leave England about Dec[ember] 5. and will come, God willing, to Naples.[a] It would be to me a great happiness to pass a time with you free from the pressure of home work. And my earnest desire is to take the help I know you would afford me.

---

[a] Note his letter to his sister Catherine Austen of 18 November 1850 in which he indicates his plans to join Gladstone on the trip and go on to Jerusalem (Purcell, i. 584; cf. an earlier letter to Robert Wilberforce [16 Oct. 1850; Bodl. MS Eng. lett. c. 656, 52–3; Purcell, i. 590]). To Purcell's statement (i. 591) that the trip did not materialize because of Gladstone's early return owing to 'illness' in his family, Gladstone writes 'No. Parl[iamen]t' (PurGl, ibid.).

I have a perfect recollection of the conversation you refer to: and I feel that what I then said is in perfect accordance with my present mind.

The lesson I trust I learned in sickness of God's mercy upon all who are faithful to their light be it what it may is still clear before me.

But it would be unreasonable to say that the facts of the Church of England or even your own estimate of them are as they were then.

I have no shame in saying that since then I have seen what I did not see before. Once I fear I surprized you by not caring to defend my consistency. I have the deepest anxiety to make clear my integrity before God & Man: but to square myself by myself is of no high importance to me. I acknowledge freely that a semblance of change, as it implies retracing confidence in past judgments imposes the duty of not being too confident in a present judgment. And that I am most willing to observe as a rule of conscience.

All that I ask is a re-examination of old evidence under the light now providentially cast upon them.

As you kindly appeal to me I will surrender myself to your appeal and go through any discipline necessary for such a testing of myself.

Will you also allow me to appeal to you for such a re-examination of your theological conclusions as you have given to your political opinions.

The duties of your political life have kept your political opinions always on the Anvil.

You have to my mind been consistent in principle & substance. Few who know you less than I do think so.

In like manner the daily, continuous action[198] & realism of theological subjects has carried my mind through matters which I pray you to look into with me.

To you I seem, what you seem to others.

I say this for a twofold purpose: First that you will not at once sentence me: but hear me: & next that you will not consider your past or present convictions as 'regula irreformabilis'.[b]

What I want is to see how you deal with facts which so far as I know have not been treated in any of your writings, or in any of our conversations.

And now I have nearly filled my paper without saying what is most urgent with me.

The Clergy of this Archd[eaconry] have desired to be convened about the R[oman] C[atholic] Hierarchy.[c]

[b] An unreformable rule.
[c] The meeting troubled Manning a good deal as is indicated in his correspondence with Priscilla Maurice (15 and 24 Nov. 1850 [Bodl. MS Eng. lett. c. 659, 189–96]) and Robert

Wilberforce (7 Nov.; Bodl. MS Eng. lett c. 656, 77–80; Purcell, i. 577–8). In 1885 he remembered the meeting thus:

Then came the Papal Aggression tumult, & in the month of November the Clergy sent me a requisition to convene them again to protest against the restoration of the Cath[oli]c Hierarchy. They had a right to ask this. I had an official duty to convene them: tho' I could not share their acts. They met I think on the 22 of November. I went over to Chichester early, & went to the Bishop (Gilbert) a kind & just man. I told him that the Clergy were assembling to protest against the Hierarchy that I must preside: that I came to clear my conscience from all participation in their act, & from all doubt of my own sincerity. I told him that I saw before me a conflict between two Supremacies, one which I was convinced was human & in violation of the Divine Office of the Church, the other Divine in its origin whatsoever be its extension or the limits of its authority: that in such a conflict I could take no part in behalf of the former; & could assume no attitude of resistance to the latter; that knowing his convictions: & how necessary it was that he should have at his side as Archdeacon some man who was of the same mind as himself, I placed my resignation in his hands.

He would not hear of it: & bound me not to say a word of this to the Clergy. I readily bound myself saying that my conscience was safe now that he knew everything.

Then I went to the meeting & opened it formally without any address. This was noted. They then passed their Address & resolutions against the Papal aggression. Finally they moved a vote of thanks to me. In answer I said: that it was the first & only time in ten years in which I had been separated in conviction & action from them: that I had no choice: that necessity was laid upon me: that I thanked them with all my heart for their brotherly love & the many acts of kindness & friendship private & public in the ten years I had held Office among them: that I should never forget it or them. My dear old friend the Dean was crying & many others. So we ended & parted. It was our last meeting & the end of my work in the Church of England: for after that I only preached once or maybe a second time at Lavington: & on Dec[ember] 8, I think I left it & never came back. ('Later Reminiscences', i. 36–8 [CP]; Purcell, i. 579–80)

On 1 December 1881 Manning noted the comment of a rural Dean who had been present at the meeting and reported to him on it thus:

Nov[ember] the 22d 1850 was the last Meeting at Chichester presided over by Archdeacon Manning—A Meeting only convened by the Archdeacon at the request of certain Clergy of the Archdeaconry for the purpose of condemning the Establishment of the Roman Hierarchy—Of what occured at this meeting I retain but a faint remembrance; though I well remember on that occasion there was a great murmur of intention to charge the Archdeacon with his Roman tendencies but no one was bold enough to realize the threat— thus manifesting that the influence which the Archdeacon had exercised over the Clergy was not diminished. On this occasion however so bitter was the hostility to Rome, that one speaker ventured to assert, that wherever the Catholic Religion was planted, vice and immorality followed in its train—to which answer was made 'that though England could not boast of the chastity of the lower orders; yet, in Catholic Ireland, female purity had grown into a proverb' (Bodl. MS Eng. lett. c. 664, 224–5).

After the fullest deliberation I am resolved to take no antagonist step on this subject.

Nevertheless I convened the Arch[deaconr]y ministerially. I have stated this to my Bishop: and my reasons.[d] I felt it also my duty to tender my resignation. But this is left for my reconsideration.

I have no words too strong to implore you not to commit yourself on this subject till we can meet. If you ever until lately thought my word worth heeding, do so once more & reserve yourself on the subject of the R[oman] C[atholic] Hierarchy. I believe it is 'set for the fall and rising again of many';[e] and that men are parting upon it for life. The country is in the worst no Popery excitement: noise without agreement or consistent meaning.[f]

Forgive me anything I ought not to have written, and with love to your wife, believe me,

Always your affect[ionat]e friend,
H. E. Manning

The Right Hon[oura]ble
W. E. Gladstone

[[Pitts; Chapeau, 181, 257–9; addressed: the Right Hon[oura]ble W. E. Gladstone Posta Restante Naples Italie Affranchiè; postmarked: PETWORTH NO 19 1850; cf. Leslie, 94]]

[[Manning confirmed his resignation to his Bishop on 21 November 1850,[g] and the following day, 22 November, chaired a meeting of Chichester clergy.[h] He left Lavington on 3 December.[i] Immediately following the meeting with the Chichester clergy Manning wrote to Hope:

---

[d] A draft of Manning's letter to his bishop is preserved in Bodl. MS Eng. lett. c. 653, 665–6. See Addenda to this Section. Note Purcell's comment with respect to Manning's relations with his bishops (i. 128): 'Mr. Gladstone told me that "Manning served under three bishops William Otter, Shuttleworth, and Gilbert with each of whom, though of different religious opinions, he was always on excellent terms." '

[e] Luke 2: 34.

[f] For details on the 'Papal Aggression' crisis see 501220gm.

[g] Bodl. MS Eng. lett. c. 654, 671; the Bishop expressed regret the following day, 22 November 1850 (ibid. 672–3). It was not until 3 January 1851, however, that the Bishop wrote, promising to send the necessary forms (ibid. 676–7).

[h] See 501117mg, note.

[i] On Manning's departure his home was rented to the Misses Brackenbury, and on 31 March 1851, Samuel Wilberforce suggested that the vacancy at Lavington be filled by Richard William Randall (1824–1906). Randall was educated at Christ Church, Oxford, and held a curacy at Binfield, Berkshire. He later served at All Saint's, Clifton, and was appointed Canon and Dean at Chichester, 1892–1902. While at Lavington and later Randall kept in contact with Manning. Manning's book and sermon manuscripts were still at Lavington on Randall's arrival. Manning returned on 1 September 1851 to pack his library and stayed a week to part with old friends. Many of his books he did not remove

Lavington. Nov[ember] 23, 1850.

My dear Hope,

Your last letter was a help to me, for I began to feel as if every man had gone to his own house & left the whole matter.

I saw Gladstone twice in London & had two jarring and useless conversations. We seemed at last to ascertain our differences to lie in the very ideas of the Church & its functions. This made me feel that all hope of our keeping together was at an end.

Since then events have driven me to a decision.

This anti-Popery cry has seized my brethren & they asked to be convened. I must either resign at once, or convene them ministerially & express my dissent, the reasons of which w[oul]d involve resignation. I went to the B[ishop]—& said this & tendered my resignation. He was very kind & wished me to take time—but I have written & made it final.

This involves the resignation of my cure of souls, which goes to my heart—but must be done & I think will be this next week.

Then I shall be able to speak my mind as to the state of things. I should be glad if we might keep together—and whatever must be done, do it with a calm & deliberateness which shall give testimony that it is not done in lightness.

I had thought of going abroad to take time to consider.[j] But the decision is made on to my Office, & I am now disposed to stay at home; especially if I c[oul]d see & consult with you. When do you come to London?

I am much afraid that this Brief & Hierarchy will set Gladstone on fire. The seat for Oxford, the crisis of public events, the material of a great movement are all against a calm, cold decision.

God grant he may rise to his own true self—for it is noble enough for anything.

Let me hear from you. This has been a sore time with me but I am lighter of heart as when someone with a long sickness is gone. Ever affect[ionate]ly y[ou]rs,

H.E.M. (NLS MS 3675, 92–5)

until 1858. For details see *DNB* and Briscoe and Mackay (1932), 51–61. On the legal case over Randall's support of Anglo-Catholic positions, brought before Randall by his curate, E. Randall (no relative), see Walter Walsh, *The History of the Romeward Movement in the Church of England 1833–1864* (London: James Nisbet, 1900), 381–4.

[j] Note his earlier letter to Robert Wilberforce (26 Sept. 1850) in which he comments: 'I have thought of going abroad for the winter, as a means of withdrawing from collision, and from embarrassing others. Gladstone's going, and the English winter would be reason' (Purcell, i. 561).

Hope responded on 28 November: 'What you say of Gladstone does not surprise me, for there is in his mind a tenacity of view, & a power of refining an argument—which work together, the one in keeping him stationary, the other in distinguishing away every fresh difficulty as it arises—But as of the day it is a noble nature, & great as the struggle may be I do not despair of the ultimate result' (Bodl. MS Eng. lett. c. 657, 83–6).[k]]]

501206mg

44. Cadogan Place. Dec[ember] 6. 1850.

My dear Gladstone,

My last letter told you that I had been compelled to resign my Office. This fact takes away the object for which I intended to leave England. And I have therefore decided to give up the rest & enjoyment of coming to you. I feel satisfied that it is better for me to remain at home in the midst of friends to whom I wish to give all evidence I can of the calmness and deliberation with which I have acted and hope to act in this hour of trial.

But my object is not to write of myself, but of you. And I will write frankly, having 'at a great price obtained this freedom'.[a]

In my last letter I prayed you not to commit yourself to any line of public policy, in haste.

You have by some 18 years of public life attained a commanding position in Parliament. You represent Oxford: and are the only man into whose hands the effectual power of one side of the House of Commons, under certain contingencies can pass. Let me say what I believe.

Parties will from this time form round two centres the one will be the Protestantism of England protecting or trying to protect[199] itself & the Church of England by legislation: the other Political Government maintaining a powerful neutrality and arbitration among all religious communions.

If you retain your seat for Oxford, and accept the leadership which is approaching you through the old Conservative & country parties you must take the former centre as your standing point.

---

[k] In his 'Later Reminiscences', i. 62, Manning noted in a series of Memoranda an 1850 Gorham reference to 'Resolutions. Gladstone' but offers no further information.

[a] 1 Cor. 7: 23.

Which God forbid.

If you take the latter centre to which all our late conferences would lead me without hesitation you know the cost.

But I believe that it is the path of Truth, peace, & Christian civilization to this great Empire.

I do not believe that the Church of England is more than a provisional institution.

It has now for 250 years[200] organized the life of England. It has become less & less commensurate. It is at this time imposed upon not incorporated with the British Empire and the spiritual life of our mixed population.

My reason for believing that it will never embrace & organize this people is because the Theology of the Church of England, which is the dynamical force of its organization is dissolved by contradictions, ambiguities, and abandonment of the principle of authority.

But the Protestantism of England will tolerate nothing higher. It does not even tolerate this. The Anglican Theology survives only in dilution with pure protestant language. Be true to it and it is denounced as worse than Popery—Romanism without its consistency.

We have descended to a lower level of popular belief and no mechanical force less than the authority of Divine Tradition teaching 'as one having authority'[b] can replace the English mind on the level of Faith.

You will think all this hard and peremptory. But it is the deep conviction of long years of patient silent thought. You thought me hasty. I may have seemed so, for events have precipitated conclusions which for long years have hung suspended waiting only for some change in the law of proportion to give them form.

May God guide you in this great crisis—on which the Faith of England and of an Empire wide as the World may be vitally touched, by your lightest[201] word.

Hampton called yesterday and gave me an excellent account of your Wife & Mary. My love to you all. Ever your affect[ionat]e friend,

H. E. Manning

[[Pitts; Chapeau, 182, 259–60; BL Add. MS 44248, 113–14 (copy); cf. Leslie, 96]]

[[On 7 December 1850, the day after he wrote his letter to Gladstone, Manning wrote to Hope, commenting on his situation in regard to Gladstone:

Your letter was a great help to me. I have resigned both Office and Benefice; and I find a common consent, including my own family, that this is final as to the future. Now

---

[b] Matt. 7: 29.

though I feel my decision to be materially complete it is not formally so and I wish to keep myself open till we can meet. I could much wish to see Gladstone; but I shall not leave England the object being gone. (NLS MS 3675, 96)

On 11 December Manning wrote again to Hope, noting the inevitability of his seeking reception in the Roman Catholic Church and the implications this would have for his friendship with Gladstone:[c]

44 Cadogan Place.
Dec[ember] 11, 1850.

Private

My dear Hope,

I feel with you that the argument is complete.

For a long time I nevertheless felt a fear lest I should be doing an act morally wrong.

This fear has passed away, because the Church of England has revealed itself in a way to make me fear more on the other side.

It remains therefore as an act of the Will.

But this I suppose it must be.

And in making it I am helped by the fact that to remain under our changed or revealed circumstances would also be an act of the Will.

And that not in conformity with but in opposition to intellectual convictions: and the intellect is Gods gift, & our instrument in attaining to knowledge of His Will.

It would be a great solace if any event were to give the momentum. And so it may be, as it was with my resignation. I seem to have been passively carried through it.

I have a sort of desire to see Gladstone once more before any final act.

Do you think this would be well?

[c] On the same day, 11 December 1850, *The Guardian*, unaware of his change in travel plans, announced Manning's resignation (892): 'Archdeacon Manning has resigned his living, and, it is said, is about to travel in the East, in company with Mr. Dodsworth. In contradiction to painful rumours afloat, it is stated, however, that they both profess their continued adherence to the Anglican Church; and their friends deny that they have any idea whatever of quitting her communion.' On 18 December the paper carried an account by the London correspondent of the *Oxford Times* (*The Guardian*, 901–2) who reported that Manning was 'in town this week. He is not looking well. He was at St. Barnabas on Sunday morning. He offered, it is said, to address the riotous mob outside the church, but was dissuaded from attempting it.' By Christmas Manning was at Abbotsford with Hope (*LD* xiv. 174).

My fear is that what he sees abroad, and this political crisis will be too strong for him.

I seem to be in this mind. To let two or three months pass, not wishing to go hastily from one Altar to Another.

And then, if no interposition seems to forbid me in the Name of God, to go in the most retired way to some Priest.

I would say, in Hill Street but that I incline to think it well to avoid the name at this stage: also I would especially desire to avoid Westminster.

I should wish it to be a simple submission to the C[atholic] Ch[urch] free from aggravations of prejudice. This is in consideration of others more than myself.

It would be to me a very great happiness if we could act together, and our names go together in the first publication of the fact. Thus far I have answered your letter drily.

As to reading I have lately done little more than look over old books: and find how great a force they have gained by the experience of the last two or three years.

The subject which has brought me to my present conviction is the Perpetual Office of the Church under divine guidance, in expounding the Faith & deciding controversies. And the book which forced this on me was Melchior Canus' Loci Theologici.[d] It is a long book but so orderly that you may get the whole outline with ease. Möhler's Symbolik[e] you know.

But, after all, Holy Scripture comes to me in a new light, as Ephes iv. 4–17. which seems to preclude the notion of a divisible unity: which is in fact Arianism in the matter of the Church.

I entirely feel what you say of the alternative.

It is either Rome or licence of thought & will.

Would to God I could help you in this great trial. My only stay is the thought that many are praying for me. I trust that God will so far hear them as to preserve me from dangerous illusions.

This may yet be: but for my whole past life, 18 years of work in the Church of England it is already cancelled by what I have done.

---

[d] Melchior Cano (1509–60), *De locis theologis, libri duodecim*... (Louvain: Exudebat Servatius Sasserus sumptibus haeredum Ioannis Stetsii, 1569).

[e] See Johann Adam Möhler, *Symbolik oder Darstellung der dogmatischen Gegensätze der Katholiken und Protestanten nach ihren öffentlichen Bekenntnisschriften* (6th, unamended edn.; Mainz: Florian Kupferberg, 1843) and John Adam Möhler, *Symbolism; Or, Exposition of the Doctrinal Differences between Catholics and Protestants, as Evidenced by Their Symbolical Writings*, trans. James Burton Robertson (2 vols.; London: Charles Dolman, 1843).

Do you think to come to London early or late in February?
Badeley seems to me much advanced.

Believe me always,
affect[ionate]ly yours,
H. E. Manning (NLS MS 3675, 98–101)]]

501220gm[a]

Num 5 Chiatamone
Naples

Dec[ember] 20. 1850

My dear Manning

I need not dwell on my disappointment at learning that we are not to see you here. If your resolution to remain in England is for your own good and that of the Church I must not grudge our particular loss. Your two letters would have suggested this matter for the conversation of weeks. On the first I must be very brief. We are sadly, strangely at issue on the *facts* of the conversation soon after your illness. If I have any one clear recollection in my mind, it is that your assurances then did not relate at all to God's mercy to those who faithfully follow their light be it what it may, but to your perfect sense of security in the Church of England from its *objective* character.

I do not appeal to consistency as such. I appeal from sentiments which appear to me partial and (forgive me) even morbid, to former convictions singularly deliberative, singularly solemn, as entitled to exercise a higher authority over your conduct in this hour (as you truly call it) of trial.

I in no degree shrink from your desire that I should review and reconsider too. As far as I know, it is not one of my besetting sins to close my mind (I do not speak of matters immediately practical) against the light: any demand of this kind: moreover, from you would and will have a peculiar authority (from you) and I will readily and anxiously accept your further[202] aid. My train of thought this year has been little less than a continued effort at such review and reconsideration: but it has brought to me no doubts as to my personal line of duty for the present circumstances: I still feel the foundation under foot and see the light overhead: laws for a future as yet undeveloped and big with scarcely imaginable dangers will I trust be supplied to us as it unfolds.

I cannot think that the Church of England in its theology *has* abandoned the principle authority. In my view it is[203] entitled to that principle *de jure*, &

---

[a] 'Wrote to H. E. Manning' (*GD* iv. 292).

holds it *de facto* in its only systematic theology. I grant with pain it is now in debate, whether this generation will be faithful to the traditions it has received: it is quite possible, God only knows, that we may witness its abandonment: from the *very* highest places of the Church it is gone. If the abandonment takes place I have the painful conviction that it will be owing not to the defective law or theology of the English Church, nor to the strength or craft of the foes of the principle, but to the errors of its friends from Newman onwards. This may be a matter of opinion: but it is one which, to me, read in the history of the time, stands out more & more, day by day, from mere colour and surface into the body and substance and relief of sheer fact.

But I am exceedingly keen to follow up with you the first part of your last letter about the probable course of public affairs. I think you know I have always deplored the late measure of the Pope. Perhaps you fear lest on that account I should leap headlong into the stream that is now setting against it and him. I can give you frankly the assurance that I will do nothing to fan those furious flames which Lord John Russell has thought fit to light.[b] Further, I do not *at present* see my way to getting rid by legislative means, of what I so much regret: & I am a little disposed God knows, to join in any attempt to prop the Church by such means. Such props will be like the

---

[b] On 29 September 1850 Pope Pius IX issued an apostolic letter, *Universalis Ecclesiae*, by which England and Wales were made an ecclesiastical province of the Roman Catholic Church and a Roman Catholic hierarchy of an archbishop and twelve suffragan bishops established therein. On 7 October 1850, Wiseman issued a Pastoral Letter, 'From without the Flaminian Gate', announcing the restoration of the hierarchy and his own new position as Cardinal Archbishop of Westminster (*EHD* 364–7; Maclear [1995], 148). A furore ensued over this 'Papal Aggression' and the resulting Ecclesiastical Titles Assumption Bill ('A Bill to Prevent the Assumption of certain Ecclesiastical Titles in respect of Places in the United Kingdom' [PP 1851 (45.) iii. 61]; 1. 14 & 15 Vict. c. 60; cf. *EHD* 369–70; Maclear [1995], 149) which forbade the acceptance of such titles. While in Italy Gladstone kept somewhat in touch with major developments in England, reading Lord John Russell's 4 November letter to the Bishop of Durham (printed in *The Times*, 7 Nov., 5a; *EHD* 367–9) which pronounced the Papal statement 'insolent and insidious' and opposed changing directions in the Tractarian movement (*GD* iv. 272) and Wiseman's *Appeal to the Reason and Good Feeling of the English People* on 5 December (ibid. 262). For an overview of the situation see Morley, i. 405–15, Ward (1915), ii. 279–93, Chadwick, i. 271–309, Machin (1974), Ralls (1974), Klaus (1987), Wolffe (1991), 243ff., Paz (1982, 1992: 8ff.), and 510306mg. Note as well Gladstone's remark to Sidney Herbert on 27 January 1851 concerning 'Lord John Russell's disgraceful letter' (Wiltshire Country Archives, Wilton Papers, 2507 F4/60).

sword of Saul on which he fell,[c] and will pierce to her very vitals. I would far rather make every effort and sacrifice towards bringing her to a new position, and adapting her to work in it: but, what is the aid on which we can count? who are men in the Church that work with us? You have a large share in the answer to that question: whether as Archdeacon or not, makes little difference.

Let me above all *retort* your apologies for seeming peremptory. You will believe me I am sure when I say that my abrupt manner of writing only comes from the confidence of old & I trust unchanging affection.

Our little Mary thank God holds well. We remain to stay even till Jan[uary] 14, later enough for the via[204] *Marseilles* letters from London of the 4th:[d] perhaps even longer. We have delightful accounts of Willy. I remain your very affectionate

W. E. Gladstone

I send this through Lincoln.

[[BL Add. MS 44248, 115–17; Purcell, i. 581–3]]

[[On 2 January 1851 Lincoln, by then in England, wrote to Gladstone commenting on Manning's situation:

Your letter to Manning, sent open to me, emboldened me to do what I have lacked courage to attempt since I returned to England—write to him. I have written to him at some length[e]—I only fear too strongly—for such is my respect for his character & admiration of his powers of mind that writing to *him* on such a subject seems almost like addressing a lecture to a Saint or offering advice to an Apostle, & the result of such restraint upon ones pen sometimes is an apparent presumption of tone which would not appear in writing to a lesser man. I fear I may have offended him but he cannot doubt the motives which alone can have induced me to write to him on such a subject & in such strong terms. I sincerely feel that *his* secession at this moment would be a blow to the Church to which all of the others of the last 10 years bear no comparison & I have tried to press upon him the awful responsibility of leading so many others into a path from which he may one day find himself obliged to secede. (University of Nottingham MS NeC 11,699)]]

510103mg

44. Cadogan Place.

---

[c] 1 Sam. 31: 4.
[d] They did remain until 26 February 1851, when they arrived back in London (*GD* iv. 310).
[e] Not located.

Jan[uary] 3. 1851.

My dear Gladstone,

Your kind letter through Lincoln has just reached me, & I write at once.

My earnest desire is to see you: and by God's will I will do nothing till[205] I have seen you. From your letter I gather that you will be at home by the meeting of Parliament.

My mind since resigning[206] has never wavered in the conviction that I could no longer with uprightness continue under oath & subscription: & that I can no longer defend or serve the Church of England within its past actual limits.

This gives me peace in the midst of a sorrow which has all but broken my heart.

This day eighteen years[207] I went to Lavington. You have never seen it, and if you had seen it you could not know what the consciousness of those eighteen years sustains like the consciousness of the present hour. It has been my only home, flock, & altar.

But as I said I feel that He who led me thither has called me away, and I am never disquieted by a doubt.

The future is not so cloudless.

Do not think that I found fault with you about foreclosing opinions. I only meant to say that your mind is not as active & apprehensive of truths which lie out of your daily path as of those which lie in it.

It seems to me that everything remands men to a re-examination of the position of the Church of England: and binds them to consider old evidences in new lights: and to take in[208] new evidences which they omitted before.

But my purpose was not to write of any details.

You have indeed a work before you for the Church of God in its relations to this World. Your first book is now come due: not in the form you thought, but in a wider, deeper & nobler.

But to do this, I fear, my last letter counted the cost: and you will have to create your men & matter.

The state of this country is mournful—or rather of the no popery class— for I believe it will be found that only a small minority has spoken.

The public opinion which carried the Bills of 1828.9 has grown and expanded since that day.

I am very thankful to hear so good an account of little Mary.

Give my love to your Wife, & tell her to think as little ill of me as she can. Believe me,

My dear Gladstone,

Always affec[tionate]ly yours,
H. E. Manning.

[[Pitts; Chapeau, 183, 261]]

[[Manning's growing concern over Gladstone's position is reflected in a letter of 9 January 1851 to Hope:

I feel what you say about Gladstone. He seems to me not to confront the evidence nor to attempt any constructive proof—but only to object and embarrass which may be done by a Deist against all revelation. This I mean is the principle not the intention of his argument. (NLS MS 3675, 103)

On 20 January 1851 Lincoln wrote Gladstone on the matter: 'I had a most kind answer from Manning. He is *staying* to see *you*. Oh that you may yet save him' (University of Nottingham MS NeC 11,700, postscript).]]

510126gm[a]

5 Chiatamone, Naples
Jan[uary] 26. 1851

My dear Manning

I sent you a few days ago a message[b] that my plans were uncertain & that I would write to you as soon as they were fixed. But upon consideration I feel as if this, though such was not my intention, had been less than kind: and I am setting about a letter although my plans are not yet settled. They are indeed rather more than not settled as active in causes of uncertainty are at work. My wife for the first time in her life has had a miscarriage, the consequence of a fright:[c] And has been thrown back in her recovery by having, though with medical sanction, made efforts too soon. It may be some weeks before she is fit to travel with perfect prudence though she is gaining ground daily.[d] Upon the whole it now seems that we must remain here and go straight home from hence. I may very probably be obliged to start within the first half of February,[e] but I hope my wife will muster

---

[a] 'Wrote to Manning' (*GD* iv. 301).

[b] Not located.

[c] 1851; 'C[atherine] refers it with much reason to the shock she got a fortnight ago from a clumsy rider on the ground opposite the house who went past her at a rapid pace very nearly knocking her down' (*GD* iv. 298). Note Catherine Gladstone's comment on a fright in a postscript to Mrs Herbert in the 27 January 1851 letter of Gladstone to Herbert (Wiltshire Country Archives, Wilton Papers, 2507 F4/60).

[d] On 2 February 1851, four days after his departure (*GD* iv. 308), Catherine wrote to Gladstone indicating that her health was improved (SDL, Glynne–Gladstone MS 612).

[e] Gladstone left on 18 February 1851 (*GD* iv. 308).

resolution to remain here, probably with her brother, in order to confirm the good which we think little Mary has thus far been realising from her stay in Italy.

We are just going to lose from this world an admirable man Mr. Charles Monsell.[f] An invalid of years' standing, he yet seemed until a fortnight or even a week ago as if he might have lived for years, and it was deeply to be desired on every one's account except his own. But the last five or six days have been an intense and continued struggle between lingering vitality & approaching death. The disease from the lungs appears to have affected the stomach and there is not a hope beyond some twelve hours more of mortal conflict. I had never known him before but have had the greatest comfort in our short acquaintance: rarely indeed have I seen either a better or wiser, or a more gentle & loving man. He had a completeness and maturity about him, which he could have learned no where especially at his time of life except under the secret and sharp discipline which cut him off from his profession and from all earthly prospects. Groaning daily in the contemplation of our disorders & convulsions in the religious sphere, of course I cannot but acknowledge the very great & peculiar blessing of being allowed in another instance to see what kind of plants they are that are reared in the atmosphere we or at least I[209] breathe while murmuring against it. His mind sympathised warmly with all the good that during his long residence he had seen in the Church of Rome: but he had a strong mild sense too that much was wrong there: he never seems to waiver respecting his own position.

Without description from you, I can too well comprehend what you have suffered in parting from Lavington: especially when it is considered not only what a mass of palpable interests clustered around your connection with it but that it likewise was the type of a system in which your whole being has long[210] been wrapped, and out of which it is now torn. Such griefs ought to be sacred to all men, of course they must be sacred to me, even did they not touch me sharply with a reflected sorrow. You can do nothing that does not reach me, considering how long you have been a large part both of my actual life and of my hopes and reckonings.

---

[f] Charles Henry Monsell (1815–51) died three days later on 29 January 1851 (ibid. 301). Gladstone visited him earlier, on 26 November 1850 (ibid. 278).

Should you do the act which I pray God with my whole soul you may not, it will not break however it may impair or strain the bonds between us. I should then earnestly pray and[211] not[212] only to obey the prompting of my own heart but to conform to a solemn conviction of duty, that you might not be as others who have gone before you, but might carry with you a larger heart and mind able to raise and *keep* you above that slavery to a system that[213] exaggeration of its forms, that disposition to rivet every shackle tighter and to stretch every breach wider, which makes me mournfully feel that the men who have gone from the Church of England after being reared in and by her are far more keen & I must add far more cruel adversaries to her, than were the mass of those whom they joined. In this I read their error, as well as in many other things. But I often wish I saw you leaning less[214] upon subjective tokens: and I must beware of doing what may seem to resemble it.

I have written thus far as if I thought you were going to follow them. It is however only because I am in doubt: and because I am too well aware that it is one of the possibilities before you. It is not I assure you because I think you have sprung to your conclusion. Even you yourself probably do not know at this moment, certainly have not known heretofore, how many & what elements of your accruing resolutions were at different stages of ripeness within you: much less could I. For my own part, my feelings towards the Church of England are no longer and cannot be a *constant quantity*, until I am brought to know whether these clouds, passing between her and my eye, are in herself or not. But the predominant feeling of my mind at this time, and that which always emerges out of the chaos of thought which a time of confusion begets, is, that no resolution involving a great and sharp change of position can be right at such a time: can be right I mean in the full and proper sense, as known to be right, as not only the right thing but done for the right reason: otherwise the man might be right who put into a lottery of religions. The materials of judgment are as it were decomposed, and in a transition state. The Divine Chemistry will before long bring them out into palpable forms. In my own case there is work ready to my hand, and much more than enough for its weakness: a great mercy & comfort. But I think I know what my course would be were there not. It would be to set to work upon the holy task of clearing, opening, & establishing positive truth in the Church of England—which is an office doubly blessed inasmuch as it is both the business of truth, and the laying of firm foundations for future union in Christendom. During the last twelve months I have in letters to you said strong things and things that startled and still startle myself upon what may come. Some things I have learned in Italy that I did not know before, one in particular. The temporal power of the Pope—that great, wonderful and ancient creation, is *gone*—the problem has been worked out—the ground is mined—the train is laid—a foreign force, in its nature transitory, alone stays the hand of those who would complete the process by applying the match. This *seems* rather than is a digression. When that event comes it will bring about a great shifting of parts, much super—and much subtler—position. God grant it may be for good. I desire it, because I see plainly that justice requires it & God is the God of justice. Not out of malice to the Popedom: for I cannot at this moment dare to answer with a confident affirmative the question, a very solemn one, 'Ten, twenty, fifty years hence, will there be any other body in Western Christendom witnessing for fixed dogmatic truth'? With all my soul I wish it well (though perhaps *not* wholly what the Consistory might think agreed with the meaning of the term—) it would be to me a joyous day in which I should see it really doing well. But I must turn off. According to what reaches us here, it is not well pleased with its handiwork in England: and I suppose has some inkling of the idea that the multiplication of individual converts is not the whole of its work nor the sole criterion of its fortunes. If it were, they would indeed be in unbounded prosperity for Lord John Russell the Archbishop of Canterbury (alas for the name) & *Co.*, are manufacturing for them at a marvellous rate. Well and is it to end in a fifteen days imprisonment?[g] If it is, I make only one condition: let the Minister, when he proposes the Bill, do it in a harlequin's jacket: & no speech will be required. I think it plain the *ius regale*[h] has been violated: plain that we should be *justified* in enforcing *it*, and forbidding all such proceedings except with consent: but also plain that they cannot be prohibited under the supremacy doctrine: and doubtful, whether it is upon the whole & now desirable to prohibit at all. On this last question however I am of course open to conviction.

I can say nothing of letters except that I hope to get here what may leave London viâ Marseilles on the 4th[i] and to recover from Rome any that may by this time have been sent off thither.

---

[g] The traditional minimal sentence in criminal law.

[h] More commonly, *iura regalia*, those rights belonging to a sovereign alone.

[i] Gladstone left later than expected, on 18 February 1851 (*GD* iv. 308).

Ever your aff[ectiona]te friend

W. E. Gladstone

The Laprimaudayes are here. I have seen (virtually) nothing of him.

[[BL Add. MS 44248, 118–19; Morley transcript; Lathbury, i. 357–9; addressed: Reverend H. E. Manning, 44 Cadogan Place, London, Gran Brittania, via Marseilles Angleterre; postmarked: cs 10 Fe 10 51; and: 8 FEVR 51 FONT DE P; cf. Morley, i. 382, 385–6, 403)]]

510221mg

44. Cadogan Place.

Feb[ruary] 21. 1851.

My dear Gladstone,

I trust that this will greet you all in safety.[a]

Let me have a word by *Post* when you will be free to see me. I will not come till I hear as you will no doubt have enough to do on first arriving.

Ever yours affect[ionatel]y,

H. E. Manning

[[BL Add. MS 44148, 120–1]]

[[Manning's desire to see Gladstone is noted in his letters to Priscilla Maurice. In a letter to her on 29 January 1851 he wrote: 'I have nothing to tell you about myself except that next week I hope to see Gladstone, and then I shall feel that I have done all that I owe to friends. Then will come my last season of trial. When and how I know not.' And on 11 February he commented to her: 'I find more winds here in a strange movement: with every sign of changes to come and they who should guide unconscious of what is at work. But I have nothing to tell you which newspapers do not. Gladstone does not come home till the end of the month. Of myself I have nothing to say that you do not know' (Bodl. MS Eng. lett. c. 659, 219–20, 223–5). Cf. as well his letter to Wilberforce, 4 February (ibid. 656, 119–22; Purcell, i. 602).

On 1 March Gladstone wrote to Catherine: 'Manning is not well & has sent to ask me to call on him which I must do tomorrow' (SDL, Glynne–Gladstone MS 772, 7–8, 8). He 'Saw Manning (Papal Aggr[ession] &c. *only*)' on 2 March (*GD* iv. 312). On 4 March he reported the meeting to Catherine, throwing light on the remark 'only' in the Diary entry:

Hope is come, looking well and I am to have an evening with him at his request. I saw him on Sunday at Manning's and I like his language but of the two will you believe I was three hours with M[anning] and he never got to the subject, shrinking from it I suppose instinctively: which is no good sign. Of course I did not think it my duty to broach the subject for every day is a day gained. He had influenza but did not look ill. (SDL, Glynne–Gladstone MS 772, 9–10, 9]]

510304mg

44. Cadogan Place.

March 4. 1851.

[a] Gladstone arrived in London on 26 February 1851 (*GD* iv. 310).

My dear Gladstone,

Our meeting on Sunday[a] was so fully bespoken by other and more fitting subjects that I made no reference to matters on which I am anxious to have an hour with you.

Would the morning i.e. from 10½ to 12 of one of the last days of this week: or the afternoon of Sunday suit you: and would your house or this be the better. Any appointment you make shall suit me.[b]

Now the subject on which I wish your mind is this. On what *principle* can the authority of the Church of England in matter[215] of Faith be maintained.

I put this *positively* and *affirmatively* because no negative or destructive arguments against any other system form a basis for us to rest on in working for souls.

Unless some affirmative position can be found or made I feel that my case is ended.

When we meet it will not be my purpose to object to anything but to possess myself of any view you will give me, that I may weigh it afterwards.

Believe me,

Always affect[ionatel]y yours,

H. E. Manning

The Right Hon[oura]ble
W. E. Gladstone
[[Pitts; Chapeau, 184, 262]]

510305gm[a]

Private

6 Carlton G[ardens]

M[ar]ch 5. [18]51.

My dear Manning

I think Sunday afternoon[b] will be best for time & my house if you are well & it suits you for place.

But I cannot accept your suggestion without some kind of *caveat*. I will waive all generalities as to personal incapacity: only saying it would be hard if the fate of the English Church with you were to be seriously touched by the casual & momentary offspring of the brain of one not intellectually alone but morally unworthy to guide anybody or to give them even the rudest material of guidance.

---

[a] 2 March 1851.   [b] See 510314gm.
[a] 'Wrote to Manning' (*GD* iv. 313).   [b] 9 March 1851.

The terms are still harder, if I am to build up a system at random[216] or to endeavour to compress & organise into one during a conversation the ideas which govern my own conduct, especially at a time like this when men are thrown back upon what lies beyond the reach of mere argument, & transcends the power of verbal expression.

And now my dear friend I must tell you that I for one at this time fundamentally mistrust the processes of your mind. I will not now refer again to your letters of last year. I am yet more struck by the issue raised between us when I was at Naples, as to a conversation[217] with you some three years ago after your return from Italy.[c] You were the speaker: I was the listener only; but a listener with eager vigilance nay at the commencement with intense anxiety. You and I are wholly at variance as to that conversation. According to me your[218] very solemn conviction, & if possible more solemn words, related to the Church of E[ngland] as she is *in herself*. You hold the negative. I cannot expect you to adopt my version if you are as assured as I am: that is so assured that (do not smile) I would tomorrow *depose* to it if needful as matter of fact. But you will not be surprised at me if I say, looking back at what I then heard, & comparing it not with your present sentiments generally but with your impressions as to what you then felt. *I* cannot explain that as a case of common forgetfulness—it affords to me a very strong presumption that your mind has broken out from the track in which it was then proceeding, & I thus[219] derive from the facts of your own mental history very strong ethical evidence in favour of the conclusions opposite to those you are embracing.

In my opinion the whole argument now applicable to this question is one not of arithmetical or mathematical precision, but of shades & colours running into one another and dependent therefore for the individual upon the freedom of the eye from discolouring influences & the judgment from the elements that disturb equilibrium. I freely own to you that in the later stages of our correspondence I think a forgone (not conclusion but) bias has been the standard by which all particular arguments have been tried in your mind. I will thus refuse nothing you bid me—but while doing it, I do it under protest—

I hope your influenza is off & you will not be sorry to learn I have good accounts from Naples.

Believe me
Ever aff[ectiona]tely yours
W. E. Gladstone

[c] See 480806mg.

Ven[erable] Archdeacon Manning
[[BL Add. MS 44248, 122–5; Morley transcript]]

510306mg

44. Cadogan Place.
March 6. 1851.

My dear Gladstone,

Sunday[a] at your house, God willing, and at about 2½.

What I ask of you is less than your letter implies. I wish only to know clearly and definitely what your own ground is.

I ask it of you for two reasons—First because I have so long confided in your mind more even, in many things, than in my own: and next because I have been engaged for some time in obtaining from other men whom I much respect the same statement of their views.

And now in turn forgive me, if I openly say that nothing has more shaken my confidence than the turning of a question so impersonal into a personal matter.

The rule of Faith is as objective as the Canon of Holy Scripture, or[220] the doctrine of the Holy Trinity.

Be my faults greater than even you think, or I know yet what I ask stands on its proper evidence.

And where is the reasonableness of tracing to personal bias a conclusion to which at the moment you see minds the most various steadily advancing? Forgive my saying this or rather writing it that I may avoid saying it: for I feel it to be an useless disturbance of a great & vital subject: useful only in my secret examinations[221] and prayers in which believe me it has been present daily for years.

May God be your guide & reward for all your friendship.

Believe me, always affect[ionatel]y yours,
H. E. Manning

The Right Hon[oura]ble W. E. Gladstone[222]

P.S. I feel a great anxiety for your course on the Aggression Bill.[b] It seems to me to be a violation of religious toleration to legislate at all.

H.E.M.

[[Pitts; Chapeau, 185, 262–3]]

[[The day following his letter to Manning, on 6 March 1851, Gladstone noted: 'with Hope I had a sad conversation that came yet nearer home. "Manning's mind I think is

---

[a] 9 March 1851.

[b] Lord John Russell introduced 'A Bill to Prevent the Assumption of certain Ecclesiastical Titles in respect of Places in the United Kingdom' on 14 February 1851 (PP 1851 [45.] iii. 61). On 7 March, Gladstone spoke at the second reading of the bill (*GD* iv. 313; Hansard, cxiv. 1144) which was postponed until 14 March. (*GD* iv. 315; Hansard, cxiv. 1323).

made up: I am not very far from the same." What piercing words. We argued for two hours, but what am I for such high work?' (*GD* iv. 313ᶜ). Manning was on Catherine Gladstone's mind on the same day when she wrote to Gladstone from Italy: 'I had some interesting talk with Lacaitaᵈ about the Roman C[atholic] system. I wish Archdeacon Manning could have heard him. He says we in England have no idea of what goes on. I drew two things particularly—1st the strong feeling he had that the system was most dangerous in its working & caused infidelism—2dly that he sighed for a pure church & in England could²²³ be no R[oman] C[atholic]—I had not before taken in that he knew Manning & upon my speaking about him he seemed to wish he could have seen him now' (SDL, Glynne–Gladstone MS 612).

As planned, on Sunday, 9 March, Gladstone saw 'Manning for three hours of discussion in which I found him unsatisfactory in his grounds as well as apparently fixed in his conclusions' (*GD* iv. 314). On 11 March he met with the Bishop of Exeter 'who told me the B[isho]ps had determined not to move in the Appeal matter this year, & showed me a paper, very ruinous in my judgment, wh[ich] they were meditating' (ibid. 314). Gladstone had hoped that the Bishops would appeal against the Gorham decision and thus possibly allow such men as Manning and Hope a way to remain within the Church of England. On 14 March he attended again to the Ecclesiastical Titles Assumption Bill in Parliament (Hansard, cxiv. 1312; *GD* iv. 315) and wrote to Catherine: 'Nothing cheering of Hope or Manning: the former the best, & much the least morbid of the two' (SDL, Glynne–Gladstone MS 772, 11–12, 12).]]

510314mg

44. Cadogan Place.
March 14. 1851.

My dear Gladstone,
  Shall you be free on Sunday at 3 ocl[ock] in the afternoon?

Ever yours Affect[ionatel]y,
H. E. Manning

[[Pitts; Chapeau, 186, 253]]

[[On 16 March 1851, Gladstone was 'With Manning 2–5. He said that he had got at my meaning about the judge in the early ages & w[oul]d consider it' (*GD* iv. 316). On the day Manning arranged this meeting with Gladstone, conversation with his friend was much on his mind. In a lengthy letter to Robert Wilberforce he wrote:

Thank God, except with my eldest brother, I have not had a word to give me pain.ᵃ My friends come about me as the Jews went to the house of Lazarus, and I never felt any love to the Church of England as impersonated in them so strong.
  Gladstone I have seen, & once talked with on viewpoints. I cannot find that he has any positive view as to the office of the Church or of the Divine Spirit in and through it. He speaks of division suspending its Office, lessening the authority of each divided

---

ᶜ On Hope's struggles at the time see Ornsby, ii. 87–100.
ᵈ James Philip Lacaita (1813–95; *DNB*) was born in Italy, served as a legal adviser to the British legation in Naples to 1852, Professor of Italian in London, 1853–6, and later served as Gladstone's secretary, 1858. Gladstone first met him 13 November 1850 (*GD* iv. 270).
ᵃ Bodl. MS Eng. lett. d. 526, 15–32, letters of November 1850 to 5 April 1851.

part, & therefore the certainty of all points disputed and decided after the division, which by exhaustion is a reductio 'visibiliter ad non esse.'[b]

Hope is minded as I am. (Bodl. MS Eng. lett. c. 656, 160–1; cf. Purcell, i. 608)]]

510317mg

44. Cadogan Place.
March 17. 1851.

My dear Gladstone,

I wish to thank you for your patience with me the last two Sundays:[a] & for the help you have given me. Our conversation yesterday was especially useful, & let me say pleasing also.

My object was to ascertain not the conclusiveness but the enunciation of your thoughts on the subject we spoke of.

In the last year I have been examining again the position of Laud, Chillingworth[b] & Stillingfleet our three best reasoners, as it seems to me: and I feel satisfied that their ultimate position is private judgment exercised upon Scripture & Antiquity. And this I find to be the case of all Anglican writers: & in the last analysis it seems to me to be the position of the Anglican Church as a whole.

It is the corporate private judgment of two Provinces against the whole Church: in many points against the Greek, in more against the Roman; in some points against the whole Church on Earth.

---

[b] Visibly to non-being. 'Omnia tendunt visibiliter at non esse', an adage taken from an Oriel Statute, claiming that the religious foundations were established since 'all things tended visibly to non-being' was widely used among nineteenth-century writers. For a comic use see Ward (1912), i. 227: 'On July 19, with some weariness, but also with a saving sense of humour, Newman relates to Faber... "Have you heard the 'last'? E. is gone! He drank too much beer, laid himself out on the kitchen dresser, packed up and went! Omnia tendunt visibiliter ad non esse, as King Edward says in our Oriel statutes." '

[a] 9 and 16 March 1851.

[b] William Chillingworth (1602–44) was educated at Trinity College, Oxford, elected a Fellow, 1629, converted to Catholicism and went to Douai, 1630, returned to England as a Protestant, 1634, and in 1638 published his highly popular *The Religion of Protestants a Safe Way to Salvation*, thereafter serving as a chaplain in the Royalist forces. Among the many editions of his major work see *The Works of William Chillingworth, M.A. of the University of Oxford: Containing his Book, intituled, The Religion of Protestants, A Safe Way to Salvation: Together with his Nine Sermons Preached before the King, or upon Eminent Occasions: His Letter to Mr. Lewgar, concerning the Church of Rome's Being the Guide of Faith and Judge of Controversies: His Nine Additional Discourses: And an Answer to some Passages in Rushworth's Dialogues, Concerning Traditions* (London: Printed for D. Midwinter..., 1742). For details see *DNB*, Pierre Desmaizeaux (1672/3–1745; *DNB*), *The Life of William Chillingworth*; ed. with notes and translations by the late James Nichols (London: Tegg, 1863), McAdoo (1965), 81–124, and Orr (1967).

Now I owe you a statement of my own thoughts in turn:—

1. It seems to me that Schlegel said most truly that 'the greatest historical[224] authority upon earth is the Catholic Church'.[c]

He meant by authority not commission but weight in evidence & decision.

2. The highest *passive* form of that authority is the universal Tradition of the Church diffused.

3. The highest *active* form is the Church in council, countersigned by the reception *of the* Church diffused.

4. The first seven Councils are examples of this greatest historical authority before the division of East & West.

5. The line of councils held in communion of which Rome was the centre, I believe to be the greatest historical authority as to the Apostolic Faith after the division of the East & West.

6. The Council of Trent received as it has been by that same world-wide communion in all matters of Faith, seems to me the greatest historical authority, as to the Apostolic Faith, now present to the World.

7. All appeals from it to antiquity will I believe be found in the last analysis to be no more than private judgment individual or corporate: I mean of private judgment in its anarchical exercise—not the use of individual intelligence & discernment to apprehend a doctrine propounded by a Teacher, but of criticism & investigation to construct a view and deduce conclusions of its own.

8. All appeals from the Council of Trent to a future general Council when the Church shall be reunited are no more than a rejection of the actual, & greatest historical authority upon earth.

It is like appealing from the actual Sovereignty to a potential which may never exist.

9. But thus far I have stated the case as a[n] historian might. I believe that this 'greatest historical authority' is the embodiment and fulfilment of our Lord's Promise by His own Presence 'always unto the end of the world'.[d] And my submission to that authority is not only upon a principle of reason but upon a principle of faith.[e]

---

[c] Cf. Friedrich Schlegel, *The Philosophy of History, in a Course of Lectures Delivered at Vienna*, trans. James Burton Robertson (2 vols.; London: 1835), ii. 83, 111, 119, 192, 200, 215, 222, 251, 264, 273, 307, 309, 322. The volume was reviewed in the *British Critic* 21 (1837), 140–67; specific reference to the role of the Catholic Church is made, 157–67.

[d] Matt. 28: 20.

[e] Note Purcell's summarization of the passage (1892, 435; cf. Purcell, i. 617): 'The last act of reason is the first act of Faith,' was a proposition which the Cardinal laid down in a private letter to Mr. Gladstone on Faith and Reason.'

This is a very imperfect outline of a subject which even to state would require a better head than mine.

I do not write this to lead to any answer but after your patience & kindness I felt it to be in your debt.

May we be guided by the Light & Spirit of our Divine Lord in this great hour. I do not believe that it is an exaggeration to call it great. It appears to me that the ways of God for a hundred years have been advancing to this point of confluence: and that the mighty frame of the British Empire is to receive a spiritual co-agent of even mightier power & sphere. If I look to the past and to the present I see one & one alone which can cope with this modern Rome and lift it above itself.

I can never tell you what your friendship has been to me. God grant that I may never lose so much of it as you have the will yet to give me.

And may you be guided & strengthened in all your great labour for His Name sake: & blessed with all good gifts in this & the life to come. Believe me,

my dear Gladstone,

Ever your affect[ionat]e friend,

H. E. Manning

The Right Hon[oura]ble
W. E. Gladstone[225]
[[Pitts; Chapeau, 187, 263–5]]

510321mg

44. Cadogan Place.
March 21. 1851.

My dear Gladstone,

If you go to St. Barnabas on Sunday,[a] you will find your refection ready for you here. Or if you *write* I will come to you by 3 ocl[ock].

Always aff[ectionatel]y yours,

H.E.M.

What a scene last night.[b] Will nothing open men's eyes?
[[Pitts; Chapeau, 188, 265]]

510321gm[a]

6 C[arlton] G[ardens] M[ar]ch 21. [18]51.

---

[a] 23 March 1851.

[b] The debate on the second reading of the Ecclesiastical Titles Bill (Hansard, cxv. 220).

[a] 'Wrote to … Manning' (*GD* iv. 317).

My dear Manning

I have wished to reply to your letter but in vain. Without going into any detail however, for the present I would only suggest, that it passes by, and does not in any manner dispose of, the statement which with so much hewing you extracted from me.

If it suits you equally well pray come on Sunday[b] at three to me.

I have to speak at the end of the debate, and am oppressed in mind with the weight of [the] case against the Bill. We expect to divide on Monday.[c] You do my puny labours honour they do not deserve. All that I feel may comfort me as a Christian is this: that without professing or pretending to see the path which is to guide us out of the labyrinth of our present embarrassments, I am reduced simply to looking for and following the will of God in the form which it never quits, that of public Justice.

I remain aff[ectiona]tely yours
W. E. Gladstone

Ven[erable] Archdeacon
Manning

[[BL Add. MS 44248, 126–7; Morley transcript]]

[[Gladstone met Manning on Sunday, 23 March 1851, '2½–4½. Not at close quarters' (*GD* iv. 317). On 27 March Gladstone 'Wrote to . . . H. E. Manning' (*GD* iv. 318; not located).]]

510328mg

44. Cadogan Place.
March 28. 1851.

My dear Gladstone,

Let me reverse my last word and ask you to come here on Sunday:[a] if equally convenient.

Ever yours affect[ionatel]y,
H. E. Manning

[[Pitts; Chapeau, 189, 265]]

[b] 23 March 1851.

[c] On 24 March 1851, Gladstone was again in the house on the Ecclesiastical Titles Assumption Bill but did not speak (Hansard, cxv. 428). The division on the second reading of the Bill occurred on 25 March (ibid. 618; *GD* iv. 316–17; *The Times*, 26 March, 3). See *Ecclesiastical Titles Assumption Bill. Speech of the Right Hon. W. E. Gladstone, M.P., in the House of Commons, on the 25th of March, 1851, on the Motion, 'That the Bill be now read a second Time'* (London: J. Bradley, 1851). Note as well his comments on the matter on 12 May (Hansard, cxvi. 382; *The Times*, 13 May, 2) and 4 July (Hansard, cxviii. 260; *The Times*, 5 July, 3).

[a] 30 March 1851.

[[On 25 March 1851 Manning signed before a Notary his resignation as Archdeacon of Chichester and Rector of Lavington. The meeting with Gladstone, earlier suggested by Manning, took place on Sunday, 30 March, and was described by Gladstone as follows: 'Wrote a paper on Manning's question & gave it to him: he smote me to the ground by answering with suppressed emotion that he is now upon the *brink*: and Hope too. Such terrible blows not only overset & oppress but I fear also demoralise me: which tends to show that my trusts are Carnal or the withdrawal of them would not leave such a void' (*GD* iv. 319). Shortly before his death in a recollection to Purcell, Manning described the meeting thus:

Shall I tell you where I performed my last act of worship in the Church of England? It was in that little chapel off the Buckingham Palace Road.[b] I was kneeling by the side of Mr. Gladstone. Just before the Communion Service commenced, I said to him, 'I can no longer take the Communion in the Church of England.' I rose up—'St. Paul is standing by his side'—and laying my hand on Mr. Gladstone's shoulder, said, 'Come.' It was the parting of the ways. Mr. Gladstone remained; and I went my way. Mr. Gladstone still remains where I left him. (Purcell, i. 617)[c]]]

510331mg

44. Cadogan Place.
March 31. 1851.

My dear Gladstone,

---

[b] The Charlotte Chapel, 12 Palace Street, was built in 1766 by Dr William Dodd; in 1923 it was rebuilt as the St James Theatre and in 1931 as the Westminster Theatre.

[c] According to Wilfrid Meynell's telling: 'The quiet state of Mr. Gladstone's conscience is illustrated by a story the Cardinal told me of the moment when his own mind was made up to submit to the Church. Mr. Manning had left his Archdeaconry and had come to London, where, as the guest of his sister in South Audley Street, he spent much time in deliberation and prayer before becoming a Catholic. It is one thing to lose faith in the Church of England; it is another thing, against the prejudices of a life, to arrive at the belief that the Roman Catholic Church, of which the Pope is the visible Head, [new page] is the one true Church of Christ upon earth. This belief was slowly maturing in his mind and heart. One Sunday Mr. Manning and Mr. Gladstone were out walking together, and they dropped into a proprietary chapel in Palace Street, close to the Buckingham Palace stables. The preacher was the Rev. Thomas Harper, who afterwards as a Jesuit Father wrote a reply to Pusey's "Eirenicon" and also an elaborate work called "The Metaphysics of the Schools." His sermon ended with a series of the solemn texts in which Our Lord bids men leave all things to follow Him. "He that loveth father or mother more than Me, is not worthy of Me." "Unless a man renounce all that he possesses, he cannot be My disciple." "If any man would come after Me, let him take up his cross daily and follow Me." "Does all that say anything to you?" This was the question that Mr. Manning put to Mr. Gladstone when they had left the chapel. "No, I cannot say it does," was Mr. Gladstone's answer. "Well, then, it does to me," said Mr. Manning, "and I am going to act upon it at once"'

I have read as carefully as I can the paper you kindly wrote for me.[a] And with some relief of mind.

If we had drawn different conclusions from the same premisses I should have been disturbed & mistrusted myself: but I find that our premisses differ to an extent I was not aware of.

It is this I think & not any fallacy which makes our conclusions to differ.

The impression I receive from what you have written is that we have a different estimate of what Holy Scripture & the Church teaches (1) as to effects[226] of the Incarnation in its relation to the mystical body of Christ (2) as to the Office of the Divine Head of the Church: (Ephes. iv. 4–16. Col. i. 15. 18. ii. 19. Ephes. v. 23. 24. 'Infallibilitas est intima atque individua Ecclesiae Sponsae, quae est corpus homogeneum et connaturale Christi, cum Eodem Sponso, et capite suo essentiali unitas et conformitas per internam Spiritus Sancti directionem &c.' as Richier says in his apology for Gerson[b]) and (3) as to the Office of the Holy Spirit from the day of Pentecost as supplying the Visible Presence of Christ on earth.

(Wilfrid Meynell in his *Memorials of Cardinal Manning* [London: Burns & Oates, 1892], unpaginated). Compare also J. R. Gasquet, *Cardinal Manning* (London: Catholic Truth Society, 1895), 105: 'One Sunday Mr. Manning and Mr. Gladstone were out walking together, and they dropped into a proprietary chapel in Palace Street, close to the Buckingham Palace stables. The preacher was the Reverend Thomas Harper, who afterwards as a Jesuit Father wrote a reply to Pusey's Eirenicon and also an elaborate work called to The Metaphysics of the Schools. His sermon ended with a series of the solemn texts in which our Lord bids men leave all things to follow Him. "He that loveth father or mother more than Me, is not worthy of Me:" "Unless a man renounce all that he possesses, he cannot be My disciple:" "If any man would come after Me, let him take up his cross daily and follow Me." "Does all that say anything to you?" This was the question that Mr. Manning put to Mr. Gladstone when they had left the chapel. "No, I cannot say it does," was Mr. Gladstone's answer. "Well, then, it does to me," said Mr. Manning, "and I am going to act upon it at once".' Note Manning's later comment as quoted by Leslie, 99–100: 'Manning gave others equal credit for their intentions. When Cardinal Gasquet reported from Oxford that Liddon was insincere, he said: "Do not say that. They used to say the same of me." Gladstone, he thought, was hindered from becoming a Catholic, not by [99] ignorance, but by invincible obstinacy.'

[a] The piece was lost later in 1851. See 611031mg.

[b] [Edmond Richer,] *Apologia pro Joanne Gersonio Pro suprema Ecclesiae & Concilii generalis Auctoritate; atque independentia Regiae Potestatis ab alio quam à solo Deo: Adversus Scholae Parisiensis, & ejusdem Doctoris Christianissimi obtrectatores* Per E. R. D. T. P. (Leiden: Apud Paulum Moriaen, 1676), axiom XVIII, sect. xxiv, pp. 99–100: 'Infallibilitas est intima atque individua Ecclesiae sponsae, quae est corpus homogeneum, & connaturale Christi, cum eodem

I do not attempt to go into these points. The two books you took[c] express my meaning: and they, after all deduction in detail, seem to me to be unanswerable.

The only remark I would make is on your reference to St. John III.8.[d]

This seems to me to unfold the cause of our whole difference.

You say if 'controverted questions go from Parish to Diocese &c. man certainly can tell whence they come and whither they go'.[e]

But surely this view of our Lord's words is not accurate.

He said to Nicodemus 'Why doubt of supernatural mysteries when even the facts of nature are beyond you?'[f] This did not make the uncertainties of the Wind, the measure or analogy of the Spirits operations.

At that very moment he was speaking of Baptism by which the work of the Spirit in regeneration is subjected to a divine and permanent order.

Your view seems to me the view of those who deny Baptismal regeneration only applied to the teaching & guiding office of the Spirit.

It seems to me that this teaching office also is subjected to a divine & permanent order in the Visible Church of which St. Cyprian says 'Unitas veritatis Sacramentum':[g] and that we do know & by the Divine instruction are taught to know how the Spirit guides & preserves the Church in the perpetual custody of the Faith once delivered to its keeping.

But I did not mean even to write as much as this for if I were to write at all I must write much more. I am in no need of the two books: keep them as long as you will. The Melchior Canus will repay all the Study you can give to it.[h]

---

sponsae, & capite suo essentiali unitas, & conformitas per internam Spiritus Sancti directionem, et observationem praeceptorum Dei, ad communionem Sanctorum, Charitatem atque unitatem Ecclesiae constituendam sub externo & visibili Papae, atque Pastorum regimine & ministerio' (Infallibility is the most intimate and individual part of the spouse of Christ, which is the homogeneous and co-natural body of Christ, a unity with its essential head and the same spouse, a conformity through the internal direction of the Holy Spirit and the observation of the commandments of God, to establish the communion of saints, charity, and the unity of the Church under an external and visible Pope and the rule and ministry of pastors).

[c] At the meeting of 30 March 1851. See 510328mg. One of these may have been by the historian Robert Hussey (1801–56; *DNB*), *The Rise of the Papal Power: Traced in Three Lectures* (Oxford: John Henry Parker, 1851) which Gladstone was reading on 30 March.

[d] 'The wind bloweth where it listeth, and thou hearest the sound thereof, but canst not tell whence it cometh, and whither it goeth: so is every one that is born of the Spirit.'

[e] Cf. John 3: 12.   [f] Cf. John 3: 1–21.

[g] Cf. Cyprian of Carthage, *On the Unity of the Catholic Church*, 7: Hoc unitatis sacramentum (this sacrament of unity), referring to the unity of the Church (PL 4. 504).

[h] At the meeting of 23 or perhaps 30 March.

Believe me, Always yours

affect[ionate]ly,

H. E. Manning

The Right Hon[oura]ble

W. E. Gladstone

[[Pitts; Chapeau, 189, 265]]

510401gm[a]

6 C[arlton] G[ardens] Ap[ril] 1. [18]51

My dear Manning,

I would not wish to press upon[227] you for your attention, but by waiting to speak to me, in a matter of such moment, you have put a responsibility upon me, which I must not evade. I therefore will remark to you that your letter of yesterday[228] does not answer my memorandum, but passes it by. If the two books you have kindly lent me[b] express your meaning, I cannot communicate with you upon it, until it has been possible for me to read them. If my representations are ignored, what was the[229] waiting to see me but another instrument of illusion?

You meet the main statement only with[230] a quotation from *Richier* (?), which stands in no contrariety to it and therefore overthrows no part of it.

Nor is my use of John. III. 8, I think, at all open to your objections. Surely I have said nothing against a divine and permanent order in the universal Church! To support this from the text I must have founded myself on a supposition that there was no fixed action of natural causes governing the winds: which you will not suppose.

What I said was this: in the case of the individual, the 'how' is concealed while the result is known: I might have carried my use of the[231] illustration further and said, known not absolutely nor always but sufficiently. I surely could not deny that the work of the Spirit is in a divine and permanent order whether in the Sacrament of Baptism or in the teaching office of the

---

[a] 'Wrote to . . . Manning' (*GD* iv. 320).

[b] See 510331mg. In Gladstone's annotations to his copy of Purcell, he writes beside this letter (PurGl i. 611), 'Ballerini Melchior Cano', indicating that he received Melchior Cano, *De locis theologis, libri duodecim* . . . (cf. Manning to Hope at 501206mg) and Pietro Ballerini (1698–1769), *De potestate ecclesiastica summorum pontificum et conciliorum generalium liber: una cum vindiciis auctoritatis Pontificiae contra opus Justini Febronii . . . Accedit appendix de infallibilitate eorumdem pontificum in definitionibus fidei* (Augsburg: Sumptibus Fratrum Veith, 1770), but there is no indication in *GD* that Gladstone consulted either of these then or ever.

Church. The want of a sensible or intelligible relation between means and ends exalts to my mind the office of Faith in regard to[232] Baptism, and likewise in regard to the maintenance of the[233] Truth in the Church. I do not wish to treat this mere illustration as if it were a demonstration or any thing like or near it. I admit that the words might in some way be satisfied by supposing our Lord simply to mean 'the facts of Nature are unintelligible therefore be not afraid if revealed truths be beyond the compass of the understanding': but this seems to me a meagre meaning, nor have you alleged any reason against believing that they teach more and show[234] that as in nature so in grace we have reality and substance of results while the causative processes are hidden. This is said of Baptism. I remark, that it is true also of the provision for maintaining the Faith in the Church, on my statement of it, but not on yours. *Valeat quantum.*[c] My present point is to show that you simply go past me now, as you did in my reference to *the* conversation of some years back:[d] Oh! look well whither you are going and what work you are marring, but most of all for God's sake look whether you are dispassionately using the means given you of holding fast or reaching the truth.

Forgive haste & believe me, aff[ectiona]tely yours,
W.E.G.

[[Pitts; Chapeau, 190a, 267–8; Purcell, i. 611–12]]

[[On Wednesday, 2 April 1851, Gladstone 'Saw Manning again: He says we differ on premises & he will not in reality discuss' (*GD* iv. 320).]]

510405mg

14. Queen Street. May Fair.
April 5. 1851.

My dear Gladstone,

Bear me in mind in your prayers tomorrow. And may God be with you always.

Ever your attached Friend,
H. E. Manning.

The Right Hon[oura]ble
W. E. Gladstone

[[Pitts; Chapeau, 191, 268; cf. Leslie, 98]]

[[On Saturday, 5 April 1851, Gladstone wrote to Manning 'in answer to his note showing that the blow was to fall tomorrow' (*GD* iv. 320; unlocated).]]

---

[c] How great an influence it [the crowd] can have [in public meetings], Cicero, *Pro Flacco*, 66.

[d] Purcell i. 612 notes that the reference here is to a conversation between the two in 1848 after Manning's return from Italy in which he stated 'a firm assurance of the unmoved and immovable title of the Church of England to her share in the one divine and catholic inheritance.'

ADDENDA TO SECTION VIII
Manning and Hope: January 1850

[[On 31 December 1849 Manning sent a brief note to Hope with enclosures (not located, but in all likelihood the same as those he sent Gladstone on the same day [491231mg]), asking that they be returned (NLS MS3675, 60–1).]]

500105hm
Private

Abbotsford
Jan[uar]y 5 [18]50

Dear Manning. I do not like to allow this post to pass without answering your letter. I do not however yet return the Enclosure because I feel unwilling without more thought, to enter upon the questions to wh[ich] it relates.

I confine myself today to the question of opportunity—I presume you intend to do something public. I know others are of the same mind & seem to feel with you that it is pending this appeal that they should speak.

But I have doubts about this. The only argument in favour of this course is that if the judgment be adverse it will be argued that it is the particular decision & not the jurisdiction wh[ich] lead to remonstrance—but the same reasoning will go further back & touch a protest made even at this stage, e.g. Why wait till the hearing of the cause & the manifestation of adverse views by some of the Judges?—And for this why come forward in this particular case when you allowed the lay baptism justices to pass without notice before the same Tribunal? &c. &c.

In short I think that neither the Church at large nor we in particular can save ourselves from the imputation of being fully committed, and this being so I think that any move wh[ich] is to be made should be much & carefully considered, & brought forward with as much unity of feeling among churchmen as possible. It is a system with which we have to contend—an old established system with many great English names to support it, & the Erastianism of all shades of politicians to render it effective. I am therefore disposed to let this case [*sic*] (Bodl. MS. Eng. lett. c. 657, 56–7).

500120hm[a]

Most Private

Abbotsford

Jan[uar]y 19[235] [18]50.

My dear Manning

I will not trouble you with my excuses for the delay attending my answer to y[ou]rs of the 31st Dec[ember] and its enclosure. The latter I now return—but to comment upon it is not easy, because a considerable part of it relates to the sense in which you individually have submitted to the Church of England, & as this varies from the ground upon which my own submission rests, we do not start from the same point. It may well be, then,[236] that I should put you in possession of my general view upon this head, & you will then be able to follow me in it's [*sic*] application to the particular cases of Hampden & Gorham.

I cannot, then, speak dogmatically of the Church of England as you do in N[umber]s. 2 & 3 of your paper—I know no theory which in strict argument will justify her present position & the attitude she has so long maintained towards the rest of the Church. The hardship of circumstances—in some sense the necessity of the case—appear to me to afford the only plea upon wh[ich] her isolation & the independence of action which (as far as the rest of the Church is concerned) she has assumed, can be defended.

Again as regards the civil power and her subjection to it, I find no other defence. The civil power has since the Reformation undoubtedly usurped part of her proper spiritual authority. Her best divines have, many of them, accepted & justified its interference, & the actual framework of her constitution perpetuates the encroachment.

On what, then, you will ask does my submission rest? I answer, on the belief, weakened but not yet destroyed, that under these heavy burthens, in her solitude & in her bonds, she yet retains the grace of the sacraments & the power of the keys. But if you sh[oul]d ask further how I am assured of this, I should hardly know what to tell you—& when others have consulted me as to remaining or going, my answer has been that I dared not advise. How indeed should I? Unless I accept the theory of development as fully as Newman, there are many things in the Church of Rome which offer difficulty—unless I turn purely Protestant it is impossible to justify all that has occurred & does daily occur in England. Many holier & wiser

---

[a] Manning responded to Hope on 9 January 1850 indicating that all correspondence should be directed to him at 44 Cadogan Place for the next three weeks (NLS MS 3675, 62–3).

men than I have deliberated and gone—but many holier & better than I deliberately remain. It is not then with me a matter which reasoning can decide. I have a conviction that I have the means of grace where I am—means far beyond the use I make of them—and till this conviction is removed I dare not venture on a change.

With these feelings my duty towards the Church of England seems to me this—To watch most jealously that her position be not made worse, & to strive, whenever there is an opportunity, to improve it; but to conceal her defects, or to seek by theory to escape from the facts of her past & present history (whatever I may have thought formerly) is not a course which I should now pursue.

And now as to the two cases of Hampden and Gorham.

Of these the first decided judicially that the Crown may force its nominee into the episcopate without any legal mode of ascertaining his fitness—but then practically we know that the Crown has since the Reformation exercised this power without resistance from the Church—we know also that no utterly unfit person need be accepted by the Church if, either[237] discipline over the priesthood in matter of doctrine keep the general body pure, or at the last moment, those who have to consecrate refuse that office.

We know also that the general practice of Ministers is to consult the Primate beforehand—& that in this case there was no objection.

Was this then a substantial alteration of the system as it existed before, or was it not merely a formal development of that Erastianism wh[ich] in substance had long been acquiesced in?

Then as to the Gorham appeal—how does it differ, except in the importance of the subject matter, from all previous appeals? Since the Reformation the jurisdiction, in the last resort, over all causes Ecclesiastical has been acknowledged in the Crown. The Delegates sat under Royal Commission, and the Judicial Committee of the Privy Council represent the same authority. There may have been more bishops concerned as judges at one time than at the other, but the *source* of jurisdiction was in law the same. This appeal then in point of jurisdiction offers nothing new to my eyes. The subject of it may indeed develop more fully the scandal of the system, but the system has long existed & been an offence in the Church.

On both these points then I would have a change if I could get it, but neither of them disturb materially the grounds of my allegiance, because that allegiance has for some time rested upon considerations, in wh[ich] these difficulties had already played their part,[238] & had allowance made for them.

But if a false judgment be pronounced in Gorham's case & that judgment be acquiesced in by the Church of England, then indeed a new
feature will arise for which I find no place. Whatever be the mouthpiece
which utters the judgment, if the Church does not repudiate it, there is an
article of the Creed struck out—And then indeed there will be a weight
thrown into the scale against my allegiance, which it would seem, ought to
prevail.

But I have already spoken too much of my own views, though you will
see that they assist[239] me, by way of contrast, to remarking on yours. You
have a theory of allegiance based upon Ecclesiastical principles, while
I have not. But when you adopted that theory had you fully considered
the facts? If you had it ought still to hold good, for I maintain that nothing,
in principle, new, has befallen us in the case of Hampden, or, as yet, of
Gorham. But if you have not hitherto read Erastianism in the history of the
Church of England since the Reformation, then I fear you & I have much
to discuss before we can meet upon common ground.

I cannot, then, advise upon your questions from your point of view
because the current of my own thoughts prevents me from entering into it,
but, from my own, I must acknowledge that the affirmance of the Royal
Supremacy by oath, if it be held to mean more than a submission de facto
to a state of things endurable under circumstances for a time, would
present serious difficulty.

And now I believe that I have said all that I can in the present stage of
our correspondence. I have written hastily & I fear in places too boldly—
but these faults I hope you will pardon. I write *for you only* & with a sincere
desire that we may understand each other, & that[240] you will help me to
correct my views where you see me to be wrong. Since Newman left us
I have had little intercourse with any one upon the great questions of
Communion. Nor have they been so much in my mind as they ought to
have been. Indeed, except with Gladstone, & now and then with persons
who have invited me to speak, I have had no inducement to discuss them.
Your letter has opened up the seam of thought again, & I would gladly
work with you in it.

Ever, my dear Manning,
yours most truly,
James R. Hope.

(Bodl. MS. Eng. lett. c. 657, 58–64; Purcell, i. 524–7)

500123mh

44 Cadogan Place
Jan[uary] 23, 1850

Private & Confidential

My dear Hope,

Although I trust to see you when you come to London I prefer to write that I may thank you for your letter which though it does not lessen my difficulties assists me in measuring them; & that I may express in writing what I had rather, for the first time, write than say.

My paper stated a Theory of our Ecclesiastical position which you are unable to receive and I am forced to admit[241] that with the knowledge I have gradually acquired I am unable to defend it.

I can say with truth that I have long believed & taught it. In the course of my time I have had to deal with dissenters. Roman Catholics, Anglicans inclining to the Roman Church, & others already reconciled to it: & I have at all times defended our position upon that statement.

Hampdens case led me to re-examine & to doubt of it. This Gorham case has led me to a fuller examination & a final conviction that of the view as stated in your letter is correct. The question is as to the *Fountain* of jurisdiction, & the *Ultimate* Judge in appeal and I am convinced that since *25* Henry VIII [c. 19][a] it has been in the Crown.

This conviction and the Ecclesiastical Theory of my letter so far as it relates to the Catholic Church are in contradiction.

But the latter has been a deep & unvarying conviction—or rather a point of Faith with me at all times.

The very change which has passed on my view of our Ecclesiastical Statutes brings it on the more openly and inevitably.

But by the Oath of Supremacy & the subscription required in the 36th Canon of 1603[b] I am bound to accept the Royal Supremacy not only as de facto but as de jure.

And this is a strait out of which you cannot help me.

I would nevertheless ask you to hear me in your mind both for counsel and for better aids that I may do nothing rash or wrong: which with my duties of a spiritual kind would be worse than death.

So much for this present about my own difficulty in this especial point.

For the rest of your letter I will say that it will be great comfort to me to share both counsel and action with you.

---

[a] See 500122mg.

[b] 'Declaration and Subscription required of such as are to be made Ministers' (Mackenzie E. C. Walcott [ed.], *The Constitutions and Canons Ecclesiastical of the Church of England* [Oxford: James Parker, 1874], 57–9).

In the Summer of 1848, when I came from Italy I told Gladstone that I did not feel any point in the Roman system to have a 'coercive jurisdiction' over my conscience—meaning that I did not feel a fear of dying in the Church of England, or compelled by any claim or conviction to submit to the Church of Rome.

This has long been my feeling: and I have held to the Church of England not through[242] repulsion from Rome but from love & a belief such as you express that the means of salvation are with us.

I must now admit to myself that the reversing of my sincere belief in our Ecclesiastical status weakens, as you say, my foundation.

What you say of your own mind you gave me fully to understand in Charles Street after you had read Newman's Book: & I have thought much of it, though I have never reopened the subject.

Our present crisis forces the whole question again upon us, for believing as I do in the infallibility of the Church as the only foundation of Faith I am unable to yield to any other authority a final source to interpret.

But I will not go in to this at present. My purpose is to convey to you that my mind is as your own: & that I desire above all things in life to see my path of duty, & to have grace to keep it. Believe me

My dear Hope,
Yours very faithfully
H. E. Manning. (NLS MS 3675, 64–7)

Resolutions Regarding the Gorham Decision: March 1850[a]

Gorham *v.* The Bishop of Exeter [Nine Resolutions as Published in the *Times* (March 20,1850), 5b.]	Resolutions for Consideration on Monday, March 18, at 8, P. M., as proposed since the meeting of March 12.	[Resolutions in Pusey's hand, March 16, 1850)	Resolutions Agreed to at a Meeting held on Tuesday, March the 12th, 1850.
1. That whatever at the present time be the force	1. That whatever at the present time be the force	That we are fully persuaded that *very many* mem-	1. That whatever, at the present time, be the force

[a] Note also among Gladstone's manuscripts the printed circular of 7 February 1850, 'To the Right Reverend the Lord Bishop of London' (BL Add. MS 44566, 89; for text of this and other Protests on the Gorham decision see W. J. E. Bennett, *The Church, the Crown, and the State: Their Junction or their Separation, Considered in Two Sermons, Bearing Reference to the Judicial Committee of the Privy Council* (3rd edn.; London: W. J. Cleaver, 1850), 36.

of the sentence delivered on appeal in the case of Gorham *u* the Bishop of Exeter, the Church of England will eventually be bound by the said sentence, unless it shall openly and expressly reject the erroneous doctrine sanctioned thereby.

of the sentence delivered on appeal in the case of Gorham *u* the Bishop of Exeter, the Church of England, by remaining silent under that sentence, or by neglecting to reaffirm the Article of the Faith therein impugned, would eventually be bound by the same sentence.

There are two other Amendments proposed to this Resolution as follows:

1. That whatever at the present time be the force of the sentence delivered on appeal in the case of Gorham *u* the Bishop of Exeter, the Church of England, will eventually be bound in the fullest manner by the said sentence,

bers of the Church of England, who *seem* to be opposed on the doctrine of baptismal regeneration, do really, (if they could but explain themselves to each other) hold one and the same faith; and for their sake as well as our own we earnestly desire to point out that our present complaint applies to our spiritual error, & not to all that may have ever been wrongly[243] taught in the Church of England concerning Baptismal regeneration.

of the sentence delivered on Appeal in the case of Gorham *u* the Bishop of Exeter, the Church of England will be fully and absolutely bound by the said sentence unless it shall openly and expressly reject the same.

except in so far as it shall openly and expressly protest against the same, by reaffirming the truths thereby impugned.

2. That whatever at the present time be the force of the sentence delivered on appeal in the case of Gorham *u* the Bishop of Exeter, the Church of England, will be bound by the said sentence, if it shall eventually accept the doctrine admitted thereby.

2. The remission of original sin to all infants in and by the grace of baptism is an essential part of the article 'One Baptism for the remission of sins.'	2. That the Article [see Codex Eccl. Afr. cap. 110] 'One Baptism for the remission of sins' as the Nicene Creed has ever been understood by the Church.	That the remission of original sin to all infants in Baptism is an essential part of the article 'One Baptism for the remission of sins' as the Nicene Creed has ever been understood by the Church.	That the said sentence places on equal ground of right two contradictory expositions of an Article of the Creed—to wit—of the Article 'I acknowledge one Baptism for the remission of sins.'

3. That—to omit other questions raised by the said sentence—such sentence, while it does not deny the liberty of holding that article in the sense heretofore received, does equally sanction the assertion that original sin is a bar to the right reception of baptism, and is not remitted, except when God bestows regeneration beforehand by an act of prevenient grace (whereof Holy Scripture and the Church are wholly silent), thereby rendering the benefits of holy baptism altogether uncertain and precarious.	That the said sentence while it does not deny the liberty of holding that article in the sense heretofore received, does equally sanction the assertion that original sin is a bar to the right reception of baptism, and is not remitted, except when God bestows regeneration beforehand by an act of prevenient grace (whereof Holy Scripture and the Church are wholly silent), thereby rendering the benefits of holy baptism altogether uncertain and precarious.

4. That to admit the lawfulness of holding an exposition of an Article of the Creed contradictory of the es-	3. That to admit the lawfulness of holding an exposition of an Article of the Creed contradictory of the es-	That the late judgment, while it does not deny to any Minister of the Church, the liberty of holding that Article in the	3. That to recognise the lawfulness of two contradictory expositions of one and the same Article of the

sential meaning of that article, is, in truth and in fact, to abandon that Article.

sential meaning of that article, is, in truth and in fact, to abandon that Article.

sense heretofore received, pronounces that it is equally admissible to hold that original sin is a hindrance to the right reception of baptism & that it is not remitted except when God bestows regeneration beforehand, by an act of prevenient grace (whereof Holy Scripture and the Church are wholly silent) thereby making the benefits of Baptism wholly uncertain & precarious. (BL Add. MS 44566, 99–100)

Creed is, in truth and in fact, to abandon that article.

5. That, inasmuch as the faith is one and rests upon one principle of authority, the conscious, deliberate, and wilful abandonment of the essential meaning of an article of the Creed destroys that divine

4. That, inasmuch as the faith is one and rests upon one principle of authority, the intelligent, deliberate, and wilful abandonment of the essential meaning of an article of the Creed destroys the divine

4. That, inasmuch as the Faith is one, and rests upon one principle of authority, the abandonment of any article of the Creed destroys the Divine Foundation upon which alone the entire Faith is pro-

foundation upon which alone the entire faith is propounded by the Church.

foundation upon which alone the entire faith is propounded by the Church.

pounded by the Church.

6. That any portion of the Church which does so abandon the essential meaning of an Article of the Creed, forfeits, not only the Catholic doctrine in that article, but also the office and authority to witness and teach as a member of the universal Church.

5. That any portion of the Church which does intelligently, wilfully and deliberately abandon the essential meaning of an Article of the Creed, forfeits, not only the Catholic doctrine in that article, but also the office and authority to witness and teach as a member of the universal Church.

5. That any portion of the Church which has so abandoned an Article of the Creed, forfeits, not only the Catholic doctrine in that Article, but also the office and authority to witness and teach as a member of the Universal Church.

7. That by such conscious, wilful, and deliberate act such portion of the Church becomes formally separated from the Catholic body, and can no longer assure to its members the grace of the sacraments and the remission of sins.

6. That by such intelligent, wilful, and deliberate act such portion of the Church becomes formally separated from the Catholic body, and can no longer assure to its members the grace of the sacraments and the remission of sins.

6. That, by so failing in its office and authority, such portion of the Church becomes formally separated from the Catholic body, and can no longer assure to its Members the Grace of the Sacraments and the Remission of Sins.

8. That all measures consistent with the present legal position of the Church ought to be taken without delay, to obtain an authoritative declaration by the Church of the doctrine of holy Baptism, impugned by the recent sentence; as, for instance, by praying licence for the Church in Convocation to give legal effect to the decisions of the collective Episcopate on this and all other matters purely spiritual.

9. That, failing such measures,

7. That all measures consistent with the present legal constitution of the Church ought first to be taken with a view to obtaining an authoritative declaration by the Church of the doctrine of the remission of sins in holy Baptism, impugned by the recent sentence; as, for instance, by praying licence for the Church in Convocation to declare that doctrine: or by obtaining an Act of Parliament, under the provisions of which the doctrine involved in the said sentence, and all matters purely spiritual, shall be submitted to the collective Episcopate, and legal effect be given to their decisions.

8. That, failing these measures,

7. That all measures within the present legal constitution of the Church ought first to be taken, with a view to an authoritative declaration by the Church of the doctrine of Holy Baptism: as, for instance, by praying licence for the Church in Convocation to declare that doctrine: or by obtaining an Act of Parliament, under the Provisions of which the Doctrine involved in the said sentence, and all matters purely spiritual, shall be submitted to the collective Episcopate, and legal effect be given to their decisions.

8. That, failing these measures,

all efforts must be made to obtain from the said Episcopate, acting only in its spiritual character, a re-affirmation of the doctrine of Holy Baptism, impugned by the said sentence.	all efforts must be made to obtain from the Episco-pate, acting only in its spiritual character, a re-affirmation of the remission of original sin to all infants in Holy Baptism, as ever held by the Church. (BL Add. MS 44566, 105)	all efforts must be made to obtain from the Episco-pate, acting only in its spiritual character, a dec-laration of the doctrine of Holy Baptism. (BL Add. MS 44566, 94)

H. E. MANNING, M.A., Archdeacon of Chichester.

ROBERT I. WILBERFORCE, M.A., Archdeacon of the East Riding.

THOMAS THORP, B.D., Archdeacon of Bristol.

W. H. MILL, D.D., Regius Professor of Hebrew, Cambridge.

E. B. PUSEY, D.D., Regius Professor of Hebrew, Oxford.

JOHN KEBLE, M.A., Vicar of Hursley.

W. DODSWORTH, M.A., Perpetual Curate of Ch. Ch., St. Pancras.

W. J. E. BENNETT, M.A., Perpetual Curate of St. Paul's, Knights-bridge.

HY. W. WILBERFORCE, M.A., Vicar of East Farleigh.

JOHN G. TALBOT, M.A., Barrister-at-Law.

RICHARD CAVENDISH, M.A.

EDWARD BADELEY, M.A., Barrister-at-Law.

JAMES R. HOPE, D.C.L.

The Scottish Bishops on the Gorham Decision: March–April 1850

8 Moray Place, March, 1850

My Lord Bishop,

We, the undersigned Bishop and Clergy of the Diocese of Glasgow and Galloway, beg leave very respectfully to tender our deep and heartfelt thanks to your Lordship for declining (so nobly and faithfully) to concur in the judgment recently pronounced by the Judicial Committee of the

Privy Council on the appeal of the Rev. Mr. Gorham against the sentence of the Court of Arches.

We are deeply impressed with a sense of the very serious consequences to the Church of England, and also (though less directly) to the Church in Scotland, of a decision, claiming to be *de facto* an authoritative decision on an appeal from the Court of His Grace the Lord Primate of All England, as to what statements are to be considered, by legal interpretation, not contrary or repugnant to the meaning of those venerable formularies which the Church receives in common with the United Church of England and Ireland.

The decision would indeed affect all Churches in communion with the Church of England more seriously than is the case at present, if the tribunal from which it had issued were in any sense a tribunal of the Church. We cannot, however, but protest against the opinion incidentally expressed, that the articles only, as distinguished from other formularies of the Church, are to be taken as the rule of doctrine; and when we call to mind that the Discipline of the Church is so greatly impeded and marred by the civil power, we find it difficult to express the feelings with which we find an argument in favour of lax interpretations, extracted from that indiscriminate use of the Burial Service, which, under heavy penalties, is compulsory on the Clergy of the Church of England, in the case of persons not excommunicate.

For these reasons alone, we should feel thankful to your Lordship for withholding your sanction and concurrence from the decision; but in the present instance we are chiefly anxious to express our grateful sense of your Lordship's firmness and faithfulness in refusing to concur with a sentence, whereby it is decreed that regeneration in Holy Baptism is not the clear and unquestionable doctrine of the Church of England, and that a Minister of the Church can reasonably, and most lawfully, deny the regeneration of infants.

With sincere gratitude to your Lordship's faithful act, with great veneration of your sacred office, and respect for your person and character, and with prayer for the divine guidance and blessing on behalf of all persons who are called to take part in this great responsibility,

We are,

My Lord Bishop,

Your Lordship's faithful servants,

Walter John,
Bishop of Glasgow and Galloway.

PS. It is proper to observe that it is proposed to send a copy of this letter to the *Guardian* newspaper.

The Right Hon. and Right Rev. the Lord Bishop of London.
Reverend Brother,

In lieu of the Pastoral Address to the Lord Bishop of London, Resolutions to the following effect will be proposed in the Synod, to be holden in the Vestry of St. Mary's, Glasgow, on Thursday next, 21st instant:—

1. That the recent decision of the Judicial Committee of the Privy Council in the case brought before them on the appeal of the Reverend Mr. Gorham, from the sentence of the Court of Arches, has a very material bearing on the doctrinal statements not only of the Church of England, but of all Churches which receive the Formularies of the Church of England, and are in communion with her.

2. That without more particular reference to the special arguments on which that decision is grounded (against which this Synod solemnly protests), the Synod has to consider the most momentous fact, that the language of Formularies, which this Church has always considered to be clear and unambiguous, on a point of the very deepest importance, is declared by the highest judicial authority in England to be so doubtful, that it is reasonable and lawful for one Minister to affirm, and another to deny, the Regeneration of Infants in Holy Baptism.

3. That the bearing of such a decision on the doctrines of the Church, whether in England or elsewhere, would indeed be more direct than in the case at present, if the Court which had issued it had by any title to be regarded as a Court of this Church; but still the fact, that the highest judicial tribunal (sitting as a Court of Appeal from the Ecclesiastical Courts, with power to compel the institution of a Priest declared heretical by these Courts) has pronounced such an opinion as to the *legal construction of those venerable Formularies which this Church receives in common with the Church of England*, demands the most prompt and determined action on the part of all those who, by their sacred office, are guardians of the Faith, and more especially on the part of the several Synods of the Church in Scotland.

4. That it is the more important that the Synods of this Church should solemnly record their sentence on this declared construction of its Formularies, inasmuch as the legal status of this Church depends on the subscription of the Thirty-Nine Articles by its Clergy; and consequently, the construction put on those Articles by the highest judicial Authority in England must most materially affect the question as to the sense in which they are received by this Church.

5. That this Synod does in the most solemn manner record its decision, that the Regeneration of infants in Holy Baptism is the natural and

legitimate meaning of the Formularies of the Church, and that no other doctrine would be consistent with the truths of Holy Scripture or the doctrine of the Primitive Church.

6. That the Synod very respectfully solicits from the Venerable Synod of the Bishops of this Church, and from the several Diocesan Synods, an attestation to the aforesaid solemn declaration; and that the Synod Clerk do communicate, the above resolutions to the Clerk of the Episcopal Synod, and to the Clerks of the several Diocesan Synods, and take all other legitimate means to give publicity to the resolutions thus solemnly adopted.

7. That the Synod has heard with joy and thankfulness, that the Right Honourable and Right Reverend the Lord Bishop of London did not concur in the decision of Privy Council; and that these Resolutions be respectfully communicated to His Lordship.

I am,

Reverend Brother,

Your faithful and affectionate servant,

W. J. Trower,

Bishop of Glasgow.

8 Moray Place, March 16, 1850 (BL Add. MS 44369, 83–4)

DECLARATION BY THE BISHOPS OF THE CHURCH IN SCOTLAND, OCCASIONED BY THE RECENT DECISION OF THE JUDICIAL COMMITTEE OF THE PRIVY COUNCIL.

Given at their Synod, on the 19th day of April, 1850.—Aberdeen.

To the Very Reverend the Deans, and the Reverend the Presbyters of the Scottish Episcopal Church: the Bishops, in Synod assembled, send greeting: Grace be with you, Brethren, and Peace from God the Father, and from our Lord Jesus Christ.

WHEREAS, certain Memorials and Addresses have been presented to us from various Diocesan Synods, expressing much uneasiness respecting the recent Decision by the Judicial Committee of Privy Council on the Appeal of the Rev. G. C. Gorham v. the Right Rev. the Lord Bishop of Exeter, and requesting our Paternal Advice for the allaying of doubts, hence arising, as to the true meaning of our Authoritative Formularies:—We, the Bishops of the Church, deeply sympathizing with our Reverend Brethren the Presbyters, in their anxiety to maintain, unimpaired, the purity of 'the Faith which was once delivered to the Saints,'[a]—declare, that We do not consider the Sentence, in the case referred

---

[a] Jude 3.

to, as having any authority to bind us, or to modify in any way the Doctrines which We, and the Episcopal Church in Scotland, hold, and have always taught, respecting the nature of Baptismal Grace. We have always held, as we were taught by those who preceded us in the Episcopate, that the Doctrine of the Church in Scotland is to be collected from the Scripture, the Creeds, the Articles, and other Formularies of the Church jointly, and not from the Articles or Formularies separately; and that, on the subject of Baptismal Grace, there is no discrepancy between the teaching of the Church in her XXVIIth Article, in the Baptismal Offices, and in the Catechism. We declare, then, that We teach, and always have taught, and We entreat, and, to the extent of our Episcopal Authority, do enjoin you, Brethren, severally to teach,—

1. In the words of our Blessed Saviour, that, 'Except a man be born of Water and of the Spirit, he cannot enter into the Kingdom of God;'[b] or, as expressed in our Office for Holy Baptism, 'None can enter into the Kingdom of God, except he be regenerated and born anew of Water and of the Holy Ghost.'

2. In the words of the Nicene Creed, with every branch of the Holy Church throughout all the world, which continues in 'the One Faith,' lives in 'the One Hope,' and acknowledges 'the One Baptism,' 'We acknowledge One Baptism for the Remission of Sins.'

3. In the words of the XXVIIth Article, that 'Baptism is a Sign of Regeneration or New Birth, whereby, as by an Instrument, they that receive Baptism rightly are grafted into the Church; the promises of forgiveness of Sin, and of our adoption to be the Sons of God by the Holy Ghost, are visibly signed and sealed; or, in the words of 'The Office for public Baptism of Infants,' that every child baptized according to that Office is then and there 'regenerate and grafted into the body of Christ's Church.'

4. With the 'Catechism, or Instruction, to be learned of every person before he be brought to be confirmed by the Bishop,' and which teaches him to say, 'In my Baptism I was made a member of Christ, a Child of God, and an inheritor of the Kingdom of Heaven.'

5. That the doctrine of Baptismal Grace is so clearly expressed in the Offices and Formularies of the Church, as they now exist, and as they were adopted by the Episcopal Church in Scotland, that We see no need of more than the present Declaration, or of adding, by any Canonical enactment of Ours, to the definitions of that doctrine, as therein set forth.

All the preceding statements, Reverend Brethren, We teach, and, by the authority committed to us, We enjoin you to teach to the Flocks under your charge, in their plain, and natural, and grammatical sense, without the intervention of any hypothesis—charitable or otherwise.

[b] John 3: 5.

And now, Brethren, beseeching you to join with us in prayer, that the Church over which the Holy Ghost hath made Us overseers, may be kept in the unity of the Spirit, and in the Bond of Peace,—We commend you to God, and to the Word of His Grace, which is able to build you up, and to give you an inheritance among all them which are sanctified.[c]

W. J. TROWER, D.D.

Bishop of Glasgow, Clerk to the Episcopal Synod.

This Paper was adopted unanimously, with the exception of Resolution V., in lieu of which the two under-signed Bishops adhere to the following Resolution:—

That the doctrine of Holy Baptism is so clearly expressed in our Formularies, that, although the fact of the late decision has given occasion for the present Declaration, We do not mean hereby to assert that the language in those documents is not precise and sufficient.

A. P. FORBES,

Bishop of Brechin

W. J. TROWER,

Bishop of Glasgow

(BL Add. MS 44566, 127; for a copy see also W. J. Trower [Bishop of Glasgow and Galloway], *A Pastoral Letter to the Clergy of the Diocese of Glasgow and Galloway in Reference to Questions Connected with the Recent Decision of the Judicial Committee of the Privy Council* [Glasgow: Maurice Ogle & Son, 1850], 42–4)

Manning and the Wilberforces on Gladstone's 'Engagement': May 1850

Lavington, May 22. 1850.

My dear Robert

First will you kindly direct the inclosed to Mr. Pope?[a] I do not know his X[Christ]ian name, or address.

Next, have you examined the B[isho]p of London's Bill?

It seems to me to be a total, & vital failure.

The Crown in Council is to possess still the absolute power of deciding whether or no any question of doctrine is involved: & of referring to the Bishops or not accordingly.

Now in the Gorham case they say that they have not touched doctrine at all.

Again & again, therefore, the same evil may be inflicted under the same disclaimer upon the other 11 articles of the Creed.

Half the Church of England, & our dear brother among the rest, maintains that doctrine has not been touched.

[c] Cf. Acts 20: 32.   [a] Not located.

This seems to me like quos deus[244] vult perdere, etc.[b]

Further, Gladstone has written to me on a scheme he says he spoke of to you (as he thinks)—an engagement to be entered into binding men not to move without two months' notice, and opportunities of discussion, etc.

I have answered that I can in no way accede. I object to all engagements: and I dread exceedingly the temptation to tamper with personal convictions, and individual conscience: and the support derived from numbers against our light before our Father which seeth in secret.

These & many more reasons make my declining final. (Bodl. MS Eng. lett. c. 655, 204–5; Purcell, i. 538)

[[On 24 May 1850 both Robert and Henry Wilberforce responded to Manning concerning the plan. Robert wrote, 'I thought Gladstone's plan therefore a good one, when it was mentioned to me, & that it might keep men together, & help in final action. I feel how much I shrink from this, & that at present I am not prepared' (Bodl. MS Eng. lett. c. 655, 207). Likewise, Henry Wilberforce commented on the plan to Manning: 'R. Cavendish told me Mr. Gladstone had a plan to prevent individual action, ab[ou]t which G[ladstone] told me he had written to you. Anything wh[ich] could secure that result would be that important of course. But how to secure it. No one I suppose moves, except under *impulsion*, and when this comes how would such a combination as G[ladstone]'s prevent it?' (ibid. 211).

Writing to Robert Wilberforce on 4 June 1850 Gladstone knew his plan lost: 'The idea of a voluntary anti-precipitation compact languishes. Manning resolutely held off: and I am exceedingly reluctant in anything to part from him. Others who had affirmed have been similarly moved by his disinclination and on the whole I can hardly think it will go on unless energetically taken up by some persons who desire it' (Bodl. MS c. 67, 22–3).

On 10 July Manning mentioned the plan to Robert once more, but then as fully rejected:

No human power or persuasion could induce me to put my hand to any such declaration, especially in combination with men who could sign it in a sense & with an animus[c] so different from my own.

But in truth, I have resolved to combine with no one. When I refused Gladstone's proposal, to whom affection and confidence bind me so closely, I refused all proposals of this kind for ever. Events have set me loose and I mean by God's help to follow what seems His guidance: taking counsel chiefly of yourself, Gladstone, & James Hope. If I might I would urge you to the same course.

It will not preclude us from aiding to the full in any reasonable plan—but it will secure us from most inconsistent and mischievous combinations, the end of which will be confusion or compromise. (Bodl. MS Eng. lett. c. 656, 5–6; Purcell, i. 539)]]

---

[b] Quos deus vult perdere, pius dementat (Whom the god wishes to destroy, he first drives mad), a common Roman adage ascribed to Euripides.

[c] Intention.

Gladstone to the Bishop of London: July 1850

500716gl

6 C[arlton] H[ouse] G[ardens] July 16. 1850

Private

My dear Lord Bishop

I think it my duty to inform your Lordship of the present state of feeling within the limited circle of my own personal acquaintance direct or indirect, with regard to the great question that agitates the Church.

The speech in which your Lordship laid such broad and solid ground for a legislative measure gave I believe the warmest satisfaction and along with that sentiment necessarily excited corresponding expectations.

Those expectations are now flagging and a dread begins to be entertained but the vital issues of the Church which are involved in the issue should be left only to the chances of a periodical struggle in Parliament which must in all probability be renewed more and more faintly in each session and must shortly cease to be renewed at all, unless there be measures taken by the bishops as shall keep the sound and warm feeling of the Church still rallied around them.

By what you and your Right Rev[erend] Brethren have already done I am convinced that you *have* prevented lamentable events which must otherwise have happened. A continuance of effort will I trust further and ever permanently prevent that scattering which seems so ever certain to ensue should a persuasion unhappily come to prevail that the protesting Bishops mean to treat the question *only* as one for Parliamentary argument in reference to the constitution of the Court of appeal.

Men feel the consultation of knowing that the formularies of the Church are properly its law: and that those formularies remain unaltered. On this account it is that they so generally admit the character of the Church not yet to have been compromised by the late Judgment.

But on the other hand that is also strongly felt which your Lordship told us with so much force of truth that much of our law is of necessity Judgemade law and it is felt that if the Judgemade law of the late decision now finally affirmed in the Courts shall govern the proceedings of the Bishops of the Church in admission whether to orders licence or benefice, that will be effectively the law of the Church of England & the mere *litera scripta*[a] of the Formularies however dear can no longer be pleaded against it.

---

[a] Written letters.

Under these circumstances men must either look to their Bishops as their natural leaders and protectors or they must act for themselves in modes more or less perilous.

In these times of mistrust it would not be difficult to lighten the present pressure & demand upon the Bishops for guidance but it would be at the cost of many lamentable occurrences and at the hazard I fear of utter disorganisation.

I suppose therefore that each man in his sphere should urge and encourage others to rely on the Bishops.

But for this it is I think extensively felt to be essential that the Bishops should not act in the Parliamentary sphere alone but should stand forth as the shepherds of the people to reassure their fainting hearts not only upon their own personal belief which is hardly in question but, in terms of whatever decorum and reserve go to the late Judgment upon the larger question whether the Church of England is to be ever again governed and administered according to the true doctrine or not.

This it has been hoped might be done by some joint proceeding such as was spoken of at an earlier stage of these sad affairs: and the hope is perhaps the more natural because no one can feel very sanguine of our attaining any effectual remedy, who calculates only on the Parliamentary force available for your Lordship's Bill.

One of the apprehensions I entertain as of a danger to the possible & proximate is this: that unless such indications as I have referred to be given, many will grow more & more afraid of seeing the Life and Faith of the Church crushed under its outer framework and will be very unwilling to rally in defence of its Civil Establishment especially on occasions when it is a favourite point of attack. I have in view particularly the Irish Church. The licence too of opinions among its clergy, the conduct of some of its Bishops in Parliament, the commencement of doubt in the minds of many whether it is really and purely teaching in the face of the Church of Rome all the articles of the Catholic Faith, its utter inaction and seeming satisfaction with the Gorham Judgment, all tend to increase the strain of the vote for the Irish Church.

Another apprehension of course is secession.

A third is this. The licence of construction has been carried up to contradiction by the recent Judgment. It has been done no doubt in favour of our particular class of opinions only. But persons of other schools will avail themselves of it should they come to believe that what has been done will be acquiesced in. Whatever amount of secessions there might be to the Church of Rome in such a case, many would remain behind even of those most vitally differing from what may be called Gorhamism: many indeed with afflicted hearts, in silence & in doubt: but many more who with avowed estrangement of affection for the Ch[urch] of England would more & more freely indulge whatever tendencies they might have acquired towards the Church of Rome and working effectively for her would nevertheless at the least plausibly maintain their position by pleading on their own behalf the principles of construction involved in the Gorham judgment.

Of all these forms of evil & perhaps of others yet more formidable I see the germs even within the circle of my own personal knowledge: and for all of them as restive there may be one and the same preventive namely evidence proceeding I will not say from all the Bishops but at least from some convincing *body* of them that they hold the doctrine of Baptism to be authoritative in the Church of England.

For I need hardly observe to your Lordship that the language adopted by some Prelates reaching apparently to this extent of meaning that the religious character of the Church never can be affected by such a Judgment even if accepted & habitually acted upon, though it may have a composing effect upon minds of a certain tone yet on the contrary alarms in the highest degree those who accept in its full & natural sense the declaration that the Church is bound to be a keeper and witness of Holy Writ & who therefore see that she cannot fail to have the doctrines of the Faith wh[ich] Holy Writ contains not for the accident only but for the law of her teaching.

Of course it is no part of my object to put your L[ordshi]p to the trouble of acknowledging this letter and I remain [*sic*] (BL Add. MS 44369, 335–8)

The Manning, Wilberforce, and Mill Declaration: August 1850

The following Declaration touching the royal supremacy in matters ecclesiastical has been put in circulation amongst the clergy.

'Whereas it is required of every person admitted to the order of deacon or priest, and likewise of persons admitted to ecclesiastical offices or academical degrees, to make oath that they abjure all foreign jurisdiction, and to subscribe to the three Articles of Canon XXXVI., one whereof touches the royal supremacy:

'And whereas it is now made evident by the late appeal and sentence in the case Gorham v. the Bishop of Exeter, and by the judgment of all the courts of common law, that the royal supremacy, as defined and established by statute law, invests the Crown with a power of hearing and deciding in appeal all matters, howsoever purely spiritual, of discipline and doctrine:

'And whereas to give such power to the Crown is at variance with the Divine Office of the Universal Church, as prescribed by the law of Christ:

'And whereas we, the undersigned clergy and laity of the Church of England, at the time of making the said oath and subscription, did not understand the royal supremacy in the sense now ascribed to it by the courts of law, nor have until this present time so understood it, neither have believed that such authority was claimed on behalf of our Sovereigns:

'Now we do hereby declare:—

'1. That we have hitherto acknowledged, and do now acknowledge, the supremacy of the Crown in ecclesiastical matters to be a supreme civil power over all persons and causes in temporal things, and over the *temporal accidents of spiritual things.*

'2. That we do not, and in conscience cannot, acknowledge in the Crown the power recently exercised to hear and judge in appeal the internal state or merits of spiritual questions touching doctrine or discipline, the custody of which is committed to the Church alone by the law of Christ.

'We therefore, for the sake of our consciences, hereby publicly declare that we acknowledge the royal supremacy in the sense above stated, and in no other.

'Henry Edward Manning, M.A., Archdeacon of Chichester.

'Robert Isaac Wilberforce, M.A., Archdeacon of the East Riding.

'William Hodge Mill, D.D., Regius Professor of Hebrew, Cambridge.'
(*The Guardian* on 21 August 1850, 602; see also Purcell, i. 540–1)

[[Note also the printed circular in response by Keble, Pusey, and Marriott:]]

Reverend Sir,

During the circulation of the statement on the Royal Supremacy recently put forth by Dr. Mill and Archdeacons MANNING and WILBERFORCE, it appeared that very many; who felt strongly about the general object, were yet, on different grounds, deterred from signing that declaration.

In order to remove these difficulties, the following declaration has been drawn up, chiefly in the words of our formularies, and confined to the one point of 'defining, explaining, or pronouncing upon the doctrine and discipline of the Church.['] For although a Court cannot define what *ought* to be the doctrine of the Church, it appears from the recent decision that it has a very large scope in defining what is, or (in its mind) is not, the Church's doctrine. It is obvious, too, that on other points (as the inspiration of Holy Scripture) there would be still more latitude for defining what need not be held by one having cure of souls. The following declaration is supplementary to the former: it is intended to give further opportunity to those who are bound by their signature in admission to maintain publicly, if they so wish, their meaning in that admission; and this because 1. The interpretation put upon it by the practice of the Court would, unless openly protested against, become its meaning; 2. Because we lie under the imputation of inconsistency, if we oppose the authority of the Privy Council in controversies of faith, and yet give no explanation of our own admission that the Queen is the Supreme Governor in all spiritual or ecclesiastical causes; 3. Because the knowledge that a considerable number of those who make this admission deny the power claimed by the Privy Council, and consider it as a grievance, might be of avail towards recovering the freedom of the Church.

The following declaration has been purposely confined to the single point which was raised by the recent decision upon a fundamental doctrine. It is not denied that the Queen's Majesty may 'refer questions touching doctrine to spiritual judges duly authorised by the Church herself;' but since 'the Church hath authority in controversies of faith' (*Art.* 20.), it is intended to deny that the Crown has that authority, directly or indirectly.

No more is here meant than to assist any who may of their own mind wish to declare that, in solemnly acknowledging the Supremacy of the Crown, they do not acquiesce in the power recently exercised by the Privy Council. Many who would gladly join in any declaration, do not yet like to frame one for themselves. Other and better might doubtless be framed. This is intended as a suggestion only.

If this declaration should receive your concurrence, and you should please to empower any of us to affix your name to it, we will take care to have it affixed to a copy lying at Mr. Stewart's, Bookseller, 11 King William Street, West Strand, London; or the name may be sent directly to

> Your faithful servants,
> J. KEBLE
> E. B. PUSEY
> C. MARRIOTT

We, the undersigned, having by subscription affirmed 'the King's Majesty, under God, is the only supreme governor of this realm, and of all other his Highness's dominions and countries, as well in all spiritual or ecclesiastical things or causes as temporal' (*Can.* xxxvi. S. 1), do accordingly acknowledge that the Queen's Majesty has 'that only prerogative, which we see to have been given always to all godly princes in Holy Scriptures by God himself; that is, that they should rule all estates and degrees committed to their charge by God" (*Art.* 37); but we deny that she has authority in controversies in faith, or may directly or indirectly define, or explain, or pronounce with authority upon the doctrine or discipline of the Church. (Bodl. MS Eng. lett. c. 654, 345–6; see also Liddon, iii. 271–2)

Manning to Maurice on the Gorham Decision: August 1850

[[The following Treatise on the Gorham Decision in Manning's hand and with it his letter to Priscilla Maurice, postmarked 20 August 1850 HURSTORRE is preserved in CP.]]
[1A—Treatise]

The substance of the able papers you sent me seems to be

1. That the present Judgment does not touch doctrine
2. That it only ascertains that the discipline of the Ch[urch] of E[ngland] is defective[245]

3. That therefore although Bishops will be compelled to institute clergymen holding the doctrine of Mr Gorham: and corruption & error of doctrine may or must ensue among the members of the Church, yet that these stains are not affixed to the Church of E[ngland] herself.

I wish I could take this view for though it would not remove difficulties of a formidable kind, it would mitigate them.

But I fear it will be found to rest on insufficient grounds.

1. For though it be true that the Judicial Committee disclaimed the power to decide whether a certain doctrine were 'theologically sound or unsound,' it claimed to judge whether the said doctrine were '*contrary or repugnant to the doctrines of the Church of England* as by law established.' See Judgment &c.

I admit that in this way it may be represented as a mere verifying of the terms of the legal establishment, or an identification of those terms.

This would hold if the controversy were between Church & State. The original covenant must be discussed & verified in such a contest.

But this is an appeal involving an internal variance in the Church. And the Church has by two Judgments: that of the Bishop, & Court of Arches pronounced on the merits of the case and the true interpretation of formularies.

The Church courts judge as to *soundness* as well as *lawfulness*. It is manifest that the Judicial committee in disclaiming to judge of *soundness* disclaimed *nothing* as to their competency to entertain questions of doctrine. They carry all power under one aspect of the question. Go through the Articles of the Creed: the J[udicial] C[ommittee] may on each say 'we pronounce nothing as to the *soundness* of contrariant expositions upon any but we declare them all to be lawful.'

It is obvious that such a power can never be entrusted to any human tribunal, for the Church is a Divine one; and the Church[246] alone determines the intentions of its own formularies.

And the rule is at this moment[247] recognized in our English Law. The Courts at Westminster in 'Quare impedit' send questions of doctrine to the Archbishop and on[248] receiving his certificate *apply* the law.

The Judicial Committee reopens the *merits* of the question being advisors of the Crown as supreme *Ecclesiastical* Judge. I believe they were wrong in statute law though I rejoice at it in disclaiming the power to pronounce on the *soundness* also. The 26 Hen[ry] VIII [c. 1] as reenacted or incorporated with 1 Eliz[abeth c. 1] gives this to be exercised through Commissioners or Delegates empowered to try the merits of the questioners.[249]

Therefore I think the J[udicia]l C[ommit]tee distinctly claims power to affix an interpretation under plea of announcing its *lawfulness*. And this proceeding seems to me to shew that the existence of such an Appellate Jurisdiction is inconsistent with the safety of the Faith, & with the Divine Office of the Church.

2. It seems to do more than shew that the Discipline of the Ch[urch] of E[ngland] is defective. It shews also that its doctrinal formularies have been tampered with so as to make them ambiguous: & that the Ch[urch] of E[ngland] has put itself at the mercy of the Civil Power. The Oath of Supremacy & subscription to the 36. Canon bind us to receive this state of the land.

3. The effect of the Judgment is (1) to bind all Bishops to institute clergymen holding Mr Gorhams doctrine & (2) all Courts to give impunity to such interpretations as the Statement of the J[udicial] C[ommittee] has declared to be lawful.

Now this seems to me to fix itself deeply into the very life of the Church of England.

1. Because the Faith of the Church is conserved & proposed in two ways 1. orally, & 2 by definitions. This judgment vitiates both. It declares the definitions to be ambiguous, and it admits false doctrine into the *oral* teaching of the Faith, which is after all the great tradition of the Church

2. Because it *destroys* the divine *authority* [double underlining] of the Faith, both written and oral, the Church of E[ngland][250] is to have[251] no doctrine on Baptism: that is it is to[252] have two:[253] both[254] equally *lawful*: neither is to be[255] propounded by the Church of England as of divine Faith. This runs through all & vitiates all other articles not touched in the present controversy. The Divine Office of the Church of England is thereby[256] annulled unless it throw off this falsehood & teach one truth as to Baptism, & that on the *authority* of God.

3. Because the supreme power of the State assumes the final office of judging of the fitness of men for cure of souls: & wrests *mission* out of the hands of the Church. This part which is little regarded is to me by itself vital. It is the whole question of Investitures. It prostrates the Church, & the succession of the Apostles at the feet of the Civil Power.

Therefore I feel that the effect of the judgment, under whatever technical or fair seeming plea on the part of the King's power:[257] is no less than a simple transfer of supreme *spiritual* authority & jurisdiction to the State: And the Church thereby descends to a place among national institutions,

& human corporations. Even sects retain more of the 'Jerusalem above' which is free.

Now I feel that this is rather a Priests answer to a Lawyers argument: therefore I will add one word. It is clear

1. That the State proposes by law the power it has been now exerting.

2. That such a power is so vitally inconsistent with the Divine Office of the Church that if it shall longer acquiesce in it, the divine Commission will be betrayed.

3. That in no Ecclesiastical Code I know is any State permitted to touch the *merits* of a question of doctrine. The Church Courts are final. See, if you can get access to it. Rechbergers Enchiridion Iuris Eccl[esiastici] Austriaci Ch VI Recursus ad Principem[a] or Orsi[b] or Ferraris.[c]

[1B—Letter]

If you can read on this thin paper I will add a few lines more. A number of our brethren think they must leave England for Rome because they cannot procure the condemnation of Mr Gorham as a heretic. Are they sure that there are not heresies on the very subject in the Romish Church, heresies which will not be condemned by Bishops & Popes, any more than Mr Gorham's are by Privy Councillors? In the Conferences, M. Lacordaire the most powerful & popular preacher in France, held before the A[rch]-b[isho]p of Paris in the Notre Dame I find a passage part of it eloquent & powerful on Baptism. Will you ask Maria what the thrust of these words. Un homme est venu; il a versé de l'eau et approncé des paroles sur votre tête; il a ordonné aux esprits ennemis de se retirer de vous; *il est entré dans votre âme pour y ôter le mal et y semer le bien* Conferences [illegible word] p. 100 [?].[d] To me they sound little less than blasphemy. Is this just because I *do* believe that the Holy Ghost is verily & indeed given in Baptism[?] If I thought with Mr Gorham I might resolve M. Lacordaire's words into

---

[a] Georg Rechberger, *Enchiridion iuris ecclesiastici Austriaci. Ed. idiomate Germanico, . . . latinitate donavit . . .* (2 vols.; Linz: Haslinger, 1824).

[b] See Giuseppe Agostino Orsi, *De irreformabili romani pontificis in definiendis fidei controversiis judicio* (4 vols.; Rome: Typis Sacrae Congregationis de Propaganda Fide, 1739), and note the use of the work by Manning in his later *Petri Privilegium: Three Pastoral Letters to the Clergy of the Diocese* (London: Longmans, 1871), often quoting the work by its running title, 'De romani pontificis auctoritate'.

[c] Lucius Ferraris (d. 1760), *Promta bibliotheca canonica, juridica, moralis, theologica.*

[d] For Lacordaire text see Henri-Dominique Lacordaire (1802–61), *Conférences de Notre-Dame de Paris. Tome troisième* (Paris: Sagnier et Bray, 1848), 263–4.

one extravagant metaphor as a bold exaggeration; holding the words of our catechism in their strict sense. I cannot read the passage without shuddering[258] But [MS damaged, 5–6 words missing] pious & able Roman Catholic; his words which give no pain to the Archbishop [MS damaged, 5–6 words missing]—of this thought nominally & formally Romanism does not [MS damaged, 2–3 words missing] insist upon the person of the Priest as necessary to a valid baptism. What does this shew [MS damaged, 1–2 words missing] there is a habit of mind among Romanists there is another habit of [mind am]ong Englishmen which is unfavourable to the full belief of God's [MS damaged, 1–2 words missing] by our Sacrament & that this like ground is to be got hold of is kept in to[259] by [illegible word] declaration of God. Truth at by or [illegible word]—we are sure of [a] written answer to procure the nominal condemnation of [illegible word] on this [illegible word] (CP).

Manning's Letter of Resignation to the Bishop of Chichester: October 1850

501023mbc

Lavington Oct[ober] 23 1850

My dear Lord

Last summer at the time when[260] I asked permission to address you in a public letter on the subject of the Royal Supremacy I stated to your Lordship that I felt guilty embarrassed & alarmed[261] by the present state of the Church of England.

Since that time I have continued to give to the subject[262] as calm, & careful examination as I am able[263] with unceasing prayer for the guidance of the[264] Holy Spirit.[265] It would be beyond my words to say what I have suffered in this season of deliberation or with what depth of pain I find myself brought to the conclusion that but[266] requires me to resign my Office into your Lordships hands.

Among many[267] sounds the thought of paining you my dear Lord, from whom I have received such great and unvarying kindness is not the least. Affections & relations dear to me as life press upon me but[268] the necessity of preserving[269] public honour & private integrity of conscience leaves me no freedom of choice.

After the fullest[270] examination I can give to the subject of[271] the Royal Supremacy as now existing in the Statute law[272] & recognized in[273] the canons of the Church of England, I am forced to the conclusion that the powers lately exercised are legal & canonical: & that by taking[274] the oath of supremacy, & by subscribing the 39 Articles of the 36 canon I am bound in conscience to recognize & accept the[275] Eccl[esiastical] prerogatives of the Crown as they have been lately exhibited.

But I feel even more certainly convinced that such prerogatives[276] are contrary to the Law of Christ & at variance with the Divine Office of the Church.

With these conclusions and with[277] public opinion every day more clearly manifested in support (with perhaps some modifications of form)[278] of the principle of the existing Royal Supremacy I feel that[279] only one course[280] is open to me. To persevere under obligations which are publicly & authoritatively interpreted in a sense contrary to conscience is impossible. Public honour is second only to private integrity and both require that a man should release himself from such a position.[281] May I then request your Lordship to appoint the manner & the time when I may with most consciousness and least pain to both execute this trying duty.

I cannot conclude without assuring you of my grateful attachment and how sincerely I shall always [illegible word] to pray that every good gift may be abundantly bestowed upon you in this & in the happier life to which we soon shall come.

Asking your forgiveness & your prayers, I am, my dear Lord,

Your faithful & affec[tiona]te Servant in Christ

H.E.M.

[[Bodl. MS Eng. lett. c. 653, 665–6 (draft)]]

ENDNOTES TO SECTION VIII

1. letter & proof] inserted
2. the] written over illegible word
3. lapsis . . . so] Morley marginalia reads: lapsis [?] of the [?] and so . . .
4. which . . . homogeneity] inserted
5. for him] inserted
6. to . . . such] inserted
7. below] according to Morley an illegible word
8. & from] inserted
9. must improve . . . be] inserted
10. is] inserted, replacing overscored: was
11. Chapeau adds: letter
12. proverbial] Chapeau omits

13. yourself] Chapeau: you
14. in] inserted, replacing overscored: of
15. mission] Chapeau: missions
16. its] inserted
17. pending] inserted
18. both] Chapeau omits
19. to try] inserted
20. And] overscored
21. I concluded . . . memorandum] at beginning of letter
22. tomorrow] inserted
23. the] Morley: these
24. therefore] inserted, replacing overscored: as
25. first] inserted
26. at any future time] inserted
27. at once] inserted
28. my] inserted
29. tenures] Chapeau: tenure
30. interested] Chapeau: interests
31. neither . . . suffice] inserted
32. on] overscored
33. Truths] Chapeau: Truth
34. My direction . . . Maidstone] at top of letter
35. they happen] happening *corrected by insertion of* they *and overcoming by* ing
36. demand] written over illegible word
37. Allies] Morley: Ellice
38. obtain] inserted
39. for] inserted, replacing overscored: 'the'
40. like it] overscored
41. she would be vitally compromised by] overscored in pencil
42. would be . . . Church] inserted in margin
43. four] *in pencil*
44. two] *in pencil*
45. two] *in pencil*
46. 2 . . . appointed] inserted in margin
47. and will . . . them] inserted
48. any] inserted
49. 'to perform' and two illegible words] overscored
50. and will make . . . relations] inserted in margin
51. including . . . Delegation] inserted
52. grave . . . his] inserted
53. Gladstone's square brackets
54. to him] inserted, replacing overscored: in respect to
55. touching] inserted

56. Gladstone's bracket
57. having] inserted
58. Gladstone's bracket
59. forthwith] inserted
60. 7. . . . Secretary] inserted in margin
61. Gladstone's square brackets
62. proposed] written over illegible word
63. so] Chapeau: as
64. the] overscoring: an
65. &] Chapeau omits
66. discussions] Chapeau: discipline
67. On] inserted, replacing overscored: By regarding
68. is] overscored
69. or need be] inserted
70. practical] written over illegible word
71. private & religious] Chapeau: religious & private
72. assemblage] inserted, replacing overscored: combinations
73. the] inserted
74. &] Chapeau: a
75. or] Chapeau omits
76. restraints] Chapeau: restraint
77. my letter] Chapeau omits
78. at least] overscored
79. think . . . to] inserted
80. the] corrected from: that
81. the] inserted, replacing overscored: of
82. doubtless] inserted
83. & cannot] inserted
84. all] overscored
85. (] overscored
86. wards] inserted
87. may] Chapeau: might
88. of E] inserted
89. I go . . . them] inserted
90. members] inserted
91. of] written over: on
92. viz] inserted
93. before] inserted
94. play] Chapeau: plays
95. spring tide] Copy: springtime
96. Resolution] corrected from: resolution
97. a] corrected from: an
98. four illegible words overscored

99. body] inserted
100. illegible word overscored
101. it] inserted
102. distinctive] inserted
103. anything] overscored
104. (for instance)] inserted
105. in the mean time] inserted
106. busied] corrected from: busy
107. in the same subject matter] inserted
108. through the evidence] overscored
109. not indeed] inserted
110. immediate...remote] inserted
111. of theirs] overscored
112. either] inserted
113. most...as] inserted
114. respect] corrected from: respects
115. and] overscored
116. as] overscored
117. do] inserted
118. and [indecipherable word]]] overscored
119. ask...to] inserted
120. correcting] inserted, replacing overscored: Legislative
121. give examples] inserted, replacing overscored illegible words
122. her] Morley: the
123. a] overscored
124. quote] overscored
125. done] inserted
126. by] overscored
127. The...Gladstone] on first page
128. This with...pact] inserted
129. settling] written over illegible word
130. on the ground] inserted
131. illegible word overscored
132. but...it] inserted
133. that] overscored
134. *per se*] inserted
135. The] Chapeau: My
136. illegible word overscored
137. seu] Chapeau: sic
138. mistrust] Chapeau: distrust
139. Here] Copy begins
140. Copy adds: that
141. Copy adds: vested not in local Episcopates severally, but

142. , and a] Copy: A
143. its judgment] Copy: the judgment of the Universal Church
144. There is . . . make it] Copy omits
145. or judgment] Copy omits
146. Copy adds: now
147. I feel] Copy: there is
148. Copy adds: as Judge of Faith against all comers
149. But . . . challenge] Copy: But can we meet the challenge which
150. is One] inserted
151. And here I feel . . . authority] Copy reads: Is not this in truth the weak point both in your Pamphlet & in my own? Both are insular: and is it possible to defend this separation from the Universal Church? The more I look into it the less I am able so to do. I fear that what you style by hupokorismos 'reattaching' the Church of England to the 'Roman obedience' is in truth reconciling the members of Christs Body in the unity of the Divine Kingdom.
      This presses me very closely. And in this form.
      Can a divided Church teach with authority, or decide with authority in controversies of faith?
152. And what security . . . yours] Copy:
      Am I the Judge?
      May it judge its own cause? If not, what Judge remains?
      What security is there for its judgment in appeal?
      Universal freedom is its *rule*. But who shall say when it applies its *rule correctly?*
      Water cannot rise above its source: & local churches may err.
      I should feel very thankful to you for your thoughts on this vital point.
153. I think] inserted
154. & is . . . authority] inserted
155. a] overscored
156. imitates &] inserted
157. ask] written over illegible word
158. (if . . . days)] inserted
159. three illegible letters overscored
160. the] inserted
161. what] inserted
162. draft] inserted
163. even] inserted
164. While] inserted, replacing overscored: After
165. good] corrected over illegible word
166. & churchman] inserted
167. but] written over illegible word
168. ill as others] written over illegible words
169. to] overscored

170. one] overscored
171. small work] inserted, replacing overscored small thin book
172. e.g.... 16] inserted
173. exclusively] Chapeau: conclusively
174. write] inserted replacing overscored illegible word
175. about her] inserted
176. their] inserted, replacing overscored: its
177. (it...pudor)] inserted
178. that even some time ago] inserted
179. taught it as the faith] inserted
180. indeed] inserted
181. (without...religious)] inserted
182. illegible word overscored
183. will] overscored
184. the] written over illegible word
185. time] inserted, replacing overscored: days
186. The...Gladstone] on first page
187. been those which] inserted
188. so] overscored
189. &] Chapeau: or
190. in my mind] inserted
191. or 2d] inserted
192. by] overscored
193. bare] inserted
194. to you] overscored
195. I know] inserted
196. to be] inserted
197. (between...house)] inserted
198. action] Chapeau: actions
199. or...protect] inserted
200. years] inserted
201. lightest] Chapeau omits
202. further] inserted
203. still] overscored
204. via] inserted
205. till] Chapeau: Until
206. since resigning] inserted
207. Chapeau adds: ago
208. to take in] inserted
209. at the least I] inserted
210. long] inserted
211. and] inserted
212. hav] overscored

213. slav] overscored
214. leaning less] MS: less leaning] marked with numerals to indicate change of reading
215. matter] Chapeau: matters
216. random] written over overscored word followed by second, illegible overscored word
217. illegible word overscored
218. story] overscored
219. thus] inserted
220. or] Chapeau: and
221. examinations] Chapeau: examination
222. The . . . Gladstone] on first page
223. could] corrected from: would
224. *historical*] inserted
225. The . . . Gladstone] on first page
226. effects] Chapeau: effect
227. upon] inserted
228. of yesterday] inserted
229. the] inserted
230. only with] corrected from: with only
231. use of the] inserted
232. regard to] inserted
233. the] inserted
234. show] corrected from: showing
235. 19] Purcell: 29
236. Illegible word overscored
237. previous] overscored
238. already played their part] inserted replacing four illegible overscored words
239. assist] Purcell: lead
240. & that] Purcell: I trust
241. Admit] replacing two illegible words overscored
242. Through] replacing overscored: from
243. wrongly] overscored in pencil and replaced by inserted: improperly
244. deus] Purcell: Deus
245. is defective] inserted
246. the Church] inserted
247. at this moment] inserted
248. on] inserted
249. to be exercised through Commissioners or Delegates empowered to try the merits of the questioners.] inserted
250. has now] overscored
251. is to have] inserted
252. to] inserted

253. &] overscored
254. Are] overscored
255. to be] inserted
256. thereby] inserted
257. on the part of the King's power:] inserted
258. Yet] overscored
259. is kept in to] inserted
260. when] inserted replacing overscored
261. alarmed & embarrassed] corrected
262. to the subject] inserted
263. to the subject] overscored
264. only right which never errs] overscored
265. Holy Spirit] inserted
266. I ought] overscored
267. [five illegible words] many thoughts of] overscored
268. *Second 'But' overscored*
269. myself from] overscored
270. and [illegible word]] overscored
271. I can give to the subject of] inserted replacing overscored: of
272. & in the C of England] overscored
273. in] inserted replacing overscored: by
274. taking] inserted
275. existing] overscored
276. as lately established] overscored
277. the manifest sense of] overscored
278. (with perhaps some modifications of form)] inserted
279. no] overscored
280. can either prevent me from the course of] overscored
281. But in coming to this deeply painful conclusion I have desired to avoid being
     either too hasty or too slow. The great and life-long sacrifices it demands of
     me have made me] overscored

SECTION IX

Epilogue

JUNE 1851–AUGUST 1853

[[On Sunday, 6 April 1851, Gladstone noted in his Diary: 'A day of pain! Manning & Hope!' and on 7 April: 'Hope too is gone.[a] They were my two props. Their going may be to me a sign that my work is gone with them. God give us daily light with daily bread. One blessing I have: total freedom from doubts. These dismal events have smitten but not shaken.' The following day, 8 April, before leaving for Paris, he 'Executed a codicil to my will striking out Hope as Ex[ecuto]r' (*GD* iv. 323).[b] In a letter to Samuel Wilberforce on 11 April he commented:

[a] Note the particular concern in Hope's case, since the two had spoken or written little of Rome's claims following Newman's conversion in 1845. (See Lathbury, i. 84.)

[b] According to a later comment by Manning: 'When I became Catholic Gladstone said to the person who told me that "he felt as if I had murdered his mother by mistake"—The Duke of Newcastles letter in April 1851 is more natural. Dr Kingsley who attended his deathbed told Lady Herbert from whom I had it, that he would see no Protestant Clergymen: that his desire was to see me: but those about him hindered it' ('Later Reminiscences' i. unnumbered page following 95; Leslie, 99; cf. Purcell i. 627). Wilfrid Meynell in his comments in 'Reminiscences of Cardinal Manning', *Contemporary Review* 61 (1892), 182, states that in 1889 Gladstone told him that with the departure of Hope and Manning 'he felt as if he had lost his two eyes'. In his annotations to his copy of Purcell's biography, Gladstone places an NB beside each of these consecutive sections:

Under a feeling or fear of desertion Manning made a compact with James Hope that they should stand together; and if so be that they were called, go together step by step on their pilgrimage to Rome.

Long ago, before the Gorham Judgment, to Robert Wilberforce Manning had acknowledged Anglicanism was a lost cause: a lost hope: a lost faith: that his destiny was Rome. (PurGl i. 552)

In 1896 Gladstone indicated to Leslie (94) that 'he could still take an oath in a court of law that Manning had said substantially, "Dying men, or men within the shadow of death, as I was last year, have a clearer insight into things unseen of others, a deeper knowledge of all that relates to Divine faith. In such a communion with death and the region beyond death I had an absolute assurance in heart and soul, solemn beyond expression, that the English Church (I am not speaking of the Establishment) is a living portion of the Church of Christ." '

I do indeed feel the loss of Manning, if and as far as I am capable of feeling anything. It comes to me cumulated, and doubled, with[1] that of James Hope. Nothing like it can ever happen to me again. Arrived now at middle life, I never can form I suppose with any other two men the habits of communication, counsel, and dependence, in which I have now for from fifteen to eighteen years lived with them both. But I will not pursue this subject. . . .

My intellect does deliberately reject the grounds on which Manning has proceeded. Indeed they are such as go far to destroy my confidence, which was once and far too long at the highest point, in the healthiness and soundness of his. To show that, at any rate, this is not from the mere change he has made, I may add, that my conversations with Hope have not left any corresponding impression upon my mind with regard to him.

I would only say, with regard to the slight indication you have given me of your train of thought, that I stop short of saying the Church of England 'has given up' a fundamental point. What I should say is, that she is critical for her life: but I think the giving up a fundamental point (otherwise than by a formal act) is a process requiring much more time & many more events to effect & substantiate it than we have yet had: to say nothing of the rather important signs in a contrary sense. (Bodl. MS Wilberforce c. 67, 26–7; cf. Morley, i. 387)

Only a few days earlier, on 9 April, Robert Wilberforce wrote to Gladstone:

There is no one perhaps who is more likely to feel the loss of our dear friend Manning than you & myself. So that I cannot help writing a few lines, even at the chance of finding you very busy, to console with you on this event.

In one respect I believe we differ. I imagine that your intellect rejects the grounds, on wh[ich] he has acted, far more than mine does. And this is a point on which I shall be very glad to have an opportunity of talking with you when I come to town . . . (BL Add. MS 44370, 66–7, 66)[c]

Gladstone's strained relationship with Hope was aided with the help of Catherine, to whom he wrote on 19 April: 'You have broken the ice for me with James Hope, which it was a little hard on you to have to do. I feel that his genial character will diminish the difficulty: but the life and soul of our intercourse are I fear gone probably[2] for ever' (SDL, Glynne–Gladstone MS 772, 20–1; a

---

[c] *The Guardian* of 9 April 1851 commented on secessions to Rome at the Church of St Saviour in Leeds (257, 263) and continued: ' Archdeacon—we should say Mr.—Manning has taken the same step in London. Painful as this intelligence must under any circumstances be, it is somewhat less so from having been so long and so reasonably apprehended. If the evil has come, we are at least relieved from the continual apprehension of it. We are informed on authority, which we fear we cannot doubt, that Mr. James R. Hope, Q. C., was received with Mr. Manning into the Roman Church. We must not disguise from ourselves the probability that such persons will not leave the English Church alone. Yet neither must we forget the hopefulness which is due to our Church and those good and noble men who stand fast in it' (257).

paragraph is cut from the last folio of the letter).[d] On 30 April from Fasque,[e] Gladstone wrote to Catherine once more, reflecting on the complexities of discussing the secession of Hope with their son: 'the telling Willy about Hope is a very serious matter. It would be a very slight one according to the views of some people who look upon the question as simply between Protestantism and Roman Catholicism, the first of course all light and the second all darkness—If he is told at present I should wish something of this kind to be said to him, that Mr Hope has left the Church of this country to which we belong, but that he believes in our Savior Christ as he did before, and that I will hereafter explain it to him more fully' (SDL, Glynne–Gladstone MS 772, 34–5, 34). On Sunday, 11 June, Gladstone 'crossed J. Hope on his stairs' and commented: 'Having mentioned that name I must here record the sad effect wrought upon me by the disasters crowned by his & M[anning']s secession: the loss of all *resolution* to carry forward the little self-discipline I ever had' (*GD* iv. 329).]]

510621mg

14. Curzon Street.[a] June 21. 1851.

My dear Gladstone,

The kind gift of your new Book[b] found me here yesterday, having first been sent to Ebury Street:[c] or I should have sooner thanked you. I do so

---

[d] Note Catherine's sensitivity regarding Gladstone's concern: on 21 April 1851 she wrote to him, indicating that a friend is 'not inclined to Rome. Wood said that y[ou]r Papal speech *converted* a very able lawyer friend of his I forget his name', and on 23 April she comments, 'You will have heard with sorrow that Mr. Simeon has been received only yesterday into the church of Rome. George wrote to Dr. Pusey about him the day before but too late. Poor James is much cut up about it. Doyle in speaking of Hope said that he felt it impossible to look upon English people who take the step but as foreigners—he feels it very much speaking of you and of him as of two such old friends of his' (SDL, Glynne–Gladstone MS 612).

[e] Gladstone was at Fasque at the time, concerned over his father's declining health (*GD* iv. 324). He would return again 29 August 1851 (ibid. 355) and remain through to his father's death, 7 December, and until after the funeral, 13 December (ibid. 378). Thereafter the Fasque property passed to his older brother, Thomas.

[a] Residence of James Hope.

[b] Luigi Carlo Farini, *The Roman State from 1815 to 1850*, trans. W. E. Gladstone (4 vols.; London: John Murray, 1851–4); the preface to the first volume is dated 3 June. Gladstone began reading Farini in Italy on 27 November 1850 (*GD* iv. 278) and completed it 12 December (ibid. 287). On 21 December he began to translate the work (ibid. 292). The fourth volume was translated by Mrs Anne (Ramsden) Bennett, Gladstone's cousin, under Gladstone's direction.

[c] The home of Monsell, 51 Ebury St., Chester Square.

now very sincerely, & yet not so much for the book as for the few words in the Titlepage in your own hand.[d] I have rested with much consolation on your last kind note and have felt no doubt that howsoever strained as you said our affection may be yet it is too mature to be now broken.

I have often wished for the fair occasion which you now kindly give me to say that I trust, if in the time of severe trial my manner or tone was for a moment sharpened you will know that my own suffering & not any diminution of affection was the cause.

God be thanked that time & trial are over and more than I ever could ask or think has been given to me. Short of this I have no will, unbidden, to write.

I am in an hour or two going into the country for a week[e] & your books will be my companions.

I hope you are all well. Give my love to Mrs. Gladstone & believe me,
Always your affect[ionat]e friend
H. E. Manning

The Right Hon[oura]ble
W. E. Gladstone
[[BL Add. MS 44248, 128–9]]

510622gm[a]

6 C[arlton] G[ardens] June 22. [18]51.
My dear Manning

Your appeal to me respecting your demeanour during the sad days[3] of our last communications together as members of the Church of England ought not to[4] go unnoticed, though I must not reciprocate it. I do not think that in reference to that or to any other period of our long friendship you have so much as a look or a syllable to regret. It is neither in retrospect nor in any sense of diminished affection that the pressure of this trial lies. It lies to me partly in my own irreparable[5] personal loss, partly in the comparison

---

[d] On the title page of the copy of the Farini translation preserved in Pitts Theology Library, Emory University is an inscription by Gladstone reading: 'H. E. Manning with W.E.G.'s affectionate regards 17 June 1851'. On the same date Gladstone noted his mailing of the volume to Manning: 'Got my first copies of Farini. Sent No 1 to the Prince: & wrote with sad feelings in those for Hope and Manning' (*GD* iv. 337; Morley, i. 405).

[e] Manning was going to Ambrose de Lisle's home, Grace Dieu. He wrote to Hope from there on 26 June 1851, describing the home and his own peaceful state (NLS MS 3675, 110–11). Note also his thanks to de Lisle on 1 October (Purcell, i. 638).

[a] 'Wrote . . . drafts & letters to Hope & Manning' (*GD* iv. 339).

between what you were and what (with or without your will) you are to the[6] Church of England.

I had not, nor have I, any foregone conclusions as to intercourse with you and Hope. As the calamity is too great for me fully to comprehend, so likewise I have not (neither probably have you)[7] attempted to argue out its consequences. Only this I can say I am not & never shall be restrained from approaching you by an alienated heart on my side or by the suspicion of it on yours.[8]

[*sic*] have wholly passed beyond the reach and measure of our own. The Lord is in His holy temple:[9] let all the[10] earth keep silence before Him![b] [11]The very afflictions of the present time are a sign of joy to follow. Thy kingdom come, Thy will be done[c] is still our prayer in common: the same prayer, in the same sense &[12] a prayer which absorbs every other.[13] That is for the future:[14] for the present we have to endure to trust & to pray that each day may bring its strength with its burden &, its lamp for its gloom.

Ever yours with unaltered affection

[[BL Add. MS 44248, 130–1; Gladstone's note: Jun. 22. Draft replies to H.E.M. and J.R.H.[d]]]

---

[b] Hab. 2: 20.   [c] Matt. 6: 10.

[d] Gladstone's reply to Hope on 22 June was verbally close at points to that which he sent to Manning:

6 Carlton Gardens
June 22 1851.

My dear Hope

Upon the point most prominently put in your welcome letter, I will only say you have not misconstrued me. Affection which is fed by intercourse, and above all by cooperation for sacred ends has little need of verbal expression: but such expression is deeply consoling, when active relations have changed. It is no matter of merit to me to feel strongly on the subject of that change. It may be little better than pure selfishness. I have too good reason to know, what this year has cost me; and so little hope have I that the places now vacant can ever be filled up for me, that the marked character of these events in reference to myself rather teaches me this lesson, the work to which I had aspired, is reserved for other and better men. And if that be the Divine Will, I so entirely recognise its fitness, that the grief would so far be small to me, were I alone concerned. The pain the wonder and the mystery is this, that you should have refused the higher vocation you had before you. The same words, & all the same words, I should use of Manning too. Forgive me for giving utterance to what I believe myself to see and know: I will not proceed a step further in that direction. There is one word, and one only in your letter that I do not interpret closely. Separated we are but I hope and think not yet estranged. Were I more estranged I should bear the

[[Throughout 1851 Manning and Gladstone continued to express interest in one another's lives. Manning, for example, wrote to Hope on 28 June: 'I have read too a few chapters of Gladstone's book with great interest. Farini is no common man—& his intellect is truly Italian' (NLS MS 3675, 112–13). Again on 4 September Gladstone asked Hope: 'Pray tell me anything you can about Manning' (ibid. 3673, 171–2), and on 14 October, writing to Badeley Gladstone spoke of 'The events of the last two years, crowned by the secession of Hope and Manning have well nigh overset me in more senses than one nor can I say that I am yet returned to my balance' (ibid. 3678, 171–2). Gladstone was still much on Manning's mind too on 21 October, when he wrote to Hope:

Have you seen the article on Anglo-Catholicism[e] in the last Edinburgh? How is it that Gladstone does not see the plain issue? How was it that we

separation better. If estrangement is to come I know not: but it will only be, I think, from causes the operation of which is still in its infancy, causes not affecting me. Why should I be estranged from you? I honour you even in what I think your error: why, then, should my feelings to you alter in anything else? It seems to me as though, in these fearful times, events were more and more growing too large for our puny grasp: and we should the more look for and trust the Divine purpose in them, when we find they have wholly passed beyond the reach and measure of our own. 'The Lord is in His holy temple: let all the earth keep silence before Him.' The very afflictions of the present time are a sign of joy to follow [cf. Rom. 8: 18]. Thy kingdom come, thy will be done, is still our prayer in common: the same prayer, in the same sense; and a prayer which absorbs every other. That is for the future: for the present we have to endure, to trust, and to pray, that each day may bring its strength with its burden, and its lamp with its gloom.

Ever yours with unaltered affection,
W. E. Gladstone.

J. R. Hope Es[quire]
(NLS MS 3673, 167–9; Ornsby, ii. 88).

    [e] Article VIII reviewing *The Two-Fold Protest: A Letter from the Duke of Argyll to the Bishop of Oxford* (London: 1851) and *Acts of the Diocesan Synod held in the Cathedral Church of Exeter* by Henry, Lord Bishop of Exeter, on...June 25, 26, 27...(London: 1851) in the *Edinburgh Review or Critical Journal* 94 (Oct. 1851), 527–57 was fiercely anti-Catholic in tone. 'The people of England are Protestant still' (ibid. 529), it commented, and went on: 'The eyes of many have been opened to the tendency and ultimate effects of Tractarian principles... [and] the Tractarians have been made to feel distrust of themselves and their position' (ibid. 530), referring with some regularity to 'Church Principles' (cf. ibid. 535–6), which, along with the previous review (ibid. 490ff.) of Gladstone's *A Letter to the Earl of Aberdeen, On the State Prosecutions of the Neapolitan Government* (London: John Murray, 1851) may have directed Manning to his reflections on Gladstone. Note also Gladstone's *A Second Letter to the Earl of Aberdeen, On the State Prosecutions of the Neapolitan Government* (London: John Murray, 1851), repr. with the first in *Gleanings*, iv. 1–69.

did not and yet when the late appeal in doctrine came we did, and still he does not. I am afraid that his notion of the Church and its office is not even what ours was.

In truth, this was the *point* brought to the test last year. And how few ever meant anything by their Cuckoo cry of the Church. (NLS MS 3675, 118–19)

Later in the same year Gladstone asked once more about Manning and was answered by Hope on 19 December, 1851 from Abbotsford:

Thanks for your last—The only news I have of Manning is negative, but a great cause of thankfullness—He has providentially been saved from what has been fatal to others—A steamer from Marseilles on which he was to sail has either been thrown up or sunk & many lives lost—His baggage was on board but he was not. (NLS MS 3674, 348)

For Gladstone the year was one of great sorrow. At its close he reflected on it, clearly mindful of the loss of his friends, perhaps especially of Manning. On 29 December he commented:

it has been to me a sad year. Almost utterly overthrown, almost a mere wreck of what might have been a Christian. If I have had in my soul any consolatory token it is this that the thought of God's presence & judgment is ever dear to me. But what things have I not done or trodden on the edge of while entertaining that thought. In truth the religious trials of the time have passed my capacity & grasp. I am bewildered, & reel under them. And this does not purify but relaxes me & leaves me more open to the invader. (*GD* iv. 382)

And again on 31 December:

It has been a sad year: I do not mean the event of the last month. He that sleeps, sleeps well. I mean the rending & sapping of the Church, the loss of its gems, the darkening of its prospects; as well as the ill fruit this has had in me individually. (ibid. 383; cf. 19 Aug. 1851)

On 29 February 1852 in a letter dated 'Rome 1 S[unday] in Lent' Manning wrote to Dodsworth: 'It would have given me pleasure if your letter had told me more of Gladstone' (CP), on 17 March 1852 he asked Hope in a postscript to 'Tell me of Gladstone and R. Cavendish' (NLS MS 3675, 122), and in July, commenting on various political matters and the state of the Church of England, stated: 'I sh[ould] much like to know what Gladstone is thinking' (ibid. 123–4).]]

521019mg

Tunbridge Wells.[a] Oct[ober] 19. 1852

My dear Gladstone,

An expression dropped from me of our Friends which led me to fear that you may have misconceived the reason of my not calling to see you. I therefore, desire before I leave England, tomorrow, to say that my heart would have drawn me to you among the first but that I hold aloof—not doubting your affection—but the outward discretion of my making any advance.

Moreover I have laid down for myself the rule to make no advance without previous intimation of a wish on the part of others.

Now I say that nothing can change in the friendship of so many years, arising at a time when we both were governed by reflection, and strengthened by trials & events out of the common way.

If I have misjudged, you will forgive it as a simple misjudgment. It would give me too much happiness to do as my heart would prompt to make such an error likely again to happen.

It is now late: & I can add no more: but I could not go abroad without writing these few words.

I trust your wife & children are well.

Hope would send his love if he knew of my writing. All is going on very well here. God be soon with you—

Believe me, always your
Attached friend
Henry E. Manning

[[BL Add. MS 44248, 132–3]]

521128gm[aa]

6 Carlton Gardens
Nov[ember] 28. 1852.

My dear Manning

You will readily believe, that I could not see your wellknown handwriting, for so many years an unfailing sign of support and consolation, on the envelope of[15] your letter of the 19th of October, without emotion. When

---

[a] Note Hope's residence there at the same time and the birth of his daughter Mary Monica on 2 October (Ornsby, ii. 169).

[aa] 'Also wrote out for post my letters [sic] to Manning' (GD iv. 473).

I opened it, it caused me but one regret, namely to find that you should have thought your conduct to me[16] could have needed explanation in my eyes. If I was so reported to you as to convey this impression,[17] be assured I was greatly misunderstood: & I hope & believe we are both long past the need of exchanging verbal pledges of that attachment, which has been & cannot cease to be. I am afraid it will sound strange, but it is the truth; I feel, with respect to the great and fearful change, which has passed upon our relations to one another,[18] as if that change had, like the Death of one dearly loved,[19] which it so much resembles,[20] finally sealed and fixed the attachment, of which it has also suspended the exercise, perhaps until the cloud of earthly life is swept away, and the new earth and new heavens, if I be found worthy,[21] are before us. I dare not indeed conjecture, what may be[22] the effect of long years yet to come:[23] it is too bold to prophesy of ourselves for the remote future: but that, which was built upon community of hopes and fears, of thoughts and feelings lying nearest the heart through the prime of life, can never in our case or in others, be unbuilt and cancelled, except it be by some like process of very[24] slow degrees.

In what I am going to say, please to[25] consider that if and when I write to you I can do it upon the old[26] footing only: that of striving to tell out my inmost thoughts: while well aware that, being so told, they cannot be understood except by one who, in order to construe[27] them, calls up & realises afresh[28] the mental habits of our relation: in which to speak or write any idea to you, was scarcely[29] more than[30] to bring[31] the offspring of one faculty of the mind under the review of another.

You have laid down then, you say, 'the rule to make no advance without previous intimation of a wish on the part of others.' I am sure you do not mean by those words to imply, that this is a matter to be governed by a mere wish, a thing lying on the surface of our being, or that it is not far deeper: it is[32] a matter, in which[33] I dare not wish anything, for we ought not to wish anything except what we feel within ourselves we have a power given us to meet and to use, but[34] I am utterly unable to tell myself how I should be able to deal with the consequences of such a wish: whether we should be reduced to the dead & cold intercourse of external life: whether every question and word would not, by the contrast with what once was, renew the inward jar: whether we should find all the living & practical points of sympathetic contact between us converted into points of acute discord, between the priest of the Roman Church, with his office & all[35] his gifts, on the one hand, & the son of the Church of England on the other, pledged[36] as deeply as faith, conviction, honour too (in my actual position),[37] and the habits of a life can pledge him to her service: both placed, or to be placed,[38] face to face in[39] the same local, & to no small degree in the same moral field of action. I cannot tell[40] what of comfort or of advantage I should gain for you, by taking it upon me[41] to bring you into such an intercourse.[42] So difficult is spontaneous action to me under our deeply painful circumstances. Nevertheless, were there the least sign, that could be[43] held a leading of Providence, my instincts would gladly follow it.

Perhaps you will smile at my speaking of faith: since you have told us that you have now found, & therefore that you had not found before, 'reality & certainty,' without which in the objects there can be no Faith. Ah my dear Friend, have you ever thought, what must[44] be the natural tendency & force of such a declaration as that, coming[45] from you, upon one like me, who have seen[46] & known you heretofore for a long course of years, in the flower & strength of your manhood, & in circumstances too the most solemn: & have thus[47] known that, until a date that could be specified, you gave every imaginable evidence of thinking then, as you think now, that you possessed[48] certainty & reality? I do not doubt that for those, who see only the outside of the facts,[49] the imposing simplicity of that declaration of yours, backed as it was by your acts, might have abundant force in the direction you devise: but for me & all in my position, compelling us to compare the past with the present, and to ask ourselves, why is his declaration now of more value, than his word & his life of so many years, so ripe & accomplished as it was in every gift of God: for us, I say, it can only have one of two effects: either it must pass by us like the wind, or it must tend to uproot the whole foundations of belief in human testimony as a means of aiding our access to Divine Revelation. And that is what wrings my heart, the conviction that it is this latter work that (far from your intention & desire,) you, & those whom you follow, & those who follow you, will chiefly do among us,[50] outcasts or pretenders[51] or whatever we may now[52] be to you,[53, 54] your fellow countrymen at large, & once your fellow Churchmen.

[55]We have not, however,[56] lost everything, though we have (as I think)[57] undoubtedly lost, in men that might be named,[58] if our treasure were only that in earthen vessels,[b] the brightest & choicest of our treasures: once

---

[b] 2 Cor. 4: 7.

perhaps too much our hope, nay our pride.[59] But what then? As God is no more tied to save by many than by few, so He may save by weak when He thinks not fit[60] to do[61] it by strong; & I see plainly, & God knows, as[62] you know, I have had need to see, that the poor Church of England as she becomes weaker in her instruments grows gradually[63] stronger in her acts. But wheresoever I, & wheresoever you may be, may every blessing of God attend you—under the shadow of His wings be our refuge, until this tyranny, the grief & strain of life,[64] be overpassed.

I am detained in London by the autumn Session.[c] The month has been one of deluge, rather than rain, & unhealthy in proportion; but my wife is well, & we have had six months of singular freedom from anxiety as to the health of children. You will be glad to hear, too, that the Herberts are as well as possible.

I remain always
Your affectionate friend
W. E. Gladstone

Rev. H. E. Manning

[[BL Add. MS 44248, 134–6; Morley transcript; BL Add. MS 44248, 137–40 (draft)]]
[[On 19 December 1852 Gladstone 'Read Manning's Lect[ure]', *The Grounds of Faith: Four Lectures Delivered at St. George's Church, Southwark* (London: Burns & Oates, 1852) (*GD* iv. 479).[d]]]

530405mg

Rome April 5. 1853.

My dear Gladstone,

Your letter of Nov[ember] 28 last reached me on the 2d of this month.

My last note needed no answer: & was written only to prevent the possibility of your thinking me to be distant and changed towards you.

My meaning in saying that I make no advance to anyone is this. Both you & I feel that we have some duties which arise from great laws & truths over which we have no authority. They govern us, not we them: & cost what it may of public or private gain they must be obeyed.

---

[c] In December Gladstone entered Aberdeen's Cabinet as Chancellor of the Exchequer, a position he would hold until February 1855.

[d] Gladstone's annotated copy is preserved at SDL, E 15/20.

But beyond the range of these there is a wide field of relations & friendships in which we have freedom of discretion & action. In this we can make concessions and allowances, & forebear, and deny ourselves. All this I simply put from me as a matter in which I desire to let others take their course.

When the Will of God required of me to withdraw from that which I had through sin and error believed to be a part of His Church & to submit myself to that which I had ever intended to obey and to serve I felt that the change in my relations to others was made not by him but by me, or more truly by Him who required so great a cost from me.

I consider them, therefore to be perfectly free and by my act I can love them still as I do you without ever seeking to meet them. And this will be my way by God's help, to the end.

Nevertheless you will believe with what sincere affection I return the expressions of your letter.

It would need another walk from the Vatican to say all I would about the certainty & reality to be found only in the Catholic Church. And I believe that if your duties required of you to verify Theology among the people of England we should not be far apart. My meaning is fully contained in two old Sermons you may remember in the IV vol. One on Ch[ris]t preached every way—& the other the Analogy of Nature.[a] God in His mercy has shewn me where they alone are verified.

I am thankful to hear that your wife & children are well.

I never go to the Altar, dearest Friend, but I bear you in my intention. May God ever bless you. Believe me as always.

Affectionately yours
H. E. Manning

The Right Hon[oura]ble
W. E. Gladstone

[[BL Add. MS 44248, 141–2; letter addressed: The Right Hon[oura]ble W. E. Gladstone MP Downing Street London]]

---

[a] See 'Christ Preached in any [sic] Way a Cause of Joy' and 'The Analogy of Nature', Henry Edward Manning, Sermons: Volume the Fourth (London: William Pickering, 1850a), 60–85, 152–75. See also 491114gm and 491230gm.

530807gm[a]

Downing Street

Aug[ust] 7. [18]53.

My dear Manning

With you, I hope, not even my date will bely me, when I say that I received with deep interest your letter of April 5, and was most thankful for the assurance with which it concluded. Indeed to express that thankfulness is the chief aim with which I write. I rejoice to be in your prayers at all times, and especially at the time you name, when Prayer assumes its vantage ground. Your intercession[65] can have no ingredient of harm for[66] me, nor even mine for[67] you. Let us continue to meet in the Presence of the Eternal. If that which was is cut away, yet this, the best part of it, invisibly[68] remains. I, indeed, shall never recover the losses I have sustained: and sustained at a time when the pressure & strain of life were becoming heavier upon me from year to year. But then I fully know it was the enjoyment, not the bereavement, that was undeserved. I never was worthy to associate with you: & now, if we could associate, perhaps you would find me less so than ever. What I still have is far more than I can appreciate or use aright,[69] what I most lament is not my[70] loss: it is that hands, once so strong to carry sword and shield, now carry them no longer in the battle, the real battle of our place & day.[71] I grudge you the rest which you say, & which I do not doubt or question, you have obtained; I would it were at an end. Never can I[72] in this world see or think of you, or[73] you of me, but this must be the pivot on which all our thoughts must turn. That I think you know well: & when you speak of the wide field of intercourse still left free to choice, as between us two—you speak what is to me a riddle. But I know also that you speak in kindness & affection, which darkens sometimes as well as sometimes clears our view.

I remain.

Ever your attached friend

W. E. Gladstone

Rev. H. E. Manning.

My house is now solitary: & in about a week I hope to make a run to Scotland.[b]

[[BL Add. MS 44248, 143–4; Morley transcript; BL Add. MS 44248, 145–6 (draft); Lathbury, ii. 287–8]]

---

[a] 'Wrote to . . . H. E. Manning (and draft)' (GD iv. 547).

[b] Gladstone left for Scotland on 17 August 1853 (GD iv. 550).

ADDENDUM TO SECTION IX

Manning, Gladstone, and Mary Stanley:
April 1853–March 1856

[[Following the correspondence of August 1853 all direct contact between Manning and Gladstone ceased for a decade. They were pressed into an engagement of sorts, however, in the autumn of 1854, when Mary Stanley (1814–79),[a] whom Manning had been serving as a spiritual adviser since their first meeting in 1848, opened correspondence regarding her religious concerns (she would eventually be received as a Roman Catholic in 1856) with Gladstone as well. Stanley had been working with Catherine Gladstone on a committee to send nurses to the Crimea, where she was soon to travel with the Sisters of Mercy under Mother Frances Bridgeman in 1854. She struggled with her attraction to Roman Catholicism and was in correspondence and personal contact with both Manning and Gladstone over her eventual decision in 1856 to be received as a Roman Catholic. Born in 1813, Mary Stanley was the second of five children to Catherine and Edward Stanley, the Bishop of Norwich, and was slightly older than her more famous brother, Arthur Penrhyn, with whom she remained in close contact to her death on 24 November 1879. Well known for philanthropic work throughout her life, she was active in the recruitment of nurses for the Crimea in 1854 and served in Westminster and Lancashire during the cotton famine of 1861. Manning first comments to Stanley on Gladstone in a letter of 1 April 1853, from Rome:

I have no thought that any Protestant argument c[oul]d weigh with you any more than with me. It all seems to me fragmentary, incoherent and irrelevant: moreover every objection carries its own answer. It is either half a truth—or altogether senseless...

---

[a] See *DNB*, Gillow, v. 524–5, Mrs Augustus Craven, *Life of Lady Georgina Fullerton*, trans. Henry James Coleridge from the French (2nd edn.; London: R. Bentley, 1888), 352ff.; A. P. Stanley, *Memoir of Edward and Catherine Stanley* (London: John Murray, 1879). Stanley's role in nursing in the Crimean War and her controversy with Florence Nightingale as a result is fully discussed by Bolster (1964) and McAuley (1962). See also Erb and Erb (1999) and Nightingale (2002), 242ff., on Nightingale's attraction to Catholicism and her correspondence with Manning on the possibility of conversion. The following addendum includes all the extant correspondence between Gladstone and Stanley, since Manning indicates that he read it (560312ms). Of the Manning–Stanley correspondence only that is included which mentions Gladstone or relates directly to her correspondence with Gladstone.

My last conferences in the A[nglican] C[hurch] were with Gladstone & Harrison. I sought them out as a duty and with great difficulty obtained an explicit, & positive statement of their own positions. They both resolved themselves into human certainty—whether of an individual or of a section, e.g. the Anglican Church. (Bodl. MS Eng. lett. c. 660, 155–6)

Late in 1854, prior to her departure for the Crimea with a band of nurses to supplement those who had earlier left with Florence Nightingale (1820–1910),[b] Stanley's attraction to Catholicism came to Gladstone's attention. Fearing her possible decision, he invited her to converse with him, sending his message through her relative, William Owen Stanley,[c] with whom he met in November. Stanley was aware of Gladstone's persuasive powers and she wrote to Manning concerning the possible discussion.[d]]]

541125ms

78 S[outh] A[udley] S[t.] Nov[ember] 25. 1854

By all means hear Gladstone. I could put down what he will say, and could almost weep over him. I have loved, & honoured him. But the last three years have been a grief to me.

I need not say—promise no one—anything.

Our Divine Lord redeemed us in His most precious blood from human authority—& the bondage of human teachers—that He alone, thro' His perpetual guidance might be our Teacher. The one, undivided, universal Church sprung from the Day of Pentecost is the organ of His voice, & thro' it He redeems us from human errors, & human authorities.

---

[b] Of the many studies on Nightingale see *DNB*, the classic biographies by Cook (1913) and Woodham-Smith (1950), and the selections of her letters, Vicinus and Nergaard (1989) and Goldie (1987).

[c] William Owen Stanley (1802–84), twin brother of 2nd Baron Stanley of Alderby, MP for Chester 1850–7 (Boase, iii. 711). Gladstone wrote to Stanley's wife, Ellen, on 19 November 1854 (*GD* iv. 661).

[d] According to Leslie, 107, Gladstone wrote to Stanley on 25 October 1854, noting 'You will see Manning soon. Pray give him my affectionate regards. I hope he knows that my feeling towards him can never alter.'

I saw Gladstone's letter to Rob[er]t Wilberforce.[a] Could you believe that he referred to Milman's Latin Christianity[b] as proof?

[a] Robert Wilberforce was received as a Roman Catholic in September 1854, following a lengthy struggle and correspondence with both Manning and Gladstone over the matter. Unfortunately little of the later correspondence remains beyond a few Manning letters in CP. The fullest version of the correspondence with Manning remains Purcell ii. 25–48. Note in particular ibid. 35–6 (cf. Leslie, 106):

paris, 26th October 1853.

MY DEAREST ROBERT—Many thanks for your kind letter, which reached me the day before I left London.

I hope you explained to Gladstone my writing last year. Your kind interpretation led me to do so, and I should wish him to know that fact.

Now for yourself, you say you do not know how it is you are so much influenced by those you are with. I have no difficulty as to the reason. First, I think you and Henry are alike *ex parte voluntatis.*

Next, . . . Anti-Catholic persuasions are especially addressed to the fear of making a mistake.

But lastly, and above all, how should you be otherwise? I was so once. Why am I not so now?

For the reason of St. Paul, in what you call my text. You have no foundation but human judgment your own on one side; Gladstone's or Keble's or Pusey's on the other.

And therefore you are 'tossed to and fro and carried about' [Eph. 4: 14] by words of men.

To me this is simply impossible, because I believe on the basis of a Divine Teacher.

There is therefore no parity or balance between Gladstone, Keble, or Pusey, and the Divine Tradition of the Church.

Your whole state verifies to me my text as well as my own experience.

Now, dearest Robert, do not go on losing yourself, as I once told you, in details. Your private judgment has convinced you of the Incarnation, Baptism, the Eucharist. Apply it now to the third and last clause of the Baptismal Creed, 'I believe in the Holy Ghost, the Holy Catholic Church.'

Write a book on this next. To go on with details of doctrine is to wink hard at the point.

I have resolved not to speak of individuals. But I find it impossible not to see that there is a key to the present conduct of many.

When you say that the Roman Church is not historically the same, is it not to say *my* view of its history differs from its own?

But may not the Catholic Church know its own history better, and by a lineal knowledge and consciousness, to which no individual can oppose himself without unreasonable-ness?

I am perfectly persuaded that the Catholic Church is historically the same in personal identity and functions.

Details are like grey hairs or wrinkles as compared with youth; or the character of the man with that of the child. But the person is the same. Dearest Robert, find the Teacher sent from God as Nicodemus did. Your Sermon on Church Authority points to the Truth. But grace only can strengthen our will to act. Ever yours most affectionately,

H.E.M.

[b] Henry Hart Milman, *History of Latin Christianity* (6 vols.; London: John Murray, 1854–5).

To this & lower than this the humanly great mind will go: unless thro' grace he becomes as 'a little child'[c] to enter the Kingdom of heaven.

F[lorence] N[ightingale] knows your state of mind perfectly.

She said to me 2 years ago when you were ill.

'Convert Ms S[tanley] quickly or there will be no Ms S[tanley] to convert.'

Also the other day she said what shewed that she perfectly knew it.

H.E.M.

[[Bodl. MS Eng. lett. c. 661, 76–7]]

[[On 25 November 1854, Gladstone 'Dined with the Herberts. Conv[ersation] on Miss Stanley' (*GD* iv. 662). On the following day, 26 November, Gladstone met with 'Miss Stanley 2 h[ours]. on the R[oman] Communion' (ibid. 663). As a result of the visit, Stanley does seem to have made some form of promise to Gladstone not to enter the Roman Church, the sort of promise that Gladstone had the habit of extracting from people.[d] The following letter appears to have been written by Mary Stanley to Catherine Gladstone on Monday, 27 November. The condition under which the meeting ended indicates that the misunderstanding which would occur a year later between the two existed already at the time of the meeting.[e]]]

541126scg

Dear Mrs. Gladstone

The result of todays deliberation was, that I said I would go on the condition of being *quite* free & under no pledge. Mr. Herbert consents to this.

I told Mr. Gladstone I would not[74] take any step without first giving him my reasons more clearly then I could do on Sunday.

I gave this promise under the impression that I was going to spend the winter at home with time to read all he might wish to put before me—

That will now be impossible—& I must go freed from any fetter or I must remain at home.—I cannot tell into what circumstances I may be thrown. I write at once to tell you[75] as in honour bound. My mother has so had a cold that I wait till tomorrow to talk over my going. It would have given her a bad night & done no good.

Ever yours with grateful affection.
M. Stanley

Monday night
6 Gros[venor] Cres[cen]t[a] [1854]

[[SDL, Glynne–Gladstone MS 802, unpaginated]]

---

[c] Matt. 18: 2ff.

[d] See the attempt made to bring Manning and Hope into a similar arrangement with Herbert and Robert Wilberforce and others in 1850. See 500520gm.

[e] On 17 December 1854 Gladstone read Mary Stanley's *Hospitals and Sisterhoods* (London: John Murray, 1854; preface dated 15 Mar.) (*GD* iv. 667).

[a] Mary Stanley's residence in London.

541127ms
>   78 S[outh] A[udley] S[t.] Nov[ember] 27. 1854

I have just read with wonder & *pain* your notes[aa] of G[ladstone]'s conversation.

1. I never heard any man assert till now that the Liturgy & articles speak 'with unfaltering voice.'

How then have two Theological & contradictory schools appealed to them equally for three hundred years?

Why is G[ladstone] right & the A[rch]b[isho]p of C[anterbury] wrong?

2. The Schools of Whitgift,[b] Abbot,[c] & Laud, & Tillotson[d] present four distinct & irreconcilable doctrines as any one read in the controversies respecting 1) Predestination & grace – 2) The Visible Church, 3) the Sacraments to name no more perfectly knows.

'Every one having access to the Liturgy' is every one going by private judgment.

The Church *is* the *living body*—not books. The *living voice* is the voice of the Church. Socinians have the Bible & the Creed.

3. Gladstone cannot produce a single difference in *doctrine of faith*. I can produce a hundred in *opinion*, in which we are all free as air.

4. The Council of Trent defines as of faith

>   1. That there is a Purgatory.

>   2. That souls therein are helped by prayers &c.

Does Gladstone mean that Döllinger (who believes the Council of Trent to be infallible) denies these two points? If not he was saying nothing.[e]

[aa] Not located. The numbered points following appear to refer to sections in Stanley's original notes.

[b] John Whitgift (1530/1–1604; *DNB*), Archbishop of Canterbury, theologically Calvinistic but opposed to Puritanism.

[c] George Abbot (1562–1633; *DNB*), Archbishop of Canterbury, Calvinistically oriented and opposed to High Church positions such as those of Laud who followed him in the office of Archbishop.

[d] John Tillotson (1630–94; *DNB*), Archbishop of Canterbury, anti-Catholic, but open to all Nonconformists, was opposed to the use of the Athanasian Creed and maintained a lower Protestant view of the sacraments.

[e] On 3 October 1845, Gladstone met with Döllinger during which the Roman Catholic doctrines of purgatory and the Blessed Virgin Mary were raised. For details see 461207gm and Addenda to Section Seven. It appears that Gladstone raised this issue in his conversation with Stanley, along with a report on two sermons he had heard in Italy on purgatory and the Virgin Mary late in 1838 that offended him greatly.

What w[oul]d Döllinger say of G[ladstone]'s theory of unity and infallibility?

5. This must be a mistake of yours. I dare not think it accurate.

Where is the Priest who denies Regeneration, the Real Presence, Absolution, Priesthood &c?

6. This is simple error.

It is no point of Faith that Popes even speaking *ex Cathedrâ* are infallible.

It is absolutely untrue that Popes *in their private capacity* are held to be infallible.

Honorius was no heretic—& if he erred (wh[ich] I do not believe) he erred only as a private Doctor of the Church: as P[ius] IX might now.

7. But I answer *is* put down because the Church of God has authority which men obey as Divine & unerring.

Nothing was ever put down in the Ch[urch] of E[ngland] because no such authority exists.

8. *No doubt*—& if *inculpable* went to heaven—as among Presbyterians, Wesleyans, Quakers, Socinians—but what then?

9. Doubt as to *Revelation?* or the Holy Trinity? the Incarnation? the Mystical Body? the Church?

Surely this is to reduce *Revelation* to *opinion?* Is God's Truth Yea & Nay?

10. But is the Church of E[ngland] in the unity & under the Guidance of the One Church, the Organ of the Holy Spirit?

All the last page is merely personal.

I have read the inclosed with great sorrow. It is not the Gladstone I remember, but the struggle of a mind, driven further, & further to declare itself simply on the side of private judgment.

In principle I see no difference between this & the Evangelical, who w[oul]d pull Anglicanism to pieces by private judgment as G[ladstone] does the Catholic Faith.

Moreover it is a studious avoiding of *principles*, & a plunging into a maze of details.

Does our Lord teach now in the world? If so by whom?

To whom shall we listen? Is there any one now of whom it can be said 'He that heareth you, heareth *Me.*'[f] If so that Body *cannot err.* For the Voice of our Lord is Divine.

H.E.M.

[[Bodl. MS Eng. lett. c. 661, 84–6]]

541129ms

Kensington Nov[ember] 29.1854

First, in promising not to see me you have done right every way.

But what a poverty of mind does the request[a] imply!

I say 'Go, & God be with you.' I need not add St Paul's words 'Be not brought under bondage to any man'[b] . . .

[[Bodl. MS Eng. lett. c. 661, 89]]

[[On the following day, 30 November, Manning wrote to Stanley, then about to leave for the Crimea, a lengthy letter summarizing her spiritual development in the previous four years (Bodl. MS Eng. lett. c. 661, 94–7). His correspondence with her during her time in the Crimea continued thereafter and on 14 April 1855 he writes, having been informed by her of her decision to be received as a Roman Catholic and supporting her in her judgement that it is best to keep silent on the matter until she returned to England[c] (ibid. 106–7). By 1 May 1855 Stanley had reached home again, and Manning advised her: 'In the Name of God, I pray you, as if it were my last word submit your aid to the guidance of any one you confide in. And do not attempt to guide yourself in this matter' (ibid. 108–9). Although Manning promised he would tell no one of her decision, rumours appear to have arisen (ibid. 114–15) and Stanley planned to meet with Manning and Robert Wilberforce sometime after 17 May (ibid. 116–17).

[f] Luke 10: 15.

[a] Possibly Gladstone's or Stanley's family's request.

[b] Cf. Rom. 8: 15 and John 8: 33.

[c] Interesting insights into Mary Stanley's life in the Crimea are available in her letters to Lady Herbert on 10 December 1854, 7, 16, 22, 28 January, 4 and 8 February 1865, as well as extracts of other letters during the time compiled by Lady Herbert in Wiltshire Country Archives, Wilton Papers, 2507 F4/64. From the 28 January letter it is already clear that Nightingale was seriously antagonistic to Stanley's presence in the war theatre and that she was involving Manning to some degree in the debate. Note as well Stanley's lengthy explanation of the strained relationships immediately after her arrival in her 23 January 1855 letter to Catherine Gladstone. (Edited and discussed in Baylen [1974].)

On 12 June 1855 Gladstone 'Worked much on arranging my letters. In selecting Manning's through the long years of our intercourse I again go through that sad experience.' The following day, 13 June, he 'Worked all day upon my letters. I find 216 of Manning's (*GD* v. 57), and several months later, on 9 September, Gladstone read the 'Manning & Meyrick Correspondence' on the moral theology of the Church of Rome[d] (ibid. 73), a task which he continued on 16 September, 'this latter with extreme pain' (ibid. 75). At some point in 1855 Gladstone is said to have commented on Manning's sincerity: 'I won't say manning is insincere. God forbid! But he is not simple and straightforward.'[e] Although, to this point Gladstone seems not to have immersed himself again in Stanley's religious concerns, he raised the matter on a visit with Arthur Stanley on 25 November 1855 (ibid. 87), and his sister felt the necessity of replying.]]

551125sg
My dear Mr. Gladstone
Arthur[a] has told me of your visit.

I decidedly felt that my promise to you was not binding when the circumstances became changed by my departure & when I wrote to say that I felt myself free.

Had I come across you on my return and you had re-opened the subject I would not have shrunk from discussion—But I never have seen you but twice & then exchanged but few words.

With regard to Lady Stratford's statement[b]—she misunder-stands my words as I have explained to Mrs. Herbert and Lady

---

[d] *Moral Theology of the Church of Rome. No. II. Certain Points in S[t]. Alfonzo de' Ligouri's Moral Theology, Considered in Nineteen Letters by the Rev. H. E. Manning and the Rev. F. Meyrick* (London: J. & C. Mozley, 1855). An unannotated copy is preserved among the Gladstone Tracts at the National Library of Wales (SDL, GTM F90/17). Note also [Frederick Meyrick], *Moral Theology of the Church of Rome. No. 1. S[t]. Alfonzo de' Ligouri's Theory of Truthfulness From the Christian Rembrancer of January, 1854* (London: J. & C. Mozley, 1854 [SDL, I/56/46 (no annotations)]), and Frederick Meyrick and H. E. Manning, *The Rambler* 16 os 4/2 (Oct. 1855), 712; short notices, 316–22, and 402.

[e] See Percy Colson (ed.), *Lord Groschen and his Friends* (London: Hutchinson, n.d.), 150.

[a] Her brother, Arthur Penrhyn Stanley.

[b] Lady Stratford de Redcliffe, wife of Lord Stratford de Redcliffe, British Ambassador to Constantinople. On 5 March 1855 Florence Nightingale wrote to Herbert: 'Lady Stratford

Canning[c]—I wrote *confidentially* to her in Sept[ember].[76]—she being
aware of my state of mind last year—to ask her whether she sh[oul]d
object to my coming out again as R[oman] Catholic in a subordinate
situation. It was an act of courtesy to her, for I know Government could
not urge it as an objection when in addition to their primary declaration
the nursing System included all opinions—the War Office declined to
accede to the 3 fold appeal of Miss Nightingale—the Commandant &
the Chaplain to have Miss Jebbatt recalled in consequence of the
declaration she made of Christian views.

Lady Stratford construed my words to mean that I had already taken
the Step—I have written to state what I did mean.

It is one year this very day since I spent 2 hours with you in Downing St.

The months which succeeded brought the stern realities of life before
me—and it was impossible to feel death so near & not to examine what
ones grounds of faith were.

I believe I could have borne the bodily fatigue. I believe that the
harassing perplexity into which I was thrown with regard to the nurses[77]

sent for Mr. Sabin, the Senior Chaplain here, over to the Embassy last week on other
business. She then exposed Miss Stanley's grievances to him "au long et au large..."
Mr. Sabin was led on (little by little) to tell Lady Stratford that Miss Stanley had
"grossly imposed upon her" & farther that he had reason to believe from putting two
& two together, & from accounts which he received from home that Miss Stanley was
only waiting to become a R[oman] Catholic & was playing the game of the R[oman]
Catholics at Koulalee—that Dr. Tice who never shewed any great love for the Nurses
at the General Hospital was encouraging the Nuns at Koulalee, being himself a R
[oman] Catholic—etc. etc. Lady Stratford was greatly alarmed "why did you not tell
this before?" & "don't tell Lord Stratford" being her chief ideas—to which Mr. Sabin
replied "he was very sorry, but he had already told Lord Stratford." Now, observe,
dear Mr. Herbert, this bother is none of my making. I have kept strict honor with
Lady Stratford, as also with Mr. Cumming about Mary Stanley's religious opinions—I
could easily have defeated her representations by "telling of her" as the children say—
and Mrs. Herbert will think that I have. But people out here do not require us at home
to tell them "things"—& Koulalee has excited suspicions, without me or in spite of
me. Cumming asked the question one day in my room whether Miss Stanley were not
a R[oman] & I put it off, in order that he might not say he heard it from me. Thus it
stands now' (Goldie [1987], 100).

[c] Charlotte Stuart, wife of Charles John Earl Canning, was, along with Elizabeth
Herbert and others, a member of the Committee of Management of the Harley Street
Institution, initially directing the Nightingale Crimean work (Goldie [1987], 186).

would not have crushed me, but the severe mental strain in addition to these two others broke me down.

I knew I was free but I felt it would be more honourable to Mr. Herbert not to profess my faith there—and so I came home & am where I was.

Many instances may doubtless be brought against[78] me of want of honesty. I am willing to bear the blame,—my only excuse is that I have *tried* to do what would cause least annoyance to my family. I have never concealed my opinions from any one who had either a right to know them, or who asked any questions—but I do shrink from bringing them forward unrequested.

The only reason for my not at once taking the step is the consideration for my family. I have never yet heard any argument which shook my increasing belief that the R[oman] Catholic Church in point of Unity— & Holiness comes nearest to the Scriptural definition of the Ch[urch] of Christ.

I have gone thro' *much* anguish of mind, & have more before me if I live to bear it. Which sometimes I think is doubtful.

I feel your kindness extremely. Believe me to be dear Mr. Gladstone

Very sincerely yours

M. Stanley

6 Grosvenor Crescent
Nov[ember] 25th
[[BL Add. MS 44384, 239–42]]

551127gs[a]

Private
Hawarden 27 [18]55

My dear Miss Stanley

Acting in the speech of frankness wh[ich] you have encouraged me to use, & wh[ich] without such encouragement might I know be justly called impertinence, I felt it just to you that you should know the state of my recollections, very fallible as they are without doubt on a matter of fact— They assure me that you did not on going to the East, retract or cancel what you had tendered & I had accepted: but you suspended its operation on the fair & obvious ground that, taking distance into view it w[oul]d amount in given contingencies to an abandonment of y[ou]r liberty instead of being what I conclude you had intended, a security taken by

---

[a] 'Wrote to . . . Miss Stanley & copy' (*GD* v. 88; cf. Lathbury, ii. 27).

y[our]self, for yourself, but by means that should be independent of your inclination at the moment, one additional opportunity of reconsidering a subject that can hardly be too fully or too often considered.

Such was my idea, not I hope despairing to you, of the original promise: & such was & is my recollection of the matter of fact. I submit them to you accordingly.

When we met upon this subject last year it struck me that your mind was in a different state from that of others which I had seen when they were meditating a similar course: that in general the arguments on the strength of wh[ich] it is designed so to act are insufficient to warrant the conclusions if only they were true: but that your arguments[79] even if they were true yet[80] did not warrant your conclusions.

And it is remarkable that I find the very same character in the letter you have now addressed to me when you say that you have heard no argument to shake 'your increasing belief that the R[oman] C[atholic] Church in point of unity & holiness comes nearest to the scriptural definition of the Church of Christ.'

I confess it seems to me that that is a question which neither of us are very competent to decide. My fixed connection has long been that the Roman Church remarkably unites within itself the opposite extremes: that it has much of the very best & a great deal of the very worst of Christianity. But I feel that this is a matter of private and personal opinion, that for me to make the little shreds and fragments of experience which I can gather within my own active sphere the ground of my hold upon the Faith and title to the reality of membership in Christ is a sad error within itself and in its consequences to me.

If it was the ordinance of God that each Christian was to institute a search and to discover for himself which of the various Christian communities came nearest in unity & holiness to the scriptural representation of the Body of Christ, it seems to me that the whole design of the historical, visible & traditional character of the Church is overthrown.

Where has God promised that in all parts of the Apostles fellowship the light sh[oul]d burn with equal purity and brightness? Even at the first the Church of Sardis[b] was not equal 'in unity & holiness' to the Ch[urch] of Ephesus, nor the Ch[urch] of Ephesus to the Ch[urch] of Smyrna;[c] but St. John did not command the Christians of Sardis to join the communion of Ephesus, nor both to leave their own & go into that of Smyrna: he bid

---

[b] Cf. Rev. 3: 1ff.   [c] Cf. Rev. 2: 8ff.

them through their rulers to amend their ways & become even like their Lord.

I avoid and eschew that question, which Ch[urch] is most holy: alas it is too sadly easy to make a case against all: but I certainly assure you, from the evidence your letter gives me, that you are bound in duty to seek to have a sound mind as well as an upright heart, & that upright as I am certain your heart is, your mind is not upon the line which leads to true conclusions & indicates the path of just and safe action.

Believe me I neither doubt nor make light of your sufferings: I trust they may be lightened, but especially that when they are lightened they may be lightened once for all; & that you will find the true solution of your present dilemma in a more just & searching examination of the whole grounds on which such a question should be handled.

I will not apologize for the manner in wh[ich] I write but I trust to your indulgence and I remain always most sincerely yours

(s[igne]d) WG

[[BL Add. MS 44384, 245–7; Lathbury, ii. 27–9]]

551130sg

6 Grosvenor Crescent
Nov[ember] 30th [1855]

My dear Mr. Gladstone

I have no copy of my letter to Mrs. Gladstone[a] in which I cancelled my promise by the circumstances which arose.

I am clear as to my own recollections & I certainly did consider myself free.

This is not of any importance now—& I will gladly hear all you have to say.

At the outset I must lay before you the difficulties I feel in entering into this correspondence.

1st I have been brought to feel that the right to private judgment is the inheritance of every English Protestant. That it is the duty of every individual who has doubts to enquire & be convinced in his own mind.

I have had the 'Popery of Protestantism' preached to me the sin of receiving Protestant faith on trust from my forefathers.

If I understand you right you do not hold this view.

[a] See 541126scg.

If so, to what extent do[81] you limit private judgment? And to whom is that judgment to be submitted?

If to the 'Church'? How?

To what phase of the Church of England—to which interpretation of the Liturgy?

2nd you must be aware of the difficulties I have in arguing any point with one whose knowledge & character has commanded my respect for so many years.

To differ appears the height of presumption—& yet to agree where I am not convinced, is not honest—

I am not young & have only come to my present opinions after years of uncertainty & doubt.

I have no wish to judge for others. Minds are so differently constituted that what brings peace to one may bring doubt to another.

Can any one take the responsibility of assuring me of my Salvation if I from earthly motives refuse to walk in the way in wh[ich] I feel I can most love & serve Christ?

It was when death was so near me that this solemn thought came across me perpetually & I felt how am I to answer this question?

Every sincerely yours
M. Stanley

[[BL Add. MS 44384, 251–2]]

[[Gladstone wrote to Miss Stanley on 1 December 1855 (*GD* v. 89; not located).]]

551204sg

6 Grosvenor Ave.
Dec 4th [1855]

Dear Mr. Gladstone

I shall be at home Thursday[aa] morning after 11 & glad to see you. Only the great difficulty I feel, and expressed in my last letter, between being honest & humble is, to me, greatly increased in a personal interview.

What you have now said has often been said to me, but I confess it is no answer to my simple questions.

Do you grant me the right of private judgment—and if not, to whom am I to submit it *practically*?

---

^{aa} 6 December 1855.

When I have your distinct answer to these two questions then I shall better understand how to proceed.

The points at issue with me are simple practical ones. I have not the mental powers to enable me to argue them except in this sense. I feel I may be left by[82] a powerful arguer such as yourself, bewildered & confused, without being convinced.

You must forgive me for writing openly
& believe me to be very sincerely yours
M. Stanley

[[BL Add. MS 44384, 258–9]]

[[On 6 December 1855 Gladstone met with Mary Stanley 'twice' (*GD* v. 90)]]

551209sg

Dear Mr. Gladstone

One thing let me assure you. I will never quote your name, if I use your arguments.

I feel it[83] would not be fair to you as I might possibly not state the cases correctly as you would.

A Catholic friend was with me today, and I asked her how it was that the German C[atholic] Church held purgatory to be an open question while the French Catholic Church made it obligatory & I mentioned the 2 books. She denied the fact & asked me the name of the German work of 17 Editions you spoke of.[a]

Will you give me the Title, that I may prove to her the correctness of the assertion?

Most sincerely yours
M. Stanley

6 Grosvenor Crescent

Dec[ember] 9th

[[BL Add. MS 44384, 265–6]]

[[Gladstone wrote to Mary Stanley on 11 December 1855 (*GD* v. 90; not located).]]

551218ms

78 S[outh] A[udley] S[t.] Dec[ember]. 18. 1855

My silence has not been from intention, but from constant work. I have been unusually occupied & overwhelmed with letters.

---

[a] Cf. 451020gm and reference to prayer book.

But for this I should have written to say that if I do not speak on matters of Faith it is because I fear to give you pain. You know that I have never done so willingly: except when I dare not do otherwise. The Church, its Truths its laws are all divine. And when they command I cannot dismiss. There is no point in what I have said on which there can be two opinions—for where the Church of God commands opinion has no place. I am therefore silent, & all I can do is to pray day by day in the Holy Sacrifice.

Some day you will know that what you call severity is fidelity to God & to you.

The Church of God requires absolute, unreasoned, & universal submission to all its Divine Laws. I render it as a child, as I would to our Lord visibly present upon earth.

It is here that we must meet. God be with you. I hope you are well: every good gift be with you this [Chris]tmas.

Believe me, always affect[ionatel]y yours
H.E.M.

[[Bodl. MS Eng. lett. c. 661, 134–5]]

551231sg

Precincts, Canterbury
Dec[ember] 31st

My dear Mr. Gladstone

I am going to tax your patience again—I wished to say that I certainly did understand you to mention the German book as a proof that the R[oman] Catholic Church was wanting in that Unity of faith wh[ich] I believed her to profess & that in that work I should see that Purgatory was in Germany an open question—in France a definite Article of Faith. I also understood you to say that change of faith was scarcely ever admissible even from dissent to the Ch[urch] of England.

Fearing lest I misunderstand other points, I mention them that you may correct me if I have overstated them myself.

—That you considered the Ch[urch] of E[ngland] had a living voice in Convocation & that had Convocation (why was it silent on such an important point) pronounced the same opinion on the Gorham question that the Privy Council did, you would have considered that the C[hurch] of E[ngland] had denied (or what you thought worse made it an open question) an Article of faith & that you c[oul]d no longer have remained in her Communion.

—That you doubted the fact of any Clergyman in the C[hurch] of E[ngland] disbelieving in Baptismal Regeneration.

—& that you considered the C[hurch] of England sanctioned Prayers for the dead.

If you remember I expressed my surprise on all these points.

—As you advised I have been reading Milman's Christianity again. In reading Ch[urch] History I am always struck by the recognition of the peculiar Catholic Doctrines in those early ages & the development of faith and discipline according to the Heresies which arose & the increase of the Church.

When I spoke to you of being strengthened in Catholic faith by Protestant writers I meant to say that when Prot[estants] & Catholics agreed in facts I believed those facts to be true.

What is the answer to the History of doctrines?

I was inclined to believe formerly that the quotations from the Early fathers given by Heylin[a] and Berington, Kirk,[b] and others were false, but on examination I found they were confirmed by almost every Protestant Historian I took up, their joint testimony proving that the Early Church held those points of faith & discipline which the development of Protestantism has cast out of the Ch[urch] of E[ngland] but which have remained from first to last in the Ch[urch] of R[ome].

I read the Arian controversy carefully—but does it prove more than that heresies were always arising & splitting away from the Church? They were not retained within her fold by declarations that they were open questions, but they were expelled by enlarged creeds were they not? That mental suffering & conflict existed then as now cannot be doubted.

I am very anxious to know exactly what you mean when you say you 'have set forth the case.' & that I 'have not put my mind into the training indispensable for this purpose.'

I am most anxious to have your outline of the case—or the first step to the outline. I have tried by giving broad questions to lay before you those

---

[a] Among the many works by Peter Heylyn (1600–62) see his *Theologia veterum: or The summe of Christian theologie, positive, polemical, and philological, contained in the Apostles creed, or reducible to it: according to the tendries of the antients both Greeks and Latines. In three books* (London: Printed by E. Cotes for Henry Seile, 1654).

[b] *The Faith of Catholics: Confirmed by Scripture, and Attested by the Fathers of the Five First Centuries of the Church*, compiled by Joseph Berington and John Kirk, rev. and greatly enlarged by James Waterworth (London: Charles Dolman, 1846).

points I most wished to have answered. I now enclose a paper found the other day written 2 years ago.[c]

My one desire is to know and follow Truth by that path which leads *me* nearest to Christ.

I cannot judge for others. I cannot end without repeating how very painful it is to me to write on these points to you feeling that to be unconvinced must appear most selfwilled—and yet what can I do unless I am truly convinced that the foundation on which I have rested & found peace for the last few years is a delusion?

I feel I cannot wish for you a greater happiness in the coming year than that you may remain satisfied and free from doubt in the Ch[urch] of England.

> dear Mr. Gladstone
> Believe me to be most sincerely yours
> M. Stanley

[[BL Add. MS 44384, 283–7]]

[[On 6 January 1856 Gladstone 'Wrote to Miss Stanley: a bewildering case. She is already in feeling Roman & something more' (*GD* v. 95). He wrote again 7 January (ibid. 100; not located).[d]]]

560110sg

> Precincts, Canterbury
> Jan[uary] 10th

My dear Mr. Gladstone

Your letter crushed and saddened me.

Believe me, it was not in a spirit of presumptuous dissatisfaction that I wrote, but in deep anxiety to know the truth, & by placing an outline

---

[c] Not located.

[d] Two days earlier, Lord Granville commented in his diary: 'A new ingredient appeared in Bruton Street—Dr. Manning, a fine-looking, intellectual priest, with good manners and agreeable. I think I should have guessed that he was an Oxford man. He has a great admiration for Gladstone, and described him very much as you or I would. He was at school with Sidney Herbert, thinks him pleasing and quick. Newcastle he has a great respect for. He believes that one of the chief causes of the Church of England clergy having lost influence with the middle classes and lower classes, is their habit of writing their sermons. He says that it is not only less interesting to the hearer, but the preacher appears less in earnest, and is absolutely himself less careful in preparing his sermon than when he is to speak it. He says the artisans are a very sceptical and a very thinking race' (Fitzmaurice [1905], i. 138).

before you, I thought to save you trouble & enable you to judge better how to deal with me, but I feel as if it was almost useless to write more.

If however you would kindly answer my first questions I should be very glad. They were

—to what extent is private judgment justifiable?

To whom is it to be submitted, If the Church—How? To what phase of the Ch[urch] of E[ngland], to what interpretation of her Liturgy & Articles?[a]

As words appeared to me I thought the view given by Church Historians of the first centuries did accord more with the faith and practice of the Ch[urch] of Rome than the Ch[urch] of England. I will mention a few who have given me this impression—Waddington,[b] Vowler Short,[c] Wheatley,[d] Neander,[e] Geissler, Hagenbach,[f] Mosheim, Milman, Bingham & others.

I have no desire to deny the merits of the Ch[urch] of E[ngland] or the corruptions of the Ch[urch] of Rome. I fully believe the former is free from much sin which exists in the latter for there is no blessing given by God which cannot be prevented by man & every doctrine is liable to abuse.

It is indeed my desire to be governed by a burning love of truth & a resolution to give up all for its sake—but it w[oul]d be untruthful to say that my education had led me to consider the Ch[urch] of E[ngland] with reverence. To enlarge upon this is needless unless you wish it.

If you can tell me what to read to contradict my conclusions, I will gladly do so. I am not likely to be in town at present, nor do I wish it.

---

[a] Cf. Manning's words in 541127ms.

[b] See George Waddington, *A History of the Church from the Earliest Ages to the Reformation* (London: Baldwin & Cradock, 1831) and *A History of the Reformation on the Continent* (3 vols.; London: Duncan & Malcolm, 1841).

[c] See the widely published Thomas Vowler Short, *A Sketch of History of the Church of England to the Revolution 1688* (2 vols.; Oxford: S. Collingwood, 1832).

[d] See James Wheatley, *The Lives, Tryals and Sufferings of the Holy Apostles, Primitive Fathers, and Martyrs* (Bristol, 1751).

[e] Note above all the highly popular and frequently reprinted Augustus Neander, *The History of the Christian Religion and Church during the Three First Centuries*, trans. Henry John Rose (2 vols.; London: C. J. G. & F. Rivington, 1831).

[f] K. R. Hagenbach, *Compendium of the History of Doctrines* (Edinburgh: T. & T. Clark, 1846).

My Protestant friends have long since condemned me. My Anglican friends look upon me with suspicion & distrust, & I have no desire to see my Catholic friends.

Believe me to be dear Mr Gladstone
very sincerely yours
M. Stanley

[[BL Add. MS 44385, 5–6]]

[[Gladstone replied on 12 January 1856 (*GD* v. 96; not located).]]

560115sg

My dear Mr. Gladstone

I am quite sure your intention was all kindness—& I feel how annoying it must be to you, to see one like myself resisting argument. But the salvation of my soul is more precious to me than any thing this world can give. For this I have sacrificed much & am prepared if needs be to sacrifice all.

I wrote shortly last time because I did not feel I c[oul]d write more. I will now go thro' the various points in both letters.

To deny the corruption of any Church—

of any institution on Earth would seem to me like denying Original sin, & as you say there is no proof of the truth of Christianity greater than the corrupt Channels thro' which that truth has flowed and existed.

On your second point one answer rises before me Mat[t]h[ew] x 34 &c.[a] But that our Lord's Words must needs be fulfilled it would be a perpetual wonder to me, why when Faith has not been the bond of social & family affection—it sh[oul]d suddenly be made the cause of scripture.

I could not answer your question—whether an answer to my enquiry about the living voice of the Ch[urch] of E[ngland] would set me at ease— till knowing where it was. I had tried it.

I feel it is scarcely fair upon you to have to undertake so hopeless a case as mine is as regards satisfaction with the Ch[urch] of E[ngland].

---

[a] Matt. 10: 34–8: 'Think not that I am come to send peace on earth: I came not to send peace, but a sword. For I am come to set a man at variance against his father, and the daughter against her mother, and the daughter in law against her mother in law. And a man's foes shall be they of his own household. He that loveth father or mother more than me is not worthy of me: and he that loveth son or daughter more than me is not worthy of me. And he that taketh not his cross, and followeth after me, is not worthy of me.'

Four or five years ago when I first began to enquire into these matters it might have been different—or even 2 or 3 years ago, when in despair at the result of communications with those I thought able to assist me, I asked a friend, to whom I c[oul]d apply for conviction, & was answered that you were best able to satisfy a doubting mind.

But how I presumed to come to you—I who only met you in society 2 or 3 times in a year.

About the 4th Century the Arian controversy—you tell me that I am wrong in saying it split away from the Church—for that it 'contended against the Truth within the Church' for whole generations.

I will give my reasons for what I said out of Milman which you recommended to me.

'At the same time, not merely on the great subject of the Trinity, had Rome repudiated the more obnoxious heresy, even on less vital questions, the Latin Capital . . . had rarely swerved from the Canon of severe orthodoxy; & if any one of her Bishops had been forced or perplexed into a rash or erroneous decision, as Liberius during his short concession to semi Arianism, . . . or Zosimus to Pelagianism; and a still later Pope, who was bewildered into Monophysitism their errors were effaced by a speedy, full, and glorious recantation'—Hist. of Latin [Christiani]ty Vol. 1.85.[b]

I asked [Benjamin][84] Harrison the question how long Arianism existed in the Church uncondemned. He answers. 'Six years from the first promulgation of his heresy by Arius to the Council of Nice.' AD 319–25. Both may be wrong—but I hope you will allow I was justified in believing what I wrote.

The sermon on Purgatory of which you spoke, did not shock me, because it has long seemed to me that an intermediate state of purification is the only way in which to reconcile God's Mercy and Justice.

All who believe in Christ are saved by Him—for He died for all.

But we find conditions of Salvation—of rewards—& we read of purification by fire—Spirits in Prison—preaching to the dead. Why should prayers have been ever offered for their dead if their eternal fate was fixed at their death, and if they are of avail—surely the benefit of a soul is of more importance than of a body.

The argument is one used at all Missionary Meetings.—I can imagine a low preacher entering into all manners of horrible & disgusting details on

[b] Henry Hart Milman, *History of Latin Christianity* (6 vols.; London: John Murray, 1854–5), bk. II, ch. 1.

the subject. Laud's Conference with Fisher[c] and Scudamore.[d] I have read Mannings Unity of Faith.[e] I have tried to read but never could fully understand.

Allies[f] and Palmer[g] I will try to get & read.

What has surprised, not to say shocked me most in the course of my enquiries & reading, on these subjects, is the want of truth & fairness in what concerns R[oman] Catholic Faith. It seems to me unjust & unreasonable not to take the R[oman] Church's own explanation of her doctrines & discipline, & it is startling to hear the avidity with which the most monstrous stories against her are believed & circulated—by wise & good people.

I had sad instances of this last winter. But you will say this is going off to another point.

Believe me to be
most sincerely yours
M. Stanley

Precincts Canterbury
Jan[uary] 15
[[BL Add. MS 44385, 16–21]]
[[On 18 January 1856 Gladstone wrote to Mary Stanley (*GD* v. 98; not located).]]

560120sg
My dear Mr. Gladstone

[c] See *A Relation of the Conference between William Laud, Late Lord Archbishop of Canterbury, and Mr. Fisher the Jesuit, by the Command of King James, of ever blessed Memory. With an answer to such exceptions as A.C. takes against it* (Oxford: Oxford University Press, 1839).

[d] John Scudamore, 1st Viscount (1601–71; *DNB*), close associate and religious confrère of Laud.

[e] That is, Manning's *Unity of the Church* (London: John Murray, 1842).

[f] Perhaps Thomas William Allies, *The Church of England Cleared from the Charge of Schism upon Testimonies of Councils and Fathers of the First Six Centuries* (London: J. Burns, 1846); note also his *The Royal Supremacy Viewed in Reference to the Two Spiritual Powers of Order and Jurisdiction* (London: William Pickering, 1850), and see 500509gm.

[g] See William Palmer, *Letters to N. Wiseman, D.D., on the Errors of Romanism in Respect to the Worship of Saints, Satisfactions, Purgatory, Indulgences and the Worship of Images and Relics. To which is added, an Examination of Mr. Sibthorp's Reasons for his Secession from the Church, with a Supplement (Comprising Observations on his Further Answer, etc.)* (3rd edn.; London, 1851), and note also his *A Compendious Ecclesiastical History from the Earliest Period to the Present Time* (new edn.; London: Edwards & Hughes, 1847).

I have to offer my most sincere apologies for any words in my last letter which implied so unjustifiable a request as to know your 'whole mind on the subject of religious Communion.'

You have been kind enough to interest yourself in my difficulties, but they would not be solved by such a course as you offer to me.

I will from hence forward avoid the course of which you complained i.e. 'flying from point,' & will hold fast to my first questions to which as yet I have received no definite answer.

When you spoke of the Arian heresy contending with truth in the Church I understood you to bring it forward as a proof that open questions existed in the Primitive Church of equal importance with those which have been the pride of the Church of England since the Reformation.

In the passage I quote from Milman, he seems to imply that such was not the case with 'obnoxious, or even less vital questions.'

Heresies, like diseases may recur again & again but are they considered as diseases to be eradicated, or as life to be sustained.

I have always gathered from history that the fierce contest with heresy was one of the complaints against the Ch[urch] of Rome.

Very sincerely yours
M. Stanley

Canterbury
Jan[uary] 20
[[BL Add. MS 44385, 24–5]]

560127gs
4, CARLTON HOUSE TERRACE,
January 27, 1856.
MY DEAR MISS STANLEY,

It will be quite as much as I can write, or as you can read with patience, if I explain upon *one sentence* of your last letter, in which you say that 'you understood me to bring forward the Arian heresy as a proof that open questions existed in the Primitive Church of equal importance with those which have been the pride of the Church of England since the Reformation.' You did not mean to impute to me this language, but how *my* language could be such as to lead you into such a statement I am at a loss to conjecture. It makes me a calumniator of the Primitive Church, and you the utterer of (in my opinion) a precipitate and untrue charge against the Church of England.

You think that I said the Arian hypothesis was an open question because I said it remained long and struggled long in the Church before the final victory of the truth.

What I have said (I speak from memory only) amounts, I believe, to this: Place yourself as an orthodox believer in the Church of the Fourth Century, and I will show you that there were times when, even as regarded the vital doctrine of the Godhead, the voice of authority was liable to the charge of a doubtful utterance, so far that the private Christian might not unreasonably doubt in what path it bid him walk.

You seem to me (forgive me) not to have considered the nature of the Church, but rather in regard to it, as it exists in England, to have rested in a creed or scheme of opinion that in other respects you have repudiated; you likewise seem to me not to have examined into the nature of the provision made by Almighty God in the Church for the establishment of the truth, and when I refer to a great case in which the horizon was long clouded, and for a time it seemed doubtful which creed would gain the mastery, you think I say it was an open question.

An open question I take to be a question which the authority ruling the Church has either by speech or general and long-continued silence, or by its falling plainly within some general rule, declared to be open—i.e., indifferent. Two men wrestle for a prize; till one wins, the question is contested. Two men agree not to wrestle for it at all, the question is open. Have I made myself clear?

Bishop Butler is not controversial; but his works are more fruitful in sound principles applicable to the mode of Providential government in the Church as well as in the world than almost any others.

Now for the Church of England. A glance at her history, in my opinion, shows the injustice of your charge and (I cannot but add) its precipitancy. The legal settlement of the Church of England dates from 1662. *She* has never retraced, never qualified any part of that settlement. Was that settlement founded on the notion of open questions? Why then did 2,000 ministers quit their benefices? The principle on which that settlement was founded was, it seems to me, the Divine Constitution of the Church; at any rate, plainly enough, it was founded upon a principle in dogma and in polity, as were the decrees of Trent. Both left open questions, but both closed some questions—the questions which they thought to be essential.

What you have to show in order to make good your charge is that the Church has left open any question which involves matter of faith properly so called. This you will find very difficult. As respects the case of Baptism which you quoted, I ask in what sense is it open? You will hardly say the language of the formularies is not clear. You will perhaps say Mr. A. and Mr. B. who deny it are unpunished. I answer Pope Liberius was unpunished when he had renounced the orthodox communion,[a] Pope Honorius remained unpunished until after his death.[b] If a Pope, then why not any man lesser than a Pope? I hope the day will come when you will regard these questions in their true light as trials of your faith.

I must not let my letter go without referring to your words, 'my first questions, to which I have received no definite answer.' I ask you plainly whether I was not justified—nay, bound—to interpose my preliminary condition? What can be the use of my answering questions until I get you to admit the principle on which we are to proceed, and the responsibility under which you have placed yourself by desiring me to enter on these subjects; for I need not say we are [as] responsible for using the light of a farthing candle when we have called for it, as we should be were it the sun.

My position is this: you are bound by duty and allegiance to the Church of England. If you have doubts in regard to her authority, you are bound (as one in the Church of Rome would be bound in the converse case) to *bring those doubts to a fair trial.* To do this you ought to state them, and to say: These and these questions being answered properly (of course without prejudice to future *lights*), my mind will be satisfied. But question after question, charge after charge, without any specification to yourself or me of the whole of what you want, is just the course which a person would take whose wounded feelings had made him determined *not* to be satisfied; it is a course into which you may unknowingly be entrapped, but into which I shall not by my conduct help to entrap you.

Some day I may ask you to let me look at these letters again. You, I know, forgive their haste, and will not make me an offender for a word.

Most sincerely yours,
W. E. GLADSTONE.

[[Lathbury, ii. 29–31]]

---

[a] Liberius, Pope, 352–66, submitted to the Emperor's demand that Athanasius be deposed. Cf. Stanley's use in 560115sg.

[b] Honorius, Pope, 625–38, supported the Monothelite position on Christ's 'one will'.

560129sg

Canterbury
Jan[uary] 29th

My dear Mr. Gladstone

I feel at a loss how to answer your last letter; It completely silences me, for I see I am quite unequal to understanding you, & I never again will presume to argue with you.

I could only state what I had learnt from books & observations, & I gave the naked results without qualification or comment to save you time and trouble.

It was your great kindness which originated these discussions, first in Nov[ember 18]54 & again in Nov[ember 18]55 & I had such a misgiving after our first interview that I could not follow your mind, that I should any how have been glad that circumstances (to my mind) cancelled the promise I gave of consulting you further. I would not willingly have renewed the subject with you.

I mention this in reference to your saying I have placed myself under responsibility by 'desiring' you 'to enter upon these subjects.'

Your refusal to answer my question till I have given you an assurance that 'satisfactory answers will set my conscience at ease' seems to me like the refusal of a D[octo]r to give medicine unless the patient will pledge himself to be cured by it.

I do not doubt that your reasons are good—& that it is my dullness which hinders my seeing them.

Believe me—it is a matter of the *deepest regret* to me to have been unable to concur in your views, & I feel that no letters or words I have received & heard on these points[85] have given me the same pain that yours have done—dating from the one to Mrs. Herbert.

To have agreed with you, or been convinced by you w[oul]d have given me sincere joy.

For the time & trouble you have spent upon me, unavailing as it has been, I am deeply grateful & if our future meetings are fewer than the past, I shall never forget your kind interest on this occasion.

Believe me to be dear Mr. Gladstone most gratefully & sincerely yours
M. Stanley

[[BL Add. MS 44385, 42–3; Stanley's annotation written over first three lines: You shall see your letters at any time, but I shall try to have them returned to me.]]

560131sg

Canterbury Jan[uary] 31

Mr dear Mr. Gladstone

I can only repeat what I have already said. I cannot say that your answer would satisfy me, *till* I know, and have proved it was satisfactory.

I thought this was equivalent to saying a *satisfactory* answer would satisfy me.

Were I on my death bed I would say I had done my utmost to know and to follow the Truth.

Very sincerely yours
M. Stanley

[[BL Add. MS 44385, 48]]

[[Gladstone wrote to Stanley on 3 February 1856 (*GD* v. 101; not located).]]

560205sg

My dear Mr. Gladstone

I have not the power of answering you—for I frankly confess I do not understand you—I know not how to word points, without apparent presumption, in wh[ich] I cannot honestly agree, & I have conscientious scruples in taking up y[ou]r time wh[ich] I feel may be well spent on the many who are able to understand you & be retained in the Ch[urch] of E[ngland] thro' your influence.

To your question about my doubts as to what the Church teaches, I could only repeat the points in wh[ich] you said I had expressed myself as one in deep dissatisfaction, venting my feelings thro' such arguments as chanced to offer.

For myself I can say no more.

For you, I rejoice that your course in life is not clouded by doubts as to the present state of the Church of England.

Believe me to be most sincerely yours
M. Stanley

Canterbury February 5

[[BL Add. MS 44385, 66–7]]

[[On 6 February 1856, Gladstone wrote to Stanley (*GD* v. 102; not located).]]

560208sg

My dear Mr. Gladstone

I would most gladly continue this correspondence if I saw any probability of its ending satisfactorily to yourself.

All minds cannot take in the same instruction & it is very possible that a very inferior mind to yourself might have had more effect upon me.

This I cannot however tell.

But I have told you the honest truth, I *do not* understand you, & I am wholly unable to argue with you.

I feel my 'duty' is to seek Christ as closely as I can. I do not feel towards the Church of England as you do, & as my reason for remaining a nominal member of her Communion for some years past has been out of consideration to my own family—I would rather believe exactly what they do—if I *may* not believe what my own convictions have led me to—& I am not sure that you would bring me to this point.

I am nearly worn out with the mental struggle.

If it is to continue I must put my soul's salvation into their hands & believe what they wish me to believe. But I trust this will not be the case & that they will set me free.

Ever most sincerely yours

M. Stanley

Canterbury
Feb[ruary] 8th.
[[BL Add. MS 44385, 75–6]]

560210gs[a]

4 C[arlton] H[ouse] T[errace]

F[ebruary] 10 [18]56
My dear Miss Stanley

I cannot control y[ou]r will but neither can I let your letter pass without an earnest remonstrance. It is to me quite unexampled in the course of my life to be either incited or allowed to enter into communications with another person on matters of vital interest, and then to have the door summarily[86] shut across the path of inquiry by a general declaration 'I do not understand you'. My experience thus concurs with reason to assure me that this method of proceeding is one which would not discharge your obligations either to truth in general or in the Church of England whose claim upon you I may observe you have always forborne to admit in any terms however you could.[87]

On the contrary I am persuaded[88] that it is one which amounts to a decision not to inquire into what may be found to[89] thwart a bias already contracted.

---

[a] 'Wrote to Miss Stanley (& draft)' (*GD* v. 103).

I have solicited you to point out what it is that you do not understand but wholly without effect.

You desired me to answer in a letter questions that have occupied volumes—is it any wonder if even irrespective of my own human faults I have been not easily intelligible?

If you say generally you do not understand what I urge[90] & yet cannot believe that my fundamental propositions are palpably irrational, how do you know but that *under* what you say you do not understand may lie the demonstration that what you desire is flatly contrary to your duty?

If you find it irksome to labour in these questions which 'the sins & infirmities of many generations have made so difficult,' why do you[91] stir them? Must the obligation manifest and absolute either to work through them, or else in the plan and calling which you are to follow Christ by the exercise of your faculties & powers, no common ones, for the fulfilment of His blessed will?

When you feel the obscurity of these controversies, & the restlessness they engender, does it ever occur to you that they may be[92] signs, sent to you[93] from God to renounce them, & to seek to fulfil His work during your day & generation in supplying the very defects which you mourn over & in bearing the odium which from the ill minded on the ill informed your good deeds might provoke?

That I may now venture to tell you is the conclusion to which my own mind has been brought in regard to you by the communications between us. It seems to me that not reason nor (even false)[94] conviction but deep discomfort has estranged you from the Church of England.

When I say to you, examine its titles you decline to examine. I rejoin this is a sign that by entering into these debates of theology you are only arousing the Tempter against yourself and that you sh[oul]d[95] seek a cure for that discomfort, but by keeping in the dark, not by praying that God may supply & may use you as an instrument[96] supplying what yet lacketh in the work of faith or[97] of Charity among us.

This is the last letter you have to fear receiving[98] from me against your will.[99] After the protestation it contains[100] my conscience is in a manner liberated. We shall[101] remember one another before His Throne & Altar of grace: I trust we shall also dwell together in the unity of the Church, the appointed[102] bond of peace.

I remain, etc.

[[BL Add. MS 44385, 77–8]]

560214sg

Feb[ruary] 14
Canterbury

My dear Mr. Gladstone

I have read & re-read your correspondence to[103] try to come to some fresh conclusion, but it is in vain.

I would only say that from those letters it would be inferred that I had *sought* your aid—& in one, you state that *I* 'tendered' & *you* 'accepted'[a] a request that you would hear me again before I took any final step—and you speak of this as 'a security taken' by myself for myself.

In another letter you speak of the 'responsibility' under which I have 'placed' myself by coming to you, and in your last you say I have acted in a way 'quite unexampled' in having 'invited or allowed' you to enter into such serious subjects and then cut you short.

May I remind you that in our first interview it was *you* who requested and I who consented.

My memory is quite clear on this point & were it not I have notes of that conversation—made at the time—wh[ich] second the fact.

What has since occurred I need not say was your seeking, not mine—& for your interest in my welfare I shall ever feel the deepest gratitude.

One thing I confess surprises me—wh[ich] is that if you understood my pledge was only temporarily suspended, 7 months should have elapsed after my return to England without your ever calling or writing.

I must say a word in conclusion on another point.

In last week's Guardian I see that Mr. Bracebridge[b] has solicited the support of the Record for Miss Nightingale 'at the expense of the character of Miss Stanley and the other devoted nurses who went with her.'[c]

---

[a] As in 551127gs.

[b] Charles Bracebridge and his wife, Selina, were long family friends of Florence Nightingale.

[c] Gladstone's letter was written only two days after Stanley's contentions with Nightingale in the Crimea became a public matter. It was voiced in the High Church paper, *The Guardian* (96) of 6 February 1856 which carried an article on the committee of the Nightingale Fund on which Gladstone served: ' Mr. Bracebridge, it appears, has been writing a letter to the *Record*, which he will not allow to be published, soliciting the support of that paper for Miss Nightingale, at the expense of the character of Miss Stanley, and the other devoted nurses who set out with her to the Crimea. The letter appears to have little effect on the question to which it is addressed, and is certainly calculated, as represented in other questions, to prove most mischievous to Miss Nightingale in an opposite direction.'

You are working on the same Committee in the same with Mr. Brace-bridge, & to you as a friend, I may say that if this is so (for I have failed in obtaining the Record) it is not generous in him to 'attack' me on points on which he knows I cannot defend myself without involving Mr. Herbert & Miss Nightingale which I will never do. I deceived no one.

Early in the matter when party spirit began to rise, I wrote to Miss Nightingale who knew my mind better than anyone, to tender my resignation of the post in which she had placed me, that of selecting her nurses.

By return of post I received her refusal of my offer—written by Mrs. Bracebridge—That I was honest to the Herberts you know.

To those of whom I had charge I would appeal to know if I had ever obtruded my opinions upon them.

When Lady Stratford questioned me at Kulalee I told her the truth & I never experienced any diminution of her kindness in consequence.

I am not afraid of any enquiry being made about me either at Therpia or Kulalee.[d]

The only complaint that could be brought against me, would be, that I would not allow charges to be made against the Sisters of mercy without instituting an enquiry. The evidence on the only charge made, is in my possession to be produced if ever called for, by either side.

Nor would I consent to take a room to myself & thus obliged 10 Nuns to sleep & live in one room.

My companions worked nobly, till they sickened one by one under the amount of work laid upon us by the Medical men—& the refusal of the Authorities at Scutari to afford us any aid, & if our system is blamed I am ready to defend it, believing that we did what England sent us out to do, & that we could not do otherwise than obey the medical men under whom we were placed.

With the most grateful sense of your kindness I shall ever remain, dear Mr. Gladstone

Most sincerely yours
M. Stanley

[[BL Add. MS 44385, 83–6]]

[[Gladstone wrote to Stanley on 15 February 1856 (*GD* v. 164; not located). Shortly thereafter Stanley wrote to Manning (correspondence not located) who responded on 22 February, directing her to a lecture of his from 1851 for her 'best answer':

---

[d] Stationed nursing sites in the Crimea, the latter the assignment of Stanley after her arrival in 1854 with the Sisters of Mercy.

You there have the simple, spontaneous witness of my whole reason & my whole heart, in the moment of my own trial. And these five years have shown me that there is One only God, one only Christ, One only Fold. For the Truth I would with joy lay down my life: a poor offering for all our Divine Lord has given for me & to me.

My Mind & Faith have been as open to you as the day and you know therefore that I speak from my soul & in the presence of God.

May God bestow upon you the gifts of His Holy Spirit, so that you may simply die to the World & to yourself. While we live to ourselves we are dead to God, & are tossed to & fro by human opinions & human influences. When we are dead to ourselves we are guided by the Holy Ghost speaking infallibly through His Church and in our hearts.

Then all the world is powerless before us, & can hold us in bondage no more.

I do not find the word miserable in the Sermon on the Mount: & it ought not to be in your mouth.

Our D[ivine] Lord says 'Blessed are they that suffer: Blessed are they that mourn.'[e] This is your true portion. God be with you. (Bodleian MS Eng. lett. c. 661, 136–7)

A second note from Stanley reached Manning on the 22 February after he sent the first and appears from the response to have focused on Stanley's 'miserable' emotional state at the time:

Your second note has just reached me.

It has gone against every natural feeling with me not to write to you words of solace & courage. And nothing, you know, but a sense of fidelity has restrained me. I feel so sure that even already you appreciate this: & that in a little while you will tell me that I have been a truthful friend, that I have waited in patience.

Yes indeed, I can give you solace: & can tell you that this light affliction which is but for a moment [illegible word] for us even in this life as inward rest in truth & in God, which is beyond all we can ask or think.[f] God knows I would go seven times thro' all for the perfect 'Truth as it is in Jesus': and it is no where but upon the altar of His Only Church.

Lay any thing at the foot of the Cross: make no shadow of plea for any thing: but make the most of every thing: & you will find the peace of perfect absolution, & perfect conformity of your whole will to the Will of God.

I never have omitted to pray for you in mass: & will do so all the more while you are passing thro' the deep waters which will not overflow Now.

On the other side you will find Jesus standing on the Shore. (Bodl. MS Eng. lett. c. 661, 138–9)]]

---

[e] Cf. Matt. 5: 10, 5: 4.   [f] Cf. Eph. 3: 20.

560223sg

Mr dear Mr. Gladstone

After your very great kindness, I feel it is due to you to tell you that the only obstacle which has stood in the way of my joining the Church of Rome is now removed. My mother has set me free and after the years of mental conflict I have had I am looking forward to rest.

I know all you will say about it—but I can do no otherwise. I can not transfer to you the responsibility of my spiritual welfare.

To God I am answerable for the use of reason He has given me, and if I have misused this gift He will judge me for it.

Amidst very great suffering attendant on this step to myself and to my family—there have been rays of comfort in the warm, & in some instances unexpected, sympathy of friends—and I never can sufficiently thank them for their endeavours to save me from what they thought a mistaken step, but more also for the comfort they have afforded my mother.

Believe me my own feeling is so far from its separating me from the friends I have loved that[104] the certainty of faith seems to enlarge my sympathies with all around me. But I know others do not feel this and I am told I must expect to lose all the friends I have had.

I would fain hope this is an exaggerated view & it will make me doubly welcome those who do not cut me off.

Many thanks for your last note.

I have nothing further to add with reference to Mr. Bracebridge. I merely wished to say what I did as members of the same Committee are in some degree connected—& are supposed to act together by an ignorant public.

Believe me to be dear Mr. Gladstone
Most sincerely yours
M. Stanley

Precincts Canterbury
Feb[ruary] 23rd
[[BL Add. MS 44385, 109–12]]

560224sg

My dear Mr. Gladstone

When I wrote last night I was not aware that my brother also intended to write.[a] I now add a line to say that I trust you will let me hear *alone* all that I know you will feel.

---

[a] On 24 February 1856, Stanley's brother, Arthur P. Stanley, Dean of Westminster, confirmed the family's decision in a letter to Gladstone marked with mixed sadness and

I ask you to spare him any severe remarks on my decision. He is not responsible for it and it is a very great sorrow both to him and my mother—and the subject is, as I have said before been too painful a one that it has not been one of family discussion.

Your letters to me have been seen by no one but myself & I consulted no one in my answers.

I wish to say this that there may be no misunderstanding.

I shall ever feel deeply grateful to you, for, as far as possible sparing my bother any additional pain which severe remarks to him about me would cause him.

Believe me to be—most sincerely yours
M. Stanley

Precincts Canterbury
Febr[uar]y 24
[[BL Add. MS 44385, 135–6]]

560227sg
My dear Mr. Gladstone

I am *most* grateful to you for your letter to Arthur[aa]—I cannot help thanking you from my heart for this as for all your kindness—do not trouble yourself to answer this—It requires none.

Ever yours most sincerely,
M. Stanley

Canterbury
Febr[uar]y 27th
[[BL Add. MS 44385, 164–5]]

[[Stanley informed Manning of her family's decision as well, requesting a meeting, and Manning replied briefly on 28 February (Bodl. MS Eng. lett. c. 661, 140–1) but, unable to meet her, sent a fuller response on 3 March.]]

anger. His family, he stated, was giving way and allowing his sister, Mary Stanley, to join the Church of Rome, adding that if Florence Nightingale's friends continued to comment on Mary's role in the Crimea, the family would be forced to tell the 'real story of my sister's relation with Miss Nightingale' (BL Add. MS 44318, 37–8).

[aa] Gladstone wrote to Arthur Penryn Stanley, 26 February 1856 (*GD* v. 108).

Pendell. Bletchingley.[a] March 3. 1856

I also wish that I could have been in London at this time: but as it is otherwise, I do not doubt that it is best.

Do not be troubled at what you are feeling.

It is inevitable. Every one has to pass thro' manifold temptations even after attaining to the truth. It is thro' these trials that God chastises & purifies. He will not accept of half our hearts: nor of mixed motives. It is moreover just that He should deal with us, as we have dealt with Him. He is generous to the generous and reserved to the tardy.

They who have kept their baptismal grace & have corresponded faithfully with His Holy Spirit from their childhood have a peace & fulness of knowledge and fervour & delicacy of love to God which satisfies their whole heart.

They who have sinned away their grace but have regained it thro' penance attain to peace, love, & joy in the measure of their mortification & contrition.

They who put God in the first place, and sacrifice what they count dearest for His love, receive love for love.

They who follow our Divine Lord with generosity, & self forgetting endurance of sorrow, loss & shame for His sake are consoled with a special peace.

They too who are deeply convinced of sin are not only patient—under the trials of loneliness, sadness, darkness, & all the things you speak of: but they acknowledge them to be just, necessary, wholesome, humbling, and blessed tokens of Gods goodness & equity in chastening them for their past infidelities to Him.

Now I would have you dismiss from your thoughts every thing but one thing. Do not ask 'what have I gained?' As if you 'carried the bag' in following Jesus. Do not complain about understanding the Divine Lordship, & supernatural order of the Catholic Church, which none can understand except by experience, and by divine illumination: and do not seek with eagerness for work, in which to lose sight of your 'own face in the glass'—but set yourself steadfastly in the light of God's presence—& let your one habitual prayer be, 'O Lord shew me my *sins* in the light of Thy Countenance'.

[a] The home of Manning's brother, Charles, and his wife, Catherine, who were received into the Roman Catholic Church on the day Manning became a priest (Purcell i. 635).

If you have ever trusted in me, trust me now. Your case is as transparent to me as the light.

Let it be enough for you for awhile to ponder on these words, 'God has saved me. I was dead—& am alive again. God has brought me out of darkness into His marvellous light. He has saved my soul out of the net of the fowler.[b] If I had died, I should have perished eternally. Except I be converted, I shall even now perish everlastingly. Let my whole life be given to humiliation, contrition, and endurance. I will never ask or seek for consolation or sweetness for I do not deserve it. It is safer & better for me to suffer with Him who suffered for me: when I have known too late and have served without fervour or fidelity.'

Do not think this severe. I pray that this may be my own state until death. God forbid that I should ask any thing of our Lord but to live the life & die the death of a fervent penitent. And if he be pleased to use me to work in Him, it is more than I deserve. And if I am ever to save a soul, it can only be by first profoundly humbling my own at the foot of the Cross.

When I entered the Church of God I thought I was some thing. I have learned that I am nothing. I have found that I neither knew God or myself: for all my knowledge was not worthy of the name. I was confident—because I was superficial, and little as I knew of other things, I knew least of myself.

Do not fear, press on in the way I have feebly, and slightly attained. It is the true way & the right—the Divine & only way of eternal life.

God be with you.

Always yours aff[ectionatel]y in J[esus] C[hrist]

H.E.M.

(Bodl. MS Eng. lett. c. 661, 142–5)

[[Shortly thereafter Stanley sent her correspondence with Gladstone to Manning. She joined the Catholic Church in March 1856.[c]]]

560312ms

Pendell. March 12. 1856.

I have read all y[ou]r letters to Mr. Gladstone and as much of his to you as I could. But I cannot follow him. I only regret that you did not in every letter repeat the first question which is the only one.

His principle is simple private judgment from first to last with freedom to revise, change, and reconstruct our religion from Baptism till death.

It is therefore never a *faith*, but only a string of variable personal opinions.

---

[b] See Ps. 91: 3, 124: 7, and Prov 6: 5   [c] See Prothero and Bradley (1894), ii.483.

In his 2d or 3d letter the words 'Certainty & reality of wh[ich] we hear so much'[a] are levelled at me. He has never forgotten or forgiven my using them. I have read his letters with sadness for more reasons than I can say.

The other two are indeed letters of fairness & justice: as well as of affection.

God grant you grace to be all your Sister desires, and you will find as she w[oul]d that there are no veils between us & the Sacred Heart: except those Sacramental Veils which declare His Very Presence. From henceforth you 'shall not learn war any more'[b] but will dwell under the Vine & under the Fig tree, in the Fruition of Truth, found, & with the certainty of the Voice of God.

Ever y[our]s affe[ctionatel]y in J[esus] C[hrist]

H.E.M.

[[Bodl. MS Eng. lett. c. 661, 146]]

[[Following her reception as a Roman Catholic Stanley asked Manning that her letters be returned. Manning responded 4 June 1856, after which only two, rather general notes from Manning to her, later in the year, are extant.]]

Pendell, June. 4. 1856

I will bring the letters to London on Friday to save Postage but I write at once.

It is certain that until the last day no words will convey to the mind of others things which are as daylight to our own mind.

There is nothing in the letters before me which is not to my mind plain as day.

I remember every passage & the moment when it was written.

The last five years are before me in these three points.

1. from 1851 to 1853 in Charles St. when I first saw with alarm, which drew from me the letter of June 7.[a]

2. From that time till you went to the East.

3. From that time till you declared yourself.

---

[a] Gladstone letter not located; cf. the use of the phrase in 521128 gm and 530405 mg.

[b] Is. 2: 4

[a] Reference perhaps to his letter of 7 June 1854:

78 South Audley St.

June 7. 1854

My dear Miss Stanley,

Saturday morning if you will I can be in Charles St. or next week as you may fix.

You are right. My wish is that you should make a perfect Sacrifice to God fixing nothing, presenting nothing, with no conditions: leaving him to dispose it as he will.

But it is simply impossible to satisfy the mind of others.

Your account of what passed in the East I take without a word. I believe that you believe what you say.

But I must add for it is fidelity to God that requires it.

1. That it is impossible that any person could without sacrilege at least on the Part of the Priest be admitted to the H[oly] Sacrament of the Body & blood of Jesus Christ, without being first, fully, formally, & universally received into the Catholic Church.

2. That I shall die without comprehending how you believed otherwise: knowing as I do all you have read: & all I have said & written to you.

3. That your not knowing cannot be without responsibility to God: for it is one of those points so primary & self evident that want of light about it cannot be inescapable.

I have now said the last word I hope ever to say on this which has been one of the greatest grief to me.

As to severity I can only leave it to the years before these things arose to speak for me. One thing I may say I have been truthful with you as in the hour of death: but I have stood between you & every one who has censured you. You alone know what I have said to you.

Such as I am you know such I must ever be. I desire to live for nothing but to save my own soul, & others by plain unbending truth.

If I find any thing to rebuke myself for in the letter you sent me it is that, I wrote so little. It was to spare you I did so. But remember what I have said. I have numberless letters written after our conversations, and you remember what they were. They began in Charles Street, on the words

It has caused the much silent wonder that this which is the first law of the life of Faith—& so [enforced?] even by the Protestants sh[oul]d come out so slowly in this matter. But it is out now in full light, & that is enough.

I shall like to hear of Ella. Every day brings new proofs of the dissolving of Anglicanism. And the alternative before people is Rome or rationalism. Two hours yesterday morning a person was saying this to me, and at night I saw a letter from another saying the same.

You shall have more letters.

Ever yours very aff[ectionatel]y

H E M

(Bodleian MS Eng. lett. c.661, 21—22)

Throughout June and to the end of July 1854 there are preserved seven letters arranging far at least four meetings between Stanley and Manning. (Ibid., 23–33)

'He that loveth Father & Mother more than me.' I have commended you to the S[acred] H[eart] & will on Friday. God be with you.

> Always yours aff[ectionatel]y in J[esus] C[hrist]
> H.E.M.

[[Bodl. MS Eng. lett. c. 661, 149–50]]

[[On 30 November and 14 December 1856 Gladstone read Manning's *Unity of the Church* (*GD* v. 175, 178), adding the annotation: 'Et tu Brute!' on the closing page (see 421021mg). On 25 January 1857, he read Manning's sermons (*GD* v. 191) and on 15 November 1857 he read 'Manning, aloud to C[atherine]' (ibid. 262). Several years later, on 19 March 1862, Mary Stanley's name came up in a conversation Gladstone held with Queen Victoria: 'I cannot quite remember when but the Queen spoke with much interest of Miss Stanley: asked me about her change of religion: and was pleased when I told her that Miss Stanley had not, as far as I knew, run into the extravagances so common among her fellow religionists in this country' (BL Add. MS 44752, 25ff. and *Autobiographica*, iii. 239). At some point in 1860 Gladstone appears to have read Manning's *A Sermon Preached at the Church of the Immaculate Conception, Lanark, on November 10th, 1859* (London: Burns & Lambert, 1860).^{b}]]

ENDNOTES TO SECTION IX

1. of] overscored
2. probably] inserted
3. days] inserted, replacing overscored: period
4. to] inserted
5. irreparable] inserted
6. illegible word overscored
7. (neither...you)] inserted
8. Last one-third of page blank. Next folio begins in middle of sentence
9. temple] written over illegible word
10. whole] overscored
11. For us] overscored
12. that too] overscored
13. That is for the end: for the day and till the end come let the Almighty direct our paths as seemeth Him good.] overscored
14. future] overscored, replacing: end
15. on the envelope of] draft: corrects from: upon
16. to me] inserted in draft
17. as to convey this impression] inserted in draft
18. relations to one another] draft corrects from: reciprocal relations
19. had...loved] draft corrects from: like Death

---

^{b} A copy of the piece is preserved with some few Gladstone Tracts at NLW (SDL GTM/F 78/21).

20. draft overscored: had
21. if . . . worthy] draft inserts
22. conjecture what may be] inserted in draft, replacing: say what
23. yet to come] inserted in draft, replacing: may be
24. very] draft inserts
25. please to] corrected in draft from: you illegible word
26. the old] draft: the one old; 'the' and 'old' inserted
27. in order to construe] draft corrects from: construes
28. calls . . . afresh] draft corrects from: calls up afresh & realises
29. scarcely] written in draft over illegible word
30. than] inserted in draft
31. of] overscored in draft
32. it is] inserted in draft, replacing overscored: &
33. and at last I feel] overscored in draft
34. but] inserted in draft, replacing overscored: &
35. all] inserted in draft
36. two illegible words in parentheses in draft overscored
37. honour . . . position)] inserted in draft with three illegible overscored words preceding: actual
38. or to be placed] inserted in draft
39. one and] overscored in draft
40. know not] inserted in draft, replacing overscored: know not
41. taking it upon me] corrected in draft from three illegible words
42. an intercourse] inserted in draft, replacing overscored: a position
43. judged] overscored in draft
44. must] inserted in draft, replacing overscored illegible word
45. coming] inserted in draft
46. you] overscored in draft
47. thus] inserted in draft
48. possessed] inserted in draft, replacing overscored: had
49. the facts] inserted in draft, replacing overscored: things
50. spiritual] inserted in draft and overscored
51. or pretenders] inserted in draft
52. now] inserted in draft
53. to you] inserted in draft
54. where] overscored in draft
55. But] overscored in draft
56. however] inserted in draft
57. (as I think)] inserted in draft
58. in men . . . named] inserted in draft
59. once perhaps . . . pride] inserted in draft
60. thinks not fit] inserted in draft replacing overscored: has not
61. do] corrected in draft from: done

62. as] inserted in draft, replacing overscored: &
63. gradually] inserted in draft, replacing inserted and overscored: a little
64. until this tyranny...life] corrected in draft from: until the grief and strain of this life, until this tyranny
65. intercession] inserted in draft replacing overscored illegible word
66. ingredient of harm for] inserted in draft
67. for] inserted in draft
68. invisibly] inserted in draft
69. aright] inserted in draft
70. own] overscored in draft
71. the real...day] inserted in draft
72. illegible word overscored in draft
73. or] draft: nor
74. not] inserted, replacing overscored: never
75. ¾ line heavily overscored & illegible
76. in Sept.] inserted
77. with regard to the nurses] inserted
78. against] inserted, replacing overscored: before
79. but that your arguments] inserted
80. yet] inserted
81. MS: to
82. illegible word overscored
83. illegible word overscored
84. Abbreviations unclear
85. on these points] inserted
86. summarily] inserted
87. me dismiss you with a free conscience but which] overscored
88. I am persuaded] inserted
89. be found to] inserted
90. urge] inserted, replacing overscored: say
91. do you] inserted
92. to you] overscored
93. sent to you] inserted
94. (even false)] inserted
95. this is a sign...shd] inserted from lower margin; the] overscored
96. for] overscored
97. faith or] inserted
98. receiving] inserted
99. against your will] inserted
100. it contains] inserted
101. my word] overscored
102. appointed] inserted
103. to] inserted
104. that] inserted